Introductory Statistics

Introductory Statistics:
A Conceptual Approach
Using R

William B. Ware
University of North Carolina at Chapel Hill

John M. Ferron
University of South Florida

Barbara M. Miller
Elon University

Routledge
Taylor & Francis Group

LONDON AND NEW YORK

First published 2013
by Routledge
711 Third Avenue, New York, NY 10017

Simultaneously published in the UK
by Routledge
2 Park Square, Milton Park, Abingdon, Oxon OX14 4RN

Routledge is an imprint of the Taylor & Francis Group, an informa business

Library of Congress Cataloging in Publication Data
    Ware, William B., author.
    Introductory statistics : a conceptual approach using R / William B. Ware,
    University of North Carolina at Chapel Hill, John M. Ferron,
    University of South Florida, Barbara M. Miller, Elon University.–1 [edition].
        pages cm
    Includes bibliographical references and index.
    1. Mathematical statistics–Textbooks. 2. R (Computer program language)
    I. Ferron, John M., author. II. Miller, Barbara Manning, author. III. Title.
    QA276.W365 2013
    519.5–dc23
    2012024922

ISBN: 978–0–8058–3651–6 (hbk)
ISBN: 978–0–415–99600–6 (pbk)
ISBN: 978–0–203–83737–5 (ebk)

Typeset in Times New Roman and Helvetica Neue
by Swales and Willis Ltd, Exeter, Devon

Printed and bound in the United States of America
by Edwards Brothers, Inc.

Dedications

To all the people from whom I've learned. In particular, I would point to my parents, Helen and Howard; my teachers in the Verona (NJ) public schools; my high school principal who encouraged me to teach, Edwin A. Willard; my professors at Dartmouth College and Northwestern University; my children, and especially my wife, Barbara. But most of all, I dedicate this book to the memory of my doctoral chair, Norman Dale Bowers; he was my teacher, my mentor, and my friend. After my final defense, he suggested that we write a book. Norman, now we have and, in this work, your spirit lives on.

WBW

I am very grateful to my major professor and mentor Dr William Ware. Over the years he has taught me a great deal about statistics and a great deal about teaching. I would also like to thank my colleagues, both faculty and students, in the Department of Educational Measurement and Research at USF. They have created a very supportive environment that has helped me continue to learn statistics and to further develop as a teacher. Finally, I would like to thank my wife, Pam, who has been so supportive over the years, my children, Emily and Anne Marie, and my parents and siblings.

JMF

I am particularly indebted to the first author of this text, Dr William Ware, who encouraged my interest and exploration of statistics. He embodies the highest ideals of teaching and is an inspiration for the professor I hope to become. To all of my teachers in the Bluefield, WV, public school system, and professors at West Virginia University and UNC-CH, thank you. Lastly, I would also like to thank my husband, Kenn Gaither, and my parents, Frazier and Phyllis Miller, from whom I learn every day.

BMM

Contents

BOOK WEBSITE (AS APPROPRIATE FOR EACH CHAPTER)
Answers to Practice Questions
Answers to Exercises
Large Data Set from the ECLS Study
Codebook for the ECLS Data Set
Other Computer Solutions: SPSS and SAS (see book website)
R Scripts
Data Files in Text Format

Illustrations

FIGURES

TABLES

BOXES

Preface

To say that this book has been a long time in coming is a major understatement. It has grown out of the development of an introductory course in applied statistics at UNC-Chapel Hill over a period of more than 30 years and has been field-tested by hundreds of students. The course at UNC-CH is offered at the graduate level and is intended to provide a sound foundation for students to proceed on to additional courses. However, it is organized and written in a style that would make the book appropriate for master's level and undergraduate courses as well. We will be up-front from the very beginning and tell you that, for many reasons, this book is very different from most books designed for a course at this level. Among the ways in which it is different are its style, its breadth of level and coverage, its organization, and its choice of computer software.

This book has been heavily influenced by the students who have taken the course over the years. They have come from many different disciplines (e.g., educational psychology, school psychology, counseling psychology, school counseling, social foundations, curriculum and instruction, educational leadership, psychology, journalism and mass communication, information and library science, public policy, business, human movement science, physical therapy, speech and hearing sciences, occupational science, health education and health behavior, maternal and child health, nutrition, and nursing). They have come from different levels (e.g., doctoral level, master's level, and even a few undergraduate students) and have represented a wide spectrum of ability, from those who avoided mathematics in high school to those who are accomplished mathematicians.

First, with regard to style, this book has been written by three people who love to teach, and who offer you over 70 years of combined experience teaching courses in applied statistics, measurement, and research methods; all three have been recognized by their respective institutions for their excellence in teaching. Consequently, this book has been written in such a way that it tries to *teach* the material to the reader, rather than simply present the material. In some ways, we believe this book could almost stand alone, without a classroom lecture experience. To that extent, instructors who adopt this book will find that they will be able to free up a lot of time to spend in class on practical applications, both the computing and interpretation of examples. Over the years, students have told us consistently that they would like more time on examples; with this book, instructors will be able to provide that experience.

Based on years of teaching, we feel that it is important for students to understand the material at a conceptual level, to be able to complete calculations without a computer, to be able to implement those calculations with the aid of a computer, and to interpret the results within an appropriate context. For that reason, we devote considerable time and space to explaining the concepts, relating new concepts to old concepts, and relying on both metaphors/analogies and mathematical formulae. Many of our colleagues have come to rely almost exclusively on computer software, but we very firmly believe that more in-depth learning occurs when one actually performs calculations with a hand-held calculator.

At this point, you may find yourself wondering how all this can be fit into one course. You are in good company, as more than one reviewer suggested that there was "just plain too much."

However, the way the material is presented affords one the opportunity to skip some of the material without losing the main ideas. As an example, at the end of several of the chapters, we provide Technical Notes that offer "proofs" of points made in the chapters. One could certainly skip those. On the other hand, they are there for those who might want to explore further. In addition, at the end of each chapter, we provide Key Terms, References, Practice Questions, and Exercises to help "nail down" the material. We also provide additional exercises and solutions to all the exercises in the supplementary materials (website) associated with this book.

With regard to organization, most books written at this level begin with descriptive statistics (univariate and bivariate) and then move to a section on the foundations of statistical inference (elements of probability, sampling distributions, and the normal distribution), completing the course by showing applications of inference using the "classical" methods of Pearson product–moment correlations, regression, t-tests, and analysis of variance. The applications are usually organized by number of groups and the attribute (mean, variance, etc.) of focal interest. Some books then cycle through the same structure again, with a section on what are called "non-parametric procedures" that may be employed when the data do not conform to the assumptions for completing the classical/traditional methods which rely on distributional assumptions in order to use mathematical probability distributions like the normal distribution, the t-distribution, the χ^2-distribution (read as "chi-squared"), and the F-distribution. Some books (very few) even go so far to introduce the newer, computer-intensive resampling methods.

We have taken a slightly different approach. Admittedly, we begin with a fairly traditional presentation of descriptive statistics, although we include correlation and regression in this section as ways to describe attributes of bivariate relationship. We follow that with a similarly traditional presentation of the tools of inference, including some basic material on probability, sampling distributions, and the normal distribution (including the central limit theorem).

We follow that material with a consideration of questions that may arise within the context of having only one group. But here we diverge; in dealing with questions of location, we present techniques for means, medians, and proportions. Right alongside, we present the analogous non-parametric procedures, as well as the appropriate resampling approaches (bootstrapping and permutation tests). Our premise is that questions arise within a context, and for that context, the researcher must be aware of the various ways that might be appropriate or inappropriate for the prevailing conditions and the particular data that are available. Thus, we organize the material by concern (location, spread, relationship) and discuss the variety of approaches that might be useful.

To provide data for most of the examples and exercises, we have included a subset of the data from the Early Childhood Longitudinal Study (ECLS), a national study developed by the National Center for Educational Statistics, a unit within the U.S. Department of Education. Starting with 21,260 kindergarten children in the fall of 1998, the study was designed to follow the cohort (or subsets of the cohort) through third grade. According to the Base Year Manual:

> The ECLS-K has several major objectives and numerous potential applications. The ECLS-K combines elements of (1) a study of achievement in the elementary years; (2) an assessment of the developmental status of children in the United States at the start of their formal schooling and at key points during the elementary school years; (3) a cross-sectional study of the nature and quality of kindergarten programs in the United States; and (4) a study of the relationship of family, preschool, and school experiences to children's developmental status at school entry and their progress during the kindergarten and early elementary school years. (p. 1-1)

The original study has been augmented to include data collection points at the end of fifth, eighth, tenth and twelfth grades. We have included only data from kindergarten and first grade. The kindergarten–first grade file contains data on 17,212 children on many, many variables. Data for all four time points were collected only on a subset of children; we have created a data set in both .exlx and .txt formats on those children ($N = 5,428$), using only a small subset of variables. The data files are on the book website, as is a modified edition of the codebook.

To eliminate some issues that are becoming increasingly important, but beyond the scope of this book, we first eliminated all cases with missing data, leaving 2,577 complete cases. In addition, we should note two other features of the full ECLS-K data file that we have ignored. First, the sampling procedure employed complex multi-stage cluster sampling. Generally, at the first stage, primary sampling units (PSU) were sampled from a list of PSUs, which are essentially geographic areas consisting of counties or groups of counties. In the second stage, schools were selected from within the selected PSUs. At the third stage, children were selected from within the selected schools. Thus, the data set has a hierarchical, or nested, structure. "Real" analyses of these data would employ more sophisticated statistical procedures than those that we discuss in this introductory course. As we describe in Chapter 18, hierarchical linear models or multi-level analyses should be used. The second issue that we have chosen to ignore is "sample weights." In creating this large, nationally representative sample, some "groups" of children were "oversampled" to provide a sufficient number of cases to yield stable statistical estimates of their characteristics. Sampling statisticians have provided sample weights to allow for over- or undersampling and non-response rates. Again, in "real" analyses of these data, these sample weights should be taken into consideration. Thus, one should be extremely cautious about generalizing any of the results we present, or any results that one might generate based on analyses of our "text book data file." Nevertheless, the data in the file allow us to conduct many different types of analyses that might be of interest.

The last major way in which this book is different is in the choice of statistical software. Over the years, we have collectively used BMD, BMDP, MYSTAT, SYSTAT, SAS, SPSS, and STATA; in this book we use R primarily, although we provide some support for SPSS and SAS users in the supplementary materials. In doing so, we are among the first to provide an introductory statistics text in the social sciences that uses R. You may wonder why.

There are actually many reasons, some from the perspective of the instructor and some from the perspective of the student. From the perspective of the instructor, R allows one to conduct simulations, complete classical/parametric and nonparametric procedures, and perform resampling analyses, all within the same environment. In addition, R is available for three platforms: PC, Mac, and Linux. R is modular in nature; it installs with a base package and several other useful packages. In addition, there are currently over 4,000 packages that programmers have contributed to complete virtually every type of analysis imaginable. Several of these add-on packages will be used in this book.

Perhaps the most important reason for using R is that is encourages students to actually think about what they are doing. Rather than simply pulling down a series of menus and clicking boxes, students have to think more deeply about the problem. In that sense, it is more like SAS in that it is syntax/code driven. However, to assist both instructors and students, we provide an R script for virtually everything presented in this book, including the figures. The script files are like templates in that they can be copied into R, edited, and used to run the analyses on the variables of interest. These script files are all available in the supplementary materials available on the website for the book. We would like to state that R is a very sophisticated programming environment. In many of our scripts, we have not employed some of these programming procedures as we wanted our scripts to be easy for students to follow. Please understand that this is a book that uses R to teach applied statistics, not a book that uses applied statistics to teach R.

From the student perspective, there is one overwhelming argument. It is free! But there is a second argument to advance. Although it is admittedly more difficult to learn R than some simple pull-down menu programs, the curve decelerates quickly, and at the end, you will have a much better understanding of statistics and statistical thinking.

In closing, we would like to thank the many people who have been instrumental in moving this project forward. There are the students, too many to name, and not wanting to risk omitting anyone, we thank them all for their constructive feedback and copy editing. This book has been through at least four or five drafts, the recent ones being read by hundreds of eyes. Yet, as we prepare the manuscript for submission, we are still finding mistakes; hopefully the errata sheet will be record-breaking short. We would also like to thank an anonymous reviewer for some very helpful feedback. We are especially grateful to John Verzani (Staten Island University) for his extensive support and help. He was most helpful from the very beginning in helping the first author get started with R, and his detailed comments and suggestions on an earlier version of this manuscript have been instrumental in improving the quality of the final manuscript. Of course, the screw-ups are all ours, not his.

Last, we would like to thank Lane Akers and Julie Ganz at Routledge for their support during this project. Lane, in particular has been the epitome of patience over the years, providing unlimited support while life happened as we tried to meet deadline after deadline, often without success. Without his support, this book would have never happened. Thanks, Lane.

Part I

Part I

1

Introduction and Background

We recognize that the word "statistics" does not elicit the same response from everyone. In fact, the range of attitudes toward a statistics class may be quite extreme, perhaps even more so than other classes you've taken in your college career. If your reaction is somewhere toward the negative end of the emotional spectrum (Think: Ugh!), don't feel bad. That's a fairly common reaction for students beginning their first course in statistics.

We know that a few of you are starting this course because you have always enjoyed mathematics. Some of you are taking this course because you are curious. You've heard about statistics and want to see what it is all about. Many of you are taking this course because it is required; you've been told that you have to take it. You are not very happy about the prospect, but you know that you will survive. And then, there are a few of you who are taking the course against your will. You are afraid to the point that you are experiencing indigestion and sleep disorders. You are thinking about dropping out of school. How will you ever survive?

We have just described the typical composition of an introductory applied statistics course for the social sciences. For just a moment, consider the plight of the unfortunate person standing at the front the class—the instructor. He or she has the difficult task of presenting the content of this course to a very diverse group of students and doing so in such a way that will not result in getting destroyed on the student evaluations of teaching at the end of the course. This book has been written to help both students and instructors. As you will soon see, it is not a typical statistics text. Rather, it is written in a style that we hope will appeal to everyone. We provide conceptual overviews, detailed step-by-step instructions on how to calculate statistics, both by hand using a calculator and using the computer statistical package R; we also provide some support for SPSS and SAS on the book website. From time to time, we will provide mathematical derivations in technical notes that you are free to ignore. Now that we've been honest up front, let's get on with it!

WHY TAKE A COURSE IN STATISTICS?

There are many different positive reasons for taking a course (or more than one) in applied statistics. Some of you are practicing professionals who will never calculate another statistic after you complete this course. But even if you do not calculate a single statistic yourself, you will need to understand what the statistics you encounter everyday—from test grades to what you read in a newspaper or at work—are telling you. As technology continues to change the way we live, you will find that researchers are using increasingly more sophisticated statistical tools to analyze their data, and the reports that appear in professional journals are becoming more and more technical and very difficult to comprehend without some understanding of statistical concepts. Thus, as practicing professionals, you need some statistical background to enable you to read, understand, and evaluate research reports. Too many consumers of research simply read an abstract and then jump to the study's conclusions and implications section without reading about the study's methods and results.

Several of you will go on to careers in which you will be designing studies, writing grant applications, and such. Hopefully, you will be very successful, in which case you will be able to employ statisticians to carry out your analyses. Even though you may not conduct the analyses, you still need to know a lot about statistics. In designing the studies, you will need to know what statistical tools are available and which ones are appropriate for answering your research questions. If you are not aware of the variety of tools available, you will tend to design your studies in overly simplified ways. There is an old saying, "If the only tool you have is a hammer, everything looks like a nail." For example, if the only statistical procedure you know is how to calculate percentages, then you may miss the opportunity to draw stronger conclusions from your research. Or, if the only statistical procedure that you know is a t-test, then you will tend to design all of your studies as consisting of two groups and analyze the data to compare the averages of the two groups. Furthermore, you will need to be able to communicate clearly with your hired statistician. Some of the most horrible mistakes are made when the principal investigator has a very limited understanding of statistics and the statistician similarly has a very limited understanding of the substantive research topic.

You should also be aware that what constitutes appropriate research methodology in the social sciences is not always a given. We have seen much controversy over the years between those who, on one extreme, believe that "if you can't measure it, it is not worth talking about" to those who, on the other extreme, believe that "the important aspects of human interaction cannot be measured." At times each group has characterized the other group unkindly. Fortunately, we seem to be progressing beyond that point as more and more researchers are employing mixed methods in their research, or a combination of both quantitative and qualitative methods in their inquiry.

Without question, the focus of this book is on quantitative methods. However, we firmly believe that the results of statistical analyses cannot be interpreted without a context. In order to conduct useful statistical analyses, one must have information about the meaning of the numbers and the conditions in which they were generated.

OUR THOUGHTS ON THE NATURE OF REALITY

We hold the belief that there is order in the universe, and that there is an external reality that exists independent of our perceptions. We believe that, in that external reality, there are cause-and-effect relationships. However, these relationships are probabilistic rather than deterministic. That is, the effect does not follow the cause every time the cause is present. We acknowledge that our ability to perceive the external world is far from perfect. Furthermore, different people can experience the same object or event and construct different perceptions. For example, many years ago, researchers looked at children's perceptions of the common silver quarter. The results indicated that children from low-income backgrounds drew quarters that were consistently larger than those drawn by children from high-income backgrounds. Other research-ers have staged events such as an automobile accident at an intersection. After the accident, inter-views of witnesses showed that, although the witnesses all experienced the same event, reports of what happened differed considerably from one person to another. Just as people construct their own meanings of their experiences, we offer a quote defining statistics as "a place where knowl-edge is neither certain nor random" (Keller, 2006, p. ix). Simply stated, there may be multiple beliefs about reality, but that does not imply that there are multiple realities.

We believe that we can build a common knowledge base. By pooling our information over time, over replications, and with input from others, we firmly believe that we can build a use-ful understanding of the world around us. We believe that our position is consistent with that of postpositivism as described by Phillips and Burbules (2000). "In short, the postpositivist sees knowledge as *conjectural*. These conjectures are supported by the strongest (if possibly imper-fect) warrants we can muster at the time and are always subject to reconsideration" (Phillips & Burbules, 2000, pp. 29–30). Similarly, "It is a confusion—and a pernicious one—to say that because a person believes X, and another doesn't, that X is both true and not true, or, relatedly, to say that there are 'multiple (incompatible) realities'" (Phillips & Burbules, 2000, p. 36). We urge you to give this well-written book a quick read. For a more extreme position on philosophy and science, we refer you to Bunge (1996). We should also note that the field of statistics predates postpositivism and that statistical arguments have been, and continue to be, used by researchers who identify with a wide variety of philosophical positions. We felt it relevant, however, to share our position in that it may help to shed light on the examples chosen and the arguments made. The remainder of this book is devoted to presenting a description of statistical methods and showing how they can be used to assist us in building an understanding of the world around us.

SCIENCE AND RESEARCH IN THE SOCIAL SCIENCES

What is Science?

The word "science" is derived from the Latin word *scientia*, meaning "knowledge." Bodies of knowledge consist of general truths and laws obtained by applying the scientific method, or agreed-upon principles and procedures for the systematic generation of knowledge. Generally, the process begins with the recognition or formulation of a problem. Based on previous knowledge, observa-tions, and experience, we develop a hypothesis, or tentative explanation. Subsequently, we collect data through observation and/or experimentation, under conditions which, as much as possible, control or rule out other explanations. Finally, the validity of the hypothesis is assessed in light of the data. When the hypothesis is in conflict with the data, the hypothesis is regarded as incorrect. However, when the hypothesis and the data are in agreement, we can say that the hypothesis is supported, although not proven. This point is somewhat subtle and often misunderstood.

Scientific research is systematic. Scientists have agreed upon what constitute legitimate ways to pursue knowledge. Scientists conduct their work in public, and their work is open to cor-rection. Perhaps most important, scientific hypotheses are both rational and testable. That is, they make sense and they are capable of being disproved.

What is Research?

We think of research as the process of building a science. There are many ways to character-ize approaches to research. Some researchers employ methods that are described as qualitative, such as observation, interviews, and focus groups. Other researchers use methods that may be described as quantitative, such as experiments, quasi-experiments, and statistics. Both approaches require creativity and rigor. Qualitative researchers collect large amounts of data; their hard work begins when they begin to analyze the data. Quantitative researchers put a lot of hard work into the development of their measures and the design of their studies; data analysis is pretty easy, relatively speaking. That said, we think that the differences between qualitative and quantitative methods have been greatly exaggerated. Indeed, one of the authors learned about experiments, observations, and interviews in a research methods course in the middle of the last century, before the term "qualitative methods" had been coined. As you might expect, however, our focus is on quantitative research. There are three main types of quantitative research: experiments, quasi-experiments, and observational studies.

Experiments

Experiments are studies in which the researcher has quite of bit of control. There is some sort of experimental treatment or intervention that is administered to a group of participants. There is also a placebo or control condition experienced by the control group. Furthermore, the researcher has the ability to determine which participants are assigned to which condition, and that assignment is made with randomization. Often, the study is completed in an isolated context, permitting the elimination of extraneous events that might influence the data.

Quasi-experiments

Quasi-experiments have many of the features of experiments, with one important difference. In typical quasi-experiments, the researcher does not have the ability to assign participants to conditions at random. Thus, quasi-experiments do not permit conclusions that are as strong as those from experiments. There are many threats, or rival explanations, that may account for the results, rather than the treatment/intervention. Much has been written about quasi-experiments, stemming from the work of Donald Campbell. The seminal work was Campbell and Stanley (1963), which was followed by an expanded coverage in Cook and Campbell (1979). The most recent and complete treatise is Shadish, Cook, and Campbell (2001). We would suggest that you check out all three references, but especially the latter; doing so will give you a sense of the development of social science methods.

Observational Studies

Observational studies are probably the most prevalent type of research in the social sciences, and perhaps the most important. As the label implies, data are collected through observation, often in an unstructured, natural setting. Observational studies are the foundation of social science research, as they provide the rich database which we may search for possible relationships among variables—relationships that can be examined and tested in subsequent studies. These non-experimental studies may be cross-sectional or longitudinal. Cross-sectional studies are those in which all of the data are collected at the same time. Longitudinal studies collect the data over an extended period of time. For example, suppose we are interested in looking at social development in secondary schools. A cross-sectional approach would collect data on freshmen, sophomores, juniors, and seniors. A longitudinal approach would start with a group or cohort of freshmen and collect data on that same group over a period of four years. Each approach has both advantages and disadvantages. In particular, cross-sectional studies can be completed in a shorter time frame, but they make the assumption that the different cohorts are equivalent. Longitudinal studies have the advantage of following a single cohort, but the study just described would require four years to collect the data.

THE CONTEXT AND NATURE OF RESEARCH IN THE SOCIAL SCIENCES

There are a number of steps in conducting research in the social sciences. First, one must come up with a research question that asks about a possible relationship between variables (e.g., Does academic motivation relate to achievement in mathematics?) or a research question about the distribution of a variable (e.g., How much variation is there in the reading comprehension of third-grade students in Florida?). Research questions may be based on our own experiences, or they may be based on our readings. Often, journal articles will end with a section that describes what steps should be taken next. Or, we may read two conflicting reports and wonder how we might explain the inconsistent results. Research questions should be worded with sufficient specificity to guide us both in our literature review and in our design of the study. Based on the research question, we begin to look into the existing literature to see what is already known about the variables we wish to examine. A good way to begin is to conduct key-word searches of relevant/appropriate databases. Nowadays, one can also get a good jump-start using Google or some other internet search engine. Eventually, we will get to the original articles, which in turn can provide additional leads in the references. After much time and thought, we become ready to frame our research hypothesis—a tentative answer to the research question. The next step is to plan, or design, our study.

Designing a Study

Many issues must be considered when designing a research study. Among the questions we must ask ourselves are: (1) who will be studied, (2) how will we obtain a sample, (3) what constructs will be studied, (4) how will the constructs be measured, (5) what kind of study will we conduct (experimental, quasi-experimental, observational), (6) how will we implement the study, (7) what statistics will be used to analyze our data, and (8) how will we interpret/generalize our results?

First, we have to decide what elements or cases we wish to study. These cases may be children, teachers, schools, newspapers, etc. Once we make this initial decision, then we must identify the collection of elements to which we wish to generalize. In other words, do we want to be able to make inferences to all schools in our state public school system? Do we want to make inferences to all newspapers owned by Knight-Ridder? This collection is called a population. Usually, we study a subset of the population, known as a sample. At this point, we must also decide what methods will be used to obtain the sample and what aspects of the elements we want to study. In short, we must identify what constructs we will study, how the constructs will be defined in terms of observable variables, and will the variables will be measured.

Next we must determine the conditions under which we will collect our data. Will we conduct an experiment, a quasi-experiment, or an observational study? Will we conduct a cross-sectional or longitudinal study? Much time is devoted to the design of the study. A part of the design should include specifying the procedures for conducting the study, particularly with regard to quality control. The more people involved (cases, colleagues, graduate assistants, data collectors, etc.), the more likely it is that something will go wrong. Checks need to be made at every step of data management. One of us can remember when the results of a final statistical analysis showed that, at the end of a preschool intervention, the children participating in the program had an average "readiness score" of just over 37. That would have been fantastic were it not for the fact that the measure employed used a stanine scale, which runs from one to nine!

Once the data have been collected and verified, they are analyzed using the appropriate statistical tests. Generally, the statistical analyses will be such that they allow one to make reasonable statements about the population based on the information available in the sample. That is, the data are examined using procedures that address the research question(s) and that are appropriate for the nature of the data collected. If the research questions are basically descriptive in nature, then one would emphasize using statistics that address certain aspects of the numbers, such as where the values tend to center, how much they differ from one another, and what is the overall shape of the collection of numbers. If the research questions address hypotheses, then the process is one of looking for patterns in the numbers to assess whether there is anything more than "random noise." Sometimes people classify statistical analyses into *descriptive statistics* and *inferential statistics*. Descriptive statistics are employed when we simply want to (literally) describe one or more of the characteristics of the data at hand. For example, where do the values tend to center? How far apart are the scores from one another or what is the spread? We may also want to describe the shape of the set of scores. Is it symmetric or not? Does the distribution tend to resemble one of the mathematical models we know? Essentially, we are only interested in the data that are available to us. In contrast, often the data available to us consist of a sample from some larger population. We want to use the data that are available to make reasonable conjectures (inferences) about the greater population. In this context, the tools and techniques that we employ are often labeled as inferential statistics.

The last step in the research process is interpreting the results of the statistical analyses. To what extent can the results be generalized to other situations: other cases, other settings, other constructs, or other time frames? One must be very careful not to generalize beyond the data—to populations not sampled, to constructs not measured, or to values of measures that are beyond the limits of that which was measured.

As you can see, several of the steps taken to ensure high-quality research do not involve statistics at all. Some statistical issues arise in selecting or developing measures of our variables, and, of course, statistical issues are involved in the analysis of the data. However, much of the hard work is just good thinking! It is important to keep in mind that a chain is only as strong as its weakest link. If the thinking processes are not done well, one cannot expect statistics to solve the problem.

The remainder of this chapter is devoted to the issues of sampling, measurement, and definitions, along with a very brief history of statistics. In Chapter 2, we will begin our more formal treatment of statistics.

POPULATIONS, SAMPLES, AND SAMPLING TECHNIQUES

Populations

A population may be conceptualized as the universe to which we want to generalize. We may wish to study the relationship between *sense of school belonging* and *achievement* in publicly supported middle schools in the United States. In this example, we would likely think of all students currently enrolled in middle schools in the United States as the population to which we wish to generalize. In an ideal world, we could look at all such children. However, studying the entire population is not feasible. In all likelihood, we would study a subset of middle school students. If the three authors of this text were going to design such a study, for example, it is highly likely that we would look at students in the central Piedmont area of North Carolina and the Tampa Bay area of Florida. At this point, we have the ideal population of all children and the realistic population in the two regions mentioned. We may refer to these as the Target Population and the Accessible Population. In order to gain access to students, Bill and Barbara might solicit school districts in central North Carolina, and John might contact school districts in the Tampa Bay area. Realistically, not all of the districts contacted would be willing to participate. At this point, you should begin to understand that the "willing population" is a subset of the Target Population, and not necessarily a representative one. Finally, not all of the "willing population" will actually provide data. Some assessment of representativeness must be made in determining the degree to which the results of our study can be generalized.

Samples

Samples are subsets of populations. There are several reasons why one might want to work with a sample. One reason is that some populations are simply not accessible, or feasible. For example, if we wanted to study the population of students in transition to secondary schools, the cost of collecting data on each and every one of them would be prohibitive. Another reason for using a sample which is related to the issue of the size of the data set is that it has been shown that one often can obtain a more accurate assessment of a population with a sample of manageable size rather than an attempted census of the population. The basic issue is one of quality control or attention to detail. The larger the data file, the more likely it is that more people will be involved. The more people involved, the more likely that errors of communication and transcription will occur. A third reason for sampling is one of practicality. For example, suppose a manufacturer of incandescent light bulbs wishes to estimate the number of hours their bulbs will burn. One approach would be to burn every bulb until it burned out. However, that would leave zero bulbs to sell, drastically reducing profits.

There are many ways to obtain a sample from a population. These will be described in the next section. But first, it is important to note that a given collection of measurements may be one researcher's population and another researcher's sample. For example, the students enrolled in our classes this semester are our populations from an instructional perspective. At the same time, these students could be considered samples of the students currently enrolled at our universities.

As you will come to see later in the text, one of the goals of statistics is to describe collections of measurements. We use the letter Y as a generic name for our variables. Thus, Y could stand for *IQ*, *GPA*, *motivation*, *attitude toward school*, etc. As noted previously, when we describe a collection of measures, we usually want to look at where the scores tend to be located (central tendency), how far apart they are from one another (dispersion or spread), and shape. Although we will offer a more formal treatment later, we would assume that all of you are familiar with the arithmetic average. In statistics, we call the arithmetic average the *mean*. When describing the dispersion of a set of scores, we tend to use a measure called a *standard deviation*, also to be more completely explained in a later chapter. Quite simply, our point at this time is that distributions of scores can be described in terms of location, spread, and shape. When we are describing populations, we refer to these characteristics as *parameters*; when describing the same characteristics in a sample, we refer to them as *statistics*. That is, parameters are characteristics of populations; statistics are characteristics of samples. We also distinguish between populations and samples in our notation. To represent parameters, we use Greek lower-case letters; when representing statistics, we use Roman Latin alphabetic characters. All of this verbiage is summarized in Figure 1.1.

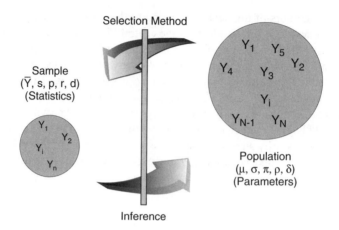

FIGURE 1.1   A conceptual diagram of the population–sample distinction, with notation.

Assuming that we are working with a sample of data drawn from a population, we are going to make conclusions based on what we see in the sample that we hope will be true for the population. Thus, on the right we have our population of scores, Y. To be able to refer to specific cases, we use subscripting notation. Thus, we use Y_i to refer to the ith case. There are N cases in the population, so i can take on any value from 1 to N. Thus, the first case in our population would be identified as Y_1, the second case as Y_2, the third case as Y_3, and so on until we have exhausted all of the cases in our population. In a sample, which is drawn from the population using one of several different sampling methods, there are n cases. Characteristics that we might want to describe in the population are the mean, the standard deviation, a proportion, a correlation or an association between two variables, or a difference between two values. The symbols we use for these are μ, σ, π, ρ, and δ, respectively. These are pronounced "mew," "sigma," "pi," "rho," and "delta." The corresponding symbols for the characteristics of a sample are $\bar{Y}$ (read as Y-bar), s, p, r, and d.

Sampling Techniques

Several methods have been developed for selecting a sample. Among them are simple random sampling, stratified sampling, cluster sampling, systematic sampling, deliberate sampling, and convenience sampling. Of course, when attempting to learn something about a population based on the information available in a sample, one would hope that the sample would be representative of the population. Before we describe several sampling techniques, we will more formally define some sampling terminology.

Sampling Terminology

When statisticians describe their sampling techniques, they employ what appears to be some jargon. Among the words they use are "element," "population," "sampling units," "sampling frames," and "sample."

Element. An element is an object or case, the unit on which a measurement is made. The unit might be an individual child, a classroom, or a school.

Population. The population is a collection of elements about which we wish to make an inference. The population could refer to all third-graders in the USA, all public kindergarten classrooms in the southeast, or all schools in West Virginia.

Sampling units. The sampling units are non-overlapping collections of elements in the population. For example, schools, which are collections of students, may be the sampling units in a study.

Sampling frame. The sampling frame is a list of the elements or, for more complex samples, a list of the sampling units.

Sample. A sample is a subset of the elements drawn from the population using one of several sampling methods.

In the next section, we describe several methods for drawing a sample from a population.

Simple Random Sampling

A random sample is sometimes defined as a sample in which all possible elements have an equal chance of occurring. While that is true, it is not a sufficient definition. The real definition of a random sample is that *all possible subsets have an equal chance of occurring.* For a simple example, suppose we have a population of eight elements and that we want to draw a sample of three elements. The possible subsets are (1, 2, 3), (1, 2, 4), (1, 2, 5), (1, 2, 6), (1, 2, 7), (1, 2, 8), (1, 3, 4), (1, 3, 5), etc. There are actually 56 different possibilities, and with simple random sampling, each of those 56 different subsets has an equal chance of becoming the sample selected. Although a random sample is the best way to ensure that a sample is representative, it is important to remember that any given random sample is not necessarily representative; it is simply a random sample. Bad random samples can (and do) happen.

Simple random sampling can be described as the statistical equivalent of drawing names out of a hat. However, it is usually done with a table of random numbers that has been generated by a computer algorithm. Basically, a computer is programmed to generate a sequence of the digits from zero up to, and including, nine, in such a way that each digit has an equal likelihood of occurring, regardless of the previous digit. Actually, the numbers are pseudo-random numbers, as the sequence will repeat after some large number of digits, perhaps 100,000,000. The sequence of digits is organized into a table such as Table A1 in Appendix A. Such tables are usually organized in columns of four or five digits. The columns have no purpose other than to make it easy to use the table. One enters the table, starting anywhere and going in any direction. For example, imagine that you have a population of 500 elements and that you want to draw a random sample of 15 cases. After numbering the elements from one to 500, you would enter the table after specifying a row and column. Look at column four and row 11. You should see "52636." Given that our population is 500 elements, it takes three digits to number all of the cases. Thus, we must read numbers from the table, three digits at a time. You could start with 526, but this case does not appear in the population. No problem. Go on to the right to 364. Note that we skip over the space as though it is not there. That element would be the first case to be sampled. Next, you see the sequence going 154, 052, 667, 492, 722, 470, etc. You would continue until you had read 15 three-digit numbers that were contained in the enumeration of the population.

As you will soon see, simple random sampling can be used in conjunction with other sampling techniques. It is the basic sampling technique that is assumed by most statistical techniques; however, most studies do not really obtain simple random samples. The implications of violating this assumption will be discussed later in this text.

Stratified Sampling

Although simple random sampling is generally considered the best way to ensure that a sample is representative of the population, there are those for whom that assurance is not sufficient. Researchers may want to be more certain that the sample is similar to the population with respect to some variable such as ethnicity. In this instance, they would use ethnicity as a stratification variable. There are two types of stratified sampling: stratified constant and stratified proportional. Although both of them employ stratification of the population on one or more variables (e.g., ethnicity or gender), they have different purposes.

STRATIFIED CONSTANT SAMPLING   Let's say that we have a population that has been stratified according to ethnicity, with 45% White, 30% African American, 20% Hispanic or Latino, and 5% Asian. In order to be certain that we had a sufficient number of Asians in the sample, we might want to over-sample that stratum. In addition, when employing some statistical procedures that allow us to compare groups, it is advantageous to have the same number of cases in each group. Thus, we might decide to employ stratified constant sampling so that a sample of 100 cases would include the same number of cases from each group. Four separate sampling frames would be constructed, and simple random sampling would be used to select 25 elements from each ethnic group or frame.

STRATIFIED PROPORTIONAL SAMPLING   Given the same population we just described, it might be our goal to describe some characteristic of the population, such as "attitude toward immigration." In this case, it would be in our best interest for the sample to represent the population. Thus, to obtain a sample of 100 cases, we would randomly select 45 Whites, 30 African Americans, 20 Hispanics, and five Asians, each from their respective stratum. In passing, we should note that experts in sampling technology can provide sampling weights associated with each case that will allow researchers to model different populations.

Cluster Sampling

Although simple random sampling may be the best way to ensure a representative sample, it is not very efficient from a logistical perspective. Suppose that we wanted to draw a random sample of children enrolled in first-grade in Florida. If we employed simple random sampling, we would probably have to devote a very large portion of the budget for travel expenses, as we would probably be collecting data from children all over the state. To make better use of our resources, we might employ cluster sampling. This method involves drawing our sample in several stages. First, we might draw a random sample of 12 school districts in Florida, after which we might draw a random sample of three schools within each district. Then, within each of the schools we would draw a random sample of two classrooms, and finally, a random sample of eight children from each classroom. Such samples are sometimes described as "complex samples." More and more often, large national studies (e.g., High School and Beyond (HSB), National Education Longitudinal Study (NELS), Early Childhood Longitudinal Study (ECLS)) are using this sampling technique. Analysis of such samples should be done with "multi-level" models, which are beyond the scope of this book. Unfortunately, many researchers are accessing these large databases and using statistical analyses that are appropriate for simple random samples. Here again, we make the case that quantitative researchers need to know a lot about statistical methods. The basic problem is that many of the formulae used in statistical procedures are based on the assumption that the measurements are independent of one another. Children within a particular school are more similar to other children in that school than they are to children in a different school. Furthermore, if data are collected on several students in the same classroom, those students are all subject to influences from the teacher, the room, etc. When this happens, our calculations are inaccurate and biased in favor of finding results that appear to be systematic; but they are not! In such situations, one should complete analyses using multi-level analyses or hierarchical linear models. Such analyses are beyond the scope of this book, but we will describe this approach in Chapter 18.

Systematic Sampling

Many researchers will use a list that enumerates the elements in the population, enter the list at random, and then select every jth case. For example, imagine that we have a population of 1000 elements and we want to obtain a sample of 100 cases. We would start anywhere in the list and select every tenth case. This technique is called systematic sampling. Unfortunately, this sample cannot be described as a random sample, although some researchers do so in error. This technique does not allow all possible subsets to have an equal chance of occurring. Indeed, adjacent elements can never be in the same sample. This procedure might result in a random sample if the cases appear on the list in a random order, but this rarely happens. This technique is frequently employed with the phone book, but therein names are listed alphabetically, not randomly.

Deliberate/Purposive Sampling

Sometimes, researchers do not select their samples at random. Rather, they select cases to study because they are of particular interest. This approach is usually employed in case study research. Some researchers, for example, will select cases that they believe will make it particularly difficult to confirm their hypothesis, thinking that their findings will be all the more impressive if their hypotheses are supported by the data.

Convenience Sampling

In actuality, convenience sampling is probably the most frequently employed sampling technique. Departments of psychology use undergraduates who must participate in one or more studies to obtain a grade in the introductory course. Introductory journalism and communication students are often used for experiments evaluating attitudes toward the media and advertising. Education professors often collect data in schools where they know the teachers or the principal, or have some other key contact. While this method of sampling may be convenient, and the only possibility in some studies with limited resources, there are serious limitations to one's ability to generalize to the population of interest based on such data.

Sampling Summary

In conclusion, deciding how to draw a sample from a population can be difficult. There are many methods to consider, each of them having its own advantages and disadvantages. The interested student may want to read more about sampling in texts devoted entirely to this topic (e.g., Henry, 1990; Kish, 1965; Levy & Lemeshow, 1999). The techniques actually used have an effect on the ways in which we analyze our data and the generalizations that we can make. Assuming that we devise an appropriate sampling plan, the next step is to select the variables that will define the constructs we wish to study.

VARIABLES

The fundamental purpose of research is to understand individual differences. That is, why are the elements in the population different from one another on some trait of interest? For example, why do some children come to school more ready to learn than others (*school readiness*)? Why do children of the same age differ with respect to their level of *social development*? The traits in which we are interested can be defined as variables, or traits that differ from case to case. Variables can be classified along a number of dimensions.

Independent versus Dependent Variables

The variables that we are interested in understanding are generally called *dependent variables*. The variables that we want to use as "explaining" variables are called *independent variables*. In a true experiment, the independent variables are under the control of the researcher and are manipulated. In contrast, in correlational studies, there is no manipulation of variables. In a correlational study, we might think of *school readiness* as the dependent variable and the *quality of the preschool experience* as the independent variable. Experiments and non-experiments differ in the degree to which we can conclude that a relationship is causal versus correlational; experiments provide a stronger basis for inferring causation.

Qualitative versus Quantitative Variables

At this point in our text, we will label variables that are categorical in nature as *qualitative*. Examples are gender, ethnicity, region of residence, and such. We may use numbers to label the categories, but the numbers have no numeric meaning. Thus, we shall refer to them as numerals, rather than numbers. In contrast, there are variables in which the numbers do have numeric meaning. These variables are labeled *quantitative variables*. We will explain this distinction in greater detail later in this chapter.

Discrete versus Continuous Variables

Not all quantitative variables are the same. A distinction can be made between *discrete* and *continuous* variables. Discrete variables are those where the possible values can assume only certain values, usually the counting numbers. Examples include number of siblings, number of automobiles owned, and number of books written. Other variables such as ability, height, and motivation are considered to be continuous in that there are an infinite number of possible values, limited only by the precision of our measurement.

We feel that this distinction is somewhat over-rated. In practice, we often treat discrete variables as though they are continuous. For example, we might find that the average number of siblings is 1.35. Do you know any child with 1.35 siblings? On the other hand, when we measure continuous variables, we put limits on the precision of our measurement. Thus, we might measure height to the nearest inch, and, as a consequence, we now have a finite number of possible values that can occur.

DEFINING THE CONSTRUCTS AND SELECTING THE VARIABLES

Much research in education and other social sciences is concerned with constructs, or underlying processes that we cannot directly observe. For example, we may wish to study the relationship between *attachment to school* and *academic achievement* in fifth-graders. But what do we mean by these labels? First, we must come up with working definitions of these constructs, often based on what other researchers have done previously. We may also come up with new definitions of the constructs. In either case, we must decide upon the variables that we can observe, from which we will make inferences about our constructs. For example, what items can we present to the students that will tell us something about their levels of achievement? What behaviors can we observe that will tell us something about the degree to which they are attached to school (*school attachment*)? That is, what observable variables will be used to assess the underlying constructs? Our decisions will, in part, affect the definitions of our constructs.

Measuring our Variables

Quantitative research involves the analysis of numbers, but where do the numbers come from? Somehow we need a way to translate our observations to meaningful numerals. The process of doing so is called *measurement*, typically defined as the operation of assigning numerals to characteristics of objects/cases, using an established rule. First, it is important to note that we measure characteristics, or attributes, of the cases, not the cases themselves. Thus, a measure of your weight is not you; it is a measure of the gravitational attraction between your body and the Earth. Similarly, your score on the quantitative portion of the Graduate Record Exam is not you; it is a measure of your ability to think quantitatively and to perform quantitative manipulations. Most importantly, the numerals are assigned according to a rule. When the first author was in elementary school, the teachers carried around a multi-purpose tool known as the ruler. Did you ever wonder why it was called such a thing? Most likely, that tool was called a "ruler" because it was the embodiment of the rule for assigning numeric values to the attribute of length. Serendipity aside, it also allowed the teacher to "rule" the classroom!

As mentioned, measurement adheres to rules. Rules for measurement differ in their nature, leading to measures that differ in the nature of the resulting numerals. These rules can be classified into categories based on the qualities of the measures, or scales, that result. There have been many such category systems devised, but the most widely used system is the one defined by Stevens (1946, 1951). Stevens defined four levels of measurement: *nominal, ordinal, interval,* and *ratio*.

Nominal Scales

Nominal scales assign numerals to categories or classes. Examples are scales that measure gender, political party preference, ethnicity, religious denomination, manufacturer of automobile driven or preferred weekly news magazine. To measure gender, we might assign the numerals "1" to females and "2" to males. The numerals are merely labels and have absolutely no numeric meaning; we cannot say that males have more gender than females.

Another example of a nominal scale of measurement is the numbers on football uniforms. The numbers on the jerseys generally are assigned according to the position played. Quarterbacks usually have numbers that are single-digit or in the teens. Running backs and defensive backs are usually numbered in the twenties, thirties, and forties. Offensive centers and defensive linebackers are assigned numbers in the fifties. Guards and tackles are assigned numbers in the sixties and seventies, respectively. Ends usually have numbers in the eighties and nineties. Thus, the players' numbers are really only numerals, indicating the position played. Thus we are limited in how we can process the values. It would make no sense to think of averaging a quarterback and a defensive end, resulting in a linebacker.

Ordinal Scales

Ordinal scales are regarded as being a higher level of measurement than nominal scales. With ordinal scales, the numerals actually have numeric meaning. Generally, larger numbers indicate more of the attribute. For example, suppose your instructor wanted to measure the physical stature of the students in your statistics class. The instructor could ask all of you to line up against a wall and then sort you visibly by height, from shortest to tallest. After ordering you, you would then be assigned a "height" of 1, 2, 3, etc., according to your position in the line. Based on this system of measurement, we can say that a "5" has more height than a "4," but we don't know how much more height. An example of an ordinal scale in educational assessment is "percentile rank." Some standardized tests report the results in terms of percentile ranks, which range from 1 to 99. A child with a percentile rank of 81 scored as high as or higher than 81 out of every 100 children in the group on which the test was normed.

Interval Scales

To describe interval scales, we will continue with the previous example of measuring physical stature. Imagine that the class is still lined up against the wall, in order of height. Rather than assigning integers indicating rank, suppose that the instructor defined the shortest person (P_1) as a reference point, assigning that person a height of 0. Using a ruler, the instructor determines that the second person (P_2) in line is one-quarter inch taller than the first person. P_2 would be assigned a height of ¼. The third person (P_3) was found to be ½ inch taller than P_2, so P_3's height would be ¾, etc. The measurements made so far would be as follows: $P_1 = 0$, $P_2 = ¼$, $P_3 = ¾$. When the measurement process was complete, we would have a scale with the following properties. Larger numbers would indicate more height. For example, if P_7 had a height of 2, P_{12} had a height of 4, and P_{16} had a height of 6, we could say that the difference between P_{12} and P_7 ($4 - 2 = 2$) is the same as the difference between P_{16} and P_{12} ($6 - 4 = 2$); a difference of two is the same, anywhere on the scale. This property is not characteristic of ordinal scales.

Although interval-level scales convey substantially more information than do ordinal scales, they do have limits. Thus, in the example above in which P_7 had a height of 2 and P_{12} had a height of 4, we *cannot* say that P_{12} is twice as tall as P_7. That is, it is not appropriate to form ratios of interval-level measures and interpret them.

Ratio Scales

Ratio scales may be viewed as interval scales with one additional property—the value of "0" is a true, or absolute zero, rather than an arbitrary one. Thus, 0 really does mean the absence of the attribute. Ratio scales in the social sciences are rare. In the physical sciences, measures of length, weight, and time have true zero points.

Keep in mind that the variables being measured exist independent of the measures used. That is, a scale of measurement is not inherent in the variable. Consider the variable of temperature. Measured on the Fahrenheit scale, we are not really sure what a value of zero indicates other than 32 degrees below the temperature at which water freezes. Measured on the centigrade scale, zero is the temperature at which water freezes. Thus, both of these scales can be considered to be interval-level scales. However, if temperature is measured on the Kelvin scale, zero really does mean "zero" in the sense that it reflects a condition of minimum molecular energy. It is not possible to go any lower.

Scales of Measurement in the Social Sciences

As noted above, ratio scales of measurement are quite unusual in the social sciences. However, we would argue that interval-level scales are not that common either. Consider the measurement of intelligence (IQ). Individual measures of IQ, such as the Weschler and Stanford–Binet scales, might be considered to be some of the most psychometrically sophisticated measures in the social sciences. If these scales are truly interval, then the difference in intelligent behavior for a child with an IQ of 100 and another child with an IQ of 75 should be the same as the behavioral difference between a child with an IQ of 150 and another with an IQ of 175. Ask a teacher. Most teachers would perceive the difference between 100 and 75 to be a lot larger than the difference between 150 and 175.

Implications of Measurement Scale for Statistics

When Stevens (1946, 1951) developed his topology of measurement scales, he introduced the notion of "permissible operations." That is, given the amount of numeric information provided by the different scales, some mathematical operations were deemed not appropriate. We have already noted the problems with calculating and interpreting ratios with interval scales. However, Stevens went further, suggesting that the level of measurement dictated the type of statistical analyses that one could perform. Thus, we find statements to the effect that one must have at least an interval level scale in order to employ *parametric* statistics (e.g., z-tests, t-tests, and analysis of variance, all of which will be presented later in the book). With ordinal scales, we are told we should employ *non-parametric* statistics or rank-order statistics. Among social scientists, you will find widespread disagreement on this issue.

Although the two specialties have much in common, we find it helpful to make a distinction between *measurement* and *statistics*. The discipline of measurement is most concerned with the rules for assigning numerals that reflect meaningful differences in reality. (For an entertaining example, see Lord (1953).) On the other hand, statistics can be divided into two subdomains: *descriptive* statistics and *inferential* statistics. The domain of descriptive statistics has much in common with measurement, in that it is important to be able to provide meaningful summaries of data. In our opinion, inferential statistics is different. The domain of inferential statistics is concerned with the differentiation between systematic patterns and random (non) patterns in data. If one examines the mathematical statistics literature that details the derivation of inferential statistical procedures, such as analysis of variance, one will not find any mention of scale of measurement. Rather, one will find that such statistical procedures make some assumptions about the distributions of the scores (spread and shape), but nothing about scale of measurement.

We take the position that the statistician must take the responsibility for determining whether the statistical procedures can be appropriately applied to a set of data. The statistician must also take responsibility for the validity of the interpretation based on the results of the analysis. As noted above, under certain conditions, it may be appropriate to statistically analyze nominal measures. That is, one could look at football jersey numbers to see if they differed systematically according to position played. They do. On the other hand, one may wind up making totally erroneous conclusions based on the analysis of ordinal data.

For example, back in the 1960s, the state of Florida required that all graduating seniors take the Florida Twelfth-Grade Exam. The exam consisted of five subtests (e.g., language arts, mathematics), with each subtest being scored on a percentile rank scale. The five scores were summed and the total was used by the state university system as a part of the admission process. To be admitted to the University of Florida in Gainesville, an applicant needed to present a score of 300 or higher. So far, we are on firm ground, even though we have added ordinal numbers, something proscribed by Stevens. Now the trouble begins.

In the early 1970s, educational accountability was gaining momentum across the nation, and Florida was no exception. A state legislator asked statisticians in the state department of education to analyze the Twelfth-Grade Placement scores, specifically to provide the average.

Keep in mind that the five subtests were each scored on a percentile rank scale. These scales are such that there is the same number of cases at each score. Distributions of this type are sometimes called *uniform* distributions. Also keep in mind that the lowest possible total would be five (assuming five scores of 1) and the highest possible score would be 495 (assuming five scores of 99). It turned out that the state average was very close to 250. The legislator reasoned that, given that the highest possible score was 495, the schools were only teaching half of the material. Actually what he had discovered was that one-half of the graduating seniors were below the state median, where the median is the point that divides a distribution into two equal parts. However, his argument was instrumental in establishing the need for accountability for the public schools in Florida. Perhaps the right decision, but for the wrong reason.

Assessing the Goodness of our Measures

At some point, decisions will have to be made about how we will measure our variables. We will either select from existing measures, or we will need to create our own measures. In either case, an important question will need to be addressed: How do we know whether our measures are any good? To answer this question, there are two issues to consider: how *reliable* is the measure, and is it *valid*?

Reliability

The reliability of measurements is usually expressed as a number between zero and one that indicates the degree to which the variability we observe with the measure is based on "true" differences on the trait or on random error. The reliability of the measurements can be conceptualized as the degree to which the measure provides consistent results. To illuminate this concept, we shall present the rudiments of classical test theory. In classical test theory, the value that we observe is thought to be made up of two components: the true score and random error. In formula form, we say:

$$O_i = T_i + E_i \tag{1.1}$$

That is, for the ith individual, the observed value (O) is equal to the true score (T) plus random error (E). Estimating the reliability of the measurements entails trying to ascertain how much of the variation in the values of O is due to variation in the values of T, and how much is due to variation in the values of E. The traditional symbol for the reliability of some measure Y is r_{yy}. Then, we say that the reliability of the measurements is:

$$r_{yy} = \frac{\text{Variation in true scores}}{\text{Variation in observed scores}} \tag{1.2}$$

If we use σ^2 as the symbol for variation, we write this expression as:

$$r_{yy} = \frac{\sigma_T^2}{\sigma_O^2} \tag{1.3}$$

In either form, one can think of the scores produced by a measure as reliable to the degree to which the individual differences that we observe are due to real differences, rather than random errors that occur in the measurement process.

Once again, a measurement that is reliable is one that is consistent. However, the consistency may be assessed over time, over forms, over raters, etc. Thus, we might expect that a measurement has more than one reliability. We should also note that whatever form of reliability we use, measurements may be reliable for some groups but not for others. That is, reliability is "population specific." Among the types of reliability are test–retest reliability, alternate form reliability, inter-rater reliability, and internal consistency.

ACROSS TIME   If we expect that a construct is relatively constant over time, then we would expect that two administrations of the measure at two different time points would provide scores that, when ranked, would put the objects in the same ordinal position at both time points. This form of reliability is called *test–retest reliability*. One of the major decisions to be made in assessing this type of stability is the length of the time interval between the two administrations of the measure.

ACROSS FORMS   Another form of reliability is *alternative-form* or *parallel-form reliability*. This type of reliability is particularly appropriate for measures that have multiple forms, such as standardized achievement tests, the SAT, the Graduate Record Exam, etc. One would want test scores to be consistent across forms, and not a function of the particular form that was administered.

ACROSS TIME AND FORMS   Essentially, this assessment of reliability involves the administration of two different forms, one at Time 1 and the other at Time 2. This is a very stringent assessment of reliability.

SPLIT-HALF   The three different types of reliability described above all involve two waves of data collection. There may be occasions in which two different forms are not available, or we don't have time to wait to assess the trait at a second time. Confronted with such constraints, some researchers turn to another form of reliability, known as *split-half reliability*. One divides the test into two separate tests; one might designate the even-numbered items to constitute one form and the odd-numbered items to constitute the second form. The consistency of the scores on the two subtests would then be assessed. It is important to be aware that the reliability of the measures generated by a test is related to the length of the test. That is, reliability estimates with short tests tend to be lower than those with longer tests. Thus, after assessing the consistency between the two "half tests," one should use a correction to estimate the reliability for the whole test. One such correction is the Spearman–Brown Prophecy Formula. As the name suggests, however, this procedure may be problematic in practice as there are some rather restrictive assumptions that need to be made.

KUDER–RICHARDSON COEFFICIENTS   Given the difficulties of constructing parallel forms and/or administering a test at two time points, Kuder and Richardson (1937) devised a way to assess reliability using one administration of one form. In the derivation of their methods, they presented two formulae for estimating the reliability, or internal consistency, of a test. It just happened that these formulae were numbered 20 and 21 in the article. Thus, the two formulae have come to be known as KR-20 and KR-21. KR-20 estimates the inter-item consistencies and then employs the Spearman–Brown formula to estimate the reliability of the entire test. If one can assume that the items are of equal difficulty, then the formula KR-20 can be simplified to yield the formula for KR-21.

COEFFICIENT ALPHA   Cronbach (1951) developed a generalization of KR-20 that is quite popular today. It can be interpreted as the average of all possible split-half estimates of reliability. We believe that its popularity may stem from the fact that it is programmed into many of the widely used statistical packages available and that it requires only one test administration. However, we believe that it may not always be the most appropriate estimate of reliability in many contexts. For example, in a large-scale testing program such as the Graduate Record Exam, it is important to have several forms available. However, as a test taker, you would not want your score to be a function of the form you took. It is important that the different forms yield equivalent measurements. Cronbach's alpha provides no information on this issue.

Validity

The second criterion employed in the assessment of the "goodness" of scores generated by a measure is the validity of the scores, or the validity of the decisions that are based on the scores. Generally, the issue of validity may be considered to be the degree to which a measure assesses what it supposedly measures. As with reliability, a measure does not have a single validity coefficient. Rather, it has a validity coefficient for a specific purpose. Most researchers would agree that the validity of score interpretation is more important than reliability. However, it turns out that reliability is a necessary, but not sufficient, condition for validity. That is, if a measure does not provide scores that are consistent, then the scores cannot be validly interpreted. As with reliability, there are several different types of validity.

CONTENT VALIDITY   This type of validity is particularly appropriate for tests that measure achievement or aptitude. Any such test can be considered to contain a sample of items taken from the population of items, or the domain. The basic question is: How well does the sample of items represent the domain of items? This assessment is usually made by a panel of experts who carefully consider the items sampled in relation to the structure of the domain.

CRITERION-RELATED VALIDITY   For many measures, the validity is assessed by looking at the relationship between the scores and some criterion. *Predictive validity* looks at the relationship between a measure and some criterion in the future. For example, in constructing a measure of aptitude, one would want there to be a strong relationship between the aptitude scores and some measure of performance. This type of validity is particularly relevant in the context of personnel selection (e.g., hiring employees, admission to college) A second type of criterion-related validity is *concurrent validity*. This form of validity is appropriate when one would like to consider substituting one measure for another. For example, most psychologists would agree that the standard for the assessment of intelligence would be an individually administered test conducted by a qualified examiner. However, such individual assessments are quite expensive. Suppose one was interested in constructing an IQ test that consisted of ratings of five behaviors made by a classroom teacher. To assess the validity of score interpretations for this measure, one would want to compare the scores from an individual IQ test to the ratings made by the teacher.

  With either of these forms of criterion-related validity, there is a common problem. The use of either predictive or concurrent validity must assume that the external criterion produces valid score interpretations. This assumption is, in practice, often difficult to justify.

CONSTRUCT VALIDITY   How well does a measure assess a specific construct such as anxiety? This is the fundamental question for construct validity, a question not easily answered. Assessing the construct validity of measurements actually involves building a logical argument over time, an argument that involves other forms of validity. The case for construct validity is made using evidence of content validity, criterion related validity, experimental results, etc.

In summary, we have tried to provide an introduction or overview of measurement. Although this book is focused on statistics, or the analysis of data, one cannot report the results of such analyses without considering the processes that generated the data. There are a number of references to which we refer the interested student. Among them are Campbell and Fiske (1959), Crocker and Algina (1986), McDonald (1999), Messick (1989), Osterlind (2006), Shepard (1993), and Thorkildsen (2005).

A BRIEF HISTORY OF STATISTICS

As a part of the study of a discipline, we think that it is important that students have some historical background. We have prepared a brief overview of the historical development of statistical methods. Because it introduces some, as yet, undefined terms, we have placed it in an Appendix 1.1 at the end of this chapter.

Uses of the Word "Statistics"

One of the first difficulties confronted by students beginning their study of statistics is that the word is used in many different ways. First, "statistics" can mean raw data. Have you even been in a heated discussion with someone who asked you for your statistics? They are asking to see your data, the information on which you are building your argument.

In a second sense, "statistics" are summaries of raw data. That is, statistics are estimates of parameters. We sometimes refer to these as descriptive statistics. A third use of the word "statistics" refers to the techniques for drawing conclusions about populations based on descriptive statistics from sample data. Here, we could use the term "inferential statistics" to refer to the rules and procedures for drawing reasonable conclusions from sample data. Finally, "statistics" may be used to refer to the discipline of mathematical statistics, in which statisticians derive new methods and models based on distribution and mathematical theory.

PLAN FOR THE BOOK

Building on topics we have discussed in this introductory chapter, we have structured this book in a manner that we hope will facilitate your learning and understanding about statistical methods. The first major section of the book will cover ways to describe raw data. That is, given a long list of numeric values, what does the set of numbers look like? From the original list, it is very difficult to know. Thus, we will describe ways in which the numbers can be processed to enable a meaningful perception of the numbers. This technique will include constructing frequency distributions and depicting them in both tabular and graphic forms. We will then present methods to further describe characteristics of the data, including location, spread, and shape. We will also present techniques for looking at the properties of the relationship between two variables. In particular, we will look at both the strength and nature of the relationship.

The second section of the book will present the fundamental tools for drawing inferences from sample data. This material will include a basic, intuitive presentation of probability theory, an examination of some important probability distributions, and the logic of statistical inference.

The third section of the book will deal with applications of statistical methods to study characteristics of the data. These methods will allow us to study location and dispersion of one variable, along with the association between two variables. Then we will present methods for comparing distributions of variables. For example, we might want to compare the scores of males and females on a measure of motivation. The comparison could be made with respect to location or dispersion.

The organization of this book will be different from that of most introductory statistics books. The traditional approach is to present the parametric methods of making comparisons, followed by a section on non-parametric procedures. We are going to do it differently. For example, in our presentation of comparing two groups with respect to location, we will present the classic t-test and its variations. Within the same section, we will present the non-parametric counterpart (Mann–Whitney U-test), followed by randomization procedures (bootstrapping and permutation tests). This format will allow you to identify the appropriate technique to employ in your analysis by specifying (1) the concern/focus (location, spread, or association), (2) the number of groups, and (3) any important subissues, including the properties of your data.

EXPECTATIONS FOR STUDENTS

When you have completed your study of the material in this book, you should have a firm grasp of the basics of statistics and statistical reasoning. You will understand a wide variety of statistical techniques, be aware of the assumptions required to use a particular technique, and be able to select the particular technique best suited to your situation. Furthermore, you will have a working knowledge of how to compute a variety of statistical values, and be able to obtain them from a computer statistical package (e.g., R, SPSS, or SAS). Last, and perhaps most important, you will be able to make appropriate interpretations of statistical results as you consider the degree to which the data meet the assumptions of the technique employed. Furthermore, you will be able to communicate the results and interpretations to others.

And now, "let the wild rumpus start."

Key Terms

Accessible population	Observational study
Alternate-form reliability	Ordinal scale
Cluster sampling	Parameter
Concurrent validity	Population
Construct validity	Predictive validity
Content validity	Qualitative variable
Continuous variable	Quantitative variable
Cross-sectional study	Quasi-experimental study
Descriptive statistics	Ratio scale
Discrete variable	Research question
Experimental study	Sample
Inferential statistics	Simple random sample

Internal consistency
Interval scale
Longitudinal study
Nominal scale

Statistic
Stratified sampling
Target population
Test–retest reliability

PRACTICE QUESTIONS

1. A researcher finds that students using a structured form of cooperative learning tend to do better than those using an unstructured form. The researcher concludes that the structured form is more effective. Which of the following research designs would typically provide the strongest support for such a conclusion?

    a. Observational.
    b. Quasi-experimental.
    c. Experimental.

2. A teacher wants to summarize how well her students did on a social studies test, and is not interested in making conclusions about a larger population of students. What type of statistics is she likely to employ?

    a. Descriptive statistics.
    b. Inferential statistics.

3. The mean for a population is

    a. a statistic referred to as $\overline{Y}$
    b. a parameter referred to as $\overline{Y}$
    c. a statistic referred to as μ
    d. a parameter referred to as μ.

4. The mean for the sample is

    a. a statistic referred to as $\overline{Y}$
    b. a parameter referred to as $\overline{Y}$
    c. a statistic referred to as μ
    d. a parameter referred to as μ.

5. Suppose we are interested in making inferences about third-grade writing achievement in Florida based on the writing scores of a subgroup of students who participated in the study. The subgroup who participated is referred to as the

    a. sample
    b. population
    c. sample population.

6. Suppose we are interested in making inferences about third-grade writing achievement in Florida based on the writing scores of a subgroup of students who participated in the study. The third-graders in Florida about whom we wish to make inferences are referred to as the

    a. sample
    b. population
    c. sample population.

7. When all possible subsets have an equal chance of becoming the sample, the sample is referred to as a

   a. convenience sample
   b. deliberate sample
   c. simple random sample
   d. cluster sample.

8. Suppose participants in a study indicate their ethnicity, and the different ethnicities are assigned numerals (e.g., Hispanic = 1, White = 2, Black = 3, Asian = 4). Ethnicity has been measured on which scale of measurement?

   a. Nominal.
   b. Ordinal.
   c. Interval.
   d. Ratio.

9. If a researcher reports Cronbach's alpha, she is reporting an estimate of the

   a. test–retest reliability
   b. internal consistency reliability
   c. content validity
   d. criterion-related validity.

10. If a researcher presents evidence about how well the sample of items on a test represents the domain of items, the researcher is documenting

   a. test–retest reliability
   b. internal consistency reliability
   c. content validity
   d. criterion-related validity.

REFERENCES

Bernstein, P. L. (1996). *Against the gods: The remarkable story of risk*. New York: John Wiley & Sons.

Bunge, M. (1996). *Finding philosophy in social science*. New Haven, CT: Yale University Press.

Campbell, D. T., & Fiske, D. W. (1959). Convergent and discriminant validation by the multitrait–multimethod matrix. *Psychological Bulletin, 56*, 81–105.

Campbell, D. T., & Stanley, J. C. (1963). Experimental and quasi-experimental designs for research. Chicago, IL: Rand McNally.

Cook, T. D., & Campbell, D. T. (1979). *Quasi-experimentation: Design and analysis issues for field settings*. Chicago, IL: Rand McNally.

Cowles, M. (2001). *Statistics in psychology: An historical perspective*. Mahwah, NJ: Lawrence Erlbaum Associates.

Crocker, L.M., & Algina, J. (1986). *Introduction to classical & modern test theory*. New York: Holt, Rinehart and Winston.

Cronbach, L. J. (1951). Coefficient alpha and the internal structure of tests. *Psychometrika, 16*, 297–334.

Henry, G. T. (1990). *Practical sampling*. Newbury Park, CA: Sage.

Kuder, G. F., & Richardson, M. W. (1937). The theory of the estimation of test reliability. *Psychometrika, 2*, 151–160.

Johnson, N. L., & Kotz, S. (1997). *Leading personalities in statistical sciences: From the seventeen century to the present*. New York: John Wiley & Sons.

Keller, D. K. (2006). *The Tao of statistics: A path to understanding (with no math)*. Thousand Oaks, CA: Sage.

Kish, L. (1965). *Survey sampling*. New York: John Wiley & Sons.

Levy, P. S., & Lemeshow, S. (1999). *Sampling of populations: Methods and applications* (3rd ed.). New York: John Wiley & Sons.

Lord, F. M. (1953). On the statistical treatment of football numbers. *American Psychologist, 8*(12), 750–751.

McDonald, R. P. (1999). *Test theory: A unified treatment*. Mahwah, NJ: Lawrence Erlbaum.

Messick, S. (1989). Validity. In R. L. Linn (Ed.), *Educational measurement* (3rd ed., pp. 13–103). New York: American Council on Education/Macmillan.

Osterlind, S. J. (2006). *Modern measurement: Theory, principles, and applications of mental appraisal*. Upper Saddle River, NJ: Pearson Education.

Phillips, D. C., and Burbules, N. C. (2000). *Postpositivism and educational research*. Lanham, MD: Rowman & Littlefield.

Salsburg, D. (2001). *The lady tasting tea: How statistics revolutionized science in the twentieth century*. New York: W.H. Freeman.

Shadish, W. R., Cook, T. D. & Campbell, D. T. (2001). *Experimental and quasi-experimental designs for generalized causal inference*. Boston, MA: Houghton Mifflin.

Shepard, L. A. (1993). Evaluating test validity. *Review of Research in Education, 19*, 405–450.

Stevens, S. S. (1946). On the theory of scales of measurement. *Science, 103*, 677–680.

Stevens, S. S. (1951). Mathematics, measurement, and psychophysics. In S. S. Stevens (Ed.), *Handbook of experimental psychology* (pp. 1–49). New York: Wiley.

Stigler, S. M. (1986). *The history of statistics: The measurement of uncertainty before 1900*. Cambridge, MA: Belknap Press/Harvard University Press.

Thorkildsen, T. A. (2005). *Fundamentals of measurement in applied research*. Boston, MA: Pearson Allyn and Bacon.

APPENDIX 1.1: A BRIEF HISTORY OF STATISTICS

Earliest Uses

It is no accident that the word "statistics" appears similar to the word "state." Indeed, statistical procedures have been used since very early in the history of human beings. One can point to the Roman Empire to find evidence of statistical activity. The government needed records that would permit taxation. The statisticians of this era maintained census records, commerce records, etc. Currently, most states have some unit equivalent to a Bureau of Vital Statistics that maintains records that can be used for formulating governmental policies and planning action. This form of statistics is essentially descriptive.

We realize that, in the material that follows, we mention many statistical techniques that we have not yet defined. We hope that the material will be informative in the historical content, while at the same time creating some curiosity.

Developments in Mathematics and Probability

In the 1600s and 1700s, there were many mathematicians generating results that shaped the development of distribution theory and probability theory. In the mid-1600s, John Graunt (1620–1674), a haberdasher by trade, was among the first to try to predict future social phenomena from an interpretation of tables of data. Early in the 1700s, John Arbuthnot (1667–1735) examined birth records in London over an 82-year period, noting that the number of male births was consistently larger than the number of female births. He concluded that this record suggested something other than chance at work. Concerned with games of chance, Huygens (1629–1695) and Bernoulli (1654–1705) both published books laying the foundations of probability theory. Subsequently, Newton (1642–1727) derived the binomial expansion, $(p + q)^n$. Practical problems, resulting from large values of n, spurred work enabling the estimation of binomial probabilities. This work was completed by De Moivre (1667–1754) and Gauss (1777–1855), leading to the normal probability distribution. A Belgian astronomer, Quetelet (1796–1874), was among the first to show the relevance of the normal distribution for modeling real-world data. He showed that the distribution of the chest circumferences of French soldiers was roughly symmetric and bell shaped, essentially normal. Galton (1822–1911), a cousin of Charles Darwin, in studying heredity in sweet peas, laid the foundation of correlation and regression, techniques that allow us to examine the strength and nature of the relationship between two variables. He was assisted by Karl Pearson (1857–1922) in the development of the mathematical formulae.

At this point, the development of statistical methods appears to have proceeded in two directions. Those working in the area of mental measurement in the early 20th century (e.g., Spearman, Burt, and Thurstone) extended the development of correlation and regression, leading to the development of factor analysis. Fisher (1890–1962), working at an agricultural experimental station, developed statistical methods for analyzing data when the independent variables were categorical, or group membership. This work resulted in the development of analysis-of-variance (ANOVA), a technique particularly appropriate for experimentation. In reality, Fisher developed ANOVA to avoid the tedious calculations that were required for regression. Unfortunately, many researchers were under the impression that the two statistical threads (correlation/regression versus ANOVA) were two distinctly different models.

Statistics in the Modern Era

Although many of the statistical methods that we use today were developed in the 1920s and 1930s, one would be hard pressed to find actual applications of multiple regression, factor analysis, or analysis of multiple dependent variables before computers. Rather, one was more likely to find analyses using two-variable correlations, t-tests, and ANOVA. Without a doubt, the development of computer technology and the availability of high-speed computers have had a dramatic effect on the application of statistical methods. With faster computers came statistical packages such as the BMDP, SPSS, SAS, Systat, Stata, and R, to name a few. More recently we have statistical packages that will permit the analysis of structural equation models (e.g., LISREL, EQS, AMOS, and Mplus) and multilevel models (HLM, MLWin). As our capacity to employ these complex procedures has increased, we are more and more likely to find such techniques being reported in the research literature. Thus, it is imperative that researchers and professionals understand both the basics of statistical reasoning and the complexities of the analyses.

An even newer variety of statistics enabled by the computer revolution is that of bootstrapping, or resampling techniques. Rather than relying on the distributional assumptions required by classical statistical methods, we can use the computer to model the statistics that we want to study.

For those of you interested in learning more about the history of statistics, there are a number of sources we would recommend. A concise and very readable history of statistics in the social sciences is provided by Cowles (2001). A more mathematical orientation is given by Stigler (1986). An entertaining treatment with an anecdotal perspective can be found in Salsburg (2001). Bernstein (1996) has given yet another entertaining presentation, but with a broader social perspective, including financial applications. For a brief biography of many people important in the development of statistics, see Johnson and Kotz (1997).

Part II
DESCRIPTIVE STATISTICS

In the first chapter we presented a case for statistics as a useful tool in the interpretation of data in the social sciences. Hopefully, our case was convincing and you are still reading the book. As we noted earlier, statistics can be used in several different ways. One of the most important uses of statistics is in the description of data. For example, imagine a superintendent of a large school district who wanted to know how her sixth-graders had scored on this year's nationally standardized achievement test. It would be very difficult for her to make much sense—or draw any conclusions about the progress of her students—from a listing of several hundred scores. Instead, there are ways to process those scores and present the results in such a way that the superintendent easily can get the information that she wants. These methods are usually labeled as *descriptive statistics*. Generally, these methods involve transforming the data into forms that can be understood more easily. These forms include tables, graphs, and measures which summarize particular characteristics of the scores.

Chapter 2 deals with the methods typically used to transform a single set of scores into tables and graphs. The methods presented in this chapter are appropriate for use with data when the scores represent a meaningful numeric scale. In Chapter 3, we deal with the methods to further reduce the information into single measures, each of which summarizes a specific characteristic of a set of numeric values. The methods for preparing tables, graphs, and summary measures when dealing with categorical data are presented in Chapter 4. All of the methods presented in Chapters 2, 3, and 4 focus on the entire set of scores. At times, we may be interested in describing the position of a specific case within the set of scores; these techniques are presented in Chapter 5.

Often, we may have more than one score on each case, such as when we have some data that might have been collected when the students were still enrolled in high school (e.g., high-school Grade Point Average, rank in class, and SAT scores) and some data collected during the first year of college (e.g., number of hours completed and Grade Point Average). In these instances, we can employ the methods described in Chapters 2, 3, 4, and 5 to each of the variables, respectively. However, we can go even further: We can describe the relationships between variables. Chapters 6 and 7 present statistical methods for describing the relationship between two variables. Once again, these methods can result in tables, graphs, and summary measures.

Thus, Part II: Descriptive Statistics covers statistical methods for processing data in a variety of different contexts. These contexts differ in terms of whether we are describing one variable (univariate statistics) or two variables simultaneously (bivariate statistics). Furthermore, the variables may be quantitative or categorical. When we want to deal with three or more variables simultaneously, we use the term "multivariable statistics." In those instances where there are two or more dependent variables, we use the term "multivariate statistics." Both multivariable and multivariate statistics are certainly beyond the scope of this book. However, a brief overview of many of these techniques is presented in Chapter 18.

2

Describing Quantitative Data with Frequency Distributions

INTRODUCTION

This chapter describes methods for processing raw data, or data in its original form, into formats that lead to clearer interpretations. Although the human brain is an amazing data processor, it does have its limits.

As we work our way through this chapter, we will consider a case study in which researchers were interested in looking at the reading skills of children entering kindergarten. In particular, they were interested in the possibility of differences between White and African American children. They drew a random sample of 100 from the 1771 records for White children and a random sample of 100 from the 224 records for African American children in the Early Childhood Longitudinal Study Kindergarten – First Grade Public-Use Child File (ECLS-K) prepared especially for this book and focused on the standardized reading scores (T-scores) collected in fall of the kindergarten year. The complete data file is available on the book website and is described in the accompanying codebook. This is an example of stratified constant sampling.

The standardized reading scores for the two samples of students are presented in Tables 2.1 and 2.2. Looking at these two groups of scores, perhaps you can begin to appreciate the problems of trying to analyze raw data. It should be clear that we need to do something with these data in order to address the issue of possible differences between the two sets of scores. But what can we do? The remainder of this chapter will describe several statistical techniques that will allow us to construct frequency distributions and present the results in a variety of tabular and graphic formats. Frequency distributions can be constructed showing raw scores (*ungrouped frequency distributions*), or the raw scores can be grouped (*grouped frequency distributions*).

UNGROUPED FREQUENCY DISTRIBUTIONS

One of the first (and most simple) methods for processing our raw data is to construct frequency distributions for the sample scores of White and African American students. A frequency distribution is a listing of all possible values and the number of times that each value occurs. In order to construct a frequency distribution, there are a number of steps to follow.

Table 2.1 Standardized reading scores for a random sample of 100 White kindergarten students

54	59	66	54	58	48	79	38	47	45
50	47	64	51	51	68	50	49	59	47
51	47	65	52	50	54	69	57	60	49
58	52	41	58	61	59	62	57	50	37
59	49	48	41	64	64	41	45	39	51
38	64	55	66	46	64	51	49	65	63
52	52	48	64	41	55	59	68	63	47
52	51	64	59	52	44	61	57	53	56
67	65	45	50	34	58	56	48	46	84
63	54	51	50	53	43	61	52	53	55

Table 2.2 Standardized reading scores for a random sample of 100 African American kindergarten students

40	42	39	51	49	51	41	42	43	52
42	49	42	55	58	54	39	55	56	34
54	68	40	42	53	59	49	63	54	64
41	37	49	70	62	43	32	51	55	52
58	49	59	41	48	52	77	29	42	46
59	52	63	35	59	30	50	54	51	49
60	39	62	61	69	49	44	61	47	41
51	59	38	37	60	42	61	39	54	62
49	48	55	42	41	64	63	53	61	48
51	47	52	38	48	50	52	51	50	64

The first step in the process is to identify both the largest and the smallest values in the set of scores. For the White students, the largest value is 84 and the smallest value is 34. The corresponding values for the African American students are 77 and 29, respectively. The next step is to list all of the possible values that might occur between the two extreme values. Such a listing for the White students is given in Table 2.3.

Now that we have listed all of the possible values that can occur within the data for the White students, we need to tally how many cases obtained each of the possible values. That is, using the scores in Table 2.1, we can produce Table 2.4.

Once the tallies have been made, we usually translate the tallies to numeric values and put the results into a table, called a "frequency distribution." The results for the White students on the reading assessment are given in Table 2.5. As you can see, we have included the

Table 2.3 A list of all possible values for the White kindergarten students

84	71	58	45
83	70	57	44
82	69	56	43
81	68	55	42
80	67	54	41
79	66	53	40
78	65	52	39
77	64	51	38
76	63	50	37
75	62	49	36
74	61	48	35
73	60	47	34
72	59	46	

Table 2.4 The number of cases having each possible value for the White students

84	/	71		58	////	45	///
83		70		57	///	44	/
82		69	/	56	//	43	/
81		68	//	55	///	42	
80		67	/	54	////	41	////
79	/	66	//	53	///	40	
78		65	//	52	///////	39	/
77		64	///////	51	///////	38	//
76		63	///	50	//////	37	/
75		62	/	49	////	36	
74		61	///	48	////	35	
73		60	/	47	/////	34	/
72		59	/////	46	//		

Table 2.5 Frequency distribution for White kindergarten students on reading (*Y*)

Y	f(Y)	Y	f(Y)	Y	f(Y)	Y	f(Y)
84	1	71	0	58	4	45	3
83	0	70	0	57	3	44	1
82	0	69	1	56	2	43	1
81	0	68	2	55	3	42	0
80	0	67	1	54	4	41	4
79	1	66	2	53	3	40	0
78	0	65	3	52	7	39	1
77	0	64	7	51	7	38	2
76	0	63	3	50	6	37	1
75	0	62	1	49	4	36	0
74	0	61	3	48	4	35	0
73	0	60	1	47	5	34	1
72	0	59	6	46	2		

entire table, even though there are many values to display. Note that all possible values should be contained in the table, even when there are no cases having that particular value. In that instance, a zero is inserted into the table. Here we have presented the table with multiple columns in the interest of saving space. Usually, frequency tables have two columns, one for the values (*Y*) and one for the frequencies (f(*Y*)). Applying that format to this example, we would have a very long table.

At this point, we know more about the distribution of the reading scores for White kindergartners than we did when we first looked at the 100 values. It should be apparent to you, however, that this level of presentation is still not particularly meaningful. That is, it is still difficult to tell how the scores are distributed within the range between 84 and 34. At this point in the process, the scores appear to be scattered across the range. Fortunately, we can do more with the data to provide more meaning to our presentation. Considering our results in Table 2.5 to be an intermediate step, we can create what is called a *grouped frequency distribution*.

GROUPED FREQUENCY DISTRIBUTIONS

Distributions such as the one in Table 2.5 are sometimes called *ungrouped frequency distributions* in order to distinguish them from grouped distributions. Given a set of scores, there is a unique ungrouped distribution; regardless of who does the analysis, the result should be the same. When we move from ungrouped to grouped distributions, we need to make some decisions, the nature of which will affect the outcome. Thus, we need some guidelines for making these decisions.

Constructing the Intervals

In essence, we are going to cluster the original possible values into groups of possible values called *class intervals*. Two major issues are: (1) how to create the class intervals, and (2) how to order them. Regarding the second issue, it is customary to put the class intervals for the largest values at the top (although very few computer programs follow this guideline). The rules for creating the class intervals are a bit more elaborate. First, the class intervals should be both mutually exclusive and exhaustive. Class intervals are mutually exclusive when a specific case can be classified into one, and only one, of the intervals. For example, we would not want to create intervals such as 10–20 and 20–30 as a case having a score of 20 could be classified into either of the intervals. Class intervals are exhaustive when every case has an interval into which it can be classified. If our highest interval is from 90–100, a case having a score of 103 would not have an interval into which it could be classified. Generally, all of the intervals should be the same width (i.e., contain the same number of possible values). One exception to this is called an *open-ended distribution*, typical for reporting incomes. Often, the upper interval for annual income will be something like "greater than $100,000."

Number of Intervals

The most complex issue to be decided is the width of the class interval, which in turn affects the number of intervals. A helpful guideline is to aim for somewhere between 10 and 20 intervals. Another guideline recommends having the number of class intervals be approximately equal to the square root of the number of cases (Howell, 2007, p. 20), with a maximum of twice the square root of n for samples sizes less than 100 (Fox, 2002, p. 21). Using fewer than 10 intervals tends to compress the information too much, and using more than 20 intervals leads to a result that doesn't sufficiently summarize the original data.

Width of the Intervals

Not all widths are equally preferred. It is usually recommended that interval widths be numbers such as 2, 3, 5, or multiples of 5, probably because we all can easily recall our multiplication tables for multiples of 2, 3 and 5. We tend to be less proficient with multiples of 7, 11, 13, etc. If we were to decide upon an interval width of 3, we might have intervals such as 12–14, 15–17, etc. At first glance, it would appear that the interval 12–14 is two units wide. However, we need to consider that the interval contains the possible values of 12, 13, and 14. When we list the intervals like 12–14, we are using the *nominal limits*. The actual, or *real limits*, are 11.5 to 14.5. Real limits are specified as having one more decimal of precision than the actual scores. The last issue to consider is how to label the intervals. By convention, the nominal lower limits of the intervals should be multiples of the interval width. These guidelines are summarized in Box 2.1.

Constructing the Grouped Frequency Distribution

In order to construct a grouped frequency distribution for the scores of the White kindergartners, we first note that the highest score is 84 and the lowest score is 34; the difference

---

Box 2.1 Guidelines for preparing a grouped frequency distribution

- Order class intervals so the largest values are at the top of the distribution.
- Make sure intervals are mutually exclusive and exhaustive.
- Include all intervals between the intervals containing the extreme scores.
- Make all intervals the same width.
- Plan for 10 to 20 intervals.
- Use widths such as 2, 3, 5, 10 and multiples of 5.
- Make the nominal lower limit of the class interval an integer multiple of the class interval width. If we select an interval width of 5, then the nominal lower limits of the intervals should be multiples of 5 (e.g., 10, 15, 20, depending where we need to begin to include our data).

---

between the two extremes is 50. If we were to use an interval width of 2, we would obtain somewhere around 25 intervals (50 ÷ 2). Thus, a width of 2 would yield too many intervals. An interval width of 3 would yield approximately 16 or 17 intervals; an interval width of 5 would result in about 10 intervals. Thus, we have two possible solutions to our problem, both of which meet the guidelines. Multiple solutions do not arise in all situations, but they occur with sufficient frequency to require a tie-breaker. The decision between multiple solutions is based upon the number of cases. When there are relatively few cases, you should pick the solution with the smaller number of intervals. With very large data sets, you may opt for the solution with the larger number of intervals. "Big" is not easy to define; as a guideline, we recommend that you select the smaller number of intervals if you are working with 100 or fewer cases. This would give us a number of intervals approximately equal to $\sqrt{100}$ or less. Thus, for the data on White kindergartners, we would select the solution that uses about 10 intervals, which would suggest a width of 5. In constructing the actual intervals, we need to go only as high and low as necessary to include the extreme scores. Given that the lowest score is 34 and that we have selected an interval width of 5, our lowest interval would be 30–34. The highest interval would be 80–84. Referring back to Table 2.3, we have counted the number of tallies in each of the class intervals and constructed the grouped frequency distribution, which is shown in Table 2.6.

If you were to construct a grouped frequency distribution for the reading scores for the African American kindergartners, your results should match the contents of Table 2.7.

Table 2.6 Grouped frequency distribution for the reading scores of White kindergartners

Y	f(Y)
80–84	1
75–79	1
70–74	0
65–69	9
60–64	15
55–59	18
50–54	27
45–49	18
40–44	6
35–39	4
30–34	1

Table 2.7 Grouped frequency distribution for the reading scores of African American kindergartners

Y	f(Y)
75–79	1
70–74	1
65–69	2
60–64	15
55–59	12
50–54	23
45–49	15
40–44	18
35–39	9
30–34	3
25–29	1

Comparing the Two Distributions

Now that we have our two sets of scores transformed into grouped frequency distributions, we can look at them in order to make comparisons. Looking at the distribution of the scores for White kindergartners in Table 2.6, we note that most of the scores appear to fall somewhere between 45 and 69. Given the clustering of scores in the midrange, we might say that the scores tend to center somewhere around the low 50s. In contrast, in the distribution of scores for the African American kindergartners, most of the values fall between 40 and 64, and they appear to center in the low 50s or high 40s.

In this section, we have shown you how to transform sets of raw data into ungrouped frequency distributions and to then move on to grouped frequency distributions. While these are the types of frequency distributions used most often, there are some other formats for results. We would be remiss if we did not show you at least two of the other forms: *relative frequency distributions* and *cumulative frequency distributions*. These two formats are described in the next section.

RELATIVE FREQUENCY DISTRIBUTIONS AND CUMULATIVE FREQUENCY DISTRIBUTIONS

Relative frequency distributions present the proportion of cases in each interval, rather than the number of cases in each interval. This form of frequency distribution is especially useful when you want to compare two sets of scores that differ in the number of cases. Relative frequency distributions are easily derived from either ungrouped or grouped frequency distributions. For example, to find the relative frequency for the interval 60–64 for the scores for the White students' data (Table 2.6), you simply divide 15 (the total number of cases in the interval) by 100 (the total number of cases in the group). To find the relative frequency for the interval 50–54 for the African American students' data (Table 2.7), you divide 23 by 100. Table 2.8 contains the relative frequency distributions for both the White and African American Fall Reading Scores.

Looking at the relative frequency distribution doesn't really give us any information that isn't apparent in the grouped frequency distribution. If you look at the number of cases in each interval, you can see fairly easily where the scores are tending to cluster. However, as previously noted, using a relative frequency distribution puts the measure of each interval on a common scale, and thus may be useful when you are trying to compare frequency distributions based on groups that are very different in size.

Table 2.8 Relative frequency distributions for the White and African American kindergarten reading scores

	White students			African American students	
Y	f(Y)	rf(Y)	Y	f(Y)	rf(Y)
80–84	1	.01			
75–79	1	.01	75–79	1	.01
70–74	0	.00	70–74	1	.01
65–69	9	.09	65–69	2	.02
60–64	15	.15	60–64	15	.15
55–59	18	.18	55–59	12	.12
50–54	27	.27	50–54	23	.23
45–49	18	.18	45–49	15	.15
40–44	6	.06	40–44	18	.18
35–39	4	.04	35–39	9	.09
30–34	1	.01	30–34	3	.03
25–29	1	.01			

Cumulative frequency distributions are a little more difficult to construct. Rather than simply converting the frequency for each interval to a proportion, you begin with the frequency distribution and add up the frequencies at or below each interval to show the accumulated number of scores. The cumulative frequency distributions for the White and African American reading scores are shown in Table 2.9.

In order to obtain the cumulative frequencies for the White scores, we started at the bottom, giving that interval its actual frequency. The next interval, 35–39, has as its cumulative frequency the actual frequency 4 plus the 1 from below, or 5. The next interval of 40–44 has the actual frequency 6 plus the accumulated 5 from below, or 11. The pattern is continued through the last interval. The cumulative frequencies for the African American scores were obtained in the same fashion. Often these cumulative frequencies are transformed to percentages. Cumulative distributions are not particularly useful for summarizing the data for a group. Rather, they are most often used to describe the position of a case (or score) within a group. They also form the foundation of comparing the distributions of two groups. These topics will be treated in Chapters 5 and 14.

Table 2.9 Cumulative frequency distributions for White and African American reading scores

	White students			African American students	
Y	f(Y)	cf(Y)	Y	f(Y)	cf(Y)
80–84	1	100			
75–79	1	99	75–79	1	100
70–74	0	98	70–74	1	99
65–69	9	98	65–69	2	98
60–64	15	89	60–64	15	96
55–59	18	74	55–59	12	81
50–54	27	56	50–54	23	69
45–49	18	29	45–49	15	46
40–44	6	11	40–44	18	31
35–39	4	5	35–39	9	13
30–34	1	1	30–34	3	4
			25–29	1	1

So far, we have discussed how you can summarize a set of scores by constructing an ungrouped frequency distribution and transforming the ungrouped distribution to a grouped distribution if there are too many intervals. Both the ungrouped and grouped distributions can be presented as either relative frequency distributions or cumulative distributions. All of these solutions have been presented in tabular form. An alternative way to present these solutions is in graphic form. Three popular forms are histograms, frequency polygons, and stem-and-leaf displays. There is another graphic form known as a box plot, but we will postpone our presentation of that form until after we have shown you how to calculate certain values that capture different aspects of frequency distributions.

HISTOGRAMS

A *histogram* of the grouped frequency distribution for the reading scores for the White children is shown in Figure 2.1. A histogram depicting the grouped frequency distribution for the reading scores for the African American children is shown in Figure 2.2.

Note that a vertical bar has been constructed, centered at the midpoint of each interval and spanning the width of the interval. Each vertical bar has a height depicting the frequency of that particular interval. In a histogram, the vertical bars touch each other unless there are no scores in the interval. In contrast, there is a similar graphic for depicting categorical data called a bar graph, in which the bars do not touch one another (see Chapter 4). Having the bars not touch one another should convey that the horizontal axis is not numeric.

There are a few conventions for constructing histograms. First, note that the values on the horizontal axis are not located in their "true" position, relative to zero (the origin). Thus, break marks, //, have been placed on the axis to call your attention to that fact. Most statistical software packages do not do this by default.

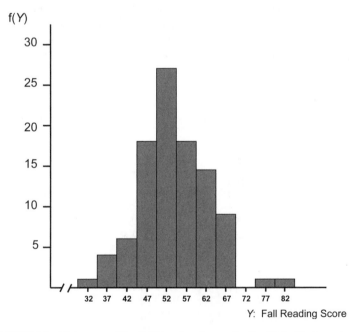

FIGURE 2.1   Histogram of the Fall Reading Scores for the White kindergarteners.

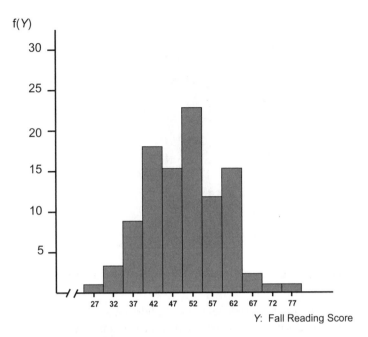

FIGURE 2.2   Histogram of the Fall Reading Scores for the African American kindergarteners.

When you do not use the true zero on the vertical axis, it is even more important to include the break marks so as not to mislead the person looking at the histogram. To elaborate on this point, suppose you were working with a simple distribution having only three possible values, 1, 2, and 3, perhaps from a three-point Likert-type scale. Suppose that the frequencies of the three intervals were 250, 240, and 210. Two different histograms depicting this distribution are shown in Figure 2.3.

Note that the two histograms of the same data present quite different impressions. The histogram on the left gives the sense that there were about five times as many 3s as 1s. The histogram on the right suggests the correct relative proportions of the intervals, but it is difficult to make fine discriminations among the heights of the bars. As an alternative, histograms can be constructed that call your attention to the "non-true" orientation relative to the origin, but do not make the bars so similar in height. Such a histogram is depicted in Figure 2.4.

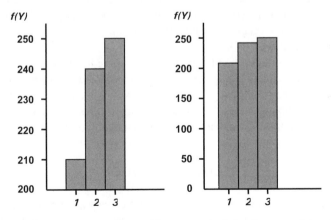

FIGURE 2.3   Two different histograms depicting the same data.

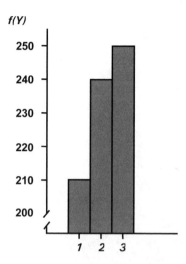

FIGURE 2.4   Histogram of the data depicted in Figure 2.3, showing the break in the vertical axis.

There is little agreement regarding the labeling of the horizontal axis in a histogram. Some authors put the labels at the edges of the bars, using either the real limits or the nominal limits as labels. We prefer to label the bars at the midpoints, as shown in Figures 2.1 and 2.2.

The last convention we will discuss pertains to the height of the histogram relative to its width. In order to make histograms comparable, one should make the height of the tallest bar somewhere between two-thirds and three-fourths of the width of the figure. Several introductory statistics books (e.g., Kirk, 1990, p. 48) cite this rule, or a similar one, without explanation. Here, we offer an example of two different graphic representations of some fictitious economic data. Suppose that unemployment rates for four consecutive years had been 5%, 6%, 8%, and 9%. The two major political parties would probably choose to chart the data in vastly different ways. Possible histograms are shown in Figure 2.5. The political party in control of the White House and/or Congress might choose to depict the data as in Figure 2.5(a). Note that the relationship between the vertical and horizontal scales gives the impression of a gradual increase in unemployment over the 4-year period. The political party not in control, but wanting to be in power, might depict the very same data as in Figure 2.5(b). The second representation seems to tell a very different story; unemployment appears to be raging out of control. A political advertisement highlighting this information may involve different layout requirements depending on the sponsoring party.

By now, you should have begun to realize that it's important to approach graphic presentations of data with a critical eye.

As noted earlier, histograms are only one form of graphic for displaying grouped frequency distributions. Historically, another popular format has been the *frequency polygon*. With the graphic capacity of modern computers, frequency polygons have been replaced with *density curves*, which may be thought of as "smoothed" frequency polygons. We discuss frequency polygons as we think that they will enhance your understanding of density curves.

FREQUENCY POLYGONS

Frequency polygons are very similar to histograms, but present a simpler visual image of a frequency distribution. In essence, there are two modifications made to move from a histogram to

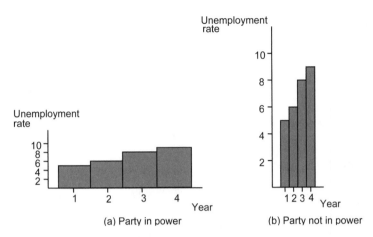

FIGURE 2.5   Two ways to present unemployment data over a 4-year period.

a frequency polygon. First, you draw lines that connect the midpoints of the tops of the vertical bars. The second change relates to the portrayal of the high and low extremes. A histogram has vertical bars only as far out in the extremes as there are data points that need to be represented. In contrast, a frequency polygon includes the intervals immediately beyond the last intervals in the histogram so that the polygon can be closed with the horizontal axis.

The relationship between a histogram and a frequency polygon is demonstrated in Figure 2.6, using the Fall Reading Scores for White kindergarteners. The frequency polygon depicting the Fall Reading Scores for the African American kindergartners is shown in Figure 2.7.

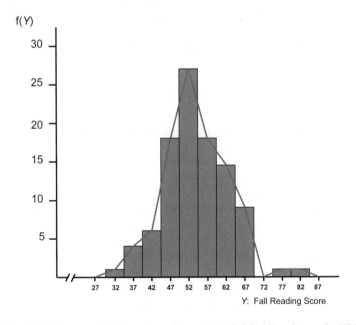

FIGURE 2.6   The histogram and frequency polygon of the Fall Reading Scores for White kindergarteners, superimposed on the same graph.

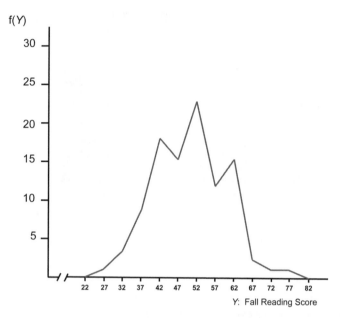

FIGURE 2.7   A frequency polygon depicting the Fall Reading Scores of African American kindergarteners.

A visual comparison of the two frequency polygons (and the two histograms) conveys much the same information that we obtained by comparing the grouped frequency distributions. Looking at the graphs of the data on White kindergarteners, we note that the scores appear to range from the low 30s to the mid-80s, with most of the scores tending to cluster between the mid-40s and the high 60s. The graphs for the African American scores suggest that the scores range from the mid-20s up to the high 70s, with the bulk of them centering between mid-30s and the mid-60s. There is a third graphic depiction of a frequency distribution called an ogive.

OGIVES

Both histograms and frequency polygons plot the frequency of each score (or interval) as a function of the values, or midpoints of the intervals. A slightly different approach would be to plot the cumulative frequencies of the values, or intervals. This procedure results in an ogive. We have plotted the cumulative frequency distributions presented in Table 2.9 in Figure 2.8.

As you can see, the pattern of round dots for the White students tends to be a little to the right of the pattern of square dots for the African American students, suggesting that the scores for the White students tend to be a little higher than those for the African American students. Later in the book, we will present a method for comparing two distributions of scores based on a comparison of their respective ogives (the Mann–Whitney U-Test).

The grouped methods we have presented so far for summarizing data (frequency tables, histograms, frequency polygons, and ogives) all help us to see patterns in the data. However, all four methods share a common liability. That is, all four methods yield results in which the individual scores are not easily seen. The fourth graphic method that we present is in essence a compromise, in that it maintains the individual scores, while at the same time, indicating groups of scores. In

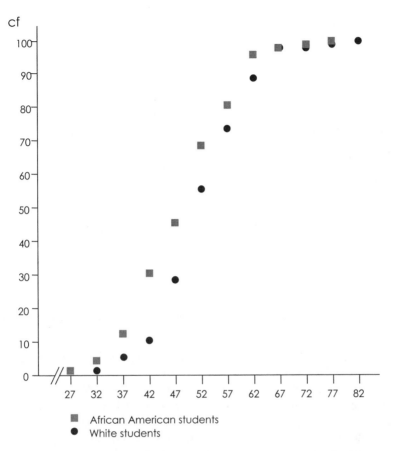

FIGURE 2.8   Ogives plotted for the White and African American students.

addition, this fourth method presents a visual pattern, much like a histogram or frequency polygon. The fourth method was described by Tukey (1977) and is called a *stem-and-leaf display*.

STEM-AND-LEAF DISPLAYS

In order to transform a set of data into a stem-and-leaf display, you begin in much the same way as you do when constructing a grouped frequency distribution. You identify the highest and lowest scores, and using those values, decide on an interval width, aiming for somewhere between 10 and 20 intervals. Here the choice of interval width is a little more restrictive. You would choose an interval width like 2, 5, or 10, values which divide evenly into 10. You would avoid interval widths like 3, which would not divide evenly into 10. For a larger scale you may choose an interval width like 20, 50, or 100, values which divide evenly into 100. Again considering the Fall Reading Scores for White kindergarteners, the highest score was 84 and the lowest score was 34, giving a range of 50. Once again, we would probably select an interval width of 5. Given that all of the values are two digit numbers, we would portray the 10s digits in the *stem* and use the units digits as the *leaves*. The stem-and-leaf displays for both the White and African American Fall Reading Scores are presented in Figure 2.9.

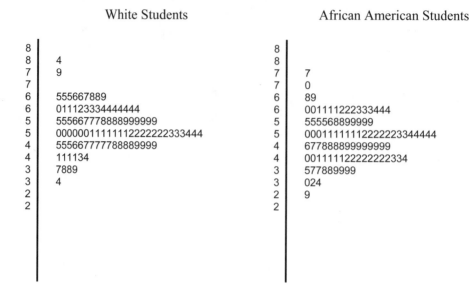

FIGURE 2.9   Stem-and-leaf displays for the Fall Reading Scores of African American kindergarteners.

Note in the display on the left, the score of 84 has been separated, with the 8 being part of one column (the stem), and the 4 being represented on the right, as a leaf. In the stem, each number is repeated twice, as the interval width is 5 units. For example, the lower 4 represents the interval from 40 to 44, while the upper 4 represents the interval from 45 to 49. Looking at the leaves for the lower 4 of the stem, we see the digits 1, 1, 1, 1, 3, and 4. Putting this all together, we can interpret the display to indicate that there are scores of 41, 41, 41, 41, 43, and 44. In a similar fashion, look at the lower 3 in the stem for the African American students. To the right, we note that there are leaves of 0, 2, and 4. Decoded, the display is telling us that there are scores of 30, 32, and 34.

As we have just described, the individual scores are represented specifically in the stem-and-leaf display, imbedded in their groups. We have followed the tradition of presenting the data with the larger values at the top of the display. Often, stem-and-leaf displays are constructed in ascending order. When that is done, the visual image presented by the display is very similar to a histogram or frequency polygon when the image is rotated 90 degrees counter-clockwise. Hence, the stem-and-leaf display contains all the desirable features of ungrouped distributions, grouped distributions, and graphs, simultaneously. They are relatively easy to construct by hand when the number of cases is relatively small but can be difficult to make when there are many cases (which is why we use computers). Comparing the displays for the White and African American Fall Reading Scores, it appears that the two distributions seem to be spread out to about the same degree, but that the scores for the African American students seem to be a little lower, overall, than the scores for the White students.

SALIENT CHARACTERISTICS OF FREQUENCY DISTRIBUTIONS

In many ways, frequency distributions are like any other object in our everyday world. Think for a moment about tables. In actuality, tables are really a construct having many different attributes. Tables differ from one another in terms of these attributes. For example, most tables have four legs, but some of them have three legs, some have more than four legs, some have two legs (trestle tables) and some even have only one leg (pedestal tables). Therefore, one way different tables can be distinguished from one another is in terms of the number of legs. Tables also can be distinguished on the basis of shape (e.g., square, rectangular, oval, circular). They can also be described in terms of the material with which they are constructed (e.g., wood, plastic, steel, glass). Thus, when we say "Go sit at the circular, wood, pedestal table in the other room," we are describing a particular table in terms of several attributes, simultaneously.

In our discussion so far, we have already suggested two attributes that can be used to describe frequency distributions, allowing us to distinguish them from one another. When we presented our initial verbal summary of the distributions of White and African American Fall Reading Scores, we noted that the distributions appeared to be similar in one way, but different in another way: both sets of scores appeared to be similarly spread out, but the scores for African American students tended to "center" at a slightly lower level. At this point, we want to make our discussion more systematic.

In Figure 2.10, we have drawn six frequency distributions that differ from one another in several different ways. Looking at the six different distributions, let's play compare and contrast. First, look at distributions A and B. In all ways except one, they appear to be identical. The only difference between A and B is that the scores in the two distributions center in different locations: the scores in A center around a lower point than do the scores in B. Thus, frequency distributions can be distinguished from each other in terms of *location*, or *central tendency*. The most widely used measures of central tendency are the mode, the median, and the mean. These measures will be defined and described in Chapter 3.

Now, turn your attention to a comparison of distributions B and C. These two distributions are centered at exactly the same location, and yet the distributions are different. The scores in C are more widely dispersed around their point of central location than are the scores in B. Thus, two distributions can be centered at the same location, but differ in terms of their *spread*, or *dispersion*. The many measures of dispersion (e.g., range, interquartile range, average deviation, variance, and standard deviation) will also be presented in Chapter 3.

Most research in the social sciences is focused on location and dispersion, particularly location. For example, appropriate questions to be asked about the White and African American students' Fall Reading Scores might be:

1. Did one of the groups tend to do better than the other? (Location)
2. Do the two groups have the same range of ability? (Dispersion)

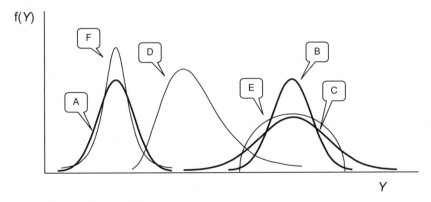

FIGURE 2.10   Several different frequency distributions.

In addition to the attributes of location and dispersion, frequency distributions can differ in other ways. Note that, in Figure 2.10, distributions A, B, C, E, and F are all symmetrical about their central point. That is, the shape of the distribution on the right side of the central point is the mirror image of the shape on the left side of the central point. In contrast, D is not symmetrical; rather, the "tail" on the right side is much longer than the one on the left side. This attribute is called *symmetry*, or *skewness*. As already noted, location and dispersion are the primary concerns in social science research. However, at times we may want to focus on skewness in its own right. For example, if an achievement test is given that is either too easy or too difficult, measures of skewness may help us detect the problem. If the test is too easy, then most of the people will score toward the top end of the possible range, with only a few people scoring toward the lower end. If you can imagine this distribution, it will have most of the scores located on the right, with a long tail trailing off to the left. If the test is too difficult, the opposite will occur. Thus, measures of skewness can help us determine whether the difficulty level of a test is appropriate.

The fourth important attribute is a bit more difficult to describe, although we will give a good try. If you compare A, B, and C with E and F, you may note a subtle difference. Distribution E appears different from distributions A, B, and C in that E appears to be "mesa-like," or flatter than A, B, or C, with shorter tails. In contrast, distribution F appears to be more pointed, or peaked, than do distributions A, B, and C. Looking specifically at distributions A and F, the distribution in F is more peaked, narrower in the shoulders, and wider in the tails, although this latter issue does not show well in the figure. This deviation in curvature is called *kurtosis*. In reality, these last two attributes (skewness and kurtosis) are characteristics that allow us to determine whether a specific frequency distribution departs from a "normal" distribution. (The notion of "normal distributions" is an underlying assumption for many of the statistical techniques that will be presented in this book.) While normal distributions are actually defined using a mathematical expression, it will be important to know whether the actual scores with which we are working can be appropriately modeled by a normal distribution. Thus, the last two characteristics of frequency distributions (skewness and kurtosis) are more important in assessing whether we are justified in applying a particular statistical treatment to our data. A more complete discussion of skewness and kurtosis will be presented in Chapter 3.

COMPUTER ANALYSIS

All of what we have presented in this chapter can be completed using computer software. For a variety of reasons, we have chosen to emphasize R in this book. Thus, our computer examples within the main body of the chapters will be completed using the R system; we provide commands for SPSS and the Statistical Analysis System (SAS) on the companion website. Fundamentals of R (basic operations, data definition, etc.) are presented in Appendix B at the end of the book. You should probably take a look at Appendix B: An Introduction to R now. (Really, we mean now!) Another good introduction to R is provided by Verzani (2005).

The four techniques which we will demonstrate are frequency distributions, histograms, density distributions, and stem-and-leaf displays. Most computer packages cannot/will not construct frequency polygons. With a little extra programming, it is possible to do so in R, but frequency polygons are approximations to density distributions, which can be easily constructed in R. We will show you how to generate the output for both the White and the African American students. The data set for this chapter (*ecls200*) is available on the website in both Excel and text format.

You should get the file and store a text version on your hard drive. If you are using a PC, we recommend that you create a folder (e.g., rbook) at the "top" of the c drive. First, we suggest that you enter your commands in a "script" file and execute them from there. You can save your "script" file, giving you a record of what you did. There are many ways in which to enter data into the R system. You can enter small sets of data directly with the **scan** or **c** function. With larger sets of data, you can enter the data into Excel, save the results as a text file, and then read the data into R with the **read.table** function. In this instance, before starting R, we took the Excel file and saved it as a tab-delimited text file with a .txt extension. We then started R, opened a new script file, and entered the commands:

```
ecls200 <- read.table("c:/rbook/ecls200.txt",
    header = TRUE)
attach(ecls200)
names(ecls200)
```

The first command reads the text file saved from Excel into a data frame in R. The first line of the text file contains the variable names; hence the "header = TRUE" part of the command. The second command, **attach( )**, makes the data frame active and allows us to access the variables by name. The use of the **attach( )** command is somewhat controversial; however, it can save a lot of typing. The third command asks R to print out all of the variable names. The output appeared in the R-console window as:

```
> ecls200 <- read.table("c:/rbook/ecls200.txt",
    header = TRUE)
> attach(ecls200)
> names(ecls200)
 [1] "id"       "childid"  "gender"   "race"     "c1rrscal"
 [6] "c1rrscal_a" "c1rrtsco" "c1rmscal" "c1rmtsco" "c1rgscal"
[11] "c1rgtsco"  "c1fmotor" "c1gmotor" "c2rrscal" "c2rrtsco"
[16] "c2rmscal"  "c2rmtsco" "c2rgscal" "c2rgtsco" "c3rrscal"
[21] "c3rrtsco"  "c3rmscal" "c3rmtsco" "c3rgscal" "c3rgtsco"
[26] "c4rrscal"  "c4rrtsco" "c4rmscal" "c4rmtsco" "c4rgscal"
[31] "c4rgtsco"  "p1learn"  "p1contro" "p1social" "t1learn"
[36] "t1contro"  "t1internp" "t1extern" "t1intern" "p1center"
[41] "p1disabl"  "p1htotal" "p1hfamil" "p1firkdg" "p1hrsprk"
[46] "wkmomed"   "wkdaded"  "eklangst" "wksesl"   "wksesq5"
[51] "s2kpupri"  "p1count"  "p1share"  "p1pencil" "p1still"
[56] "p1letter"  "p1verbal" "p1expect" "p1readbo" "p1tellst"
[61] "p1singso"  "p1helpar" "p1chores" "p1games"  "p1nature"
[66] "p1build"   "p1sport"  "p1chlboo" "p1chsesa" "p2librar"
[71] "p2safepl"  "p2parbag" "p2drug"   "p2burglr" "p2violen"
[76] "p2vacant"  "p2bktog"  "ses_orig"
```

As you can see, the file contains many variables. For a description/explanation of the variables, see the codebook on the website. We are going to focus on the standardized reading scores collected during the fall of kindergarten, *c1rrtsco*. Given that we want to analyze the data for White and African American students separately, we created separate data frames. There are several different ways in which to analyze subsets in a data frame, and we show these in Appendix B. To create the separate data frames, we entered the following commands in the script file:

```
ecls200.white <- ecls200[ecls200$race == "1",]
ecls200.aa <- ecls200[ecls200$race == "2",]
```

In Appendix B, we show you how to use the **subset( )** command to accomplish the same end. At this point, we now have three separate data frames: *ecls200*, *ecls200.white*, and *ecls200.aa*. First, let's look at the data for the White students. To do this, we first will make the *ecls200* data frame inactive with the **detach( )** command, and make the data frame for the 100 White students active with the **attach( )** command. If we do not do this, we may analyze the wrong data. We will then instruct R to construct a frequency distribution for these scores, using the **table( )** command.

```
detach(ecls200)
attach(ecls200.white)
table(c1rrtsco)
```

The output appears as:

```
> table(c1rrtsco)
c1rrtsco
34 37 38 39 41 43 44 45 46 47 48 49 50 51 52 53 54
 1  1  2  1  4  1  1  3  2  5  4  4  6  7  7  3  4

55 56 57 58 59 60 61 62 63 64 65 66 67 68 69 79 84
 3  2  3  4  6  1  3  1  3  7  3  2  1  2  1  1  1
```

The output is organized into paired rows; the top row consists of the values of the variable, the second row contains the number of cases having that value, the third row continues the values of the variable, and the fourth row contains the number of cases having that value, etc. We can see that the smallest value is 34 and the largest value is 84, as we saw earlier in this chapter. Also note that, like most other statistical packages, R does not list values that do not appear in the data. For example, the 34 appears right next to the 37, giving the appearance that there is no break in the distribution. Thus, you need to be careful when you read the output from the **table( )** function.

Using the rules for constructing grouped frequency distributions and histograms, we might reason that the class interval width should be five points, with the lowest interval beginning at 29.5 and the highest interval should end at 84.5. Within the **hist( )** command, R allows us to set the real limits of the class intervals and the interval width using the **breaks( )** specification (see Verzani (2005, pp. 56–59)). The **xlab( )** specification allows us to label the X axis. The **rug( )** command shows the location of the cases on the horizontal axis. We can implement these decisions with the following commands:

```
hist(clrrtsco, breaks = seq(29.5, 84.5, 5),
  xlab = "Pre-K Reading Scores for Whites")
rug(clrrtsco)
```

The resulting histogram is shown in Figure 2.11.

As with many computer graphics procedures, the default is to show only one "mark" at a given location, even if there are several points at that location. That is, they are over-plotted. We can modify this by "jittering" the points. That is, we can add a little "fuzz" so that we can see where there are several points. To accomplish this, we modify the **hist( )** and **rug( )** commands as follows:

```
hist(clrrtsco, breaks = seq(29.5, 84.5, 5),
  xlab = "Pre-K Reading Scores for Whites")
rug(jitter(clrrtsco))
```

The modified histogram is shown in Figure 2.12.

If we want, we can impose an approximation to the density distribution on the histogram, as a substitute (or improvement) for a frequency polygon. To do this, we add a command to our file and modify our **hist( )** command so that it does not use the frequency on the vertical axis; rather, it uses a "relative frequency" scale:

```
hist(clrrtsco, prob = TRUE, breaks = seq(29.5,
  84.5, 5),
  xlab = "Pre-K Reading Scores for Whites")
lines(density(clrrtsco))
rug(jitter(clrrtsco))
```

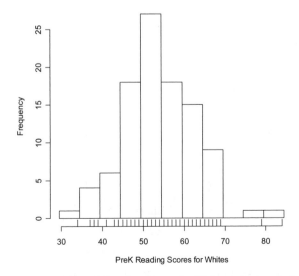

FIGURE 2.11   Histogram of the Fall Reading Scores for White students entering kindergarten.

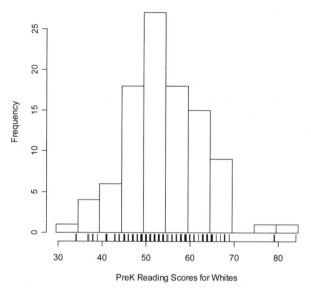

FIGURE 2.12   Histogram of the Fall Reading Scores for White students entering kindergarten, with jittering.

The result is shown in Figure 2.13.

Last, we might want to produce a stem-and-leaf display for these scores. It is a very simple command. If we use the default, the stem will be displayed in groups of 10 units for this particular set of data. If we want more groups, we can insert a "scale" factor:

```
stem(c1rrtsco, scale = 2)
```

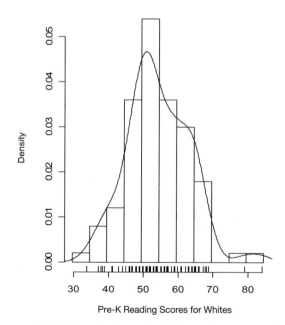

FIGURE 2.13   Histogram of the Fall Reading Scores for White students entering kindergarten, with jittering and the density distribution.

The output is:

```
> stem(clrrtsco, scale = 2)
  The decimal point is 1 digit(s) to the right of the |

  3 | 4
  3 | 7889
  4 | 111134
  4 | 555667777788889999
  5 | 00000011111122222223334444
  5 | 555667778888999999
  6 | 011123334444444
  6 | 555667889
  7 |
  7 | 9
  8 | 4
```

All of these commands can be repeated for the African American students. We simply need to **detach( )** the file for White students and **attach( )** the file for African American students, and then run the same commands.

```
detach(ecls200.white)
attach(ecls200.aa)
table(clrrtsco)
```

The output is:

```
> table(clrrtsco)
clrrtsco
29 30 32 34 35 37 38 39 40 41 42 43 44 46 47 48 49 50 51 52 53
 1  1  1  1  1  2  2  4  2  5  8  2  1  1  2  4  8  3  7  6  2

54 55 56 58 59 60 61 62 63 64 68 69 70 77
 5  4  1  2  5  2  4  3  3  3  1  1  1  1
```

Here, we can see that the lowest score is 29 and the highest score is 77. Thus, we would want to modify our **hist( )** command accordingly.

```
hist(clrrtsco, breaks = seq(24.5, 79.5, 5),
   xlab = "Pre-K Reading Scores for African Americans")
rug(jitter(clrrtsco))
```

The result is shown in Figure 2.14.

To generate the plot of the estimated density distribution:

```
hist(clrrtsco, prob = TRUE, breaks = seq(24.5, 79.5, 5),
```

```
    xlab = "Pre-K Reading Scores for African Americans")
lines(density(clrrtsco))
rug(clrrtsco)
```

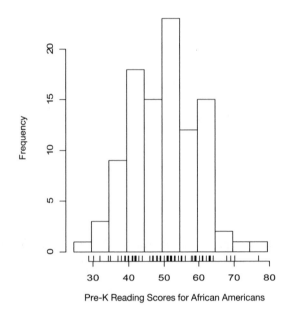

Pre-K Reading Scores for African Americans

FIGURE 2.14   Histogram of the Fall Reading Scores for African American students entering kindergarten, with jittering.

The result is shown in Figure 2.15.

And last,

```
    stem(clrrtsco)
```

In this command, we did not have to add the scale factor. The output is:

```
> stem(clrrtsco)
  The decimal point is 1 digit(s) to the right of the |

  2 | 9
  3 | 024
  3 | 577889999
  4 | 001111122222222334
  4 | 677888899999999
  5 | 0001111111222223344444
  5 | 555568899999
```

```
6 | 001111222333444
6 | 89
7 | 0
7 | 7
```

As an alternative to the **attach/detach** sequence, we could have used the **with( )** command, which is equivalent.

```
with(ecls200.white, table(c1rrtsco))
```

There are a number of R programmers who prefer this to the **attach/detach** sequence. There is yet another way to access directly variables that are within different data frames. For example, imagine that we have three data frames that have been created within the same session. In order to find the means for different data frames, we could use commands such as:

```
mean(ecls200$c1rrtsco)
mean(ecls200.white$c1rrtsco)
mean(ecls200.aa$c1rrtsco)
```

Obviously, as with most statistical programs, there is more than one way to accomplish the same goal. Different approaches work better or worse for different tasks for different people. Over time, you will find what works best for you in different situations.

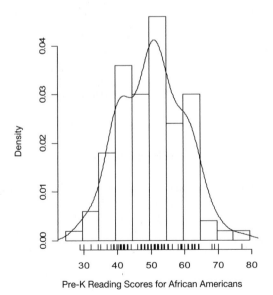

Pre-K Reading Scores for African Americans

FIGURE 2.15   Histogram of the Fall Reading Scores for African American students entering kindergarten, with jittering and the density distribution.

CHAPTER SUMMARY

In this chapter, we have presented several different methods for transforming a set of raw quantitative data into a more meaningful format. The initial step nearly always consists of preparing a frequency distribution of raw scores in table form. Sometimes, these distributions are further processed to construct grouped frequency distributions, again in table form. These tables are usually accompanied by, or even replaced by, presentations in graphic form. Most often, these graphic presentations take the form of histograms or frequency polygons. With the increasing use of computer programs to process data, we are noting an increase in the use of stem-and-leaf displays, a format which includes the valuable aspects of both the tabular and graphic displays for giving meaning to sets of raw scores.

After considering both tabular and graphic depictions of distributions of data, we looked for attributes that might be useful in distinguishing one distribution from another. Based on an examination of Figure 2.10, we were able to identify several relevant attributes or concepts that could be helpful. Specifically, we noted (1) the location of the scores, or where the scores tend to center, (2) the dispersion of the scores, or how far apart the scores are from one another, and (3) shape, which involves two matters—the symmetry of distribution of scores (skewness) and the curvature of the distribution of scores (kurtosis).

In the next chapter, we present specific measures of each of these attributes. In looking at the issue of central tendency, we describe three measures (mode, median, and mean). In our discussion of dispersion, we explain many measures (range, interquartile range, average deviation, variance, and standard deviation).

Key Terms

Bivariate statistics	Nominal limits
Central tendency	Ogive
Class interval	Real limits
Cumulative frequency distribution	Relative frequency distribution
Dispersion	Shape
Frequency polygon	Skewness
Grouped frequency distribution	Spread
Histogram	Stem-and-leaf display
Interval width	Ungrouped frequency distribution
Kurtosis	Univariate statistics
Location	

REFERENCES

Fox, J. (2002). *An R and S-PLUS companion to applied regression*. Thousand Oaks, CA: Sage.

Howell, D. C. (2007). *Statistical methods for psychology* (6th ed.). Belmont, CA: Thomson Wadsworth.

Kirk, R. E. (1990). *Statistics: An introduction* (3rd ed.). Fort Worth, TX: Holt, Rinehart and Winston.

Tukey, J. W. (1977). *Exploratory data analysis*. Reading, MA: Addison-Wesley.

Verzani, J. (2005). *Using R for introductory statistics*. Boca Raton, FL: Chapman & Hall/CRC Press.

PRACTICE QUESTIONS

1. Which statistical method shows a distribution's shape while also providing information on all the individual values in the distribution?

   a. Frequency polygon.
   b. Histogram.
   c. Stem-and-leaf display.
   d. Ungrouped frequency distribution.

2. Which of the following presentations would be most useful in quickly communicating how the values from a variable are distributed?

   a. Cumulative frequency distribution.
   b. Histogram.
   c. Ordered list of the scores.
   d. Unordered list of the scores.

3. In creating a grouped frequency distribution, which of the following interval widths would be the easiest for the reader to process?

   a. 7
   b. 8
   c. 9
   d. 10

4. When creating a grouped frequency distribution, about how many groups would you want to create?

   a. 1 to 2
   b. 5 to 8
   c. 10 to 20
   d. 30 to 50

5. The highest bar in a histogram corresponds to the group that:

   a. Contains the lowest score in the distribution.
   b. Contains the highest score in the distribution.
   c. Contains the fewest scores in the distribution.
   d. Contains the most scores in the distribution.

6. Which two techniques are most similar in the information they provide?

   a. Histogram and frequency polygon.
   b. Histogram and stem-and-leaf display.
   c. Histogram and ungrouped frequency distribution.
   d. Frequency polygon and stem-and-leaf display.

7. If a researcher refers to one distribution as symmetric and another as asymmetric, she is referring to differences in:

   a. central tendency
   b. dispersion
   c. skewness
   d. kurtosis.

8. If a researcher says one distribution tends to have higher scores than another, she is referring to differences in:

    a. central tendency
    b. dispersion
    c. skewness
    d. kurtosis.

9. If a researcher says one distribution tends to be flat while another is peaked with thick tails, she is referring to differences in:

    a. central tendency
    b. dispersion
    c. skewness
    d. kurtosis.

10. If a researcher says the values are much more spread out in one distribution than another, she is referring to differences in:

    a. central tendency
    b. dispersion
    c. skewness
    d. kurtosis.

EXERCISES

2.1. For each of the following sets of conditions, give (a) the number of class intervals, (b) the size of the class interval, and (c) the nominal limits of the lowest class interval.

	Largest Score	Smallest Score	Number of Scores
a.	78	24	57
b.	276	122	32
c.	37	8	112
d.	510	390	200

2.2. A sample of public school teachers was administered a job satisfaction questionnaire at the beginning of the school year, while the State Legislature was still in session, haggling over the State Budget. A major point of contention between the House and Senate was how much of a raise to give school teachers. The instrument consisted of six 5-point Likert-type items with a 1 representing "extremely dissatisfied" and a 5 representing "extremely satisfied" for each of the six items. The responses on the six items were summed, yielding a total score. Their scores were as follows:

8	7	4	25	9	7	6	15	11	9
6	12	22	7	18	13	4	10	13	17
12	11	19	8	16	14	11	17	10	22
21	9	12	22	17	9	5	16	23	29
7	5	6	6	7	13	6	5	5	9
15	21	5	11	6	9	18	12	10	8

Using these scores, construct both an ungrouped and grouped frequency distribution.

2.3.   A test of computer aptitude was given to a sample of professors at a prestigious university in the Mid-Atlantic States. The test consisted of 100 items, scored right or wrong. Using the data as given below, construct a grouped frequency distribution. When you have your solution, describe the distribution of scores.

77	62	81	72	45	51	54	93	55	76	75
42	48	51	57	66	69	53	17	58	67	72
69	70	49	60	35	69	57	63	59	26	71
64	45	64	58	54	49	66	71	59	66	51
97	83	79	61	83	72	68	70			

2.4.   Using a traditional six-sided die, roll it 60 times and prepare a frequency distribution indicating how many times each of the sides (1–6) appeared.

2.5.   Using your "grouped" solution for Exercise 2.2, construct a histogram.

2.6.   Using your "grouped" solution for Exercise 2.3, use R to construct a histogram with a density curve imposed over the histogram.

2.7.   Using R with the data in Exercise 2.3, construct a stem-and-leaf display. Do one for each class interval equal to 5 and 10.

3

Describing Quantitative Data: Summary Statistics

INTRODUCTION

In the previous chapter, we described procedures that could be used to process data in ways that would enable us to better understand a distribution of the scores in a holistic fashion. Specifically, we looked at tabular presentations (ungrouped and grouped frequency distributions, relative frequency distributions, and cumulative frequency distributions) and graphic presentations (histograms, frequency polygons, and stem-and-leaf displays). Toward the end of this chapter, we present another graphic format (box-and-whisker plots), which assumes an understanding of some of the material developed in this chapter.

In the previous chapter, we also examined score distributions from a more global perspective, identifying several dimensions that are useful for distinguishing one set of scores from another. That is, we looked at how distributions of scores could differ in several ways. The first dimension we considered was *location* or *central tendency*. Next, we considered *dispersion* (spread/variability) or how much the scores differed from one another. Last, we looked at *shape*, which involves two considerations, symmetry and curvature.

In this chapter, we present a variety of methods to capture the essence of each of these three characteristics for a particular set of scores, using a single value to describe each of the three attributes, respectively. Actually, we will use two values to describe the shape of a distribution. Thus, we continue our journey away from the most complete, detailed form of data to higher levels of abstraction. We do so as researchers, not as clinicians. That is, a classroom teacher might have measures for evaluating learning style for each of his/her students. As a teacher, one would want to be able to link the scores with specific students. However, at a different level, a teacher might also be interested in comparing different classrooms (or schools) with respect to the distributions of learning styles. At this level, the link between scores and students is of little relevance. Or consider a physician. A database includes measures of systolic and diastolic blood pressures of patients in her practice. She would want to link specific scores to particular patients; knowing the average blood pressures across the entire practice would not be all that helpful. On the other hand, researchers might be interested in comparing different clinics (e.g., general medicine, general surgery, dermatology, and oncology) with regard to average blood pressures.

In the previous chapter, we focused on two distributions of scores, standardized reading scores of 100 White and 100 African American students collected at the beginning of kindergarten. Acknowledging that these two distributions are really samples drawn from the large Early Childhood Longitudinal Study Kindergarten ECLS-K/1 data file described on the book website, we will consider these two data sets to be two populations. That is, the primary focus of this chapter is to develop methods for describing characteristics of populations of measurements. Consequently, we will use Greek letters to denote that parameters are being calculated. When necessary, we will discuss the population/sample paradigm.

CENTRAL TENDENCY

There are three measures of central tendency in common practice: the *mode*, the *median*, and the *mean*. Each of these measures represents a slightly different way to represent the attribute of centrality, and each has its advantages and limitations.

The Mode

The mode of a distribution of scores is simply the value that occurs most often. Thus, going back to Table 2.5 in which the frequency distribution of reading scores for White kindergarten students is presented, you can determine that the scores of 64, 52, and 51 each appear seven times in the 100 cases. Although the scores for the African American students are not presented in a table, a similar examination of those 100 scores would show that the scores of 49 and 42 both occur eight times in the set of 100 scores. Thus, for each set of scores, our analyses show that each distribution is characterized by multiple modes. We will address this issue again later when we summarize the properties of the three measures of central tendency.

In a similar fashion, we can determine the mode for a grouped frequency distribution. Looking at Table 2.6 in which the grouped frequency distribution for White students is depicted, we can see that the class interval 50–54 contains 27 scores, more than any other class interval. Thus, we would say that the modal class interval is 50–54. Sometimes, the midpoint of the interval is used to describe the modal class, resulting in a statement to the effect that 52 is the modal class. Applying the same process to the grouped frequency distribution for the scores of African American students in Table 2.7, we note that the class interval 50–54 contains 23 scores, more than any other class interval. Thus, we would say that the modal class interval for the African American students is 50–54, or 52.

The Median

The median is the point on a scale that separates a distribution of scores into two parts; one half of the scores are above the median and the other half are below the median. It may be helpful to associate the median of a distribution of scores with the median of a four-lane, divided highway. Just as half the lanes of the highway are on either side of the median, half the scores in a distribution are on either side of the median.

There are many simple, short-cut rules that have been offered to find the median of a set of scores, but these rules generally apply to special cases. There are rules for dealing with an odd number of cases as opposed to an even number of cases. There are other rules for dealing with situations where there is only one case at the median value as opposed to several cases at that value. We think that it is worth taking the time to present one general process for finding the median and explaining how it works. For one reason, it always works! In addition, knowledge of this process will help you better understand future statistical concepts, particularly the interquartile range and percentile ranks. However, at first look, we admit that the formula looks pretty scary. The expression that is used to find the median of a set of scores is:

$$\text{Median} = \left(\frac{(n/2) \ - \ \Sigma f_b}{f_i} \right) i + Y_{ll} \tag{3.1}$$

Once you have recovered from the shock of this expression, take a look at the meaning of each of the terms. After defining each of the terms, we will show you how the expression is applied to find the median, using several examples.

First, the n in the numerator is the number of scores in the set. For our case study, there are 100 scores in each of the files for the White and African American students, respectively. The second term in the numerator, Σf_b, is equal to the number of cases below the interval containing the median, or the "sum of frequencies below." The term in the denominator, f_i, is equal to the number of scores in the interval containing the median. The i just outside of the parentheses is equal to the width of the class interval. If you are working with an ungrouped distribution, i is equal to one (1.0). The last term, Y_{ll}, is equal to the lower limit of the interval containing the median.

To demonstrate how the process works, let's take a look at the frequency distribution of the reading scores for White students given in Table 2.5. Remember that there are 100 scores in this distribution, so that the median will be the point that separates the largest 50 values from the smallest 50 values. The cumulative frequencies are not displayed in this table, but you could start at the lower end of the distribution and create them. Were you to do so, you would find that when you included the seven scores having a value of 52, you would have a cumulative frequency of 49. That is, there are 49 scores at or below 52. If you were to now include the three scores having a value of 53, you would see that you would have 52 scores at or below a score of 53; you would have "crossed the median!" Thus, we know that the median is somewhere between 52.5 and 53.5. That is, Y_{ll} is equal to 52.5, and f_i is equal to 3. The interval width is 1. Substituting these values into the expression for the median, we would determine the median for these scores as follows:

$$\text{Median} = \left[\frac{(100/2)-49}{3} \right] 1 + 52.5 \tag{3.2}$$

Evaluating this expression, we would find the median of the White students' scores to be 52.83.

One way to conceptualize how the formula works is to picture the score interval containing the three scores of 53. The median has to fall between the first and second score of 53 so that there are a total of 50 scores on either side of the median. This implies the median is 1/3 of the way through the interval, and thus 1/3 of the way between 52.5 and 53.5, which can be shown visually as shown in Figure 3.1.

In a similar fashion, we could find the median of the African American scores. Creating an ungrouped frequency distribution for these 100 scores, you would find that there are 49 scores at or below 50. There are seven scores of 51. Thus, the median is somewhere between 50.5 and 51.5. Substituting these values into the expression for the median,

$$\text{Median} = \left(\frac{(100/2)-49}{7} \right) 1 + 50.5 \tag{3.3}$$

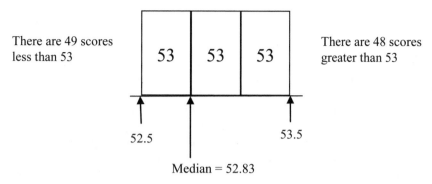

There are 49 scores less than 53

53 53 53

There are 48 scores greater than 53

52.5

53.5

Median = 52.83

FIGURE 3.1   Separating the scores within an interval to find the median.

and we find that the median score for the African American students is 50.64, slightly below that for the White students. If you request the medians from computer programs such as R, the values that you will obtain are 53.0 for the White and 51.0 for the African American students. Most programs use an approximation or a different definition. The values obtained are quite similar to those we derived, and in fact are what would be obtained if we were to round our results to integers. We consider this "close enough for government work."

This same process also can be applied to grouped frequency distributions. Consider the values in Table 2.9, which contains the cumulative frequency distributions for both the White and African American grouped frequency distributions. Applying the same logic as before to the White distribution, we see that we can go up to the interval 45–49 inclusive and have the sum of the frequencies below equal to 29. If we were to include the scores in the next interval, we would have to include a total of 56 scores, once again having crossed the median. Thus, we would set up the expression for the median as follows, keeping in mind that the interval width is now 5:

$$\text{Median} \quad = \quad \left(\frac{(100/2) - 29}{27} \right) 5 + 49.5 \qquad (3.4)$$

We would find the median for the White distribution to be 53.39. Likewise, we could find the median for the African American scores:

$$\text{Median} \quad = \quad \left(\frac{(100/2) - 46}{23} \right) 5 + 49.5 \qquad (3.5)$$

The resulting median is 50.37. You will note that the values obtained from the grouped frequency distributions are slightly different from those obtained from the ungrouped distributions; this discrepancy is attributed to grouping error. That is, implicit in this process, it is assumed that the scores are uniformly distributed within the class intervals. Usually, this is not the case, and the degree to which they are not uniformly distributed affects the magnitude of the discrepancy. But, not to worry. Remember that we are showing you the details to help you better understand the concepts. These numeric summaries are designed to help you obtain meaningful insights. Thus, roughly similar values convey essentially the same information. In reality, you will soon be relying on computer programs like R to analyze the numbers for you.

The Mean

There are several ways in which to combine a set of numbers to represent a central point. For now, we will define the mean as the arithmetic mean, or the sum of the scores divided by the number of scores. We agree with Huck (2009) that is important to acknowledge that the arithmetic mean is only one way to combine a set of values to present a description of centrality, albeit the most common way. However, there are other ways to "average" a set of numbers (e.g., geometric means, harmonic means, trimmed means). For example, when an investment advisor talks about the "3-year annualized gain" of a mutual fund, she is giving you the geometric mean, which equals the cube root of the product of the respective 3-yearly gains.

Given that we are describing the scores available to us, we will consider the scores to be a population, using the symbol μ (read "mu") to denote the mean. Thus, for the reading scores for White students contained in Table 2.1, we would define the arithmetic mean as:

$$\mu = \frac{54+50+51+58+...+84+55}{100} = \frac{5421}{100} = 54.21 \tag{3.6}$$

In a similar fashion, we can calculate the arithmetic mean of the reading scores for the African American students in Table 2.1:

$$\mu = \frac{40+42+54+51+...+48+64}{100} = \frac{5038}{100} = 50.38 \tag{3.7}$$

As you can see, there is not much more we can say about how to find a mean; it is a concept with which you were most likely quite familiar before you started this course. Now, we will take the opportunity to introduce some ideas about the mean and its attributes. We will start with some notation.

Summation Notation

At this point, it is appropriate to introduce you to some notation. You don't really need it right now, but you will soon, and it is never too early to begin. Let's say we are working with the numbers 4, 6, 3, 7, and 2. Given those five numbers, we could represent the mean as:

$$\mu = \frac{4+6+3+7+2}{5} \tag{3.8}$$

Based on years of experience, you know how to decode that symbol into a set of instructions, leading you to see that:

$$\mu = \frac{22}{5} = 4.4 \tag{3.9}$$

That is, you know that the symbol is telling you to add the five numbers in the numerator and then divide the total by five. So, in reality, the visual symbol presented in Equation 3.8 literally only works if you are working with those specific five numbers. We need another symbol that would work with any five numbers:

$$\mu = \frac{Y_1 + Y_2 + Y_3 + Y_4 + Y_5}{5} \tag{3.10}$$

We have now introduced subscript notation, along with a generic name for the variable, Y. The general form of subscript notation is Y_i. The i is an indeterminate value. Thus, we are now working with a symbol that can be used for any five values, which is somewhat limited. Yet, suppose that we are working with a set of scores that has more or fewer than five values. We will use n to denote the number of scores in the data set, revising our symbol to:

$$\mu = \frac{Y_1 + Y_2 + \ldots + Y_i + \ldots + Y_n}{n} \tag{3.11}$$

Given our penchant for brevity, we can simplify this symbol even further. The numerator of the symbol is telling us to sum the n numbers. We can substitute some shorter notation by using the symbol Σ, which is an upper-case Greek sigma, the summation operator. Thus we wind up with:

$$\mu = \frac{\sum_{i=1}^{n} Y_i}{n} \tag{3.12}$$

The $i = 1$ beneath the summation operator is telling you to start with the first value; the n above the summation operator is telling you to stop when you get to and include the last value.

With the intent to make this clearer, we mention the idea of a "trimmed" mean. Although it is more complex than this, the basic idea is to eliminate extreme values so that they do not affect the mean adversely. It is rumored that the Geography Department at UNC-Chapel Hill has reported that graduates of their department have a very large average annual income. (Of course, Michael Jordan graduated from that department in the 1980s.) If you wanted to write a symbol for the mean that instructed you to drop the three lowest scores and the three highest scores, you could write:

$$\mu_{\text{trim}} = \frac{\sum_{i=4}^{n-3} Y_i}{n-6} \tag{3.13}$$

Notice what we have done? Assuming that the Y_i values are in rank order, we have instructed you to skip the three lowest scores and the three highest scores. When working with a sample of data, the notation is slightly different:

$$\bar{Y} = \frac{\sum_{i=1}^{n} Y_i}{n} \tag{3.14}$$

Instead of using the symbol μ (mu), we have used the generic name of the variable, Y. Note that where the subscript i had been, there is now a dot. The dot notation indicates that the summation has taken place. The bar over the Y indicates that a division has taken place.

The mean has a number of interesting properties, two of which we will explain: the mean is a product-moment statistic, and the mean is a "least-squares" estimator.

The Mean as a Product-Moment or Balance Point

By virtue of the way it is derived, the mean can be considered the balance point of a distribution, such that the products of the deviations from the mean multiplied by the number of times each occurs must sum to zero. One might think of the mean as the center of gravity. Consider that we might be working with the three values 5, 8, and 14. Hopefully, without too much difficulty you can see that the mean of these three numbers is 9. Now consider what we have depicted in Figure 3.2.

Think about the figure as being like a scale. We have located "weights" at the three values, 5, 8, and 14. In order for the scale to balance, we would have to place the fulcrum at 9, so that the sum of the deviations on the left side $[(5 - 9) + (8 - 9) = -5]$ is equal in magnitude but opposite in sign to the sum of the deviation(s) on the right side $[(14 - 9) = 5]$. Stated differently, the mean is the point in a distribution about which the sum of the deviations of the scores from that point equals zero. We offer a proof of this in Technical Note 3.1 at the end of this chapter. You can skip this note if you wish, but trying to follow the proof and the explanations should enhance your understanding of summation notation.

The Mean as a Least-Squares Estimate

When we calculate the mean as a descriptive statistic to represent central tendency, in a sense we are saying that the mean is a representative score. Unless all of the scores are identical, we can anticipate that most, if not all, of the scores will be different from the mean. The differences between the actual scores and the mean can be considered errors in our estimate for each case. Clearly, we would like to keep those errors small. Furthermore, we feel that it is better to be off a small amount for many scores, so as not be off a lot on any score. This is the principle of least squares, and the mean is the least-squares estimate of central tendency. That is, the function

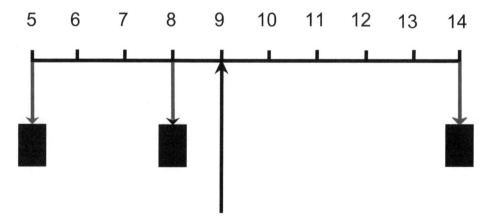

FIGURE 3.2   The mean as a product-moment statistic.

$$\sum_{i=1}^{n}(Y_i - a)^2$$

takes on its minimum value when the value of the constant a is equal to μ. If the scores are considered to be a sample from the population, we would substitute the sample mean. We show you the proof of this in Technical Note 3.2 at the end of this chapter, but it requires the use of calculus, so many of you may wish to skip it.

Properties of the Measures of Central Tendency

We have described three different measures of central tendency—the mode, the median, and the mean. Each of these involves a slightly different definition of "representative" and each has its advantages and disadvantages.

The Mode

First, the mode can be used with both quantitative and categorical variables. In fact, it is the only measure of the three that can be used with categorical variables. It is the most typical or frequently occurring value in the distribution. Unfortunately, it can be relatively unstable in that minor shifts of scores within a distribution can change the mode dramatically. Furthermore, distributions can have multiple modes, which can be both bad and good. If the intent is to be able to summarize a distribution with one value, having multiple modes can be problematic. On the other hand, knowing that a distribution has more than one mode can be informative; it might suggest that there are meaningful subgroups of cases within the distribution.

Finally, the mode does not readily fit into a system of advanced statistical procedures.

The Median

The median can be used only with quantitative data. It is the point on the scale that separates the highest 50% of the scores from the lowest 50% of the scores. As such, it is not sensitive to extreme values; shifts in the tails of the distribution do not affect the median. Thus, it may be the most appropriate measure to describe the central tendency of a skewed distribution or one that has some extreme values, particularly if they are all on the same side of the central point. Despite the appearance of the formula/expression for the median, we believe that it is fairly simple to calculate, once you understand the process. When you are working with an open-ended distribution (a distribution where one end or the other is expressed as "less than Y" or "greater than Y"), it is the only quantitative measure of central tendency that can be used. However, like the mode, the median does not fit easily into any simple mathematical system.

The Mean

As noted earlier, the mean can be thought of as the "center of gravity" of a distribution; it is the balance point. It uses information from each and every observation in the data set; that is generally a good thing. However, in the presence of outliers or skewness, it can lead to a misleading result. Consider once again the income distribution of geography majors at UNC-Chapel Hill. Michael Jordan's many, many millions of dollars in income draw the average up, especially when you consider that geography is a fairly small major at UNC. Also, as noted earlier, the mean is a balance point, or a product-moment statistic. As such, it is "compatible" with other product-moment statistics within advanced mathematical systems. We will have more to say about that shortly. Also noted earlier, the mean is a "least-squares" estimate.

Sampling Stability of the Three Measures of Central Tendency

Although the present discussion is focused on describing the characteristics of populations of data, we would be remiss if we did not point out another comparison that can be drawn among the three measures. Once again, we need to digress from the population description mode to the population/sample paradigm, the primary focus of this book. The basic idea is rather simple: when we draw samples from a population, we would like the results to be fairly consistent. That is, we would prefer that the statistics from the various samples be fairly similar. For example, if we were to draw a sample from a population and calculate the mean of the sample data, we would like the means of other drawn samples to be close. We can compare the sampling behavior of the mode, the median, and the mean using a simulation in R. In passing, R does not have a function for finding the mode as the mode is not used in inference. With some assistance from John Verzani (personal communication), we were able to write a function. One of the many strengths of R is the ability to create functions on your own. These functions are stored in a text file which is executed when the script file is executed.

The logic of the simulation is fairly straightforward; we first defined a population to be the set of integers one to 100, inclusive. Then we drew 20,000 random samples of 100 cases from the population of integers from 1 to 100, with replacement. For each of the 20,000 samples, we asked the program to calculate the mode, the median, and the mean. When the program was finished, we had 20,000 modes, medians, and means. We then asked the program to find the largest and smallest value of each statistic. The results were 30 and 1 for the mode, 23.50 and 8 for the median, and 20.20 and 11.08 for the mean. Thus, you can see that the mode jumps around more than the median and, in turn, the median more than the mean. For the skeptics who might be thinking that there is a unique finding, we ran the script again, getting a different set of 20,000 samples. The results were virtually the same: 30 and 1 for the mode, 23.0 and 8.5 for the median, and 20.52 and 11.20 for the mean. We have depicted these finding in Figure 3.3, in which we have constructed a histogram for the 20,000 means with the corresponding density distribution. We have also imposed the density distributions for the median and mode in the same figure. Note that, in the figure, the density distribution for the mode is a little higher in the middle than it is on the sides. This result is an artifact of our having used the "middle" mode (median of the modes) when there were multiple modes.

These findings support our assertion that the mean has the most sampling stability of the three statistics, with the median being second. We find this to be the case for the types of distributions typically encountered in behavioral research. There are exceptions, however. For example, the median becomes more stable than the mean in an extremely skewed distribution.

In making the point about the relative sampling stability of the three measures of central tendency, we implicitly relied on the notion of spread, the second distinguishing characteristic of distributions of scores. We now turn to a more formal treatment of the issue of dispersion, also called "spread" or "variability."

VARIABILITY

As we noted before, two distributions can be centered at the same point, but still be different from one another in terms of the spread, or variability, of the scores. For example, see Figure 3.4.

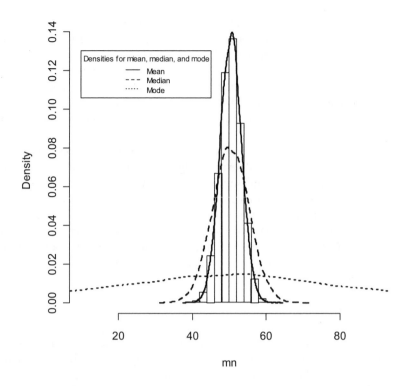

FIGURE 3.3   Comparing the density distributions for the mean, median, and mode.

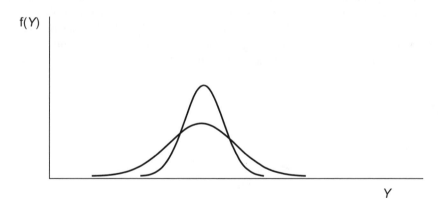

FIGURE 3.4   Two distributions having the same center, but different variability.

Measures of variability address the question, "How spread out are the scores from one another?" Measures that describe this attribute are the *range*, the *interquartile range*, the *average deviation*, and the *variance* with its associated *standard deviation*.

The Range

The range is the most simple of the measures of dispersion; it is the difference between the largest score and the smallest score in the distribution. For the reading scores of the White students in Table 2.1, it is 84 – 34, or 50. The range of the reading scores of African American students in Table 2.2 is 77 – 29, or 48. These two values appear quite similar, suggesting that the amounts of variability in the two sets of data are quite comparable. On occasion, you may see some texts suggest adding one point to the difference between the maximum and minimum values, making the two ranges 51 and 49, respectively. We fail to find any compelling reason to do so. We suppose that one could argue that there are really 51 different possible values in the scores for the White students. However, we would argue that the range is a distance, not the number of possible values.

The advantage of the range is that it is relatively easy to understand. Indeed, it is essentially what we employed in discussing the relative sampling stability of the three measures of central tendency when we reported the largest and smallest values. On the other hand, the range has some limitations. First, it tends to change systematically as a function of the sample size. That is, the larger the sample size, the more likely you will sample cases from the tails of the distribution, increasing the range. Second, the range tends to be unstable. A large change in only one case, either the maximum or the minimum value, will result in a large change in the range, even though the rest of the scores remain unchanged. This limitation leads us to the interquartile range as a possible solution to this problem.

The Interquartile Range

During our earlier explanation of summation notation, we referred to trimmed means as a way to reduce the influence of outliers. This feat would be accomplished by deleting the same, small percentage of the highest and lowest scores. Employing this idea in calculating a measure of variability, we could find the point that separates the lowest 25% of the scores from the highest 75% of the scores. We could also find the point that separates the bottom 75% of the scores from the top 25% of the scores. These two points are called *quartiles*, the first quartile (Q_1) and the third quartile (Q_3), respectively. The median is the second quartile (Q_2). The distance between Q_3 and Q_1 is the interquartile range (IQR), the range on the scale within which the middle 50% of the cases fall. The definition of the IQR is depicted in Figure 3.5.

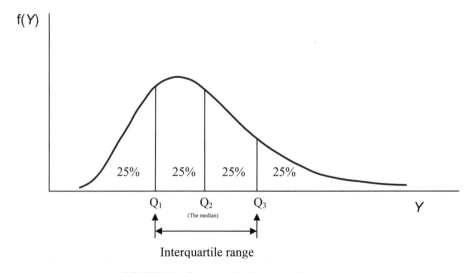

FIGURE 3.5   Depicting the interquartile range.

As you might have already imagined, the calculation of the quartile points is very similar to the calculation of the median. It employs virtually the same formula, but rather than using $n/2$, it uses the formula twice, once with $\frac{1}{4}n$ and again with $\frac{3}{4}n$. The minor changes are as follows:

$$Q_1 = \left(\frac{\frac{1}{4}n - \Sigma f_b}{f_i} \right) i + Y_{11} \tag{3.15}$$

$$Q_3 = \left(\frac{\frac{3}{4}n - \Sigma f_b}{f_i} \right) i + Y_{11} \tag{3.16}$$

The basic meaning of the various terms within the formulae is similar to those in the expression for the median. We illustrate the use of these formulae (Equations 3.15 and 3.16) using the grouped frequency distributions for the reading scores for the White and African American students, specifically the cumulative frequency distributions in Table 2.9. In both distributions, there are 100 scores.

First, for the White students, we want to find both Q_1 and Q_3. We know that we want to find the points below which 25 and 75 scores fall. We can see that we can go up to the point 44.5 without crossing Q_1. We can also see that there are 18 scores in the interval 44.5–49.5, the interval containing Q_1. Thus,

$$Q_1 = \left(\frac{(100/4) - 11}{18} \right) 5 + 44.5 \tag{3.17}$$

In a similar fashion, we can proceed up to the point 59.5 without crossing Q_3. We also note that there are 15 scores in the next interval, 59.5–64.5. Substituting the values into the expression appropriately:

$$Q_3 = \left(\frac{(3 \times 100/4) - 74}{15} \right) 5 + 59.5 \tag{3.18}$$

When we evaluate these two expressions, we find that $Q_1 = 48.39$ and $Q_3 = 59.83$. Thus, the IQR for the White students' scores is the difference, or 11.44 points. In a similar fashion, using the cumulative frequency distribution for the African American students in Table 2.9, we find:

$$Q_1 = \left(\frac{(100/4) - 13}{18} \right) 5 + 39.5 \tag{3.19}$$

and

$$Q_3 = \left(\frac{(3 \times 100/4) - 69}{12} \right) 5 + 54.5 \tag{3.20}$$

Thus, for the African American students' scores, $Q_1 = 42.83$ and $Q_3 = 57.0$, and the IQR = 14.17 points. Although the range suggested about the same or slightly less variability in the distribution of the African American scores, the IQR would suggest that the range for the middle 50% of the scores is perhaps slightly greater for the African American scores. Now let's learn about the next measure of dispersion, the mean deviation or average deviation.

The Average Deviation

The average deviation or mean deviation has been around for a very long time, although it is not used much in practice, having been replaced by the standard deviation as computational effort has been reduced by having access to computers. However, for the sake of completeness, we will describe it here. Furthermore, it has been extended to be the basis of one of the statistical procedures that we will present later in the book, Levene's test for the equality of variances. Once again, the idea is fairly simple. If a set of scores has very little variability, then the scores should all be quite close to the mean. As the variability increases, the distances from the mean will increase. We face a fundamental problem: as proved in Technical Note 3.1, the sum of the deviations around the mean will always sum to zero, no matter what the distribution looks like. To get around this problem, we can consider the deviations from the mean without regard to direction by taking the absolute values of the deviations before summing them. Thus, the average deviation (AD) can be defined as:

$$AD = \frac{\sum_{i=1}^{n} |Y_i - \mu|}{n} \tag{3.21}$$

For the reading scores of the White students in Table 2.1, recall that the mean was 54.21. We would compute the average deviation as:

$$AD = \frac{|54 - 54.21| + |50 - 54.21| + ... + |84 - 54.21| + |55 - 54.21|}{100} = \frac{705.52}{100} = 7.06 \tag{3.22}$$

For the reading scores of the African American students in Table 2.1, the mean was 50.38. In a similar fashion, we would find the average deviation to be:

$$AD = \frac{|40 - 50.38| + |42 - 50.38| + ... + |48 - 50.38| + |64 - 50.38|}{100} = \frac{755.24}{100} = 7.55 \tag{3.23}$$

A comparison of the two average deviations would suggest a little more spread in the scores of the African American students, consistent with the finding from the IQR.

The fundamental "trick" to finding the average deviation is to use the *absolute value* function to convert all the deviations from the mean to positive values, resulting in deviations from the mean that are meaningful distances, disregarding direction. There is also another way to get around the problem that the sum of the deviations from the mean is equal to zero. We can square the deviations from the mean and, as we shall see shortly, this strategy will result in a measure of dispersion that is compatible with the mean.

The Variance

The variance is defined quite simply as the "average squared deviation from the mean." In formal notation:

$$\sigma^2 = \frac{\sum_{i=1}^{n}(Y_i - \mu)^2}{n} \tag{3.24}$$

Note that we have used the Greek letters for the variance (σ^2) and for the mean (μ). At this point, we are still describing the characteristics of a population of scores. The numerator of the formula, the sum of squared deviations from the mean, is called the *sum-of-squares*. The sum-of-squares divided by the number of scores (n) is sometimes called a *mean square*. This particular form of the formula is called the "definitional formula;" it suggests that one first finds the value of μ, subtracts it from each and every value of Y, squares those differences, adds up the squared differences, and then divides by the number of cases. There are two liabilities imbedded in this process. First, it requires that the data be entered twice, first to find μ, and then re-entered a second time to find the deviations from μ. The second problem is related to the first; to find μ, one has to divide, and division can be a major source of rounding error.

There is a better way. As we show in Technical Note 3.3, the numerator (sum-of-squares) can be calculated without dividing to find the mean first. That is, the sum-of-squares (SS) can be written as:

$$SS = \sum_{i=1}^{n}Y_i^2 - \frac{\left(\sum_{i=1}^{n}Y_i\right)^2}{n} \tag{3.25}$$

The two terms, ΣY_i^2 and ΣY_i, can usually be derived by entering the data only once into most hand-held calculators. (Thus, you can use the time for the second data entry to enter the data again, to check if you did it correctly the first time!) We will show you toward the end of this chapter how to generate these quantities in R.

To demonstrate the difference between the two formulae, let's consider that we have the four numbers: 3, 4, 7, and 10. To use the definitional formula, we first find μ to be 6, which does not have any rounding error, which is obviously not usually the case. Then we substitute the values into Equation 3.24:

$$\sigma^2 = \frac{\sum_{i=1}^{n}(Y_i - \mu)^2}{n} = \frac{(3-6)^2 + (4-6)^2 + (7-6)^2 + (10-6)^2}{4} \tag{3.26}$$

Evaluating this expression, the result is 30/4, or 7.5. On the other hand, if we use Equation 3.25, we would proceed as follows:

$$SS = \sum_{i=1}^{n}Y_i^2 - \frac{\left(\sum_{i=1}^{n}Y_i\right)^2}{n} = \left(3^2 + 4^2 + 7^2 + 10^2\right) - \frac{(3+4+7+10)^2}{4} = 174 - \frac{24^2}{4} = 30 \tag{3.27}$$

Having found the sum-of-squares to be 30, we would divide by 4 to obtain the variance. The complete computational formula for the variance is:

$$\sigma^2 = \frac{\sum_{i=1}^{n} Y_i^2 - \left[\left(\sum_{i=1}^{n} Y_i \right)^2 / n \right]}{n} \tag{3.28}$$

We realize that we have presented many different formulae in this section, and we know that you will be moving away from hand computation to using a computer package to complete the calculations, R in our case. Nevertheless, we think that it is important that you see the actual formulae being used and have a little experience using them; it will make the concepts more meaningful. For example, if you look back at the definitional formula for the variance (Equation 3.24), you can see that it involved squaring the deviations from the mean. Thus, the variance is defined on a different scale than the original scores; if you consider the original scores to be on a linear scale, then variance is an area concept. To be able to use a measure of dispersion to describe the spread of a set of scores that is on the same scale as the original scores, we will use the *standard deviation*.

The Standard Deviation

Quite simply, the standard deviation is defined as the positive square root of the variance. By definition,

$$\sigma = \sqrt{\frac{\sum_{i=1}^{n} (Y_i - \mu)^2}{n}} \tag{3.29}$$

and the computational formula for the standard deviation would be:

$$\sigma = \sqrt{\frac{\sum_{i=1}^{n} Y_i^2 - \left[\left(\sum_{i=1}^{n} Y_i \right)^2 / n \right]}{n}} \tag{3.30}$$

Thus, for our small set of four scores used above, the standard deviation would be $\sqrt{7.5}$, or 2.74. Applying the same process to the White students' reading scores in Table 2.1,

$$\sigma = \sqrt{\frac{\sum_{i=1}^{n} Y_i^2 - \left[\left(\sum_{i=1}^{n} Y_i \right)^2 / n \right]}{n}} = \sqrt{\frac{54^2 + 50^2 + 51^2 + \ldots + 84^2 + 55^2 - \frac{5421^2}{100}}{100}} \tag{3.31}$$

$$= \sqrt{\frac{301,645 - 293,872.41}{100}} = \sqrt{77.7259} = 8.82$$

In a similar fashion, you can substitute the African American students' reading scores, and find

$$\sigma = \sqrt{\frac{\sum\limits_{i=1}^{n} Y_i^2 - \left[\left(\sum\limits_{i=1}^{n} Y_i\right)^2 / n\right]}{n}} = \sqrt{\frac{40^2 + 42^2 + 54^2 + \ldots + 48^2 + 64^2 - \dfrac{5,038^2}{100}}{100}} \tag{3.32}$$

$$= \sqrt{\frac{262,688 - 253,814.44}{100}} = \sqrt{88.7356} = 9.42$$

Interpreting the Standard Deviation

The standard deviation is a measure of dispersion, and two standard deviations may be compared if the two variables are measured on the same scale. If so, the set of scores with the larger standard deviation is more spread out than the one with the smaller standard deviation. But, what if the two sets of measures are not on the same scale? To address this issue, we can use the *coefficient of variation* (*CV*). The coefficient of variation is defined as:

$$CV = \frac{\text{Standard deviation}}{\text{Mean}} = \frac{\sigma_y}{\mu_y} \times 100 \tag{3.32}$$

Sets of measures with larger *CV*s are considered to be more spread out, or variable, than those with smaller *CV*s, regardless of scale.

SUMMARIZING OUR DESCRIPTIVE STATISTICS

We have completed our presentation of ways in which to summarize the characteristics of central tendency and variability, using the reading scores of the White and African American kindergarten students. Our results are presented in Table 3.1.

What can these scores tell us about the scores for both White and African American students? At this point, we certainly know a lot more about the two sets of scores than we did when

Table 3.1 A summary of the descriptive statistics for location and dispersion for both White and African American students

Characteristic	White students	African American students
Mode	64, 52, 51	49, 42
Modal class	50–54	50–54
Median	52.83	50.64
Mean	54.21	50.38
Range	50.00	48.00
Interquartile range	11.44	14.17
Average deviation	7.06	7.55
Variance	77.73	88.74
Standard deviation	8.82	9.42

they were first presented in Tables 2.1 and 2.2. With regard to the measures for central tendency, the mode is not very helpful; there are multiple modes for both groups. The mode may be useful for describing categorical data (as in Chapter 4), but it is not used very much with quantitative data. Looking at both the median and the mean, our calculations suggest that the scores for the White students may tend to be a little higher than those for the African American students. With the exception of the range, all of the measures of dispersion suggest that the scores for the White students may be little less widely dispersed than those for the African American students.

THE VARIANCE OF A SAMPLE

At this point, we digress to introduce a sometimes confusing concept. Until now, we have primarily been describing statistical techniques to summarize the data at hand. In effect, the data have been the population, the only data of interest. However, most applications of statistics in research occur within a different context. That is, we are using data available to us as a sample, upon which we can base inferences made to a population to which we do *not* have access. When we summarize the data with regard to central tendency (the mean), we calculate the sample mean and that is our estimate of the population mean. Calculating the variance on a sample is not quite that simple, however. Recall that we defined the variance as the average squared deviation from the mean. Referring back to Equation 3.24,

$$\sigma^2 = \frac{\sum_{i=1}^{n}(Y_i - \mu)^2}{n} \tag{3.34}$$

Note that we use μ in our calculations. That is, when we are working with a population and we calculate the mean, we actually have calculated μ. When we calculate the mean of a sample, we do not have μ; we only have an estimate of μ. Thus, we substitute our estimate of μ into the equation and indicate that we are estimating the variance by placing the "hat" symbol over σ^2.

$$\hat{\sigma}^2 = \frac{\sum_{i=1}^{n}(Y_i - \bar{Y})^2}{n} \tag{3.35}$$

What are the implications of this substitution? There are mathematical statisticians who can help us here. If we were to draw many, many samples for a defined population, we could calculate the variance on every one of them. Obviously, they would differ from sample to sample. Imagine that we drew one million samples and then averaged the million variances. That long-range average variance would give us some indication of the value being estimated by our "estimator." Statisticians have a tool that permits them to algebraically determine that value or long-range mean without actually drawing many, many samples. The tool is "expectation algebra," which can be used to find the long-range mean, or expected value. Applied to Equation 3.34, we can show that the expected value of our estimator can be determined as:

$$E\left(\hat{\sigma}^2\right) = \sigma^2 - \frac{\sigma^2}{n} \tag{3.36}$$

Looking at Equation 3.36, we see that our estimator tends to underestimate σ^2. Luckily, now that we know what is being estimated and what we want to estimate, we can use a little algebra to correct our estimator.

$$E\left(\hat{\sigma}^2\right) = \sigma^2 - \frac{\sigma^2}{n} = \frac{n\sigma^2}{n} - \frac{\sigma^2}{n} = \frac{n\sigma^2 - \sigma^2}{n}$$
$$= \frac{\sigma^2 (n-1)}{n}$$

(3.37)

We can see that our estimate is $(n-1)/n$ times the value we would like it to be. Thus, if we multiply our estimator by $n/(n-1)$, we should have an estimator that estimates our "target," σ^2. We will correct our estimator as follows:

$$\left(\frac{n}{n-1}\right)\hat{\sigma}^2 = \left(\frac{n}{n-1}\right)\frac{\sum_{i=1}^{n}(Y_i - \bar{Y})^2}{n} = \frac{\sum_{i=1}^{n}(Y_i - \bar{Y})^2}{n-1}$$

(3.38)

Thus, when we are using a sample of data to estimate the variance of a population, we use the sample mean as an estimate of the population mean to calculate the sum-of-squares, and then we divide by $n-1$ rather than n. This estimator is called the *unbiased estimate of the population variance* and is denoted by s^2. Note that we have changed from a Greek letter, σ, to its Latin counterpart, s:

$$s^2 = \frac{\sum_{i=1}^{n}(Y_i - \bar{Y})^2}{n-1}$$

(3.39)

There is another way to think about this. Suppose we were to ask you to write down five numbers. You could write down any five numbers you wanted. Now suppose we asked you to write down five numbers that have a mean of 20. Given the restriction that we have imposed, that the mean be equal to 20, you can only freely specify four of the five numbers; the fifth number is not free to vary as there is only one value, given the first four values, that will result in a mean of 20. This concept is called "degrees of freedom (*df*)." Thus, we will modify our definition of the variance. The variance is the sum of squared deviations from the mean divided by the number of independent observations (*df*). If we are working with a population, all of the observations are independent and we can divide by n. However, if we are using a sample of data to estimate the variance of the population, we use the mean of the sample as an estimate of the mean of the population. We lose one degree of freedom, and we divide by $n-1$.

A Simulation with R

We conducted a simulation with R to demonstrate that this really works. First, we established a population of the integers from 1 to 30, inclusive. The variance of this population is $\sigma^2 = 74.917$. Then we drew 15,000 samples, with replacement, for several different sample sizes (5, 10, 15, 20, 25, 30, 40, and 50). For each sample size, we calculated the expected value of the biased estimate (Equation 3.36), the average of the 15,000 biased estimates (Equation 3.35), and the average of the 15,000 unbiased estimates (Equation 3.38.) The results are presented in Table 3.2.

Table 3.2 Results from simulating the biased and unbiased estimates of the population variance ($\sigma^2 =$ 74.917)

Sample size	Expected value of biased estimates	Average of biased estimates	Average of unbiased estimates
5	59.933	60.192	75.239
10	67.425	67.342	74.824
15	69.922	70.101	75.108
20	71.171	71.289	75.041
25	71.920	71.940	74.938
30	72.419	72.356	74.851
40	73.044	72.928	74.979
50	73.418	73.520	75.020

After examining the contents of the table, you should be able to see several patterns. First, looking at the first column, you can see that the expected value of the biased estimate changes with the sample size. As the sample size increases, the amount of bias decreases. Second, comparing the first and second columns, we can see that the means of the 15,000 biased estimates are quite close to what we would expect them to be, based on the algebraically derived expected values. This finding supports the mathematical statisticians who derived the formula (Equation 3.36) for the expected value of the biased estimate. Third, and last, looking at the values in the third column, we see that the means of the 15,000 unbiased estimates of the population variance are all quite close to the actual population variance (74.917), regardless of the sample size. There is some regularity in this universe!

The Standard Deviation of a Sample

As noted previously, the standard deviation is the positive square root of the variance. When working with a sample, the standard deviation, which is denoted with an s, can be found by first finding the sample variance and then taking the square root.

$$s = \sqrt{s^2} = \sqrt{\frac{\sum_{i=1}^{n}(Y_i - \bar{Y})^2}{n-1}}$$

(3.40)

Now, we turn our attention to the matter of the shape of a distribution.

THE SHAPE OF A DISTRIBUTION

In order to describe the shape of a distribution of scores, we use two concepts—symmetry and curvature. This material was first discussed in Chapter 2, but it is appropriate to review some of the ideas here. To assist with this discussion, we present a modified version of Figure 2.9 in Figure 3.6.

The Symmetry of a Distribution

First, let's look at distributions A, B, and C. Distribution A is symmetric about its central point. However, neither distribution B nor C is symmetric. Most of the scores in distribution B are

f(Y)

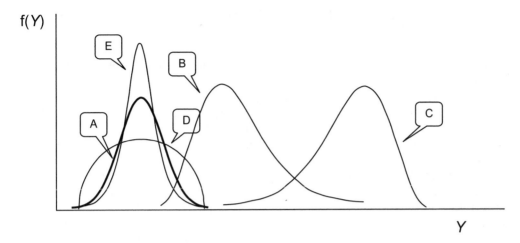

FIGURE 3.6   Several distributions for discussing the shape of a distribution.

toward the low end of the range, with a tail of scores trailing off to the high end. This departure from symmetry is called "skewness;" the scores in B are said to be skewed to the right, or positively skewed. In reverse, the scores in distribution C seem to cluster toward the upper end of the distribution; the scores in C would be described as skewed to the left, or negatively skewed. The particular label for the type of skewness is conveyed by the atypical scores. We will discuss how to measure/assess symmetry later in this chapter.

The Curvature of a Distribution

Consider distributions A, D, and E. All three of the distributions are symmetrical and centered at the same location. However, the three distributions are different. They differ in terms of the nature of the curvature. In this context, the standard is the normal distribution. We're assuming that you have some awareness of the normal or bell-shaped curve, although we will discuss it in much greater detail later in the book. Distribution A is a normal distribution. Departures from the curvature of a normal distribution are measured by the *kurtosis* of a distribution; derived from the Greek word *kyrtos* for "convex." Distributions that are flatter than normal with short tails are said to be platykurtic (depicted by distribution D). Distributions similar to E are peaked, with narrow "shoulders" and longer, heavy tails; they are said to be leptokurtic. Some practical examples: The heights of people tend to be normally distributed, income and family housing prices tend to be positively skewed, and the prices of futures in the financial markets tend to be leptokurtic.

In summary, thus far we have presented ways to summarize or describe the three characteristics of a distribution of scores: center, spread, and shape. In considering the central tendency, or location of a distribution of scores, we describe and defined three measures: the mode, the median, and the mean. For dispersion, we considered the range, the interquartile range, the average deviation, the variance, and its square root, the standard deviation. Last, we elaborated on the shape of a distribution, discussing skewness and kurtosis. We will now show how the mean, the variance, and measures of skewness and kurtosis are related to one another, making them mathematically compatible, or tractable. The vehicle for showing these interrelationships is known as *moment-generating functions*.

THE RELATIONSHIPS BETWEEN THE MEAN, THE VARIANCE, AND MEASURES OF SKEWNESS AND KURTOSIS

As it turns out, the mean, the variance, and the two measures of shape (skewness and kurtosis) can be derived within a common process. The core of the process is to subtract some value from each score and then raise the deviation to some power. For example, if we begin by subtracting the constant zero from each score, raise that deviation to the first power, and then sum the results, we wind up with the total sum of the scores, albeit in a rather long way. From that sum, we can derive the mean by dividing the sum by the number of scores. In like fashion, we could subtract the mean from each of the values, raise the deviations to the second power, and then sum the resulting values. Hopefully, you recognize this as the sum-of-squares, from which you can obtain the variance by dividing by the degrees-of-freedom. We have described the process in much greater detail in Technical Note 3.4 at the end of this chapter. In a similar way, deviations from the mean can be raised to the third power to obtain a measure of skewness and to the fourth power to obtain a measure of kurtosis. The specific formulae are presented in Technical Note 3.4.

A GRAPHIC TECHNIQUE FOR DEPICTING LOCATION, DISPERSION, AND SHAPE SIMULTANEOUSLY: BOX-AND-WHISKER PLOTS

To summarize, to describe a distribution of quantitative scores, it is important to present information about location, spread, and shape. In most situations, the mean, the standard deviation, and measures of skewness and kurtosis are the most appropriate information to provide. An alternative graphic depiction, the *box-and-whisker plot*, was devised by Tukey. It is sometimes called simply a *box plot*, and sometimes the "five-point summary." Contained in the figure are the median, the first and third quartiles, and the maximum and minimum values. A prototypic box plot is shown in Figure 3.7.

The ends of whiskers mark the most extreme cases that are not outliers. The maximum length of the whisker is $1.5 \times$ IQR. O (for outlier) is used to denote the position of an observation that falls between $1.5 \times$ IQR and $3 \times$ IQR from the ends of the box. E (for extreme) is used to denote any observation that falls more than $3 \times$ IQR from the ends of the box. Box plots are often shown in a vertical orientation. In either case, the box plot usually contains a scale for the variable being depicted, either at the side or along the bottom.

COMPUTER CASE STUDY

The purpose of this case study is to demonstrate how to use R to generate most, if not all, of the information that we have presented in this chapter. We will focus on a different variable, producing frequency distributions, histograms, and descriptive statistics that in turn will address questions about location, dispersion, and shape. Last, we will present box plots for the variables. We will focus on the item response theory (IRT) math scales scores for White and African American

FIGURE 3.7   A generic box-and-whisker plot.

students (*c1rmscal*) collected at the beginning of kindergarten for the same samples of 100 of each of the two groups. First, let's look at another way to create subgroups, using the **subset( )** command. In addition, rather than creating subfiles that contain all of the variables, we use the **select( )** option to include only the variable of interest, *c1rmscal*. We also include the entering kindergarten reading score expressed in T-score units.

```
ecls200 <- read.table ("c:/rbook/ecls200.txt",
  header = TRUE)
attach(ecls200)
ecls200.white <- subset(ecls200, race=="1",
  select = c(c1rrtsco, c1rmscal))
ecls200.aa <- subset(ecls200, race=="2",
  select = c (c1rrtsco, c1rmscal))
```

First, let's look at central tendency. R does not have a function to find the mode but, as noted earlier in this chapter, we have one to do so. Even so, the mode is not very useful in most situations. We can also locate the mode with R using the **table( )** function or by constructing a histogram. For the White students:

```
attach(ecls200.white)
table(c1rmscal)
```

We could also have requested this analysis by writing:

```
with(ecls200.white, table(c1rmscal)
```

The output follows:

```
> table(c1rmscal)
c1rmscal
  8   9  11  13  14  15  16  17  18  19  20  21  22  23  24  25  26  27
  1   1   3   2   1   1   6   4   6   6   2   8   8   4   4   9   9   5

 28  29  30  31  32  33  34  35  36  40  46  49
  2   2   2   3   1   3   1   1   2   1   1   1
```

Scanning the values in the table, we can see that the mode is 25 or 26, as each value appears nine times. After examining the results from **table( )**, we note that the range is 41 and that there are 100 cases. We decide that the class interval width should be 5 units, so that the lowest class interval should be 4.5–9.5, with the highest interval going up to 49.5. Thus, we write our **hist( )** command:

```
hist(c1rmscal, prob = TRUE,
  breaks=seq(4.5, 49.5, 5),
  xlab = "Pre-K IRT Math Scores for Whites")
lines(density(c1rmscal))
rug(jitter(c1rmscal))
```

The results are shown in Figure 3.8.

Looking at the histogram, we can see that the "tallest" bar is over the class interval 25–29. More often, we are interested in finding the median and the mean. The commands in R are **median( )** and **mean( )**. Our command for the mode is **mode( ).**

```
> mode(c1rmscal)
[1] 25 26
> median(c1rmscal)
[1] 23
> mean(c1rmscal)
[1] 23.31
```

Thus for the White students, we can see that there are two modes at 25 and 26, just as we noted in the table, and that the median and mean are both quite close to 23. We again note that the function used by R to find the median is slightly different from the one we presented earlier in this chapter, but it is close enough. To assess dispersion, R has several commands: **range( )**, **IQR( )**, **var( )**, and **sd( )**. There is no command to find the average deviation, but a function could be written if needed. We should point out that R, like most statistical programs, returns the unbiased sample estimate of variance ($n-1$) rather than the population variance (n). We have written a function (**var.pop( )**) that returns the value of the population variance.

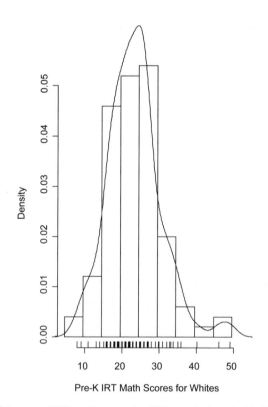

FIGURE 3.8   Histogram of IRT math scores for White students entering kindergarten.

```
> range (clrmscal)
[1]  8 49
> IQR(clrmscal)
[1] 7.5
> var.pop(clrmscal)
[1] 50.2139
> var(clrmscal)
[1] 50.72111
> sd(clrmscal)
[1] 7.121876
```

R also has several commands that provide information regarding location and dispersion at the same time. They are the commands **quantile( )**, **summary( )**, and **fivenum( )**. The default values returned by the **quantile( )** function are the minimum, maximum, first quartile, median, and third quartile. The values returned by the **summary( )** function are the same, but it also provides the mean. The **fivenum( )** function provides basically the same values as the default values from the **quantile( )** function, but instead of the first and third quartiles, it reports the Tukey hinges, which are essentially the same values.

```
> quantile(clrmscal)
   0%    25%    50%    75%   100%
 8.00  18.75  23.00  26.25  49.00
> summary(clrmscal)
   Min. 1st Qu.  Median    Mean 3rd Qu.    Max.
   8.00   18.75   23.00   23.31   26.25   49.00
> fivenum(clrmscal)
[1]   8.0 18.5 23.0 26.5 49.0
```

In a similar fashion, we can generate descriptive statistics for the African American students. First, we need to detach the subfile for White students and attach the data file for African American students. If we had used the **with( )** command, we would not have to detach the subfile for White students.

```
detach(ecls200.white)
attach(ecls200.aa)
> table(clrmscal)
clrmscal
  8  9 10 11 12 13 14 15 16 17 18 19 20 21 22 23 24
  2  2  2  5  3  6  8  2  8  6  5 11  9  7  2  5  2

 25 26 28 29 31 33 43
  6  1  1  3  1  2  1
```

We can see that the mode minimum value is 8, the maximum value is 43, and the mode is 19. If we construct the histogram, we see that the modal class interval is 15–19.

```
hist(c1rmscal, prob = TRUE,
  breaks=seq(4.5, 44.5, 5),
  xlab = 'Pre-K IRT Math Scores for African
     Americans')
lines(density(c1rmscal))
rug(jitter(c1rmscal))
```

The results are shown in Figure 3.9.

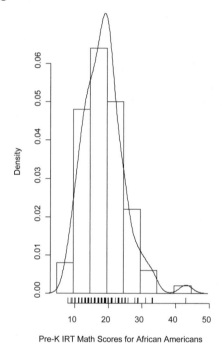

Pre-K IRT Math Scores for African Americans

FIGURE 3.9   Histogram of IRT math scores for African American students entering kindergarten.

Producing the descriptive statistics for the African American students:

```
> mode(c1rmscal)
[1] 19
> median(c1rmscal)
[1] 19
> mean(c1rmscal)
[1] 18.59
> range(c1rmscal)
[1]   8 43
> IQR(c1rmscal)
```

```
[1] 7
> var.pop(c1rmscal)
[1] 35.4619
> var(c1rmscal)
[1] 35.8201
> sd(c1rmscal)
[1] 5.98499
> quantile(c1rmscal)
   0%  25%  50%  75% 100%
    8   14   19   21   43
> summary(c1rmscal)
   Min. 1st Qu.  Median    Mean 3rd Qu.    Max.
   8.00   14.00   19.00   18.59   21.00   43.00
> fivenum(c1rmscal)
[1]   8 14 19 21 43
```

Looking over the results for the two groups, we can see that the scores for the White students tend to be a little higher than those for the African American students and they also tend to be a little more variable.

R does not have preprogrammed functions for describing the shape (skewness, kurtosis, and their standard errors) of a distribution. Later in this chapter (Technical Note 3.4) we present Fisher's statistics for calculating these statistics. We have used those formulae to create functions in R to return Fisher's coefficients of skewness and kurtosis, and their respective standard errors. The code for these functions, as well as that for the mode, is executed by the **source( )** function at the beginning of the script; the code is presented on the companion website for this book. In order to generate the statistics describing shape, we use the following code, executed from a script file:

```
attach(ecls200.white)
skewness(c1rmscal)
SEsk(c1rmscal)
kurtosis(c1rmscal)
SEku (c1rmscal)
detach(ecls200.white)
attach(ecls200.aa)
skewness(c1rmscal)
SEsk(c1rmscal)
kurtosis(c1rmscal)
SEku(c1rmscal)
detach(ecls200.aa)
```

Of course, we could have used the original data.frame (*ecls200*) with the **tapply( )** command. We obtained output as follows:

```
> attach(ecls200.white)
> skewness(c1rmscal)
[1] 0.741362
> SEsk(c1rmscal)
[1] 0.2413798
> kurtosis (c1rmscal)
[1] 1.681191
> SEku(c1rmscal)
[1] 0.4783311
> detach(ecls200.white)
> attach(ecls200.aa)
> skewness(c1rmscal)
[1] 0.9165493
> SEsk(c1rmscal)
[1] 0.2413798
> kurtosis(c1rmscal)
[1] 2.015073
> SEku(c1rmscal)
[1] 0.4783311
> detach(ecls200.aa)
```

Rounding to two decimal places, we can see that the measures of skewness and kurtosis for the White students are .74 and 1.68, respectively. For the African American students, the comparable measures are .91 and 2.01, respectively. Our functions for the standard errors with 100 cases in each group return values of .24 and .48 for skewness and kurtosis, respectively.

What do the measures of skewness and kurtosis suggest? The measure of skewness can range from $-\infty$ to $+\infty$. When a distribution is leptokurtic, the measure of kurtosis is bounded by $+\infty$. Interestingly, when a distribution is platykurtic, the measure of kurtosis is bounded on the lower end by -6 for small samples; kurtosis in a population can never be less than -2. We elaborate on these limits in Technical Note 3.5. There are two perspectives from which to evaluate information about skewness and kurtosis. From one perspective, the degree to which the non-normality is substantial depends on context, and consequently differing guidelines have been presented by authors. For example, Kline (2005) cited West, Finch, and Curran (1995) who suggested that as long as the measures of skewness are within the range of ±2 and the measures of kurtosis are less than 7, the distributions are "relatively close" to normal, whereas Hopkins and Weeks (1990) have labeled a skewness of 1 to be substantial.

From another perspective, you can divide the measure of skewness by its standard error. For the White students' scores that would be .74/.24, or approximately 3. Likewise, you could divide the measure of kurtosis by its standard error, resulting in a value a little larger than 3. Thus, both skewness and kurtosis are both about three standard deviations from the expected value of zero, if the scores are being sampled from a normal population. Were we to do the same thing with the scores for African American students, we would find similar results, although slightly more skewed and leptokurtic. Both distributions appear to be positively skewed and leptokurtic. But, before we come to any conclusions, we should probably look at some visual displays of the data, along with the possibility of outliers. And once again, the answer to whether or not the measures of skewness and kurtosis are within "acceptable limits" is, like so many other things in life, "it depends. "

At this time, we can show you how to use R to produce a figure that will display the box-and-whisker plots for the two groups of students with the **boxplot( )** function. To do this, we need to go back to the data frame that contains all of the cases, both White and African American students.

```
attach(ecls200)
boxplot(c1rmscal ~ race)
```

When we run this set of commands, we obtain the graphic shown in Figure 3.10.

These plots are consistent with our finding that both sets of scores are positively skewed. Note the "trailing" cases in the upper part of the box plots. If we want to know which specific cases are in the tails, we can employ the **which( )** function. For example, we might want to know which cases had values greater than 35:

```
which(c1rmscal > 35)
```

The output is:

```
> which(c1rmscal > 35)
[1]   19   20   36   61   77 134
```

To summarize our findings, it appears that the scores for the White students tend to be a little higher and more variable than those for the African American students. Both distributions are slightly positively skewed and leptokurtic; both have some outliers at the high ends of the distributions.

FINDING THE SUM OF Y AND THE SUM OF Y² WITH R

When calculating the mean and the variance, preliminary calculations involve finding the sum of the set of scores and also the sum of the scores squared (before summing). As you can see in Equations 3.12 and 3.25, these two values are the essential ingredients. To do this with R is a very simple matter. Let's draw a random sample of 10 values from the integers from 1 to 20 inclusive.

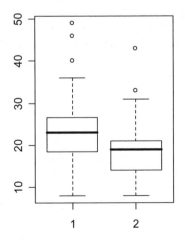

FIGURE 3.10   Box plots of the IRT math scores for White (1) and African American (2) students.

In our R script below, we will store the 10 random values in a vector *Y*, print them out, and then develop the two quantities we need:

```
# Script 3b
# Define the population
pop <- 1:20
y <- sample(pop, size = 10, replace = TRUE)
y
sum.y <- sum(y)
sum.y
sum.y2 <- sum(y*y)
sum.y2
```

The result is:

```
> y
 [1] 18 19 15 19 10  8  6  4 14 19
> sum.y <- sum(y)
> sum.y
[1] 132
> sum.y2 <- sum(y*y)
> sum.y2
[1] 2044
```

CHAPTER SUMMARY

In this chapter, we have presented several different measures that can be used to describe distributions of data. To describe location or central tendency, we have presented the mode, the median, and the mean. For dispersion, we have presented the range, the interquartile range, the average deviation, the variance, and the standard deviation. Describing the shape of a distribution quantitatively is best done with a computer program. In particular, we can use measures of skewness and kurtosis and their respective standard errors (standard deviations). In conclusion, when describing a set of scores, we refer to the "four-S" principle; one should address the issues of size, "s"enter, spread, and shape.

Key Terms

Average deviation	Mode
Central tendency	Quartiles
Coefficient of variation	Range
Degrees of freedom	Sampling stability
Dispersion	Skewness
Interquartile range	Standard deviation
Kurtosis	Summation notation

Least-squares principle

Mean

Mean square

Median

Sum-of-squares

Unbiased estimate of σ^2

Variability

Variance

REFERENCES

Hopkins, K. D., & Weeks, D. L. (1990). Tests for normality and measures of skewness and kurtosis: Their place in research reporting. *Educational and Psychological Measurement*, *50*, 717–729.

Huck, S. W. (2009). *Statistical misconceptions*. New York: Routledge.

Kline, R. B. (2005). *Principles and practice of structural equation modeling* (2nd ed.). New York: Guilford Press.

West, S. G., Finch, J. F., and Curran, P. J. (1995). Structural equation models with non-normal variables: Problems and remedies. In R. H. Hoyle (Ed.), *Structural equation modeling: Concepts, issues, and applications*. Thousand Oaks, CA: Sage.

PRACTICE QUESTIONS

1. In a box plot, what percent of the observations fall in the box?

    a. 25%.
    b. 50%.
    c. 75%.
    d. depends on the distribution's shape.

2. Which of the following measures of central tendency indicates the point that divides the upper and lower 50% of the scores?

    a. Mean.
    b. Median.
    c. Mode.

3. If the mean is 35 and the median is 30, the distribution is likely to be:

    a. positively skewed
    b. negatively skewed
    c. symmetric
    d. bimodal.

4. Variance can be thought of as:

    a. half the range
    b. the sum of squared deviations from the mean
    c. the average deviation
    d. the average squared deviation from the mean.

5. Consider the following set of scores, 1, 5, 6, 7, 8, and 10. What is the median?

    a. 5.5.
    b. 6.0.
    c. 6.5.
    d. 7.0.

6. Say a distribution has $Q_1 = 10$, $Q_2 = 16$, and $Q_3 = 20$. Where would a score of 39 fall on the box plot?

    a. Inside the box.
    b. As part of the upper whisker.
    c. As an outlier.
    d. As an extreme.

7. What would happen to the mean of a distribution of test scores if a teacher adds 10 points to each score?

    a. It stays the same.
    b. It increases by 10 points.
    c. It becomes 10 times as large.
    d. It will increase, but the amount depends on the shape of the distribution.

8. What would happen to the standard deviation of a distribution of test scores if a teacher adds 10 points to each score?

    a. It stays the same.
    b. It increases by 10 points.
    c. It becomes 10 times as large.
    d. It will increase, but the amount depends on the shape of the distribution.

9. What would happen to the mean of a distribution of test scores if a teacher multiplies each score by 2?

    a. It stays the same.
    b. It increases by 2 points.
    c. It becomes twice as large.
    d. It will increase, but the amount depends on the shape of the distribution.

10. What would happen to the variance of a distribution of test scores if a teacher multiplies each score by 2?

    a. It stays the same.
    b. It becomes twice as large.
    c. It becomes four times as large.
    d. It will increase, but the amount depends on the shape of the distribution.

11. Suppose you have a sample of 28 scores. Consider the deviation of individual scores from the sample mean and from the population mean. Which of the following statements is true?

    a. The scores tend to deviate more from the population mean.
    b. The scores tend to deviate more from the sample mean.
    c. The scores deviate the same amount from each mean.

12. If the interquartile range is 12, what is the maximum length of the lower whisker on the box plot?

    a. 12.
    b. 18.
    c. 24.
    d. 36.

EXERCISES

3.1. Find the mode, the median, and the mean for the following scores:

Y	f(Y)
6	2
5	4
4	3
3	2
2	1
1	2

3.2. Find the mode, the median, and the mean for the following scores:

2 4 3 4 1 5 6 5 4 3 5 7 9

3.3. Find the modal class, median, and mean for the results from Exercise 2.3. (Use the keyed solution—Part B). What do the results tell you about the relative values?

3.4. Compute the range and interquartile range for the data in Exercise 2.2 (ungrouped) and Exercise 2.3 (grouped).

3.5. Compute the standard deviation for the data in Exercise 3.2.

3.6. Using R, generate descriptive statistics and graphs for the data in Exercise 2.2.

TECHNICAL NOTES

Technical Note 3.1: Proving that the Sum of the Deviations Around the Mean is Equal to Zero

1. $$\sum_{i=1}^{n}(Y_i - \mu) = \sum_{i=1}^{n}Y_i - \sum_{i=1}^{n}\mu \qquad \text{Why?}$$

The rules of summation tell us that the summation operator can be "distributed" across the terms of a linear combination $(Y_i - \mu)$.

2. $$\sum_{i=1}^{n}Y_i - \sum_{i=1}^{n}\mu = \sum_{i=1}^{n}Y_i - n\mu \quad \text{Why?}$$

The second term, $\sum_{i=1}^{n}\mu$, is telling us to sum the constant μ n times. That is like adding the number 3 n times. The result would be $3n$.

3. $$\sum_{i=1}^{n}Y_i - n\mu = \sum_{i=1}^{n}Y_i - n\left(\frac{\sum_{i=1}^{n}Y_i}{n}\right) \qquad \text{Why?}$$

We just substituted the expression for μ.

4. $\sum_{i=1}^{n} Y_i - n\left(\dfrac{\sum_{i=1}^{n} Y_i}{n}\right) = \sum_{i=1}^{n} Y_i - \left(\sum_{i=1}^{n} Y_i\right) = 0$ Why?

The n terms divide out, and the rest should be obvious.

Technical Note 3.2: Proof that the Sum of Squared Deviations from a Point is a Minimum when that Point is Equal to the Mean

First, let's start with the expression:

$$S = \sum_{i=1}^{n}(Y_i - a)^2$$

We want to find the value of a at which the value of S is at its minimum possible value. Those of you who have taken one semester of calculus will probably recognize this problem as one involving differential calculus. Those of you not having had any calculus may wish to stop reading this note here.

If you are still reading, here we go. First, we expand the expression for S by squaring the binomial.

$$S = \sum_{i=1}^{n}(Y_i - a)^2 = \sum_{i=1}^{n}\left(Y_i^2 + a^2 - 2aY_i\right)$$

Next, we will take the derivative of S with respect to the variable a.

$$\frac{dS}{da} = \sum_{i=1}^{n}(2a - 2Y_i)$$

The next step is to distribute the summation operator.

$$\frac{dS}{da} = \sum_{i=1}^{n}(2a - 2Y_i) = 2\sum_{i=1}^{n}a - 2\sum_{i=1}^{n}Y_i = 2na - 2\sum_{i=1}^{n}Y_i$$

Last, we set the derivative of S with respect to a equal to zero, and solve for a.

$$2na - 2\sum_{i=1}^{n}Y_i = 0$$

$$2na = 2\sum_{i=1}^{n}Y_i$$

$$na = \sum_{i=1}^{n}Y_i$$

$$a = \frac{\sum_{i=1}^{n}Y_i}{n}$$

Thus, you can see that the function S, the sum of squared deviations from some point, takes on its minimum value when the deviations are taken about the mean.

Technical Note 3.3: Deriving the Computational Formula for the Sum-of-Squares

1. $SS = \sum_{i-1}^{n} (Y_i - \mu)^2$ Why?

That is the definition!

2. $\sum_{i-1}^{n} (Y_i - \mu)^2 = \sum_{i=1}^{n} \left(Y_i - \dfrac{\sum_{i=1}^{n} Y_i}{n} \right)^2$ Why?

Substituting the formula for the mean μ.

3. $\sum_{i=1}^{n} \left(Y_i - \dfrac{\sum_{i=1}^{n} Y_i}{n} \right)^2 = \sum_{i=1}^{n} \left(Y_i^2 + \left(\dfrac{\sum_{i=1}^{n} Y_i}{n} \right)^2 - 2Y_i \left(\dfrac{\sum_{i=1}^{n} Y_i}{n} \right) \right)$ Why?

Expansion of a binomial.

4. $\sum_{i=1}^{n} \left(Y_i^2 + \left(\dfrac{\sum_{i=1}^{n} Y_i}{n} \right)^2 - 2Y_i \left(\dfrac{\sum_{i=1}^{n} Y_i}{n} \right) \right)_i = \sum_{i=1}^{n} Y_i^2 + \sum_{i=1}^{n} \left(\dfrac{\sum_{i=1}^{n} Y_i}{n} \right)^2 - \sum_{i=1}^{n} 2Y_i \left(\dfrac{\sum_{i=1}^{n} Y_i}{n} \right)$ Why?

Using the rules of summation to distribute the summation operator.

5. $\sum_{i=1}^{n} Y_i^2 + \sum_{i=1}^{n} \left(\dfrac{\sum_{i=1}^{n} Y_i}{n} \right)^2 - \sum_{i=1}^{n} 2Y_i \left(\dfrac{\sum_{i=1}^{n} Y_i}{n} \right) = \sum_{i=1}^{n} Y_i^2 + \sum_{i=1}^{n} \dfrac{\left(\sum_{i=1}^{n} Y_i \right)^2}{n^2} - 2 \sum_{i=1}^{n} Y_i \dfrac{\sum_{i=1}^{n} Y_i}{n}$ Why?

The second term is derived simply by squaring both numerator and denominator of the fraction inside the parentheses. The third term is derived by pulling the constant 2 outside the summation sign (rules of summation).

6. $\sum_{i=1}^{n} Y_i^2 + \sum_{i=1}^{n} \dfrac{\left(\sum_{i=1}^{n} Y_i \right)^2}{n^2} - 2 \sum_{i=1}^{n} Y_i \dfrac{\sum_{i=1}^{n} Y_i}{n} = \sum_{i=1}^{n} Y_i^2 + n \dfrac{\left(\sum_{i=1}^{n} Y_i \right)^2}{n^2} - 2 \dfrac{\left(\sum_{i=1}^{n} Y_i \right)^2}{n}$ Why?

The second term can be simplified, as the term following the first summation sign is constant with regard to the subscript i. Thus, we are adding the "constant" n times. The third term is simplified using basic laws of algebra.

7.
$$\sum_{i=1}^{n} Y_i^2 + n\frac{\left(\sum_{i=1}^{n} Y_i\right)^2}{n^2} - 2\frac{\left(\sum_{i=1}^{n} Y_i\right)^2}{n} = \sum_{i=1}^{n} Y_i^2 + \frac{\left(\sum_{i=1}^{n} Y_i\right)^2}{n} - 2\frac{\left(\sum_{i=1}^{n} Y_i\right)^2}{n} \quad \text{Why?}$$

The second term simplifies with one of the *n* terms dividing out. Note that the second term in the result now looks very much like the third term. This result simplifies to:

$$\sum_{i=1}^{n} Y_i^2 - \frac{\left(\sum_{i=1}^{n} Y_i\right)^2}{n}$$

Technical Note 3.4: Moment Generating Functions: The Relationships Between the Mean, the Variance, and Measures of Skewness and Kurtosis

The starting point for our discussion is an ungrouped frequency distribution for a set of *n* scores Y_i. In summation notation, the values of the subscript *i* range from 1 to *n*. In presenting the ungrouped frequency distribution, we are going to modify the notation slightly to Y_j, where Y_j is a value that Y_i can assume. For example, suppose that the first, seventh, and thirteenth scores in a distribution all have the value 17. In our modified notation, $Y_j = 17$ and has a frequency of 3.

An ungrouped distribution, much like the one in Table 2.5, is shown in Table 3.3.

We could represent the sum of the observations as:

$$\sum_{i=1}^{n} Y_i = 20 + 19 + 18 + 18 + 17 + 17 + 17 + \ldots + 15 + 15 + 14 = 234 \tag{3.41}$$

With our modified notation, we could also represent the sum of the observations as:

$$\sum_{j=1}^{k} Y_j \times f\left(Y_j\right) = (20 \times 1) + (19 \times 1) + (18 \times 2) + \ldots + (15 \times 2) + (14 \times 1) = 234 \tag{3.42}$$

Just for fun, see if you can use the information in Table 3.3 to replicate what we just did. Now let's use a mathematical trick of rewriting the first part of Equation 3.40, without really changing anything.

$$\sum_{j=1}^{k} Y_j \times f\left(Y_j\right) = \sum_{j=1}^{k} \left(Y_j - 0\right)^1 \times f\left(Y_j\right) \tag{3.43}$$

As you well know, subtracting zero from each value, Y_j, and then raising the difference to the first power makes not a bit of difference. However, we now have an expression for the sum

Table 3.3 An ungrouped frequency distribution

Y_j	$f(Y_j)$
20	1
19	1
18	2
17	3
16	4
15	2
14	1

of a set of numbers in a form that can be tweaked to yield other interesting results. This form is a variation of a moment-generating function. Its number is conveyed by the exponent, and it is said to be "about some point." Specifically, Equation 3.41 defines the "first moment about the origin" and it simply defines the sum of a set of scores. Furthermore, we know that the sum of a set of scores can be transformed to the mean by dividing by the number of scores. Now consider the next equation:

$$\sum_{j=1}^{k}\left(Y_j - \mu\right)^1 \times f\left(Y_j\right) \tag{3.44}$$

This expression is the "first moment about the mean." It is the sum of the deviations from the mean, which we know to be zero for all distributions. As a result, this moment is not going to permit us to differentiate one distribution from another. Moving on, what can we say about the "second moment about the mean"?

$$\sum_{j=1}^{k}\left(Y_j - \mu\right)^2 \times f\left(Y_j\right) \tag{3.45}$$

Hopefully, you can recognize the "second moment about the mean" as just another way to represent the sum of the squared deviations from the mean, or the sum-of-squares. And you should recall that the sum-of-squares divided by n (or $n-1$) is the variance. Thus, the second moment about the mean yields a value that can be transformed into the variance. Now that we are on a roll, let's look at the "third moment about the mean."

$$\sum_{j=1}^{k}\left(Y_j - \mu\right)^3 \times f\left(Y_j\right) \tag{3.46}$$

What is accomplished by raising the deviations from the mean to the third power is not so obvious. But think for a moment. Some of the deviations are positive and some are negative. When raised to the third power, they retain their original sign. Now think about a distribution that is positively skewed. With a long tail to the right, there are some scores that will yield large, positive deviations. When cubed, they get really large and positive. They will overwhelm the smaller negative deviations, giving a net result that is a positive number. What about a negatively skewed distribution? Given the long tail to the left, there are some scores that will have relatively large negative deviations. When cubed, they result in very large, negative values, which will overwhelm the smaller positive deviations. Thus, the net result across the entire set of scores will be negative. With a symmetric distribution, the cubed deviations should add to something close to zero. As you probably already suspect, the third moment about the mean can be transformed into a measure of skewness. There is more than one way to do this, but two formulae, derived by Karl Pearson and Sir Ronald Fisher, are the ones primarily used. At one time, the Pearson formula was used by the SYSTAT and STATA computer programs, while the Fisher formula was used by SPSS, SAS, and Excel. Given that many researchers are likely to use SPSS or SAS, we will provide the Fisher formula:

$$g_1 = \frac{n\sum_{i=1}^{n}\left(Y_i - \bar{Y}\right)^3}{(n-1)(n-2)s^3} \tag{3.47}$$

As you can see, this measure, g_1, is based on raising the deviations from the mean to the third power. It also involves the sample size n and the standard deviation s, effectively removing the sample size and the scale/metric from the results. Now, imagine that you repeatedly draw random samples from a symmetric population. The measure of skewness, g_1, is zero for a symmetric distribution. Thus, you would expect the different samples to have different measures of skewness, but they should be fairly close to zero. How close? Fisher also gave us an expression for the standard error (standard deviation) for his measure of skewness:

$$SE_{g_1} = \sqrt{\frac{6n(n-1)}{(n-2)(n+1)(n+3)}} \tag{3.48}$$

Some authors give an approximate formula for the standard error of skewness, saying that it is approximately the square root of $6/n$ ($\sqrt{(6/n)}$). In most instances, that is close enough for government work. Looking at Equations 3.47 and 3.48, no one in his or her right mind would willingly calculate these values. We present the formulae for your understanding, but we will rely on a computer program to do the work.

Let's take it one more step.

$$\sum_{j=1}^{k} (Y_j - \mu)^4 \times f(Y_j) \tag{3.49}$$

Of course, we would call this expression the "fourth moment about the mean." Difficult to explain conceptually, it actually captures the curvature of a distribution and can be transformed into a measure of kurtosis. There are symmetrical, unimodal distributions that are not normal distributions. Deviations from normality are measured by Fisher's formula for kurtosis, used by SPSS and SAS:

$$g_2 = \frac{n(n+1)\sum_{i=1}^{n}(Y_i - \bar{Y}.)^4}{(n-1)(n-2)(n-3)s^4} - \frac{3(n-1)^2}{(n-2)(n-3)} \tag{3.50}$$

As you can see, at the heart of it is the sum of the deviations from the mean, raised to the fourth power. Furthermore, the various terms involving n and s^4 remove both sample size and scale/metric from the measure. You also see a term subtracted at the end of the expression. In a *perfectly* normal distribution, the first term in the measure is equal to 3.0. The term that is subtracted is adjusted for sample size and re-centers the distribution of measures of kurtosis to be zero for normally distributed variables. Again, measures of kurtosis for samples drawn from normally distributed populations should be close to zero. Fisher also provided a formula for the standard error (standard deviation) for his measure of kurtosis:

$$SE_{g_2} = \sqrt{\frac{24n(n-1)^2}{(n-3)(n-2)(n+3)(n+5)}} \tag{3.51}$$

As with the measure of skewness and its standard error, we will rely on a computer program to calculate the values for us.

If you are like most people, it will take a little while to get comfortable conjuring up what non-zero values for skewness and kurtosis are telling you about a distribution's shape. What does a distribution with skewness of .49 and kurtosis of .56 look like? To what degree would that distribution look different than a normal distribution or a distribution with skewness of 1.77 and a kurtosis of 3.93? These things will get clearer with experience, if each time you examine a distribution you do so both graphically and in terms of the summary statistics. To help you get started we have included histograms along with skewness and kurtosis values for a wide variety of distributions in Figure 3.11. In examining these histograms you will notice that the lack of normality

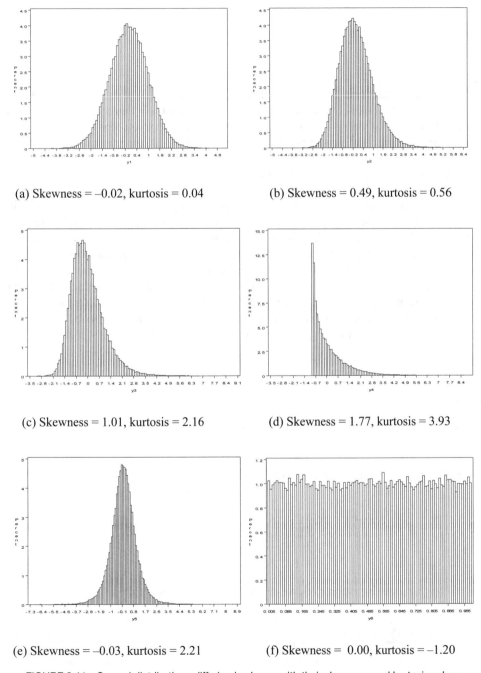

(a) Skewness = –0.02, kurtosis = 0.04   (b) Skewness = 0.49, kurtosis = 0.56

(c) Skewness = 1.01, kurtosis = 2.16   (d) Skewness = 1.77, kurtosis = 3.93

(e) Skewness = –0.03, kurtosis = 2.21   (f) Skewness = 0.00, kurtosis = –1.20

FIGURE 3.11   Several distributions differing in shape, with their skewness and kurtosis values.

in the distribution with skewness of .49 and kurtosis of .56 is barely perceptible, but the lack of normality in a distribution with skewness of 1.77 and kurtosis of 3.93 is visually quite obvious.

To summarize, we have just shown you that a measure of central tendency (the mean), a measure of variation (the variance and standard deviation), and measures of shape (skewness and kurtosis) can all be derived from the same process, raising deviations from some value to a power. The general form is:

$$\sum_{j=1}^{k} (Y_j - a)^m \times f(Y_j)$$ (3.52)

For us, the constant being subtracted will either be the origin (0) or the mean (μ). The exponent m will be 1, 2, 3, or 4. Obviously, there are possibilities other than the four we have presented, but the four that we have presented tell you virtually all that you need to know to describe a distribution of scores. Taken together, they are like the DNA of a distribution!

Technical Note 3.5: Limits on the Measure of Kurtosis

Kurtosis provides an indication of how much farther some observations are from the mean than others. When we have some observations that are much farther from the mean than others (e.g., outliers) the kurtosis value is large. There is no limit to how much further these outlying observations may be from the mean relative to the other observations and thus no upper bound on kurtosis.

The minimum value for kurtosis is obtained when no observations are farther from the mean than any others. This happens when exactly half the observations are at the minimum and half the observations are at the maximum (e.g., 0, 0, 100, 100, or 49, 49, 51, 51). In this case all deviations from the mean are equal in magnitude, with half being positive and half negative.

To derive the minimum value of kurtosis that can be calculated under this condition, let

$$D_i = Y_i - \overline{Y}.$$

However, since all of the deviations are equal, we will define:

$$\sum_{i=1}^{n} (Y_i - \overline{Y})^4 = nD^4$$

In a similar fashion, we can determine that:

$$s^4 = \left(s^2\right)^2 = \left(\frac{\sum_{i=1}^{n}(Y_i - \overline{Y})^2}{n-1} \right)^2 = \left(\frac{nD^2}{n-1} \right)^2 = \frac{n^2 D^4}{(n-1)^2}$$

Now referring back to Equation 3.50, we can make substitutions as follows:

$$g_2 = \frac{n(n+1)\sum_{i=1}^{n}(Y_i - \overline{Y}.)^4}{(n-1)(n-2)(n-3)s^4} - \frac{3(n-1)^2}{(n-2)(n-3)} = \frac{n(n+1)(nD^4)}{(n-1)(n-2)(n-3)\left(\frac{n^2 D^4}{(n-1)^2}\right)} - \frac{3(n-1)^2}{(n-2)(n-3)}$$

which can be simplified to:

$$g_2 = \frac{n(n+1)\left(nD^4\right)}{(n-1)(n-2)(n-3)\left(\dfrac{n^2D^4}{(n-1)^2}\right)} - \frac{3(n-1)^2}{(n-2)(n-3)} = \frac{(n-1)^2 n^2 (n+1)D^4}{(n-1)(n-2)(n-3)n^2D^4} - \frac{3(n-1)^2}{(n-2)(n-3)}$$

In turn, this expression can be simplified by dividing the numerator and denominator of the first term by common terms, obtaining:

$$g_2 = \frac{(n-1)(n+1)}{(n-2)(n-3)} - \frac{3(n-1)^2}{(n-2)(n-3)}$$

At this point, we can see that, under the condition yielding a minimum value for kurtosis, we have an expression that depends only on sample size. In order for the expression to be defined, n must be four or greater. When sample size is at the smallest possible value (4), the expression for g_2 evaluates to –6. As sample size approaches "infinity" (i.e., we have the population), $g_2 = 1 - 3 = -2$.

Thus, when working with a sample, we can be confident that the measure of kurtosis (g_2) can never be less than –6.0; in a population the minimum value of kurtosis is –2.0.

4

Describing Categorical Data: Frequency Distributions, Graphics, and Summary Statistics

INTRODUCTION

In Chapters 2 and 3 we presented techniques for aggregating and describing sets of quantitative measurements, focusing on the properties of centrality, dispersion, and shape. In this chapter we present techniques for summarizing the properties of nominal measurements, where the numerals have no numeric meaning and are simply labels for the categories into which our observations may be classified. For example, in the two previous chapters, we have been working with a data set including data for 200 children entering kindergarten, 100 of which were White and 100 of which were African American. These data were randomly sampled from the larger data file described in the codebook contained on the book website. In the larger file of 2,577 cases, there are several other racial/ethnic groups represented. If you look at the codebook as related to the variable "race," you will note that values of one (1) refer to "White, Non-Hispanic," values of two (2) refer to "Black or African American, Non-Hispanic," values of three (3) refer to "Hispanic, Race Specified," etc. Looking at the column of values for "race" in the data file, you will see integer values 1 through 8, with –9 for missing values. The integer simply informs you of the race/ethnic group of that particular case.

We gave considerable thought to integrating the material in this chapter within the previous two chapters. Ultimately, however, we felt that there is a sufficient difference between quantitative variables and nominal/categorical variables that a separate chapter on describing nominal/categorical variables is warranted. In showing you how to prepare tabular and graphic depictions of the data, some of the work from previous chapters will be repeated. We will revisit the issues of central tendency and dispersion, but the property of shape is not appropriate for categorical measures.

FREQUENCY TABLES

We will continue to work with the smaller data set with information on the White and African American entering kindergarteners. In that data file, there are data regarding several categorical variables such as gender, family type, and parental educational level. First, let's focus on the gender variable, which is coded 1 for "male" and 2 for "female." We might want to compare the two

Table 4.1 Gender distribution within each of the two racial groups

	White	African American
Male	54	50
Female	46	50

Table 4.2 Distribution of family type within each of the two racial groups

	White	African American
Two parents, plus siblings	90	73
Two parents, no siblings	8	20
One parent, plus siblings	2	5
One parent, no siblings	0	1
Other	0	1

racial groups to see if they are similar or different with regard to the distribution of gender. To do that, we would simply count up the number of 1s and 2s within each racial group, presenting our results in a table like Table 4.1.

Examining the numbers in the table, it would appear that the gender variable is fairly evenly distributed, especially in the African American group. Later in the book, we will show you how to more directly address the question of whether the distribution of gender is the same in both groups. The real question is not whether the distributions are "identical." Clearly, they are not. But are they sufficiently similar so that we could consider the differences to be the result of random sampling error?

Let's take a look at another of the categorical variables, family type or structure. It is the variable *p1hfamil* in the data file, and it is coded with the integers 1 through 5. Rather than explain the coding here, we will label the values in the frequency table and refer you to the codebook in Appendix B. Once again, counting the number of times each integer occurs within each of the racial groups, we would arrive at the results presented in Table 4.2.

Once again, the two racial groups appear to be rather similar with regard to "family type." Over 90% of the children in each of the groups are living with two parents. You can see that constructing frequency distributions for categorical variables is very similar to constructing such distributions for quantitative variables. The only difference is that, with quantitative variables, there is a natural ordering of the values. With categorical variables, you need to give some thought as to how you are going to order/present the categories in the table. There may be more than one way to do it, but you should have a reason in mind. In both Table 4.1 and Table 4.2, we have chosen to follow the lead of the codebook's author. In Table 4.1, males are coded as ones and females as twos. In Table 4.2, two-parent families are listed before one-parent families, and within each of those groups, "with siblings" precedes "no siblings." Like many category systems, we also need an "other" category. As with quantitative variables, these tabular presentations of data can also be depicted in graphic form.

GRAPHIC DISPLAYS

When working with quantitative variables, we could choose to present our data graphically in the form of histograms, frequency polygons, stem-and-leaf displays, and box plots. When working with categorical variables, we are somewhat more limited in our choices. The two most popular forms of presentation are *bar charts* and *pie charts*.

Bar Charts

In many ways, bar charts are similar to histograms. However, there is one important difference. In histograms, the vertical bars depicting the frequency of values or class intervals are adjacent to one another, touching, unless there is an interval in which there are no scores. Having the bars touch in histograms conveys a sense of continuity. In bar charts, the vertical bars are separated by space to convey the categorical nature of the data. A bar chart for the gender distribution in the White students sample is shown in Figure 4.1.

Sometimes, bar charts are constructed in a more complex fashion, to show the frequency distribution of the categorical variable in more than one group. An example is given in Figure 4.2, which shows the distribution of gender for both White and African American children entering kindergarten.

There are different ways to use colors to label your variables. Sometimes, in contrast to Figure 4.2, the males may share a color distinct from that shared by the females. These decisions are really a matter of taste.

Pie Charts

Pie charts are an alternative way to graphically depict frequency distributions of categorical variables. They are circles that look like "pies," with the slices representing the relative proportions of the different categories. Bar charts can be drawn manually using any of several different

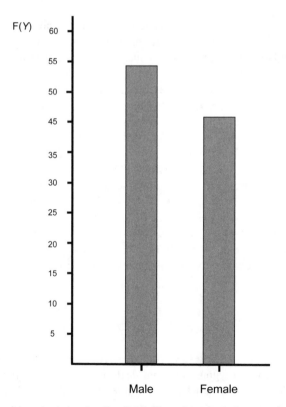

FIGURE 4.1   A bar chart showing the distribution of gender in the sample of White students.

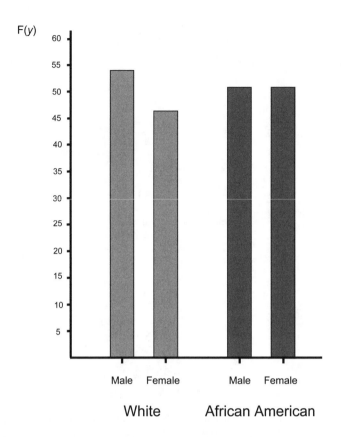

FIGURE 4.2   Bar chart showing the distribution of gender for both White and African American students entering kindergarten.

graphic computer programs. The bar charts in Figures 4.1 and 4.2 were drawn using Microsoft PowerPoint. Drawing pie charts manually is difficult. In addition to the difficulty, there is a broad consensus among statisticians that they should not be used (Verzani, 2006, p. 36). In a bar chart, the number of cases in a category is depicted as length, whereas in a pie chart the number of cases is represented by area. Generally, human beings are much more adept at judging length than they are at judging area. Nevertheless, in Figure 4.3 we show some examples of pie charts, prepared using R, depicting the distribution of family type.

As you can see, the distributions of family type for White and African American students are slightly different, although both pie charts are predominantly white in color, showing "children living with two parents plus siblings." In the next section we'll describe these distributions in greater detail, developing indices to describe aspects of the frequency distributions.

DESCRIBING FREQUENCY DISTRIBUTIONS OF CATEGORICAL VARIABLES

As we noted earlier, it is possible to summarize the characteristics of central tendency and dispersion of nominal measurements, although our options are much more limited than those available to us when working with quantitative variables. Descriptions of shape are more difficult, if not impossible, as most definitions of shape require quantification.

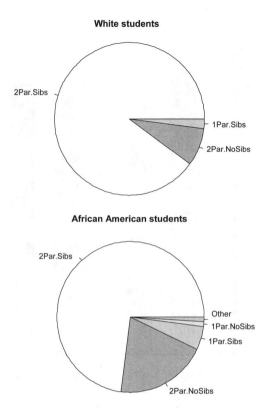

FIGURE 4.3   Pie charts depicting the distribution of family type for White and African American students.

Describing Central Tendency or Location

The only measure of central tendency appropriate for nominal measurements is the mode, which we have described previously. In describing the distributions of gender presented earlier in this chapter, we might say that the "modal gender" for White students is "male." Describing the distributions of "family type" for White and African American students, we could say that the "modal family type" for both groups is "two-parent families, with siblings." If we wished to provide more detailed information, we could use proportions. For example, we could say that 54% of the White students are male and 46% of them are female. In describing "family type" for the African American group, we might say that 73% live in two-parent families with siblings, 20% of them live in two-parent families without siblings, 5% of them live in one-parent families with siblings, 1% of them live in one-parent families without siblings, and 1% of them live in some sort of other arrangement.

Describing Dispersion or Variability

Recall that the notion of variability addresses the degree to which the observations differ from one another. When dealing with quantitative variables, the measures of dispersion are all based on some definition of distance (i.e., range, interquartile range, average deviation, variance, standard deviation). When you are dealing with nominal level measurements, the property of distance is not present. Rather, a measure of variability for nominal measurements must be based on the notion of differentiation.

Consider the distribution of gender for White students described earlier. Fifty-four of them are male; 46 of them are female. None of the males can be distinguished from any of the other males, nor can any of the females be distinguished from any of the other females. However, each of the 54 males can be distinguished from each of the 46 females. That is, within this sample of 100 students, you can make 54 × 46, or 2,484 differentiations. If the males and females were equally distributed, as they are in the African American group, there would be 50 in each gender group. In that case, we can make 50 × 50, or 2,500 differentiations. Actually, given two groups with 100 observations, that is the maximum number of differentiations that can be made. Thus, we might think that the variable of gender is more variable for African American students than it is for White students. Recall that variability was defined previously as cases being "different" from each other with regard to distance. With a categorical variable, we cannot use a "distance" metric but must rely on differentiation. As there are 2,500 possible differentiations in the African American group and only 2,484 possible differentiations in the White group, we can say that the African American group is more differentiated, or variable. Now consider another set of observations, where there are 20 males and 80 females. In this case, we can make 1,600 distinctions. At the extreme, imagine a set of observations in which all of the cases are male; there are no distinctions possible with regard to gender. Returning to our data set of 200 cases, we can directly compare the number of gender distinctions because both the White and African American groups have the same number of observations (100) classified into the same number of groups (2).

When there are more than two categories—as with family type—things get a little more complex. With five categories and 100 cases, the maximum number of distinctions would be obtained if there were 20 cases in each category. Given five groups, we could distinguish the 20 cases from the 20 cases in each of the other groups; there are 10 such comparisons (groups 1 to 2, 1 to 3, 1 to 4, 1 to 5, 2 to 3, 2 to 4, 2 to 5, 3 to 4, 3 to 5, and 4 to 5), each yielding 400 distinctions. Thus, the maximum number of distinctions possible would be 4,000. Now, let's consider the distribution of family type for the White students presented in Table 4.2. The frequencies of the five family types were 90, 8, 2, 0, and 0, respectively. In this instance we can distinguish each of the 90 cases from each of the 8 cases (720), each of the 90 cases from each of the 2 cases (180), and each of the 8 cases can be distinguished from each of the 2 cases (16). Thus, we can make a total of 916 distinctions in the actual data (720 + 180 + 16 = 916). Given that there would be 4,000 possible distinctions under the condition of maximum dispersion, we could create an index of variation of 916/4000, or .229. Kirk (1990) has described just such a process, labeling it as *the index of dispersion*, sometimes called the *index of qualitative variation*. He described the index as the ratio of "the number of distinguishable pairs to the maximum possible number of distinguishable pairs for *c* categories" (p. 125).

Our presentation above would lead you to believe that calculating the index of dispersion requires a lot of thinking and calculating. Fortunately, Kirk (1990) also presented a formula for calculating the index:

$$\text{Index of dispersion} = \frac{c\left(n^2 - \sum_{j=1}^{c} n_j^2\right)}{n^2(c-1)} \tag{4.1}$$

where *c* is the number of categories, *n* is the total number of cases, and n_j is the number of cases in the *j*th group. For *family type* within the group of White students, we would calculate the index as:

$$\text{Index of dispersion} = \frac{5\left[100^2 - \left(90^2 + 8^2 + 2^2 + 0^2 + 0^2\right)\right]}{100^2\left(5-1\right)} = .2290 \tag{4.2}$$

Referring back to Table 4.2, we could calculate the index for the African American students as:

$$\text{Index of dispersion} = \frac{5\left[100^2 - \left(73^2 + 20^2 + 5^2 + 1^2 + 1^2\right)\right]}{100^2\left(5-1\right)} = .5305 \tag{4.3}$$

Comparing the two results, you can see that there is more variability in "family type" for African American students than there is for White students. To make things a bit easier, we have written a function in R that is contained in the "functions.txt" file. Now, let's try to pull all of this together by using R to describe the distribution of "Mother's Educational Level" for both the White and African American kindergarten students.

DESCRIBING CATEGORICAL VARIABLES USING R

According to the codebook on the website, the variable of Mother's Educational Level (*wkmomed*) for both White and African American students is coded from 1 to 9, with 1 = Eighth Grade Education or Below and 9 = Doctoral or Professional Degree. This variable could be seen as quantitative; specifically, an ordinal variable, where a 9 indicates a higher educational level than a 1. A careful look at the coding, however, shows that 4 = Vocational/Technical Program. Given where that stands relative to High School/GED and Some College, one could argue with ordinal position. We will therefore treat this variable as categorical. Given that the variable is categorical, the values have no numeric meaning; rather they are nominal in nature. Thus, we will want to create value labels for the categorical variables. Other categorical variables include Father's Educational Level (*wkdaded*), *gender, race*, whether or not the child was ever in childcare (*p1center*), family type (*p1hfamil*), and socioeconomic status (*wksesq5*). In order to do this, we first create a data frame (*ecls200*) by reading the text file (ecls200.txt). Then, for each of the categorical variables of interest, we used the factor( ) function to create value labels as shown in the R script. In R, categorical variables are stored as factors. Note that in declaring variables to be factors and providing labels for the numeric values, we have created new variables. For example, *gender* has been mapped onto a new variable, *f.gender*. We do this so as to preserve the original variables and their values. You might want to take a look at the script now. We have included a part of that script here for your reference:

```
# Make labels for race
ecls200$f.race <- factor(ecls200$race,
   levels = 1:2, labels = c("White", "AA"))
# Code WKMOMED and WKDADED by reusing labels,
# helpful when many variables have the same value
# labels. Again, note the use of the decimal to
# avoid blanks
```

```
ednames <- c("8th.Grade.or.Less",
  "9th.to.12th Grade", "HS.Grad/GED",
  "Voc/Tech.Prog", "Some.College",
  "Coll.Grad", "Some.Grad/Prof.School",
  "Master's", "Doctoral/Prof.Deg")
ecls200$f.momed <- factor(ecls200$wkmomed,
  levels = 1:length(ednames),
  labels = ednames)
ecls200$f.daded <- factor(ecls200$wkdaded,
  levels = 1:length(ednames),
  labels = ednames)
```

After creating and assigning the labels for the values, things can get a little messy. Once the value labels are linked to the levels of the original categorical variables, you would like to keep the "order" of the levels consistent. R does not make this easy. Your first thought might be to write out the file and then read it back in when you need it. You could do this with:

```
write.table(ecls200,file="c:/rbook/f.ecls200.txt")
```

This command would write a new text file, f.ecls200.txt. However, when you read the file back in, any commands involving the categorical factors may result in output having the labels sorted in an unexpected way; the "ordered" property is not retained. We offer two solutions to this. First, you could use an "ordered prefix" for your labels. Rather than using "Male" and "Female," you could use "(1) Male" and "(2) Female." Another option is to save the script file that you used to create the value labels, and always use it to read in the original text file which did not have the labels, recreating them. As long as you stay in R, the order of the labels will be maintained. We prefer the latter option. There are additional, more complex, options available in R (e.g., dump( )/source( ) and save( )/load( )), but they are beyond the scope of this book. You may choose to pursue those options on your own at this point.

At last, we are ready to proceed with the analyses. In the body of the chapter, we present only the commands to complete the desired analyses. Let's look at the distribution of Mother's Educational Level for each of the racial groups.

```
# Looking at the distribution of Mother's
# educational level for each race
t <- with(ecls200, table(f.momed, f.race))
```

The output from R is:

```
> t <- with(ecls200, table(momed, race))
> t
                      race
momed                 White  AA
  8th Grade or Less       2   0
  9th to 12th Grade       7   9
  HS Grad/GED            26  35
```

Voc/Tech Prog	8	4
Some College	23	30
Coll Grad	22	16
Some Grad/Prof School	5	3
Master's	7	3
Doctoral/Prof Deg	0	0

We might choose to create a more appealing table, like Table 4.3.

We have written a function **indexdisp( )** to calculate the index of dispersion with R. It is contained in the "functions" file that is read at the beginning of the script. Given that we have obtained the tabled values, we can use the function as follows:

```
# Obtaining IoD for White subsample
w.vals <- c(2,7,26,8,23,22,5,7,0)
indexdisp(w.vals)
# Obtaining IoD for AA subsample
aa.vals <- c(0,9,35,4,30,16,3,3,0)
indexdisp(aa.vals)
```

The program returns:

```
> indexdisp(w.vals)
[1] 0.9135
> indexdisp(aa.vals)
[1] 0.8442
```

On the other hand, we could create an R object containing the tabled values and then extract the values for input to the indexdisp( ) function. In our script, we stored the tabled values in "t."

```
# Given the we know that the object "t" will have 9
# rows and 2 columns,
# we could also construct the script as follows:
w.vals1 <- c(t[1,1], t[2,1], t[3,1], t[4,1],
  t[5,1], t[6,1], t[7,1], t[8,1], t[9,1])
aa.vals1 <- c(t[1,2], t[2,2], t[3,2], t[4,2],
  t[5,2], t[6,2], t[7,2], t[8,2], t[9,2])
indexdisp(w.vals1)
indexdisp(aa.vals1)
```

In either case, it would appear that the educational level of the White mothers is slightly more widely dispersed than is that of the African American mothers.

If we want to obtain bar charts for each of the two racial subgroups, we will use the subfiles as before. The commands for producing these plots are given below. To make the two plots comparable, we plotted proportions, rather than raw counts. Of course, in this situation, both groups are of the same size.

Table 4.3 Frequency distributions of Mother's Educational Level for White and African American students

Mother's educational level	White	African American
Eighth Grade or Below	2	0
Ninth to Twelfth Grade	7	9
High School Graduate/GED	26	35
Vocational/Technical Program	8	4
Some College	23	30
Bachelor's Degree	22	16
Some Graduate/Professional School	5	3
Master's Degree	7	3
Doctoral/Professional Degree	0	0

```
# Obtaining a bar plot for the White subsample
with(subset(ecls200, subset = f.race == "White"),
  barplot(table(f.momed)/length(f.momed),
  xlab = "EDLEVEL for White Mothers",
  ylab = "Proportions"))
# Obtaining a bar plot for the African American
# subsample
with(subset(ecls200, subset = f.race== "AA"),
  barplot(table(f.momed)/length(f.momed),
  xlab = "EDLEVEL for African American Mothers",
  ylab = "Proportions"))
```

The results are shown in Figures 4.4 and 4.5. Note that R, like most other computer programs, does not place "blank spaces" where there are no observations, making a direct comparison of the two plots a little difficult.

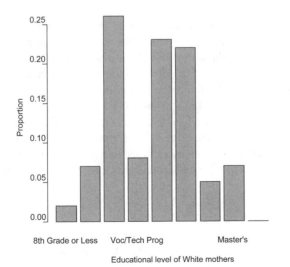

FIGURE 4.4   Bar chart depicting educational level for White mothers.

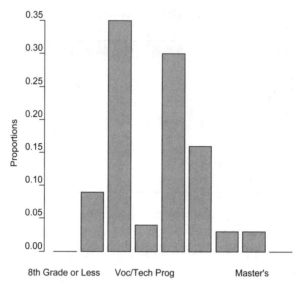

FIGURE 4.5 Bar chart depicting educational level for African American mothers.

What can we say at this point? An examination of Table 4.3 would suggest that the modal category for both groups is High School Graduate or Equivalent. For both groups, there also appears to be a concentration of cases who attended some college or graduated with a Bachelor's degree. What about spread? We can calculate the index of dispersion for each of the two groups. In the case of the White mothers we find the index to be .9135; for African American mothers it is .938. (We'll leave it to you as an exercise to verify our calculations.) Overall, the two distributions appear to be fairly similar.

CHAPTER SUMMARY

In this chapter we have presented some ways to describe and summarize frequency distributions for categorical or nominal level measurements. Obviously, we can create frequency distributions and table the results, just as we did for quantitative variables. If we choose to display the results in graphic form, we may use bar graphs and/or pie charts. In summarizing what we see in the tables and graphs, we are typically limited to describing the central tendency and dispersion of the distributions. For describing central tendency, the only measure available to us is the mode. However, we may provide more detail by noting the proportion of cases in each of the categories. For describing variability, we presented the index of dispersion, a measure based on the number of cases that can be distinguished from other cases, relative to the maximum number of distinctions that might be made, given a particular number of categories and number of cases.

Key Terms

Bar chart
Pie chart

Index of dispersion
Index of qualitative variation

REFERENCES

Kirk, R. E. (1990). *Statistics: An introduction* (3rd ed.). Fort Worth, TX: Holt, Rinehart, and Winston.
Verzani, J. (2005). *Using R for introductory statistics*. Boca Raton, FL: Chapman & Hall/CRC Press.

PRACTICE QUESTIONS

1. Which of the following variables is categorical?

   a. Religious affiliation.
   b. Number of hours studied.
   c. Score on a state achievement test.
   d. Attitude about school.

2. Bar charts differ from histograms in that the bars:

   a. are horizontal
   b. are colored
   c. touch
   d. do not touch.

3. Which of the following visual displays could be used for a categorical variable?

   a. Box-and-whisker plot.
   b. Stem-and-leaf display.
   c. Bar chart.
   d. All of these displays could be used.

4. Suppose we are looking at whether or not students graduate from high school. At Westside High, 200 students graduated and 100 did not. At Eastside High, 250 graduated and 50 did not. What is the modal class of the graduation variable at Westside High?

   a. Not graduated.
   b. Graduated.

5. Suppose we are looking at whether or not students graduate from high school. At Westside High, 200 students graduated and 100 did not. At Eastside High, 250 graduated and 50 did not. For which school is there more variation in the graduation variable?

   a. Westside.
   b. Eastside.

EXERCISES

In this chapter, we have relied heavily on R to examine sets of nominal level measurements. We have shown you how to use R to construct frequency tables and create graphic displays (bar charts and pie charts). Then we showed you how to summarize the information in terms of central tendency (the mode) and variability (the index of dispersion). Using the same data file, available on the book website with the materials for Chapter 4, we would like you to do the same.

Compare the White and the African American students on two categorical variables: Father's Educational Level (*wkdaded*) and socio-economic status (*wksesq5*).

5

Describing the Position of a Case within a Set of Scores

INTRODUCTION

Until now we have focused on procedures for describing sets of scores in terms of their general properties: size (n), location, spread, and shape. At times, the value of a score for a particular individual may also be of concern, particularly within a clinical context. In an example given in Chapter 3, we referred to blood pressures and patients. From a database of systolic and diastolic blood pressure readings, a physician would certainly want to link specific scores to individual patients. In that case, the actual value and its link to the case are meaningful.

In the social sciences, we may be less concerned about the actual value than its relative placement within the overall distribution of scores. We commented in Chapter 3 that outliers or extreme observations could influence statistics like the mean and standard deviation, which are used to summarize a distribution of scores. We also showed in Chapter 3 how outlying values could be represented visually in a box plot. We did not, however, provide a measure indicating the degree to which an observation was extreme or unusual. To do so we need statistics that describe the position of an individual score relative to the larger distribution. Such statistics are also useful when we want to compare two scores within a distribution, such as comparing one child's reading score of 26 to another child's reading score of 31. Obviously, they are different scores, but just how different are they? Or we might want to compare two scores in two different distributions, such as comparing a child's reading score of 26 to the same child's math score of 35.

In this chapter we show you how such comparisons are made. Our discussion is limited to ways of dealing with quantitative variables. Central to this idea is the notion of standard scores, which come in two varieties. Some standard scores express the position of a specific case in terms of relative position within the group. Other standard scores express the position of the case relative to a point, usually the mean of the distribution.

The Problem

Suppose that you and a friend are enjoying a cup of coffee at a local cafe. Midterm exams have been graded and returned in class earlier that day. Your friend tells you that she got an 83 on the statistics midterm and a 72 on the measurement midterm.

The Question

In which course is she doing better? At this point, we do not have enough information to answer the question in a meaningful way.

The Solution

We need to obtain additional information so that we interpret the two scores within their relative contexts, or distributions. As noted earlier, this additional information can be presented in one of two ways, although the distinction may be somewhat artificial. One way to "locate" the scores is to provide their ranks, relative to the other scores. For example, we often hear high school students describing their academic performance in terms of "rank in class." For instance, we imagine that some of you reading this book may have graduated in the "top quarter" of your class. Recall our presentation of ways to divide a distribution into four parts in Chapter 3—Q_1, the median, and Q_3. Common ways of expressing these types of standard scores are quartiles, quintiles, deciles, and centiles. As the names would suggest, the distributions are divided into 4, 5, 10, and 100 parts, respectively.

Another way to situate a particular score is to describe the position of the score relative to the mean. For example, we might say that a score is a standard deviation above the mean. First, we will elaborate on the "rank" type of standard scores.

EXPRESSING THE ORDINAL POSITION OF A SCORE: PERCENTILE RANKS

As we have already noted, there are several schemes for dividing a distribution of scores into parts. However, the most common of these is to divide the scores into centiles, or 100 parts. In Chapter 3, we presented a formula for finding the median:

$$\text{Median} = \left[\frac{(n/2) - \Sigma f_b}{f_i} \right] i + Y_{ll} \tag{5.1}$$

We then showed how the formula could be modified to find the quartile points by simply changing the $\frac{1}{2}n$ to $\frac{1}{4}n$ and $\frac{3}{4}n$, respectively. This thinking can be extended easily to find the centile points. For example, one could use the same process, substituting $1/100 \times n$, $2/100 \times n$, $3/100 \times n$, ... $99/100 \times n$, respectively. The resulting values are the centiles, or percentiles.

At this point, we should make a distinction. There is a subtle difference between *percentiles* and *percentile ranks*. The process we described in the paragraph above yields percentiles, or the points on the original scale that divide the distribution. To illustrate what we mean, in Table 5.1 we have modified Table 2.5 by including the cumulative frequency distribution.

Let's say we want to find the point that separates the lower 62% of the scores from the upper 38% of the scores. In this distribution there are 100 scores. Thus $n = 100$. Applying the modified formula:

$$P_{62} = \left[\frac{(62/100) \times 100 - \Sigma f_b}{f_i} \right] i + Y_{ll} \tag{5.2}$$

Looking at the point 56.5 in the Y column in Table 5.1, we can see that we have a total of 61 scores below, as shown in the cf column. Note that there are three scores in the interval 56.5 to 57.5. Thus,

Table 5.1 Frequency distribution for White kindergarten students on reading (*Y*)

Y	f(Y)	cf	Y	f(Y)	cf	Y	f(Y)	cf	Y	f(Y)	cf
84	1	100	71	0	98	58	4	68	45	3	14
83	0	99	70	0	98	57	3	64	44	1	11
82	0	99	69	1	98	56	2	61	43	1	10
81	0	99	68	2	97	55	3	59	42	0	9
80	0	99	67	1	95	54	4	56	41	4	9
79	1	99	66	2	94	53	3	52	40	0	5
78	0	98	65	3	92	52	7	49	39	1	5
77	0	98	64	7	89	51	7	42	38	2	4
76	0	98	63	3	82	50	6	35	37	1	2
75	0	98	62	1	79	49	4	29	36	0	1
74	0	98	61	3	78	48	4	25	35	0	1
73	0	98	60	1	75	47	5	21	34	1	1
72	0	98	59	6	74	46	2	16			

$$P_{62} = \left[\frac{(62/100) \times 100 - 61}{3} \right] 1 + 56.5 = 56.8\overline{3} \tag{5.3}$$

We would probably round the result to 57. Given this result, we could say that that the 62nd percentile is 57; the percentile rank for a score of 57 is 62.

There is another way to find the percentile rank of a score. Equation 5.2 can be rewritten more generally as:

$$\text{Percentile} = \left[\frac{(P_r/n) \times 100 - \Sigma f_b}{f_i} \right] i + Y_{ll} \tag{5.4}$$

With a little algebra, one can solve for P_r and rewrite the formula as

$$P_r = \frac{100}{n} \left[\Sigma f_b + \frac{f_i (\text{Percentile} - Y_{ll})}{i} \right] \tag{5.5}$$

This new formula can be used to find the percentile rank of a score. To find the percentile rank of a score of 57, we would use the cumulative frequency distribution in Table 5.1 and plug in the numbers:

$$P_r(57) = \frac{100}{100} \left[61 + \frac{3(57 - 56.5)}{1} \right] = 62.5 \tag{5.6}$$

Using this approach, we confirm that the percentile rank for a score of 57 is 62 (62.5 rounded to 62.0).

We are going to calculate several more values in order to make a point about percentile rank scores. We have just seen that the percentile rank of 57 is 62. Let's find the percentile rank for a score of 60:

$$P_r(60) = \frac{100}{100} \left[74 + \frac{1(60 - 59.5)}{1} \right] = 74.5 \tag{5.7}$$

We would probably round this outcome to 74. As you can see, in the middle of the distribution where the scores seem to cluster, a raw score increase of 3 points (60 – 57) results in an increase of 12 points on the percentile rank scale. Now, let's compute the percentile ranks for raw scores of 68 and 81:

$$P_r(68) = \frac{100}{100}\left[95 + \frac{2(68-67.5)}{1}\right] = 96 \tag{5.8}$$

$$P_r(81) = \frac{100}{100}\left[99 + \frac{0(81-80.5)}{1}\right] = 99 \tag{5.9}$$

Out in the upper tail of the distribution, a raw score increase of 13 points is equivalent to an increase of only 3 points on the percentile rank scale. An analogous situation occurs in distance track events. A runner at the back of the pack can make a move, passing all the runners as she moves to the head of the pack, vastly improving her position. However, she has to run a lot faster and cover more ground to catch the two leaders. Now consider the leader. No matter how far she gets ahead of the person in second place, she cannot better her position. Her percentile rank is limited in communicating the distance between her and the other runners. Similarly, percentile ranks are limited in communicating the degree to which an outlying score deviates from the other scores in a distribution. The general message is that percentile ranks are purely ordinal scales and that one needs to be careful in their use and interpretation.

Misinterpretations of Percentile Rank Scores

In addition to being careful how you treat percentile ranks in calculations, you also need to be very careful that you understand what they mean. Two classic examples come to mind. In the first, all of the school principals in a large district were called to a summer workshop to discuss district-wide issues and policies. When it was announced that the average salary for principals in the district was at the 53rd percentile rank nationally, one of the principals stood up and loudly stated that is was most unfortunate that principals in their county were paid only half as much as other principals.

Another classic misunderstanding of the nature of percentile ranks was made by a state legislator. In a Southeastern state, the higher education system did not use the SAT to make admissions decisions. Rather, the state had contracted with a testing organization to construct a Twelfth Grade Placement Exam consisting of five subtests (Reading, Math, Science, Social Studies, and Writing), each of which was scored on a percentile rank scale. Thus the total score ranged from 5, which corresponded to a percentile rank of 1 on each subtest, to a 495, which corresponded to a percentile rank of 99 on each subtest. All students in the state seeking a high school diploma had to take the exam. The flagship university in the state required a total score of 300 for admission. So far, so good. Unfortunately, the legislator got someone in the state department of education to calculate the state average, thinking that the scores reflected the amount of material mastered, rather than relative position. It turned out to be right at 250. Knowing that the scores could range from 5 to 495, the legislator concluded (erroneously) that the children in the public schools were only mastering about half of the material. In fact, he had discovered that exactly half of the students were below the state median!

In summary, there are several types of scores that are based on relative position within a group. While we find percentile ranks to be a somewhat useful way in which to convey achievement scores, as we noted there are other scores that are used to show position within a group in relation to some point, usually the mean. These will be more useful for indexing the extremeness of an outlier. We turn our attention to a discussion of this approach.

THE POSITION OF A SCORE RELATIVE TO THE MEAN

In Chapter 3, we presented a number of ways in which to describe frequency distributions, two of which can be used to standardize a set of scores. In particular, we can use the mean and the standard deviation to situate scores within a distribution. The mean of the distribution serves as the reference point, and the standard deviation is used to express how far the score is from the mean. Assume that we are starting with a set of scores Y with a mean (μ) of 50 and a standard deviation (σ) of 10. Such a distribution might be depicted as in Figure 5.1.

Now, imagine that we subtract 50 from each and every score in the distribution. What would be the result? If a set of scores had a mean of 100 and we subtracted 5 from each of the scores, then on average the scores would be five less, and the new mean would be 95. In our case, if the original mean is 50 and we subtracted 50 from each score, the new mean would be zero. In essence we would have shifted the distribution of Y to the left, as in Figure 5.2. The location

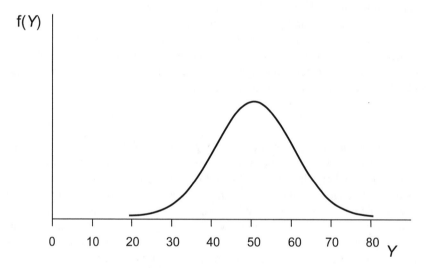

FIGURE 5.1   A distribution of scores with a mean of 50 and a standard deviation of 10.

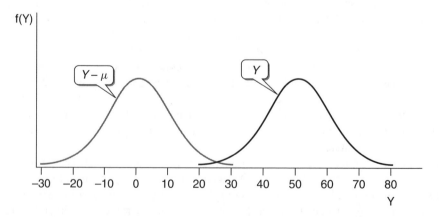

FIGURE 5.2   The distribution of $(Y - \mu)$ in relation to the distribution of Y.

would change, but the spread and shape would not. In effect, we can make a generalization about the result when we add a constant to each value of a variable Y. Remember that the mean of a random variable is sometimes called its "expected value," written as $E(Y)$. Assume that we start with a random variable Y with $E(Y) = \mu$ and $var(Y) = \sigma^2$. If we derive a new random variable $(Y + c)$, we can expect that $E(Y + c) = \mu + c$ and $var(Y) = \sigma^2$. When the value of the constant is subtracted, $E(Y - c) = \mu - c$, but the variance is unaffected, just as before.

Now, what happens to a distribution when we multiply the values by a constant? Let's start with a very simple set of scores: 1, 2, 3, 4, and 5. It should be pretty easy to see that the mean of these five scores is 3. What is its variance, σ^2? In order to find the variance, we'll use the definitional formula. The process is depicted in Table 5.2.

Table 5.2 Finding the variance of the integers 1 through 5, inclusive

	Y	$(Y - \mu)$	$(Y - \mu)^2$
	5	2	4
	4	1	1
	3	0	0
	2	−1	1
	1	−2	4
Sum	15	0	10
Mean	3	0	$\sigma_Y^2 = 2$

As you can see, for our random variable Y, the mean is 3 and the variance is 2. What do you think would happen if we generated a new random variable, $2Y$? Let's see what happens in Table 5.3.

Table 5.3 Finding the variance of the integers 1 through 5 multiplied by 2, inclusive

	$2Y$	$(2Y - \mu_{2Y})$	$(2Y - \mu_{2Y})^2$
	10	4	16
	8	2	4
	6	0	0
	4	−2	4
	2	−4	16
Sum	30	0	40
Mean	6	0	$\sigma_{2Y}^2 = 8$

As you can see, the mean of $2Y$ is 6, and the variance is 8. What if we try $3Y$ as in Table 5.4?

Table 5.4 Finding the variance of the integers 1 through 5 multiplied by 3, inclusive

	$3Y$	$(3Y - \mu_{3Y})$	$(Y - \mu_{3Y})^2$
	15	6	36
	12	3	9
	9	0	0
	6	−3	9
	3	−6	36
Sum	45	0	90
Mean	9	0	$\sigma_{3Y}^2 = 18$

You can see that the mean of $3Y$ is 9, and the variance is now 18. Do you see the pattern? When you multiply a random variable by a constant, the new mean is the old mean multiplied by the constant (3, in this case), and the new variance is the old variance multiplied by the square of the constant $(2*3^2)$. More formally, $E(cY) = cE(Y) = c\mu$ and $\text{var}(cY) = c^2\text{var}(Y) = c^2\sigma^2$. Now, you may think that this result is a function of our having picked a special set of numbers. To validate our point, we used R to generate 10 random integers between 1 and 15. The values generated were 13, 1, 8, 10, 3, 15, 7, 4, 15, and 1. The mean, μ, of these 10 values is 7.7. The variance, σ^2, is 26.61. Now, if we multiply each of the 10 values by 2, we would have the values 26, 2, 16, 20, 6, 30, 14, 8, 30, and 2. For these values, we find that $\mu = 15.4$, exactly twice the value of μ for the original values. Furthermore, we find that $\sigma^2 = 106.44$, exactly four times the value of σ^2 for the original values.

What are the implications for our deriving standard scores? We have already seen that subtracting μ from every value in a distribution of scores has the effect of changing the location of the distribution, centering it at zero. However, neither the variance nor the shape is changed. Now, suppose that we take these "deviation scores" and divide each of them by the standard deviation, σ. First, recall that division is really multiplication by the inverse. So we are multiplying the deviation scores by $1/\sigma$. Based on what we have just seen, we will expect the new mean to be equal to the old mean times $1/\sigma$. Given that the old mean was zero, the new mean will also be zero. Furthermore, we would expect the new variance to be the old variance multiplied by the square of the constant, or σ^2 times $(1/\sigma)^2$. As you can see, the result is 1.0. Thus, anytime you transform a set of values by first subtracting the mean and then dividing the results by the standard deviation, you will always obtain a set of values with a mean of zero and a variance of one. Thus, the standard deviation is also one.

This transformation is called the *z-transformation*. In effect, we are transforming the values to values on a new scale, The resulting values will express the position of each of the original scores in terms of its distance from the original mean in standard deviations. If the result is negative, the original score is below the mean; if it is positive, the original scores is above the mean. Specifically, a *z*-score of 1.5 means that the score is one-and-one-half standard deviations above the mean. A *z*-score of $-.75$ tells you that the score is three-quarters of a standard deviation below the mean. The distribution of *z*-scores, relative to the distributions of the original scores and the deviation scores is shown in Figure 5.3.

Note that the distributions of Y and $(Y - \mu)$ are the same in spread and shape; they differ only in location. In geometry, we would say that the distributions are congruent. Furthermore, note that the distribution of *z*-scores has the same proportional shape as both the original distribution and the distribution of deviation scores. In geometry, we would say the distributions are similar.

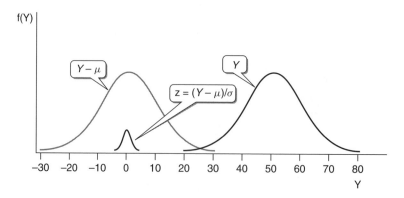

FIGURE 5.3   The distributions of Y, Y − μ, and z = (Y − μ)/σ

We make this point so that you will not confuse this z-transformation with another transformation that actually changes the shape of the distribution, making the distribution of the z-scores a normal, bell-shaped, distribution. We will explain the difference in a later chapter. For now, know that the z-transformation results in a new distribution that looks like a miniature edition of the original scores when $\sigma > 1.0$. When $\sigma < 1.0$, the new distribution will look like an enlargement.

Why is it important to know about z-transformations? Returning to the problem posed at the beginning of the chapter, we presented a student who had obtained a score of 83 on the statistics midterm and a score of 76 on the measurement midterm. Without additional information, we could not determine how her performance in the two courses compared. However, let's supply some additional information. The mean on the statistics midterm was 80; the mean on the measurement midterm was 70. At this point, we can say that she scored 3 points above the mean on the statistics exam and 6 points above the mean on the measurement exam. What can we say now? Not much, until we know the spread of the scores. The standard deviation on the statistics midterm was 3 points, while the standard deviation on the measurement exam was 12 points. Now we can see that our student was one standard deviation above the mean on the statistics midterm and only one-half a standard deviation above the mean on the measurement exam. What we have just expressed in text form can be expressed in formulae:

$$z - \text{score} = \frac{\text{Obtained score} - \text{Group mean}}{\sigma} = \frac{Y - \mu}{\sigma}$$

$$z_{\text{statistics}} = \frac{83 - 80}{3} = 1.0 \tag{5.10}$$

$$z_{\text{meas}} = \frac{76 - 70}{12} = .5$$

As you can see, converting raw scores to z-scores permits us to draw conclusions about differential performance. It also provides a way to index the degree to which an outlying score is extreme. Suppose that we found the highest math score in our data set had a z-score of 2.13, whereas the highest reading score in our data set had a z-score of 6.24. This is illustrated in Figure 5.4. Clearly the highest reading score is much more extreme. Maybe we should revisit the reading scores to make sure that the test was scored and recorded accurately. In the next section, we will look at how z-scores can be transformed to other scales.

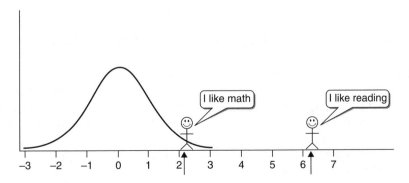

FIGURE 5.4   Illustration of the position of the highest math score and highest reading score relative to a distribution of z-scores.

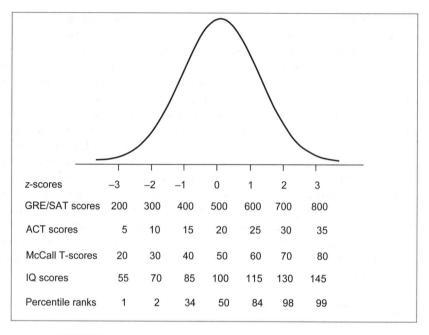

FIGURE 5.5   The relationships between several standardized scales.

Using z-Scores to Derive New Metrics

Once the z-scores have been derived from the original (raw) scores, they can be converted to any scale. For example, Graduate Record Exam (GRE) subtest scores are standardized to have a mean of 500 and a standard deviation of 100. Thus, an applicant scoring 1.5 standard deviations above the mean on the Verbal subtest would be assigned a GRE score of 650. For another example, measures of intelligence (IQ) are standardized to have a mean of 100 and a standard deviation of 15 (on the Wechsler tests). The equivalence of several standardized scales (measures) is depicted in Figure 5.5. In particular, we show z-scores in relation to GRE/SAT scores, ACT scores, McCall T-scores, IQ scores, and percentile rank scores (assuming a bell-shaped, normal distribution). To obtain the derived scores, one would simply multiply the desired standard deviation times the z-score and then add the result to the desired mean.

AN EXAMPLE OF CONVERTING A SET OF RAW SCORES TO STANDARD SCORES

Now that we have some understanding of the meaning of different types of standard scores, let's take a look at how one might standardize a set of scores. For our example, we will consider that large Early Childhood Longitudinal Study (ECLS) data set as being a nationally representative sample of children. We have a sample of 2,577 cases in that file. Suppose we were interested in standardizing the reading (*c1rrscal*) and math (*c1rmscal*) Item Response Theory (IRT) scores that were obtained when the children entered kindergarten. We could do this in two different ways. We could convert the raw scores to percentile ranks, or we could find the respective means and standard deviations of the two variables and then convert the raw scores to z-scores. First, let's look at how to convert the scores to percentile ranks.

Converting a Set of Raw Scores to Equivalent Percentile Ranks

The first step in transforming the raw scores to equivalent percentile rank scores was to use R to derive a frequency distribution of the 2,577 scores. First, we will present the results in detail for the math test. Using the **table( )** command in R, we generated the frequency distribution:

```
> table(clrmscal)
clrmscal
   7    8    9   10   11   12   13   14   15   16   17   18   19
   1   17   37   25   54   76   85  125  121  133  145  145  177

  20   21   22   23   24   25   26   27   28   29   30   31   32
 177  153  157  119  102  110   70   52   53   53   64   51   44

  33   34   35   36   37   38   39   40   41   42   43   44   45
  40   35   29   18   23   13    9   10   11    9    4    3    3

  46   47   48   49   51   52   54   57
   4    3    2    5    4    1    4    1
```

Take a moment to familiarize yourself with the distribution of these scores. The scores range from a high score of 57 to a low score of 7. The frequency distribution from R is presented in Table 5.5.

Table 5.5 Frequency distribution for the 2,577 math scores for the entering kindergarteners

Y	f(Y)	Y	f(Y)	Y	f(Y)	Y	f(Y)	Y	f(Y)
57	1	46	4	35	29	24	102	13	85
56	0	45	3	34	35	23	119	12	76
55	0	44	3	33	40	22	157	11	54
54	4	43	4	32	44	21	153	10	25
53	0	42	9	31	51	20	177	9	37
52	1	41	11	30	64	19	177	8	17
51	4	40	10	29	53	18	145	7	1
50	0	39	9	28	53	17	145		
49	5	38	13	27	52	16	133		
48	2	37	23	26	70	15	121		
47	3	36	18	25	110	14	125		

We then wrote an R script that employed the **ecdf( )** function to construct the cumulative frequency distribution, from which we extracted the set of percentile ranks for the observed scores. The script appears in the supplementary materials on the book website.

The results of running this script are:

```
> pr.table
        val  pr
  [1,]    7   0
  [2,]    8   1
  [3,]    9   2
  [4,]   10   3
```

```
 [5,]  11    5
 [6,]  12    8
 [7,]  13   11
 [8,]  14   16
 [9,]  15   21
[10,]  16   26
[11,]  17   32
[12,]  18   37
[13,]  19   44
[14,]  20   51
[15,]  21   57
[16,]  22   63
[17,]  23   68
[18,]  24   72
[19,]  25   76
[20,]  26   79
[21,]  27   81
[22,]  28   83
[23,]  29   85
[24,]  30   87
[25,]  31   89
[26,]  32   91
[27,]  33   93
[28,]  34   94
[29,]  35   95
[30,]  36   96
[31,]  37   97
[32,]  38   97
[33,]  39   98
[34,]  40   98
[35,]  41   98
[36,]  42   99
[37,]  43   99
[38,]  44   99
[39,]  45   99
[40,]  46   99
[41,]  47   99
[42,]  48   99
[43,]  49  100
```

```
[44,]   50 100
[45,]   51 100
[46,]   52 100
[47,]   53 100
[48,]   54 100
[49,]   55 100
[50,]   56 100
[51,]   57 100
```

Given the large size of the sample, one of the values at the low end was 0 and several of the values at the high end were 100. As percentile rank scores go from 99 down to 1, we would want to change the 100s to 99s and the 0s to 1s. The final results for the math scores are presented in Table 5.6.

Table 5.6 Math raw scores and their percentile rank equivalents

Y	P_{rY}	Y	P_{rY}	Y	P_{rY}	Y	P_{rY}	Y	P_{rY}
57	99	46	99	35	95	24	72	13	11
56	99	45	99	34	94	23	68	12	8
55	99	44	99	33	93	22	63	11	5
54	99	43	99	32	91	21	57	10	3
53	99	42	99	31	89	20	51	9	2
52	99	41	98	30	87	19	44	8	1
51	99	40	98	29	85	18	37	7	1
50	99	39	98	28	83	17	32		
49	99	38	97	27	81	16	26		
48	99	37	97	26	79	15	31		
47	99	36	96	25	76	14	16		

We followed the same process with the reading scores for the entering kindergarteners. The highest reading score was 81 and the lowest was 11. Again, we used the **ecdf( )** function in R to construct the cumulative frequency distribution and used Script 15.2 to derive the percentile rank equivalents for the raw scores. The final results are displayed in Table 5.7.

Table 5.7 Reading raw scores and their percentile rank equivalents

Y	P_{rY}	Y	P_{rY}	Y	P_{rY}	Y	P_{rY}	Y	P_{rY}
81	99	66	99	51	98	36	91	21	40
80	99	65	99	50	98	35	90	20	33
79	99	64	99	49	97	34	88	19	28
78	99	63	99	48	97	33	86	18	24
77	99	62	99	47	97	32	83	17	22
76	99	61	99	46	97	31	81	16	18
75	99	60	99	45	97	30	79	15	13
74	99	59	99	44	97	29	76	14	9
73	99	58	98	43	96	28	74	13	5
72	99	57	98	42	96	27	70	12	2
71	99	56	98	41	95	26	67	11	1
70	99	55	98	40	95	25	63		
69	99	54	98	39	94	24	58		
68	99	53	98	38	94	23	53		
67	99	52	98	37	92	22	48		

What can all of this information tell us about individual scores? Let's look as some specific records in the data set. In the *ecls2577* data, there are actually two "ID" variables: *childid* that was created when the data set was created and *caseid* that we created. We will use the ID that we created, *caseid*. To find the values for that case:

```
> which(caseid == "1303")
[1] 1303

> ecls2577[1303,1:7]
      caseid childid gender race clrrscal clrrtsco clrmscal
1303    1303     177      2    1       26       56       23
```

Child 1,303 scored 26 on the reading test and 23 on the math test. Using Tables 5.6 and 5.7, we can see that that child is reading at the 67th percentile rank (see Table 5.7) and is performing at the 68th percentile rank in math (see Table 5.6). We might conclude that that child is performing similarly in reading and math. Let's look at a different child, Child 342:

```
> which(caseid == "342")
[1] 342
> ecls2577[342,1:7]
      caseid childid gender race clrrscal clrrtsco clrmscal
342     342   1,410      1    2       35       65       22
```

We can see that Child 342 scored 35 on the reading test and 22 on the math test. As shown in the same tables, this child has percentile rank scores of 90 in reading and 63 in math, respectively. How might we describe these same two children using standard scores?

Converting Raw Scores to Standard (z) Scores with R

In order to convert raw scores to z-scores, we need to find the group means and standard deviations. Using R with the complete data file of 2,577 cases we found the mean and standard deviation of the reading scores to be 24.89 and 9.66, respectively. We found the comparable values for the math scores to be 21.54 and 7.52.

```
> mean(clrrscal)
[1] 24.8929
> sd(clrrscal)
[1] 9.659668
> mean(clrmscal)
[1] 21.53512
> sd(clrmscal)
[1] 7.524419
```

Using Equation 5.10, we can then convert the raw scores for Child 1,303 to z-scores, obtaining values of $z_{read} = .11$ and $z_{math} = .19$. Thus, we can see that this child is above average in reading and above average in math. Regarding Child 342, the comparable z-scores are $z_{read} = 1.04$ and $z_{math} = .06$. In comparison, this child is quite a bit above average in reading and just above average in math.

We have written Script 5.3 to show you how to complete this process with R (see the book website). The first part of the script shows the translation of the formula into R syntax. The second part of the script shows you how to use the **scale( )** function to convert the raw scores to z-scores and then request the specific scores for particular cases.

CHAPTER SUMMARY

In this chapter we have presented several ways to transform raw scores to derived scores that convey some meaning about the position of the scores within the overall distribution. The two methods that we have emphasized are percentile ranks and z-scores. Percentile ranks fall on a scale from 1 to 99 and tell you the position of a case in terms of its ordinal position within the distribution. On the other hand, z-scores inform you about the position of scores relative to the mean of the distribution in terms of the number of standard deviations below or above the mean. Each form of standard score has its advantages and disadvantages.

Key Terms

Percentile	z-score
Percentile rank	z-transformation
Standard score	

PRACTICE QUESTIONS

1. Which of the following z-scores indicates the most extreme observation?

   a. −4.3.
   b. 0.0.
   c. 1.9.
   d. 3.4.

2. A score of 84 separates the lowest 75% of the scores from the highest 25% of the scores, and a score of 65 separates the lowest 25% of the scores from the highest 75% of the scores. What is the percentile rank of a score of 84?

   a. 25.
   b. 65.
   c. 75.
   d. 84.

3. A score of 84 separates the lowest 75% of the scores from the highest 25% of the scores, and a score of 65 separates the lowest 25% of the scores from the highest 75% of the scores. What is the 25th percentile?

   a. 25.
   b. 65.
   c. 75.
   d. 84.

4. Assume you have a normal distribution of scores. Imagine four scores which have corresponding z-scores of $-.5$, 0, .5, and 1.5. If the raw score of each of these is increased by 10, which score's percentile rank would change the least?

    a. $z = -.5$.
    b. $z = 0.0$.
    c. $z = .5$.
    d. $z = 1.5$.
    e. They would all change the same amount.

5. Assume you have a normal distribution of scores. Imagine four scores which have corresponding z-scores of $-.5$, 0, .5, and 1.5. If the raw score of each of these is increased by 10, which z-score would change the least?

    a. $z = -.5$.
    b. $z = 0.0$.
    c. $z = .5$.
    d. $z = 1.5$.
    e. They would all change the same amount.

6. Assume you are dealing with a positively skewed distribution, with a mean of 60 and a standard deviation of 10. Suppose that for each score in the distribution we subtract 60 and then divide by 10. The distribution of the transformed scores will be:

    a. positively skewed
    b. negatively skewed
    c. normal
    d. platykuric.

7. Assume you are dealing with a positively skewed distribution, with a mean of 60 and a standard deviation of 10. Suppose that for each score in the distribution we subtract 60 and then divide by 10. What will be the mean and standard deviation of the distribution of transformed scores?

    a. Mean = 60 and standard deviation = 10.
    b. Mean = 60 and standard deviation = 1.
    c. Mean = 0 and standard deviation = 10.
    d. Mean = 0 and standard deviation = 1.

EXERCISES

5.1. Using the large ECLS data file ($N = 2{,}577$), convert the General Knowledge IRT Scale Scores at the end of first grade (*c4rgscal*) to a set of percentile ranks. Find the percentile ranks of the following scores: 41, 38, 26, and 31.

5.2. Consider four children scoring 41, 38, 26, and 31, respectively. Convert their scores to z-scores.

5.3. Given your results from Exercises 5.1 and 5.2, what can you say about the performance of these four children on the test of general knowledge?

6

Describing the Relationship between Two Quantitative Variables: Correlation

INTRODUCTION

In the previous chapters, we have presented a variety of ways to describe distributions of data for both quantitative and categorical measures. In this chapter, we begin our discussion dealing with quantitative variables in situations in which we have more than one measure on each case. With two measures on each case, the measures are said to be paired; such distributions are also called *bivariate* distributions. For example, for a set of athletes, we might have measures of height and weight. For a set of patients, we might have measures of cholesterol and blood pressure. And for a set of newspapers, we might identify measures of circulation and advertising revenue. With three or more variables, we have multivariate distributions. An example of a *multivariate* distribution might include measures of motivation, intelligence, and school achievement on a set of students. The possibilities abound!

In situations like these, it would still be possible (and appropriate) to employ the procedures that we have already discussed for situations in which there might be only one variable. That is, we could construct frequency distributions; create graphic displays such as histograms, frequency polygons, box plots, and stem-and-leaf displays; and calculate descriptive measures of location, dispersion, and shape. Describing data is a very important activity. Indeed, describing the amount of variability in a set of measures is the first step to building a science.

Few, if any, research questions in the social sciences have been stimulated by the observation of a constant. If all of the children in the Paris schools had been achieving at the same level, Binet would not have been commissioned to construct a measure to predict how well children would do in school, a measure we now know as "intelligence." Rather, the first step in building a science is to observe variation, or individual differences between cases. Once we establish the presence of variation, human beings seem to have an innate need to understand why the cases vary. One way to approach the problem is to find other measures which seem to move in concert with the variable we are trying to understand. We call this "co-movement" *covariation*. That is, in situations having two or more variables measured on each case, it is possible that two variables might tend to move together. For example, children who score higher on measures of intelligence tend to achieve at higher levels in school, children who are taller tend to also be heavier, and newspapers with wider circulation tend to have higher advertising revenues. For a visual image, think about dancing. Consider how Ginger Rogers and Fred Astaire in *Shall We Dance* – or John Travolta and Olivia Newton John in *Grease* – covaried in their movements. (Most people would agree that Fred and Ginger covaried more strongly than did John and Olivia.) Of course, variables can also move in opposite directions. In the world of investments, when interest rates go up, bond prices tend to go down. We have just introduced you to the notion of a *bivariate distribution*, which can be viewed in two different ways or models. One aspect of bivariate distributions is the strength of the linear relationship between the two variables. This perspective is called the "correlational approach." If it can be established that two variables are related, then one might want to describe how one variable varies as a function of the other; this perspective is the regression model.

It is important to note that the discussion in this book will be restricted to linear relationships. There are many instances in which a relationship may be non-linear, and it is possible to modify the methods that follow to deal with these relationships. The specific modifications for dealing with non-linear relationships, however, are beyond the scope of this book.

The Correlation Model

Given situations in which there are at least two variables, we may be interested in describing the relationship between two of the variables. In our large Early Childhood Longitudinal Study (ECLS) data file, we have measures of reading and math taken during the fall of kindergarten. We also have measures of Mother's Educational Level and Father's Educational Level. We might want to look at the relationship between these two variables in each of these pairs. Here, the question is simply whether the two variables are related or not and, if so, how strong the relationship is. Both of the variables are free to vary, and we are making no assumptions about how they might be related in terms of which variable might be the cause of the other. That is, neither variable is said to *depend* on the other.

The Regression Model

The regression model is appropriate for experiments and, to some degree, for non-experiments. For example, let's assume that we want to look at the relationship between the number of math homework problems completed and achievement in math. If we were designing an experiment, we would decide ahead of time the different number of problems to assign for each experimental condition, and we would randomly assign students to the different conditions. Thus, we might decide to look at no homework problems per week, five problems per week, 10 problems per week, and 15 problems per week. Note that we have set up the different conditions in advance; the number of problems assigned is not free to vary. Rather, the possible values are pre-specified. Furthermore, we have set up the study as an experiment as we have total control over which students are assigned to which conditions. In addition, it is clear that we want to look at math achievement as a function of amount of homework. In this situation, we would label amount of homework as the *independent variable* and math achievement as the *dependent variable*, since we're examining whether math achievement *depends* on the amount of homework. As we have described the situation, it is appropriate for a regression model.

Contrast the situation we just described with a different approach. Suppose that we administered a survey to students in which they were asked about how much math homework they completed in an average week. Then, we matched the survey results with their actual level of math achievement. This approach is quite different from the regression approach, although we are studying the relationship between the same two variables. As just described, we are operating within the correlational model. It is still possible to apply a regression approach in the analysis of the data, however, and it is frequently done in practice. For example, we could declare that math achievement is the dependent variable and that the survey result regarding amount of math homework completed is the independent variable. We should point out that the assumptions of the regression model are not fully satisfied and we should therefore exercise some caution in the interpretation of our results.

For those of you who may be somewhat confused, we promise that we will explain what we are talking about in this chapter and the next. In this chapter, we devote our attention to the notion of correlation. In Chapter 7, we will treat the issue of regression in considerable detail.

MOVING FROM UNIVARIATE DISTRIBUTIONS TO BIVARIATE DISTRIBUTIONS

As noted earlier in this chapter, we have already spent a lot of time and space presenting ways in which to describe a single set of measurements. The basic idea is depicted in Figure 6.1. We begin with a list of the data, organize it into a frequency distribution, depict it in a graphic form, and finally calculate some values that describe attributes of the distribution (location, dispersion, and shape).

There is a similar progression when working with bivariate distributions, as we are now. That is, we begin with a listing of the data, convert it to a bivariate distribution, and then present it in graphic form. The first part of the progression is depicted in Figure 6.2.

Note the question mark underneath the "Graphic display" heading. In part, we have included it to pique your curiosity, but also because it is very difficult to draw a bivariate distribution free-hand. Instead, we have resorted to using the **perscp( )** function in R to do it for us. In the large ECLS data file, two of the variables are Mother's Educational Level (*wkmomed*) and Father's Educational Level (*wkdaded*). In Script 6.1 (see the book website), we first asked the program to draw the bivariate frequency distribution as is, with all its bumps and irregularities. Then we asked the program to smooth the surface. These two graphics are presented in Figure 6.3.

Given the difficulty involved in drawing a three-dimensional graphic, we provide several alternatives for representing a bivariate distribution. One possibility is similar to the contour maps used in cartography to depict terrain. For example, consider that you are looking at the distribution on the right in Figure 6.3, but from above. For a population, it might look like Figure 6.4.

The most frequent approach employed when using a computer program to depict the bivariate distribution of a sample is the *scatterplot*. It is a two-dimensional representation that puts the X variable on the horizontal axis, the Y variable on the vertical axis, and places markers at the coordinates of the data points. In Figure 6.5, we include, as an example, a scatterplot of mother's educational level with Father's Educational Level using the data file of 200 cases employed in

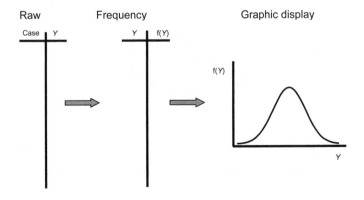

FIGURE 6.1   The progression from raw data, to frequency distribution, to graphic.

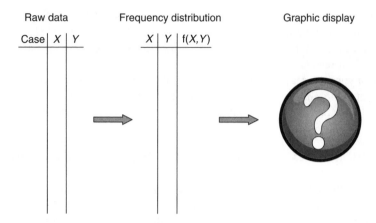

FIGURE 6.2   Moving from raw data for a bivariate distribution to a bivariate frequency distribution.

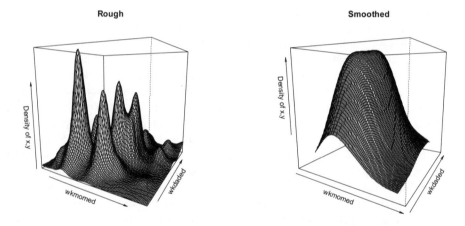

FIGURE 6.3   Rough and smoothed bivariate frequency distributions of Mother's and Father's Educational Level.

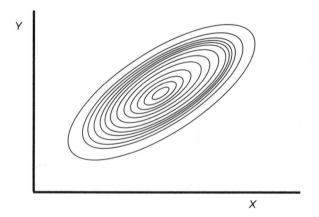

FIGURE 6.4   A contour map approach to depicting a bivariate frequency distribution.

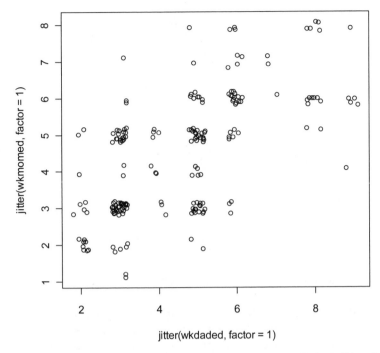

FIGURE 6.5   Scatterplot from R of Mother's Educational Level with Father's Educational
Level with jittering ($n = 200$).

previous chapters. We will discuss the details of how to create such a scatterplot in the computer example presented later in this chapter. We now turn our focus to the correlational model.

THE CORRELATIONAL MODEL: ASSESSING THE STRENGTH OF LINEAR ASSOCIATION

One of the first steps in assessing the strength of an association between two variables is to examine a scatterplot of the data. Rather than show plots of actual data at this point, we present some prototypic patterns in Figure 6.6. In our plots, we have denoted the variables as Y_1 and Y_2, to convey that neither of them is the independent or the dependent variable.

One way to think about the strength of a linear relationship or association is the degree to which the data points fall on a line. In part (a) in Figure 6.6 we have depicted a fairly strong relationship. Given that it shows a situation where Y_2 increases as Y_1 increases, we describe it as a direct or positive relationship. The relationship shown in part (b) is also positive, but it is not as strong as the one in part (a). In part (c) we have shown a pattern that indicates little, if any, relationship between the two variables. As you move left or right on the Y_1 scale, there is no systematic change in Y_2. In part (d) the pattern suggests a fairly strong relationship, but it is negative or inverse. As the values of Y_1 increase, the values of Y_2 tend to decrease. The pattern in part (e) also suggests a negative relationship, but not as strong a relationship as the pattern in part (d). The pattern in part (f) is perhaps the most interesting of the lot. Clearly, there is a relationship between Y_1 and Y_2, but it is not linear. As Y_1 increases, Y_2 increases at first, reaches a maximum, and then decreases. We refer to this type of relationship as "non-linear," or "curvilinear."

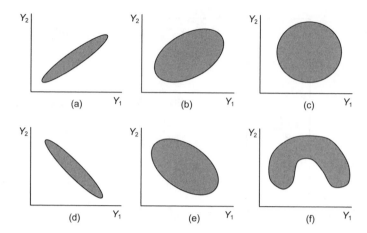

FIGURE 6.6   Some typical patterns of association between two variables.

Early Work on Describing Linear Relationships between Variables

The first clear attempts to describe linear association can be traced back to Sir Francis Galton, a younger cousin of Charles Darwin. Galton began breeding sweet peas in the 1870s, examining the characteristics of the peas over generations. In comparing the size of the parent seeds to the size of the offspring seeds, he noted what he called "reversion to the mean." That is, the offspring of large seeds tended to be large, but not as large as the parent seeds. The offspring of small seeds tended to be small, but not as small as the parent seeds.

He also examined human traits over generations. He noted that very tall parents produced tall children who tended to be not quite as tall as their parents. Similarly, very short parents produced short children, but not quite as short as their parents. He noticed the same phenomenon with regard to "genius." Galton described this tendency as reversion, or regression to the mean.

In light of his observations, he began to explore ways in which to measure the degree of association between his sets of observations. His first attempts relied on ranking techniques, along with tabular presentations. It remained for his protégé, Karl Pearson, to develop the mathematical basis for the way in which we now measure covariation, the Pearson Product-Moment Correlation coefficient. To explore how this was done, let's start by revisiting the definition of variance.

Moving from Variance to Covariance to Correlation

The definition of variance, first presented in Chapter 3, is repeated here.

$$\sigma_Y^2 = \frac{\sum_{i=1}^{n}(Y_i - \mu_Y)^2}{n} \tag{6.1}$$

This expression can be rewritten as:

$$\sigma_Y^2 = \frac{\sum_{i=1}^{n}(Y_i - \mu_Y)(Y_i - \mu_Y)}{n} \tag{6.2}$$

We are dealing with two variables, Y_1 and Y_2, in a correlation model, but we will rename the two variables X and Y, respectively, to present more conventional notation. Given that there are two different variables, we will rewrite Equation 6.2 as:

$$\sigma_{XY} = \frac{\sum_{i=1}^{n}(X_i - \mu_X)(Y_i - \mu_Y)}{n} \tag{6.3}$$

First, note that we have changed the term on the left side of the equal sign. For the variance, the deviation from the mean is used twice, so we write the symbol as σ_Y^2. With the modification, there are two different deviations, one on the X variable and the other on the Y variable. Thus, we use the symbol σ_{XY} and call it the covariance. Let's take a look at how this formula would work with several typical, moderate positive relationships as depicted in Figure 6.7. In addition to the usual oval representing the scatterplot, we have added reference axes at μ_x and μ_y.

First, let's focus on the point in quadrant 1. It is above the mean on both X and Y. Thus, the two deviations are both positive, as is their product. Next, consider the point in quadrant 2; it is below the mean on X but above the mean on Y. One of the deviations is positive and the other is negative; their product will be negative. In quadrant 3, both deviations will be negative, but their product will be positive. Quadrant 4 is similar to the situation in quadrant 2, but reversed. Nevertheless, one deviation is positive and the other is negative; their product will be negative. After having found the two deviations for each of the data points and multiplied them together, the products are summed. Looking at Figure 6.7, you should be able to see that most of the points are in quadrants 1 and 3, where the products are positive. Furthermore, the deviations in those quadrants would tend to be larger than those in quadrants 2 and 4. Larger deviations result in larger products. Looking at the big picture, a scatterplot like the one in Figure 6.7 would result in a large, positive sum in the numerator of σ_{XY}. In Figure 6.8 we repeat Figure 6.6 with reference axes.

Let's say that we have computed the covariance for (a) in Figure 6.8. Now look at (b). The pattern is still such that the two positive quadrants (1 and 3) are going to outweigh the two negative quadrants, but the imbalance in the number of points and the magnitude of the products is not as large. Thus, we would still obtain a positive result, but it would not be as large as in (a).

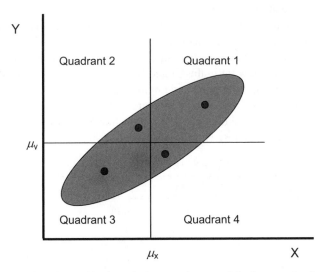

FIGURE 6.7   The formula for covariance and the four quadrants.

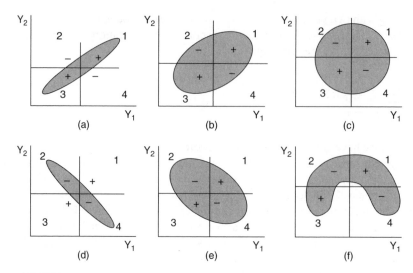

FIGURE 6.8   How the formula for covariance works with different scatterplots.

Looking at (c), we note that the two positive quadrants are similar to the two negative quadrants; we should expect a sum of products close to zero. Considering (d), we might expect a sum of products similar to that in (a), with a negative value. Similarly, the result for (e) should be about the same magnitude as that in (b), but reversed to a negative sign. Last, consider (f). Quadrant 1 should produce products about the same magnitude that quadrant 2 yields. Thus, their sum should be close to zero. In a similar fashion, the products from quadrants 3 and 4 should be about the same magnitude, but reversed in sign. Consequently, the numerator of the formula for the covariance should be close to zero, as with (c). However the reason is quite different. In (c), there is no relationship at all. In (f), there is a relationship, but it is non-linear. Thus, obtaining a covariance close to zero should be interpreted as no *linear* relationship, not as no relationship.

At this point, we can see that the covariance has two desirable properties. First, its magnitude tells us something about the strength of the relationship, all other things being equal. Second, its sign tells us whether the relationship is positive or negative.

It does have one very unfortunate property, however. Consider the data in Table 6.1. Two different residents in neonatology were conducting a study of newborns in the Neonatal Intensive Care Nursery. In particular, they were both interested in looking at the relationship between length and weight. Dr. Smith grew up in the United States and obtained his medical training at Harvard. Dr. McDowell grew up in London and obtained her training at the University of Edinburgh. The data they collected (on the same infants) are presented in Table 6.1.

Each of the residents enters the data into a program like R, SPSS, or SAS, requesting the covariance between the two measures. The residents are only interested in these four infants so

Table 6.1 Data on length and weight collected by Drs. Smith and McDowell

	Dr. Smith			Dr. McDowell	
Child	*Length (in.)*	*Weight (oz)*	*Child*	*Length (cm)*	*Weight (g)*
1	17.0	64.0	1.0	42.2	1,816
2	18.5	72.0	2.0	47.0	2,043
3	16.0	62.0	3.0	40.5	1,759
4	19.0	80.0	4.0	48.3	2,270

they ask the program to use Equation 6.3. (If they wanted to estimate the population covariance from a sample, they would use the sample means in the computation and the denominator would be changed to $n-1$, just like we did for the variance). Using Equation 6.3, the computer program provides a value of 8.06 to Dr. Smith, but returns a value of 584.44 to Dr. McDowell. How can this be? The two residents took the same measurements—only one measured the variables in inches and ounces, while the other expressed them in centimeters and grams. As you can see, the "amount of covariation" depends on the scales on which the two variables are measured. This can be quite problematic if we wish to be able to present a meaningful descriptive statistic.

If metric is the problem, however, the situation is easy to remedy. We can solve the problem by putting all variables on the same scale prior to calculating the covariance. As discussed in Chapter 5, we can accomplish this by converting both X and Y respectively to z-scores. After the transformations, both variables are on a scale with a mean of zero and a standard deviation of one. We could then rewrite our expression for the covariation between X and Y as:

$$\sigma_{z_x z_y} = \frac{\sum_{i=1}^{n} z_x z_y}{n} \tag{6.4}$$

Thus, we could present a "standardized" covariance by standardizing both variables before computing the covariance. This standardized covariance is called the correlation coefficient and is denoted as ρ_{XY}.

Despite the simplicity of Equation 6.5, most people don't want to go to the trouble of standardizing the variables prior to calculation. Rather, they would prefer to work with raw scores in the original metric. Fortunately, there is also a simple way to do that. Let's rewrite Equation 6.4, expanding the z-score notation and substituting ρ_{XY} for the σ:

$$\rho_{XY} = \frac{\sum_{i=1}^{n}\left(\frac{X_i-\mu_X}{\sigma_X}\right)\left(\frac{Y_i-\mu_Y}{\sigma_Y}\right)}{n} = \frac{1}{n}\sum_{i=1}^{n}\left(\frac{X_i-\mu_X}{\sigma_X}\right)\left(\frac{Y_i-\mu_Y}{\sigma_Y}\right) \tag{6.5}$$

With a little algebraic manipulation, this expression can be changed to:

$$\rho_{XY} = \frac{\left[\frac{\sum_{i=1}^{n}(X_i-\mu_X)(Y_i-\mu_Y)}{n}\right]}{\sqrt{\left(\left[\frac{\sum_{i=1}^{n}(X_i-\mu_X)^2}{n}\right]\right)\left(\left[\frac{\sum_{i=1}^{n}(Y_i-\mu_Y)^2}{n}\right]\right)}} = \frac{\sigma_{XY}}{\sqrt{\sigma_X^2\sigma_Y^2}} \tag{6.6}$$

Looking carefully at Equation 6.6, you can see that the numerator is the covariance, and the denominator is the square root of the product of the variances. We spent time in Chapter 3 discussing the arithmetic mean along with other measures of location; the denominator above is sometimes called the geometric mean of the two variances. That is, the nth root of the product of n things is the geometric mean, yet another way to express a representative value. Thus, the denominator has the effect of standardizing the covariance. So, you can either standardize the variables and compute the covariance of the standardized variables, or you can calculate the covariance and then standardize it. In both cases, you obtain the standardized covariance, or the correlation coefficient.

Note that if you were estimating the population correlation from a sample, you would substitute the sample means for the population means and use $n - 1$ instead of n in Equation 6.6. This change occurs in both the numerator and denominator, which ends up dividing out. Therefore the process of computing the correlation is identical whether you are working with a sample or a population. This consistency in the process of computation mirrors what we saw when we calculated a mean, but differs from what we saw when we computed a standard deviation, a variance, or a covariance. When we estimate the correlation from a sample, we tend to use the symbol r, instead of ρ.

The correlation coefficient, r, can take on any value from -1 to $+1$, with a value of zero indicating no linear relationship. However, this "full range" is possible only when both the distributions of X and Y are the same (Huck, 2009, p. 42). Note that the reported correlation coefficient should be decoded in terms of its magnitude and sign separately. That is, a correlation of $-.80$ is larger than one of $+.70$. The sign merely tells you whether the relationship is direct or inverse. Of course, a correlation coefficient of either -1.00 or $+1.00$ indicates a perfect linear relationship, one in which the points in a scatterplot fall on a line.

For computing the correlation coefficient, most people would not use Equation 6.6, which is in definitional form. Rather, they would employ an algebraically identical equation, in computational form:

$$r_{XY} = \frac{n \sum_{i=1}^{n} X_i Y_i - \left(\sum_{i=1}^{n} X_i \right)\left(\sum_{i=1}^{n} Y_i \right)}{\sqrt{\left[n \sum_{i=1}^{n} X_i^2 - \left(\sum_{i=1}^{n} X_i \right)^2 \right]\left[n \sum_{i=1}^{n} Y_i^2 - \left(\sum_{i=1}^{n} Y_i \right)^2 \right]}} \tag{6.7}$$

Although this form looks rather messy, it is actually quite easy to use, as we will demonstrate in the next section.

Calculating the Correlation Coefficient: An Example

Earlier in the this chapter, we showed you a computer-drawn bivariate distribution of Mother's and Father's Educational Level (see Figure 6.3) using data from the full ECLS data set. In this section, we use a small, random sample of data ($n = 20$) from the larger data set. The data are presented in Table 6.2. See the codebook on the book website for the value labels.

Table 6.2 A random sample of 20 cases from the ECLS data set: Mother's Educational Level (MomEd) and Father's Educational Level (DadEd)

Case	MomEd	DadEd	Case	MomEd	DadEd
1	6	9	11	6	6
2	4	5	12	4	5
3	6	6	13	3	5
4	5	3	14	1	3
5	5	3	15	3	5
6	3	3	16	5	5
7	3	3	17	3	3
8	6	6	18	5	3
9	3	3	19	5	6
10	7	7	20	3	3

Table 6.3 A correlation table of Mother's Educational Level (MomEd) and Father's Educational Level (DadEd)

				DadEd						
		1	2	3	4	5	6	7	8	9
MomEd	9									
	8									
	7							1		
	6						3			1
	5			3		1	1			
	4					2				
	3			5		2				
	2									
	1			1						

An examination of the data as presented in the table is not very informative regarding the strength of the relationship between the two variables. We have the same basic problem that we had when we looked at a long list of values to try to assess location, dispersion, and shape. We need to process the data in order to better understand how the variables are related. First, let's take a look at graphic depictions of the bivariate relationship with the data presented in a correlation table (Table 6.3). The format is similar to the one used by Galton to look at the heritability of stature. An inspection of Table 6.3 contents shows a trend; as Mother's Educational Level increases, so does Father's Educational Level, and vice versa.

Another graphic presentation is the scatterplot. Using R (Script 6.2), we first produced a standard scatterplot, which is presented in Figure 6.9. The data had been saved in a text file named *chap6.ex1*. The R commands that were executed are:

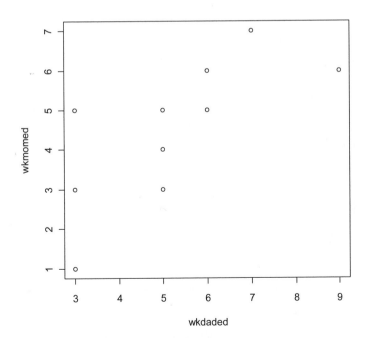

FIGURE 6.9   A scatterplot of Mother's Educational Level and Father's Educational Level produced by R (*n* = 20).

```
chap6.ex1 <- read.table("c:/rbook/chap6.ex1.txt",
  header = TRUE)
attach(chap6.ex1)
plot(wkdaded, wkmomed)
```

Looking at the plot, you will notice that there are only 10 dots in the plot. That is because R, like most programs, by default only places one symbol at each set of coordinates, regardless of how many data points are located at that position. Thus, you do not really get a true sense of where the cases are tending to concentrate. We offer two ways to address this issue by modifying the plot command:

```
# Using the jitter option
plot(jitter(wkdaded, factor = 1), jitter(wkmomed,
  factor = 1))
# Using the sunflowerplot option
sunflowerplot(wkdaded, wkmomed)
```

The modified scatterplots obtained using the jitter option and sunflower plot command are shown in Figures 6.10 and 6.11.

Given what we have seen in all three presentations, it seems there is a positive relationship between Mother's Educational Level and Father's Educational Level, although it is far from perfect. There is an additional option for plotting, which represents the density with shading, but it does not really show much when there are only 20 cases:

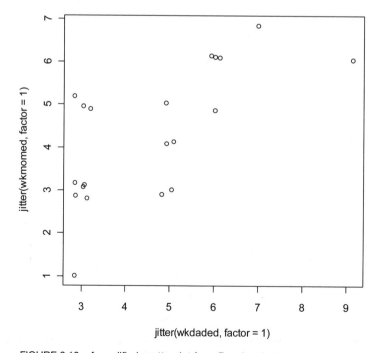

FIGURE 6.10   A modified scatterplot from R, using the jitter option ($n = 20$).

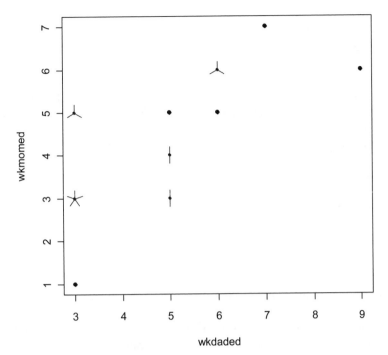

FIGURE 6.11   A modified scatterplot from R, using the sunflower plot command ($n = 20$).

```
plot(wkdaded, wkmomed, pch = 16,
  col = rgb(0, 0, 0, alpha = 0.25))
```

We now show you how to calculate the correlation coefficient. Returning to the data in Table 6.2, we will designate Father's Educational Level as the X variable and Mother's Educational Level as the Y variable. Looking at Equation 6.7, we can see that there are a number of quantities that we need to calculate from the data. Two of them simply involve finding the sums of the X and Y variables, and two of them involve squaring the values before summing. Based on our work in Chapter 3, these calculations should pose no problem. Do note, however, that there is a new entity in the situation: ΣXY. To find that value, we multiply the X value times the Y value for each case and then sum the products. For the data in Table 6.2, we would proceed as $(6 \times 9) + (4 \times 5) + (6 \times 6) + \ldots + (3 \times 3)$. Given the data in the table, we would find:

$$\sum_{i=1}^{20} X_i = 92 \qquad \sum_{i=1}^{20} X_i^2 = 480$$

$$\sum_{i=1}^{20} Y_i = 86 \qquad \sum_{i=1}^{20} Y_i^2 = 414$$

$$n = 20 \qquad \sum_{i=1}^{20} X_i Y_i = 429$$

On the book website we show you how to use R (Script 6.3) to generate these numbers. We would then substitute these values into Equation 6.7 as follows:

$$r_{XY} = \frac{20 \times 429 - 92 \times 86}{\sqrt{\left(20 \times 480 - 92^2\right)\left(20 \times 414 - 86^2\right)}} = .6665936 = .67 \tag{6.8}$$

We have provided a very precise result and then rounded to two decimal places. The precise result will be used to make a point in Chapter 7 regarding the fact that r^2 can be interpreted as the proportion of variance explained.

To calculate the correlation coefficient in R, we use the **cor( )** function:

```
cor(wkdaded, wkmomed)
```

The program returns:

```
> cor(wkdaded, wkmomed)
[1] 0.6665936
```

Several Issues in the Interpretation of the Correlation Coefficient

We have just calculated the value of r to be .67. But what does it mean? Among the issues to consider when interpreting a correlation coefficient are magnitude, linearity, possible restriction in range, potential outliers, presence of subgroups, and causality.

Magnitude

The size of the correlation coefficient informs us about the strength of the linear association between the two variables. There are some people who like to discuss "cutpoints" between small correlations, modest correlations, and large correlations. We do not. The size of a correlation is context specific. That is, what might represent a large correlation in one context might be a small correlation in another. In that sense, correlations are similar to reliability coefficients. Correlation coefficients also tell us something about the amount of shared variance between two variables. If you take the value of r and square it ($.67^2 = .449$), you will know that these two variables share approximately 45% of their variation. The value, r^2, is sometimes called the *coefficient of determination*. Its counterpart, $1 - r^2$, is called the *coefficient of alienation*. We will discuss this further in Chapter 7.

Linearity

The interpretation of r also assumes that the relationship is linear. Recall part (f) of Figure 6.8, in which the relationship was non-linear. When you obtain a value of r close to zero, you should not jump to the conclusion that the two variables are not related. The only conclusion to be made is that they are not linearly related. A look at a scatterplot can be very helpful in sorting out the possibilities.

Restriction in range

Another issue to consider in interpreting r is the possibility of a restriction in the range of one or both variables. In this context, we are not referring to the size of the variance, but rather to the degree to which the variables actually vary across their potential range. Remember that the

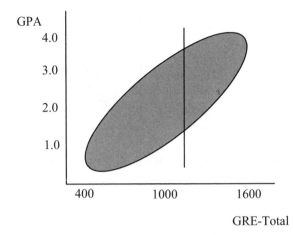

FIGURE 6.12   The effect of restriction of range on the correlation coefficient.

correlation coefficient is a measure of covariation. If one of the variables does not vary very much, it cannot covary with another variable. For example, graduate students have been known to put forth the argument that the Graduate Record Exam (GRE) should not be used as a criterion in the application/acceptance process for graduate programs. After all, it does not correlate that well with success in graduate school. But let's think about this argument. Does everyone who applies to graduate school get accepted? Of course not. The GRE–Total of the Verbal and Quantitative subtests could range from a low of 400 to a high of 1,600. Assuming that a particular graduate program requires a minimum GRE score of 1,100, all of those below 1,100 in the computation of the correlation between GRE and Grade Point Average (GPA) are eliminated. They don't have GPAs. The effect of this can be seen in Figure 6.12

Looking at the entire oval/ellipse, it would appear that there is a degree of correlation between the two variables, perhaps in the range .60 to .70. Now look at the figure, erasing in your mind the part of the plot to the left of the vertical line above 1,100 on the horizontal axis. The remainder of the plot looks like a much weaker association. In considering the possibility of restricted range, compare the range of possible scores on a measure with the actual range of scores in the data. If the actual range is considerably smaller, that becomes a possible explanation for a lack of correlation.

The Presence of Outliers

Another issue to consider in the interpretation of the correlation coefficient is the possible presence of outliers. The specific nature of their effect on the value of r depends on their location. This point is illustrated in Figure 6.13.

In part (a), the overall relationship between X and Y is not very strong. However, given that there is an outlier, the dot, the strength of the relationship will be overestimated as the outlier is along the trajectory of the pattern. In part (b), the overall relationship is fairly strong, but the location of the outlier will effectively weaken our estimate of the correlation coefficient. In order to detect an outlier, you should look at both descriptive statistics and scatterplots. The outlier in part (a) is much higher than any of the other X and Y scores and thus should be detected in the univariate distributions. In part (b), the outlying point is within the range of both X and Y; it is an outlier by virtue of its position, not its values of X and/or Y. It would probably only be detected by looking at the scatterplot.

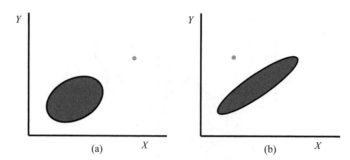

FIGURE 6.13   The potential effect of outlying observations.

The Presence of Subgroups

Imagine that you are going to look at the correlation between foot length and the number of vocabulary words in the pre-school and elementary school population. We believe that you would find a fairly substantial correlation between these two variables in this situation. But what does it mean? We've depicted our view of a possible explanation in Figure 6.14.

Each of the different ovals represents a different age group. Within each age group, there is a rather weak relationship between vocabulary size and foot size, probably due to an age range of almost a year within a grade. As age increases, feet grow and so does the size of the vocabulary. If you think about examining all of the data points as one group, the correlation would appear to be very strong. Thus, the observed correlation between vocabulary size and foot size in the population of young children is an artifact of age differences. When a correlation coefficient can be explained by a common third variable, as in the example just presented, we say that the correlation is *spurious*. We will show you a way to use scatterplots in R to assess the effects of subgroups.

Causality

Last, how can we interpret a correlation coefficient within the context of possible causal relationships? If we observe that two variables are correlated, that finding is consistent with a number of possibilities. First, it might be that X causes Y. Or it might be that Y causes X. A third pos-

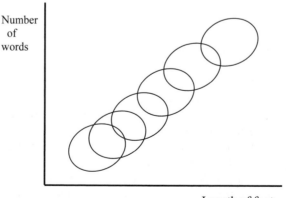

FIGURE 6.14   The effect of subgroups on the correlation coefficient.

sibility is that X and Y cause one another. At first, that last possibility sounds impossible, but such relationships do exist. Consider the relationship between the thermostat (on/off) and the room temperature. In the winter, when the temperature drops to a certain level, the thermostat goes to "on" and causes the temperature of the room to rise. That is, the temperature affects the thermostat, and the thermostat affects the temperature. Another example is the financial health of corporations and stock prices.

Finally, there is the possibility that the correlation we observe results from both variables having a common cause, similar to the situation we described with vocabulary and foot size. Another example: Do you know that the amount of damage done by a house fire is positively related to the number of firefighters on the scene? Before you conclude that we would be better off sending fewer firefighters, think for a moment. The magnitude of the fire affects both the amount of damage and the number of firefighters dispatched to the fire. If you can hold the magnitude of the fire constant (like looking at vocabulary and foot size within grade level), you will find that the more firefighters on the scene, the less the amount of damage done by the fire. Indeed, systems of correlations can be very tricky to interpret, and we should be careful to consider all possibilities. This situation is sometimes called Simpson's paradox.

We will now present another case study of correlation, using R to look at the relationship between reading scores at the beginning of kindergarten and reading scores at the end of first grade.

A COMPLETE EXAMPLE OF A CORRELATIONAL ANALYSIS WITH R

For this example, we will use the data set of 200 cases that was used in Chapters 3 and 4. We will describe the relationship between reading scores measured at the beginning of kindergarten and those measured at the end of first grade. There are a number of steps in this analysis. First, we will generate some descriptive statistics. We will look at the output for reasonable means, minimums, and maximums. We will also inspect the standard deviations with a concern for possible restrictions in range. Second, we will produce a scatterplot of the two variables, displaying multiple cases at the same coordinates. The scatterplot will be examined for a possible non-linear relationship and the presence of outliers. We will also produce a scatterplot that has plots for White students and African American students superimposed on the same plot. We will then use R to calculate the correlation coefficient, after which we will assess the impact of the outliers. Finally, we will make some concluding statements.

Descriptive Statistics

To examine the characteristics of the two variables, *c1rrscal* and *c4rrscal*, we executed the R commands:

```
table(c1rrscal)
table(c4rrscal)
summary(c1rrscal)
summary(c4rrscal)
sd(c1rrscal)
sd(c4rrscal)
boxplot(c1rrscal,c4rrscal)
```

The output from R is:

```
> table(c1rrscal)
c1rrscal
11 12 13 14 15 16 17 18 19 20 21 22 23 24 25 26 27
 1  2  4 10  6 14  4  6  4 13 16 18 16  8  8  5  3

28 29 30 31 32 33 34 35 36 38 39 40 41 43 56 61 71
 7 10  6  6  5 10  1  2  1  2  1  1  1  1  3  3  2
> table(c4rrscal)
c4rrscal
19 21 25 27 30 31 34 35 36 38 39 41 42 43 44 45 46
 1  1  1  1  1  1  3  3  1  1  6  5  1  3  2  5  6

47 48 49 50 51 52 53 54 55 56 57 58 59 60 61 62 63
 3  4  5  6  5  5  4  9  4  9  5  7  1  7  5  4  5

64 65 66 67 68 69 70 71 72 73 74 75 76 77 78 79 81
 5  5  6  5  4  4  8  4  4  2  4  4  4  4  2  2  2

86
 1
> summary(c1rrscal)
   Min. 1st Qu.  Median    Mean 3rd Qu.    Max.
  11.00   19.00   23.00   24.23   29.00   71.00
> summary(c4rrscal)
   Min. 1st Qu.  Median    Mean 3rd Qu.    Max.
  19.00   49.00   57.00   57.29   67.00   86.00
> sd(c1rrscal)
[1] 8.30191
> sd(c4rrscal)
[1] 12.94736
> boxplot(c1rrscal,c4rrscal)
```

The box plot from this output is shown in Figure 6.15.

Without knowing too much about these two scales, we will assume that the means are reasonable, that the minimum and maximum values are within range (indicating no gross coding errors), and that the standard deviations reflect a reasonable amount of variation. We could calculate the coefficients of variation (CV) for each measure, finding that $CV_1 = 34.26$ and $CV_2 = 22.26$. The boxplots suggest that there may be three high scores for *c1rrscal* and two low scores for *c4rrscal*. On *c1rrscal*, the values (71, 61, 56) are quite a bit above the next value, 43, after which the scores drop to several 41s. If converted to z-scores, the values would be 5.63, 4.43, and 3.83, indicating each is over 3 standard deviations from the mean. The rest of the table looks fairly reasonable. We will make note of these three cases for possible problems in the analysis.

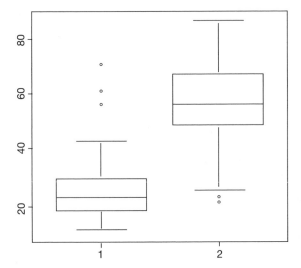

FIGURE 6.15   Box plot of reading score at the entry to kindergarten (1) and at the end of first grade (2).

Linearity, Outliers, and Subgroups

At this point, it is appropriate to produce a scatterplot to inspect the data for a possible violation of the assumption of linearity; we will also be able to look at the plot for bivariate outliers. At the same time, we will calculate the value of the correlation coefficient:

```
plot(jitter(c1rrscal, factor = 1),
  jitter(c4rrscal, factor = 1))
cor(c1rrscal, c4rrscal)

> cor(c1rrscal, c4rrscal)
[1] 0.6105477
```

The scatterplot from this output is shown in Figure 6.16.

Given the results from R, we can see that the three top scores, flagged earlier, seem to be unusual cases and perhaps may influence the calculation of the correlation coefficient, which we found to be .611. The inclusion of the three points suggests that the relationship might be slightly non-linear; assessing this is beyond the scope of this book. However, we have looked at the possibility. Briefly, if the three data points remain in the file, one could argue that there is a curvilinear trend in the data. However, if the three outliers on *c1rrscal* are removed, there is virtually no evidence for curvilinearity.

Dealing with the Outliers on c1rrscal

There are several ways to explore the effects of those three cases. A very popular option is to delete those cases and recalculate the correlation between the two variables. In R, it is possible to exclude cases from an analysis without actually deleting them from the file. Recall that the three outlying cases were much higher than the next case, which had a value of 43. To temporarily exclude those three cases, try the statement below:

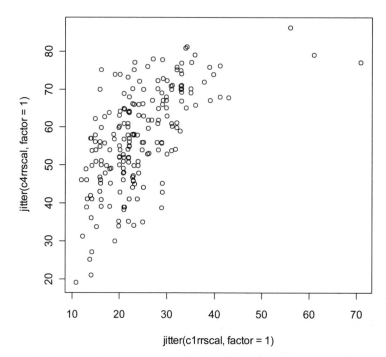

FIGURE 6.16   Scatterplot of reading score at the beginning of kindergarten (*c1rrscal*) and at the end of first grade (*c4rrscal*) for 200 children.

```
with(subset(chap6.case, subset = c1rrscal < "45"),
    cor(c1rrscal, c4rrscal))
```

This statement instructs R to only use cases having a value of 44 or below on the *c1rrscal* variable.

```
> with(subset(chap6.case,
    subset = c1rrscal < "45"),
    cor(c1rrscal, c4rrscal))
[1] 0.6120354
```

As you can see, excluding the three cases changed the correlation coefficient to .612. It should be rather obvious that those three cases do not have a very large impact on the magnitude of *r*. This does not mean, however, that all outliers will typically have little to no effect on the correlation. It may be good to explore why the effect was so small in this data set. In this case, we removed three observations which had large positive deviations on each variable, which tends to reduce a positive correlation. By removing these three points, we made the relationship more linear, which tends to increase the magnitude of the correlation. In this particular data set, these two effects almost canceled each other out.

We have now computed two different correlations, .611 and .612. Which should be reported? Some would recommend reporting the correlation for the full data set (outliers included), but this leaves one open to critiques that the results are too heavily influenced by a few cases. One approach to addressing these concerns is to note the outliers and the impact that their removal would have on the reported correlation. Others may recommend dropping or deleting the "problematic" cases. This can also leave one open to being criticized for manipulating the data to make things look better. Rather than dropping the cases, we would recommend a less "severe" solution. We suggest that the cases remain in the data file, but that they be recoded to reduce their potential influence (Tabachnick & Fidell, 2007, p. 77). Thus, case 165 would have its value of 56 recoded to a value of 44, one above the real value of 43. Case 61 would be recoded to a 45, and case 99 would be recoded to a value of 46. In this way, the cases remain in the file and they are still at the extreme of the distribution, yet their potential influence would be reduced. (If you choose to do this, we recommend that you code the data into a new variable so that you retain the original data.)

When we recoded the cases and recomputed the correlation coefficient, we obtained a value of .636, which we feel might be the most appropriate value to report, along with an explanation of how it was obtained. (Of course we recognize that not everyone would choose this option.)

Last, let's look at the possibility of racial effects on the computation of the correlation coefficient. To accomplish this, we used the following commands:

```
# Produce a scatterplot with subgroups
# Set plotting character to 1 for all cases
pchval <- rep(1, length = length(f.race))
# Set plotting character to 18 for AA
pchval[f.race == "AA"] <- 18
plot(jitter(c1rrscal, factor = 1),
  jitter(c4rrscal, factor = 1), pch = pchval)
legend(50, 30, c("White", "AA"), pch = c(1, 18))
with(subset(chap6.case,
  subset = f.race == "White"),
  cor(c1rrscal,c4rrscal))
with(subset(chap6.case, subset = f.race=="AA"),
  cor(c1rrscal, c4rrscal))
```

Looking at the resulting scatterplot (Figure 6.17), you can see that the cases in the two different groups are quite interspersed; it is unlikely that there are differences between the two groups of any substance.

We then calculated the two correlation coefficients:

```
> with(subset(chap6.case,
    subset = f.race == "White"),
    cor(c1rrscal,c4rrscal))
[1] 0.563217
> with(subset(chap6.case, subset = f.race == "AA"),
    cor(c1rrscal,c4rrscal))
[1] 0.6286595
```

As you can see, R returned a value of $r = .563$ for White students and $r = .629$ for African American students. These values were obtained leaving the three problem cases in their original form.

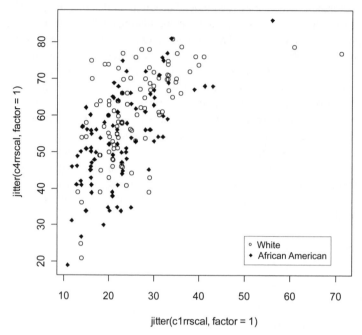

FIGURE 6.17   Scatterplot of reading score at the beginning of kindergarten (*c1rrscal*) and at the end of first grade (c4rrscal) for 200 children, disaggregated by race.

The two correlation coefficients are somewhat different, but not by much. In Chapter 15, we will show you how to assess whether the difference is "real" or whether differences of that magnitude can be reasonably expected to occur by chance.

SUMMING IT UP

We have looked at the relationship between reading scores measured at the beginning of kindergarten and similar scores measured at the end of first grade. In our analysis, we examined the descriptive statistics for possible anomalies in the data, finding some outlying cases. We suggested two different ways to deal with the outliers. The correlation coefficient with the original data was .611. When we dropped the outliers, it was .612. Recoding the outliers yielded a result of .636. In any of the results, it would appear that the correlation between these two variables is about .6. Thus, we can say that the two variables share about 36% (.602) of their variation. Before we end the chapter, we should point out that the Pearson Product-Moment correlation is not the only way to examine the relationship between two variables.

OTHER APPROACHES TO DESCRIBING CORRELATION

In this chapter, we have spent a considerable amount of time describing ways in which to describe the relationship between two quantitative variables. Specifically, we introduced you to the Pearson Product-Moment Correlation (PPMC) coefficient. In this section, we introduce you to several other procedures for describing the relationship between two variables. The PPMC coefficient is appropriate when both variables are quantitative, continuous, and measured on a ratio, interval, or approximately interval scale. From time to time, other conditions arise that require us to consider alternatives to the PPMC, such as when variables are measured as a dichotomy, are rank ordered, or when you have qualitative/categorical variables. The procedures we present in this section should be considered representative rather than exhaustive. These techniques can be classified roughly into several categories: Substitutes for PPMC (the Spearman Rank Correlation, the point-biserial correlation coefficient, and the phi coefficient), Non-Product-Moment Coefficients for quantitative variables (the biserial correlation coefficient and the tetrachoric correlation coefficient), Non-Product-Moment Coefficients for categorical variables (the Contingency Coefficient and Cramer's V), and standardized mean differences, which are conceptually different than correlation coefficients, but commonly used to describe the relationship between a categorical and quantitative variable (Cohen's d).

In order to demonstrate some of the techniques, we have drawn a random sample of 15 cases from the data file of 200 cases. In this small data set, we have included gender (0 = male, 1 = female), race (0 = White, 1 = African American), and the fall kindergarten test scores for reading and math. The data are presented in Table 6.4.

Other Product-Moment Correlation Coefficients

In addition to the PPMC coefficient, several other coefficients have been developed for situations where the two variables are not continuous. It may be helpful to think of these procedures as short cuts for PPMC for specific conditions, making computation easier before the availability of computers. Essentially, these procedures differ in terms of the types of variables for which they were intended. One of the more well-known alternatives to PPMC is the Spearman Rank Correlation coefficient.

Spearman Rank Correlation

The Spearman Rank Correlation coefficient was developed for situations where both variables were measured on ordinal (rank-type) scales, such as the *U.S. News & World Report's* rankings

Table 6.4 Gender (0 = male, 1 = female), race (0 = White, 1 = African American), reading, and math scores for 15 cases from the ECLS data file

Case	Gender	Race	Reading	Math
1	0	1	17	14
2	0	1	14	9
3	0	1	28	28
4	1	1	14	11
5	1	1	20	14
6	1	1	16	22
7	1	1	22	17
8	0	0	24	49
9	0	0	21	20
10	0	1	33	20
11	1	1	32	19
12	1	1	22	20
13	0	1	11	11
14	0	0	20	26
15	0	1	14	12

of 25 colleges and universities on two different occasions. It might also be recommended for situations in which there might be one or more outlying cases or a relationship that is monotonic but not linear (i.e., higher values of one variable tend to be associated with higher values of the other variable, but in non-linear fashion). To apply this procedure, the two variables are each converted to ranks, thus reducing the influence of the potential outliers or non-linearity. Assuming no ties, the differences between the ranks for each pair were entered into the equation:

$$r_{ranks} = 1 - \frac{6\sum_{i=1}^{n} D_i^2}{n(n^2 - 1)} \tag{6.9}$$

Let's look at the relationship between the reading and math scores for these 15 cases. Table 6.5 is a modification of Table 6.4 to include the ranks of the reading and math scores, along with the differences between ranks. Where there are several scores of the same value (tied), they are each given the average of the ranks for the positions occupied. We should also point out that scores are ranked from smallest to largest, with the smallest score being assigned a rank of 1.

If we apply the formula for PPMC to the actual reading and math scores, the result of the computation is $r = .465$. On the other hand, if we apply the formula for PPMC to the ranked reading and math scores, the result is $r = .658$. Alternatively, if we square the differences in Table 6.5 and insert them into Equation 6.9, we obtain:

$$r_{ranks} = 1 - \frac{6(175.5)}{15(15^2 - 1)} = .687 \tag{6.10}$$

The difference between the values for PPMC for the ranked scores and the Spearman coefficient is due to the presence of tied scores. If there are no ties, the two values will be the same, and thus Equation 6.9 is a short-cut way of computing the PPMC when the scores are ranked and there are no ties. There is a correction to Equation 6.9 for ties, but Kirk (1990, p. 186) noted that

Table 6.5 Gender, race, reading scores, math scores, ranked reading scores, ranked math scores, and differences between ranks for 15 cases from the ECLS data file

Case	Gender	Race	Reading	Math	Rank reading score	Rank math score	Difference
1	0	1	17	14	6.0	5.5	0.5
2	0	1	14	9	3.0	1.0	2.0
3	0	1	28	28	13.0	14.0	−1.0
4	1	1	14	11	3.0	2.5	0.5
5	1	1	20	14	7.5	5.5	2.0
6	1	1	16	22	5.0	12.0	−7.0
7	1	1	22	17	10.5	7.0	3.5
8	0	0	24	49	12.0	15.0	−3.0
9	0	0	21	20	9.0	10.0	−1.0
10	0	1	33	20	15.0	10.0	5.0
11	1	1	32	19	14.0	8.0	6.0
12	1	1	22	20	10.5	10.0	0.5
13	0	1	11	11	1.0	2.5	−1.5
14	0	0	20	26	7.5	13.0	−5.5
15	0	1	14	12	3.0	4.0	−1.0

it is rather complex and tedious and recommended that more effort be devoted to avoiding ties. Most statisticians today would simply recommend the use of PPMC for ordinal data.

Point-Biserial Correlation

Occasionally, one might want to correlate a dichotomous variable with a continuous variable. This situation occurs more often in the area of measurement, where one might be interested in the relationship between getting an item correct and the total score on the test. The formula for the point-biserial correlation coefficient is:

$$r_{pb} = \frac{\bar{Y}_{.1} - \bar{Y}_{.2}}{s_Y} \sqrt{\frac{n_1 n_2}{(n_1 + n_2)(n_1 + n_2 - 1)}} \tag{6.11}$$

Let's consider the relationship between race and math score. Applying the formula for PPMC, we obtain a result of $r = -.638$, suggesting that low on race (White is coded as 0) is associated with higher scores on math. If we apply Equation 6.11 to our data,

$$r_{pb} = \frac{\bar{Y}_{.1} - \bar{Y}_{.2}}{s_Y} \sqrt{\frac{n_1 n_2}{(n_1 + n_2)(n_1 + n_2 - 1)}} = \frac{16.42 - 31.67}{9.891} \sqrt{\frac{12 \times 3}{15 \times 14}} = -.638 \tag{6.12}$$

As you can see, the results are identical.

The Phi Coefficient

The last product-moment correlation coefficient that we present is the phi coefficient (ϕ). It was developed for describing the relationship between two variables, each dichotomous. For example, in our data set for this chapter, we have the two variables of gender and race, each on a dichotomous scale. In order to compute the phi coefficient, we can organize the data in Table 6.4 into a 2 × 2 table as shown in Figure 6.18. Classifying our 15 cases into the table, we obtain a result shown in Figure 6.19.

The formula for calculating the phi coefficient is:

$$r_\phi = \frac{bc - ad}{\sqrt{(a+c)(b+d)(a+b)(c+d)}} \tag{6.13}$$

Applying the values in Figure 6.19, we obtain:

$$r_\phi = \frac{6 \times 3 - 0 \times 6}{\sqrt{(0+3)(6+6)(0+6)(3+9)}} = \frac{18}{\sqrt{3 \times 12 \times 6 \times 9}} = .408 \tag{6.14}$$

If we apply the formula for PPMC, we obtain exactly the same result.

As you can see, with the exception of the Spearman coefficient, the results of these special procedures are identical to those obtained with the formula for PPMC. We have described these

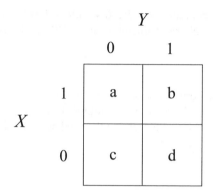

FIGURE 6.18   Arrangement of data in a 2 × 2 table to calculate the phi coefficient.

Race

	0	1
1	0	6
0	3	6

Gender

FIGURE 6.19   Classifying our data into a 2 × 2 table to calculate the phi coefficient.

special procedures as you may encounter them in the literature. That said, we would recommend the PPMC for situations involving two quantitative variables, one quantitative variable and one dichotomy, or two dichotomies.

Non-Product-Moment Correlation Coefficients

The three procedures we have just presented are all modifications of the formula for PPMC to be applied in special situations. There are several other ways to describe the relationship between two variables which are not based on the PPMC formula. Broadly speaking, we can divide these methods into two classes: those that are designed for use with quantitative and dichotomous variables, and those that are appropriate for use with categorical (qualitative) variables.

Non-Product-Moment Correlation with Quantitative and Dichotomous Variables

Earlier in the chapter, we presented the point-biserial correlation coefficient and the phi coefficient for dealing with special situations. With both of those coefficients, the dichotomous variables were regarded as true dichotomies (e.g., gender, race). There are other situations in which the dichotomous variable may be regarded as a "forced" split on a variable that has an underlying continuous distribution. For example, when correlating success on a test item (correct/incorrect), we might be willing to assume that success on the item is based on the amount of knowledge a student has about the content of the item. When the knowledge reaches a certain threshold, the student tends to get the item correct.

While there are other non-product-moment correlations, we are only going to describe two of the more frequently encountered procedures. The biserial correlation coefficient may be used to correlate a continuous variable with a dichotomous variable when the dichotomy is assumed to be an arbitrary cut on an underlying distribution that is normal in shape. (We will not spend much time on the biserial correlation coefficient as it calls for an understanding of the normal distribution, which we discuss in more detail in Chapter 11.) The tetrachoric correlation coefficient is used to correlate two dichotomous variables, assuming that the distributions underlying both dichotomies are normal.

THE BISERIAL CORRELATION COEFFICIENT   The biserial correlation coefficient (r_{bis}) may be used to describe the strength of the relationship between a continuous variable (Y) and a dichotomous variable $(0, 1)$. The formula for computing r_{bis} is:

$$r_{bis} = \frac{\overline{Y}_1 - \overline{Y}_0}{s_y} \left(\frac{pq}{y} \right)$$

(6.15)

Given the new notation, we have some explaining to do. First, let $\overline{Y}_1$ be the mean of the group with the larger mean on the continuous variable Y. Thus, $\overline{Y}_0$ is the smaller mean on the continuous variable. In the denominator, s_y, is the standard deviation of the entire sample on the variable Y. Within the parentheses, p is the proportion of cases in Group = 1, and q is the proportion of cases in Group = 0. The last term, y, is found in a table of the unit-normal distribution. Given that we have not yet made a formal presentation of the normal distribution, we will simply say that y is the ordinate (or height) of the normal distribution at the point that divides the normal distribution into the two proportions, p on one side and q on the other side. We will not present an example of the calculation as we do not want to digress further into a discussion of the normal distribution at this point.

However, we would like to mention that the use of the biserial correlation makes the assumption that the dichotomized variable is an artificial division of the underlying variable, which is further assumed to be normally distributed. This assumption is often unjustified, and in extreme cases, the resulting coefficient may fall outside the range ± 1.0. For this reason, we hesitate to recommend its use.

THE TETRACHORIC CORRELATION COEFFICIENT   The tetrachoric correlation coefficient (r_{tet}) may be used to correlate two dichotomous variables. The difference between r_{tet} and the phi coefficient (r_{ϕ}) presented earlier is that the tetrachoric correlation coefficient assumes that both dichotomous variables represent the artificial splitting of two underlying, normally distributed variables. The actual formula for calculating r_{tet} is quite complex, and several approximations have been offered. We will stop here and leave the computational details to a more advanced statistics book.

Non-product-Moment Correlation for Categorical Variables

There are numerous procedures for looking at the degree of association between categorical variables. The phi coefficient may be regarded as a special case when both categorical variables are dichotomous. However, there are many research situations where one or both categorical variables have more than two categories, or levels. For these situations, one may wish to apply Pearson's Contingency Coefficient (*C*) or Cramer's *V*. The computation of both of these coefficients is based on Pearson's Chi-Squared statistic (χ^2), which will be described later in the book. Thus, at this time, we present the formulae with very little discussion.

THE CONTINGENCY COEFFICIENT Let's assume that we have two categorical variables. Variable *X* has *i* levels and variable *Y* has *j* levels. Thus, the observations may be classified into one of the *i* × *j* cells in the table, with the table being finalized by counting the number of observations/cases classified into each cell, respectively. Based on the cell counts, it will be possible to calculate Pearson's χ^2 statistic, which then forms the basis for our two measures of association. The expression for Pearson's contingency coefficient is:

$$C = \sqrt{\frac{\chi^2}{n+\chi^2}}$$ (6.16)

where *n* is the total number of classified cases. The values for this coefficient can range between 0 and close to 1, but for some contexts (combinations of row and column totals in the *i* × *j* table) the upper bound of the Contingency Coefficient is considerably less than 1, making it rather difficult to interpret the result. Thus, we do not recommend use of the Contingency Coefficient.

CRAMER'S *V* The formula for Cramer's *V* was designed so that the upper bound of 1 would be attainable regardless of the row and column totals. The formula for Cramer's *V* is:

$$V = \sqrt{\frac{\chi^2}{n(q-1)}}$$ (6.17)

where *q* is the lesser of *i* and *j*. For 2 × 2 tables, Cramer's *V* also has the nice property of being equal to the phi coefficient, which is easily interpreted as a correlation coefficient. For these reasons, we would tend to recommend Cramer's *V* for summarizing the relationship between two categorical variables.

Standardized Mean Differences

When researchers look at the relationship between a categorical variable and a quantitative variable they often summarize the relationship between the two variables using a standardized mean difference. This approach is conceptually very different than using a correlation coefficient. In general, a difference in means between groups suggests some association between group membership and the quantitative variable. As the mean differences increase, the association gets stronger. We will spend our time focusing on the simplest of these measures, Cohen's *d*, which is used to summarize the relationship between a dichotomous variable and a quantitative variable. We should mention that there are more general measures, such as Cohen's *f*, which are appropriate for any number of groups, but we save discussion of these until later in the book where they can be more easily defined.

Cohen's *d* is the most commonly used standardized mean difference and can be thought of as the distance between two means in standard deviation units. The equation for defining Cohen's *d* is:

$$d = \frac{\bar{Y_1} - \bar{Y_0}}{s_p} \tag{6.18}$$

where $\bar{Y_1}$ is the greater of the two means, $\bar{Y_0}$ is the lesser of the two means, and s_p is the pooled standard deviation. The pooled standard deviation is a weighted-average standard deviation that takes into account that there may be different numbers of observations in the different groups. More formally, the pooled standard deviation can be computed by going back to the sum-of-squares for each group and aggregating, then finding the pooled variance by averaging, and then taking the square root to obtain the pooled standard deviation. This process is summarized in the following equation:

$$s_p = \sqrt{\frac{SS_1 + SS_0}{n_1 + n_0 - 2}} \tag{6.19}$$

where SS_1 and SS_0 are the sum-of-squares for the two groups, and n_1 and n_0 are the sample sizes of the two groups.

If we look at the relationship between race and math score, we find that:

$$d = \frac{\bar{Y_1} - \bar{Y_0}}{s_p} = \frac{31.667 - 16.417}{7.9012} = 1.930 \tag{6.20}$$

This indicates the mean for the White children in this sample was a little less than two standard deviations greater than the mean for African American children. Note that this is a different interpretation than we would make for a correlation coefficient, which couldn't possibly exceed 1.0.

You may suspect, however, that there should be some relationship between Cohen's *d* and the point-biserial correlation because they can both be used to index association between a dichotomous and quantitative variable. If you were thinking along these lines, your suspicions were correct. The mathematical relationship is shown in Equation 6.21. The magnitude of the point-biserial correlation that we found before (see Equation 6.12) can be obtained by substituting into Equation 6.21 the values of 1.93 for Cohen's *d*, 15 for *N*, the total sample size, 3 for n_1, the sample size for the African American students, and 12 for n_0, the sample size of the White students.

$$r_{pb} = \sqrt{\frac{d^2}{d^2 + \left[(N^2 - 2N)/n_1 n_0\right]}} = \sqrt{\frac{1.93^2}{1.93^2 + \left[(15^2 - 2\times15)/(3\times12)\right]}} = .638 \tag{6.21}$$

CHAPTER SUMMARY

In this chapter, we have introduced bivariate distributions and the ways in which they can be described, both in terms of the strength of the relationship (correlation) and the nature of the relationship (regression). This chapter has focused on the correlational approach, moving from bivariate frequency distributions through covariance and on to the standardized covariance, or the correlation coefficient. We have also described several alternatives to the PPMC coefficient. Our primary purpose for doing so was to introduce you to some of these methods, so that you don't assume that PPMC is the only technique available. Some of these techniques, particularly the ones for dealing with quantitative variables (e.g., Spearman Rank Order and point biserial) were developed as shortcut formulae, or substitutes for the more tedious PPMC formula. As such, they are not currently used very much given the availability of statistical software that calculates PPMC quickly and easily.

Several of the techniques introduced in this chapter (e.g., biserial, the Contingency Coefficient, and Cramer's V) require some understanding of methods that we will discuss in more detail later in this book (e.g., the unit-normal distribution and Pearson's χ^2). Consequently, we acknowledge that you may not feel that you have the same level of understanding of these methods as you do about others presented in earlier chapters. For those of you wanting to read more about these correlational techniques, we have listed several references at the end of this chapter.

In the next chapter, we turn our attention to using regression analysis to describe the nature of the relationship between two quantitative variables.

Key Terms

Bivariate distribution	Karl Pearson
Correlation table	Linear relationship
Correlational model	Pearson Product-Moment Correlation
Covariance	Regression model
Covariation	Scatterplot
Dependent variable	Sir Francis Galton
Independent variable	

REFERENCES

Huck, S. W. (2009). *Statistical misconceptions*. New York: Psychology Press.
Kirk, R. E. (1990). *Statistics: An introduction*. Fort Worth, TX: Holt, Rinehart and Winston.
Tabachnick, B. G., & Fidell, L. S. (2007). *Using multivariate statistics* (5th ed.). Boston: Pearson Education.

PRACTICE QUESTIONS

1. If the covariance between two variables is positive, one can conclude that the correlation will be:

   a. zero
   b. positive
   c. negative
   d. undefined.

2. Which of the following correlations is the strongest?

    a. −.81.
    b. −.02.
    c. .23.
    d. .74.

3. If the correlation between X and Y is positive, can one comfortably conclude that increasing X will increase Y?

    a. No.
    b. Yes.

4. Small children and the elderly tend to have less manual dexterity than 20 and 30 year olds. Is it appropriate to use the Pearson Product-Moment Correlation to describe the relationship between age and manual dexterity?

    a. Yes, because there is no relationship between these two variables.
    b. Yes, because there is a linear relationship between these two variables.
    c. No, because these two variables are categorical.
    d. No, because the relationship is not linear.

5. If outliers are removed, the correlation:

    a. will increase
    b. will decrease
    c. will remain the same
    d. may increase, decrease, or remain the same.

6. Some educational researchers decide to take a break from their statistical analyses to do some bungee jumping off a 100 meter cliff. While jumping, they consider two variables: (1) the distance below the bottom of the cliff (0 meters when they first jump), and (2) the distance above the ground (100 meters when they first jump). What would the correlation between these two variables be?

    a. 1.0.
    b. .5.
    c. 0.
    d. −.5.
    e. −1.0.

7. If two variables share 25% of their variation, the correlation between the two variables is:

    a. 0
    b. .25
    c. .50
    d. .75
    e. 1.0.

EXERCISES

6.1. In the table below are measures of IQ and GPA for 20 college freshmen.

Case	IQ	GPA	Case	IQ	GPA	Case	IQ	GPA
1	110	1.8	8	120	2.5	15	119	2.4
2	124	3.1	9	127	3.1	16	128	2.6
3	137	3.0	10	118	2.1	17	124	3.2
4	122	2.5	11	131	2.8	18	132	3.5
5	126	3.1	12	111	1.6	19	121	2.7
6	122	2.6	13	119	2.0	20	134	3.6
7	115	2.0	14	139	3.8			

Enter the data into R and construct a scatterplot of these data. Does the relationship appear linear or non-linear?

6.2. Using Script 6.3 as a model, find ΣX, ΣX^2, ΣY, ΣY^2, ΣXY, and n for the data in the table.

6.3. Calculate r.

6.4. Confirm your results with R.

APPENDIX 6.1: USING R TO GENERATE THE VALUES NEEDED TO CALCULATE PEARSON'S PRODUCT-MOMENT CORRELATION

In addition to the statistical capabilities of R, it can also be used as a calculator. We have written Script 6.3 to show you how to generate the values that you need to calculate correlation coefficients. Recall that in order to calculate a correlation coefficient, you need a number of values: ΣX, ΣX^2, ΣY, ΣY^2, ΣXY, and n. To generate these values, we followed the steps described below.

1. Read in the data for X (*daded*) and for Y (*momed*).
2. Use the **sum( )** function to find the ΣX and ΣY.
3. Use the **sum( )** function to find ΣX^2 and ΣY^2, the trick being to square the values within the parentheses before summing them.
4. Use the **sum( )** function to find ΣXY, again multiplying the two values within the parentheses before summing.
5. Use the **length( )** function to find the sample size.
6. Print out the results.

7

Describing the Relationship between Two Quantitative Variables: Regression

INTRODUCTION

In the Chapter 6, we introduced situations in which there are two or more variables measured on each case, such as height and weight measures for athletes, and moved from descriptions of univariate distributions to descriptions of bivariate distributions. In considering the possibility that two variables might "move together," or correlate, we assumed that the relationships being described were linear. We traced the development of a measure of the strength of the linear relationship, or the degree to which the data points in the scatterplot appeared to fall on a line. In particular, we showed you how to calculate the Pearson Product-Moment Correlation coefficient. We also described other ways to measure the strength of the relationship between two variables. In this chapter, we will describe the process of regression, or how one variable changes as a function of the other.

The correlation coefficient gives you some sense of the degree to which two variables move together; it does *not* tell you *how* they move together. Given the assumption of linearity, it might seem reasonable to describe the nature of the relationship between the two variables with a line. When we discussed using the mean as a measure of central tendency, we noted that the mean might not describe any case exactly, but that it was a value that minimized the sum of the squared "errors of prediction." In a similar fashion, when we fit a line to a scatterplot of data, it is possible to draw a line on which no single data point falls, but the line still serves as a global description of the general trend of how one variable might change with another. That is, we might use a line to describe how one variable varies as a function of the other. This is the essence of regression analysis.

Linear regression provides us with a way to describe the nature of the linear relationship between two variables. In order to complete a regression analysis, we must make a decision regarding which variable will be plotted on the vertical axis and which variable will be plotted on the horizontal axis. Borrowing from the mathematics of functions, we will employ the standard notation as shown in Equation 7.1.

$$y = f(x) \tag{7.1}$$

In this notation, the variable y is plotted on the vertical axis, which is sometimes called the "ordinate." The variable x is plotted on the horizontal axis, or the "abscissa." We think in terms of y

varying as a function of x; y is called the "dependent variable" while x is called the "independent variable." In experimental situations, we think about the independent variable (manipulated) as being a possible cause of the dependent variable (observed). In reality, in most social science research both variables are observed. This can lead to some problems, which we will address later in this chapter. In correlational data, we may think in terms of using the X variable to predict the Y variable. For example, we might want to use SAT total score to predict freshman Grade Point Average (GPA).

Two points should be made at this juncture. First, when describing how one variable changes with another, the notion of prediction might seem out of place. That is, if we have a bivariate distribution with X and Y measured on each case, it might seem odd to predict Y from X; we already know the values of Y. In this context, the word "predict" may be interpreted in the sense of "model"—a model of the relationship between X and Y, or an exploration of how variation in the independent variable coincides with variation in the dependent variable. Second, in the example of using SAT scores to predict freshman GPA, there is a clear temporal sequence making it obvious which variables should serve as the dependent and independent variable. In other cases, it might not be so clear. Suppose we want to look at the relationship between reading achievement and mathematics achievement. In this situation, which variable should be the independent variable? It is not apparent, so a decision might be made based on a researcher's interests.

Consider another situation in which a physiologist might be interested in the relationship between stature and weight. Most physicians would think of looking at weight as a function of height so that they might identify patients whose weights are not well predicted from their heights. Those patients whose weights differ greatly from what would be predicted may be suffering from eating disorders—those whose weights are much less than predicted may suffer from anorexia or bulimia, while those whose weights are much greater than predicted may be on their way to obesity. (One may also argue that the relationship should be considered in the reverse, looking at height as a function of weight. At the time of his annual physical, the first author usually points out to his physician that he is a bit short for his weight!)

In this chapter, we will discuss the methods of fitting a line to describe a bivariate relationship. First, we will review the logic and notation that is usually employed in high-school algebra. Building on the notion of linear functions, we will present the logic of finding the "line of best fit" from a conceptual perspective, with the mathematical derivation presented in a technical note. We will then show you how to calculate the expression for the best line based on the data used in Chapter 6, after which we will show you how to use R to find the regression line. Next, we will use some data from the Early Childhood Longitudinal Study (ECLS) file to demonstrate how to find the regression line and to examine the data and solution in light of outliers and other influential cases. Last, we will show you some data that demonstrate the importance of using graphic depictions of your data in conjunction with computer analyses.

REVIEWING THE ALGEBRA OF LINES

One topic covered in high-school algebra is functions. Within that topic is a subset of functions, labeled "polynomial functions," which looks at functions where y varies as a first degree function of x (linear function), a second-degree function of x (quadratic function), a third-degree function of x (cubic function), etc. In our discussion, we will focus primarily on linear functions, although we will reference quadratic functions at one point in our presentation. In high-school algebra, linear functions are typically presented in a slope-intercept format as:

$$y = f(x) = mx + b \tag{7.2}$$

Remember that two points determine a line. That is, if you plot two points, there is only one line that can be drawn between the two. Another way to determine a line is with one point and a "direction." Equation 7.2 is of the latter form. The coefficient of x, m, is the slope or direction, and b is the intercept. That is, when x is equal to zero, the value of the function is b. Thus, b is the point on the vertical axis where the line crosses the axis. The situation is more clearly presented in Figure 7.1.

In Figure 7.1, we have depicted a proxy for a scatterplot in which Y is plotted as a function of X. Note that above the origin, where both Y and X are equal to zero, we have shown the line crossing the vertical axis (ordinate) at the point b. The point b is the Y-intercept. We have also drawn a line through the scatterplot, and using part of the line between the two points as the hypotenuse, we have constructed the legs of a right triangle. These legs have been labeled, Δx and Δy, respectively. The Δ is an upper-case Greek "delta" and is used as the mathematical symbol for change. Δy is sometimes called the "rise," while Δx is sometimes called the "run." That is, as you move from point 1 to point 2 on the X axis, you "run" over a distance of Δx. As you move from point 1 to point 2 on the y axis, you "rise" a distance of Δy. For this line, as you move from point 1 to point 2, Y changes Δy and x changes Δx. Thus, the change in y relative to the change in x could be described as $\Delta y/\Delta x$, or "rise over run." The resulting value is called the slope and is labeled m. Thus, Equation 7.2 is sometimes called the "slope-intercept form" for a line.

Moving from Algebraic Notation to Statistical Notation

In statistics, most authors employ a slightly different notation. Rather than use m and b as in the high-school context, many books use a slightly different set of symbols, which can be confusing at first as the b takes on a different meaning. In addition, in statistics, we are dealing with random variables, so we move to uppercase X and Y. A fairly popular notation in statistics is:

$$\hat{Y} = f(X) = a + bX \tag{7.3}$$

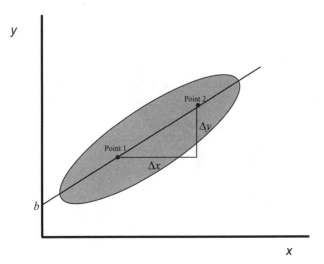

FIGURE 7.1   Explanation of the notation for a line in high-school algebra.

Note that in Equation 7.3, b, which had been the intercept, is now the coefficient for X, which means that b is now the value of the slope. The a in Equation 7.3 is the constant, or Y-intercept. The little symbol over the Y is a "hat" to denote that we are predicting Y. Thus, Equation 7.3 would be read as, "Y-hat equals a plus b times X."

Just to confuse you a little bit more, we actually prefer the notation depicted in Equation 7.4.

$$\hat{Y} = f(X) = b_0 + b_1 X \tag{7.4}$$

This expression would read as, "Y-hat equals b-sub-zero plus b-sub-one times X." In this notation, b_0 is the intercept and b_1 is the slope.

THE NOTION OF PREDICTING Y FROM X

There are several ways we could approach the problem of depicting the form of the relationship between Y and X. We will describe several of them, starting with the most intuitive but least appropriate. We will then take a conceptual–visual–quasi-mathematical approach, which will be followed by a description of the mathematical solution to our problem.

A Simple Approach

Imagine that you have a bivariate distribution and that it has been depicted as a scatterplot. Now imagine that you sorted the data file by the X variable, so that all of the cases having the same value of X would be contiguous. It would be a fairly simple matter to find the average of the Y values for each value of X. Then, you plot the average of the Y values as a function of the X values. The result might look like Figure 7.2.

The dots in the figure represent the means of Y at the various values of X. We could then connect the dots to depict the way in which Y changes as a function of X. The result is a series of line segments—a picture which shows how Y changes with X. But this solution is not particularly appealing. It has different slopes, depending where you are on the X variable. It would seem

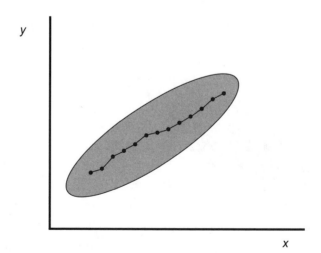

FIGURE 7.2   A simplistic solution to modeling Y as a function of X.

reasonable to assume that the slope for the line would be constant; thus, we could represent the relationship with one common line, which is just what regression analysis does.

Regression Analysis: A Visual, Conceptual Approach

The situation: We would like to fit one line to our scatterplot. The problem: There is an infinite number of different lines that could be drawn through the scatterplot. It should be obvious that some lines are much better than others. For example, in Figure 7.3, line 1 would appear to be a much more appropriate description of the relationship than is line 2.

Visually, we can differentiate reasonable lines from preposterous lines. But is there a way that we can compare one reasonable line to another? Here we turn to the "principle of least-squares" to assist us. Given any scatterplot, we could draw a line through the plot and think about how far the observations deviate from the line. For any given value of X, the vertical height of the line above that particular value of X would be Y-hat, the predicted value of Y. However, a case with that value of X might have a different value of Y, either above or below the line. The situation is depicted in Figure 7.4. In this figure, we have represented the general scatterplot with the ellipse, and shown a specific case i as a dot. The actual values of X and Y for this case are (X_i, Y_i). If we were to use the regression line as shown in the figure, we would "predict" that the ith case would have a Y value of $\hat{Y}_i$. The vertical distance between Y_i and $\hat{Y}_i$ is an error. In statistics, the term "error" does not mean that you did something wrong. It simply indicates the inability to be exactly correct. In this case, the error is simply called an *error of estimation*.

For each data point in the distribution and a given regression line, we can find the amount of error, or the error of estimation for that case. Unless there is a perfect linear relationship and all of the data points fall on the line, there will be errors; of course we would like to keep the amount of error for the line as small as possible. We will invoke the least squares principle to do this. That is, we want the value of Equation 7.5 to be as small as possible.

$$SS_{\text{error}} = \sum_{i=1}^{n} \left(Y_i - \hat{Y}_i \right)^2 \tag{7.5}$$

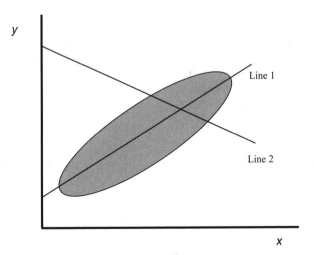

FIGURE 7.3   Two different lines describing the relationship between Y and X, one good (line 1) and the other quite bad (line 2).

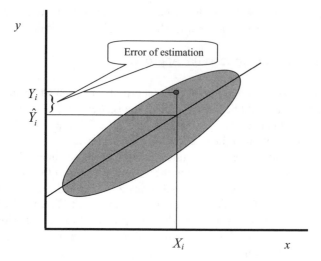

FIGURE 7.4   The logic of finding the best regression line.

Before we see how this is actually done with a little help from our more mathematically inclined colleagues, let's engage in a little trial and error using the data set we used in Chapter 6, presented in Table 6.2. (At this point, we will not repeat the table.) First, let's use R to produce a scatterplot for the 20 cases. The resulting plot, editing the axes, is presented in Figure 7.5.

Now suppose we took Figure 7.5 out on campus, lurking around the entrance to the undergraduate library. At random, we stop a student, asking him to draw a line through the points that he thinks best describes how Mother's Educational Level (*wkmomed*) varies as a function of Father's Educational Level (*wkdaded*). Imagine that he drew the Line 1 as shown in Figure 7.6. (After the line was drawn, we confirmed that the student was an undergraduate.)

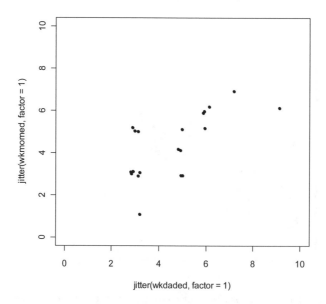

FIGURE 7.5   Scatterplot of Mother's Educational Level as a function of Father's Educational Level.

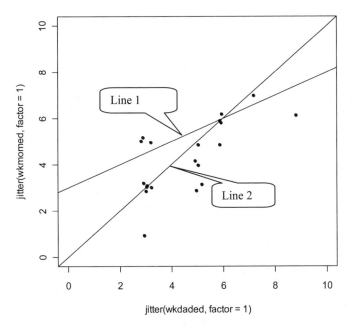

FIGURE 7.6   Lines drawn by an undergraduate student (line 1) and a graduate student (line 2) to describe the relationship between Mother's Educational Level and Father's Educational Level.

Looking at the line as drawn in Figure 7.6, we can see that the intercept is 3.0 and that the slope is .5. Thus, the student has drawn a line as:

$$\hat{Y}_i = 3.0 + .5 \times X_i \tag{7.6}$$

Now we are going to present the data in Table 7.1 with some modifications. In addition to the actual values of Mother's Educational Level and Father's Educational Level, we are going to use the line depicted in Figure 7.6 to find $\hat{Y}_i$ (predicted value) and the error of estimation (error) for each case.

If you square the values in the error column and add them up, you should obtain a value of 45.00. In an absolute sense, this value does not tell us very much; it can only be evaluated in

Table 7.1 The original data, predicted values, and errors for modeling Mother's Educational Level as a function of Father's Education Level, using the line drawn by an undergraduate (line 1 in Figure 7.6)

Case	MomEd	DadEd	$\hat{Y}_i$	Error	Case	MomEd	DadEd	$\hat{Y}_i$	Error
1	6	9	7.5	−1.5	11	6	6	6.0	0.0
2	4	5	5.5	−1.5	12	4	5	5.5	−1.5
3	6	6	6.0	0.0	13	3	5	5.5	−2.5
4	5	3	4.5	0.5	14	1	3	4.5	−3.5
5	5	3	4.5	0.5	15	3	5	5.5	−2.5
6	3	3	4.5	−1.5	16	5	5	5.5	−0.5
7	3	3	4.5	−1.5	17	3	3	4.5	−1.5
8	6	6	6.0	0.0	18	5	3	4.5	0.5
9	3	3	4.5	−1.5	19	5	6	6.0	−1.0
10	7	7	6.5	0.5	20	3	3	4.5	−1.5

relation to values obtained in a similar fashion using different lines. For example, suppose we had lingered by the door of the graduate library and randomly selected a student about to enter the building. After verifying that the student was enrolled in a graduate program, we asked her to perform the same task we had posed to the undergraduate student—drawing a line through the picture that represents how Mother's Educational Level varies as a function of Father's Educational Level. Imagine that this student drew the line that we have labeled as line 2. Looking closely at line 2, we can ascertain that this line has an intercept of 0.0 and a slope of 1.0. That is, the line could be stated as:

$$\hat{Y}_i = 0.0 + 1.0 \times X_i \tag{7.7}$$

Using the same process used to construct Table 7.1, we could construct Table 7.2. By squaring the values in the error column and adding them, you obtain a result of 36 for line 2. Comparing the results of line 1 (45) and line 2 (36), we can see that line 2 is a better line from a "least squares" perspective. What we have just seen is that the sum of the squared errors is different for different lines; different lines are specified by having different intercepts and different slopes.

To explore this, we applied different functions for $\hat{Y}_i$ to the 20 cases and used each one to calculate SS_{error} for different combinations of intercepts and slopes. We varied the intercepts from one to eight in increments of 1.0 and varied the slopes from .1 to 1.6 in increments of .1. For each combination of intercept and slope, we recorded the SS_{error} and created a data set consisting of the values of b_0, b_1, and SS_{error} for each variation. Examining each case, we eliminated cases having very large SS_{error} as they caused our plots to be scaled to accommodate the large SS_{error} (and thus made the part of the plot in which we were interested quite small). We then plotted SS_{error} as a function of b_0 and b_1, simultaneously. The plot produced by R is shown in Figure 7.7. If you have trouble imagining what this plot may look like in three dimensions, visualize a king-size bed sheet being held at the four corners. Although the particular shape of the sheet may vary as a function of how the sheet is held, all of the different shapes share in common the fact that there is some place over the floor where the sheet is closer to the floor than at any other point. The floor is the analogue of the two-dimensional plane determined by b_0 and b_1. The vertical dimension is SS_{error}.

If we could actually look at the sheet, we could probably identify the point (b_0, b_1) over which the sheet was at its lowest point. Having binocular vision, we have depth perception. However, we could also find the low point by looking for the low point of the contour from each of the two dimensions, b_0 and b_1. Looking at the plot in Figure 7.7, we might guess that the contour

Table 7.2 The original data, predicted values, and errors for modeling Mother's Educational Level as a function of Father's Educational Level, using the line drawn by a graduate student (line 2 in Figure 7.6)

Case	MomEd	DadEd	$\hat{Y}_i$	Error	Case	MomEd	DadEd	$\hat{Y}_i$	Error
1	6	9	9.0	−3.0	11	6	6	6.0	0.0
2	4	5	5.0	−1.0	12	4	5	5.0	−1.0
3	6	6	6.0	0.0	13	3	5	5.0	−2.0
4	5	3	3.0	2.0	14	1	3	3.0	−2.0
5	5	3	3.0	2.0	15	3	5	5.0	−2.0
6	3	3	3.0	0.0	16	5	5	5.0	0.0
7	3	3	3.0	0.0	17	3	3	3.0	0.0
8	6	6	6.0	0.0	18	5	3	3.0	2.0
9	3	3	3.0	0.0	19	5	6	6.0	−1.0
10	7	7	7.0	0.0	20	3	3	3.0	0.0

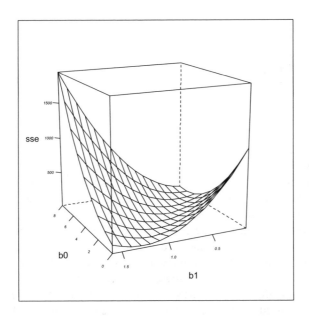

FIGURE 7.7   A three-dimensional perspective of a plot of SS_{error} as a function of different combinations of intercept and slope using the 20 cases having measures of Mother's Educational Level and Father's Educational Level.

reaches its low point somewhere around b_0 a bit lower than 2.0 and somewhere around b_1 close to .5 or a little more. Thus, we might estimate that the SS_{error} is minimized when we fit a line at approximately:

$$\hat{Y}_i = 1.5 + .55 \times X_i \tag{7.8}$$

Regression Analysis: The Mathematical Approach

There is actually a branch of mathematics that does mathematically and more precisely what we just did conceptually. In particular, differential calculus can be used to find minimum and maximum values of mathematical functions. This approach is detailed more completely in Technical Note 7.1, but we will cover the main points here in the text. In the previous section, we saw that, for a particular set of paired X, Y values, the sum of the squared errors (SS_{error}) varied as a function of both b_0 and b_1. Referring back to Equations 7.4 and 7.5, note that they can be combined by substituting the equation for $\hat{Y}_i$ (Equation 7.4) into Equation 7.5, resulting in:

$$SS_{error} = \sum_{i=1}^{n}\left[Y_i - \left(b_0 + b_1 X_i\right)\right]^2 = \sum_{i=1}^{n}\left(Y_i - b_0 - b_1 X_i\right)^2 \tag{7.9}$$

For any given set of data, it should be clear that the SS_{error} is going to change as a function of both b_0 and b_1. Glossing over the specifics (which are detailed in Technical Note 7.1), the calculus is used to find the two partial derivatives with respect to b_0 and b_1. The two partial derivatives are both set equal to zero and the resulting simultaneous equations are solved, resulting in the expressions for b_0 and b_1 as follows:

$$b_1 = \frac{n\sum_{i=1}^{n} X_i Y_i - \left(\sum_{i=1}^{n} X_i\right)\left(\sum_{i=1}^{n} Y_i\right)}{n\sum_{i=1}^{n} X_i^2 - \left(\sum_{i=1}^{n} X_i\right)^2} \tag{7.10}$$

$$b_0 = \bar{Y} - b_1 \bar{X} \tag{7.11}$$

The calculus yields expressions for both the slope and intercept that will provide us with the smallest sum of squared errors possible.

Note that Equation 7.10, which defines the slope, has some similarities with Equation 6.6, which defines the correlation coefficient. In the special case where we work with standardized variables (z-scores), Equation 7.10 becomes identical to Equation 6.6 (see Technical Note 7.2), and thus the slope is equal to the correlation coefficient. Also note that when working with z-scores, Equation 7.11 has to equal zero, because each mean is equal to zero. When we conduct a regression with z-scores, we refer to the solution as the "standardized solution" and refer to the slope as the "standardized regression coefficient," which is commonly symbolized as β_{yx}. Reports of regressions will often include both the raw score solution (containing b_0 and b_1) and the standardized solution (containing β_1). We suggest you start by working with raw scores.

Let's take a look at how the expressions in Equations 7.10 and 7.11 can be applied to our 20 cases from Chapter 6. We will repeat the initial summaries of the paired data:

$$\sum_{i=1}^{20} X_i = 92 \qquad \sum_{i=1}^{20} X_i^2 = 480$$

$$\sum_{i=1}^{20} Y_i = 86 \qquad \sum_{i=1}^{20} Y_i^2 = 414$$

$$n = 20 \qquad \sum_{i=1}^{20} X_i Y_i = 429$$

Applying these values to our expressions for the slope (Equation 7.10), we find:

$$b_1 = \frac{20 \times 429 - 92 \times 86}{20 \times 480 - 92^2} = \frac{668}{1,136} = .588028 \approx .588 \tag{7.12}$$

and

$$b_0 = \frac{86}{20} - .588 \times \frac{92}{20} = 4.3 - .588 \times 4.6 = 4.3 - 2.7048 = 1.5952 \approx 1.595 \tag{7.13}$$

Thus, we can write the line that describes the relationship of Mother's Educational Level as a function of Father's Educational Level as:

$$\hat{Y}_i = 1.595 + .588 X_i \tag{7.14}$$

Comparing this result to our estimate in Equation 7.8, we can see that our conceptual approach resulted in a solution quite close to the exact solution produced by the calculus. The expression in 7.14 is called the "least-squares regression line," or the "line of best fit."

Now, let's look at how this expression can be applied to our data, using the same process that we used to produce Tables 7.1 and 7.2. In doing so, we are going to employ a level of precision beyond that which is used in practice. We do so in order to show you some numeric relationships later in this chapter. The values of the residuals in Table 7.3 were extracted by R; we will show you how shortly.

Looking at the errors in Table 7.3, we see that there are no errors of zero. That is, there are no cases for which there is perfect prediction. Yet, the "least-squares" principle asserts that this is the best line. From this we might conclude that using that principle is predicated on the assumption that it is preferable to make lots of little errors rather than a few large errors.

Now that we have a line that fits better than any other line, we turn our attention to describing how well the line fits. One way of doing this is to describe how far observations tend to deviate from the regression line. Recall that in Chapter 3 we computed a standard deviation to describe how far observations tended to deviate from the mean. To do so we found all the deviations, squared them, averaged the squared deviations, and then took the square root. We can go through the same process but, instead of finding deviations from the mean, we could find deviations from the regression line. We call this statistic the *standard error of estimate*, which is defined mathematically as:

$$SE_{est} = \sqrt{\frac{\sum_{i=1}^{n}(Y_i - \hat{Y}_i)^2}{n-2}} = \sqrt{\frac{SS_{error}}{n-2}} \tag{7.15}$$

Note that when we average the squared deviations we divide by $n - 2$. When we were computing the standard deviation for the *sample* we suggested you divide by $n - 1$, because one degree of freedom was lost by taking deviations from the sample mean instead of the population mean. Now we are taking deviations from the regression line, which is defined by two sample statistics, the intercept and the slope, and thus we lose two degrees of freedom. Another way to think about this is to consider that the calculation of the intercept and slope requires that the means on both X and Y must be estimated. Either way, it takes two degrees of freedom to estimate the errors from the regression line.

Table 7.3 The original data, predicted values, and errors for modeling Mother's Educational Level as a function of Father's Educational Level, using the least-squares regression line

Case	MomEd	DadEd	$\hat{Y}_i$	Error	Case	MomEd	DadEd	$\hat{Y}_i$	Error
1	6	9	6.887	−0.887	11	6	6	5.123	0.876
2	4	5	4.535	−0.535	12	4	5	4.535	−0.535
3	6	6	5.123	0.876	13	3	5	4.535	−1.535
4	5	3	3.359	1.640	14	1	3	3.359	−2.359
5	5	3	3.359	1.640	15	3	5	4.535	−1.535
6	3	3	3.359	−0.359	16	5	5	4.535	0.464
7	3	3	3.359	−0.359	17	3	3	3.359	−0.359
8	6	6	5.123	0.876	18	5	3	3.359	1.640
9	3	3	3.359	−0.359	19	5	6	5.123	−0.123
10	7	7	5.711	1.288	20	3	3	3.359	−0.359

Using the errors in Table 7.3, we find the *SS* for the errors to be about 24.56, and then compute the standard error of estimate to be 1.17, which indicates the deviations between the observations and the regression line tend to be about 1.17 points. Of course some observations are closer than this and some are a bit further, but this gives us a measure of the typical distance from the regression line. Recall that to really make sense out of the value for a standard deviation we had to think about the scale of the variable. The same is true here. Mother's Educational Level is measured on a nine-point scale, so the value of 1.17 tells us that our observations tend to be a little over a point away from what we would predict on a nine-point scale. The 1.17 would lead us to different impressions if we were predicting something on a different scale. For example, if we were predicting Graduate Record Exam (GRE) scores (scaled from 200 to 800) and obtained a standard error of estimate of 1.17 we would likely be amazed by how small the errors tended to be. But if we were predicting GPAs (scaled from 0 to 4) and we tended to be off 1.17, we would probably be disappointed in the size of our errors.

Although the standard error of estimate is a very useful summary statistic it is also helpful to have a standardized measure of how well the line fits the scatterplot. Let's look at the entries in Table 7.3 from another perspective. The original variables were *wkmomed* and *wkdaded*. First, consider the values for the dependent variable, *wkmomed*. Using the data, we can find the SS_{MomEd} to be 44.20 ($414 - (86)^2/20$). Now, if you take the time to calculate the *SS* for $\hat{Y}_i$, you will find that value to be about 19.64 ($389.4623 - (86.00258)^2/20$). Note that the sum of *Y* (86) is very, very close to the sum of $\hat{Y}_i$ (86.00258). In fact, it differs only because of rounding error. This implies that the average of the errors should be zero. Recall that we previously found the *SS* for the errors, and obtained a value of about 24.56. Now, if you are paying particularly close attention, you will see the *SS* for $\hat{Y}_i$ (19.64) and the *SS* for the errors (24.56) sum to the *SS* for *wkmomed* (44.20). We have partitioned the variability (*SS*) in the dependent variable (*wkmomed*) into two parts, that which can be predicted by the independent variable (*wkdaded*) and that which cannot be predicted by the independent variable, the unexplained variation.

Furthermore, consider the proportion of variability in *wkmomed* that can be predicted by *wkdaded*, which is 19.64/44.20, or .444344. If you take the square root of .444344, you will obtain about .666, which is the value of *r* that we found when analyzing this data in Chapter 6. Turning that around, if you find the value of *r* and square it, you will know what proportion of the variability in the dependent variable is shared with the variability in the independent variable. As a proportion, the value of r^2 gives us a standardized measure of how well the line fits. When r^2 is 1.0, its maximum, the line goes through all the points in the scatterplot, which implies there are no errors and thus all the variation in the dependent variable is associated with the independent variable. When r^2 is 0, its minimum, the line fits horribly. The slope will be zero and thus none of the variation in the dependent variable is shared with the independent variable. The line does not help us predict the dependent variable, and we would be just as well off predicting the group mean for every case.

Before moving on, we wish to make a few additional points using the information in Table 7.3. What do we know about the correlation between *wkdaded* and $\hat{Y}_i$? With just a little bit of thinking, you should be able to conclude that the correlation between these two variables is 1.0. Why? Because $\hat{Y}_i$ is a linear function of *X* (*wkdaded*), nothing more, nothing less. The variation in the $\hat{Y}_i$ column is entirely the result of the variation in the *wkdaded* column. In order to confirm this conclusion, try plotting the $\hat{Y}_i$ values as a function of *wkdaded*; the points should fall on a line. Now, think about the relationship between *wkmomed* and $\hat{Y}_i$. If $\hat{Y}_i$ is nothing more than *X* (*wkdaded*), then the correlations between *wkmomed* (*Y*) and $\hat{Y}_i$ should be the same as that between *wkmomed* and *wkdaded* (.67). Now for the clincher. What is the correlation between *wkdaded* (*X*) and Error? It has to be zero. Why? Because the regression analysis has used as much of the information in X as is possible to predict Y. Thus $(Y_i - \hat{Y_i})$ should be totally independent of X. We will now use R to show that what we have just asserted is actually the case.

Using R to Find the Line of Best Fit

Using the data file of 20 cases with measures of Mother's Educational Level and Father's Educational Level, we followed the sequence below to regress *wkmomed* on *wkdaded*, using the **lm( )** function to complete the regression.

```
chap7.ex1 <- read.table("c:/rbook/chap6.ex1.txt",
  header = TRUE)
attach(chap7.ex1)
reg <- lm(wkmomed ~ wkdaded)
reg
```

When the **lm( )** function is executed, R creates an object (*reg*) containing the results. The results are:

```
Coefficients:
(Intercept)       wkdaded
      1.595         0.588
```

You can see that these values agree with the "hand computed" results. In addition to the regression equation, *reg* contains the predicted values ($\hat{Y_i}$), which can be extracted with the **fitted( )** command. It also contains the unstandardized residuals which can be extracted with the **resid( )** command, which is how we found the residuals in Table 7.3. For example:

```
#Adding the predicted values and residuals to the data frame
chap7.ex1$pred <- fitted(reg)
chap7.ex1$res <- resid(reg)
names(chap7.ex1)
attach(chap7.ex1)
pred
res
```

Printing out the predicted values and residuals so that you can see them:

```
> pred
      1       2       3       4       5       6       7       8
  6.887   4.535   5.123   3.359   3.359   3.359   3.359   5.123
      9      10      11      12      13      14      15      16
  3.359   5.711   5.123   4.535   4.535   3.359   4.535   4.535
```

17	18	19	20
3.359	3.359	5.123	3.359

```
> res
```

1	2	3	4	5	6	7
-0.887	-0.535	0.876	1.640	1.640	-0.359	-0.359
8	9	10	11	12	13	14
0.876	-0.359	1.288	0.876	-0.535	-1.535	-2.359
15	16	17	18	19	20	
-1.535	0.464	-0.359	1.640	-0.123	-0.359	

These results agree with those in Table 7.3. Furthermore, we can verify our assertions about the correlations among the original variables (*wkmomed*, *wkdaded*) and the added variables, *pred* and *res*.

```
#Looking at the intercorrelations
cor.mat <- cov2cor(cov(chap7.ex1))
print(cor.mat, digits = 3)

> print(cor.mat, digits=3)
         wkmomed  wkdaded      pred       res
wkmomed    1.000 6.67e-01  6.67e-01  7.45e-01
wkdaded    0.667 1.00e+00  1.00e+00  1.41e-17
pred       0.667 1.00e+00  1.00e+00 -2.19e-17
res        0.745 1.41e-17 -2.19e-17  1.00e+00
```

At this point, we need to explain the notation used by R. After several of the entries in the table of correlation coefficients, there is some "scientific" notation. For example, look at the entry in the top row, second column: 6.67e-01. The "e-01" means that you should move the decimal point one place to the left, making the value .667. Of course, that is the correlation coefficient that we saw in Chapter 6. Now, consider the correlation between *wkdaded* and *pred*, $r = 1.00$. The correlation between *wkmomed* and *pred* is .667, the same as the correlation between *wkmomed* and *wkdaded*. In addition, the correlation between *wkdaded* and *res* is reported as 1.41e-17, which for all intents and purposes is zero.

An Aside: Reversing The Roles of the Independent and Dependent Variables

Just for fun, let's take a look at what would happen if we were to reverse the roles of the independent and dependent variables. Recall that in the correlational model, it does not make any difference which variable is labeled X and which is labeled Y. The correlation coefficient is the same.

Using R, we reversed the roles and obtained the following:

```
> reg.rev <- lm(wkdaded ~ wkmomed)
```

```
> reg.rev
Coefficients:
(Intercept)        wkmomed
     1.3507         0.7557
```

Note that we have obtained a different regression equation; both the intercept and the slope are different. When *wkdaded* was the independent variable, we obtained a slope of .588. When *wkmomed* was the independent variable, we obtained a slope of .756. What if we were to average these two values? We would find the arithmetic mean to be .672, which is quite close to the correlation coefficient. But remember, we also have talked about another type of mean—the geometric mean. In this case, it would be the square root of the product of the two values, or $\sqrt{(.588)(.756)}$ = .6667, which is exactly equal to the correlation coefficient! Those clever statisticians …

Another Aside: The Standardized Regression Solution

Earlier in the chapter, we talked about regression analysis using standardized variables, z_x and z_y. Let's take a look at how this might be done with R. First, we will need to convert the original variables to z-scores using the **scale( )** function and then complete the regression analysis with the standardized values.

```
chap7.ex1$z.wkmomed <- scale(wkmomed)
chap7.ex1$z.wkdaded <- scale(wkdaded)
attach(chap7.ex1)
z.reg <- lm(z.wkmomed ~ z.wkdaded)
z.reg
```

The results are:

```
Call:
lm(formula = z.wkmomed ~ z.wkdaded)

Coefficients:
(Intercept)        z.wkdaded
  1.981e-17        6.666e-01
```

As you can see from the results, the intercept is virtually zero, and the slope is .666, the same as the correlation coefficient.

THE USE OF REGRESSION FOR PREDICTION

At the beginning of this chapter, we said that we would be using regression to describe the nature of the relationship between two variables. In this sense, we are using the word "predict" in the sense of "model." We must also acknowledge, however, that regression analysis is often used to actually "predict" in the more common sense. In an overly simplified example, a college admissions officer might want to look at the relationship between SAT-Total score and GPA at the end of the freshman year (FGPA). She might collect data on last year's freshmen, obtaining the SAT and FGPA scores from student records. Subsequently, she could regress FGPA on SAT and obtain a regression equation. After showing that the regression lines obtained were similar across several cohorts, she might think about using a regression line predicting FGPA as a part of the admissions process. That is, for next year's applicants, she might predict what the FGPA would be a year later. However, we have seen that individual cases have errors associated with them. Said differently, we would expect that predictions would not necessarily be the same as the actual FGPAs that students would obtain. The standard error of estimate (SE_{est}) becomes crucial at this point.

Earlier, we noted that the SE_{est} is the standard deviation of the errors of prediction, or estimation, and provided an expression for the SE_{est} in Equation 7.15. We later defined r^2, and can thus provide an alternative expression:

$$SE_{est} = \sqrt{\frac{(1-r^2)SS_Y}{n-2}} \qquad (7.16)$$

As a rule of thumb (which will be more fully explained later in this book), it is reasonable to assume that most values of a variable will fall within ±2 standard deviations of the mean. Thus, we could set up what might be called a "prediction interval" for $\hat{Y}_i$, suggesting that a reasonable guess for a predicted value would be within a range of ±$2SE_{est}$ of $\hat{Y}_i$. We have shown how that might work in Figure 7.8.

We must now very quickly point out that, while it may appear reasonable, this is not the correct way to do this. The amount of error is not constant across the range of X. Recall that we noted earlier that the mean of $\hat{Y}_i$ is the same as the mean of Y. This implies that there is one point that the regression line must always pass through, the sample mean of X and the sample mean of Y (see Technical Note 7.3). In the real sense of prediction (sample to population), getting the intercept a little bit different than the "true" intercept simply raises or lowers the regression line. However,

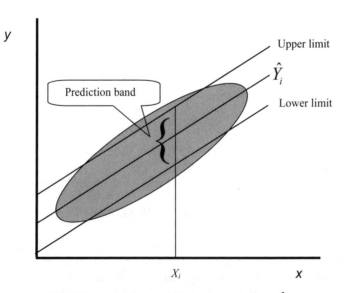

FIGURE 7.8   Building a prediction interval around $\hat{Y}_i$, the incorrect way.

if the slope is off a bit and the line must pass through the center of the scatterplot, then the regression line "wags." The errors in the extremes of X will be greater than those in the midrange of X, which must be considered. The effect of doing so is to produce a prediction interval that, rather than looking like two parallel lines as in Figure 7.9, looks more like a hyperbola. We can't draw that very easily, but we can demonstrate our meaning with R.

Before doing so, we should note that there is a difference between predicting the mean value of Y for all cases having a particular value of X and predicting the value of Y for one case having a particular value of X. In a situation in which you want to develop a prediction interval for the mean value of Y for all cases at a particular value of X, you would use the following formula:

$$SE_{prediction} = SE_{est} \sqrt{\frac{1}{n} + \frac{\left(X_i - \bar{X}_.\right)}{(n-1)s_x^2}} \qquad (7.17)$$

If you want to predict the value of Y for a single case at a particular value of X, then Equation 7.16 is modified to be:

$$SE_{prediction} = SE_{est} \sqrt{1 + \frac{1}{n} + \frac{\left(X_i - \bar{X}_.\right)}{(n-1)s_x^2}} \qquad (7.18)$$

To produce a scatterplot that includes the original data, *wkdaded* and *wkmomed*, along with the regression line and the "intervals" just described, we executed the following commands, contained in Script 7.1:

```
interval.frame <- data.frame(wkdaded = 0:10)
pp <- predict(reg, int = "p",
  newdata = interval.frame)
pc <- predict(reg, int = "c",
  newdata = interval.frame)
plot(jitter(wkdaded), jitter(wkmomed),
  ylim = c(0, 10), xlim = c(0, 10), pch = 16)
pred.wkmomed <- interval.frame$wkdaded
matlines(pred.wkmomed, pc, lty = c(1, 2, 2),
  col = "black")
matlines(pred.wkmomed, pp, lty = c(1, 3, 3),
  col = "black")
```

We need to explain. The first line creates a data frame called *interval.frame*. We establish the values of *wkdaded* from zero to 10 for plotting the intervals. We want to be able to plot two different intervals, which we will call *confidence intervals* (for the mean) and *prediction intervals* (for individual scores). The second and third lines of commands above create these values and add them to *interval.frame*. The last two lines create the lines for *pc* and *pp*. The "lty" option specifies what line type to use. The first option is for the regression line; the second and third are for the interval lines. The intervals produced by R are shown in Figure 7.9.

Looking at Figure 7.9, two features should be readily apparent. First, the prediction bands

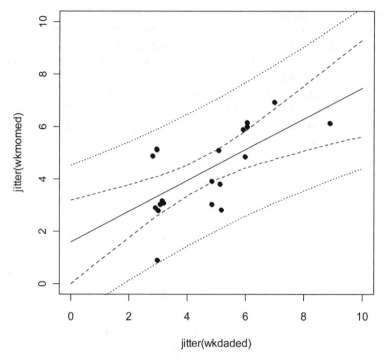

FIGURE 7.9 Prediction bands for predicting the mean value of *Y* (inner band) and an individual value of *Y* (outer band).

are curved, as we suggested, being wider at the extremes of *X* than they are at the midrange of *X*. Second, the prediction band for an individual case is considerably wider than the prediction band for the mean.

We are now ready to work through a complete example of regression with R. We will look at the regression of reading scores at the end of first grade (*c4rrscal*) on the general knowledge scores at the beginning of kindergarten (*c1rgscal*), using the data file of 200 cases. Remember the language of regression; *c4rrscal* is the dependent variable, and *c1rgscal* is the independent variable. However, rather than looking at the regressions within each racial group, we will explore the relationship between the two variables for males and females separately.

A COMPLETE EXAMPLE OF REGRESSION ANALYSIS USING R

In this example, we demonstrate a complete analysis addressing the question of whether reading scores at the end of first grade can be explained (statistically) by general knowledge scores at the beginning of kindergarten. We describe the relationship separately for males and females. In doing so, we start by screening the data, looking for reasonable amounts of variability, outliers, and the existence of a linear relationship. We then perform the regression analyses, giving some attention to cases for which the model may not be appropriate, and we consider the possibility that there may be cases that exert a large influence on the regression solutions. We then conclude with an interpretation of our findings.

Creating Subfiles

After opening the data file in R, we create two data frames, one for females and one for males.

```
# Read in the data
ecls200 <- read.table("c:/rbook/ecls200.txt",
  header = TRUE)
attach(ecls200)
# Create factor variable with labels
ecls200$f.gender <- factor(gender, levels = 1:2,
  labels = c("Male", "Female"))
# Create separate data frames by gender
ecls200.female <- subset(ecls200,
  f.gender == "Female")
ecls200.male <- subset(ecls200,
  f.gender == "Male")
```

Screening the Data

Within each gender group, we want to examine each of the two variables separately and look at the scatterplots. In the univariate analyses, we will assume that the means are reasonable and that all of the values are within the possible ranges of the variables. We also want to look for possible outliers and reasonable amounts of variation. In order to do this, we are going to use the **tapply( )** function. Given that it basically is the same command for every statistic and that the commands will be repeated in the output, we are not going include a block of commands prior to looking at the output. At this point, there are three data frames in the R workspace; we will **attach( )** the *ecls200* frame, which includes both genders. At the end, we created box plots, side by side, with **boxplot**(*varname ~ f.gender*). The output from R:

```
> # Looking at General Knowledge measured Fall-K
> tapply(c1rgscal, f.gender, length)
  Male Female
   104     96
```

Although there are slightly fewer females, the two groups are basically the same size.

```
> tapply(c1rgscal, f.gender, table)
$Male

 9 10 11 12 13 14 15 16 17 18 19 21 22 23 24 25 26
 2  2  1  1  3  1  6  5  4  3  5  7  4  8  6  5  6

27 28 29 30 31 33 34 35 37 38 39 41
 5  5  3  6  3  1  4  2  2  2  1  1
```

```
$Female

 8 10 11 12 13 14 15 16 17 18 19 20 21 22 23 24 25
 1  2  4  1  1  5  5  3  3  2  5  9  5  3  3  6  2


26 27 28 29 30 31 32 33 34 35 36 37 40
 5  6  4  4  5  2  1  3  1  2  1  1  1
```

Looking at the two frequency tables, they appear to be quite similar; the males range from 9 to 41, the females from 8 to 40. Neither gender group seems to have any outliers in the tails of the distributions.

```
> tapply(clrgscal, f.gender, summary)
$Male
   Min. 1st Qu.  Median    Mean 3rd Qu.    Max.
   9.00   18.00   23.50   23.55   28.00   41.00
$Female
   Min. 1st Qu.  Median    Mean 3rd Qu.    Max.
   8.00   17.00   22.00   22.56   28.00   40.00
```

An examination of the descriptive statistics also suggests that the two distributions are quite similar. The scores for the males appear to be ever so slightly higher than those for the females.

```
> tapply(clrgscal, f.gender, sd)
    Male   Female
7.292608 7.087146
```

With regard to dispersion, the **summary( )** function suggested that the interquartile ranges for the two distributions were similar, which is confirmed by the two standard deviations being quite similar. Given the means and standard deviations, we can calculate the two coefficients of variation: $CV_{male} = 30.97$ and $CV_{female} = 31.41$.

```
> tapply(clrgscal, f.gender, skewness)
     Male      Female
0.1337754   0.1067506


> tapply(clrgscal, f.gender, SEsk)
     Male      Female
0.2368232   0.2462100


> tapply(clrgscal, f.gender, kurtosis)
      Male       Female
-0.4559947   -0.6224874
```

```
> tapply(c1rgscal, f.gender, SEku)
        Male      Female
   0.4694546   0.4877319
```

An inspection of the two groups with regard to the measures of shape (skewness and kurtosis) and their respective standard errors suggests that the two groups are similar. Furthermore, both groups would be reasonable samples to have come from normally distributed populations.

```
> boxplot(c1rgscal ~ f.gender,
    ylab = "Fall-K General Knowledge Scores")
```

The box plot is shown in Figure 7.10.

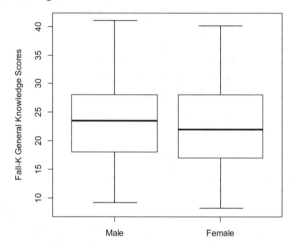

FIGURE 7.10   Box plot of fall general knowledge scores for males and females.

The box plots for the two genders are consistent with the previous findings; the two distributions are very similar. Now, we turn our attention to an examination of the Spring-1 reading scores.

```
> # Looking at Reading Scores measured Spring-1
> tapply(c4rrscal, f.gender, length)
  Male Female
   104     96
```

We note that the sample sizes for the end-of-first-grade reading scores are the same as they were for the beginning-of-kindergarten general knowledge scores, suggesting no missing data.

```
> tapply(c4rrscal, f.gender, table)
$Male

19 21 25 30 31 34 35 39 41 42 43 44 45 46 47 48 49
 1  1  1  1  1  2  1  4  3  1  3  2  1  3  2  3  3
```

```
50 51 52 53 54 55 56 57 58 59 60 61 62 63 65 66 67
 4  2  2  1  6  2  6  2  5  1  1  4  2  2  4  2  3

69 70 71 72 73 74 75 76 77 78 79 86
 2  4  1  4  1  1  3  1  2  1  1  1
$Female
27 34 35 36 38 39 41 45 46 47 48 49 50 51 52 53 54
 1  1  2  1  1  2  2  4  3  1  1  2  2  3  3  3  3

55 56 57 58 60 61 62 63 64 65 66 67 68 69 70 71 73
 2  3  3  2  6  1  2  3  5  1  4  2  4  2  4  3  1

74 75 76 77 78 79 81
 3  1  3  2  1  1  2
```

The frequency tables for females and males, respectively, indicate that the females might have one low score and the males might have one high score. Also, the scores for the males seem to be a little more spread out than those for the females.

```
> tapply(c4rrscal, f.gender, summary)
$Male
   Min. 1st Qu.  Median    Mean 3rd Qu.    Max.
  19.00   47.00   56.00   55.73   66.00   86.00

$Female
   Min. 1st Qu.  Median    Mean 3rd Qu.    Max.
  27.00   51.00   60.00   58.98   68.00   81.00

> tapply(c4rrscal, f.gender, sd)
    Male   Female
13.48443 12.18453
```

The descriptive statistics for the two gender groups suggest that the scores for the males may tend to be slightly lower than those for the females, as seen in both the means and the medians. Both the interquartile range and the standard deviation for the males indicate slightly more spread in the scores than the corresponding values for the females' scores. Given the descriptive statistics above, we can calculate the coefficients of variation for the two groups: $CV_{male} = 24.20$ and $CV_{female} = 20.66$.

```
> tapply(c4rrscal, f.gender, skewness)
      Male     Female
-0.2856082 -0.3192164

> tapply(c4rrscal, f.gender, SEsk)
     Male    Female
0.2368232 0.2462100
```

```
> tapply(c4rrscal, f.gender, kurtosis)
     Male      Female
-0.1208287 -0.5017706
> tapply(c4rrscal, f.gender, SEku)
      Male     Female
  0.4694546 0.4877319
```

The measures of shape (skewness and kurtosis) and the respective standard errors suggest that the two distributions of scores are quite similar, although the scores for the females might be a little more platykurtic than those for the males. However, both sets of scores might be reasonable expectations from a normal population.

```
> boxplot(c4rrscal ~f.gender,
    ylab = "Spring-1 Reading Scores")
```

The result is shown in Figure 7.11.

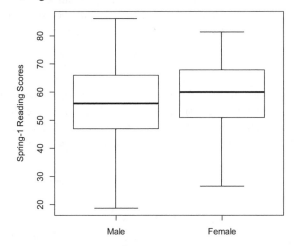

FIGURE 7.11   Box plot of spring reading scores for males and females.

The two box plots confirm our previous findings. The scores for the females tend to be a little higher than those for the males; the scores for the males tend to be a little more spread out than those for the females. Interestingly, the "Tukey criteria" that are built into the **boxplot( )** function did not identify any outliers.

Here we want to take a look at the relationship between the two variables within each of the two groups. We could do that separately for each group, but we would rather look at the two bivariate distributions in the same graphic in order to make a direct comparison. In order to do that, we used the following commands:

```
# Produce a scatterplot with subgroups
# Set plotting character to 1 for all cases
pchval <- rep(1, length = length(f.gender))
# Set plotting character to 18 for Males
```

```
pchval[f.gender == "Male"] <- 18
plot(jitter(c1rgscal, factor = 1),
  jitter(c4rrscal, factor = 1), pch = pchval)
legend(32, 28, c("Male", "Female"), pch = c(18, 1))
legend(32, 40, c("Male", "Female"), lty = c(1, 2))
with(ecls200.male, abline(lm(c4rrscal ~ c1rgscal),
  lty = 1))
with(ecls200.female, abline(lm(c4rrscal~c1rgscal),
  lty = 2))
```

The results are shown in Figure 7.12.

Looking at the chart, we see that the markers for males and females seem quite interspersed. Although the two regression lines have slightly different intercepts and slopes, they are generally quite similar. Later in the book, we will consider ways to compare the lines beyond what we can do visually. We do not spot any bivariate outliers, or cases with unusual combinations of values on the variables. Finally, we explored the possibility of curvilinear relationships by trying to fit quadratic functions. Although the visual graph showed some curvilinearity, the increases in r^2 for both groups were very small. We concluded that it would be appropriate to fit lines for both groups.

Fitting the Regression Lines

In addition to fitting the regression lines for the two groups separately, we also want to explore the possibility that there might be some cases for which the linear models did not fit well. We can identify these cases by calculating standardized residuals. Standardized residuals are the errors of prediction divided by the standard error of estimate, putting them into a z-score metric. Standard-

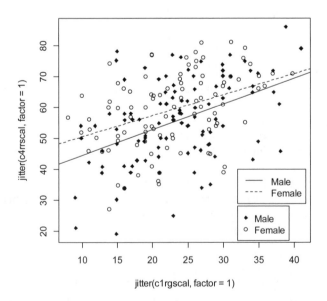

FIGURE 7.12   Scatterplot of spring reading scores and fall general knowledge scores for males and females.

ized residuals in excess of ±2.5 might be considered large. Further, we want to consider whether some cases were exerting a disproportionately large influence on the location of the regression lines. To do this, we loaded the **car** package in our R session so that we can examine a diagnostic called Cook's Distance. Cook's D is a measure of the influence of a case that is computed by dropping each case in turn, calculating the regression on the remaining $n-1$ cases, and comparing those two solutions. Cook's D is a global measure, indicating the effect of an observation without specifically indicating whether it is the intercept or slope that is affected. Although there is no clear set of criteria for evaluating Cook's D, some authors suggest that values greater than 1.0 are noteworthy (e.g., Howell, 2007). Based on his interpretation of the work of Chatterjee and Hadi (1988), Fox (1991) suggested that values greater than $4/(n-2)$ should be examined more carefully (values greater than .039 in this instance). Yet another group of people are only concerned with cases for which the values appear considerably larger than for others (e.g., Agresti & Finlay, 1997; Fox, 1997). A large Cook's D suggests that a case has had a substantial influence on the solution. First, let's look at the results for the females. We ran the following commands.

```
attach(ecls200.female)
mod.female <- lm (c4rrscal ~ c1rgscal)
mod.female
ecls200.female$res <- resid(mod.female)
attach(ecls200.female)
ecls200.female$z.res <- scale(res)
attach(ecls200.female)
range(z.res)
# Look at residuals)
plot(z.res, ylim = c(-5, 5))
abline(h = 2.5)
abline(h = - 2.5)
which(z.res < -2)
which(z.res > 2)
# Look at Cook's D
denom <- length(res) - 2
plot(cooks.distance(mod.female))
abline(h = 4/denom, lty=2)
which(cooks.distance(mod.female) > (4/denom))
```

The regression equation for females gives:

```
> mod.female
Coefficients:
(Intercept)      c1rgscal
    43.6631        0.6788
> range(z.res)
[1] -2.337454  1.861028
```

From this output, we can see that the regression line for females is $\hat{Y}_i = 43.66 + .679 \times$ General Knowledge Test, and that the residuals are within the ± 2.5 limit. The plot of the residuals is shown in Figure 7.13.

If we use the **which( )** command to identity residuals in excess of ± 2.0, we find that cases 11, 31, 63, and 84 are less than -2, and that there are no cases with residuals greater than 2.0. Thus only four cases out of the 100 are in excess of ± 2.0, about what we would expect.

Now, let's look at the values of Cook's D; the plot is shown in Figure 7.14.

We note that there are four values of Cook's D that exceed $4/(n - 2)$. To find out which cases, we can use the command **which(**cooks.distance (mod.female) > 4/denom)**)**. The output from R indicates that the cases are 11, 31, 63, and 84. Given that cases 11, 31, and 63 were also identified

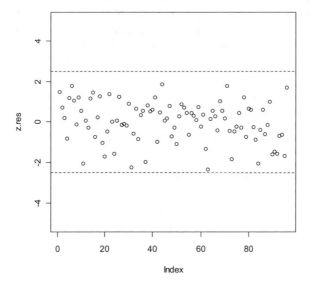

FIGURE 7.13   Plot of the residuals for females for each case.

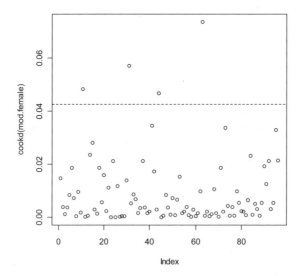

FIGURE 7.14   Plot of Cook's D for females for each case.

as having relatively large residuals, we might consider rerunning the analysis without those three cases. We'll leave that up to you.

Now, let's repeat the analysis for the males:

```
attach(ecls200.male)
mod.male <- lm (c4rrscal ~ c1rgscal)
mod.male
ecls200.male$res <- resid(mod.male)
attach(ecls200.male)
ecls200.male$z.res <- scale(res)
attach(ecls200.male)
range(z.res)
#Look at residuals)
plot(z.res, ylim = c(-5, 5))
abline(h = 2.5, lty = 2)
abline(h = - 2.5, lty = 2)
which(z.res < -2)
which(z.res > 2)
#Look at Cook's D
denom <- length(res) - 2
plot(cooks.distance(mod.male))
abline(h = 4/denom, lty = 2)
which(cooks.distance(mod.male) > (4/denom))
detach(ecls200.male)
```

First, the regression equation gives:

```
> mod.male

Coefficients:
(Intercept)      c1rgscal
    36.1996        0.8294
```

We can see that the regression line for males is $\hat{Y}_i = 36.2 + .829 \times \text{GKT}$. These values are not exactly the same as those obtained for the females. (Later in the book we will show you how to compare the values to see if they differ by more than you would expect by chance.)

Now, consider the residuals:

```
> range(z.res)
[1] -2.512187  2.436096
```

You can see that there are some cases with rather large standardized residuals. Let's look at the plot, shown in Figure 7.15.

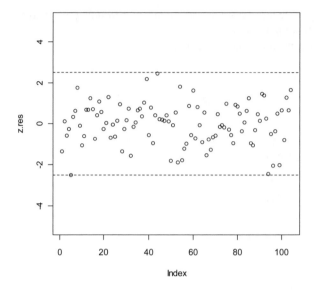

FIGURE 7.15   Plot of the residuals for males for each case.

```
> which(z.res < -2)
[1]   5 94 96 99
> which(z.res > 2)
[1] 39 44
```

In the males sample, six of the 100 cases have residuals in excess of ±2.0, again about what we would expect. Next, let's look at the Cook's D values for males, shown in Figure 7.16.

In the plot, we can see that there are several cases having values of Cook's D larger than the threshold:

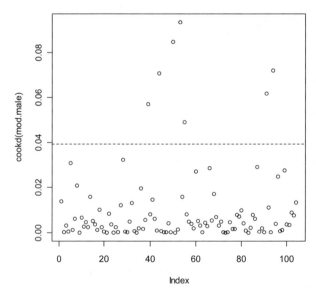

FIGURE 7.16   Plot of Cook's D for males for each case.

```
> which(cooks.distance(mod.male) > (4/denom))
39 44 50 53 55 91 94
```

Three of those cases (39, 44, and 94) also have large residuals. Again, one might consider rerunning the analysis without including those particular cases in order to see what effect there might be on the solution.

At this point, we have looked at the separate regression lines for females and males, for which the two solutions appear to be quite similar. If we are willing to assume that they are basically the same, we might choose to run one analysis, pooling the males and females into one data set. If we were to do this, we would get the following results:

```
> mod.ecls200
Coefficients:
(Intercept)      clrgscal
    40.2095        0.7402
```

We can see that the regression solution is part way in between the two separate solutions, which is what we would expect.

```
> range(z.res)
[1] -2.737973  2.261304
```

When we fit separate regression lines within each gender group, we were optimizing the fit for each group. When we "force" one solution for both groups, the fit will not be quite as good. Thus, we note that the range of residuals for the common solution is a little larger.

As we have proceeded through this example, we have noted that there may be cases which might exert an influence on the solution(s). Assuming that we've piqued your curiosity, we'll leave it to you, the reader, to explore the possibility in your own re-analyses.

CHAPTER SUMMARY

In this chapter, we have presented methods for describing the nature of the linear relationship between two variables. We began by reviewing some high-school algebra, followed by a transition from algebraic notation to statistical notation. We then presented several ways to find the line of best fit. First, we looked at partitioning the data file on X and then plotting the means of the Y values at each value of X, as a function of X. We then used a little trial-and-error to give you a feel for the process from a conceptual perspective. After that, we showed you the "real" way to find the regression line, using expressions derived from the calculus. This was followed by a complete example in R, including screening the data, finding the regression solution(s), and checking for potential problematic cases. This completes our presentation of descriptive statistics, and techniques for characterizing attributes of univariate and bivariate distributions. In summary, the characteristics of univariate distributions are size, location, spread, and shape. The characteristics of bivariate distributions are the strength of the linear relationship and the nature of the linear relationship.

We will now turn our attention to the topic of inferential statistics, procedures that will permit us to make reasonable inferences about population characteristics (parameters) based on sample characteristics (statistics). In the next section of the book, we will cover the foundations of inference, in particular the basics of probability and sampling distributions.

Key Terms

Error of prediction   Residual
Intercept   Slope
Least-squares regression line   Standard error of estimate
Line of best fit   Standardized regression coefficient
Prediction intervals $\hat{Y}_i$
Regression coefficient

REFERENCES

Agresti, A., & Finlay, B. (1997). *Statistical methods for the social sciences* (3rd ed.). Upper Saddle River, NJ: Prentice Hall.

Chatterjee, S., and Hadi, A. S. (1988). *Sensitivity analysis in linear regression*. New York: John Wiley.

Fox, J. (1991). *Regression diagnostics*. Newbury Park, CA: Sage.

Fox, J. (1997). *Applied regression analysis, linear models, and related methods*. Thousand Oaks, CA: Sage.

Howell, D. C. (2007). *Statistical methods for psychology* (6th ed.). Belmont, CA: Thomson Wadsworth.

PRACTICE QUESTIONS

1. A group of researchers has just run a regression and found the following values in the output: $SS_{tot} = 300$, $SS_{error} = 100$, $SE_{est} = .88$, intercept = 2.5, and slope = .90. How much does the predicted value change for each unit change in the predictor variable?

    a. .67.
    b. .33.
    c. .88.
    d. .90.
    e. 2.50.

2. A group of researchers has just run a regression and found the following values in the output: $SS_{tot} = 300$, $SS_{error} = 100$, $SE_{est} = .88$, intercept = 2.5, and slope = .90. What is the size of a typical prediction error?

    a. .67.
    b. .33.
    c. .88.
    d. .90.
    e. 2.50.

3. A group of researchers has just run a regression and found the following values in the output: $SS_{tot} = 300$, $SS_{error} = 100$, $SE_{est} = .88$, intercept = 2.5, and slope = .90. What proportion of the variability in the dependent variable is associated with the independent variable?

a. .67.

b. .33.

c. .88.

d. .90.

e. 2.50.

4. A group of researchers has just run a regression and found the following values in the output: $r^2 = .40$, $SE_{est} = 5.1$, intercept $= 4.4$, and slope $= 2.0$. What would be the predicted value for someone who scored a zero on the predictor?

a. 5.1.

b. 4.4.

c. 2.0.

d. 10.4.

e. 13.2.

5. A group of researchers has just run a regression and found the following values in the output: $r^2 = 0.40$, $SE_{est} = 5.1$, intercept $= 4.4$, and slope $= 2.0$. What would be the predicted value for someone who scored a 3 on the predictor?

a. 5.1.

b. 4.4.

c. 2.0.

d. 10.4.

e. 13.2.

6. Two observations have the same size errors. One has a predictor value equal to the mean value of the predictor, and the other has the minimum predictor value. What can you conclude about the Cook's D values associated with these two observations?

a. They will be equal.

b. The one with the minimum predictor value will have a smaller Cook's D.

c. The one with the minimum predictor value will have a larger Cook's D.

d. The one with the minimum predictor value may have a larger or smaller Cook's D.

7. After running a regression analysis a researcher notes there is an observation with a standardized residual that is much larger than the others. If this outlying observation is removed and the analysis rerun, the standard error of estimate would be expected to:

a. increase

b. decrease

c. remain the same.

EXERCISES

7.1. At the end of Chapter 6, the first exercise provided data consisting of IQ and GPA data for 20 first-year college students. You were asked to enter the data into R to develop the "summary" data needed to calculate the Pearson correlation coefficient (ΣX, ΣX^2, ΣY, ΣY^2, ΣXY, and n). Assuming that you completed that assignment correctly, you have the values necessary to calculate the least-squares regression line. If not, compute these summary values. The data are repeated here.

Case	IQ	GPA	Case	IQ	GPA	Case	IQ	GPA
1	110	1.8	8	120	2.5	15	119	2.4
2	124	3.1	9	127	3.1	16	128	2.6
3	137	3.0	10	118	2.1	17	124	3.2
4	122	2.5	11	131	2.8	18	132	3.5
5	126	3.1	12	111	1.6	19	121	2.7
6	122	2.6	13	119	2.0	20	134	3.6
7	115	2.0	14	139	3.8			

7.2. Using those summary data, calculate the regression line for predicting GPA from IQ with a hand-held calculator.

7.3. For all 20 cases, construct a table that includes the original values of IQ and GPA, the predicted values, the residuals, and the squares of the residuals. Find the sum of the GPA scores, the sum of the predicted values, the sum of the residuals, and the sum of the squared residuals.

7.4. Enter the data into R and confirm all of your work above.

TECHNICAL NOTES

Technical Note 7.1: The Mathematical Basis For Regression

The least-squares regression line, or line of best fit, is based on the minimization of the sum of squared error of estimation. That is, given a regression line of the form:

$$\hat{Y}_i = b_0 + b_1 X_i$$

We want to minimize the sum of squared differences between the actual values of Y_i and $\hat{Y}_i$. We will define our "error function" to be minimized as:

$$S = \sum_{i=1}^{n} (Y_i - \hat{Y}_i)^2 = \sum_{i=1}^{n} \left[Y_i - \left(b_0 + b_1 X_i \right) \right]^2 = \sum_{i=1}^{n} \left(Y_i - b_0 - b_1 X_i \right)^2$$

We want to minimize this function with respect to b_0 and b_1. Thus we will take the partial derivative of S with respect to b_0 and b_1:

$$\frac{\partial S}{\partial b_0} = -2 \sum_{i=1}^{n} (Y_i - b_0 - b_1 X_i)$$

and

$$\frac{\partial S}{\partial b_1} = -2 \sum_{i=1}^{n} X_i (Y_i - b_0 - b_1 X_i)$$

Analogous to rotating our plot so that we could look at it from the perspectives of b_0 and b_1, we set both partial derivatives equal to zero to find the low points:

$$-2\sum_{i=1}^{n}\left(Y_i - b_0 - b_1 X_i\right) = 0$$

and

$$-2\sum_{i=1}^{n}X_i\left(Y_i - b_0 - b_1 X_i\right) = 0$$

We can now divide both sides of both expression by -2 and simplify:

$$\sum_{i=1}^{n}\left(Y_i - b_0 - b_1 X_i\right) = \sum_{i=1}^{n}Y_i - nb_0 - b_1\sum_{i=1}^{n}X_i = 0$$

and

$$\sum_{i=1}^{n}X_i\left(Y_i - b_0 - b_1 X_i\right) = \sum_{i=1}^{n}X_iY_i - b_0\sum_{i=1}^{n}X_i - b_1\sum_{i=1}^{n}X_i^2 = 0$$

First, let's solve the first expression for b_0.

$$nb_0 = \sum_{i=1}^{n}Y_i - b_1\sum_{i=1}^{n}X_i$$

$$b_0 = \frac{\sum_{i=1}^{n}Y_i}{n} - b_1\frac{\sum_{i=1}^{n}X_i}{n}$$

or

$$b_0 = \bar{Y} - b_1\bar{X}$$

Now we can substitute the expression for b_0 into the second expression and solve it for b_1:

$$\sum_{i=1}^{n}X_iY_i - b_0\sum_{i=1}^{n}X_i - b_1\sum_{i=1}^{n}X_i^2 = 0$$

Making the substitution for b_0:

$$\sum_{i=1}^{n}X_iY_i - \left(\frac{\sum_{i=1}^{n}Y_i}{n} - b_1\frac{\sum_{i=1}^{n}X_i}{n}\right)\sum_{i=1}^{n}X_i - b_1\sum_{i=1}^{n}X_i^2 = 0$$

Carrying out the implied multiplication:

$$\sum_{i=1}^{n} X_i Y_i - \left(\frac{\sum_{i=1}^{n} Y_i \sum_{i=1}^{n} X_i}{n} - b_1 \frac{\sum_{i=1}^{n} X_i \sum_{i=1}^{n} X_i}{n} \right) - b_1 \sum_{i=1}^{n} X_i^2 = 0$$

Removing the parentheses:

$$\sum_{i=1}^{n} X_i Y_i - \frac{\sum_{i=1}^{n} Y_i \sum_{i=1}^{n} X_i}{n} + b_1 \frac{\sum_{i=1}^{n} X_i \sum_{i=1}^{n} X_i}{n} - b_1 \sum_{i=1}^{n} X_i^2 = 0$$

Multiplying both sides of the equation by –1:

$$-\sum_{i=1}^{n} X_i Y_i + \frac{\sum_{i=1}^{n} Y_i \sum_{i=1}^{n} X_i}{n} - b_1 \frac{\sum_{i=1}^{n} X_i \sum_{i=1}^{n} X_i}{n} + b_1 \sum_{i=1}^{n} X_i^2 = 0$$

Moving all terms not containing b_1 to the right side:

$$-b_1 \frac{\sum_{i=1}^{n} X_i \sum_{i=1}^{n} X_i}{n} + b_1 \sum_{i=1}^{n} X_i^2 = \sum_{i=1}^{n} X_i Y_i - \frac{\sum_{i=1}^{n} Y_i \sum_{i=1}^{n} X_i}{n}$$

Factoring the b_1 from both terms on the left side:

$$b_1 \left(\sum_{i=1}^{n} X_i^2 - \frac{\sum_{i=1}^{n} X_i \sum_{i=1}^{n} X_i}{n} \right) = \sum_{i=1}^{n} X_i Y_i - \frac{\sum_{i=1}^{n} Y_i \sum_{i=1}^{n} X_i}{n}$$

Dividing both sides by the "coefficient" of b_1:

$$b_1 = \frac{\sum_{i=1}^{n} X_i Y_i - \dfrac{\sum_{i=1}^{n} Y_i \sum_{i=1}^{n} X_i}{n}}{\sum_{i=1}^{n} X_i^2 - \dfrac{\left(\sum_{i=1}^{n} X_i \right)^2}{n}}$$

Multiplying both numerator and denominator by n:

$$b_1 = \frac{n\sum_{i=1}^{n} X_i Y_i - \sum_{i=1}^{n} Y_i \sum_{i=1}^{n} X_i}{n\sum_{i=1}^{n} X_i^2 - \left(\sum_{i=1}^{n} X_i \right)^2}$$

Voilá!

Technical Note 7.2: Regression with Standardized (z) Scores

When working with standardized scores (z-scores), the slope of the regression line takes on the value of r. In this note, we will show why this is so. First, we begin with a modified version of Equation 7.10:

$$b_1 = \frac{n\sum_{i=1}^{n} X_i Y_i - \left(\sum_{i=1}^{n} X_i\right)\left(\sum_{i=1}^{n} Y_i\right)}{n\sum_{i=1}^{n} X_i^2 - \left(\sum_{i=1}^{n} X_i\right)^2} \tag{7.10}$$

Dividing both the numerator and the denominator by n,

$$b_1 = \frac{\left[n\sum_{i=1}^{n} X_i Y_i - \left(\sum_{i=1}^{n} X_i\right)\left(\sum_{i=1}^{n} Y_i\right)\right]/n}{\left[n\sum_{i=1}^{n} X_i^2 - \left(\sum_{i=1}^{n} X_i\right)^2\right]/n}$$

Based on material from earlier in the book, we recognize the numerator as the covariance of X and Y, and the denominator as the variance of X. Thus, we can write:

$$b_1 = \frac{\text{cov}(X,Y)}{\text{var}(X)}$$

Now, consider the case when X and Y are in z-score form.

$$b_1 = \frac{\text{cov}(z_x, z_y)}{\text{var}(z_x)}$$

First, we note that the denominator will be equal to 1.0, the variance of a standardized variable. Thus,

$$b_1 = \text{cov}(z_x, z_y)$$

However, in Chapter 6, we showed that the covariance between two standardized variables is equal to the correlation coefficient (Equations 6.4 through 6.7). Therefore,

$$b_1 = \text{cov}(z_x, z_y) = r_{xy} = \beta_{y.x}$$

In conclusion, the slope of the regression line when the two variables are in standardized form is equal to the correlation coefficient, and is denoted as $\beta_{x.y}$.

Technical Note 7.3: Proof that the Regression Line must Pass through the Point $\overline{X}$, $\overline{Y}$

The givens: $\hat{Y}_i = b_0 + b_1 X_i$ and $b_0 = \overline{Y} - b_1 \overline{X}$.

Substitute the expression for b_0 into the first expression:

$$\hat{Y}_i = \bar{Y}_. - b_1 \bar{X}_. + b_1 X_i$$

Now we have a slightly more complex expression for predicting Y from X. What would one predict for Y for a case at the mean of X? Substitute $\bar{X}$ for X_i in the expression above:

$$\hat{Y}_i = \bar{Y}_. - b_1 \bar{X}_. + b_1 \bar{X}_. = \bar{Y}_.$$

Part III

THE FUNDAMENTALS OF STATISTICAL INFERENCE

In the previous seven chapters, we have been concerned with describing sets of scores, both individually (univariate distributions) and jointly (bivariate distributions). We began by looking at ways to summarize sets of scores with frequency distributions and corresponding graphics (histograms and density curves). After identifying the salient characteristics that allow us to differentiate one distribution of scores from another (size, location, spread, and shape), we then focused on the presentation of single values that could convey a meaningful summary of those characteristics. In addition to reporting the number of cases in the distribution, we looked at the mode, median, and mean as measures of location; the range, interquartile range, average deviation, variance, and standard deviation as measures of spread; and skewness and kurtosis as measures of shape. With regard to bivariate distributions we looked at correlation as a measure of strength of linear association and regression as a description of the nature of the linear association. All of this was accomplished as though the data with which we were concerned constituted a population. Thus, the measures generated would be considered parameters. That is, when we calculate the mean of a population we know with absolute certainty, discounting data entry errors and/or computational errors, that the value we obtain is the mean of the population.

Most statistical analyses, however, are completed within the population/sample paradigm. In these situations, the data under investigation consist of a subset of some population of scores to which we want to generalize. Thus, when we calculate the mean of a sample, in addition to the errors mentioned above (i.e., data entry errors), other uncertainties also enter our statistical world. We know that the sample mean is an estimate of the population mean, but we do not know how far off our estimate might be. To cope with this uncertainty, we introduce the notion of "probability."

In order to draw reasonable conclusions about populations based on our observation of samples, we need to examine the fundamental tools of statistical inference. These tools include a basic understanding of probability, which is covered in Chapter 8; probability distributions and sampling distributions, which are covered in Chapter 9; and some mathematical probability distributions (e.g., the binomial and normal probability distributions), presented in Chapters 9 and 10.

PART III
THE PLURALIST CRITIQUE OF
DELIBERATIVE DEMOCRACY

8

The Essentials of Probability

It has been said facetiously that in life the only certainties are death and taxes; all else is uncertain. In statistics, as in life, there are few certainties. The notion of uncertainty is essential to an understanding of inferential statistics. We will be using the descriptive statistics that we have already learned in the first seven chapters to describe the data to which we have immediate access—the sample data. Based on what we see in the sample, we want to be able to make reasonably valid statements about the population, to which we do not have immediate access. Furthermore, we want to minimize the likelihood that our generalizations are way off target. *Probability* is one of the tools that will assist us in this task.

THREE VIEWS OF PROBABILITY

There are several definitions or types of probability; we present three here. These views of probability are the personal/subjective view, the classical/logical view, and the empirical/relative frequency view.

The Personal/Subjective View

As we noted above, our lives are filled with uncertainty every day. Our language has many words that suggest uncertainty: likely, probably, perhaps, maybe, etc. On a hot summer day in the South, consider that it *often* rains in the mid- or late-afternoon. Of course it doesn't *always* rain. Thus, when we leave for work or school in the morning, we must make a decision as to whether we should take an umbrella. We may look at the weather forecast online, consider the consequences of not having an umbrella if it does rain, or consider old sayings like, "Red sky at night, sailors' delight; red sun at morn, sailors take warn." Eventually we come to a conclusion and we either do or do not carry an umbrella. If you were to assemble a group of friends after lunch and ask who was carrying an umbrella, you would "probably" find that some of your friends had umbrellas and some did not. Why the difference? Because we differ from one another in the way we assess the likelihood of rain. Thus, while "probability" is used here in a subjective way, which is likely the most prevalent use of the term, it is fraught with problems as we disagree in our own determination of the probabilities of events. Within the context of our research activities, we need a more systematic approach to assessing probability. There are two additional views of probability that will serve us in this regard.

The Classical/Logical View

The classical/logical conceptualization of probability is central to the understanding of statistical inference and hypothesis testing. It consists of a logical/conceptual analysis of a situation, one that enumerates all the possibilities and asserts some assumptions about the likelihood of each possibility of occurring. For example, consider the act of flipping a coin, perhaps a U.S. quarter, and letting it fall on a hard surface. In thinking about what might happen, we would note that there are two distinct possible outcomes: "heads" or "tails." (Of course, the coin could stand on edge, but we will not consider that possibility as an admissible outcome.) If we assume that both outcomes are equally likely, then we would expect to see "heads" half of the time and "tails" half of the time. For another example, consider the dice that are a part of many board games. Let's say we take one of them and roll it. A traditional die is cubic in form, with six sides, each having one of the numbers one through six on it; sometimes the numbers are numerals and sometimes they are represented as dots. If we assume we're working with a fair die, then we are asserting that each of the six sides is equally likely to occur in a single roll, so that we might expect to see each side about one-sixth of the time.

We can make this explanation more formal. In the first step, we consider the action to be taken and enumerate the possible outcomes. In the case of the six-sided die, the outcomes are "one," "two," "three," "four," "five," and "six." Then we define the outcome of interest, for example "three." Now, we can present a more formal definition of probability:

$$P(A) = \frac{n_A}{n_S} \tag{8.1}$$

where n_A is the number of outcomes satisfying the condition A, and n_S is the total number of enumerated possibilities. Thus, for our die-rolling example, if we wanted to find the probability of seeing a "one," we would note that there is only one outcome satisfying the "one" condition, and there are six possible outcomes. Therefore the probability of seeing a 1 would be 1/6. On the other hand, if we wanted to find the probability of seeing an outcome of "four or less," we would note that there are four outcomes satisfying the "four or less" condition, and six possible outcomes. Thus, we find the result to be 4/6 or 2/3.

Checking it Out with R

Let's go back to the probability of seeing a 1 in a single roll of a die. We noted above that it is equal, logically, to 1/6 or about .1666. We could ask each of you reading this to find a six-sided die, roll it many times, and report to us the number of times you rolled the die and how many 1s you observed. But thankfully, there is an easier way with R. We can write a short script to simulate this situation. To begin, we are going to set the number of rolls to a rather large number: 360,000. If the probability of seeing a 1 is 1/6, we would intuitively expect to see 1 about 60,000 times. Let's see what happens when we run the R commands that follow:

```
# Script 8.1 - Simulating a 6-sided die
# Establish the six values
die <- 1:6
die
# Perform the simulation
# Set the number of rolls
n <- 360000
sim <- sample(die, 360000, replace = TRUE)

# Table the results
tab <- table(sim)
tab
freq1 <- tab[1]
freq1
prob1 <- freq1/n
prob1
```

The salient results are:

```
> die <- 1:6
> die
[1] 1 2 3 4 5 6

> tab
sim
    1     2     3     4     5     6
60063 59936 59761 60314 59813 60113

> freq1
    1
60063
> prob1 <- freq1/n
> prob1
        1
    0.1668417
```

We can see that the results of the simulation are quite close to what we expected; instead of see-ing 60,000 "ones," we saw 60,063 "ones," yielding a probability of .16684 rather than .16666. Later, we will more formally attribute this discrepancy to sampling error. For now, know that two of the three authors are employed at public universities, and these results are "close enough for government work." Just for fun, try to write an R script to simulate a large number of tosses of a fair coin.

The Empirical/Relative Frequency View

The third type of probability we wish to present is sometimes described as the empirical/relative frequency view. Rather than logically enumerating the possible outcomes and looking at them, we observe the process and simply count how many times we obtain the desired outcome within the number of times we repeat the process. For example, suppose that we had a six-sided die and we rolled it six times, observing the outcome 1 two times. Based on our observation, we would say that the probability of a 1 is 2/6 or 1/3. Let's say we now roll the die 12 times and observe only one "one." With this result we would say that the probability of a 1 would be 1/12. More formally, if we complete the process n times, and we see our desired outcome n_A times, we would say that:

$$P(A) = \frac{n_A}{n} \quad \text{as } n \to \infty \tag{8.2}$$

Thus, we can estimate the probability of A through observation. Our estimate should then become closer and closer to the "true" value as the number of trials becomes larger and larger, approaching infinity. Let's see how this works with R, and let's assume that we had not already engaged in the logical determination of the probability of a "one."

Checking it Out with R

In this series of simulations, we are going to roll the die different numbers of times. We will start with a small value such as six, and gradually increase the number of rolls, seeing what happens as the number of trials increases.

LOOKING AT SIX TRIALS   The R script is as follows:

```
die <- 1:6
n <- 6
sim <- sample(die, n, replace = TRUE)
tab <- table(sim)
freq1 <- tab[1]
freq1
prob1 <- freq1/n
prob1
```

The salient results are:

```
> freq1
1
3
> prob1 <- freq1/6
> prob1
  1
0.5
```

We see that, for this simulation, there were three "ones," yielding a probability of 3/6 or .5.

LOOKING AT 12 TRIALS   The R script is as follows:

```
die <- 1:6
n <- 12
sim <- sample(die, n, replace = TRUE)
tab <- table(sim)
freq1 <- tab[1]
freq1
prob1 <- freq1/12
prob1
```

The salient results are:

```
> freq1
1
1
> prob1 <- freq1/12
> prob1
        1
0.08333333
```

In this simulation of 12 rolls, we note that there was only one 1 observed, yielding a probability of 1/12, or .0833.

At this point, rather than take up space by repeating the simulation while increasing the number of trials, we will summarize the results. The values in the following table were generated by running the basic R script shown above, only changing the number of rolls.

As you can see from the results in the Table 8.1, as the number of trials increases, the probability of seeing a 1 gets closer and closer to the value that we obtained through our logical/classical analysis.

A Real-Life Application of the Empirical/Relative Frequency View

Earlier in this chapter, we used the example of uncertainty about the possibility of rain and how there are individual differences in "umbrella carrying" behavior. Most of us have had the

Table 8.1 The results from simulating the rolling of a six-sided die for various numbers of trials

Number of trials	Number of 1s	P(1)
36	3	.0833
360	56	.1555
3,600	619	.1719
36,000	5,987	.1663
360,000	59,845	.1662
3,600,000	599,277	.1665

experience of consulting the National Weather Service, the Weather Channel, Weather.com, or any of several locally available services that provide weather forecasts. For example, while this chapter was being written, the forecast for the Raleigh/Durham area from the National Weather Service indicated a 20% chance of scattered showers during the evening. Meanwhile, the Weather Channel, which provides hourly details, showed between a 20% chance and 10% chance of scattered showers for the same time frame. (In the next section, we address the limitations of such scales and take both services "to task" for the scales they use; nevertheless, it's important to understand where they obtain their numbers.) Weather forecasts employ the empirical/relative frequency view of probability. What they are really saying is that over all of the records that they have available, when the conditions have been as they currently are (i.e., fronts, isobars, locations of high and low pressure areas, humidity, etc.), it has rained 20% of the time.

We will now provide some more formal definitions of terms associated with probability.

SOME BASIC DEFINITIONS OF TERMS RELATED TO PROBABILITY

Up to now, we have been discussing probability in a rather informal, intuitive fashion. In order to proceed further, we need to define some terms in a more formal way.

Experiment

Our use of the term "experiment" is much broader than usually comes to mind. An experiment can be any process, in a laboratory or otherwise, where we can observe the result of a process and the result of that process is uncertain. Thus, rolling a die or flipping a coin would be considered an experiment.

Events and Sample Spaces

In our presentation of the logical/classical view of probability, we talked about listing all the possible outcomes that might be observed; these outcomes are called *events*. A listing of all possible events constitutes the *sample space*. One can consider two possible ways to enumerate the outcomes. We can list them at the most elemental, atomistic level. With a six-sided die, the outcomes are "one," "two," "three," "four," "five," and "six." Listed at this level, we refer to these outcomes as *simple events*. On the other hand, we could enumerate the possibilities as "seeing an even number," "seeing an odd number," "seeing an outcome less than or equal to two," etc. When the outcomes are listed in such a way that more than one simple event can meet the criteria, we refer to the outcomes as *compound events*. As another example, consider the experiment to be defined as tossing a coin three times (H = heads; T = tails). The simple events would be HHH, HHT, HTH, HTT, THH, THT, TTH, and TTT. On the other hand, we could enumerate the possibilities as seeing "no heads," "one head," "two heads," or "three heads." The compound event "two heads" would be obtained by observing any one of the three simple events HHT, HTH, or THH.

Probability Functions

Way back in Chapter 1, we presented a very brief, fairly traditional, definition of measurement: Measurement is the assignment of numerals to attributes of objects to express amount of the attribute, according to a rule. One way to think about a probability function is as a "theoretical" measurement rule. A *probability function* is a rule that assigns a value $P(A_i)$ to each simple event A_i such that:

1. $P(A_i)$ is greater than or equal to zero,
2. $P(A_i)$ is less than or equal to one, and
3. the sum of all $P(A_i)$ over *all simple events* is equal to one for a finite sample space.

We'll now provide some examples of these definitions as we show you ways to find probabilities for well-defined experiments.

RULES FOR FINDING PROBABILITIES

We have already presented two useful ways to find probabilities for experiments when the outcomes are enumerated at the simple level. However, there are times when things are just not that simple. Consider the typical deck of cards; there are four suits (spades, hearts, diamonds, and clubs), and each suit consists of 13 cards numbered two through 10, along with an ace, jack, queen, and king. The spade and club suits are black in color, while the heart and diamond suits are red. Some typical problems/questions: If you were to draw one card at random from the 52-card deck, what is the probability that: (1) the card would be a "ten" or that it would be red; (2) the card would be a "two" or a "ten"; (3) the card would be a red "ten"?

We will start with a slightly more simple experiment: rolling a fair 12-sided die. (Note: The traditional die found in most board games is a six-sided cube. However, dice come in other forms. Several years ago, the first author was presented with a bagfull of dice, including one that was eight-sided and another that was 12-sided. He will always be indebted to Adrienne Belafonte Biesemeyer, a most delightful visiting student, for opening up new horizons.) First, let's enumerate the possibilities. The sample space is presented in graphic form in Figure 8.1.

Now, let's define some events:

Let A = "Observe an odd number"
Let B = "Observe a number less than five"

These events are depicted graphically in Figures 8.2 and 8.3.

In Figure 8.2, we note that of the 12 possible outcomes, six of them are "odd." Thus, the probability of the event A, observing an odd number, is 6/12, or .50. Similarly, in Figure 8.3, we

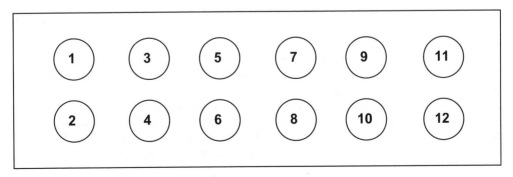

FIGURE 8.1   Diagram of the simple outcomes (sample space) for rolling a 12-sided die.

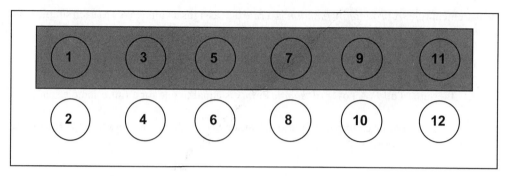

FIGURE 8.2   A Venn diagram of the event "observing an odd number."

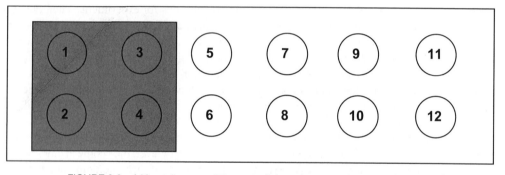

FIGURE 8.3   A Venn diagram of the event "observing a number less than five."

note that of the 12 possible outcomes, four of them are "less than 5." Thus, we can say that the probability of event B, observing a number less than five, is 4/12, or .33. So far, so good. However, we are often presented with more complex problems. For example, what is the probability of rolling the die once and observing an outcome that is "odd *or* less than five?" Another question might ask about the probability of the outcome being "odd *and* less than five?" We have emphasized the words "or" and "and" as they are key to finding the answers to these questions. We have two different rules for finding the probabilities of these more complex outcomes. When the question poses the "or" option, we should use the "Additive Rule," and when the question poses the "and" option, we should use the "Multiplicative Rule." We proceed to define and demonstrate these rules for these examples.

The Additive/Union Rule

When the question asked uses the "or" conjunction (e.g., $P(A$ or $B)$), we should use the Additive Rule, sometimes called the "Union Rule" as it is based on the "union" principle in set theory. We have diagrammed the situation is Figure 8.4.

In this situation, any outcome that satisfies the condition "odd" or "less than 5" would meet the criteria. Looking at Figure 8.4, we can look in the shaded area and see that there are eight of the simple events that fall within the shading. Thus, we can see that the probability that the outcome is either "odd" or "less than 5" is equal to 8/12, or .667. We can state this more formally:

$$P(A \text{ or } B) = P(A) + P(B) - P(A \text{ and } B)$$

$$(8.3)$$

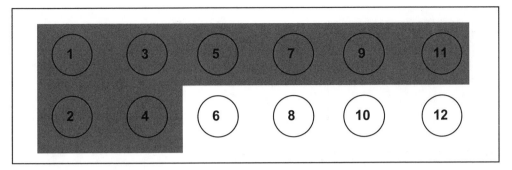

FIGURE 8.4   A Venn diagram depicting the outcome for *P*(A or B).

The last part of the expression is the result of having counted some of the elements twice. In Figure 8.4, we can see that when we count the "odd" events, count the events "less than 5," and then add the two counts, the events "1" and "3" will have been double-counted. The last part of Equation 8.3 corrects for this. Thus, working through Equation 8.3:

$$P(\text{A or B}) = P(\text{A}) + P(\text{B}) - P(\text{A and B}) = \frac{6}{12} + \frac{4}{12} - \frac{2}{12} = \frac{8}{12} \tag{8.4}$$

It is always reassuring when a mathematical rule yields the same results that we can see in the diagram! At this time, we should point out that there are special occasions when Equation 8.4 can be simplified. Specifically, when the two events, A and B, are mutually exclusive, then the equation becomes:

$$P(\text{A or B}) = P(\text{A}) + P(\text{B}) \tag{8.5}$$

The term "mutually exclusive" simply means that the outcome cannot possibly satisfy both events simultaneously. For example, suppose we define another outcome C, "greater than 10." In this case, the outcome cannot be "less than 5" and "greater than 10" at the same time. Thus, there is no double-counting. For this reason, we strive to define our complex outcomes to be comprised of mutually exclusive events.

The Multiplicative/Intersection Rule

When the question posed uses the "and" conjunction, we should apply the Multiplicative Rule, sometimes called the Intersection Rule as it is based on the intersection principle in set theory. Specifically:

$$P(\text{A and B}) = P(\text{A}) \times P(\text{B}|\text{A}) = P(\text{B}) \times P(\text{A}|\text{B}) \tag{8.6}$$

As you quickly see, we've added a new notation, $P(\text{B}|\text{A})$. This notation refers to "conditional" probability. We would read Equation 8.6 as saying, "The probability that the outcome is both A and B is equal to the probability that it is A multiplied times the probability that it is B, given that it is A." Good gracious, what is that all about? It is probably most easily seen by going straight to the example.

What is the probability of observing an outcome that is both "odd" and "less than 5"? Looking at Figure 8.5, you will see that we have boxed in the "odd" numbers and boxed in the numbers

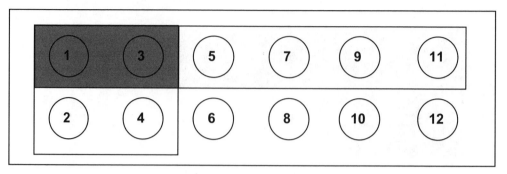

FIGURE 8.5   A Venn diagram depicting the Multiplicative Rule for P(A and B).

"less than 5." The only two simple events that fall in both boxes are "1" and "3." Thus, only two of the 12 simple events satisfy the condition so that we can say that the probability that the outcome is *both* "odd" and "less than 5" is 2/12, or .167.

Now, let's work through the logic of Equation 8.6. To find the probability that the outcome is both "odd" and "less than 5," we can multiply the probability that it is "odd" (6/12) times the probability that it is "less than 5," given that it is "odd." Looking at Figure 8.5, we can see that if we confine ourselves to the "odd" numbers, only two of them are "less than 5." Thus, we could multiply 6/12 times 2/6 and obtain 12/72, or .167. Working the problem the other way, we could find the probability that the outcome is "less than 5" (4/12) and multiply that times the probability that the outcome is "odd" given that it is "less than 5." Looking at the diagram, we can see that if we confine ourselves to the outcomes that are "less than 5," two out of the four outcomes "less than 5" are "odd." We can then find the final answer by multiplying 4/12 times 2/4, yielding 8/48, or .167.

As with the Additive/Union Rule, there is a special condition that leads to a simplification of Equation 8.6. If the two events A and B are independent, then P(A) is not affected by the condition B and we can assert that P(A|B) = P(A) and likewise, P(B|A) = P(B). Thus:

$$P(\text{A and B}) = P(\text{A}) \times P(\text{B}) \tag{8.7}$$

For this reason, statisticians like to define their outcomes as independent events as it greatly simplifies the calculations of probabilities.

More about Independence and Conditional Probability

The notion of conditional probability has been used to determine the independence or non-independence of events. Years ago, before we knew as much as we now know, there was a raging debate about whether smoking cigarettes was related to lung cancer. To establish a clear causal link, one could consider an experiment in which people were randomly assigned to a "smoking" or "non-smoking" condition. As we now know, that would not have been good for the "smokers."

Instead, epidemiologists were able to employ the notion of conditional probability to establish a link. Using large databases, they were able to determine the probability that someone in the general population would contract lung cancer (A). If smoking (B) is unrelated to lung cancer (A), then P(A) should be equal to P(A|B). However, in data that were collected, it was found that P(A|B), the probability of contracting cancer given that the patient was a smoker, was substantially larger than $P(A)$, the probability of contracting cancer. Thus, they were able to argue that there was a relationship between smoking and lung cancer.

At this juncture, we have made the point that the logical/classical view of probability will be central to our building a system that will allow us to make reasonable inferences from sample results to populations. After looking at our simple examples with the 12-sided die, it should be apparent that finding/calculating probabilities relies heavily on counting the possibilities. We assume that each and every one of you is a competent counter. Nevertheless, we are going to spend the remainder of this chapter showing you some rules for counting things more quickly.

RULES FOR COUNTING

This final section of this chapter will focus on ways to count quickly. Specifically, we will explain the Fundamental Counting Rule and how it can be applied to two particular situations: (1) finding the number of ways to order a set of objects (permutations), and (2) finding the number of ways to select a number of subsets, where order does not make any difference (combinations).

The Fundamental Counting Rule

The *Fundamental Counting Rule* is just that, fundamental and fairly intuitive. It states that if one experiment has n_1 possible outcomes and another experiment has n_2 possible outcomes, then the first experiment, followed by the second experiment will have $n_1 \times n_2$ possible outcomes. For example, if we were to toss a coin and then roll a six-sided die, there are 12 possible outcomes that might be obtained. Without too much difficulty, you should be able to enumerate them: H1, H2, … H6, T1, … T6. This rule forms the basis for much of what we will be doing, hence the label "fundamental."

Next, let's consider how we might count the number of ways to arrange a set of n objects, when order makes a difference (and sometimes it does). If you doubt that, try a little experiment. Drink a tall glass of orange juice, followed immediately by a tall glass of milk. Wait a while and then try the two again, reversing the order, milk followed by orange juice. Ordered arrangements are called *permutations*.

Permutations

Suppose that we have three different balls: lined, cross-hatched, and spotted. How many ways are there to arrange them in order? The first one could be any one of the three possibilities. But once the first ball is placed, there are only two left over. Therefore, the second ball can only be one of two possibilities. After the first two balls are placed, we only have one left, so that the third ball can only be the one ball we have left. Thus, there are three ways to do the first, two ways to do the second, and one way to do the third. Applying the Fundamental Counting Rule, there are $3 \times 2 \times 1$ ways to arrange the three; the answer is six. (If you can find a seventh way to arrange the balls that is different from these six ways, you may have a dissertation topic for a PhD in mathematics!) We have shown the six arrangements in Figure 8.6.

As you can imagine based on our previous presentations, we have a notation for this concept of permutations:

$$P_n^n = n(n-1)(n-2)\ldots(3)(2)(1) = n! \tag{8.8}$$

Question: How many ways are there to arrange three different balls?

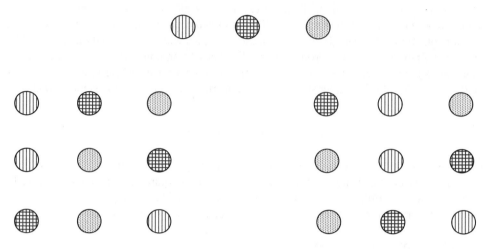

FIGURE 8.6   The six permutations of three balls.

This notation is read, "The number of permutations of *n* objects using all *n* of them is *n* times *n* minus 1 times *n* minus 2, continuing down to 2 times 1. This product is equal to *n* factorial."

Let's apply this idea to a real-world example. Have you ever wondered how many different ways there are to put away a standard croquet set? In a standard set, there are six balls, each a different color. Each ball has a mallet of matching color. There is also a set of wickets, of course, but since they all look alike, we will not deal with them. Usually, the set comes with a rack that has a cylinder in the center in which to stack the balls; the mallets are placed in the top of the rack, left to right, or right to left if you prefer. Now, the balls can be ordered in the cylinder 6! different ways, or 720 ways. The mallets can also be ordered in 6!, or 720 different ways. Applying the Fundamental Counting Rule, the set can be put away in 720 × 720 different ways, or 518,400 different arrangements. Wow, did you know that you could count that fast?

Sometimes, we are concerned with the number of arrangements when we are not going to use all of them. For example, there is a retail chain that advertises that it has 31 different flavors of ice cream. Have you ever wondered how many different triple-decked choices there are, assuming that you do not choose the same flavor twice? (After all, who would ever pick vanilla-vanilla-vanilla?) In this case, we are talking about the number of arrangements of *n* objects, using only *r* of them. This is not so hard to figure out. The first flavor in the cone could be any one of the 31 flavors, the second flavor could be any one of the remaining 30 flavors, and the third flavor could be any one of the remaining 29 flavors. Thus, the answer is 31 × 30 × 29, or 26,970 different orders. Of course, we have a notational representation of this process. First think of 31! as 31 × 30 × 29 × 28!. So,

$$P_r^n = n(n-1)(n-2)\ldots(n-r+1) = \frac{n!}{(n-r)!} \tag{8.9}$$

Permutations with R

Of course, R can be used to calculate these results. For example,

```
# How to find 6!
prod(6:1)
# The croquet problem
prod(6:1)*prod(6:1)
# The ice cream problem, finding the number of
# permutations of 31 flavors, using only three of
# them
prod(31:1)/prod(28:1)
# Another way
prod(31:29)
```

The results are:

```
> # How to find 6!
> prod(6:1)
[1] 720
> # The croquet problem
> prod(6:1)*prod(6:1)
[1] 518400
> # The ice cream problem, finding the number of
> # permutations of 31 flavors, using only three of
> # them
> prod(31:1)/prod(28:1)
[1] 26970
> # Another way
> prod(31:29)
[1] 26970
```

At this point, you should (hopefully) be feeling comfortable with the notion of permutations. However, in practice we are interested in situations where order does not make a difference. That is, we are interested in the number of subsets, disregarding the order within the subset. This notion is called *combinations*.

Combinations

One way to think about the idea of combinations is to think about the number of permutations, and then take the number of different orders into account. For example, consider the number of permutations of the three balls if we use only two of them. The six permutations are depicted in Figure 8.7.

Looking more carefully at the picture, we can see that the combination of "Line and Screen" appears twice, first as "Line and Screen" and again as "Screen and Line." That particular combination has been counted twice when listing out the permutations. That is because the two different balls can appear in two different orders. More generally, if we have counted the number of permutations

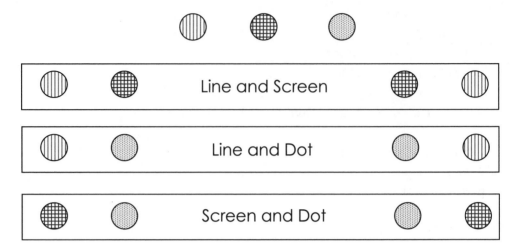

FIGURE 8.7 The number of permutations of three balls, using only two of them.

of *n* objects using only *r* of them, we know that each of those combinations will appear as *r*! different permutations. Thus,

$$C_r^n = \frac{P_r^n}{r!} = \frac{n!}{(n-r)!\,r!} \tag{8.10}$$

As an example, how many different five-card poker hands are possible from a standard 52-card deck? Once we have the five cards, it does not matter in which order we received them.

$$C_5^{52} = \frac{52!}{(52-5)!\,5!} = 2{,}598{,}960 \tag{8.11}$$

As an aside, there are only four possible "royal flushes" (ace, king, queen, jack, and 10 of the same suit). Thus, going back to our understanding of the logical/classical view of probability, the probability of being dealt a royal flush is 4/2,598,960, or .0000015. So, even if you are a full-time professional poker player, do not expect to see very many of those hands in your lifetime!

Combinations with R

Finding combinations with R is a little easier than finding permutations. With permutations, you have to represent the formula to R. For combinations, you can represent the formula, or you can use the **choose( )** function.

```
#Combinations: The poker hand problem by formula
prod(52:1)/(prod(47:1)*prod(5:1))

#Combinations with the choose function
choose(52,5)
```

The results are:

```
> prod(52:1)/(prod(47:1)*prod(5:1))
[1] 2598960
 > #Combinations with the choose function
> choose(52,5)
[1] 2598960
```

CHAPTER SUMMARY

In this chapter, we have introduced many new ideas and terms. After defining three views of probability, we focused on the logical/classical view and showed you ways to calculate probabilities for outcomes defined in different ways: the Additive or Union Rule, and the Multiplicative or Intersection Rule. Subsequently, we presented the Fundamental Counting Rule and applied it to assist us in counting the number of permutations (arrangements in order) and combinations (subsets without regard to order). These ideas will be applied in the next chapter as we begin to define and work with probability and sampling distributions.

Key Terms

Probability	Additive Rule
Classical/logical probability	Multiplicative Rule
Empirical/relative frequency probability	Mutually exclusive
Experiment	Conditional probability
Simple event	Independent
Compound event	Fundamental Counting Rule
Sample space	Permutations
Probability function	Combinations

PRACTICE QUESTIONS

1. While hiking along a high mountain ridge one member of the group suggests the trail is getting a bit too precarious, the chance of injury too high, and thus they should head back. Another member disagrees with this assessment and urges the group to move on. This discussion is based on:

    a. classical/logical probabilities
    b. empirical/relative frequency probabilities
    c. personal/subjective probabilities.

2. Suppose a statistics class has 11 female and 10 male students. Suppose that one student will be randomly selected to work a problem. The probability that the selected student will be a female is:

    a. higher than the probability that the selected student will be a male
    b. lower than the probability that the selected student will be a male
    c. equal to the probability that the selected student will be a male.

3. Suppose a statistics class has 11 female and 10 male students. Suppose that the first student selected to work a problem was a female. If a second student is randomly selected from the students who have not worked a problem, the probability that this next student will be a female is:

    a. higher than the probability that the selected student will be a male
    b. lower than the probability that the selected student will be a male
    c. equal to the probability that the selected student will be a male.

4. Suppose the instructor of the high-school statistics course wanted to determine how many different ways her 21 students could be lined up to go to the computer lab. Which of the following methods would be the most appropriate way to count the possibilities?

    a. Listing every possibility and then counting them up.
    b. Using the permutation formula.
    c. Using the combination formula.

5. Suppose the instructor of the statistics class randomly selected 10 of the 21 students to try out a new study guide, while the remaining students used the old study guide. The instructor wanted to know how many different possible subsets of 10 students could have been selected. Which of the following methods would be most appropriate for determining this?

    a. Listing every possibility and then counting them up.
    b. Using the permutation formula.
    c. Using the combination formula.

6. Suppose a statistics class has both male and female students, and that some of each group like their statistics book, while others dislike their statistics book. Which of the following probabilities would be the greatest?

    a. Randomly selecting a student that was female.
    b. Randomly selecting a student that was female AND liked the book.
    c. Randomly selecting a student that was either female OR liked the book.

EXERCISES

8.1. Suppose that you draw one card at random from a thoroughly shuffled deck of cards.

    a. How many simple events are associated with this experiment?
    What is the probability of drawing
    b. The two-of-hearts?
    c. A diamond?
    d. A red card?
    e. A black queen, given the card is a face card?

8.2. Consider the experiment composed of one roll of a fair die, followed by one toss of a fair coin. List the simple events, assigning a logical probability to each. Determine the probability of observing each of the following events:

    a. 6 on the die, heads on the coin

b. even number on the die, tails on the coin
c. even number on the die
d. tails on the coin.

8.3. What is the probability of randomly picking a 6 or a 9 in one draw from an ordinary deck of cards? What is the probability of drawing a card which is either a black card or a face card in one draw?

8.4. Experiment 1 has two outcomes: A and ~A. Experiment B also has two outcomes: B and ~B. The two experiments are independent. $P(A)=.5$ and $P(B)=.9$. What is the probability that both will occur? That neither will occur? That one or the other or both will occur?

8.5. Imagine yourself sitting at home some evening, feeling guilty that you are not studying your statistics. Looking at your computer guide, text, course pack, and your notebook, you decide to stack them neatly in the center of your coffee table. If you were to decide which of all possible arrangements was most complementary to your interior decorating theme, how many arrangements would you need to try?

8.6. How many different study groups with five members could be formed from a section of introductory statistics that has 40 students enrolled?

8.7. Given that a student is enrolled in a small college offering 15 different programs, in how many ways can the student select a major and minor area? A major and a primary minor and a secondary minor? A major and two minors? (Hint: When considering primary and secondary minors, order makes a difference.)

8.8. Suppose a certain rock band has a repertoire of 18 songs that they can perform very well. With these 18 selections, how many different CDs can they market, if they put 12 selections on each CD? Two CDs are considered to be the same if they have the same 12 selections, regardless of order.

9

Probability and Sampling Distributions

INTRODUCTION

In the previous chapter, we introduced some definitions of probability, some basic concepts related to probability, and showed you different ways to count the number of possibilities (e.g., the Fundamental Counting Rule, permutations, and combinations). In this chapter, we are going to begin to apply some of those ideas as we start to build a system that will allow us to test hypotheses about populations using data available from samples from those populations. We will begin with a very simple experiment, tossing a coin four times.

TOSSING A FAIR COIN FOUR TIMES

Based on our definition of an experiment in Chapter 8, the process of tossing a coin four times qualifies as an experiment; we can observe the outcome of each toss, and the outcome is uncertain. First, let's look at possibilities. On the first toss, we could observe an outcome of heads (H) or tails (T). On each of the remaining three tosses, we could observe an H or a T. Thus, the possibilities for four tosses can be enumerated as follows: HHHH, HHHT, HHTH, HHTT, HTHH, HTHT, HTTH, HTTT, THHH, THHT, THTH, THTT, TTHH, TTHT, TTTH, and TTTT. We can see that there are 16 different possible outcomes when listed as simple events. We could have anticipated this result by using the Fundamental Counting Rule from Chapter 8. There are two possible outcomes on each of the four tosses, so the number of possibilities should be $2 \times 2 \times 2 \times 2$, or 2^4.

In many situations, we are not interested in the order in which things appear, but rather we are interested in the overall value. Consider dealing a hand in a game of bridge or poker. Once the dealer has finished, each player takes some time to sort the hand. If one player winds up with all four aces, it really doesn't matter when those particular cards were dealt. In the same sense, in our experiment of four tosses of the coin, we may not be interested in the particular order of the outcomes, but rather we might be interested in the number of times H appears in the four tosses. Assuming that the coin is fair ($p = .5$) and that the tosses are independent (the probability of H on the second toss is not affected by the outcome of the first toss), we can assert that the probability of each of the 16 simple events is 1/16. Can you explain why?

Let's focus on one of the simple events: HTHH. The probability of H on the first toss is ½. The probability of T on the second toss is $P(T|H)$, but since they are independent, that is simply $P(T)$. So, $P(HTHH)$ is $P(H$ and T and H and $H)$. Given that we are looking at an "and" conjunction, we apply the Multiplicative Rule and find that the probability is $½ \times ½ \times ½ \times ½$, or 1/16. We'll leave it up to you to work through the other 15 simple events, should you feel the need to do so. We have summarized the results in Table 9.1, in which we have also included a column indicating the number of Hs in the four tosses. In doing so, we have defined a quantitative measure describing each of the simple outcomes. That is, we have defined a *random variable*. A random variable is somewhat like a measurement rule in that it assigns a value to each of the experimental outcomes. In most cases, the value is numeric. In this experiment, the number of Hs in the four tosses can range from zero to four, and we do not know what sequence we will get in any four tosses of the coin.

Now, let's talk about the probability of observing three Hs in four tosses of the coin. An examination of Table 9.1 indicates that there are four different ways of obtaining three Hs: HHHT, HHTH, HTHH, and THHH, each having a probability of 1/16. So we could write:

$$P(Y=3)=P(\text{HHHT or HHTH or HTHH or THHH})$$

Here we are using the "or" conjunction so we should apply the Additive Rule from Chapter 8. Given that the four possible simple events that satisfy the compound event are mutually exclusive, we can simply add up the probabilities to obtain 4/16 or ¼. Following through with the other possible outcomes ($Y=0, 1, 2,$ and 4), we can create Table 9.2. In doing so, we have constructed a

Table 9.1 Enumerating the simple events, and their probabilities, and the number of heads in four tosses of a fair coin

Simple event	Probability	Number of heads (Y)
HHHH	1/16 = .0625	4
HHHT	1/16 = .0625	3
HHTH	1/16 = .0625	3
HHTT	1/16 = .0625	2
HTHH	1/16 = .0625	3
HTHT	1/16 = .0625	2
HTTH	1/16 = .0625	2
HTTT	1/16 = .0625	1
THHH	1/16 = .0625	3
THHT	1/16 = .0625	2
THTH	1/16 = .0625	2
THTT	1/16 = .0625	1
TTHH	1/16 = .0625	2
TTHT	1/16 = .0625	1
TTTH	1/16 = .0625	1
TTTT	1/16 = .0625	0

Table 9.2 The probability distribution for the number of heads observed in four tosses of a fair coin

Number of heads (Y)	P(Y)
4	1/16
3	4/16
2	6/16
1	4/16
0	1/16

rule that associates the probability of observing that particular value with each value of a random variable. This rule or "function" is called a *probability distribution*.

Simulating Four Tosses of a Fair Coin with R

To simulate four tosses of a fair coin, we could ask you to round up many, many of your friends and throw a coin-tossing party, where each of you tosses a coin four times and you count the number of Hs observed in the four tosses. Or, we can simulate this process with R. To make the arithmetic easy, we are going to program R to simulate 16,000 of your nearest and dearest friends. That is, we are going to replicate four tosses of a coin 16,000 times. Intuitively, if the probability of observing four Hs in the four tosses is 1/16, we might reasonably expect to see four Hs in about 1,000 of the 16,000 replications. Similarly, we would expect to see four Ts in about 1,000 of the replications. Based on the probability distribution we constructed in Table 9.2, we would also expect to see three Hs about 4,000 times, two Hs about 6,000 times, and one H about 4,000 times. Here is the R script:

```
# Script 9.1 - Simulating Four Tosses of a Fair
# Coin
# Define number of replications
N <- 16000
# Define number of tosses
n <- 4
stat <- numeric(N)
for (i in 1:N) {
  sam <- sample(0:1, n, replace = TRUE)
  num <- sum(sam)
  stat[i] <- num
}
table(stat)
```

After we run this script, we can use the table command in R to generate a frequency table for the results of the 16,000 replications:

```
> table(stat)
stat
   0    1    2    3    4
 975 4042 6016 3968  999
```

While the results are not *exactly* what we predicted, they are "close enough for government work." Note that if you run the simulation in R yourself, the numbers will come out a little differently, but again close to what we predicted. In general and as noted specifically in Chapter 8, the simulations will tend to produce results that are closer to the expected proportions as the number of simulated experiments increases. Let's take a look at another experiment. Suppose we want to look at the outcomes that might occur if we roll a fsair die four times.

ROLLING A FAIR DIE FOUR TIMES

Let's assume that we are working with a traditional die, having six sides, with each side equally likely. In this experiment, we are going to count the number of 2s seen in the four rolls. As with the coin tossing experiment, we will list the simple events. We will indicate "two" with a 2 and a "not two" with an X. (This example may not be necessary, but we believe that it will help you better understand a short cut that we will explain soon.) For each toss there are two outcomes (2 or X) and there are four rolls, thus there are 16 possible outcomes, just as we had with four coin tosses. Asserting that the die is fair establishes that $P(2)$ is 1/6 and that $P(X)$ is 5/6. From here, we proceed to construct Table 9.3.

In Table 9.3, we have shown the probability of any single event by explicitly noting the probability in the second column as the product of the four probabilities of the outcomes (2 or X) involved in that simple event, where $P(2)=1/6$ and $P(X)=5/6$. Now, we are in a position to construct Table 9.4 which contains the probability distribution of the random variable, the number of 2s observed in four rolls of a fair die.

In doing so, we see that there is only one simple event in which four 2s are observed, with a probability of 1/1296. We then see that there are four simple events in which three 2s are observed, each with a probability of 5/1296. Given that these simple events are mutually exclusive, we can add the four probabilities to obtain 20/1296. In similar fashion, we see that there are six simple events that reflect seeing two 2s, each with a probability of 25/1296. Thus the probability of observing two 2s in the four rolls is 150/1296. We can see that there are four simple

Table 9.3 Enumerating the simple events, their probabilities, and the number of 2s observed in four rolls of a fair die

Simple event	Probability	Number of 2s (Y)
2222	$(1/6)^4 = 1/1296$	4
222X	$(1/6)^3(5/6) = 5/1296$	3
22X2	$(1/6)^2(5/6)(1/6) = 5/1296$	3
22XX	$(1/6)^2(5/6)2 = 25/1296$	2
2X22	$(1/6)(5/6)(1/6)^2 = 5/1296$	3
2X2X	$(1/6)(5/6)(1/6)(5/6) = 25/1296$	2
2XX2	$(1/6)(5/6)^2(1/6) = 25/1296$	2
2XXX	$(1/6)(5/6)^3 = 125/1296$	1
X222	$(5/6)(1/6)^3 = 5/1296$	3
X22X	$(5/6)(1/6)^2(5/6) = 25/1296$	2
X2X2	$(5/6)(1/6)(5/6)(1/6) = 25/1296$	2
X2XX	$(5/6)(1/6)(5/6)^2 = 125/1296$	1
XX22	$(5/6)^2(1/6)^2 = 25/1296$	2
XX2X	$(5/6)^2(1/6)(5/6) = 125/1296$	1
XXX2	$(5/6)^3(1/6) = 125/1296$	1
XXXX	$(5/6)^4 = 625/1296$	0

Table 9.4 The probability distribution for the number of 2s observed in four rolls of a fair die

Number of 2s (Y)	P(Y)	Decimal equivalent
4	1/1296	.00077
3	20/1296	.01543
2	150/1296	.11574
1	500/1296	.38580
0	625/1296	.48225

events in which one 2 is observed, each with a probability of 125/1296. Combining them, we find that the probability of observing one 2 is 500/1296. Last, there is only one simple event reflecting zero 2s observed in the four rolls, with a probability of 625/1296. If we add up the five probabilities we have just derived, we obtain 1296/1296, or 1.0, just as it should be.

Simulating Four Rolls of a Fair Die with R

The probability distribution in Table 9.4 is based on a logical analysis of the process of rolling a fair die four times and observing the number of 2s that might be observed in the sequence of four rolls. As with the coin-tossing example, we can simulate this "experiment" using R to replicate the four rolls 129,600 times. (In this case, we'll not suggest a die rolling party as we assume you don't have that many friends.) The script we have written has two loops. The first loop draws four numbers from the numbers 1 through 6; within each of those 129,600 iterations, there is a nested loop that counts the number of 2s contained within that particular iteration. At the end of the process, we construct a frequency table. Again, intuitively, if $P(Y=4)$ is 1/1296, in the 129,600 iterations, we could expect to see about 100 of them that contain four 2s, etc. Let's look first at the R script and then at the results.

```
# Script 9.2 - Simulating Four Rolls of a Fair Die
# Define the number of replications
N  <- 129600
# Define the number of rolls
n <- 4
stat1 <- numeric(N)
for (i in 1:N){
  counter <- 0
  sam <- sample(1:6, n, replace = TRUE)
  for (j in 1:n) {
  if (sam[j] == "2") counter = counter + 1
}
  counter
  stat1[i] = counter
}
table(stat1)
```

The results are:

```
> table(stat1)
stat1
     0     1     2     3     4
62273 50241 15002  1981   103
```

If intuition serves us correctly, we would expect to have seen the results as follows:

0	1	2	3	4
62500	50000	15000	2000	100

As you can see, the results of the empirical simulation are quite similar to what we would have expected. Perhaps the world is not such an unpredictable place after all.

It turns out that the examples just presented (coin tossing and die rolling) are similar in that each of them was defined in such a way that there were only two possible outcomes on each trial. That is, the outcome is binary. Think of each toss or roll as an experiment repeated four times. When we define a random variable as the "number of heads" or the "number of 2s" observed in a series of two or more trials, the probability distribution for that random variable is called the *sampling distribution* for that random variable. That is, a sampling distribution is a probability distribution for a statistic based on repeated samples. In the remainder of this book, we will look at the sampling distributions of many random variables (statistics). Some of them will be discrete variables, such as the number of siblings in a family or the number of heads observed in several tosses of a coin. Others will be continuous variables, such as the time it takes to complete a task or the degree of positive affect in a classroom. We are going to start with a discrete distribution that is relatively simple; both of the examples presented previously in this chapter are examples of the binomial distribution.

BERNOULLI TRIALS AND THE BINOMIAL DISTRIBUTION

Experiments that have only two possible outcomes (e.g., heads or tails, 2 or not 2, etc.) are called Bernoulli trials. A series of two or more independent Bernoulli trials constitutes a binomial experiment, and the sampling distribution of the random variable can be derived using the binomial expansion. Binomial experiments are characterized by the following attributes:

1. Each trial can have only two outcomes, often called *success* and *failure*.
2. The experiment has a specified number of trials, usually denoted by *n*.
3. The probability of a *success* is usually denoted by *p* and the probability of a *failure* by *q*; thus, the sum of *p* and *q* is equal to 1.0.
4. The trials are independent of one another. That is, the value of *p* on later trials is not affected by the outcomes of previous trials.
5. The random variable is defined as the number of *successes* observed in the *n* trials.

There are many examples of binomial "experiments" in real life. In the health sciences, researchers may be interested in studying processes that lead to one of two outcomes. The patient shows a positive response to the treatment or not. Insurance underwriters may be looking at whether a client has an automobile accident or not. Newspaper publishers might want to examine whether an advertiser continues to place ads or not after some change in policy. Researchers in educational measurement might want to look at performance patterns on some assessment where the student gets each of a series of test items correct or not.

As we have already seen (think coins and dice), we can go through the process of enumerating the sample space at the level of simple events and construct the sampling distribution as in Tables 9.2 and 9.4, respectively. When the number of trials is fairly small, this is not difficult to manage. Of course when the number of trials is larger, such as listing all possible simple events for 100 tosses of a fair coin, the process becomes much more difficult. Thankfully, there is an easier solution. First, let's take a look at what happens when we start raising $(p+q)$ to increasing powers. Remember that $(p+q)$ is equal to 1.0, so that $(p+q)^n$ will always equal one, regardless of the value of n.

$$(p+q)^2 = p^2 + 2pq + q^2 \qquad (9.1)$$

$$(p+q)^3 = p^3 + 3p^2q + 3pq^2 + q^3 \qquad (9.2)$$

$$(p+q)^4 = p^4 + 4p^3q + 6p^2q^2 + 4pq^3 + q^4 \qquad (9.3)$$

Let's stop here and look at what happened when we raised $(p+q)$ to the fourth power. First, there are lots of terms in p and q. But look at the coefficients moving from left to right. They are, respectively, 1, 4, 6, 4, and 1. Now, look at the values in Table 9.2. It's more difficult to see in Table 9.3, but there is only one simple event with four 2s, four simple events with three 2s, six simple events with two 2s, four simple events with one 2, and one simple event with no 2s. Do you see the pattern? This process of raising $(p+q)$ to different powers generates what are called the binomial coefficients. These coefficients can also be seen in what is commonly referred to as Pascal's Triangle, which we have started in Table 9.5.

Again, do you see the pattern? Starting with the single 1 at the top, we then put two 1s in the next row. In the third row, again put two 1s with a space between them. Looking above the space in the third row to row two, we see a 1 to the left of the space and a 1 to the right of the space. We add them together and get a 2. Now, put two 1s in the fourth row with two spaces between them. Looking above the left space to row three, we see a 1 to the left and a 2 to the right. Add them together and put a 3 in the space. Do the same for the second space. Looking above, we see a 2 to the left and a 1 to the right. Add them together and put the sum of 3 in the space. We'll leave it to you to see if you can do the remaining rows on your own. The mathematical pattern is typically attributed to the mathematician Blaise Pascal, although it had been studied by mathematicians in the middle East (Persia) and the far East (India and China) for many centuries. For more information, see http://en.wikipedia.org/wiki/Pascal%27s_triangle. All of this can be put together into what is called the binomial expansion.

$$P(Y = r) = C_r^n p^r q^{(n-r)} \qquad (9.4)$$

Table 9.5 The binomial coefficients displayed in Pascal's triangle

						1								
					1		1							
				1		2		1						
			1		3		3		1					
		1		4		6		4		1				
	1		5		10		10		5		1			
1		6		15		20		15		6		1		
1		7		21		35		35		21		7		1	
						Etc.								

At first glance, Equation 9.4 appears rather scary. Let's take a closer look. The left side of the expression is simply read, "The probability that the value of the random variable Y takes on the value r" where r is the number of successes observed in the n trials. In both of our earlier examples, r could take on the values of 0, 1, 2, 3, or 4. In general, r can run from 0 to n. Now, let's look at the right side of the expression. The first term you encounter, C_r^n, is the number of combinations of n things, taking r of them. If you can't remember this, refer back to Chapter 8. Then you note p raised to the rth power followed by q raised to the $(n-r)$th power. How does this work? Let's run through the coin tossing example where $p = q = .5$ and n was equal to 4.

$$P(Y = 4) = C_4^4 (1/2)^4 (1/2)^0 = \frac{4!}{0!4!}(1/2)^4 = 1/16 \tag{9.5}$$

$$P(Y = 3) = C_3^4 (1/2)^3 (1/2)^1 = \frac{4!}{1!3!}(1/2)^4 = 4/16 \tag{9.6}$$

$$P(Y = 2) = C_2^4 (1/2)^2 (1/2)^2 = \frac{4!}{2!2!}(1/2)^4 = 6/16 \tag{9.7}$$

$$P(Y = 1) = C_1^4 (1/2)^1 (1/2)^3 = \frac{4!}{3!1!}(1/2)^4 = 4/16 \tag{9.8}$$

$$P(Y = 0) = C_0^4 (1/2)^0 (1/2)^4 = \frac{4!}{4!0!}(1/2)^4 = 1/16 \tag{9.9}$$

If you compare these results to the entries in Table 9.2, they should match. Now, let's do the same thing for the die rolling example, where $p = 1/6$ and $q = 5/6$. Before we start, consider the four simple events that contain three 2s. Each of them contains three factors of 1/6 and one factor of 5/6, although they appear in different orders. Of course, since multiplication is commutative, we can rearrange the order, grouping like terms, and representing the multiplication by exponents. Here we go:

$$P(Y = 4) = C_4^4 (1/6)^4 (5/6)^0 = \frac{4!}{0!4!}(1/6)^4 = 1/1,296 \tag{9.10}$$

$$P(Y = 3) = C_3^4 (1/6)^3 (5/6)^1 = \frac{4!}{1!3!}(1/6)^3 (5/6)^1 = 4 \times (5/1296) = 20/1,296 \tag{9.11}$$

$$P(Y = 2) = C_2^4 (1/6)^2 (5/6)^2 = \frac{4!}{2!2!}(1/6)^2 (5/6)^2 = 6 \times (25/1296) = 150/1,296 \tag{9.12}$$

$$P(Y = 1) = C_1^4 (1/6)^1 (5/6)^3 = \frac{4!}{3!1!}(1/6)^1 (5/6)^3 = 4 \times (125/1296) = 500/1,296 \tag{9.13}$$

$$P(Y = 0) = C_0^4 (1/6)^0 (5/6)^4 = \frac{4!}{4!0!}(1/6)^0 (5/6)^4 = 1 \times (625/1296) = 625/1,296 \tag{9.14}$$

As you can see, the "combinatorial" part of the expression calculates the number of paths that satisfy the outcome, "*r* successes," and the part of the expression that involves *p* and *q* calculates the probability of each of those outcomes. Then, we can multiply as a quick way to add the equal probabilities together.

Another Example: Tossing a Fair Coin 12 Times

Let's take a look at another binomial experiment, tossing a fair coin 12 times. Intuitively, we might reasonably expect to see six Hs and six Ts, but we also know that we would not expect to see a 6/6 split every time. Sometimes we might see a 7/5 or 5/7 split. Other times, we might see an 8/4 or 4/8 split. However, we might suspect that it would be unlikely for us to see 12/0 or 0/12 split. Suppose that we are interested in determining the probability of seeing 0, 1, 2, 10, 11, or 12 Hs in 12 tosses of the coin. We could evaluate each of these outcomes, but since we are asserting that $p = q = .5$, the results will be symmetric. So we really only need to do the "low" side.

$$P(Y = 0) = C_0^{12}(1/2)^0(1/2)^{12} = \frac{12!}{12!\,0!}(1/2)^{12} = 1 \times (.0002441406) \tag{9.15}$$

$$P(Y = 1) = C_1^{12}(1/2)^1(1/2)^{11} = \frac{12!}{11!\,1!}(1/2)^{12} = 12 \times (.000244) = .002929688 \tag{9.16}$$

$$P(Y = 2) = C_2^{12}(1/2)^2(1/2)^{10} = \frac{12!}{10!\,2!}(1/2)^{12} = 66 \times (.000244) = .01611328 \tag{9.17}$$

If we add these three results together, we obtain a value of .01928 for the probability of $P(Y \leq 2)$. Given that $P(Y \geq 10)$ is also .01928, we now know that the probability of seeing 0, 1, 2, 10, 11, or 12 Hs in 12 tosses of a fair coin is equal to .03856. Thus, if we were to see any of those results, we might suspect that the coin is not a fair one. A result of 0, 1, 2, 10, 11, or 12 would be so far away from what we expected that it would not be very likely to happen.

DEFINING THE EXPECTED VALUE OF A RANDOM VARIABLE

In the second part of this book, we learned how to describe real data in terms of a number of salient attributes. The characteristics of central tendency, spread, and shape are also relevant to sampling distributions. In this section, we will focus on the notion of central tendency. Think about the binomial distribution for four tosses of a fair coin. Intuitively, we see that, on average, we would expect to see about two heads and two tails in any sequence of four trials. Imagine that we were to replicate the four tosses many, many times and take note of the number of heads in each of the series of four tosses. After many, many series, we could find the mean number of heads across the large number of series; it would seem reasonable to expect that the mean should be quite close to two. We can formalize this notion of expectation with a definition of *expected value*. For a discrete random variable, *Y*, with a known probability distribution $P(Y)$ and where Y_j is the *j*th outcome in the set of *k* simple events:

$$E(Y) = Y_1 \times P(Y_1) + Y_2 \times P(Y_2) + \dots + Y_k \times P(Y_k) = \sum_{j=1}^{k} Y_j \times P(Y_j) = \mu \tag{9.18}$$

For a binomial random variable, it can be shown/proved that:

$$E(Y) = n \times p \tag{9.19}$$

As a practical example, consider a well known game of chance, roulette. (There are many variations of roulette; we are describing one of the more common ones.) The game is played by tossing a small ball onto a wheel that is spinning; the wheel typically has 38 slots. The ball bounces around, eventually coming to rest in one of the slots. Usually, the 38 slots are numbered from 1 to 36; half of those slots are red and half are black. In addition, there are two green slots numbered 0 and 00. There are many different ways to place a bet, one of which challenges you to guess the correct slot in which the ball will come to rest. With a bet of $1, you get a payoff of $35 if you guess the correct slot. Sounds like a good deal, right? Well, before you "bet the ranch," let's apply the notion of expected value to the situation. There are two outcomes; you net either $34 or –$1. Remember that if you win, one of the dollars coming back to you was yours at the start of the spin. Now the probability that you correctly guess the slot (and win) on a fair wheel is 1/38. Correspondingly, the probability that you lose your dollar is 37/38.

$$E(Y) = (\$34) \times \frac{1}{38} + (-\$1) \times \frac{37}{38} = -\$.0789 \tag{9.20}$$

As you can see, for every dollar you bet, over the long haul you can expect to lose nearly eight cents. Not in your best interest. In another example, Trosset (2009) has presented a detailed description of another popular game of chance, craps. He calculated the probability of a player winning in a fair game of craps to be .4929, close to 50/50, but once again, not in your favor. While we are not opposed to gambling, we would urge you to think of it as entertainment rather than a way to make money. In passing, we should point out that insurance underwriters use the notion of expected value to set rates in a way that "assures" the company that it will make a profit over the long term.

Now that we have defined *expected value*, think back to our definition of the variance as the average squared deviation from the mean. We will now use the notion of expected value to define the variance of a random variable.

DEFINING THE VARIANCE OF A RANDOM VARIABLE USING EXPECTED VALUE

Let's consider once again a random variable, Y, with a known probability distribution $P(Y)$. In Chapter 3, we defined the variance as:

$$\sigma^2 = \frac{\sum_{i=1}^{n}(Y_i - \mu)^2}{n} \tag{9.21}$$

Given that the variance is the average of the squared deviations from the mean, μ, we can use the definition of expected value to derive the variance, given the probability distribution $P(Y)$. That is:

$$\sigma^2 = E\left[(Y-\mu)^2\right] = [Y_1 - E(Y)]^2 \times P(Y_1) + \dots + [Y_k - E(Y)]^2 \times P(Y_k)$$

$$= \sum_{j=1}^{k}[Y_j - E(Y)]^2 \times P(Y_j) \tag{9.22}$$

Just to make the point clear, for a discrete random variable with known probability distribution $P(Y)$, we can define its mean ($E(Y)$) and its variance ($E[Y-E(Y)]^2$). Summing it up, if we know the probability distribution of a random variable, or we are willing to assume it, we know the mean and variance of the random variable, and hence, the standard deviation of the random variable. Thus, we can make predictions about where the values should center and how spread out they should be. If the random variable Y is a continuous variable, then we would need to modify Equations 9.18 and 9.22, replacing the summation operator Σ with the integration symbol, $\int$, and employ the calculus, which is beyond the scope of this book.

For a binomial random variable, it can be shown that var(Y)=npq. Recall our experiment of tossing a fair coin four times where we defined a random variable as the number of Hs in the four tosses. The expected value of this random variable would be $E(Y)=n\times p=4\times.5=2$, suggesting that we would expect two Hs in four tosses. The variance of the random variable would be var(Y)=$n\times p\times q = 4\times.5\times.5=1$, and the standard deviation of the random variable would be the square root of the variance, or 1. If we turn to the experiment where we rolled the die four times, the expected value should be smaller than it was in the coin tossing experiment, because the probability of getting a 2 when rolling a die is less than the probability of getting an H when tossing a coin, so the expected number of 2s should be less. In fact, $E(Y)=n\times p = 4\times(1/6)=.6666667$. The variance in the number of 2s would be var(Y)=$n\times p\times q =.5555556$, which shows that there would be less variability in the number of 2s in replications of the second experiment than in the number of Hs in replications of the first.

THE BINOMIAL DISTRIBUTION WITH R

With R, it is quite a simple task to derive the probabilities for the values of binomial random variables. Let's look at the examples in this chapter (tossing a fair coin four times, rolling a fair die four times, and tossing a fair coin 12 times) using R. For each of these examples, we will follow the same process. First, we will define a variable (vector) with the number of possible successes (r). Then we will use the **dbinom( )** function to find the probability for each of the possible values of r. Last, we will find the expected value and the variance. In the case of the 12 tosses of a fair coin, we will show you how to find the probability that the number of Hs observed will be less than or equal to 2 or greater than or equal to 10, results relatively far away from our expectation of 6.

Four Tosses of a Fair Coin

First, consider a script to look at the binomial distribution for four tosses of a fair coin.

```
# Script 9.3 - Using R to look at Four Flips of a
# Fair Coin
# Define the number of trials/flips
n <- 4
# Define the vector of possible values, from
# largest to smallest
num.success <- n:0
num.success
```

```
# Define the probability of a success
p <- 1/2
prob.success <- dbinom(num.success, n, p)
# Provide names for num.success
names(prob.success) <- num.success
prob.success
# Find the expected value
EV <- sum(num.success*prob.success)
EV
# Find the variance
VAR <- sum(((num.success-EV)^2)*prob.success)
VAR
```

Here are selected results:

```
> num.success
[1] 4 3 2 1 0
> prob.success <- dbinom(num.success,n,p)
> prob.success
     4      3      2      1      0
0.0625 0.2500 0.3750 0.2500 0.0625
> #Find the expected value
> EV <- sum(num.success*prob.success)
> EV
[1] 2
> # Find the variance
> VAR <- sum(((num.success-EV)**2)*prob.success)
> VAR
[1] 1
```

You may wish to compare these probability results to those in Table 9.2. You may also want to note that the expected value of 2 and variance of 1 matches what we had calculated by hand in the last section.

Four Rolls of a Fair Die

Now let's look at four rolls of a fair die, where we count the number of 2s observed in the four rolls.

```
# The Die
# Define the number of rolls
n <- 4
```

```
# Define the vector of possible values, from high to low
num.success <- n:0
num.success
# Define the probability of a success
p <- 1/6
prob.success <- dbinom(num.success, n, p)
prob.success
names(prob.success) <- num.success
# Find the expected value
EV <- sum(num.success*prob.success)
EV
#Find the variance
VAR <- sum(((num.success-EV)^2)*prob.success)
VAR
```

Selected results are:

```
> num.success
[1] 4 3 2 1 0
> prob.success <- dbinom(num.success,n,p)
> prob.success
        4         3         2         1         0
0.0007716 0.0154320 0.1157407 0.3858024 0.4822530
> #Find the expected value
> EV <- sum(num.success*prob.success)
> EV
[1] 0.6666667
> # Find the variance
> VAR <- sum(((num.success-EV)^2)*prob.success)
> VAR
[1] 0.5555556
```

These probability results look rather similar to those in Table 9.4, as they should, and again the expected value and variance match what was presented in the last section.

Twelve Tosses of a Fair Coin

Now, let's look at the 12 tosses of a fair coin. Recall that we were interested in finding the probability that the number of Hs observed was 0, 1, 2, 10, 11, or 12. We translated this statement into $P(Y \leq 2) + P(Y \geq 10)$. How could we find the answer with R? Building on what we have just done, we will define a vector/variable of the values 0 through 12. We will then use the **dbinom( )** function in R to find the probability of each of the 13 possible outcomes, after which we will sum the appropriate values. (In the vector, prob.success, the probabilities for $r=0$, 1, and 2, respectively, are in positions 1, 2, and 3.)

```
# Script 9.4 - Twelve Tosses of a Fair Coin
# Define the number of trials
n <- 12
# Define the probability of a success
p <- .5
# Define the vector of possible values
num.success <- 0:12
# Find the probability of each outcome
prob.success <- dbinom(num.success,n,p)
# Finding the sum of the three lower values
# (0, 1, & 2)
ple2 <- sum(prob.success[1:3])
# Finding the sum of the three largest values
# (10, 11, & 12)
pge10 <- sum(prob.success[11:13])
prob <- ple2 + pge10
prob
# An alternative way, using the pbinom function
prob1 <- pbinom(2, 12, 0.5, lower.tail = TRUE) +
  pbinom(10-1, 12, 0.5, lower.tail = FALSE)
prob1
```

According to the results that appear in the R console,

```
> prob
[1] 0.03857422
> prob1
[1] 0.03857422
```

Once again, the result from R is very close to the one obtained in our hand calculation. The difference here can be attributed to rounding differences as R is using the same formula that we used. If we had used R to arrive at the result through simulation, then the accuracy would also have depended on the number of simulated experiments. At this point, we are ready to present a very important concept, the relationship between probability distributions, area, and probabilities.

PROBABILITY AND AREA

Let's depict the probability distribution for four tosses of a fair coin (see Table 9.2) in a graphic format. The possible values of the random variable are 0, 1, 2, 3, and 4. Rather than plot the number of cases having each value on the vertical axis, we are going to represent the probability of each outcome on the vertical axis. In addition, we have added some lines to the figure. The results of our efforts are displayed in Figure 9.1. Looking carefully at Figure 9.1, you will note that the histogram is composed of 16 rectangles. If we think of the area within the histogram, we might say that it equals 16 units. However, if we define the total area within the histogram as being equal to 1.0, then each of the rectangles has an area of 1/16 and we can equate area with probability. For example, consider P(num.success$\geq$3). Given that we are working with a discrete random variable, we will make a slight correction and assert that P(num.success$\geq$3) is the same as P(num.success$>$2.5). Looking at Figure 9.1, you can see that five of the 16 rectangles are located above (to the right of) 2.5. Thus, we can see graphically that P(num.success$>$2.5) is equal to 5/16.

For most of the remainder of this book, we will be concerned with continuous probability distributions rather than discrete ones. Continuous probability distributions will be graphically represented by the smooth curve of the density distribution, as opposed to the discrete bars of a histogram. Instead of thinking about "area within the histogram," we will be thinking in terms of "area under the curve." In the next section, we will give a very brief introduction to the "distributions in our future" and more fully explain what we mean by area under the curve.

SOME CONTINUOUS PROBABILITY DISTRIBUTIONS

As we have suggested, inferential statistics involve making inferences about populations based on sample data; probability will be an indispensable tool in this process. The probability distributions which we will find useful include the z-distribution, the t-distribution, the χ^2-distribution (read "chi-squared"), and the F-distribution. Arguably, the z-distribution, also known as the unit-normal distribution, is the most important of these; it is the topic of the next chapter.

Before we move on, we should explain what we mean by "area under the curve." The curve to which we are referring is the smooth line of the density distribution. If we want to find the probability associated with obtaining a value greater than some specified value, say a, we find the proportion of the area under the curve that is beyond a. In Figure 9.2, we have displayed

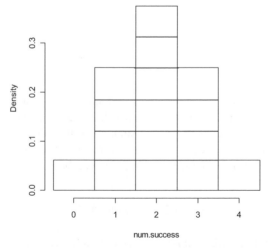

FIGURE 9.1   Depicting the probability distribution of four tosses of a fair coin as a histogram.

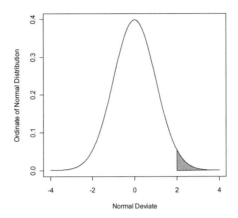

FIGURE 9.2   Depicting $P(z > 2.0)$ as a shaded area under the normal probability density function.

the density distribution for the z-distribution. Although in theory the possible values of this random variable go from $-\infty$ to $+\infty$, realistically nearly all of the values will be between $+3$ and -3. Suppose we are interested in $P(z > 2.0)$. As before, we define the entire area under the density function as being equal to 1. In addition, we have shaded the area under the curve that falls above 2.0. Those of you who have taken a course or two in calculus may recall that we could find this area using integration, which is the analog of addition as employed in the case of a discrete distribution.

CHAPTER SUMMARY

In this chapter, we have introduced the idea of a random variable and shown how some of the basic definitions of probability introduced in Chapter 8 can be used to build an understanding of the probability distribution of a random variable. We have focused in particular on a discrete random variable, a binomial random variable, which is based on the notion of counting the number of successes in a number of trials. Toward the very end of the chapter, we introduced you to the notion of a continuous random variable and very briefly mentioned four of the probability distributions that we will be using during much of the remainder of this book.

Key Terms

Bernoulli trial
Binomial coefficients
Binomial distribution
Binomial expansion
Expected value

Pascal's Triangle
Probability distribution
Random variable
Sampling distribution

REFERENCES

Trosset, M. W. (2009). *An introduction to statistical inference and its applications with R*. Boca Raton, FL: CRC Press.

PRACTICE QUESTIONS

For questions 1 through 8, suppose you have four children in a reading group (Larry, Cindy, Sherona, and Pablo) and you randomly pick one child to lead the discussion in the group each day of a 5-day week. Furthermore, we define the outcome of each day's selection to be binary, Pablo leads the discussion or he doesn't.

1. The number of times Pablo leads the discussion in a week would be the:

    a. probability distribution for this experiment
    b. probability of an outcome
    c. constant in this experiment
    d. random variable in this experiment.

2. The probability that Pablo leads the discussion all five days in a week is the:

    a. expected value
    b. probability distribution
    c. probability of a simple event
    d. random variable.

3. If we could replicate this experiment many, many times, the average number of times that Pablo leads the discussion in a week would be the:

    a. expected value
    b. probability distribution
    c. probability of an outcome
    d. random variable.

4. If we found the probability of Pablo leading the discussion zero times, one time, two times, three times, four times, and five times, the set of six probabilities would be the:

    a. expected value
    b. probability distribution
    c. probability of an outcome
    d. random variable.

5. Monday's selection of a discussion leader could be considered a:

    a. binomial experiment
    b. Bernoulli trial
    c. neither binomial experiment nor a Bernoulli trial.

6. The selections of discussion leaders for the week constitute a:

    a. binomial experiment
    b. Bernoulli trial
    c. neither binomial experiment nor a Bernoulli trial.

7. What is the probability that Pablo would be selected all 5 days of the week?

    a. .0000000000.

   b. .0009765625.
   c. .0039065500.
   d. .2500000000.

8. What is the expected number of times that Pablo would be selected?

   a. 0.00.
   b. 1.00.
   c. 1.25.
   d. 2.50.

EXERCISES

9.1. Let Y be a random variable having the following probability distribution:

Y	0	1	2	3	4	5	6
$P(Y)$	.05	.10	.10	.20	.30	.15	.10

Determine the following probabilities:
a. $P(Y \leq 1)$
b. $P(Y > 2)$
c. $P(Y > -1)$
d. $P(2 < Y < 6)$
e. $P(Y = 4)$
d. $P(Y < 1)$.

9.2. Suppose that you are employed by a life insurance company and that you sell a $20,000 whole-life policy for an annual premium of $600. The actuarial tables indicate that the probability of death during the next year for a client similar to yours in age, gender, etc. is .01. What is the insurance company's expected first-year profit for a policy of this type?

9.3. Imagine that you have a biased coin, weighted such that the probability of obtaining a heads is .25. Using the binomial expansion, generate the probability distribution for eight tosses of the coin. What is the probability of observing seven or eight heads? Verify your results with R.

10

The Normal Distribution

INTRODUCTION

The normal probability distribution should need no introduction. Some of you may already know it as the "bell-shaped curve." Actually, the normal probability distribution is a family of distributions; the members of the family can differ in mean and standard deviation, but all have their shape in common. That is, they are similar in shape in the same sense that two triangles are similar in geometry, up to a point. As it turns out, it is extremely difficult to determine by visualization whether a distribution is normal or not. Indeed, some normal distributions appear "tall and skinny," while others appear "wide and flat." However, as we will highlight, they all share certain characteristics. To illustrate our point, consider some "typical" normal distributions depicted in Figure 10.1. The three distributions have different means and standard deviations, making them appear different. However, these distributions are all normal distributions. Normal distributions are all unimodal and symmetric, sharing in common their basis in the density function for the normal probability distribution, which we will describe soon.

Our knowledge of the normal probability distribution is due to the contributions of many mathematicians. Extending the work of Jacob Bernoulli, Abraham De Moivre published the second edition of *The Doctrine of Chances; or a Method of Calculating the Probabilities in Events in Play* in 1738. In this edition appeared the first English translation in which the density distribution of the normal probability distribution was described (Seneta, 1997). This work was further advanced by Pierre Simon Laplace (Grattan-Guinness, 1997) and Carl Friedrich Gauss (Stigler, 1986). As is so often the case in history, the normal distribution is sometimes referred to as the "Gaussian distribution," ignoring the contributions of the earlier mathematicians.

THE NORMAL PROBABILITY DISTRIBUTION AND ITS IMPORTANCE

As noted above, the normal probability distribution is a family of distributions, linked together by the density function for normal distributions:

$$F(y) = \frac{1}{\sqrt{2\pi\sigma^2}} \; e^{-\frac{1}{2}\frac{(y-\mu)^2}{\sigma^2}} \tag{10.1}$$

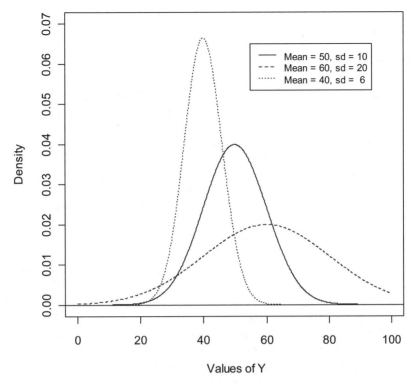

FIGURE 10.1   Three normal distributions with different means and standard deviations.

At first glance, this appears to be a formidable and strange expression. Let's break it down into small steps. First, think of it simply as a mathematical function such as those you encountered in your first algebra course. The specific result of the equation is a function of the variable Y. Looking at the right side of the equation, we see the numbers 1 and 2, where the 2 appears in the denominator with π and σ^2, all under the square root sign. Hopefully, you should have no fear of 1 and 2. We also recall that σ^2 is the variance. The symbol π refers to the mathematical constant, the ratio of the circumference to the diameter of a circle, approximately 3.1416. Just to the right, you see the letter e. Aside from being the fifth letter of our alphabet, e is another mathematical constant, approximately 2.718. You may have learned that it is the base of natural logarithms. Actually it can be defined as:

$$e = \lim_{n \to \infty}\left(1 + \frac{1}{1!} + \frac{1}{2!} + \frac{1}{3!} + \frac{1}{4!} + \dots + \frac{1}{n!}\right) \tag{10.2}$$

Now, we note that e is being raised to a power, albeit a rather complex one. We see the fraction ½ with a minus sign, followed by $(y - \mu)^2/\sigma^2$. Of course, we recall that μ is the symbol for the mean. Putting it together, we see that everything in Equation 10.1 is known, except for the values of y, μ, and σ. Thus, for every combination of the population parameters μ and σ that we might specify, we could run through values of y and evaluate the function. If we were to plot $F(y)$ as a function of y, we would obtain a normal distribution that would be centered at whatever value of μ we specified. Furthermore, it would have a standard deviation equal to σ. For example, if we specified that μ equaled 50 and that σ equaled 10, we would obtain the normal curve that is depicted in

Figure 10.1. If we were to specify different values for μ and σ, respectively, we would obtain a different normal curve, located at a different center, with a different amount of spread.

The Importance of the Normal Distribution

One can argue that the normal probability distribution is the most important probability distribution in statistics. To begin, there are many variables that have distributions that closely resemble normal distributions. For example, if you were to collect a large number of measurements on a random sample from the population—measurements of height, weight, intelligence, mechanical aptitude, etc.—you would see that their frequency distributions appear to be very similar to a normal distribution. (Actually, the introduction of "fast food" has resulted in a tendency for weight to now be positively skewed.) Historically, Adolphe Quetelet was one of the first to apply statistics to social phenomena (Stigler, 1986, 1997). Several of his contributions include the concept of the "average man" ("*l'homme moyen*") and the idea that natural variables tend to follow a normal distribution. In a book published in 1846, he showed that measures of the heights of conscripts in the French army and measures of the chest girths of Scottish soldiers were distributed essentially as normal distributions. He also demonstrated the relationship between the binomial ($p = .5$) and normal distribution, showing the close correspondence when the number of trials was large ($n = 999$). For a more contemporary example, check out http://www.youtube.com/watch?v=AUSKTk9ENzg. This short video shows that investment portfolio returns seem to follow a normal distribution, suggesting that "timing the market" may be futile!

As just noted, Quetelet demonstrated the similarity between the binomial distribution and the normal distribution. Indeed, the normal probability distribution can be used to derive probabilities for other probability distributions, though this is not as valuable as it was before computers. However, it is still worth noting. In Figure 10.2, we show the relationship between the binomial distribution for $n = 4$, 8, 12, and 16 trials and the corresponding normal distributions. In each of the charts, the "solid" circles depict the densities for the binomial distributions, and the solid "lines" depict the densities for the appropriate normal distributions. The normal distributions were derived from material presented in Chapter 9, where we noted that, for a binomial random variable Y, $E(Y) = np$ and var(Y) = npq. As you can see in Figure 10.2, with only four trials, there are some differences between the binomial distribution and the normal distribution. With 12 or 16 trials, however, the two probability distributions, one discrete and the other continuous, are virtually identical. We provide a numeric example later in this chapter.

There are two other reasons that support the argument for the central importance of the normal distribution in statistics. As we have already noted, many natural variables tend to be normally distributed. In addition, many sample statistics tend to be normally distributed. Specifically, sample means tend to follow a normal probability distribution, even if the population of measurements does not. That is, the normal probability distribution provides a good model for the sampling distribution of many of the statistics that we will use. We will elaborate on this point later in the chapter. Finally, the normal distribution is central to the study of statistics as many of the mathematical derivations invoke the assumption of normally distributed variables. However, we do not elaborate on this aspect as this book is applied in focus.

Some Characteristics of Normal Distributions

As we suggested earlier in this chapter, normal distributions may differ in terms of their means and standard deviations, but they all share some common attributes. As we noted earlier, substituting different values for μ and σ into Equation 10.1 would yield curves that were literally

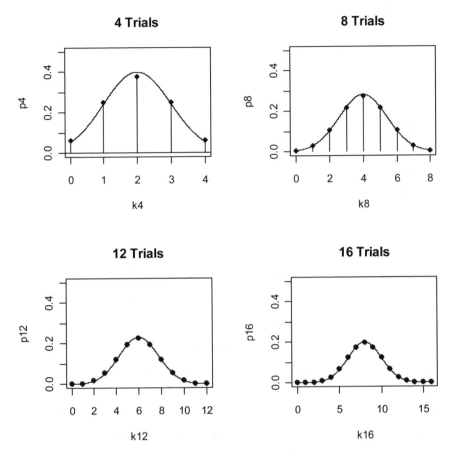

FIGURE 10.2   The correspondence between the binomial distribution and the normal distribution for 4, 8, 12, and 16 trials.

different: located at different centers and having different standard deviations. Let's look at Figure 10.3; the horizontal axis is labeled with values from –4 to +4.

The curve represents the density of the normal distribution with $\mu = 0$ and $\sigma = 1.0$. Look at the two vertical lines that are located above –1 and +1 on the horizontal axis. If you look carefully, you will note that they intersect the curve at the points of inflection. Think of the curve as the "profile" of a mountain. If you were to start climbing from the "trail head" at –4, you would experience the mountain becoming steeper and steeper as you proceeded. However, when you got to the point above –1 (one standard deviation below the mean), you might note that the climb would start to become easier as the mountain began to level off. That point is called the point of inflection. If you were to proceed over the summit and down the other side, as you began the descent, you would feel that the trail was becoming steeper and steeper, until you got to the point above +1, one standard deviation above the mean. Then the trail would seem to level out as you approached the bottom. This point is the other point of inflection. All normal distributions, regardless of mean and variance, have their points of inflection one standard deviation below and above the mean.

More importantly, regardless of the specific mean and variance, all normal distributions share the same amount of area between standard deviations. We have noted the approximate

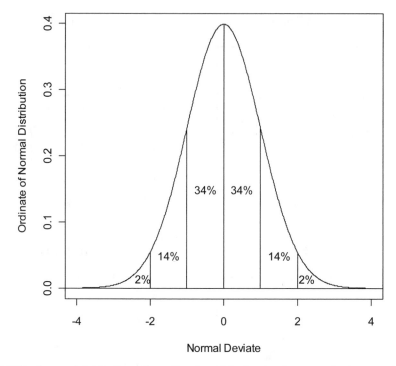

FIGURE 10.3   A normal distribution with $\mu = 0$ and $\sigma = 1.0$, showing the approximate amount of area between standard deviations.

values in Figure 10.3. For all normal distributions, there is approximately 34% of the area between the mean and one standard deviation away from the mean. Between one and two standard deviations from the mean, on either side, is approximately 14% of the area. In each tail, more than two standard deviations from the mean, is the final 2%. Again, remember that if we define the entire area under the curve as being equal to 1.0, we can equate area and probability. Putting this together, if it were not for the constant relationship between area and standard deviations, to find the area under a curve, we would need a separate probability table for each of the different normal distributions. However, because of this property, we can convert any normal distribution to a normal distribution with $\mu = 0$ and $\sigma = 1.0$ (the unit-normal distribution) and use the same table of probabilities for all normal distributions.

Transforming any Normal Distribution to the Unit-Normal Distribution

Earlier in the book (Chapter 5), we talked about locating scores within a distribution of scores. We described two different types of references: percentile ranks scores and what some people call standard scores. In the discussion of standard scores, we presented the z-transformation. We now repeat that presentation of the transformation. In doing so, we give a summary of Tables 5.2, 5.3, and 5.4 in Table 10.1, and then show a generalization of the transformation graphically. As you recall, we started with a contrived, simple set of numbers—the integers 1 through 5, inclusive. We noted that the variance of these five values was equal to 2. These values are presented in Table 10.1 in which we also calculate the mean and the variance of the five scores, considering them as a population of values.

Table 10.1 Calculating the mean and variance of a set of numbers, and then calculating the mean and variance of different multiples of the original numbers

Y	$(Y-\mu)$	$(Y-\mu)^2$	$2Y$	$(2Y-\mu_{2Y})$	$(2Y-\mu_{2Y})^2$	$3Y$	$(3Y-\mu_{3Y})$	$(3Y-\mu_{3Y})^2$
5	2	4	10	4	16	15	6	36
4	1	1	8	2	4	12	3	9
3	0	0	6	0	0	9	0	0
2	−1	1	4	−2	4	6	−3	9
1	−2	4	2	−4	16	3	−6	36
	$\mu = 3$	$\Sigma = 10$		$\mu = 6$	$\Sigma = 40$		$\mu = 9$	$\Sigma = 90$
		$\sigma^2 = 2$			$\sigma^2 = 8$			$\sigma^2 = 18$

Working with the original numbers, we find that $\sigma_Y^2 = 2$. Next, we multiplied the original values of Y by 2, creating a new variable $(2Y)$ having values of 10, 8, 6, 4, and 2. When we calculated the variance of the new random variable, we found that $\sigma_{2Y}^2 = 8$. Finally, we multiplied the original values by 3, creating a new random variable $(3Y)$. When we found the variance of $3Y$, we found that $\sigma_{3Y}^2 = 18$. Remember the pattern? Think for a moment … What do you think the variance of $4Y$ might be?

Perhaps we can refresh your memory. When we multiplied by 2, the variance was increased by a factor of 4. When we multiplied by 3, the variance was increased by a factor of 9. It would appear that when we multiply a variable by a constant, the variance of the new variable is the "constant squared" times the old variance. Thus, we would predict that the variance of $4Y$ should be 32. Let's put this together in a more formal fashion. When you add a constant to a random variable Y:

$$E(Y+c) = E(Y)+c$$
and
$$\text{var}(Y+c) = \text{var}(Y)$$

(10.3)

When we multiply a constant times a random variable:

$$E(cY) = c \times E(Y)$$
and
$$\text{var}(cY) = c^2 \times \text{var}(Y)$$

(10.4)

With this information, we can now look at what really happens when we employ the z-transformation that we presented in our discussion of standard scores.

The Mathematics of the z-Transformation

We begin with a random variable Y, which is normally distributed with mean μ and variance σ^2. That is, $Y \sim N(\mu, \sigma^2)$. First, we subtract the mean of Y, μ, from each of the values of Y. By Equation 10.3,

$$E(Y-\mu) = E(Y)-\mu = \mu - \mu = 0$$

(10.5)

Thus, we see that the effect of subtracting μ is to center the distribution of $(Y-\mu)$ at zero. That is:

$$(Y-\mu) \sim N(0, \sigma^2)$$

(10.6)

Now, we will divide each value of $(Y - \mu)$ by σ. Remember that dividing by σ is the same as multiplying by $1/\sigma$. Thus, by Equation 10.4,

$$\frac{(Y-\mu)}{\sigma} \sim N(0,1) \tag{10.7}$$

For those of you feeling mystified by the algebra, the variance specified in Equation 10.6 is σ^2. But when we multiply the random variable $(Y - \mu)$ by $1/\sigma$, the new variance will be $(1/\sigma)^2$ times the old variance, or $\sigma^2 (1/\sigma^2)$, or 1. Graphically, in Figure 10.4, we have depicted what happens when we start with a random variable $Y \sim N(8, 4)$.

The distribution of the original variable Y is depicted in Figure 10.4(a). Immediately to the right, we show the distribution of the variable $(Y - \mu)$ in relation to the original variable. In the lower left panel of Figure 10.4, we show all three distributions Y, $(Y - \mu)$, and $(Y - \mu)/\sigma$. The last stage is called the z- or unit-normal distribution, which is depicted in the last panel of Figure 10.4(d). In the last panel, we have shown as a shaded area $P(z > 2.0)$. It is the z-distribution that is presented in table format in most statistics books. We now turn our attention to Table A.2, in Appendix A. We have formatted the table in a traditional form used in most books. Although z-values can be negative, the table contains only the positive values as the distribution of z is symmetric. The first column contains the values of z, the second column contains the amount of area

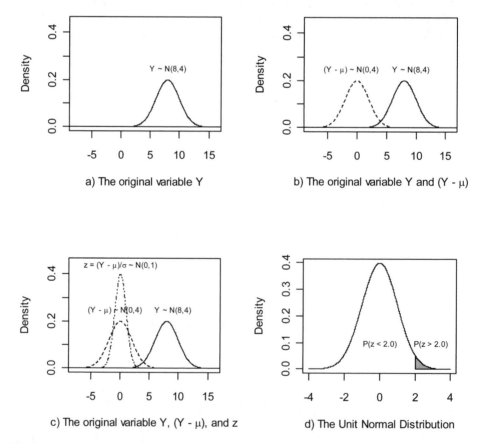

FIGURE 10.4   The three stages of the z-transformation with the unit normal distribution as the end result.

between the mean of z (zero) and the particular z value, the third column contains the amount of area from the particular z value to infinity, and the last column provides the ordinate, or density (height), of the distribution for the particular value of z. The ordinate is not used very often in statistics, but if you look at any of Figures 10.3, 10.4(c), or 10.4(d), you can see that the height of the curve when $z = 0$ appears to be around .40. If you look at the value in Table A.2, when $z = 0$, the ordinate is .39894. Pretty close!

Using the Table for the Unit-Normal Distribution to Find Areas

Now, let's look more closely at Table A.2. Look for the row with $z = 1.0$. Immediately to the right you will see that the "area to mean" is .34134. As we noted in Figure 10.3, approximately 34% of the area lies between ± 1 standard deviation from the mean. Now look for the row with $z = 2.0$. You should see that the "area to mean" is .47725. The difference between that value and .34134 is .13591, or rounded off, approximately .14. Hence, our assertion that approximately 14% of the area lies between 1 and 2 standard deviations from the mean. Furthermore, note in the row with $z = 2.0$, the "area beyond" is .02275. Thus, only about 2% of the area lies beyond either ± 2 standard deviations from the mean.

In order to become more familiar with Table A.2, let's try a few problems. For example, what proportion of the area in a normal distribution falls below a z-score of 2.57? Looking at the table, we find $z = 2.57$ and note that the "area to mean" is .49492. Now, we have to consider the entire part of the distribution that lies below the mean. It is .50000. Thus, the answer is .49492 + .50000, or .99492. We have depicted the solution in Figure 10.5(a). Here's another question: What proportion of the area in a normal distribution falls below a z-score of $-.62$. Looking at $z = .62$ in Table A.2, we see that the "area beyond" is .26763. Because the distribution of z is symmetric, we know that 26.763% of the area falls below $z = -.62$. We have shown this in Figure 10.5(b).

What about something a little different: What proportion of the area in a normal distribution falls between a z-score of 1.14 and a z-score of -1.42? This one is going to take a little more work. Looking at Table A.2, we find $z = 1.14$ and note that the "area to mean" is .37286. Then we find $z = 1.42$ and note that the "area to mean" is .42220. When in doubt, always draw a picture. We have depicted the solution to this problem in Figure 10.5(c). Given the figure, we can see that we should add those two areas together, to get .79506.

Let's try one more problem. What proportion of the area in a normal distribution falls between a z-score of $+.62$ and a z-score of $+1.78$? You may want to look at Figure 10.5(d) as you think about this. Although there are several different ways to find the answer, we think of it as finding the "area to mean" for $z = 1.78$ and then subtracting the "area to mean" for $z = .62$. Thus, the correct answer is .46246 − .23237, or .23009. Now, we'll try a little variation. Given a random variable $Y \sim N(70, 9)$, what proportion of the area falls between 66 and 75? Your first thought may be that we don't have a table for this member of the family of normal distributions, and you are correct. However, we can use the z-transformation to convert the values of 66 and 75 to z-scores and then use the table for the unit-normal distribution.

$$z_{66} = \frac{66 - 70}{3} = -1.33$$

$$\text{(10.8)}$$

and

$$z_{75} = \frac{75 - 70}{3} = 1.67$$

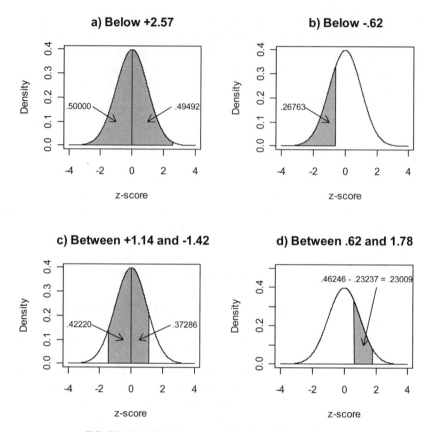

FIGURE 10.5   Finding areas under the unit-normal curve.

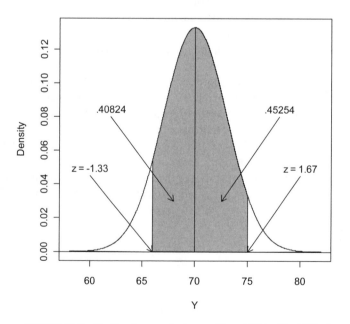

FIGURE 10.6   Finding the area between 66 and 75 for $Y \sim N(70, 9)$.

Now, we have a problem like the one depicted in Figure 10.5(c). We find the two respective values for "area to mean" (.40824 and .45254) and add them together to obtain .86078. We have shown the process in Figure 10.6. Now that you have a sense of how to find values based on Table A.2, let's take a look at how we might use R to solve the same problems.

Using R to Find Areas Under the Normal Curve

R has several variations for many of the mathematical probability distributions. For the normal distribution, they are **dnorm( )**, **pnorm( )**, **qnorm( )**, and **rnorm( )**. Respectively, these functions allow you to find the density/height, the cumulative probability, the quantiles, and to generate random variates. For our purposes now, we will use **pnorm( )**. This function will return the cumulative probability from $-\infty$ to the argument supplied to **pnorm( )**. First, the R script:

```
# Finding the area below z = 2.57
pnorm(2.57)
# Finding the area below z = -.62
pnorm(-.62)
# Finding the area between z = 1.14 and z = -1.42
pnorm(1.14) - pnorm(-1.42)
# Finding the area between z = .62 and z = 1.78
pnorm(1.78) - pnorm(.62)
# Finding the area between 66 and 75 for Y ~ N(70,9)
pnorm(75, mean = 70, sd = 3) - pnorm(66, mean = 70, sd = 3)
```

The corresponding results from the R console are:

```
> # Finding the area below z = 2.57
> pnorm(2.57)
[1] 0.994915
> # Finding the area below z = -.62
> pnorm(-.62)
[1] 0.2676289
> # Finding the area between z = 1.14 and z = -1.42
> pnorm(1.14) - pnorm(-1.42)
[1] 0.795053
> # Finding the area between z = .62 and z = 1.78
> pnorm(1.78) - pnorm(.62)
[1] 0.2300909
> # Finding the area between 66 and 75 for
> # Y ~ N(70,9)
> pnorm(75, mean = 70, sd = 3)
> - pnorm(66, mean = 70, sd = 3)
[1] 0.8609984
```

As you can see, the results are nearly identical to those we obtained using the table. Any differences are the result of our rounding, particularly in the last problem.

Hopefully, you now have an understanding of the unit-normal distribution and how any normal distribution can be converted to the unit-normal distribution by using the z-transformation. You might have obtained a sense that extreme values of z are rather unlikely. In particular, we noted earlier that the area beyond a z-score of 2 is .02275. Thus, we can say that the probability of seeing a z-score more extreme than ± 2 is equal to $2 \times .02275$, or .0455. Thus, if we were randomly sampling from a normal distribution, we might expect to see a value two or more standard deviations from the mean only about one time in 20.

Using the Normal Distribution to Approximate the Binomial Distribution

As we noted earlier in this chapter, the normal distribution can be used to approximate several other probability distributions. Let's take a look at how it can be used to approximate the binomial distribution. You may recall from Chapter 9 that we employed the binomial distribution to find the probability of observing 2 or fewer heads in 12 tosses of a fair coin; the result was .01928. You may also recall that the expected value of a binomial random variable is np, and the variance of a binomial random variable is npq. Thus, in an experiment tossing a fair coin 12 times, we can find the expected value as $12 \times .5 = 6$ and the variance as $12 \times .5 \times .5 = 3$. Thus, the standard deviation is $\sqrt{3} = 1.732$. We now have the information we need to approximate the binomial probability for $P(Y \leq 2)$ with the normal distribution. All we need to do is to convert 2 to a z-score. In doing so, we need to consider that we are using a continuous distribution to approximate a discrete distribution. That is, $P(Y \leq 2)$ for a binomial distribution is logically equivalent to $P(Y \leq 2.5)$ for a continuous distribution. It may help you to recall the difference between nominal limits and real limits that we noted in our presentation of frequency distributions. Thus, we proceed to convert 2.5 to a z-score:

$$z = \frac{Y - \mu}{\sigma} = \frac{2.5 - 6}{1.732} = -2.02 \tag{10.9}$$

We find the area below a z-score of -2.02 to be equal to .0217. The exact binomial probability was .0193. The difference is a mere .0024. Not bad! Let's see how it works with a larger number of trials. For example, let's consider tossing a fair coin 100 times. What is the probability of seeing 45 or fewer heads? First, let's use R to find the binomial probability.

```
# Finding the binomial probability of 45 or fewer
# heads
# in 100 tosses of a fair coin
# Create a vector to hold the values of the
# sampling distribution.
num.success<- 0:100
prob.success <- dbinom(num.success,100,0.5)
prob.le.45 <- sum(prob.success[1:46])
prob.le.45
# Alternative way
pbinom(45, size = 100, prob= 0.5)
```

The results are:

```
> prob.le.45
[1] 0.1841008
> pbinom(45, size = 100, prob= 0.5)
[1] 0.1841008
```

Now, let's use the normal approximation. First, we find $\mu = np = 100 \times .5 = 50$ and $\sigma = \sqrt{npq} = \sqrt{100 \times .5 \times .5} = 5$. Correcting for continuity, we change $P(Y \le 45)$ to $P(Y < 45.5)$ and find the corresponding z-score:

$$z = \frac{Y - \mu}{\sigma} = \frac{45.5 - 50}{5} = -.9 \tag{10.10}$$

We now find the area below a z-score of $-.9$ to be $.1841$. Note, that to four decimal places, the results from the "exact" binomial and the normal approximation are identical!

Earlier in this chapter, we noted that the normal distribution could also be used to describe the sampling distribution of many statistics. In particular, we want to look at the distribution of sample means.

THE NORMAL DISTRIBUTION AND THE SAMPLING DISTRIBUTION OF THE MEAN

In Chapter 9, we noted that the probability distribution for a random variable is called the *sampling distribution* for that random variable. That is, a sampling distribution is a probability distribution for a statistic based on repeated samples. Consider the situation in which we have a population defined as $Y \sim N(\mu, \sigma^2)$. If we were to repeatedly draw many, many random samples of n cases from that population and then calculate the mean of each sample, we would wind up with a large number of sample means. It would be highly unlikely that all of the sample means would be equal to the same value. Rather, each of the sample means would be an estimate of the population mean, μ, but they would be different from one another. In this section, we are going to show you that we have reason to anticipate how the distribution of sample means might look. In our presentation of descriptive statistics, we noted that important characteristics of a distribution are center, spread, and shape. We will address each of the three attributes in turn.

But first, let's enumerate some sampling experiments. Imagine that we have a population consisting of the integers 1, 2, 3, 4, and 5. Imagine that we are going to draw samples of size 2 from this population, with replacement. In the same way that we described the possibilities for tossing a coin, we will list all of the possible samples. The first observation in the sample could be any one of the five values; the second could be any one of the five values as well. Thus, there are 25 different samples that might be obtained. We have listed the 25 different samples in Table 10.2, along with the sample means that would result.

Under the assumption of random sampling, we can assert that each one of the 25 possible samples is equally likely. Now, looking at the sample means, we can see that there is only one of the possibilities that yields a sample mean of 1.0. Similarly, there is only one of the possibilities that yields a sample mean of 5.0. We can continue to examine the simple events and construct the probability distribution for the statistic, the sample mean, as displayed in Table 10.3.

Table 10.2 Possible samples of size 2 from the population (1, 2, 3, 4, and 5) with the sample mean

Sample	Mean	Sample	Mean
1, 1	1.0	3, 4	3.5
1, 2	1.5	3, 5	4.0
1, 3	2.0	4, 1	2.5
1, 4	2.5	4, 2	3.0
1, 5	3.0	4, 3	3.5
2, 1	1.5	4, 4	4.0
2, 2	2.0	4, 5	4.5
2, 3	2.5	5, 1	3.0
2, 4	3.0	5, 2	3.5
2, 5	3.5	5, 3	4.0
3, 1	2.0	5, 4	4.5
3, 2	2.5	5, 5	5.0
3, 3	3.0		

Table 10.3 The sampling distribution of the means from Table 10.2

Mean	Frequency	P(Mean)
1.0	1	.04
1.5	2	.08
2.0	3	.12
2.5	4	.16
3.0	5	.20
3.5	4	.16
4.0	3	.12
4.5	2	.08
5.0	1	.04

We know that, for the population, each of the five values is equally probable. However, we can see in Table 10.3, the sample means are not. Let's use R to simulate our experiment a large number of times. First, we will define the population as the integers 1 through 5 and draw random samples of $n = 1$. We will then repeat the process, drawing random samples of $n = 2$, calculate the mean for each of the random samples, and then look at the distribution of the sample means. Here is the R script for 500,000 random samples:

```
# Simulating the sampling distribution of the mean
# for n = 2
# From the population of 1, 2, 3, 4, and 5.
pop <- 1:5
N <- 500000
stat1 <- numeric(N)
stat2 <- numeric(N)
for (i in 1:N) {
```

```
    sam1 <- sample(pop,1,replace=TRUE)
    stat1[i] <- mean(sam1)
    sam2 <- sample(pop, 2, replace = TRUE)
    stat2[i] <- mean(sam2)
}
par(mfrow=c(1,2))
hist(stat1, prob = TRUE, breaks = seq(-.5, 5.5, 1))
hist(stat2, prob = TRUE, breaks = seq(-.5, 5.5, .5))
par(mfrow = c(1, 1))
# Finding the means and the variances
mean(stat1)
var(stat1)
mean(stat2)
var(stat2)
```

The results are depicted in Figure 10.7.

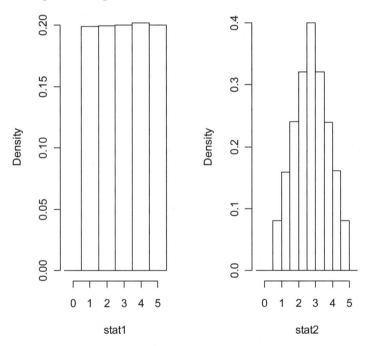

FIGURE 10.7   The distribution of the population (*stat1*) and 500,000 sample means for *n* = 2 (*stat2*).

The histogram of *stat1* is essentially a model of the population of integers 1 through 5, as *stat1* is based on 500,000 samples of size 1. The histogram of *stat2* is the sampling distribution of 500,000 sample means of size 2, drawn from the population. It should be obvious to you that the sampling distribution does not look like the distribution of the population. It is probably not clear to you how they differ. Before we elaborate on that issue, let's repeat the simulation, but this time we will draw samples of $n = 5$. The results are shown in Figure 10.8.

There are several points we would like to make. Earlier in this chapter, we noted that the mean of the integers 1 through 5 was 3, and the variance was 2.0. In our simulation, when the sample size was 2, R generated 500,000 observations (*stat1*) and 500,000 sample means for $n = 2$.

```
> mean(stat1) = 3.00185 and > var(stat1) =  2.001203
> mean(stat2) = 2.99809 and > var(stat2) =  0.999748
```

We can see that the means of both *stat1* and *stat2* are very close to the actual mean, 3.0. On the other hand, we see that the variance of *stat1* is very close to the variance of *Y*, but that the variance of *stat2* is approximately half of the variance of *Y*. When we look at the results for the second simulation in which the sample size was increased to 5, we see:

```
> mean(stat1) = 2.996834 and > var(stat1) = 1.998008
> mean(stat5) = 3.000348 and > var(stat5) = 0.398741
```

Again, the mean and the variance of *stat1* remain quite close to the mean and the variance of the population. However, while the mean of *stat5* remains close to the mean of *Y*, the variance of *stat5* is approximately one-fifth of the variance of *Y*. Do you see the pattern? It appears that the mean of the sample means remains close to the mean of the population, but that the variance of the sample means seems to decrease as the sample size increases. Later in this chapter, we will

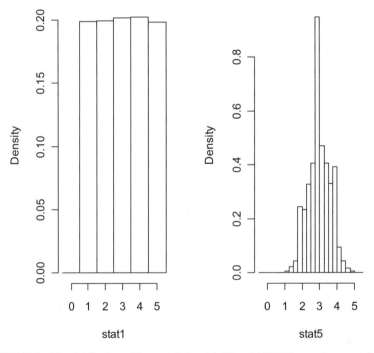

FIGURE 10.8   The distribution of the population (*stat1*) and 500,000 sample means for $n = 5$ (*stat5*).

make a more formal presentation of these points, though we also want to make an observation concerning the shape. Drawing random samples of single observations results in a frequency distribution that is quite similar to the shape of the population. When the sample size is greater than one, however, things appear to change. If you look more carefully at Figure 10.7, you will see that the shape of the distribution of *stat2* is rather triangular. That is, if you visually connect the midpoints of the tops of the bars of the histogram, the lines would be nearly straight going up on the left side and nearly straight going down on the right side. If you were to do that same thing for *stat5* in Figure 10.8, you would see some curvature. Before we elaborate, let's look at some more simulations.

Simulating the Sampling Distribution of the Sample Mean with R

We will consider three different types of populations: normal, uniform (like the numbers 1 through 5), and exponential (positively skewed). For each type of population, we will draw 100,000 random samples of varying sample sizes: 1, 5, 10, and 25. Let's first select a particular normal distribution, one with $\mu = 50$ and $\sigma = 10$. We used an R script that appears in the supplementary materials for this chapter that are on the book website. The descriptive statistics are presented in Table 10.4, and the results are depicted graphically in Figure 10.9, with the expected normal distribution superimposed. Looking at the descriptive statistics in Table 10.4, we note that the mean of the means is very close to 50, regardless of sample size. The standard deviations of the means are also quite close to what would be expected based on the respective sample sizes. Second, the standard deviation of the distribution of sample means appears to decrease with increased sample size. With regard to the pattern of the standard deviations of the means, the standard deviations appear to be equal to the standard deviation of the population divided by the square root of the size of the sample. The "expected standard deviations" in the table are based on this formula, which we present a little later in this chapter. Perhaps most important, the values for skewness and kurtosis suggest that the sampling distribution of the mean is normal when sampling from a normal population, regardless of sample size. These distributions are shown graphically in Figure 10.9 and confirm our impressions based on the values in Table 10.4.

Before we leap to any generalization, let's look at a different type of population—one that is symmetric but not normal. For this purpose, let's look at a population of the integers from 1 to 30. For this population, we can ascertain that $\mu = 15.5$ and $\sigma^2 = 74.9167$. (Can you confirm this? Give it a try.)

We used another R script that is contained on the book website in the supplementary materials for this chapter. The descriptive statistics for the population and the four simulations ($n = 1, 5, 10,$ and 25) are presented in Table 10.5 Again, there are several patterns worth noting. First, the

Table 10.4 The results from simulating the sampling distribution of the mean for a population that is defined as the normal distribution (50, 100), based on 100,000 replications

	Mean	Standard deviation	Expected standard deviation	Skewness	Kurtosis
Population	50.000	10.000	NA	.000	.000
n = 1	49.992	9.960	10.000	.002	−.005
n = 5	50.006	4.464	4.472	.004	.012
n = 10	49.999	3.153	3.162	−.003	−.001
n = 25	49.993	1.996	2.000	.008	−.011

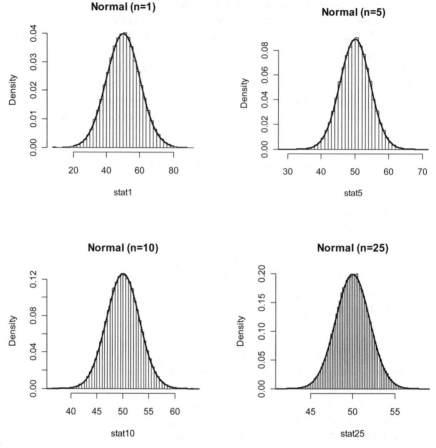

FIGURE 10.9   The sampling distribution of 100,000 means from a normal population with μ = 50 and σ^2 = 100 for n = 1, 5, 10, and 25, with the "expected" normal distribution superimposed.

means of the 100,000 random samples remains very close to the mean of the population, 15.500. Second, the values of the standard deviations of the means are quite close to what we would expect. Third, and perhaps most important, look at the changes in skewness and kurtosis. The values for skewness seem to stay close to zero as the uniform distribution is symmetric. However, as sample size increases, the values for kurtosis seem to converge on the value that characterizes a normal distribution (0).

Table 10.5 The results from simulating the sampling distribution of the mean for a population that is defined as the discrete uniform distribution (1, 30), based on 100,000 replications

	Mean	*Standard deviation*	*Expected standard deviation*	*Skewness*	*Kurtosis*
Population	*15.500*	*8.655*	*NA*	*.000*	*−1.200*
$n = 1$	15.533	8.685	8.655	−.006	−1.207
$n = 5$	15.463	3.870	3.871	.003	−.229
$n = 10$	15.502	2.730	2.737	.018	−.131
$n = 25$	15.502	1.729	1.731	−.006	−.035

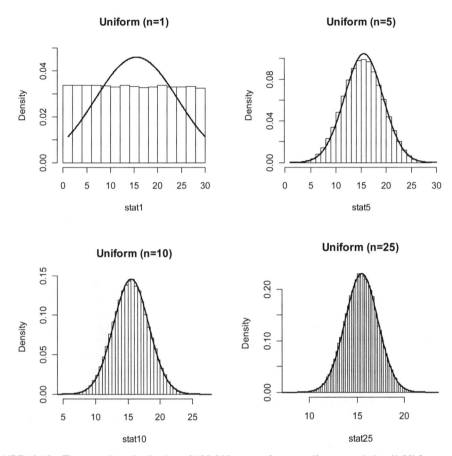

FIGURE 10.10   The sampling distribution of 100,000 means from a uniform population (1:30) for n = 1, 5, 10, and 25.

Just to be careful, let's look at a simulation in which the population is not symmetric. We generated a population from the exponential distribution, with rate equal to 2.0. We began by generating 10,000 random variates from an exponential distribution; the mean of the variates was .49644, and the standard deviation was .49573. We then followed the same pattern of generating 100,000 samples of size 1, 5, 10, and 25. The R script for this simulation is given on the book website. The descriptive statistics are presented in Table 10.6, and the distributions are shown in Figure 10.11.

Table 10.6 The results from simulating the sampling distribution of the mean for a population that is defined as the exponential distribution (rate = 2), based on 100,000 replications

	Mean	*Standard deviation*	*Expected standard deviation*	*Skewness*	*Kurtosis*
Population	*.496*	*.496*	*NA*	*1.981*	*5.918*
$n = 1$	.498	.496	.496	1.979	5.935
$n = 5$	.496	.221	.222	.865	1.130
$n = 10$	.497	.157	.157	.609	.559
$n = 25$	.496	.099	.099	.392	.227

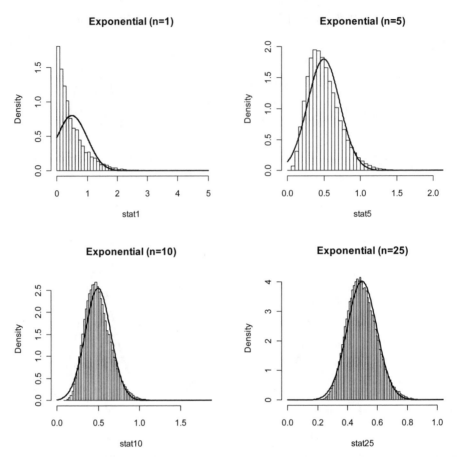

FIGURE 10.11   The sampling distribution of 100,000 means from an exponential population (rate = 2) for n = 1, 5, 10, and 25.

As you can see, the pattern for the exponential distribution is similar to that for both the normal and the uniform distributions. The means of the sample means stay very close to the mean of the population, and the standard deviations of the sample means follow the predicted pattern very closely. Most important, both the values of skewness and kurtosis decrease as the sample size increases. With a sample size of 25, they are still a bit away from 0 and 0, respectively, but they are getting close. Indeed, if you look at the histogram for n = 25 in Figure 10.11 without the expected normal distribution superimposed, we believe that you would be hard pressed to detect the non-normality. These ideas are generally packaged together in what is called the Central Limit Theorem.

THE CENTRAL LIMIT THEOREM

The Central Limit Theorem is one of the most fundamental ideas underlying applied statistics based on classic distribution theory. Many of the techniques that we will present in this book are based on the assumption of a normal population. The results of our simulations suggest that the expected value of the sample mean is equal to the population mean and that the variance of the distribution of sample means follows a predictable pattern; it is equal to the variance of the population divided by the sample size. This appeared to be true, no matter what the shape of the population. The important part of the Central Limit Theorem is that the distribution of sample means will tend to be normal with sufficient sample size, even if the population is non-normal. Furthermore, assuming the random variable $Y \sim N(\mu, \sigma^2)$, we can state the following:

$$E(\bar{Y}) = E(Y) = \mu$$

$$\text{var}(\bar{Y}) = \frac{\text{var}(Y)}{n} \tag{10.11}$$

We have observed these two assertions in our simulations, and they are proved in Technical Note 10.1.

The Implications

To put these ideas together in a specific situation, let's go back and consider a population such as was described earlier in this chapter. Consider a random variable Y that is normally distributed with a population mean (μ) of 50 and a standard deviation of 10 ($\sigma^2 = 100$). Imagine a situation in which we were going to draw random samples of 25 values from such a population. What might we expect in such a situation? If you have no idea, then you have not been reading this chapter very carefully! First, we know that we would expect the mean of any sample to be some-

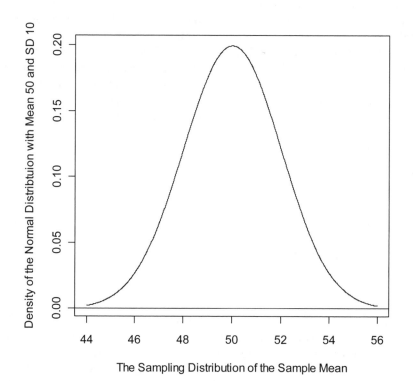

The Sampling Distribution of the Sample Mean

FIGURE 10.12   The sampling distribution of the mean for $\mu = 50$, $\sigma^2 = 100$, and $n = 25$.

where around 50. Furthermore, we know that on repeated samplings, we would not expect all the sample means to have the same value; we would expect some variability due to random sampling. But how much? Given what we have presented, we would expect the variability in the sample means to be approximately 100/25, or about 4. Thus, the standard deviation of the distribution of sample means should be about 2. The standard error of the distribution of sample means is also known as the *standard error of the mean*. Given the results of our simulations, we might also reasonably expect the distribution of the sample of sample means to be fairly close to a normal distribution. We have depicted our "expectation" in Figure 10.12. As you can see in the figure, 46 is two standard deviations below the mean and 54 is two standard deviations above the mean. Based on what we have seen earlier in this chapter, we would expect to see means more extreme than that a little less than 5% of the time, not a very likely outcome. Thus, if we were to draw a random sample of 25 cases from a population which we assumed was normally distributed with a population mean (μ) of 50 and a standard deviation of 10 ($\sigma^2 = 100$), and the mean of that sample was say, 56.2, we might have reason to wonder what went wrong. One of three things might have happened: (1) we have seen a very unusual event, (2) our sampling procedure was flawed, or (3) perhaps the mean of the population from which we drew the sample is not equal to 50!

CHAPTER SUMMARY

In this chapter, we have focused on the probability distribution of a continuous random variable, the normal probability distribution. There are other continuous probability distributions that we will encounter in later chapters; we began with the normal distribution as it is so central to the study and understanding of applied statistics. Not only are many real-world variables approximately normally distributed, but the normal distribution can also be used to approximate the probability distributions of other random variables. Furthermore, the assumption of normally distributed random variables is fundamental in the derivation of many statistical formulae. From our applied perspective, the major reason for having a sound understanding of the normal probability distribution is linked to the Central Limit Theorem. The means of random samples drawn from non-normally distributed populations may be expected to be normally distributed if the sample size is sufficiently large. Furthermore, if the random variable Y is assumed to be

$$Y \sim N\left(\mu, \sigma^2\right) \tag{10.12}$$

then we can assert that

$$\bar{Y} \sim N\left(\mu, \frac{\sigma^2}{n}\right) \tag{10.13}$$

Even when we do not know the distribution of Y

$$Y \sim \text{??}\left(\mu, \sigma^2\right) \tag{10.14}$$

the result in Equation 10.13 still pertains with a sufficiently large sample size. As a rule of thumb, a sample size of 25 or more will yield a distribution of sample means that is approximately normally distributed, at least "close enough for government work." We are aware of only one type of distribution for which this does not hold, the Cauchy distribution, which is defined as the ratio of two independent normal deviates. The Central Limit Theorem does not apply to variables that follow a Cauchy distribution. On the other hand, let it be said that in our accumulated experience, we have never seen such a variable in practice.

Key Terms

Abraham De Moivre	Normal probability distribution
Adolphe Quetelet	Standard error of the mean
Carl Friedrich Gauss	Unit-normal distribution
Central Limit Theorem	z-Transformation

REFERENCES

Grattan-Guinness, I. (1997). Pierre Simon Laplace. In N. L. Johnson & S. Kotz (Eds.), *Leading personalities in statistical sciences: From the seventeen century to the present* (pp. 15–20). New York: John Wiley.

Seneta, E. (1997). Abraham De Moivre. In N. L. Johnson & S. Kotz (Eds.), *Leading personalities in statistical sciences: From the seventeen century to the present* (pp. 26–27). New York: John Wiley.

Stigler, S. M. (1986). *The history of statistics: The measurement of uncertainty before 1900* (pp. 139–158). Cambridge, MA: Belnap Press/Harvard University Press.

Stigler, S. M. (1997). Lambert Adolphe Jacques Quetelet. In N. L. Johnson & S. Kotz (Eds.), *Leading personalities in statistical sciences: From the seventeen century to the present* (pp. 64–66). New York: John Wiley.

PRACTICE QUESTIONS

1. The normal distribution can be described as:

    a. asymmetric and bimodal
    b. asymmetric and unimodal
    c. symmetric and bimodal
    d. symmetric and unimodal.

2. Consider randomly selecting a single value from a normal distribution with a mean of 0 and a variance of 1. Which of the following selections is more probable?

    a. A value between 0 and 1.
    b. A value between 1 and 2.
    c. A value between 2 and 3.
    d. A value greater than 3.

3. Consider randomly selecting a single value from a unit normal distribution. Which of the following selections would be most rare?

    a. A value between −1 and +1.
    b. A value between −2 and +2.
    c. A value between 0 and +.5.
    d. A value between −5 and −3.

4. Suppose you had a normal distribution with a mean of 47.189 and a standard deviation of 4.323. If you subtracted 47.189 from each value and then divided the resulting values by 4.323, you would get a new distribution, which could be described as:

    a. normal, with a mean of 1 and standard deviation of 0

b.   normal, with a mean of 0 and standard deviation of 1
c.   maybe not normal but with a mean of 1 and standard deviation of 0
d.   maybe not normal but with a mean of 0 and standard deviation of 1.

5.   Suppose you repeatedly sample from a negatively skewed distribution samples of size 30, compute the means of those samples, and then look at the distribution of those sample means. The distribution of sample means would be expected to be:

a.   negatively skewed
b.   positively skewed
c.   normal
d.   uniform.

6.   Suppose you repeatedly sample from a negatively skewed distribution samples of size 25, compute the means of those samples, and then look at the distribution of those sample means. If the variance in the population is 250, the expected variance in the distribution of sample means is:

a.   0
b.   10
c.   25
d.   250.

7.   If the distribution of sample means has the same variance as the population distribution the sample size is:

a.   0
b.   1
c.   10
d.   100
e.   cannot be determined.

EXERCISES

10.1. Using the unit-normal probability distribution, find the following areas:

a.   between 0 and 2.00
b.   between -1.69 and 0
c.   beyond -2.15
d.   between -1.50 and .33
e.   between 1.12 and 1.98.

10.2. It is known that the scores on a test designed to measure public school teachers' attitudes toward "mainstreaming" are normally distributed with a mean of 65 and a standard deviation of 11.5. If one teacher is drawn at random, what is the probability that his/her score will be above 80?

10.3. Assume that Y is a binomial random variable with $n = 12$ and $p = .60$. Use the binomial expansion and the normal approximation to the binomial distribution to find the following:

a. $P(Y \leq 2)$
b. $P(Y = 10)$.

TECHNICAL NOTES

Technical Note 10.1: The Expected Value and the Variance of the Sample Mean

The Givens

THE POPULATION

$$Y \sim N(\mu, \sigma^2) \rightarrow E(Y) = \mu, \text{ var}(Y) = \sigma^2 \qquad (10.15)$$

THE RULES OF EXPECTATION ALGEBRA

$$E(Y + c) = E(Y) + c \qquad (10.16)$$

$$E(cY) = c \times E(Y) \qquad (10.17)$$

$$E(X + Y) = E(X) + E(Y) \qquad (10.18)$$

THE RULES OF VARIANCE

$$\text{var}(Y + c) = \text{var}(Y) \qquad (10.19)$$

$$\text{var}(cY) = c^2 \times \text{var}(Y) \qquad (10.20)$$

$$\text{var}(X + Y) = \text{var}(X) + \text{var}(Y) + 2\text{cov}(X, Y) \qquad (10.21)$$

$$\text{var}(X - Y) = \text{var}(X) + \text{var}(Y) - 2\text{cov}(X, Y) \qquad (10.22)$$

If X and Y are independent:

$$\text{var}(X + Y) = \text{var}(X) + \text{var}(Y) \qquad (10.23)$$

Definition of $\bar{Y}$ and the Proofs

Given a sample of n independent observations from the population, Y:

$$\text{var}(X + Y) = \text{var}(X) + \text{var}(Y) \qquad (10.24)$$

EXPECTED VALUE OF THE MEAN

$$\bar{Y} = \frac{Y_1}{n} + \frac{Y_2}{n} + \frac{Y_3}{n} + \cdots + \frac{Y_n}{n} \tag{10.25}$$

$$E\left(\bar{Y}\right) = E\left(\frac{Y_1}{n} + \frac{Y_2}{n} + \frac{Y_3}{n} + \cdots + \frac{Y_n}{n}\right) \tag{10.26}$$

$$E\left(\bar{Y}\right) = E\left(\frac{Y_1}{n}\right) + E\left(\frac{Y_2}{n}\right) + E\left(\frac{Y_3}{n}\right) + \cdots + E\left(\frac{Y_n}{n}\right) \tag{10.27}$$

$$E\left(\bar{Y}\right) = \frac{1}{n}E\left(Y_1\right) + \frac{1}{n}E\left(Y_2\right) + \frac{1}{n}E\left(Y_3\right) + \cdots + \frac{1}{n}E\left(Y_n\right) \tag{10.28}$$

$$E\left(\bar{Y}\right) = \frac{1}{n}\mu + \frac{1}{n}\mu + \frac{1}{n}\mu + \cdots + \frac{1}{n}\mu \tag{10.29}$$

$$E\left(\bar{Y}\right) = \frac{1}{n}\left(n\mu\right) = \mu \tag{10.30}$$

THE VARIANCE OF THE MEAN FOR INDEPENDENT, IDENTICALLY DISTRIBUTED RANDOM VARIABLES

$$\mathrm{var}\left(\bar{Y}\right) = \mathrm{var}\left(\frac{Y_1}{n} + \frac{Y_2}{n} + \frac{Y_3}{n} + \cdots + \frac{Y_n}{n}\right) \tag{10.31}$$

$$\mathrm{var}\left(\bar{Y}\right) = \mathrm{var}\left(\frac{Y_1}{n}\right) + \mathrm{var}\left(\frac{Y_2}{n}\right) + \mathrm{var}\left(\frac{Y_3}{n}\right) + \cdots + \mathrm{var}\left(\frac{Y_n}{n}\right) \tag{10.32}$$

$$\mathrm{var}\left(\bar{Y}\right) = \frac{1}{n^2}\mathrm{var}\left(Y_1\right) + \frac{1}{n^2}\mathrm{var}\left(Y_2\right) + \frac{1}{n^2}\mathrm{var}\left(Y_3\right) + \cdots + \frac{1}{n^2}\mathrm{var}\left(Y_n\right) \tag{10.33}$$

$$\mathrm{var}\left(\bar{Y}\right) = \frac{1}{n^2}\sigma^2 + \frac{1}{n^2}\sigma^2 + \frac{1}{n^2}\sigma^2 + \cdots + \frac{1}{n^2}\sigma^2 \tag{10.34}$$

$$\mathrm{var}\left(\bar{Y}\right) = \frac{1}{n^2}\left(n\sigma^2\right) = \frac{\sigma^2}{n} \tag{10.35}$$

Part IV
STATISTICAL INFERENCE

Let's take a moment to review what we have covered so far. After a brief introduction, we discussed ways to describe various attributes of quantitative data. We identified several characteristics that could be used to differentiate one set of data from another and provided several different measures of each characteristic. In addition to providing information about the number of data points (sample size), we considered location or central tendency (mode, median, and mean), dispersion or spread (range, interquartile range, average deviation, variance, and standard deviation), and shape (skewness and kurtosis).

Then, after providing some basic definitions and examples related to probability, we introduced the concepts of probability distributions and sampling distributions, suggesting that sampling distributions are rather like abstract sets of scores in that they, too, may be described in terms of location, spread, and shape. We then focused on the sampling distribution of the mean, presenting the Central Limit Theorem (CLT). Based on the CLT, we showed you that, if you are willing to make some assumptions about the population from which the sample is drawn, you can reasonably predict what sample means might be expected to be observed when drawing random samples.

We are now ready to put these ideas together in a way that will allow us to make reasonable inferences about a population based on what we observe in a sample presumably drawn from that population. The remainder of the book will be concerned with *inferential statistics*, organized in a different way than most applied statistics texts.

Most texts present the different techniques in the order in which they were developed historically. They begin with what we describe as the "classical tests," most of which assume randomly drawn samples from normally distributed populations. These tests examine hypotheses about population parameters (μ, σ^2, π, ρ, δ, etc.) and belong to the family of *parametric statistics*. Most of these procedures were developed in the late 1800s and into the 1900s. Generally, these procedures involve working with the data to calculate a value (*test statistic*) which, if the assumptions are met, may be compared to values obtained from one of several different mathematical probability distributions. We have already considered the unit-normal distribution (z). Other distributions that we will introduce and employ are the t-distribution, the χ^2-distribution, and the F-distribution.

In the early to mid-1900s, statisticians began to raise questions about the validity of the normality assumption, particularly in situations with relatively small samples. Subsequently, a number of statistical procedures were developed to apply in these situations. Most of these procedures convert the scores to ranks and then work with the ranks, which consist of consecutive integers. The probability distributions of the different test statistics were derived by systematically enumerating the different ways (permutations) in which the ranks could be arranged. These procedures do not involve estimates of parameters, but rather compare the cumulative frequency distributions to assess whether two (or more) sets of scores might have come from the same population. These procedures are known as *non-parametric statistics*.

The third phase in the development of statistics was made possible by the availability of high-speed, inexpensive computing. Indeed, the computer used by the first author in writing this text has more computing capacity than Northwestern University did in the 1960s when he was a graduate student. These newer procedures may be considered a blending of parametric and non-parametric statistics, in that they may be concerned with using the data to test hypotheses about parameters; but rather than invoking normal distribution theory, they actually generate different arrangements of the data to simulate the probability distribution of the test statistics. These newer procedures are described with a variety of different labels: *bootstrapping procedures*, *resampling procedures*, *randomization tests*, and *permutation tests*. Following Good (2006), we will refer to this set of procedures as *resampling methods*.

Most introductory texts in applied statistics first present the parametric procedures, running through a variety of different contexts. Then they recycle through the same contexts, presenting the non-parametric procedures that might be applied when the assumptions for the parametric procedures may not apply. Very few current texts even introduce the newer resampling procedures. This book is different, in that we cycle through the various contexts only once. For example, when considering a particular context (e.g., comparing two groups with respect to location), we first present the traditional "two-sample *t*-test," followed by the non-parametric alternative (Mann–Whitney *U*-test), in turn followed by approaches that rely on randomization procedures. With the flexibility of the randomization procedures, we need not confine ourselves to questions about means. We can also pose questions about other estimators of location (medians, trimmed means, etc.).

In Chapter 11 we describe the traditional way to draw inferences about populations based on samples, employing methods based on the distributional assumption of a normal population. This approach is sometimes called *hypothesis testing*. In Chapter 11 we focus on questions regarding location which involve only one sample. We openly admit that this approach is not without its critics; it is seen as controversial by many. We consider some of the criticisms and identify some of the limitations of hypothesis testing, noting two types of error that may result, and we integrate these ideas with the concept of *statistical power*.

In Chapters 12 and 13 we describe other procedures appropriate for questions involving only one sample. These procedures address questions concerning location, spread, shape, and association (correlation and regression) with quantitative data, and distribution and association with count data. We also introduce the concept of confidence intervals as an alternative to hypothesis testing. Furthermore, we present an alternative to traditional confidence intervals based on distribution theory, describing procedures that result in *bootstrapped confidence intervals*. These procedures are computer intensive and were not possible 100 years ago. Given current computer capabilities, however, we suggest these procedures may be preferable to those involving classical distributional assumptions.

In Chapter 14, similar to in Chapter 11, we focus on questions regarding location (means, medians, and proportions), presenting methods for dealing with two samples rather than just one sample. After presenting the classical methods based on distributional assumptions (*parametric statistics*), we describe alternative methods that were developed to apply to situations in which the assumptions for parametric statistics could not be justified (*nonparametric statistics*). Last, we show how the same questions can be addressed with resampling methods. We describe procedures for both *independent* and *dependent samples*. Samples are considered independent when the two sets of scores have been collected on two totally independent sets of cases (e.g., females and males); samples are considered dependent when the two sets of scores have been collected on cases that have been matched on some variable or one set of cases that has been measured on more than one occasion (e.g., pretest and post-test).

In Chapter 15, we continue our presentation of methods appropriate for two samples, discussing both independent and dependent samples as appropriate. We extend the system beyond location, dealing with other characteristics such as variances, correlations, and regression coefficients. Again, we show how resampling methods can be used to replace the classical approaches.

In Chapter 16, we extend the context to consider methods for dealing with questions about three or more groups (*k*-sample procedures). These methods will be concerned primarily with issues of location. We first describe the traditional approach, analysis-of-variance (ANOVA), which focuses on means. Next, we consider the non-parametric alternative, the Kruskal–Wallis test. Finally, we show how resampling procedures can be employed. Also, in Chapter 16, we briefly present methods for focusing on other attributes in the *k*-sample context: proportions and variances. The material in Chapter 16 is extended in Chapter 17 to deal with procedures that allow us to examine specific questions within the *k*-sample context (e.g., Does group 1 differ from group 4?).

Finally, in Chapter 18, we look beyond the material presented in this text. We provide conceptual descriptions of multiple regression, analysis-of-variance for two or more independent variables, multivariate analysis-of-variance, linear discriminant function analysis, canonical correlation/variate analysis, log-linear analysis and logistic regression, cluster analysis, structural equations, and multi-level analyses.

11

The Basics of Statistical Inference:
Tests of Location

INTRODUCTION

Earlier in the book, we devoted considerable time and space to a discussion of ways to describe sets of scores in meaningful ways. At that point, our focus was only on the scores at hand; they constituted our population of interest and the quantities derived could be considered parameters. Specifically, we described ways to summarize and present information about location, spread, and shape, with size (n) being a given. Such activity is often described as *descriptive statistics*. Exploring/describing data is an essential activity. Through exploration and description, we may see patterns and relationships and begin to wonder if these patterns might be generalized beyond the data at hand. That is, we question whether what we are seeing in our data might also be seen in other sets of data. These questions are often called *research questions*. Based on our knowledge and/or previous experience, we might formulate tentative answers to our questions. These tentative answers are called *research hypotheses*. As the term implies, these answers are hypothetical and need to be supported or refuted based on new data. To address this concern, we engage in *inferential statistics*.

In order to test the validity of our research hypotheses, we no longer consider the scores to be a population, but rather a sample of scores from some population of interest to us. We can use the same computational processes/routines to derive descriptions of the scores in the sample, but the results are no longer considered to be parameter values. Rather, they are sample statistics that estimate, under an assumption of random sampling, the parameters of the population. In this chapter, we begin to examine procedures that can help us draw appropriate conclusions (inferences) about the state of matters in the population, based on the information available in our sample. The information available in the sample can be represented in several different ways to provide useful information about the population. Within the set of techniques of inferential statistics, we will show you how to use null hypothesis testing, confidence intervals, and effect sizes to support or refute your hypotheses. Up front, we need to tell you that inferential statistics is *not* the path to Eternal Truth, not even with a lower-case "t." Rather, we think of it as "quantified common sense."

Inferential statistics is important as it is characterized by prediction, rather than description. It just so happens that the first author wrote this sentence (4 February 2010) on the day after a major upset in college basketball. If he were to try to impress you with his extensive knowledge of college basketball by telling you that the University of South Florida Bulls (visiting and unranked) beat the Georgetown University Hoyas (home and ranked No. 7) by 8 points, would you be impressed? Hopefully not, as you might correctly surmise that he simply read it in the morning newspaper. However, what if he had predicted the 8-point win on 2 February 2010? You might first consider that he got lucky, but if he could accurately predict other games before they were played, you might soon begin to believe that he knows something about college basketball. So, too, it is with science. Showing the ability to predict accurately is more impressive than simply describing after the fact. In this chapter, we will focus on the technique of making predictions and then examining their plausibility by looking at data. This process is called *null-hypothesis testing*.

AN OVERVIEW OF THE PROCESS OF NULL HYPOTHESIS TESTING

One of the earliest documented instances of the application of inferential logic appeared in a book by Graunt (1662). Graunt was a haberdasher in London with an interest in statistical records. Based on his examination of parish death records, he reasoned (predicted?) that it was highly unlikely that anyone currently "sound of mind" would die in the asylum at Bedlam, as only one in approximately 1,500 had done so. According to Cowles (2001), an even more systematic approach was evidenced in the work of John Arbuthnot, a Scottish physician who was also interested in mathematics. He examined data on christenings over an 82-year span (1629–1710), noting that in every one of those years there were more christenings of males than females. Applying the logic of the binomial theorem, he concluded that this inequality was so extreme that it could not likely have occurred by chance. Rather, he attributed it to Divine Providence.

The process of hypothesis testing is much more fully developed than it was in the times of Graunt and Arbuthnot. The conventional approach currently employed by most researchers represents a blended process, combining recommendations made by Fisher (1959, 1960) which built on earlier work by Neyman and Pearson (1928). For a detailed presentation of the process, we refer you to Chow (1996). We also want to acknowledge that hypothesis testing has been criticized by many scholars on many different issues. Indeed, an edited work by Harlow, Mulaik, and Steiger (1997) detailed many of the issues with a balanced perspective, presenting arguments both in favor and against the practice of hypothesis testing. We will not summarize the various positions here; suffice it to say that we believe that, when used properly, hypothesis testing is one of several useful techniques for assisting us in making reasonable inferences about populations based on sample data.

Before we launch into a more detailed presentation of hypothesis testing, let us point out that the method is based on the logic of "proof-by-counterexample." That is, suppose that we assert a mathematical equality:

$$2 \times x = x^2 \tag{11.1}$$

As a "proof" of our assertion, we offer the following. Let $x = 2$; therefore,

$$2 \times 2 = 2^2$$
$$4 = 4 \tag{11.2}$$

But, you are skeptical. So we come back with another example. Let $x = 0$; therefore,

$$2 \times 0 = 0^2$$
$$0 = 0$$

(11.3)

Now do you believe? Of course not! Our point is simple; as soon as you find another value of x such as 1, 3, 4, etc. for which the equality does not hold, you have disproved it. Such is the logic that is central to hypothesis testing, as you will soon see.

A CLOSER LOOK AT THE PROCESS

Null hypothesis testing is a process that involves several different stages. Most scientific endeavors begin with observation, namely examining the data and looking for possible patterns. The data we examine may come from any of several different sources. For example, a classroom teacher may notice that the children who raise their hands to answer questions tend to sit toward the front of the room. Healthcare workers may have noted that the group of patients being treated for lung cancer seems to contain a higher percentage of cigarette smokers than does the general population. In examining the research literature, you might notice that many studies find a relationship between two variables, but many others do not. This might lead to a controversy within a discipline. Taking a closer look, you might note that the studies finding a relationship were all carried out using samples of White participants, while the studies not finding the relationship were completed with primarily African American participants. For example, studies in which the relationship between "school belonging" and achievement is examined may find a strong positive relationship when looking at data collected on White students; studies looking at the same relationship in the African American population may find considerably weaker relationships. In each of these situations, questions might emerge. We call these questions *research questions*.

In the first case, we might ask whether children who tend to volunteer responses to teacher questions tend to sit toward the front of the room. In the second case, we might ask whether smoking cigarettes is related to lung cancer. And, in the third situation, we might wonder if the presence or absence of the relationship is possibly related to ethnicity. Generally, research questions are concerned with possible relationships between independent variables and dependent variables. For example, we might be concerned with the population of fourth-grade children who indicate that they would like to be astronauts when they grow up. Specifically, we might wonder if they are different in regard to intelligence than the general population of fourth-grade children. Though it might not be immediately apparent, we are asking a rather specific question about a possible relationship between career aspirations and intelligence.

The more carefully worded are your research questions, the more likely you are to be successful in your research efforts. Fraenkel and Wallen (1996) stipulated four aspects of good research questions. First, it should be possible to examine the question within reasonable limits of time, effort, and money. Second, the question should be stated in such a way that informed people in the field would agree on the meanings of the key terms used. Third, the question should be one that is worthy of the resources to be used as the answer will add to the knowledge base. Last, the question should be stated in such a way that the investigation can be completed without psychological or physical harm to the participants.

Once we are satisfied with the wording of our research question, we provide a tentative answer to the question. In this example, we have several possibilities. For example, we might conjecture that fourth-graders who aspire to be astronauts would tend to be *more* intelligent than the general population of fourth-graders. On the other hand, we might believe that these aspiring astronauts would tend to be *less* intelligent than the general population. A third possibility would be to say that they are *different* in intelligence than the general population. Any of these three possibilities would be considered a *research hypothesis*. Your research hypothesis can be derived from your personal experience, previous research, or some combination of the two. Within our three possible hypotheses, we have actually framed two different types of hypotheses, one-tailed and two-tailed hypotheses. The first two possibilities suggest a direction (i.e., *more* or *less*) and are called one-tailed, or directional, hypotheses. The third alternative does not specify direction. Rather, it simply asserts that the two groups are *different*. This possibility is called a two-tailed, or non-directional, hypothesis. At another level, all three possibilities share a common characteristic in that they are inexact hypotheses. An example of an exact hypothesis would be to assert a specific value as an alternative. For more information about exact alternate hypotheses, see Hays (1963).

Regarding the characteristic of intelligence, let's assume that we will be working with a standardized test of intelligence. Most of these tests are nationally standardized to have a population mean (μ) of 100, with a standard deviation (σ) of 15. An example of an exact hypothesis would be to specify the actual magnitude of the difference. For example, we might specify that the mean intelligence of fourth-grade aspiring astronauts is equal to 107, rather than the national mean of 100. However, in the social sciences, nearly all hypothesis testing involves inexact hypotheses.

Suppose we believe that aspiring astronauts are different than the general population in average intelligence. First, we translate our research hypothesis into a statistical hypothesis:

$$\mu \neq 100 \tag{11.4}$$

At this point, we state a contradiction to our research hypothesis and label it as our *null hypothesis*:

$$\mu = 100 \tag{11.5}$$

Note that our two statements are mutually exclusive and exhaustive. That is, they cannot both be true at the same time, and one of them must be true.

Imagine that we want to set up a process to compare the two hypotheses to assess which one of them is more believable. This process is called *hypothesis testing*; it is based on proof by counterexample. We suspect that aspiring astronauts are different in intelligence, but we negate what we believe by assuming the null hypothesis. Then we collect data on a random sample of aspiring astronauts, measuring them on the attribute of intelligence. We hope that our data will indicate that the mean intelligence of our sample is so far from 100 that it would be unreasonable to think that the mean intelligence of the population of aspiring astronauts is equal to 100.

How does this work? To compare our two hypotheses, we need to establish some conditions. For the purpose of testing our research hypothesis, we will assume that the null hypothesis ($\mu = 100$) is true. Furthermore, we will draw a random sample of 25 participants from the population of aspiring astronauts. Based on concepts we have already discussed earlier in this book, we know that if the null hypothesis is true, the sample mean of these 25 cases should be an estimate of 100, the mean of the population. We also know that we can expect some sampling error. That is, we would not expect the sample mean to be exactly equal to 100. Sometimes it will be less than 100 and sometimes it will be greater than 100. Once in a while, it might be very far from 100, but most of the time it should be close. We know this because we know that the distribution of the sample mean is normal in shape.

What else do we know? We know that the variable of intelligence is normally distributed in the population, with a standard deviation (σ) of 15. Given our earlier discussion, we would expect the standard deviation of the distribution of sample means (standard error of the mean), with a sample size of 25, to be equal to $15/\sqrt{25}$, or $15/5 = 3$. We know that, even if the true mean is 100, sometimes we are going to obtain a sample mean rather far away from 100. Therefore, we need to set up a decision rule to guide us. In lay terms, we must draw a line in the sand where we can decide which of the two competing hypotheses is more reasonable. To accomplish this, we must first decide what constitutes a reasonable risk. Based on the Central Limit Theorem, we know something about the sampling distribution of the mean and we can use this knowledge to develop a reasonable expectation of what we may observe. Based on that range of "reasonable expecta-tion," we might deduce that is unlikely that we would obtain/see data that are very far from our expectation based on the distribution under the null hypothesis. That is, when we obtain a sample mean far away from 100, we are going to reject the null hypothesis as untenable, and favor the alternative. This level of reasonable risk is called the *level of significance.* "Significance" comes from the same root as "sign," as in "indicative of something"; in this case indicative of a non-ran-dom event. In the social sciences, it is usually set at a probability of .05. Why .05? Salsburg (2001) cited an article by Fisher that appeared in the *Proceedings of the Society for Psychical Research* in 1929. He quoted from the article, "It is a common practice to judge a result significant, if it is of such a magnitude that it would have been produced by chance not more frequently than once in twenty trials." Of course, one-twentieth is .05. If that does not convince you, try this "experi-ment." Take a coin and flip it 10 times with a friend; you flip it 10 times and then have your friend flip it 10 times. Every time you flip it, say "heads" no matter what the outcome. After you have "observed" four heads in a row ($p = .0625$), we predict that your friend is going to start to have a "funny look" on his/her face. Flip it for a fifth trial and "observe" another head ($p = .03125$). Somewhere around four, five, or six heads in a row ($p = .016$), we predict that your friend is going to ask if you are telling the truth. (When the first author does this experiment in front of a class, he uses a two-headed coin so that he can always tell the truth!) Thus, a probability of .05 would seem to be a reasonable standard for doubt. Using this standard of .05, we will reject the null hypothesis when the sample data that we actually obtained, or sample data that are less consistent with the null hypothesis than the data we actually obtained, would have occurred by chance, given the null hypothesis, with a probability of .05 or less. Thus, the statistical analysis reduces the data to a probability, the probability of obtaining data as discrepant or more discrepant than observed, given the validity of the null hypothesis. This probability is called a *p*-value and can be interpreted as a conditional probability: $(P(\text{Observed data}|H_0) + P(\text{More discrepant data}|H_0))$.

THE EXAMPLE IN DETAIL

Let's take a more detailed look at the example in the previous section. We have decided to test the null hypothesis (H_0) against the alternate hypothesis (H_1) as follows:

$$H_0: \mu = 100$$
$$H_1: \mu \neq 100$$

(11.6)

As noted earlier, if we assume that the variable (IQ) is normally distributed in the population, we can be quite certain that the distribution of sample means drawn from such a population will be normally distributed. We have assumed (based on the null hypothesis) that $\mu = 100$, we know that the variance of the population (σ^2) is 225, and we specified that we would work with a sample size (n) of 25 aspiring fourth-grade astronauts. If we specify that our level of significance will be .05, then we can set up our decision rule as shown in Figure 11.1.

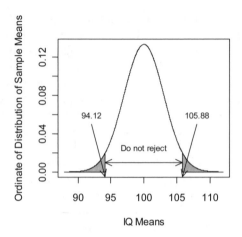

FIGURE 11.1   The decision rule for testing the hypotheses in the astronaut example.

According to the null hypothesis, we would expect the mean of our sample of 25 cases to be an estimate of $\mu = 100$. Given that we have specified a level of significance of .05 and that we are assuming the sample means to be normally distributed, we obtain the values of ± 1.96 from the table of the unit-normal (z) distribution. These values "cut off" an area of .025 in each tail of the z-distribution. We also know that the distribution of sample means should have a standard deviation of 3 points (i.e., the standard error of the mean). Thus, we add and subtract 3×1.96 from the mean of 100, obtaining the values of 105.88 and 94.12, respectively. To sum it up, if we are drawing a random sample of 25 cases from the population specified, only 5% of the time would we expect to see a sample mean so far from 100 (less than 94.12 or greater than 105.88) by chance. (The region defined by ≤ 94.12 or ≥ 105.88 is called the *region of rejection*.) Thus, were we to observe a sample mean so far from 100, we might reasonably suspect that the mean of the population from which we sampled was not equal to 100.

Given this decision rule, if we were to observe a sample mean of 106, we would reject the null hypothesis in favor of the alternate hypothesis. If we observed a sample mean of 92, we would also reject the null hypothesis. If we were to observe the sample mean to be 105, we would not reject the null hypothesis. This event raises two issues. First, one might think that 106 and 105 are not that different. So what's the deal here? Granted, they are not that different, but in the procedures for inferential statistics, one has to draw the line somewhere. Thus, we take the position that the results of a statistical analysis are either significant or they are not. Stated simply, "close" counts in the game of horseshoes but not in statistics. As we will see shortly, if you thought that 105 was a big difference from 100, then you should have planned the study differently so that you would be able to reject the null hypothesis with an observed difference of 5 points.

Second, we must consider what it means not to reject the null hypothesis. This question has been controversial among statisticians. One school of thought says that we "accept the null hypothesis." Another school of thought notes that we "fail to reject the null hypothesis." Although you may not see much difference between the two statements, the first seems to say that we believe the null hypothesis is true. The second is more consistent with the notion that we did not have sufficient evidence to reject the null hypothesis; it has survived this test. This notion is consistent with Popper's (1959) concept of "yet to be disconfirmed," and it is the position that we support. However, we would admit openly that, in the event of a non-rejection of H_0, we may act as though it is true, at least until proven otherwise.

One- vs. Two-Tailed Hypotheses

Earlier in this chapter, we mentioned that there is a difference between one-tailed and two-tailed hypotheses. That is, one could state the research hypothesis as a "difference" without specifying the direction, or one could state the expected direction of the difference in the research hypothesis. In the example that we presented for the aspiring astronauts, we conducted a two-tailed statistical test as you can see in Equation 11.6. However, imagine that we actually believed that aspiring astronauts are more intelligent than the general population. In that instance, we would have formed our set of hypotheses a little differently. For example, see Equation 11.7:

$$H_0: \mu \leq 100$$
$$H_1: \mu > 100$$

(11.7)

On the other hand, you might really believe that aspiring astronauts are less intelligent than the general population. In that case, you would state your hypotheses as in Equation 11.8:

$$H_0: \mu \geq 100$$
$$H_1: \mu < 100$$

(11.8)

These two possibilities have been depicted in Figure 11.2.

If we are going to test a one-tailed alternative at the .05 level, the z-score that cuts off 5% of the area in one tail of a normal distribution is 1.645. Thus, we would multiply 1.645 by 3, the standard error of the mean, and obtain 4.935. To define the critical area in the upper tail, we would add 100 and 4.935 to obtain 104.935; to define the critical area in the lower tail, we would subtract 4.935 from 100 and obtain 95.065. At this point, we would like to describe some common mistakes that people make in considering the issue of one- versus two-tailed hypotheses.

Some Common Mistakes with One- vs. Two-Tailed Hypotheses

In our previous discussion of the two-tailed situation, we noted that an observed mean of 106 would be sufficient evidence to reject H_0, while an observed mean of 105 would not be sufficient. It is our belief that one should use two-tailed hypotheses in most circumstances, as they are more conservative and allow for the detection of unintended effects in the "wrong" direction. One-tailed tests might be appropriate when there is some compelling reason. However, imagine that

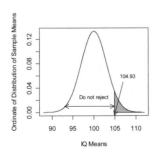

a) For an Upper One-Tailed Alternate

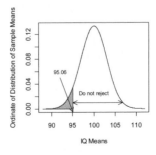

b) For a Lower One-Tailed Alternate

FIGURE 11.2   Setting the regions of rejection for one-tailed hypotheses: (a) for an upper one-tailed alternate; (b) for a lower one-tailed alternate.

we had completed the two-tailed test as before, and we had observed a sample mean of 105. At first glance, we note that we cannot reject H_0, though it would probably not take us long to realize that *had we run a one-tailed test*, our results would have allowed us to reject H_0. Nevertheless, we did *not* run a one-tailed test. We need to keep in mind that hypothesis testing is rather like a game of chance. We specify our hypotheses before we look at our data. Imagine that you had placed a $2 bet on a 100:1 long shot in the last Kentucky Derby. Now, imagine that your horse won. When you go back to the window to collect, you cannot tell the bookie that you bet $1,000. (Well, you can, but bad things might happen to you!) The second mistake that people tend to make is to run a one-tailed hypothesis test in one tail, find that they picked the wrong tail, and then re-run a one-tailed test in the other tail or a two-tailed test. Again, you should not change your hypothesis after looking at the data.

A MORE CONVENTIONAL APPROACH TO HYPOTHESIS TESTING

In our description of the process of hypothesis testing, we have explained how we can derive what might be reasonably expected to be seen in a sample from some population, given some assumptions. The approach we took was intended to explain the underlying logic, and we will use that logic again when we explain some issues—types of decision errors and statistical power—toward the end of this chapter. In this section, we will present a more conventional approach to hypothesis tests, using data from the Early Childhood Longitudinal Study (ECLS) data set of 2,577 cases that accompanies this book. We turn our attention to several of the variables that were assessed at the beginning of kindergarten, in particular the reading, math, and general knowledge measures expressed in McCall T-score units. T-scores are standard scales that are normally distributed with a mean (μ) of 50 and a variance (σ^2) of 100 (see Chapter 5 and Figure 5.5).

To begin, let's take a look at how Asian students perform relative to the general population. For each of the three variables (*reading*, *math*, and *general knowledge*), we will be testing the hypotheses as follows:

$$H_0: \mu = 50$$
$$H_1: \mu \neq 50$$

(11.9)

To obtain the data, we read the *ecls2577.txt* file into a **data.frame** in R. We then drew a random sample of 20 records from the subset of Asian students.

Testing the Hypotheses on Reading

The data for the 20 reading scores were: 65, 28, 49, 70, 87, 52, 50, 73, 68, 52, 74, 41, 50, 58, 57, 30, 70, 66, 53, and 43. (We have included the actual scores in the event that you would like to reproduce our analysis.) The mean of these 20 scores is 56.8. Given that $n = 20$ and $\sigma^2 = 100$, we will test the hypothesis by transforming the data to a z-score and use the .05 level of significance:

$$z_{obs} = \frac{\bar{Y} - \mu}{\left(\sigma / \sqrt{n}\right)} = \frac{56.8 - 50}{\left(10 / \sqrt{20}\right)} = \frac{6.8}{2.236} = 3.04$$

(11.10)

As we are testing a two-tailed hypothesis at the .05 level, the value of z that cuts off .025 in each tail is ±1.96. Given that the z_{obs} is +3.04, we note that we have a value in the region of rejection, so we reject H_0. In testing the hypotheses for math and reading, we will be a little briefer.

Testing the Hypotheses on Math

The math scores for our sample of 20 Asian students were 56, 38, 51, 66, 76, 61, 50, 76, 63, 52, 66, 48, 56, 48, 43, 38, 56, 55, 49, and 47. The mean of these 20 scores is 54.75. Thus,

$$z_{obs} = \frac{\bar{Y} - \mu}{\left(\sigma / \sqrt{n}\right)} = \frac{54.75 - 50}{\left(10 / \sqrt{20}\right)} = \frac{4.75}{2.236} = 2.12 \tag{11.11}$$

Once again, given the critical values of z of ±1.96, we are in the region of rejection and thus should reject the H_0 with respect to math, as we did with reading.

Testing the Hypotheses on General Knowledge

The scores of the 20 Asian students on the general knowledge variable are 63, 42, 39, 46, 71, 42, 38, 46, 64, 48, 71, 53, 49, 45, 46, 34, 43, 51, 44, and 55. The mean of these 20 scores is 49.5. As before,

$$z_{obs} = \frac{\bar{Y} - \mu}{\left(\sigma / \sqrt{n}\right)} = \frac{49.5 - 50}{\left(10 / \sqrt{20}\right)} = \frac{-.5}{2.236} = -.22 \tag{11.12}$$

Unlike the results obtained for the reading and math variables, this time our result falls in the region of non-rejection; there is insufficient evidence to reject H_0.

Summary of the Example of Hypothesis Testing

Considering our three analyses independently, we would tentatively conclude that Asian students seem to come to school better prepared than the general population in both reading and math, but appear to be similar to the general population with regard to general knowledge. Though these decisions are based on our analyses, they are also based on sample data; we do not really know the "truth" in the population. Thus, we need to consider the possibility that our decisions might be wrong, noting particular kinds of errors we might make.

POSSIBLE DECISION ERRORS IN HYPOTHESIS TESTING

The unfortunate reality of the situation is that no matter what decision you make about the tenability of H_0, your decision may be wrong. On the one hand, if you reject H_0 when testing at the .05 level, it may be that the null hypothesis is actually true. That is, you may have obtained one of those "bad" random samples (i.e., non-representative) that you will get 5% of the time. Recall that random samples are simply random samples; we hope they are representative, but we know that any one random sample is not necessarily representative. If this is the case, you will have made a Type I error. On the other hand, you may find that while your data provide insufficient evidence to reject H_0, it may be the case that H_1 is actually true and H_0 is not true. For one reason or another, however, you have been unable to reject H_0. In this case, you will have made a Type II error. The possibilities are depicted in Table 11.1.

Table 11.1 Possible outcomes when testing a null hypothesis against an alternative hypothesis: Type I and Type II errors

		The "truth" in the population	
		H_0 true	H_0 false
Your decision	Reject H_0	Type I error (α)	Good decision ☺
	Do not reject H_0	Good decision ☺	Type II error (β)

The probability of making a Type I error is set at α, which is also called the *level of significance*. The probability of making a Type II error is β. In discussing each of these types of errors and their interrelationship, we will return to the first example in this chapter, the aspiring astronaut example. As you may recall, the process of hypothesis testing consists of a number of steps: specifying H_0, setting the significance level, and examining the distribution of the sample statistic under H_0, which is based on the sample size (n). When you set the level of significance to α, the probability of making a Type I error is whatever you set as α; you have total control over the probability of making a Type I error. If making a Type I error 5% of the time is unacceptable to you, then you can set α at 0.01, knowing that you will make Type I errors about 1% of the time. Note that in making these statements we are assuming you will conduct your tests in an appropriate manner. If you compute things incorrectly or use a test that assumes a random sample when you don't have a random sample the actual Type I error rate may not be equal to α.

Based on the conditions established for testing H_0 in this example, we derived a decision rule as depicted in Figure 11.1. If we were to observe a sample mean between 94.12 and 105.88, we would not reject H_0. However, if the sample mean we observed was either ≤94.12 or ≥105.88, we would reject H_0. If we were to reject H_0, we would have to consider the possibility that we might be making a Type I error.

However, what if we found a sample mean somewhere between 94.12 and 105.88? Although we would not reject H_0, that does not necessarily mean that H_0 is true; we might be making a Type II error. Determining the probability of a Type II error (β) is not quite as simple as determining the probability of a Type I error. To determine the actual value of β, we need to consider several things simultaneously. To take you through the logic of the process, we have constructed Figure 11.3.

There are four panels in Figure 11.3. The first panel (a) is actually a repeat of Figure 11.1; it shows the distribution of the sample mean under the assumption of the null hypothesis, along with the two-tailed decision rule for rejecting H_0. We will reject H_0 if the observed sample mean is ≤94.12 or ≥105.88. When thinking about a Type II error, it is important to understand that two things must happen. First, H_0 must be false, and second, the decision must be not to reject H_0. Let's deal first with H_0 being false. In panel (b), we have removed the distribution under H_0, but we still show the decision rule derived under H_0; it remains in place. A Type II error will occur anytime we fall in the region of non-rejection established under H_0 when, in fact, we are actually drawing our sample from a population with a mean different from that specified in H_0. For now, let's assume μ is not equal to 100; rather it is equal to 104. Thus, H_0 is false. We have depicted this in panel (c). In this specific situation, the probability of a Type II error (β) would be equal to the likelihood of observing a sample mean between 94.12 and 105.88 when sampling from a distribution with a mean of 104. We have shaded that area in panel (d). If you recognize this problem as being similar to those depicted in Figure 10.5(c) and 10.5(d), good for you! To put things in a positive light, we talk about the *power* of a statistical test as being the probability of rejecting a false H_0. Power is defined as follows:

Power $= 1 - \beta.$ (11.13)

We can easily find this probability with some simple statements in R:

```
# Finding beta and power when alpha is .05
s <- 3
mu0 <- 100
mu1 <- 104
lcv05 <- qnorm(.025, mean = mu0, sd = s)
ucv05 <- qnorm(.975, mean = mu0, sd = s)
upper05 <- pnorm(ucv05, mean = mu1, sd = s)
lower05 <- pnorm(lcv05, mean = mu1, sd = s)
beta05 <- upper05 - lower05
beta05
power05 <- 1 - beta05
power05
```

The results are shown below:

```
> beta05
[1] 0.7340542
> power05 <- 1 - beta05
> power05
[1] 0.2659458
```

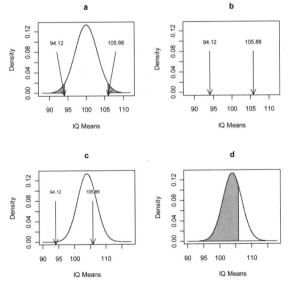

FIGURE 11.3   Type I and Type II errors, finding β.

As you can see, β is equal to .734. That is, in this situation, if the real mean is 104 rather than 100, you have a probability of making a Type II error equal to .734. The corresponding power is .266.

It may not be obvious to you but, in order to find β, we had to specify a particular value of the "true" μ. Actually, that is only one of several factors that affect β and, in turn, power. We now turn our attention to those issues.

FACTORS THAT AFFECT THE VALUES OF β/POWER

Determining the value of β is much more complex than determining α, the level of significance. There are several factors that affect the value of β, some of which you completely control (in an ideal world), one you must consider and may control to some degree, and one over which you have no control. You have total control over the level of significance; it is whatever you decide. In an ideal world, you also should have control over the sample size, but we acknowledge that this world is far from ideal and, at times, you have to work with whatever is available. Another factor is the reliability of the measure of the dependent variable. Last, the magnitude of β is affected by the true value of μ, which you do not know. We now consider each of these issues in turn.

How β is Affected by α

In the example we just worked, we had originally set .05 as the level of significance. In that instance, we found β to be equal to .734, with a corresponding power of .266. Suppose we had decided to set the level of significance at .01. We can use the R script below to find β. First, we determine the decision rule under H_0. Once we have obtained the region of rejection, we can find β and power.

```
# Finding beta when alpha = .01
s <- 3
mu0 <- 100
mu1 <- 104
lcv01 <- qnorm(.005, mean = mu0, sd = s)
ucv01 <- qnorm(.995, mean = mu0, sd = s)
upper01 <- pnorm(ucv01, mean = mu1, sd = s)
lower01 <- pnorm(lcv01, mean = mu1, sd = s)
beta01 <- upper01 - lower01
beta01
power01 <- 1 - beta01
power01
```

The results for $\alpha = .01$ are:

```
> beta01
[1] 0.8929269
```

```
> power01 <- 1 - beta01
> power01
[1] 0.1070731
```

As you can see, when we move from $\alpha = .05$ to $\alpha = .01$ the value of β increases to .893 and power decreases to .107. Let's see what happens if we set α to .10.

```
# Finding beta when alpha = .10
s <- 3
mu0 <- 100
mu1 <- 104
lcv10 <- qnorm(.05, mean = mu0, sd = s)
ucv10 <- qnorm(.95, mean = mu0, sd = s)
upper10 <- pnorm(ucv10, mean = mu1, sd = s)
lower10 <- pnorm(lcv10, mean = mu1, sd = s)
beta10 <- upper10 - lower10
beta10
power10 <- 1-beta10
power10
```

The results for $\alpha = .10$ are:

```
> beta10
[1] 0.6208476
> power10 <- 1 - beta10
> power10
[1] 0.3791524
```

If we increase α to .10, then the value of β decreases and power increases. Do you see the pattern? The value of β varies inversely with the value of α. One way to think about this is to imagine what happens to your region of non-rejection when you change α. If you decrease the value of α, the region of rejection gets smaller and the region of non-rejection gets larger, which makes it harder to reject a true null hypothesis (fewer Type I errors) but also makes it harder to reject a false null hypothesis (less power and more Type II errors). As you try to protect yourself against making a Type I error, you increase the likelihood that you will make a Type II error, all other things held constant. Let's now take a look at how the sample size (n) affects the values for β and, in turn, power.

How β is Affected by n

In our original example we specified a sample size of 25. When testing at $\alpha = .05$, we found that β was .734 and the power was .266. What if we were to redo the analysis, but specify a sample size of 100? We need to go back to the material presented in Chapter 10 and recall that the standard error of the mean is equal to $\sigma/\sqrt{n}$. If we increased the sample size from 25 to 100, we should note that the standard error of the mean will decrease from 3 to 1.5. With that value, let's re-evaluate the situation for $\alpha = .05$. Note that all we needed to do was to edit the earlier script, changing the standard deviation from 3 to 1.5.

```
# Finding beta and power when alpha is .05
# and n = 100
s <- 1.5
mu0 <- 100
mu1 <- 104
lcv05 <- qnorm(.025, mean = mu0, sd = s)
ucv05 <- qnorm(.975, mean = mu0, sd = s)
upper05 <- pnorm(ucv05, mean = mu1, sd = s)
lower05 <- pnorm(lcv05, mean = mu1, sd = s)
beta05 <- upper05 - lower05
beta05
power05 <- 1 - beta05
power05
```

The results for $\alpha = .05$ and $n = 100$ are:

```
> beta05
[1] 0.2398738
> power05 <- 1 - beta05
> power05
[1] 0.7601262
```

As you can see, by increasing the sample size from 25 to 100, we reduced the standard error of the mean from 3 to 1.5. This reduction has the effect of narrowing the region of nonrejection and the variability of the sample means, thus decreasing the likelihood of falling in that region when $\mu = 104$. Consequently we see β drop from .734 to .240, with power increasing from .266 to .760. We could employ other values of n to solidify our argument, but we'll leave that up to you. We can say with confidence that increasing the sample size will lead to a reduction in β with a corresponding increase in power. Now, we will turn to a brief discussion of how reliability affects the magnitude of β.

How β is Affected by Reliability (r_{yy})

Very early in this book, we presented a brief discussion of measurement, defining reliability and validity. Recall that reliability refers to the notion of error of measurement. In particular, reliability was defined as the ratio of "true score" variance to "total" variance. The higher the reliability, the more consistent are the scores. If a measure is not reliable, the scores contain a lot of error, which will increase the variability of our measure. In the z-test for a mean, you should recall that our measure of error goes in the denominator of the formula. Thus, low reliability will tend to inflate the denominator, which, in turn, will decrease the quotient. Consequently, lower reliability will deflate our computed z-values, therefore reducing our chances of obtaining a z-value in the region of rejection. As a result, we reduce our chances of rejecting H_0 when it should be rejected; an instance of inflated β and reduced power. The message should be clear; in designing your research studies, you should spend some time trying to identify the most reliable measures of the variables you want to study. Finally, we are ready to confront the "fly in the ointment," the true value of μ.

How β is Affected by the True Value of μ

We refer to the true value of μ as the "fly" as we will never know the true value of μ. (If we did, we would not be testing hypotheses about it!) It is the one thing over which you have no control. Before we propose some resolution to this problem, let's look at how the value of μ affects β. Once again, in our first example in this section, we specified $\mu = 104$, testing at a two-tailed level of α of .05. This situation resulted in a $\beta = .734$ and a power of .266. Now let's redo that example, changing the value of μ to 102.

```
# Finding beta and power when mu = 102
s <- 3
mu0 <- 100
mu1 <- 102
lcv05 <- qnorm(.025, mean = mu0, sd = s)
ucv05 <- qnorm(.975, mean = mu0, sd = s)
upper05 <- pnorm(ucv05, mean = mu1, sd = s)
lower05 <- pnorm(lcv05, mean = mu1, sd = s)
beta05 <- upper05 - lower05
beta05
power05 <- 1 - beta05
power05
```

The results are:

```
> beta05
[1] 0.8977341
> power05 <- 1 - beta05
> power05
[1] 0.1022659
```

You can see that when $\mu = 102$ rather than 104, our power to detect it has decreased from .266 to .102. Now, let's see what might happen if μ were actually 110.

```
# Finding beta and power when mu = 110
s <- 3
mu0 <- 100
mu1 <- 110
```

```
lcv05 <- qnorm(.025, mean = mu0, sd = s)
ucv05 <- qnorm(.975, mean = mu0, sd = s)
upper05 <- pnorm(ucv05, mean = mu1, sd = s)
lower05 <- pnorm(lcv05, mean = mu1, sd = s)
beta05 <- upper05 - lower05
beta05
power05 <- 1 - beta05
power05
```

The results are:

```
> beta05
[1] 0.08481872
> power05 <- 1 - beta05
> power05
[1] 0.9151813
```

The pattern should be obvious. When the true mean is very close to the one hypothesized in H_0, the power is very low. When the true mean is far from the value specified in H_0, the power is greatly increased. Perhaps to overstate it, it is a lot easier to see a large difference than it is to see a small difference. By analogy, go outside on a clear night with a full moon. It is much easier to see the moon than it is to see the former planet Pluto; we'd be willing to bet you won't be able to find Pluto.

A Proposed Solution

We have seen that there are three primary factors that affect our ability to control the probability of a Type II error: level of significance, sample size, and the difference between the true mean and the one hypothesized in H_0. What to do? First, we recommend that researchers decide what is the minimum difference they want to detect. This difference is called the *effect size*. If we are working with a planned intervention to increase children's likelihood of doing well in school and using IQ as the dependent variable, would we be satisfied with an average increase of 1 IQ point? Probably not! After consulting with the experts, we might decide that we think that a minimum difference of 15 points would be of interest. If we were working in an internal medicine clinic in a program to reduce hypertension, how much of a decrease in both systolic and diastolic pressure would we want to observe? Though we are not physicians, we would be willing to bet that a decrease of one or two points would not cut it. As you can see, the size of the effect may vary from scale to scale. Cohen (1992) has simplified things for us by proposing .2 standard deviations as a small effect, .5 standard deviations as a medium effect, and .8 standard deviations as a large effect.

After deciding on the minimal effect size, we would set our minimum "desired" power to detect that difference. Just as .05 has become the conventional maximum level of α, .20 is emerging at the maximum level of β, which converts to a minimum power of .80. Last, we need to specify the risk we are willing to take on making a Type I error, the level of significance. Once these three values are specified, it is possible to use them in a formula that will derive the sample size needed to give you what you want. Rather than give you the formula, we would refer you to several books (e.g., Cohen, 1988; Murphy & Myors, 1998), and later we will show you some "power calculators" that are out on the Web. If you just cannot wait, try a Google search for "G power."

CHAPTER SUMMARY

In this chapter, we have outlined the process of hypothesis testing, using an example in which we are interested in whether the mean of a sample is a reasonable estimate of a hypothesized population mean. The process is based on proof by counterexample. That is, we formulate a research hypothesis, contradict it (H_0), and then try to show that the data are inconsistent with the contradiction, providing indirect support for our research hypothesis. In order to employ this process, we need to set a level of significance, typically $\alpha = .05$. Recall that, in this context, "significant" connotes a "sign of something interesting," not necessarily important. Based on a comparison of our data with the hypotheses, we make a decision about which hypothesis (H_0 or H_1) we will consider to be more tenable.

We must keep in mind that no matter what we decide, we may be making a mistake. If we decide to reject H_0, we may be making a Type I error. If we decide not to reject H_0, we might be making a Type II error. Last, we tried to pull all of this together with a discussion of statistical power. We recommended that the researcher consider all of this in the design of the study. Such consideration involves a decision about what size difference is substantially important (effect size), what level of risk of a Type I error is acceptable (level of significance, typically .05), and how much power is desired to find the effect if it is indeed present. All of this leads to a calculation of the sample size necessary to achieve the conditions specified.

In the next chapter we provide more examples of the application of this process to other one-sample contexts, where we will consider questions that deal with location (means and medians, and proportions). In Chapter 13 we will address variances, shape (e.g., possible departures from normality, distributions of categorical variables), bivariate situations for quantitative variables (correlation and regression), and association for categorical variables. In many of these applications, in addition to the classical tests based on normal distribution theory, we will also present non-parametric approaches, along with resampling methods.

Key Terms

Alpha	One-tailed hypothesis
Alternative hypothesis	Parametric statistics
Beta	Research hypothesis
Dependent samples	Research question
Hypothesis testing	Statistical hypothesis
Independent samples	Statistical power
Inferential statistics	Two-tailed hypothesis
Level of significance	Type I error
Non-parametric statistics	Type II error
Null hypothesis	

REFERENCES

Chow, S. L. (1996). *Statistical significance: rationale, validity, and utility.* London: Sage.

Cohen, J. (1988). *Statistical power analysis for the behavioral sciences* (2nd ed.) Hillsdale, NJ: Erlbaum.

Cohen, J. (1992). A power primer. *Psychological Bulletin, 112*, 155–159.

Cowles, M. (2001). *Statistics in psychology: An historical perspective.* Mahwah, NJ: Lawrence Erlbaum Associates.

Fisher, R. A. (1959). *Statistical methods and scientific inference* (2nd ed.). New York: Hafner.

Fisher, R. A. (1960). *The design of experiments* (7th ed.). New York: Hafner.

Fraenkel, J. R., & Wallen, N. E. (1996). *How to design and evaluate research in education.* (3rd ed.). New York: McGraw-Hill.

Good, P. I. (2006). *Resampling methods* (3rd ed.). Boston, MA: Birkhäuser.

Graunt, J. (1662). *Natural and political observations. Mentioned in a following index, and made upon the bills of mortality.* London: Martin, Allestry, and Dorcas.

Harlow, L. L., Mulaik, S. A., & Steiger, J. H. (Eds.). (1997). *What if there were no significance tests?* Mahwah, NJ: Lawrence Erlbaum Associates.

Hays, W. L. (1963). *Statistics for psychologists.* New York: Holt, Rinehart, and Winston.

Murphy, K. R., & Myors, B. (1998). *Statistical power analysis: A simple and general model for traditional and modern hypothesis tests.* Mahwah, NJ: Erlbaum.

Neyman, J., & Pearson, E. S. (1928). On the use and interpretation of certain test criteria for purposes of statistical inferences (Part I). *Biometrika, 20A*, 175–240.

Popper, K. R. (1959). *The logic of scientific discovery.* London: Hutchinson.

Salsburg, D. (2001). *The lady tasting tea: How statistics revolutionized science in the twentieth century.* New York: W. H. Freeman.

PRACTICE QUESTIONS

1. The hypothesis that contradicts the research hypothesis is called the:

   a. null hypothesis
   b. alternate hypothesis
   c. directional hypothesis.

2. In hypothesis testing, researchers may gain support for their research hypothesis by showing that the data are:

   a. consistent with the alternate hypothesis
   b. inconsistent with the alternate hypothesis
   c. consistent with the null hypothesis
   d. inconsistent with the null hypothesis.

3. A researcher conducting a hypothesis test will typically reject the null hypothesis if the probability obtained is:

   a. greater than .05
   b. less than .05.

4. Suppose a researcher tests a null hypothesis and obtains a probability of .03. This implies that:

    a. there is a .03 probability that the null hypothesis is true.
    b. if the null hypothesis is true, there is a .03 probability that the researcher would obtain a sample that is less consistent with the null hypothesis than the sample obtained.
    c. if the null hypothesis is false, there is a .03 probability that the researcher would obtain a sample that is less consistent with the null hypothesis than the sample obtained.
    d. if the alternate hypothesis is true, there is a .03 probability that the researcher would obtain a sample that is less consistent with the alternate hypothesis than the sample obtained.

5. A colleague suggests running a statistical test at $\alpha = .01$, as opposed to $\alpha = .05$, to reduce the chances of a Type I error. What effect will this have on the chance of a Type II error?

    a. It will increase.
    b. It will decrease.
    c. It will remain the same.

6. A colleague suggests that you plan the study with a larger sample size. What effect will this have on the chance of a Type I error?

    a. It will increase.
    b. It will decrease.
    c. It will remain the same.

7. A colleague suggests that you plan the study with a larger sample size. What effect will this have on the chance of a Type II error?

    a. It will increase.
    b. It will decrease.
    c. It will remain the same.

8. A statistical test will tend to have more power if the effect size is:

    a. zero
    b. small
    c. medium
    d. large.

EXERCISES

11.1 Suppose that the average height of the population of adult males in Great Britain is 68.5 inches with a standard deviation of 2.5 inches. A random sample of 20 gifted adult males was selected and the average height was found to be 67 inches. Using a level of significance of .05, does the observed mean suggest that gifted adults differ from the general population of males?

12

Other One-Sample Tests for Location

INTRODUCTION

In the previous chapter, we explained the logic underlying the process of hypothesis testing and gave you several examples. All of the examples shared some common properties: all were concerned with one sample, specified a hypothesis about a population mean, and used variables for which we knew the variance of the population. Beginning in this chapter, we are going to expand the possibilities to deal with a mean when we do not know the population variance, and with other measures of location (proportions and medians). In Chapter 13, we will address situations that are concerned with measures of variability and with measures of relationship (correlations and regression coefficients). In this chapter and thereafter, we will also present an alternative to hypothesis testing usually referred to as "confidence intervals," and we will describe both the traditional methods of constructing confidence intervals and the newer, computer-intensive, resampling methods.

ANOTHER TEST ON A MEAN: THE t-TEST

When testing a hypothesis about a population mean based on sample data, more often than not we will not know the variance of the population. Rather, we will use the sample data to estimate that variance. As presented in the previous chapter, for testing hypotheses of the form:

$$H_0: \mu = \mu_0$$
$$H_0: \mu = \mu_0$$

(12.1)

We presented a formula that transforms our data into a z-statistic:

$$z_{obs} = \frac{\bar{Y} - \mu}{\sigma / \sqrt{n}}$$

(12.2)

When we do not know the value of σ, we must substitute an estimate of σ. We learned much earlier in the book that the sample value of s^2 was an unbiased estimate of σ^2. Thus we may want to use s as an estimate of σ. Recall that:

$$s^2 = \frac{\sum_{i=1}^{n}\left(Y_i - \overline{Y}_.\right)^2}{n-1} \tag{12.3}$$

Thus, our expression for transforming our data would be:

$$\hat{z}_{obs} = \frac{\overline{Y} - \mu}{s/\sqrt{n}} \tag{12.4}$$

We have placed a "hat" over the z_{obs} as we are not really certain that this statistic will be distributed as z. To demonstrate this point we can look at the sampling distribution of s^2 using simulations with R. Let's assume that we are working with a random variable that is normally distributed with a mean of 50 and a variance of 25 ($Y \sim N(50, 25)$). We used the R script (Script 12.1) that is contained in the supplementary materials for this chapter (see book website), repeating it with sample sizes of 2, 5, 10, and 25. The descriptive statistics are presented in Table 12.1, and the results are depicted graphically in Figure 12.1.

Table 12.1 Descriptive statistics for the distribution of 100,000 sample variances ($\sigma^2 = 25$) with sample sizes of 2, 5, 10, and 25

	Sample size			
	$n = 2$	$n = 5$	$n = 10$	$n = 25$
Mean	24.787	24.983	24.951	24.991
Median	11.345	20.967	23.120	24.313
Skewness	2.786	1.416	.928	.577
Kurtosis	11.596	3.019	1.246	.502

As you can see, both in the table and the figure, the sampling distribution of s^2 is very positively skewed and leptokurtotic for small samples. As the sample size increases, the distribution becomes more symmetric. The implications are rather subtle, but important. With smaller sample sizes, the distribution of sample variances can be expected to be positively skewed. The implications are depicted graphically in Figure 12.2, in which we depict a "smoothed" version of the sampling distribution for $n = 12$ (see Script 12.2). With simulation, we found the median to be 23.51, less than the expected mean of 25.

As you can see, with the median less than the mean, you would expect s^2 to be less than its expected value (σ^2) more than 50% of the time. Thus, substituting s for σ in Equation 12.2, as in Equation 12.4, would yield a quotient (z_{obs}) that would tend to be too large (positive or negative). Thus, if we were to proceed in this way and use the z-distribution as a criterion, we would expect to exceed ±1.96 more than 5% of the time, increasing our actual risk of a Type I error.

Let's take a look at a simulation (see Script 12.3) of this problem, drawing random samples of size 4, 9, 16, and 25 from a normally distributed population with a mean of 50 and a variance of 100. For each of the samples drawn, we will use Equation 12.4 to calculate an estimate of z and then look at the distributions of our four estimates. For each of the four distributions, we have calculated descriptive statistics including means, standard deviations, skew, and kurtosis. The results are presented in Table 12.2 and depicted graphically in Figures 12.3 through 12.6, along with a graphic of the unit-normal distribution.

Looking at the figures, you should be able to see easily that when the sample size is small ($n = 4$), the distribution of $\hat{z}_{obs}$ is symmetric and quite leptokurtic. As the sample size increases, the

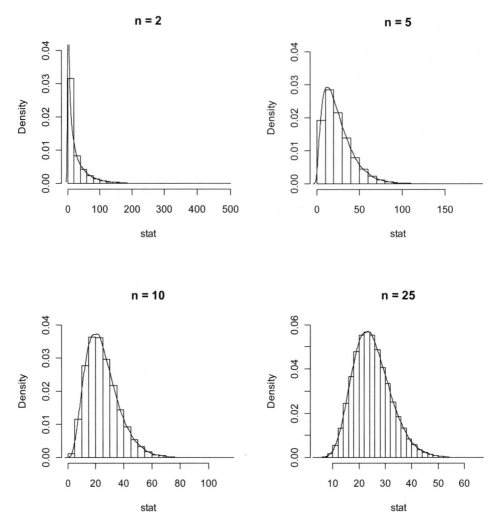

FIGURE 12.1   The sampling distribution of the variance (s^2) for $n = 2$, 5, 10, and 25, sampling from a normally distributed population with $\mu = 50$ and $\sigma^2 = 25$.

distribution of $\hat{z}_{obs}$ remains symmetric but becomes less leptokurtic, approaching the unit-normal distribution when $n = 25$. These impressions are verified by looking at the contents of Table 12.2. First, note that, regardless of sample size, the mean of $\hat{z}_{obs}$ remains quite close to zero. Second, note that the variance of $\hat{z}_{obs}$ becomes smaller as n increases. In fact, it is very close to 1.0 when $n = 25$. We may recall another probability distribution that has a mean of zero and a variance of 1.0, the *unit-normal distribution*.

   Also note that we have included two rows in Table 12.2 that contain "Lower .025" and "Upper .025." These rows contain the values of $\hat{z}_{obs}$ that cut off the lower and upper 2.5% of the simulated values. When the sample size is small, these values are in excess of ±3.0, but as the sample size increases to 25, they are close to ±2.0, values quite close to ±1.96. We have also included rows labeled "Percent ≤1.96" and "Percent ≥1.96." You can see that, if we were working with a sample size of 4 and using our formula with critical values of ±1.96, as we erroneously thought we were doing a two-tailed z-test at the .05 level, we would reject the null hypothesis about 14%

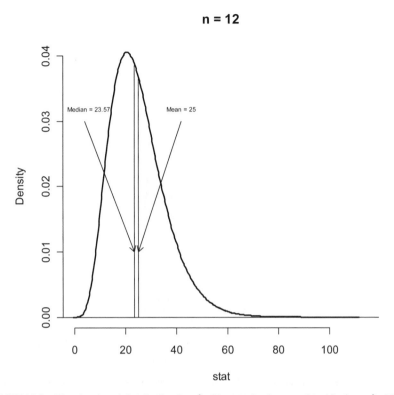

FIGURE 12.2   The simulated distribution for s^2 with sample size equal to 12 when $\sigma^2 = 25$.

Table 12.2 Results from the simulation of $\hat{z}_{obs}$ for samples sizes of 4, 9, 16, and 25

	Sample size			
Characteristic	*n = 4*	*n = 9*	*n = 16*	*n = 25*
Mean	−.0199	0.0154	−.0034	−.0059
Variance	2.8881	1.3613	1.1402	1.0550
Skewness	.0742	.0755	−.0216	.0229
Kurtosis	18.3263	2.4363	.4621	.3005
Lower .025	−3.3687	−2.2868	−2.1005	−2.0194
Upper .025	3.1645	2.2866	2.1033	2.0340
Percent ≤ 1.96	.0778	.0403	.0344	.0283
Percent ≥ 1.96	.0734	.0418	.0332	.0287

of the time. Similarly, with a sample size of 9, our actual Type I error rate would be about .08; with sample sizes of 16 and 25, the error rates would be about .065 and .056, respectively. Thus, when we do not know the variance of the population, it is inappropriate to use the formula for a z-test, substituting s for σ.

The t-Distribution

At this point, we might suspect that we are dealing with another probability distribution that is asymptotic to the unit-normal probability distribution as the sample size increases. Indeed we

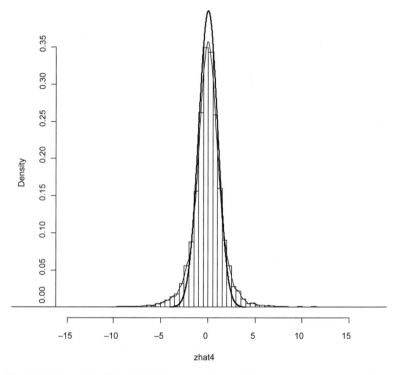

FIGURE 12.3   The distribution of $\hat{z}_{obs}$ ($N = 10,000$) for a sample size (n) of 4; the unit-normal distribution is shown by the darker "line."

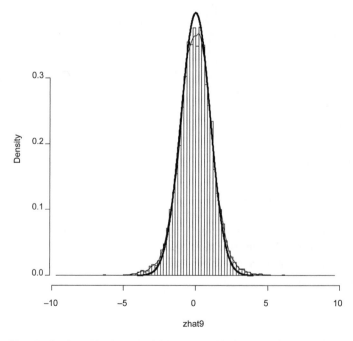

FIGURE 12.4   The distribution of $\hat{z}_{obs}$ ($N = 10,000$) for a sample size (n) of 9; the unit-normal distribution is shown by the darker "line."

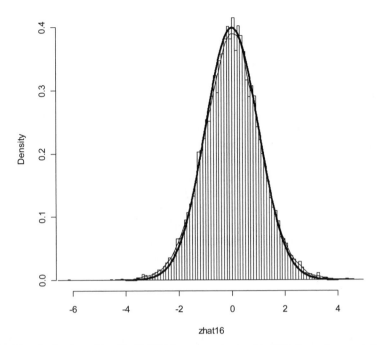

FIGURE 12.5   The distribution of $\hat{z}_{obs}$ ($N = 10,000$) for a sample size (n) of 16; the unit-normal distribution is shown by the darker "line."

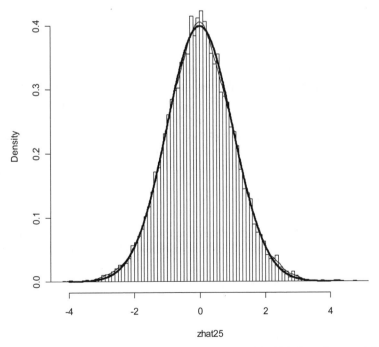

FIGURE 12.6   The distribution of $\hat{z}_{obs}$ ($N = 10,000$) for a sample size (n) of 25; the unit-normal distribution is shown by the darker "line."

are; we are looking at the t-distribution. "The t-distribution" is actually a family of distributions, with a separate member for each sample size. Although with today's computers, we could simulate the distribution for each sample size, we fortunately have a solution based on the work of William Sealy Gosset completed early in the 20th century.

With an Oxford degree in chemistry and a minor in mathematics, Gosset was an employee of the Guinness brewery, concerned with quality control. The very nature of quality control makes it economically inadvisable to use large samples; if General Electric tested 90% of its light bulbs for burn-out time, it would have only 10% of the bulbs available for sale. In the context of brewing stout, the delicate and dynamic nature of the brewing process makes it even more inadvisable to use large samples. Thus, Gosset found it necessary to employ small samples. According to Cowles (2001, p. 117), Gosset studied the distribution of the mean and s by drawing sample sizes of 4 from a population of approximately 3,000 measurements. Although he did not provide a conclusive mathematical proof, he did the basic work that later stimulated Fisher to derive the mathematical basis for the t-distribution (Fisher, 1925). Due to Guinness policies in reaction to an incident of industrial espionage, employees were not allowed to publish anything based on their work at the brewery. Thus, Gosset published under the pseudonym, A. Student. For more information, see Read (1997).

The t-Test

As noted previously, the t-distribution is a family of distributions, a subset of the gamma (γ) probability distribution (Evans, Hastings, & Peacock, 1993). Although it can be defined very generally, for our purposes we can define it more specifically as the distribution of the following test statistic:

$$t_{obs} = \frac{\bar{Y}_{.} - \mu}{s / \sqrt{n}} \tag{12.5}$$

Assuming that the null hypothesis is true, that the random variable Y is normally distributed, and that the observations are independent, this test statistic will be distributed as t with $df = n-1$, an expected value of zero and a variance of $df/(df-2)$. We have depicted several different t-distributions for various sample sizes in Figure 12.7 (see Script 12.4). As you can see, the pattern is virtually identical to the results for our simulations depicted in Figures 12.3 through 12.6 – symmetric but rather leptokurtic (heavy tailed) for smaller sample sizes. We have included selected values of t in Table A.3 in Appendix A.

Example 12.1: An Example of a t-Test

Using the ECLS2577 data file, we can determine that, for the entire file, the mean of the Item Response Theory (IRT) scaled reading scores at entry to kindergarten is 24.89, or approximately 25.0. We might be interested in knowing if children identified as Native Hawaiian, Other Pacific Islanders are different from the general population. We would be interested in contrasting the hypotheses:

$$H_0: \mu = 24.89$$
$$H_1: \mu \neq 24.89 \tag{12.6}$$

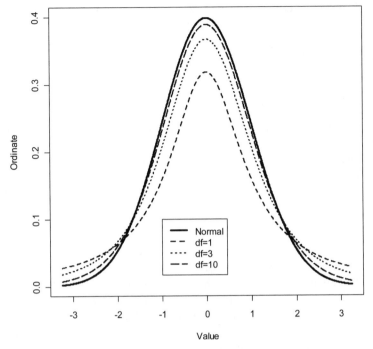

FIGURE 12.7   The *t*-distributions for *df* = 1, 3, and 10, with the unit-normal distribution.

Suppose we draw a random sample of 12 children from the Native Hawaiian, Other Pacific Islander group and find their entry level IRT reading scores to be 13, 19, 15, 19, 30, 29, 13, 14, 14, 14, 15, and 33. Given these data, what should we conclude?

First, we need to generate some preliminary statistics: $\Sigma Y = 228$, $\Sigma Y^2 = 4928$ and $n = 12$. Based on these figures we find the sample mean to equal 19.0 and the sample variance to equal 54.18. Thus, $s = 7.36$. Plugging these results into Equation 12.5, we obtain:

$$t_{obs} = \frac{\bar{Y}_\cdot - \mu}{s/\sqrt{n}} = \frac{19 - 24.89}{7.36/\sqrt{12}} = \frac{-5.89}{2.12} = -2.78 \tag{12.7}$$

Since we are testing a two-tailed hypothesis with $n = 12$ ($df = n - 1 = 11$), we can use Table A.3 to find the critical values of t: ±2.2010. Given our calculated result of –2.78, we would conclude that the evidence favors the alternate hypothesis. That is, if we have met the assumptions, including the null hypothesis, we would expect to see a value of t_{obs} in excess of ±2.2010 less than 5% of the time. But we did see such a value. Thus, we should reject the null hypothesis, keeping in mind that we may be making a Type I error.

COMPLETING THE EXAMPLE IN R   We can use R in at least two different ways to complete this example. After reading the data into R with a **c( )** function, we can use R as a calculator or we can use the **t.test( )** function. The script appears on the book website with the supplementary materials for this chapter (Script 12.5). The relevant output is:

```
> t.obs
[1] -2.77191
```

Rather than obtaining the critical values from Table A.3, we can use the **qt( )** function in R to find them:

```
> critical.values <- qt(p=c(.025, .975), df=11)
> critical.values
[1] -2.200985  2.200985
```

Or, we can use the **pt( )** function in R to find the *p*-value for the observed value of t_{obs}:

```
> # Observed t is negative and two-tailed test
> p.value <-2*pt(t.obs, df=n - 1)
> p.value
[1] 0.01816484
```

Whether we use the critical-value approach or the *p*-value approach, we reach the same conclusion. The probability of observing a sample mean of 19, or further from 24.89 than 19, when sampling from a population having $\mu = 24.89$ with a sample of 12 cases is sufficiently low (less than .05) that we have reason to challenge the null hypothesis, rejecting it in favor of the alternate hypothesis. Yet another way to use R to complete the test is to use the **t.test( )** function:

```
> # The t.test function in R
> t.test(irt, alternative="two.sided",
>   mu=24.89)


        One Sample t-test

data:  irt
t=-2.7719, df=11, p-value=0.01816
alternative hypothesis: true mean is not equal to 24.89
95 percent confidence interval:
 14.32315 23.67685
sample estimates:
mean of x
      19
```

Part of the output immediately above reports that the "95 percent confidence interval:" is from 14.32 to 23.67. At this point, we are going to defer an explanation of confidence intervals until we have presented several other one-sample tests. Before we move on to other tests, we should briefly mention the assumptions for a one-sample *t*-test on a mean.

Assumptions for a t-Test

Once again, the assumptions for a *t*-test are that the data represent independent observations and that they come from a population that is normally distributed. Remember that means tend to be normally distributed if the sample size is sufficiently large. Thus the t-test tends to be *robust* with respect to the assumption of normality. That is, departures from a normally distributed population tend to have very little effect on the results, specifically the derived p-values. There are statistical tests for departures from normality, but at this point we will simply state that when the coefficient of skewness is within the range of ±2 and kurtosis is less than 5, you are probably alright to proceed with a t-test.

Designing a Study to be Analyzed with a t-Test

Toward the end of the previous chapter, we introduced the topic of statistical power, an issue that, ideally, should be considered in the design of a study before data are collected. Recall that the issue of power involves the dynamic relationship between α, β, n, and the "true" difference. There is a function in R, **power.t.test( )**, which will enable you to do this rather easily. The structure of the syntax is:

```
power.t.test (n = value, delta = value, sd = value,
sig.level = value, power = value,
type = "one.sample",
alternative = c("two.sided", "one.sided"))
```

where you supply the particulars for four of the five values, and the function calculates the value for the omitted *value*. Specifically, "n" is the sample size, "delta" is the difference between the sample and population means that you wish to detect, "sd" is your estimate of the standard deviation of the population, "sig.level" is α, and "power" is $1-\beta$.

Continuing our previous example, H_0 specified that $\mu = 24.89$, or approximately 25. Our data suggest that the standard deviation is around 7 or 8; we'll go with 8. Furthermore, let's say that we want to be able to detect a 4-point difference, or what Cohen labeled a "medium" effect. In addition, we will set α at .05, and we want a minimum power of .80. Supplying those values to the **power.t.test** function:

```
> power.t.test(delta = 4, sd = 8, sig.level = .05,
>   power = .8, type = "one.sample",
>   alternative = "two.sided"

    One-sample t test power calculation

          n = 33.36720
       delta = 4
          sd = 8
   sig.level = 0.05
       power = 0.8
 alternative = two.sided
```

As you can see, the function has returned a value of 33.37 for the value of n. Thus, we would want to use 34 cases in our study to meet our conditions. Of course if we had the resources to sample more than 34 cases that would be desirable because it would increase the power.

Now, we move on to discuss other tests. One such procedure is the one-sample test for a proportion; it is closely related to a test on a mean.

A TEST ON A PROPORTION

Pollsters live and die reporting proportions. What proportion of likely voters favors a particular candidate? What proportion of voters opposes a specific legislative issue? What proportion of the electorate is in favor of a government policy, such as the "big bank" bailouts toward the end of the first decade of the 21st century? A proportion is nothing more than a mean when the possible values are 0 and 1. Now, doesn't that sound like something familiar? The binomial distribution, perhaps?

Let's pursue that for a bit, combining what we know about binomial distributions with what we know about the effects of multiplying a random variable by a constant. First, let's make sure that you recall the binomial distribution. Hopefully, you remember a binomial "experiment" as one in which the number of "successes" (r) is counted in a series of trials (n). Furthermore, we hope that you remember that the expected value of a binomial random variable is np, the number of trials multiplied by the probability of a success. Also recall that the variance of a binomial random variable is npq, where $q = 1 - p$.

Now, consider that a hypothesis about a proportion π might be stated as in the following equation, where π_0 is some particular value of π:

$$H_0: \pi = \pi_0$$
$$H_1: \pi \neq \pi_0 \tag{12.8}$$

For example, we might be interested in whether the proportion of people in favor of some issue was equal to or different from .50. Translating our notation for the binomial into the notation for testing hypotheses about parameters of populations,

$$E(Y) = np = n\pi$$
$$\mathrm{var}\,(Y) = npq = n\pi(1 - \pi) \tag{12.9}$$

A binomial random variable is actually the sum of a series of 1s and 0s. A proportion is simply of the average of the 1s and 0s, or the sum (Y) divided by the number of trials (n). Thus, if the random variable Y is binomial, then the observed sample proportion is simply:

$$p = \frac{Y}{n} \tag{12.10}$$

That is, an observed proportion p is simply an observed binomial random variable Y multiplied by $1/n$. Based on our earlier work regarding the effects of multiplying a random variable times a constant,

$$E(p) = E\left[\left(\frac{1}{n}\right)Y\right] = \left(\frac{1}{n}\right)E(Y) = \left(\frac{1}{n}\right)n\pi = \pi \tag{12.11}$$

and

$$\text{var}(p) = \text{var}\left[\left(\frac{1}{n}\right)Y\right] = \left(\frac{1}{n}\right)^2 \text{var}(Y) = \left(\frac{1}{n}\right)^2 n\pi(1-\pi) = \frac{\pi(1-\pi)}{n} \qquad (12.12)$$

At this point, we find ourselves in the position of wanting to test a hypothesis about a proportion (which is actually a mean) where, based on the null hypothesis, we know both the expected value and the variance of the population. If you are thinking that sounds like the conditions for a z-test, you are correct. To test a hypothesis about a proportion, we can construct a z-test:

$$z_{obs} = \frac{p - \pi_0}{\sqrt{[\pi_0(1-\pi_0)]/n}} \qquad (12.13)$$

Example 12.2: A One-Sample Test on a Proportion

Let's continue pursuing our interest in Native Hawaiian, Other Pacific Islander children. Again, based on our data file ECLS2577, we can determine that 75% of the children were reported as having spent some time in day care prior to beginning school. Thus, $\pi = .75$ and $(1-\pi) = .25$. Suppose we are interested in determining whether the population of Native Hawaiian, Other Pacific Islander children had similar pre-school experience. We draw a random sample of 20 children from this subpopulation and find the data to show (1, 1, 1, 1, 0, 1, 1, 0, 1, 0, 0, 1, 1, 0, 1, 0, 0, 0, 0, and 0) where 0 = "yes" and 1 = "no." Looking at the data, we can see that 10 of the children spent some time in day care and that 10 of the children did not; $p = .50$. Thus, our hypotheses to contrast are:

$$\begin{aligned} &H_0: \pi = 0.75 \\ &H_1: \pi \neq 0.75 \end{aligned} \qquad (12.14)$$

We would proceed as follows:

$$z_{obs} = \frac{p - \pi_0}{\sqrt{[\pi_0(1-\pi_0)]/n}} = \frac{.50 - .75}{\sqrt{[0.75(1-.75)]/20}} = \frac{-.25}{.0968} = -2.58 \qquad (12.15)$$

Given that this is a two-tailed z-test, the critical values are ± 1.96. We find that our observed value is in the region of rejection. We reject H_0 in favor of H_1; it would appear that fewer Native Hawaiian, Other Pacific Islander children experienced some form of day care.

Completing Example 12.2 in R

Once again, there is more than one way to complete this example in R. We can use R as a calculator, or we can use the **prop.test( )** function. First, let's look at a way to use R as a calculator. The R script appears in the supplementary materials for this chapter (Script 12.6 on the website). The most relevant output is:

```
> z.obs = (p - pi)/sqrt((pi*(1 - pi))/n)
> z.obs
```

```
[1] -2.581989
> critical.values <- qnorm(p=c(.025, .975))
> critical.values
[1] -1.959964  1.959964
> # Observed z is negative and two-tailed test
> p.value <- 2*pnorm(z.obs)
> p.value
[1] 0.009823275
```

As you can easily see, the results agree with our hand calculations in Equation 12.15. To use the **prop.test( )** function, we simply provide the number of successes, the number of trials, and the null value for π. In addition, you may specify the form of the alternate hypothesis as "two. sided," "less," or "greater." We should mention that some statisticians recommend using Yates' Correction for Continuity, similar to what we did when we used the normal approximation to the binomial distribution. However, there is some evidence that the correction is overly conservative, and it is not generally employed. Unfortunately, it is the default in R, so we need to turn it off.

```
> prop.test(10, 20, p=.75,
>   alternative="two.sided", correct=FALSE)

        1-sample proportions test without continuity
correction

data:  10 out of 20, null probability 0.75
X-squared=6.6667, df=1, p-value=0.009823
alternative hypothesis: true p is not equal to 0.75
95 percent confidence interval:
 0.299298 0.700702
sample estimates:
  p
0.5
```

R uses a slightly different formula for the test and reports the result as a chi-squared (χ^2) statistic. Shortly we will show you that a χ^2-value with one degree of freedom is simply a z-value, squared. Thus, 6.6667 equals $(-2.58)^2$, and you can see that the p-values are identical. Once again, the R function produces a confidence interval, which we will explain shortly.

Assumptions for a One-Sample Test on a Proportion

The assumptions for a one-sample test on a proportion are very similar to those for a one-sample test on a mean, which should come as no surprise. However, in this special case, the assumption of normality needs some additional discussion. Proportions can vary from 0 to 1. If the population proportion is .50, the sampling distribution of p will be symmetric and sufficiently close to normal to meet the assumption. However as π departs from .50, the sampling distribution of p

will become more and more skewed. Given the Central Limit Theorem, we know that the distribution of sample means will approach a normal distribution with sufficient sample size. How big is sufficient in the case of a proportion? If both $n\pi$ and $n\pi(1-\pi)$ are greater than or equal to 5, the sampling distribution of p should be sufficiently close to normal to justify the use of the z-test.

Designing a Study to be Analyzed with a z-Test on a Proportion

Just as there was a function in R to address the issue of power with respect to a t-test, so too there is a function to do the same thing with a z-test on a proportion: **power.prop.test( )**. This function only deals with two-sample tests, however, which we will not discuss until Chapters 13 and 14.

In the meantime, there is an R package (**pwr**) that you can install and load with a library command. Within the package, there is a **pwr.p.test( )** function, which has a syntax structure:

```
pwr.p.test(h=value, n=value, sig.level=value, power=value,
    alternative=c("two.sided", "less", "greater"))
```

where you supply three of the four values. The value for h is the effect size, which for a proportion can be found with the command "h <- ES.h(p,π)," where you supply the values for p and π. The effect size h is defined using an arc sine transformation ($\sin^{-1}$),

$$h = 2 \times \sin^{-1}\left(\sqrt{p_1}\right) - 2 \times \sin^{-1}\left(\sqrt{p_2}\right) \tag{12.16}$$

where p_1 is the larger of the two proportions (p or π) and p_2 is the smaller of the two proportions (p or π). In our example, the value of π specified in H_0 is .75. Given the skewed nature of the sampling distribution of proportions, we would recommend that you think about size of the difference you wish to detect separately for each direction. Let's say we are interested in detecting a difference if the population proportion is actually as high as .85 or as low as .65. We would then calculate the effect size in each direction. Although these could turn out to be the same, they will often be a little different. We would recommend that you find the sample size needed for the smaller of the two effect sizes.

Thus, after loading the **pwr** package with a **library** command, we would use R as follows:

```
> h1 <- abs(ES.h(.65, .75))
> h1
[1] 0.2189061
> h2 <- abs(ES.h(.85, .75))
> h2
[1] 0.2517987
> h <- min(h1, h2)
> h
[1] 0.2189061
> pwr.p.test(h=h, sig.level=.05, power=.8,
>   alternative ="two.sided")
```

```
      proportion power calculation for binomial distribution
(arcsine transformation)

               h = 0.2189061
               n = 163.7913
       sig.level = 0.05
           power = 0.8
     alternative = two.sided
```

Thus, if we were designing this study prospectively, we would want to collect data on approximately 164 cases in order to meet our conditions.

ANOTHER TEST ON A MEASURE OF LOCATION: THE MEDIAN

As we noted earlier in our discussion of descriptive statistics, the mean is not always the most appropriate measure of central tendency; with scores that are particularly skewed, the median may be more appropriate. Though, in some ways, a one-sample test on a median is a bit out of place at this point, as the sampling distribution of the median can be quite difficult to calculate (thus, we cannot construct a "parametric" test for the median), we can use the discrete binomial distribution to construct a test based on a proportion.

Example 12.3: A One-Sample Test on a Median

In most locations, the prices of homes are quite skewed. Frequently, realtors talk about the median cost of housing, rather than the average cost of housing. For example, on a recent visit to http://realestate.yahoo.com/North_Carolina/Raleigh, we learned that the median price of houses for sale in the Raleigh market is $213,900. In an issue of the *Raleigh News and Observer* (1 May 2010), an advertisement appeared for a local real estate agency listing a number of houses for sale. We might be interested in assessing whether the houses listed were representative of the Raleigh market at large. We entered the house prices into R and then proceeded to determine the number of listings that were above and below the purported median ($213,900). The entire script is given on the website in the materials for this chapter (see Script 12.7). This procedure is sometimes called a *Sign Test* (Howell, 2007).

There were 36 listings with a median of $424,900. If the median listing is the same as the median house price in Raleigh, then we would expect one-half of the prices to be above $213,900 and one-half of the prices to be below $213,900. After examining the 36 listings, it turned out that 28 prices were above the Raleigh median and eight listings were below. This problem is logically equivalent to finding the probability of 28 or more heads in 36 tosses of a fair coin. The results from **prop.test( )**, where "counter.m" and "tot" are derived in the script, are:

```
> prop.test(counter.m, tot, p = .50,
>    alternative = "two.sided", correct = FALSE)

        1-sample proportions test without continuity
correction
```

```
data:   counter.m out of tot, null probability 0.5
X-squared=11.1111, df=1, p-value=0.0008581
alternative hypothesis: true p is not equal to 0.5
95 percent confidence interval:
 0.6191530 0.8828367
sample estimates:
      p
0.7777778
```

As you can see, the probability (*p*-value) of obtaining a 28/8 split under an assumption that the listed properties are randomly sampled from the Raleigh area is .0008581. Thus, it would appear that this particular set of listings featured in the advertisement in the *Raleigh News and Observer* has a median different from the actual Raleigh median. Either the agency lists primarily up-scale housing or it chose to include only more expensive homes in the advertisement.

At this point, we have described several tests to address questions/hypotheses about location. Now, we are going to present an alternative to hypothesis testing known as "interval estimation." Hypothesis testing is based on point estimation; a sample statistic is used as an estimate of a population parameter. Then, as we described at the beginning of Chapter 11, the value stated in H_0, combined with some distribution theory, is used to construct a range of values that would be reasonable to observe given that the null hypothesis is true. This range of reasonable values was called the *region of non-rejection*. The sample statistic is then evaluated in light of the region of non-rejection. If the sample value falls within that range, we do not reject H_0. If instead, it falls outside the region of non-rejection (i.e., in the *region of rejection*), we reject H_0 in favor of H_1. We may even provide a *p*-value, which is the probability of observing a sample value as extreme or more extreme than the one we did obtain, given that H_0 is true. The information provided in the results is limited to the sample value, the decision (reject or not reject), and perhaps a *p*-value. As an alternative, interval estimation provides values that allow for a reject/not-reject decision not only for the value hypothesized in H_0 but also for other hypothesized values. In addition, information about the precision of the estimate is included. All of this information is provided in a *confidence interval*.

CONFIDENCE INTERVALS BASED ON DISTRIBUTION THEORY

As just noted, in traditional hypothesis testing, an interval of reasonable values is constructed around the value hypothesized in H_0; this interval is known as the region of non-rejection. With interval estimation, an interval of reasonable values is constructed around the sample estimate; this region is known as the *confidence interval*. If we are testing a hypothesis at the .05 level, we would construct the corresponding 95% confidence interval. Generally, a level of significance (α) would be equivalent to a $(1-\alpha)\%$ confidence interval. Confidence intervals can be constructed with traditional distribution theory, or they may be constructed with resampling methods. First, we will describe how confidence intervals are constructed using traditional methods. Then we will describe how they may be interpreted. Last, we will show you how confidence intervals can be constructed using resampling techniques, not only for means and proportions, but also for medians.

Constructing Confidence Intervals

The process of constructing a traditional confidence interval is virtually the same as constructing a region of non-rejection, except that the interval is constructed around the sample statistic rather than the hypothesized population parameter. Let's return to Chapter 11 and consider the example in which we tested a hypothesis regarding the mean entering-kindergarten reading scores for Asian students. The givens of the situation were a sample mean of 56.8, a sample size of 20, and a population variance of 100. Given that the population variance is known, we can use the z-distribution to construct our interval as follows:

$$\bar{Y} - z_{\alpha/2} \frac{\sigma}{\sqrt{n}} \leq \mu \leq \bar{Y} + z_{\alpha/2} \frac{\sigma}{\sqrt{n}}$$

$$56.8 - 1.96 \frac{10}{\sqrt{20}} \leq \mu \leq 56.8 + 1.96 \frac{10}{\sqrt{20}} \tag{12.17}$$

$$52.42 \leq \mu \leq 61.18$$

First, note that although the first line of Equation 12.17 looks complex, it is nothing more than an algebraic manipulation of the formula for z_{obs} (Equation 11.9). The results suggest that, given our sample mean of 56.8, any values of μ between 52.42 and 61.18 are reasonable values of μ for populations from which this sample might have been drawn. Recall that, in the example in Chapter 11, the value of μ hypothesized in H_0 was 50. Given the confidence interval, a value of 50 is not reasonable and should be rejected. Thus, confidence intervals can be used to test hypotheses. Furthermore, they can be used to test hypotheses other than the one specified in H_0. For example, if we reported this confidence interval in a research report, another investigator who hypothesized (H_0) that the value of μ for the population of Asian children might be 60 would be able to look at our interval, note that 60 is within our confidence interval, and come to a decision *not* to reject that particular null hypothesis.

Now, let's reconsider a situation presented in Example 12.1 earlier in this chapter. Based on the data available in the sample of 12 Native Hawaiian, Other Pacific Islander children, we found that the sample mean was 19 and the sample standard deviation (s) was 7.36. The null hypothesis was that μ was equal to 24.89. In this example, though we did not know the population variance; we estimated it from the sample data. Thus, we used a t-test rather than a z-test. We can make the same accommodation in calculating our confidence interval, using the t-distribution rather than the z-distribution:

$$\bar{Y} - t_{\alpha/2} \frac{s}{\sqrt{n}} \leq \mu \leq \bar{Y} + t_{\alpha/2} \frac{s}{\sqrt{n}}$$

$$19 - 2.201 \frac{7.36}{\sqrt{12}} \leq \mu \leq 19 + 2.201 \frac{7.36}{\sqrt{12}} \tag{12.18}$$

$$14.32 \leq \mu \leq 23.68$$

Given that the hypothesized value of 24.89 is not contained within the interval, we would reject it as an unreasonable value for the population mean, reaching the same conclusion as when using the t-test. In passing, it is worth noting that the result in Equation 12.18 is the same as the one reported in the R output.

As you might suspect, we can also construct a confidence interval for a proportion. There are at least seven different recommendations for constructing such intervals (Newcombe, 1998). The simplest approximation which is based on the normal distribution works relatively well when the proportion is not too far from .5 and when the sample size is relatively large. As a general guideline, if both np and $n(1-p)$ are ≥ 10, then the simple asymptotic method can be used:

$$p - z_{\alpha/2}\sqrt{\frac{p(1-p)}{n}} \leq \pi \leq p + z_{\alpha/2}\sqrt{\frac{p(1-p)}{n}} \tag{12.19}$$

If not, then use of the more complex score method is justified. This approach, which is also based on the normal distribution, makes fewer simplifications in the approximation and consequently it does not force the sample proportion to be at the center of the interval. This is particularly helpful when the sample proportion is near a boundary (i.e., 0 or 1) and the sample size is relatively small. For example, if the sample proportion was .95 we wouldn't want the upper limit of the confidence to exceed 1.0 (a proportion over 1.0 simply isn't possible), but with a small sample we may need the lower limit to fall below .90, which leads to the need for an interval that isn't centered around the sample proportion of .95. In such situations the score method is preferred. The expression for the score method is:

$$\frac{2np + z_{\alpha/2}^2 \pm z_{\alpha/2}\sqrt{z_{\alpha/2}^2 + 4npq}}{2(n + z_{\alpha/2}^2)} \tag{12.20}$$

Returning to Example 12.2 in which n was 20 and p was .5, one could use Equation 12.19, as both np and $n(1-p)$ are ≥ 10:

$$.5 - 1.96\sqrt{\frac{.5(1-.5)}{20}} \leq \pi \leq .5 + 1.96\sqrt{\frac{.5(1-.5)}{20}} \tag{12.21}$$

$$.281 \leq \pi \leq .719$$

If we use Equation 12.20 instead, we get an interval that ranges from .299 to .701, which is similar to what we obtained from the simpler approximation and matches exactly the interval reported by R.

As an alternative to using approximations based on the normal distribution, one can obtain a confidence interval using the binomial distribution. Switching to the binomial distribution relieves the need for approximations, and thus the resulting intervals are often referred to as "exact" intervals. It should be noted, however, that this approach tends to be a bit conservative, which means that more than 95% of our 95% confidence intervals will contain the population proportion. It also means that you should anticipate intervals based on the binomial distribution to be a little wider than those based on approximations to the normal distribution. You can use the **binom.test( )** function to get an "exact" confidence interval:

```
> binom.test(10, 20)

        Exact binomial test

data:  10 and 20
number of successes=10, number of trials=20, p-value=1
```

```
alternative hypothesis: true probability of success is not
equal to 0.5
95 percent confidence interval:
 0.2719578 0.7280422
sample estimates:
probability of success
               0.5
```

Interpreting Confidence Intervals

Given the similarity between probability and level of significance, it would seem natural to say the there is a probability of .95 that the value of μ is contained within the confidence interval. From a mathematical perspective, however, the value of μ is either in the interval or it is not. Rather, we can say that we are 95% confident that the interval contains the true value of μ. The difference may seem very subtle to you, but it is a big deal for mathematical statisticians. We have constructed Figure 12.8 to help make the distinction. In this case, we will talk about a 90% confidence interval, as we did not want to draw 20 lines rather than 10. Looking at Figure 12.8, the heavy horizontal line toward the top of the figure represents the continuum of the random variable Y. The heavy vertical line in the center of the figure is the true location of the population mean, μ. Imagine that we were to draw 10 random samples from the population, and for each of them, construct a 90% confidence interval. The appropriate interpretation of confidence intervals would suggest that 90% of the intervals so constructed would contain μ. Note that nine of the 10 intervals around the 10 means span/contain the value of μ.

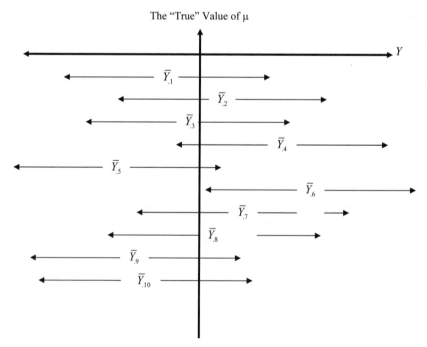

FIGURE 12.8 The logic of constructing and interpreting 90% confidence intervals for the sample mean.

At this point, if we were to follow the structure earlier in this chapter, we would construct a confidence interval for a median. However, the median is not a mathematically tractable statistic; its sampling distribution is not well known. That is, the distribution theory to guide us in determining which mathematical probability distribution to use is not well established. However, there is hope!

We now turn to an alternative process for constructing confidence intervals based on the available data rather than distribution theory. As we have already noted, confidence intervals based on distribution theory can only be constructed for statistics that have a known sampling distribution. We would also point out that the legitimate interpretation of such confidence intervals is predicated on the data meeting assumptions. For example, in dealing with means (and proportions), we have to assume that the random variable Y is normally distributed or that the sample size is sufficiently large to yield a statistic with a sampling distribution that is approximately normal. This alternative process relies on resampling methods. The particular method is called *bootstrapping*.

CONSTRUCTING CONFIDENCE INTERVALS EMPIRICALLY: BOOTSTRAPPING

When we test hypotheses, we make the assumption that the data contain information about the population. In addition, we make other assumptions about the distribution of the population. Suppose we are not willing to make those other assumptions. We can still assume that the sample data are a reasonable facsimile of the population, modeling that sampling distribution by repeatedly drawing samples from our sample and then looking at the distribution of our sample statistics. The trick is to "sample with replacement." This technique is called "bootstrapping." In this technique, we are not making assumptions about the sampling distribution. Rather, we are "pulling ourselves up by our bootstraps." Let's go back to revisit Example 12.1.

In this example, we had a random sample of 12 *irt* scores from Native Hawaiian, Other Pacific Islander children. Using distribution-based methods, we found a confidence interval from 14.32 to 23.68. Using a different approach, we can repeatedly draw a random sample of 12 values from our sample, with replacement. Suppose we repeated this process 100,000 times and calculated the mean on each of the 100,000 re-samplings. We could then look at the actual distribution of our 100,000 re-sampled means. If we were to delete the lowest and highest 2.5% of those 100,000 re-sampled means, the outer limits of the remaining re-sampled means could be considered an estimate of the 95% confidence interval. As funky as this may sound, it is becoming increasingly accepted in the world of applied statistics, especially with the easy access to high-speed computers and programs like R. For more information, see Davison and Hinkley (1997), Edgington and Onghena (2007), Efron (1982), Efron and Tibshirani (1993), Good (2000, 2006), Lunneborg (2000), Mooney and Duval (1993), and Simon (1997).

A Bootstrapped Confidence Interval for Example 12.1 with R

We have applied these ideas in taking another look at Example 12.1. The R script is included on the website (Script 12.8). In order to demonstrate the basic technique, we first re-sampled our sample of 12 observations with replacement; we did this 100,000 times. The results are:

```
> quantile (stat,probs=c(.025,.975))
    2.5%    97.5%
15.33333 23.25000
```

First, note that this result is not exactly the same as that from distribution-based theory methods. Also, note that the interval is not perfectly symmetric around the mean of 19.0. There are many different ways to construct bootstrapped confidence intervals; Lunneborg (2000) labeled this approach the "nonsymmetric percentile confidence interval estimate." Although it is a logical approach, it has a tragic flaw. Recall that in our discussion of the range as a descriptive statistic for dispersion/variability, we noted that the range tends to be a function of the sample size. The larger the sample size, the larger the range tends to be. We noted something similar when we looked at the sampling distribution of s^2 in our introduction to the t-distribution. There is a tendency for s^2 to underestimate σ^2 more than half of the time, but this tendency decreases as the sample size increases. Thus, with small samples, the variability present in the sample tends to be less than the variability in the population. That said, the variability of our re-sampled means could be expected to be less than the variability of the means in the population of sample means, resulting in confidence intervals that are too narrow. Both Lunneborg (2000) and Good (2006) have recommended the *bias corrected and accelerated* (BC_a) method (Efron & Tibshirani, 1993, pp. 178–188) as an improvement over the percentile methods. The computation of BC_a confidence intervals is rather complicated; fortunately it is available in the **boot** package in R. After loading the **boot** package with a **library( )** command, the output from R reports the results from four different methods of estimation; we present only two of them here:

```
> library(boot)
> f.mean<-function( y, id ){
>   mean(y[id])
> }
> boot.ci(boot(irt, f.mean, 100000), conf=.95)
Based on 100000 bootstrap replicates

Intervals :

Level      Percentile              BCa
95%    (15.33, 23.25 )     (15.67, 23.92 )
```

Based on the literature, we recommend the BC_a results for your consideration.

A Bootstrapped Confidence Interval for Example 12.2 with R

Example 12.2 was concerned with testing a hypothesis about a proportion. We now repeat this example, first with our own syntax for a non-symmetric percentile confidence interval estimate, and then with the BC_a estimate (Script 12.9).

```
> quantile (stat,probs=c(.025,.975))
   2.5% 97.5%
   0.3   0.7

library(boot)
f.mean<-function( y,id ){
```

```
  mean(y[id])
}
boot.ci(boot(day.care, f.mean, 100000), conf=.95)

BOOTSTRAP CONFIDENCE INTERVAL CALCULATIONS
Based on 100000 bootstrap replicates

boot.ci(boot.out=boot(day.care, f.mean, 1e+05), conf=0.95)

Intervals :

Level     Percentile              BCa
95%    ( 0.30,  0.70 )     ( 0.25,  0.65 )
```

Note that the BC_a interval is different from those constructed with either distribution theory or the percentile method. It is the one that we would recommend.

A Bootstrapped Confidence Interval for Example 12.3 with R

Example 12.3 was concerned with testing a hypothesis about a median. It is at this point that the advantages of bootstrapped confidence intervals become even more apparent. Even if we assume a normal population, the sampling distribution is somewhat complex, as its distribution depends on the underlying distribution, not just its standard deviation. However, we can still find a bootstrapped estimate of the confidence interval with resampling methods. Indeed, if a quantity can be calculated, it can be bootstrapped to find a confidence interval. The R script is available on the website in the supplementary materials for this chapter (Script 12.10). The results from our percentile confidence interval and the BC_a estimate are:

```
> quantile (stat,probs=c(.025,.975))
  2.5%  97.5%
284950 550000

> boot.ci(boot(house.price,f.median,100000),conf=.95)
BOOTSTRAP CONFIDENCE INTERVAL CALCULATIONS
Based on 100000 bootstrap replicates
CALL :
boot.ci(boot.out=boot(house.price, f.median, 1e+05),
conf=0.95)

Level     Percentile              BCa
95%    (284950, 550000 )    (280450, 538750 )
Calculations and Intervals on Original Scale
```

By now you should be relatively convinced that the results of our syntax for the percentile method and the results from the **boot.ci( )** function in R agree. Thus, in the future, we will rely on the results from the **boot.ci( )** function whenever possible.

CHAPTER SUMMARY

We started with an alternative to the one-sample z-test for a mean. In situations in which we must estimate the population variance from the sample data, it is appropriate to use the one-sample t-test. There are some who advocate using a z-test when the sample size is 30 or greater; we do not. We then presented the one-sample test on a proportion as a special case of a test on a mean. Next, we considered the sample median as a measure of location that is, at times, more appropriate than the mean. We constructed a way to test a hypothesis by applying the binomial distribution; this procedure is sometimes called the Sign Test.

After presenting several different examples of testing hypotheses, we introduced you to an alternative approach, constructing confidence intervals. We demonstrated ways to construct them with distribution-theory-based methods and then introduced empirically based resampling methods with bootstrapping. These methods may be more appropriate for situations where traditional assumptions are in doubt, and may be the only methods available for estimates that have no known sampling distribution, such as the median, the interquartile range, etc.

In the next chapter we will consider other one-sample procedures for dealing with situations in which we might be concerned with variability, relationships (correlation and regression), and distributions of categorical data, both univariate and bivariate

Key Terms

Bootstrapping   Sign Test
Confidence interval   Statistical power
Fisher's Exact Test t-Distribution
Robust   William Sealy Gosset

REFERENCES

Cowles, M. (2001). *Statistics in psychology: An historical perspective* (2nd ed.). Mahwah, NJ: Lawrence Erlbaum Associates.

Davison, A. C., & Hinkley, D. V. (1997). *Bootstrap methods and their application.* Cambridge, UK: Cambridge University Press.

Edgington, E. S., & Onghena, P. (2007). *Randomization tests* (4th ed.). Boca Raton, FL: Chapman & Hall/CRC.

Efron, B. (1982). *The jackknife, the bootstrap and other resampling plans.* Philadelphia, PA: Society for Industrial and Applied Mathematics.

Efron, B., & Tibshirani, R. J. (1993). *An introduction to the bootstrap.* New York: Chapman & Hall.

Evans, M., Hastings, N., & Peacock, B. (1993). *Statistical distributions* (2nd ed.). New York: John Wiley.

Fisher, R. A. (1925). Applications of "Student's" distribution. *Metron, 5,* 90–104.

Good, P. (2000). *Permutation tests: A practical guide to resampling methods for testing hypotheses.* New York: Springer.

Good, P. I. (2006). *Resampling methods: A practical guide to data analysis* (3rd ed.). Boston: Birkhäuser.

Howell, D. C. (2007). *Statistical methods for psychology* (6th ed.). Belmont, CA: Thomson Higher Education.

Lunneborg, C. E. (2000). *Data analysis by resampling: Concepts and applications.* Pacific Grove, CA: Duxbury.

Mooney, C. Z., & Duval, R. D. (1993). *Bootstrapping: A nonparametric approach to statistical inference.* Newbury Park: CA: Sage.

Newcombe, R. G. (1998). Two-sided confidence intervals for the single proportion: Comparison of seven methods. *Statistics in Medicine*, *17*, 857–872.

Read, C. B. (1997). Gosset, William Sealy ("Student"). In N. L. Johnson & S. Kotz (Eds.), *Leading personalities in statistical sciences: From the seventeenth century to the present* (pp. 327–329). New York: John Wiley.

Simon, J. L. (1997). *Resampling: The new statistics* (2nd ed.). Arlington, VA: Resampling Stats, Inc.

Student, A. (1908). The probable error of the mean. *Biometrika*, *6*, 1–25.

PRACTICE QUESTIONS

1. Suppose we wish to test the null hypothesis that the population mean is equal to 50. If we do not know the population standard deviation and thus estimate it using the sample standard deviation, which sampling distribution would be most appropriate for the test?

   a. z.

   b. t.

   c. χ^2.

   d. p.

2. Suppose we wish to test the null hypothesis that the population mean is 50 and that we have observed a sample mean of 55. We also note there is an outlying score of 35. After further checking we find that this score was entered incorrectly and that it should have been a 53. If we correct this data entry mistake, the t-value:

   a. will increase

   b. will decrease

   c. will remain the same

   d. may increase or decrease.

3. A researcher testing the null hypothesis that the population proportion is .50 obtains a p-value of .0023. Using a conventional α of .05, the researcher should conclude that:

   a. the population proportion is .50

   b. the population proportion differs from .50

   c. the population proportion may or may not differ from .50.

4. Two researchers each conduct a study and construct a confidence interval around the obtained sample mean. Everything is the same in the two studies except that the second researcher has a sample size that is twice as large as the first researcher's. Relative to the first researcher, the second researcher should expect the confidence interval she constructs to be:

   a. wider than the first researcher's

   b. narrower than the first researcher's

   c. the same size as the first researcher's.

5. As variation increases, one anticipates the confidence interval to be:

   a. wider

   b. narrower

   c. unchanged.

6. A researcher constructs a 95% confidence interval for a proportion that runs from .44 to .52. Which of the following statements is an accurate interpretation?

   a. The population proportion is between .44 and .52, 95% of the time.

   b. We are 95% confident that the population proportion is .48.

c. We are 95% confident that the sample proportion is between .44 and .52.

d. We are 95% confident that the population proportion is between .44 and .52.

EXERCISES

12.1. Prior to the institution of a new safety program, the mean number of on-the-job accidents per day on a particular automobile assembly line was 4.5. A new safety-education program was implemented to reduce the number of accidents. A random sample of 30 days was taken from a 2-year period following the implementation of the program, and the number of accidents per day was recorded. The sample mean and standard deviation were determined as 3.7 and 1.3, respectively. Is there sufficient reason to conclude at the .01 level that the number of accidents has decreased since the beginning of the safety program?

12.2. In 1991, the proportion of new car buyers who were women was .32. In a random sample of 150 new car buyers in 2001, 64 were women. Do these data indicate that the true proportion of new car buyers in 2001 who were women is different from the 1991 proportion? Test at $\alpha = .05$.

12.3. According to http://www.city-data.com, the estimated median of housing prices in Chapel Hill was $356,878 (retrieved on 18 August 2010). The advertisement placed by The Home Team in the *Chapel Hill News* on 15 August 2010 listed 29 homes (houses and condos) for sale. The prices were (in dollars): 659,000, 399,000, 222,500, 599,000, 350,000, 295,000, 495,000, 384,900, 219,000, 599,000, 349,000, 269,500, 489,900, 335,000, 189,000 439,750, 335,000, 268,500, 475,000, 264,500, 189,500, 375,000, 300,000, 199,000, 449,000, 252,500, 178,900, 369,000, and 299,000. Given these prices, do you think that these listings are representative of the homes in Chapel Hill, NC?

13

More One-Sample Tests

INTRODUCTION

In this chapter, we will present other one-sample procedures for addressing concerns related to variability, relationships, and categorical variables. Within the context of the test for variance, we will also consider tests of shape, with respect to departures from normality. Specifically with categorical variables, we will address the issue of shape with what is called a "chi-squared (χ^2) goodness-of-fit test;" the basic idea of which is whether the numbers of observations (counts) within the categories depart from some expected counts for the corresponding categories.

A TEST ON ONE VARIANCE

While it is true that most research questions focus on location and relationships, there are times when we might be concerned with variability. For example, we might suspect that children referred for individual assessment by a school psychologist might be more heterogeneous than the general population with regard to measured intelligence. Given that the Weschler series of intelligence (IQ) tests is standardized to have a variance of 225, we would be interested in contrasting the hypotheses:

$$H_0 : \sigma^2 \leq 225$$
$$H_1 : \sigma^2 > 225$$

(13.1)

Consider another example; it would be reasonable to suspect that experiencing a course in driver's education might reduce the variability in the time spent "not moving" at the stop sign at an intersection.

In our previous examples of hypothesis testing, we have applied linear transformations to our data to "reduce" the data to an observed test statistic that can then be compared to a mathematical probability distribution to obtain an estimate of the probability of observing the data at hand, given that the null hypothesis is true. Linear transformations involve addition/subtraction and multiplication/division; they change the scaling of the data, but not the shape of the distribution. In working with means (and proportions), it is reasonable to suspect that the sampling distribution of the statistics will be symmetric, and we are able to use the z-distribution or t-distribution as the situation requires. Both of these probability distributions are symmetric. However, recall that in our introduction to the t-test, we examined the sampling distribution of the sample variance, finding that it is positively skewed, particularly with small samples. Thus, using the z- or t-distribution to model the sampling distribution of variances would require a non-linear transformation of the data. As an alternative, perhaps we should consider a different probability distribution. As you will see, the latter is the way to go.

To help build an understanding of the non-symmetric probability distribution that we will be employing, we first need to call your attention to the formula for the sample variance:

$$s^2 = \frac{\sum_{i=1}^{n}\left(Y_i - \overline{Y}_.\right)^2}{n-1} \tag{13.2}$$

Now, because all three authors of this text have tenure, we are going to multiply both sides of the expression by $(n-1)$:

$$(n-1)s^2 = \sum_{i=1}^{n}\left(Y_i - \overline{Y}_.\right)^2 \tag{13.3}$$

And since both Bill and John are both full professors and Barbara is an associate professor, they all want to divide both sides by σ^2:

$$\frac{(n-1)s^2}{\sigma^2} = \frac{\sum_{i=1}^{n}\left(Y_i - \overline{Y}_.\right)^2}{\sigma^2} \tag{13.4}$$

Now, concentrate your attention on the right side of Equation 13.4. With a stretch of the imagination, hopefully you can see a sum of what resembles squared z-scores. That is:

$$\frac{(n-1)s^2}{\sigma^2} = \frac{\left(Y_1 - \overline{Y}_.\right)^2}{\sigma^2} + \frac{\left(Y_2 - \overline{Y}_.\right)^2}{\sigma^2} + \ldots + \frac{\left(Y_i - \overline{Y}_.\right)^2}{\sigma^2} + \ldots + \frac{\left(Y_n - \overline{Y}_.\right)^2}{\sigma^2} \tag{13.5}$$

If we were to subtract the population mean, μ, rather than the sample mean, it would be, literally, the sum of independent squared z-scores. We are going to pursue this thought, doing a little simulation with R.

Simulating the Sum of Squared z-Scores with R

To simulate the sum of squared z-scores with R, we have drawn random samples of size $n = 1$, 2, 5, and 10 from the unit-normal distribution, squared the elements, and summed them. The R script appears on the website in the supplementary materials for this chapter (Script 13.1 on the website). The results are displayed in Table 13.1 and Figure 13.1. Those of you astute at seeing patterns need no help; the rest of us may have to look at the results for a bit. After sufficient time, we should all be able to see that there are some patterns with respect to the means and variances in Table 13.1. As the sample size increases, both the means and variances increase. In fact, the means are very close to the size of the sample, and the variances are very close to twice the size of the sample. Furthermore, as the sample size increases, both skewness and kurtosis decrease, making the shape closer to a normal distribution. We did not include the results in Figure 13.1, but we ran the simulation for $n = 20$ and found the mean, variance, skewness, and kurtosis to be, respectively, 19.9948, 39.8697, .6130, and .5306. The pattern seems to be reliable! And guess what … there is actually a mathematical probability distribution that models this pattern very closely: the chi-squared (χ^2) distribution.

Table 13.1 Means, variances, skewness, and kurtosis for z-scores, squared and summed, for $n = 1, 2, 5$, and 10, based on 100,000 replications

	Sample size			
	n = 1	*n = 2*	*n = 5*	*n = 10*
Mean	1.0029	1.9999	5.0082	9.9964
Variance	2.0163	3.9702	9.9855	19.8648
Skewness	2.8595	2.0007	1.2637	.8675
Kurtosis	12.5162	6.0458	2.4538	1.0765

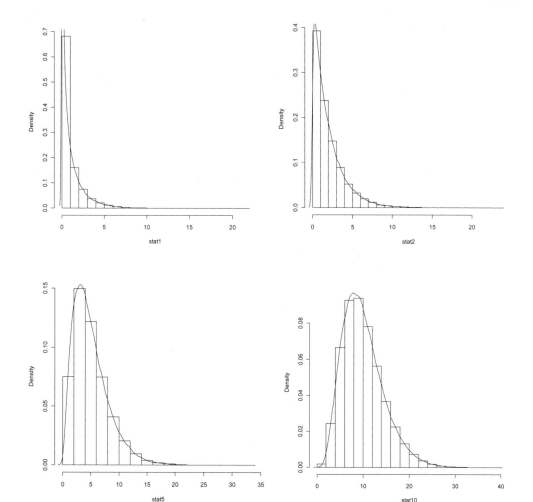

FIGURE 13.1   The sum of squared z-scores for $n = 1, 2, 5$, and 10, based on 100,000 replications.

The χ^2 Distribution

The χ^2 distribution is actually a family of distributions; like the t-distribution, there is a different member for each number of degrees of freedom. The χ^2 family can be defined in different ways. Though it can be derived as a member of the gamma (γ) distribution (like the t-distribution), the easiest way is to think about it is as the sum of independent squared z-scores. In order for this to be true, the z-scores *must* be from the unit-normal distribution, not just any set of raw scores transformed to z-scores. That implies that the distribution of the random variable Y must be normal. The degrees of freedom (df) for χ^2 is equal to the number of independent z-scores and is denoted ν (a lower case Greek "n" and read as "nu"); the expected value of χ^2 is equal to the number of degrees of freedom, and the variance of χ^2 is equal to twice the number of degrees of freedom. More formally, assuming normality and independence:

$$\sum_{i=1}^{n} z_i^2 \sim \chi^2 (\nu, 2\nu) \tag{13.6}$$

A number of different χ^2 distributions are shown in Figure 13.2, for df = 3, 6, 10, and 15 (see Script 13.2).

Returning to a consideration of Equations 13.4 and 13.5, remember that we are substituting the sample mean for the population mean. Thus, only $n - 1$ scores are free to vary. Stated differently, if we want to test a hypothesis about a population variance, we can calculate the sample variance and transform it as follows:

$$\chi^2_{obs} = \frac{(n-1)s^2}{\sigma_0^2} \tag{13.7}$$

The result should be approximately distributed as χ^2 with $df = n - 1$ as long as the null hypothesis is true and the population values are normally distributed.

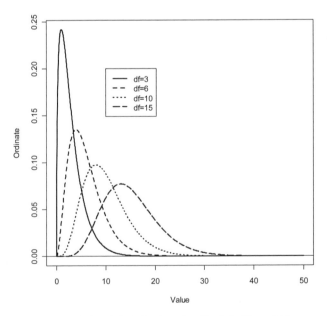

FIGURE 13.2 χ^2 distaributions for df = 3, 6, 10, and 15.

An Example of a One-Sample Test on a Variance

Let's continue with our interest in children from the Native Hawaiian, Other Pacific Islander population considered in Chapter 12. We are going to focus on the entering kindergarten T-scores on general knowledge. Given that they are T-scores, we know that the variance in the general population is 100 (see Chapter 5). Let's test the hypothesis that this subpopulation is different in variability from the general population. We would set up our null and alternate hypotheses as:

$$H_0 : \sigma^2 = 100$$
$$H_1 : \sigma^2 \neq 100$$

(13.8)

We draw a random sample of 20 children from the population of Native Hawaiian, Other Pacific Islander children and find their general knowledge T-scores to be 48, 30, 47, 53, 55, 56, 41, 32, 36, 35, 39, 39, 33, 49, 35, 61, 26, 47, 33, and 41. Rather than do all of the calculations "by hand," we will use R to help us. The R script appears in the supplementary materials for the chapter (Script 13.3 on the book website).

As we noted previously, in order to employ the χ^2 test, it is imperative that the scores be drawn from a population that is normally distributed. Thus, in our script, we examine the statistics for skewness and kurtosis, and introduce you to another R package, **nortest**, which contains several tests of departures from normality. At the end of our treatment of testing hypotheses about variances, we will introduce you to some other tests of departure from normality. Although the issue of normality is an important assumption when testing hypotheses about variances, we will not state the null hypothesis in a formal fashion. (Suffice it to say that the H_0 for each of these tests is that the population from which the scores are drawn follows a normal probability distribution.) Given that the most popular of these tests of normality is the **shapiro.test( )**, it is the only one we will report.

A quick check on the descriptive statistics for normality shows us that it would be reasonable to assume that these scores came from a normal population:

```
> skewness(gk)
[1] 0.3673274
> SEsk(gk)
[1] 0.5121033
> kurtosis(gk)
[1] -0.8204306
> SEku (gk)
[1] 0.9923836
```

That is, for both skewness and kurtosis, the data are within what one would expect from a normal population (less than one standard error from expectation). This conclusion is supported by the results of the **shapiro.test( )**; the *p*-value is greater than .50.

```
> shapiro.test(gk)
        Shapiro-Wilk normality test
data:  gk
W = 0.9596, p-value = 0.5365
```

Thus, we are justified in using our χ^2 test for contrasting the hypotheses about the variance (see Equation 13.7).

```
> s2 <- var(gk)
> s2
[1] 94.58947
> chi.obs<-df*s2/sigma2
> chi.obs
[1] 17.972
```

The results from R indicate that the sample variance is 94.59 and the observed value of χ^2 is 17.92. Now, we need to figure out what this means. A table of the critical values of χ^2 is included in Table A.4 in Appendix A.

Unlike the z and the t tables, which are symmetric, the tails of the χ^2 must be tabulated separately, as the distribution is not symmetric. Given that we are testing a two-tailed hypothesis at the .05 level, we will put .025 in each of the two tails. Looking at the lower tail in Table A.4 with $n = 20$ ($df = 19$), we see that the value that cuts off .025 is 8.9065. Similarly, the value that cuts off .025 in the upper tail is 32.8523. Although we think there is some value in being able to find values in the table, we can also get R to provide them with a **qchisq( )** function. In either case, we would set up our regions of rejection and non-rejection as shown in Figure 13.3 (see Script 13.4). Given that our observed value of 17.97 falls in the region of non-rejection, we would fail to reject H_0 in this case.

Constructing a Confidence Interval for this Example

As an alternative to testing the hypothesis, we could construct a confidence interval. Based on classical distribution theory, we construct the 95% confidence interval as follows:

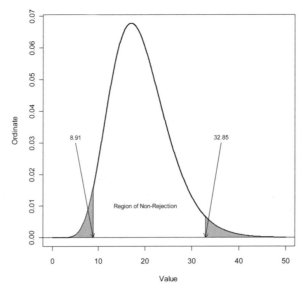

FIGURE 13.3   Regions of rejection and non-rejection for one sample test on a variance ($df = 19$).

$$\frac{(n-1)s^2}{\chi^2_{\frac{\alpha}{2},v}} \leq \sigma^2 \leq \frac{(n-1)s^2}{\chi^2_{1-\frac{\alpha}{2},v}} \tag{13.9}$$

Using the data from our example, we would substitute values as follows:

$$\frac{(20-1)94.59}{32.85} \leq \sigma^2 \leq \frac{(20-1)94.59}{8.91} \tag{13.10}$$

$$54.70 \leq \sigma^2 \leq 201.70$$

Or, we could find the BC$_a$ bootstrapped estimate in R:

```
> f.var <- function(y,id) {
>    + var(y[id])
>    + }
> boot.ci (boot(gk, f.var, 100000), conf = .95)
BOOTSTRAP CONFIDENCE INTERVAL CALCULATIONS
Based on 100000 bootstrap replicates
CALL :
boot.ci (boot.out = boot(gk, f.var, 1e+05),
    conf = 0.95)

Intervals :
Level       Percentile               BCa
95%     ( 49.38, 134.87 )     ( 61.63, 154.41 )
```

In all cases the hypothesized value (100) falls within the confidence interval.

Another Example of a One-Sample Test on a Variance

Let's look at another example of the one-sample test on a variance. Recall that earlier we gave as an example the situation where one might want to test whether children referred to a school psychologist for individual assessment were equivalent to the general population of children with respect to variability in IQ scores. We have used R to simulate data that would characterize what we believe might be happening. What we have done is to simulate what is called a "mixture distribution," or a distribution composed of two different distributions. We believe that children who are referred may actually represent two distinctly different subpopulations. On the one hand, some of those children may be toward the low end of the distribution and are having difficulty keeping up. On the other hand, some of the children may be coming from the high end of the distribution and are bored and acting out. Both subsets are likely to be restricted in range. (You don't have to agree, but that is how we constructed the fictitious data set.) The script appears on the book website in the supplementary materials for this chapter (Script 13.5). We believe that the students who are referred for assessment are more variable than the general population. The hypotheses to be contrasted are:

$$H_0 : \sigma^2 \leq 225$$
$$H_1 : \sigma^2 > 225$$

(13.11)

First, we should look at the data:

```
> mean(both)
[1] 100.3333
> sd(both)
[1] 25.90345
> skewness(both)
[1] -0.0400426
> SEsk(both)
[1] 0.4268924
> kurtosis(both)
[1] -1.568425
> SEku(both)
[1] 0.8327456
```

We note that the mean is about what we would expect for the general population; however, the standard deviation is, as we predicted, larger than that for the general population ($\sigma = 15$).

Checking for Normality

Looking at the measures of skewness and kurtosis, we can see that the distribution is essentially symmetric, but that it is nearly two standard errors negatively kurtotic. Perhaps we should complete a **shapiro.test( )**:

```
> shapiro.test(both)

        Shapiro-Wilk normality test

data:  both
W = 0.9033, p-value = 0.01013
```

The p-value is rather small. The data depicted in the histogram in Figure 13.4 do not look very normal. Thus the data give us reason to question the assumption of normality, which is essential for the χ^2 one-sample test on a variance. (Should you wish to replicate our analyses, the actual data are given immediately below. Or you could use the script to generate your own data.)

```
> both
 [1]  88  79  64  79  78  78  84  73  69  94  56  71  75  73
[15]  85 128 121 119 125 132 131 122 114 116 122
[26] 139 111 120 124 140
```

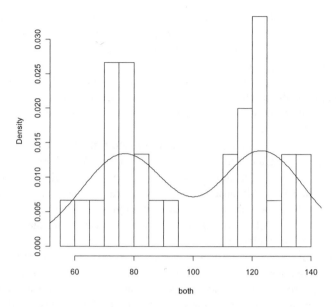

FIGURE 13.4   Histogram and density distribution of the data for the one-sample test on a variance with school psychology referrals.

Given that the assumption of a normally distributed population is rather tenuous, what should we do? Bootstrap, of course! The actual variance for our data is $s^2 = 670.99$. If we want to do a one-tailed test at the .05 level, we should do a two-tailed confidence interval at the 90% level and only use the lower-tailed value for our decision. Can you explain why?

To demonstrate the difference, we will actually do both a 95% and 90% confidence interval:

```
> boot.ci(boot(both,f.var,100000), conf=.95)

Level      Percentile              BCa
95%    (482.1, 827.3 )     (533.8, 899.9 )

> boot.ci(boot(both,f.var,100000), conf=.90)

Level      Percentile              BCa
90%    (507.8, 796.0 )     (558.3, 864.8 )
```

Note that the 90% BC_a confidence interval is narrower than the 95% interval, as you would expect. Any value outside of the interval may be rejected as untenable. Our hypothesized value was 225, and the lower value of the 90% BC_a interval is 558.3. Thus, we should reject.

OTHER TESTS OF DEPARTURES FROM NORMALITY

The first two authors of this text have been involved in developing other tests for departures from normality. Ware and Ferron (1995) developed a test modeled after the K^2 test of D'Agostino and

Pearson (1990). Using the Fisher estimates for skewness and kurtosis and their respective errors, they developed a test statistic which they named g^2. The test statistic is formed by taking the indices of skewness and kurtosis, dividing each by its respective standard error, squaring the two values and adding them together. The distribution of g^2 was approximated by extensive simulation. Their work was extended by Althouse, Ware, and Ferron (1998) in a study which refined the estimated sampling distribution of g^2 and compared it to several other tests of normality. The test has been programmed in R as described in Script 13.6 in the supplementary materials for this chapter (see the book website).

Ware and Althouse (1999) continued to develop and test procedures for testing departures from normality, developing a test modeled after the Shapiro–Wilk (1965) test (W). At that time, the W test was available only for sample sizes of 50 or less. Although approximations had been developed (Royston, 1982), Althouse (1997) showed that the approximation may not provide adequate control of the Type I error rate. Again employing Monte Carlo simulation to explore the sampling distribution, Althouse and Ware developed a procedure that they called the "line test." The test statistic is developed as follows: Order the observed values, convert their ranks to percentile ranks, convert the percentile ranks to z-scores under an assumption of normality, and then correlate the original scores with the corresponding z-scores. If the distribution of data were perfectly normal, the resulting r would be 1.00. As the original data depart from normality, the values of r will decrease. They found that line test was similar in power to W for small sample sizes, equivalent in power to W for large sample sizes, and did not manifest an inflated Type I error rate. The line test statistic has been programmed in R and appears in Script 13.7 in the supplementary materials for this chapter (see book website).

Implementing the g.square and line.test Functions

The mixture distribution from the previous example has been implemented using Script 13.8:

```
> g.square(data)
[1] "The value of g-squared"
[1] 3.556138
[1] "The sample size"
[1] 30
[1] "p > .10"
> line.test(data)
[1] "The correlation between actual cdf and normal cdf"
[1] 0.9557293
 [1] "Significant at the .05 level"
```

As you can see, the **g.square( )** test does not find that the data depart from normality, but the **line.test( )** finds a difference at the .05 level.

OTHER ONE-SAMPLE TESTS

Thus far in this chapter we have considered tests of hypotheses and confidence intervals for one-sample situations with the variability of only one *quantitative* variable. Now, we will consider other one-sample situations. First, we will consider a one-sample test that deals with only one *categorical* variable, focusing not on attributes of the distribution, but rather on the overall distribution. Then we will consider situations that involve two quantitative variables, looking at tests of correlation and regression. Finally, we will look at the issue of relationship between two categorical variables.

The Distribution of One Categorical Variable: Pearson's χ^2 Goodness-of-Fit Test

There are occasions when we are interested in testing the hypothesis about the distribution of a categorical variable, somewhat like using the **shapiro.test( )** function for looking at the normality of a quantitative variable. For example, we might be interested in assessing preference for each of three weekly news magazines (*Newsweek*, *Time*, and *U.S. News and World Report*), based on the responses of a sample from some population. If they are equally preferred, then if we were to take a sample of 300 cases, we would expect to see approximately 100 respondents indicate that they preferred each of the magazines. Another popular example of this type of test is concerned with the distribution of the colors in packages of M&Ms. According to the company website, one should expect to see 14% brown, 14% yellow, 14% red, 18% blue, 21% orange, and 18% green morsels in a package of plain candies (which only add to 99%). (See http://joshmadison.com/article/mms-color-distribution-analysis for an amusing treatment of this problem.) How might we proceed in a situation in which we want to compare actual counts to expected counts? The data consist of counts per category and some basis for "expectation" per category. It turns out that Pearson was able to show that the χ^2 probability distribution could be used to conduct a test of observed counts versus expected counts. Indeed, this test is what jumps into the minds of most statistics students when they hear the term "chi squared."

The Basis for Pearson's χ^2 test

In introducing the concept of probability earlier in this book, we considered the binomial distribution as an example of a discrete probability distribution. The binomial distribution provides a model for considering the number of "successes" versus "failures" in a set of n trials. In fact there is another discrete probability distribution we should also consider, the Poisson distribution. (Yes, we have the name correct.) Siméon Poisson was a French mathematician who studied the binomial distribution under conditions of large n (approaching infinity) and very small values of p (approaching zero). In doing so, he derived what we now know as the Poisson distribution:

$$P(Y) = \frac{\lambda^Y e^{-\lambda}}{Y!} \tag{13.12}$$

where $Y = \{0, 1, 2, 3 \ldots\}$, the counting integers. The distribution is useful in modeling the number of events within a time frame, particularly rare events. The distribution has the interesting property that both its expected value (μ) and its variance (σ^2) are equal to λ (Evans, Hastings, & Peacock, 1993). We have simulated the Poisson distribution for values of $\lambda = .5$, 1, 3, and 5 (Script 13.9). The results, including means, variances, skewness, and kurtosis are displayed in Table 13.2 and are depicted graphically in Figure 13.5.

As you can see in both the table and the figure, the means and the variances are both very close to what is expected. Furthermore, as the value of λ increases, the distributions of the Poisson random variates decrease in both skewness and kurtosis; when $\lambda = 5$, the distribution is quite close to normal, as can be seen in the last panel of Figure 13.5.

Table 13.2 Descriptive statistics for the Poisson distribution of 100,000 random variates with lambda (λ) = .5, 1, 3, and 5

	Sample size			
	$\lambda = .5$	$\lambda = 1$	$\lambda = 3$	$\lambda = 5$
Mean	.5012	.9970	3.0031	5.0063
Variance	.5045	1.0031	3.0345	5.0131
Skewness	1.4176	1.0111	.5795	.4468
Kurtosis	1.9789	1.0228	.3221	.1978

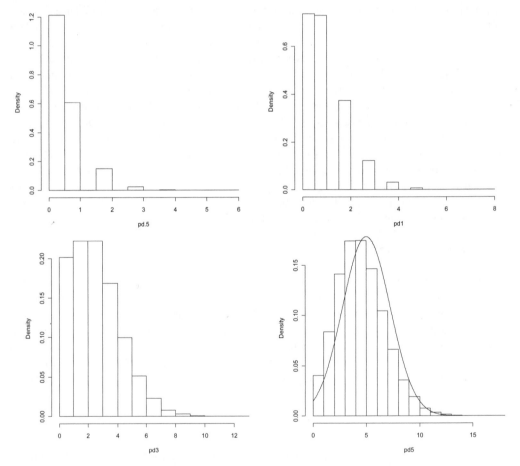

FIGURE 13.5   Histograms of 100,000 Poisson random variates for lambda (λ) = .5, 1, 3, and 5, with normal density distribution for $\lambda = 5$.

We cannot reconstruct Pearson's thinking as he derived the test statistic, but we can reverse-engineer it for you. Pearson's test statistic is:

$$\chi^2 = \sum_{j=1}^{k} \frac{\left(O_j - E_j\right)^2}{E_j} \tag{13.13}$$

Let's express Equation 13.13 in a form based on Poisson notation:

$$\chi^2 = \sum_{j=1}^{k} \frac{\left(Y_j - \lambda\right)^2}{\lambda} \qquad (13.14)$$

However, given that λ is both the mean and the variance of the Poisson distribution, we can substitute as follows:

$$\chi^2 = \sum_{j=1}^{k} \frac{\left(Y_j - \mu\right)^2}{\sigma^2} \qquad (13.15)$$

Thus, Pearson's formula (Equation 13.13) can be considered a sum of squared z-scores. If the random variable Y is normally distributed, then that sum should be distributed as χ^2. Given that the Poisson distribution appears to be quite close to a normal distribution for values of $\lambda \geq 5$, we can use this expression to test hypotheses about distributions of categorical variables when the expected cell counts are five or greater.

An Example of the χ^2 Goodness-of-Fit Test

Let's take a look at the racial composition of the ECLS2577 data file, using a random sample of 300 cases. One might ask if the racial composition of the sample is similar to the population at large. According to the 2000 U.S. Census (as reported at: http://factfinder.census.gov/servlet/QTTable?_bm=y&-geo_id=01000US&-qr_name=DEC_2000_SF1_U_QTP5&-ds_name=DEC_2000_SF1_U), the racial composition of the population in the United States was as follows:

Racial group						
White	Black	American Indian	Asian	Native Hawaiian	Other	Multiple
75.1%	12.3%	.9%	3.6%	.1%	4.3%	3.7%

In our sample, the 300 children were classified as:

Racial group						
White	Black	American Indian	Asian	Native Hawaiian	Other	Multiple
147	53	18	12	11	48	11

Given the category percentages provided by the Census Bureau, we can derive our "expected" values by multiplying the percentages by 300 and dividing by 100, obtaining the following values:

Racial group						
White	Black	American Indian	Asian	Native Hawaiian	Other	Multiple
225.3	36.9	2.7	10.8	.3	12.9	11.1

Now that we have both the "expected" and the "observed" counts, we can plug the numbers into Equation 13.15 as shown below. In passing, we note that the computations are always completed on the "counts," not on the percentages.

$$\chi^2 = \frac{(147-225.3)^2}{225.3} + \frac{(53-36.9)^2}{36.9} + \frac{(18-2.7)^2}{2.7} + \frac{(12-10.8)^2}{10.8} +$$

$$\frac{(11-0.3)^2}{.3} + \frac{(48-12.9)^2}{12.9} + \frac{(11-11.1)^2}{11.1} \qquad (13.16)$$

$$= 27.212 + 7.024 + 86.700 + .133 + 381.633 + 95.505 + .001$$

$$= 598.201$$

Given that the sample size is known to be 300, only six of the seven category counts are free to vary. That is, the number of degrees of freedom for this analysis should be $7 - 1$, or 6. In general, the number of degrees of freedom for a one-sample goodness-of-fit χ^2 test will be the number of categories minus 1. When we consider the location of the region of rejection, we should note that any difference between "observed" and "expected," no matter which direction, will increase the observed value of χ^2. Thus, we want to consider only the upper-tailed value of χ^2 for 6 degrees of freedom. Whether we use Table A.4 or the **qchisq( )** function in R, we obtain a critical value of 12.59. Given our observed value of 598.2, we would reject H_0. (Back in Equation 13.6, we noted that the expected value of χ^2 was equal to the number of degrees of freedom, and the variance of χ^2 was equal to twice the number of degrees of freedom. Given that the number of degrees of freedom for this is 6, it should be pretty obvious that 598.2 is very far from what we might expect under H_0.)

It would appear that the racial composition of our sample of 300 children is different from that reported in the 2000 Census. Given that the calculated values for each of the categories are squared z-scores, we can compare the results within each cell to a value of 3.84, or approximately 4. Looking at Equation 13.16, it would appear that Whites have been undersampled, while the Black, American Indian, Native Hawaiian, and Other categories have been oversampled. (This practice of oversampling some groups and undersampling other groups is fairly common in large-scale research. At the same time, survey statisticians also compute "sample weights" for each category so that one can construct a "representative" sample. That is, some small groups are oversampled in order to have a sufficient number of cases to analyze. This problem can be corrected by weighting the cases by the sample weights.)

COMPLETING THE EXAMPLE WITH R   In order to complete this example with R, we used Script 13.10 included on the book website. The results are:

```
> result <-chisq.test(obs, p = prob)
Warning message:
In chisq.test(obs, p = prob) : Chi-squared approximation may
be incorrect
> result

        Chi-squared test for given probabilities

data:  obs
X-squared = 598.209, df = 6, p-value < 2.2e-16
```

```
> qchisq(.95,6)
[1] 12.59159
>
> # Obtaining the residuals
> residuals (result)
[1] -5.216523  2.650407  9.311283  0.365148 19.535437
9.772648
[7] -0.030015
```

As you can see, when R provides the residuals, it is giving us the square roots of the calculated values for each cell. These are z-scores, rather than squared z-scores. Thus, we would use a "critical value" of approximately 2 to identify which cells are contributing to the "significant" χ^2.

A PROBLEM WITH THE DATA IN THE EXAMPLE   As you may have noticed in the R output, there is a warning message. In our explanation of χ^2 earlier in the chapter, we noted that the use of Pearson's χ^2 statistic assumes that the random variable (the observed) must be normally distributed, stating that when the observed values are counts (following a Poisson distribution), this assumption is considered justified. Typically, this logic is summarized by a statement to the effect that the procedure is justified as long as all of the expected cell counts are 5 or greater. In looking at our data, even though the sample size was 300, two of the categories (i.e., American Indian and Native Hawaiian) had expected cell frequencies of less than 5, which could be problematic. To investigate this possibility, we have written an R script (Script 13.11) to simulate the population, repeatedly resampling 300 cases with replacement, calculating the χ^2 statistic on each resample, and counting the number of times the computed value exceeded the actual value from the real data. Though the script took a very long time to run, the results finally appeared:

```
> counter
[1] 0
> p.value = counter/N
> p.value
[1] 0
> crit.vals <- round(quantile(stat,
>    probs = c(.005, .025, .05, .95,.975,.995)), 3)
> crit.vals
   0.5%    2.5%     5%    95%   97.5%   99.5%
  0.782   1.259  1.646 13.441  15.735  23.467
```

As you can see, the resampled χ^2 never exceeded the actual χ^2 (598.209) in 100,000 replications. That might have been expected, given that the distribution-based p-value was $2.2e^{-16}$. Of some interest are the quantile values provided by the simulation. The distribution-based values are, respectively, .676, 1.237, 1.635, 12.592, 14.449, and 18.5476. As you can see, the lower-tailed simulated values are relatively similar, but the upper-tailed values are somewhat different, perhaps because of the low expected values in two of the cells.

We offer Script 13.11 for those of you who wish to read it carefully to better understand the process. However, we also know that some of you may just want a solution to the problem so that you can move on. For you we have added some statements at the end of Script 13.11 that employ the ability of the **chisq.test( )** function to resample:

```
# Resampling with the simulation capacity of the
# chisq.test function
# Provide the observed counts
obs <- c(147, 53, 18, 12, 11, 48, 11)
sum(obs)
# Find the expected probabilities for each cell
ratios <- c(75.1, 12.3, 0.9, 3.6, 0.1, 4.3, 3.7)
prob <- ratios/sum(ratios)
result <-chisq.test(obs, p = prob,
   simulate.p.value = TRUE, B = 100000)
result
```

The results are:

```
> result
Chi-squared test for given probabilities with simulated p-
value (based on
        1e+05 replicates)
data:  obs
X-squared = 598.209, df = NA, p-value = 1e-05
```

As you can see, in this case, the results are not very different. In the conventional approach the p-value was 2.2×10^{-16}; with the resampling approach the p-value is 1×10^{-5}. Our main reason for showing the resampling approach is to allow you to bypass our own resampling script if you wish.

All of the examples in this chapter have, so far, been addressing hypotheses about one variable for one group. At this point, we continue to deal with one-group hypotheses, but will be concerned with two variables and the relationship between them. You may wish to refer back to the chapters on correlation and regression to refresh your memory. First we will deal with situations in which the variables are quantitative and can be considered quasi-continuous. There are two such situations that we will cover: (1) when H_0 states that ρ equals zero, and (2) when H_0 states that ρ equals some particular value not equal to zero. Last, we will address the matter of relationships between two categorical variables.

OTHER ONE-SAMPLE TESTS: BIVARIATE RELATIONSHIPS

In this section, we will discuss three different situations concerned with the relationship between two variables: (1) testing whether there is a relationship or not between two quantitative variables; (2) testing whether the relationship between two quantitative variables is different from some specified, non-zero relationship; and (3) testing whether there is a relationship or not between two categorical variables. In each of these three situations, we will present the traditional, distribution-based approach and the resampling approach.

One-Sample Test for Relationship: H_0: $\rho = 0$

The first situation investigates whether two variables are linearly related or not. The hypotheses to be contrasted are:

$$H_0: \rho = 0$$
$$H_0: \rho \neq 0$$
(13.17)

One might want to know whether the SAT-Total score obtained as a high-school senior is related to end-of-year first-year Grade Point Average in college. Or, one might be interested in looking at the possible relationship between the number of books in the home and reading ability at the beginning of kindergarten. As an example, let's look at a possible relationship between socioeconomic status (SES) and reading ability at the beginning of kindergarten. A random sample of 30 cases was drawn from the ECLS2577 data file; the SES and Item Response Theory (IRT) scaled reading scores are presented in Table 13.3. The scores were entered into R with Script 13.12, which is given on the book website.

Before we proceed with calculating the correlation coefficient, we should first examine the scatterplot for linearity and potential outliers. The default plot is presented in the top of Figure 13.6. An examination of the scatterplot does not indicate any systematic departure from a linear relationship, nor do we see any bivariate outliers. Thus, we are assured that it is appropriate to use Pearson's r to assess the degree of the relationship. To employ Pearson's r as an appropriate measure of linear relationship, we need only assume that the relationship is linear. However, to test it for significance, we need to assume that the two variables are distributed as a bivariate normal distribution.

For purposes of review, we will calculate the correlation coefficient, r, using:

$$r = \frac{n\sum_{i=1}^{n} XY - \left(\sum_{i=1}^{n} X\right)\left(\sum_{i=1}^{n} Y\right)}{\sqrt{\left[n\sum_{i=1}^{n} X^2 - \left(\sum_{i=1}^{n} X\right)^2\right]\left[n\sum_{i=1}^{n} Y^2 - \left(\sum_{i=1}^{n} Y\right)^2\right]}}$$
(13.18)

Considering SES as the X variable and IRT as the Y variable, we can develop the preliminary calculations: $\sum X = 1,397$, $\sum Y = 743$, $\sum X^2 = 66,617$, $\sum Y^2 = 19,955$, $\sum XY = 35,208$, and $n = 30$.

Table 13.3 SES and reading IRT data for a one-sample test on a correlation coefficient

Child	SES	IRT	Child	SES	IRT	Child	SES	IRT
1	60	25	11	57	38	21	50	22
2	48	22	12	48	33	22	39	15
3	58	28	13	42	29	23	40	17
4	44	22	14	38	20	24	40	34
5	41	28	15	42	20	25	54	35
6	40	29	16	48	23	26	59	24
7	41	14	17	40	21	27	38	31
8	55	23	18	44	12	28	52	36
9	38	13	19	49	33	29	40	16
10	60	23	20	42	23	30	49	34

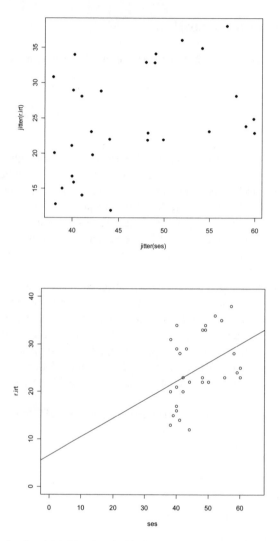

FIGURE 13.6   Scatterplot (without and with the regression line) of SES and IRT, $n = 30$.

Thus,

$$r = \frac{30(35,208) - (1,397)(743)}{\sqrt{\left[30(66,617) - (1,397)^2\right]\left[30(19,955) - (743)^2\right]}}$$

$$= \frac{18,269}{\sqrt{(46,901)(46,601)}} = 0.3907 \tag{13.19}$$

The question is now framed as, "Is the value of .3907 sufficiently different from 0 so that it is reasonable to doubt H_0, or is it within the range of what might be reasonable to expect due to sampling error?" Although there are tables for the critical values of r, we prefer to use a transformation of r into a t-statistic. (If nothing else, it means one less table to figure out.) The transformation is:

$$t_{obs} = r\sqrt{\frac{(n-2)}{1-r^2}}$$

(13.20)

$$t_{obs} = 0.3907\sqrt{\frac{28}{1-0.3907^2}} = 2.246$$

At this point, we need to determine the appropriate value of df to use to enter the t table. There are 30 paired observations. In order to calculate the value of r, we need to estimate the mean values for both SES and IRT. Thus, there are two restrictions, and $df = n - 2$, or 28. Going to Table A.3, we find the two-tailed critical value for $df = 28$ and $\alpha = .05$ to be 2.048. Thus, we would reject H_0. All of this can be done very easily in R:

```
> cor(ses, r.irt)
[1] 0.3907744
> cor.test(ses, r.irt)

        Pearson's product-moment correlation

data:  ses and r.irt
t = 2.2464, df = 28, p-value = 0.03275
alternative hypothesis: true correlation is not equal to 0
95 percent confidence interval:
 0.03550350 0.65835744
sample estimates:
      cor
0.3907744
```

Enough said? Well, not quite. We'd also like to point out that the test of the correlation coefficient is the same as the test on the slope of the least-squares regression line, although the assumptions about the population are different. You might want to go back to Chapter 6 to refresh your memory about the difference between the correlation and regression models. In R,

```
> lm.reg <- lm(r.irt ~ ses)
> summary(lm.reg)

Call:
lm(formula = r.irt ~ ses)

Residuals:
    Min      1Q  Median      3Q     Max
-11.767  -5.170  -1.598   7.162  11.791

Coefficients:
        Estimate Std. Error t value Pr(>|t|)
```

```
(Intercept)    6.6279      8.1710    0.811    0.4241
ses            0.3895      0.1734    2.246    0.0327
```

```
Residual standard error: 6.856 on 28 degrees of freedom
Multiple R-squared: 0.1527,     Adjusted R-squared: 0.1224
F-statistic: 5.046 on 1 and 28 DF,   p-value: 0.03275
```

Note that the *p*-value for the test on the correlation (.03275) is virtually the same as the *p*-value for the slope (.0327) in the regression equation. The plot of SES and IRT is repeated in the lower part of Figure 13.6, with the "true" origin and the regression line overlaid.

Of course, we can also use a resampling approach to testing H_0. Unfortunately, the **boot.ci( )** function can only deal with one-variable situations, but there are several other ways to do this. We chose to use the "percentile" method to bootstrap the confidence interval with 100,000 replications. Given that we want to resample the bivariate observations, R selected a random sample of 30 cases, with replacement. Then the respective SES and IRT values are selected in pairs for those cases:

```
> round(quantile(stat, probs = c(.005, .025, .05, .95, .975,
    .995)), 3)
 0.5%  2.5%    5%    95% 97.5% 99.5%
0.004 0.106 0.155 0.606 0.643 0.711
```

As you can see, the 95% confidence interval is (.106, .643), a little different from that provided by the **cor.test( )** function, (.036, .658), but not very different.

Power Calculations for Testing Hypotheses about Correlation Coefficients

Once again, we employ the **pwr** package, which includes a function **pwr.r.test( )**. The syntax is somewhat similar to the previous examples:

```
pwr.r.test (n = value, r = value,
  sig.level = value, power = value,
  alternative = c("two.sided", "less", "greater")))
```

Again, by specifying all but one of the values, the function will solve for the remaining one. In our example, let's say we are interested in detecting a correlation of .30 or greater, at the .05 level two-tailed, and with a power of .90. In this case,

```
> pwr.r.test(r = .3, sig.level = .05, power = .90,
>   alternative = "two.sided")
```

approximate correlation power calculation (arctangh transformation)

```
              n = 112.3961
              r = 0.3
```

```
    sig.level = 0.05
        power = 0.9
  alternative = two.sided
```

As you can see, if we wanted to meet our conditions, we would need approximately 110 to 115 cases.

When the null hypothesis asserts that $\rho = 0$, then it is reasonable to think that the sampling distribution of r would be symmetric around zero. With very small samples, it is conceivable that r could be ±1.0, but that it not very likely with any reasonably sized sample. Thus, we are able to use the symmetric, mathematical probability distribution (t) to derive our p-values.

What if the null hypothesis states that $\rho = \rho_0$, where ρ_0 is some value other than zero? For example, imagine that you are drawing samples from a bivariate population (X, Y) where $\rho_{XY} =$ .80. The values of r based on repeatedly sampling the population should average to .80, but with very small samples, any particular r could be different as +1.00 or −1.00. Such a sampling distribution would not be symmetric. Thus, in such situations, the conversion of r to a t would not be appropriate. However, there is a solution.

One-Sample Test for Relationship: H_0: $\rho = \rho_0$, where $\rho_0 \neq 0$

Given that the sampling distribution of r is not symmetric when $\rho \neq 0$, we have a minor problem. Indeed, the sampling distribution of r becomes more and more skewed as ρ is increasingly different from zero. One solution would be to find a probability distribution that would "behave" in a similar fashion. An alternative approach would be to find a non-linear transformation that would make the sampling distribution of the transformed values of r symmetric. This was the approach taken by Fisher (1921) in the following transformation:

$$r' = z_r = \frac{1}{2}\log_e(1+r) - \frac{1}{2}\log_e(1-r) \tag{13.21}$$

Originally called "Fisher's transformation of r to z," we prefer the alternate "r to r'" to avoid confusion with the (unit-normal) z-distribution. As formidable as Equation 13.21 appears, we have done two things to make it easy for you. First, we have constructed a table of the transformed values (Table A.5), and second, we have provided an R script that does the transformation and all of the rest of the computation for you.

Before moving through an example, let's take a look at Table A.5 in Appendix A. The values in the column on the left margin are the first two decimal places of the correlation to be transformed. The column headings are the third decimal place. Thus, if you wanted to transform a value of .362, you would go to the row labeled ".36," and then go to the third column in that row labeled ".002." In that location you should see .3792. Now, let's transform a value of .786. Go to the row labeled ".78" and the column labeled ".006." There you will find the value 1.0609, which is what you would obtain if you were to use Equation 13.21 with $r = .786$. Notice that the effect of the transformation is greater with .786 than it is with .362. This is as it should be, as .786 is further from zero than is .362. Thus, the sampling distribution of r would be more skewed for $\rho = .786$ than for $\rho = .362$.

As an example, let's use the ECLS data file. Considering the entire data file as a population, we can find that the correlation between the Time1 (fall-K) IRT reading score and the Time4 (spring-First Grade) IRT reading score is .65. Now, suppose we look at a subsample ($n = 28$) of female, Native American students and we find $r = .75$. We might ask if the strength of association is stronger for this group than it is for the general population. Restating the issue in terms of hypotheses:

$$H_0: \rho \leq 0.65$$
$$H_1: \rho > 0.65$$

(13.22)

The givens of the situation are $\rho_0 = .65$, $r = .75$, and $n = 28$. We proceed by transforming both ρ and r, using Table A.5 in Appendix A. The values returned are .7753 and .9730, respectively. We then substitute those values into the formula provided by Fisher (1921):

$$z_{obs} = \frac{r'_r - r'_\rho}{\sqrt{1/(n-3)}}$$

(13.23)

The result is distributed as z, as the transformed values in the numerator are both normally distributed, and the standard error in the denominator is known, not estimated from sample data as soon as the sample size is specified. Substituting our values:

$$z_{obs} = \frac{r'_r - r'_\rho}{\sqrt{1/(n-3)}} = \frac{.9730 - .7753}{\sqrt{1/(28-3)}} = \frac{.1977}{.2} = .988$$

(13.24)

Noting in Equation 13.22 that this is a one-tailed z-test in the upper tail, the critical value is 1.645. Given that the result does not fall in the region of rejection, we would not reject H_0.

We have written Script 13.13 to complete this analysis in R. All you need to do is to supply the correct values for ρ, r, and n. Then run the script.

```
> rho.z
[1] 0.7752987
> r.z
[1] 0.972955
>
> z.obs <- (r.z - rho.z)/sqrt(1/(n-3))
> z.obs
[1] 0.9882818
```

As you can see, the results agree with our hand calculations. We can also use this transformation to construct a confidence interval for r. More specifically, we transform r to r', build the confidence interval around r', and then transform the limits back to r. The confidence interval for r' can be constructed using the process illustrated in Equations 12.16, 12.17, and 12.18:

$$r' \pm z_{\alpha/2} \frac{1}{\sqrt{n-3}}$$

At the end of Script 13.13, we have written the code to calculate the 95% confidence interval:

```
> # Finding the confidence interval
> r.prime.low <- r.prime - qnorm(.975)/sqrt(n - 3)
> r.prime.up  <- r.prime + qnorm(.975)/sqrt(n - 3)
> r.low <- round(atan(r.prime.low), 3)
> r.up  <- round(atan(r.prime.up), 3)
> cat("95% CI is",r.low,"-",r.up,"\n")
95% CI is 0.526 - 0.939
```

With raw data, it would also be possible to use a resampling approach to construct a confidence interval around the observed value of r.

Both of the examples described immediately above are concerned with looking at a relationship (linear) between two quantitative variables. We now turn our attention to the matter of association between two categorical variables.

One-Sample Test for Relationship: Categorical Variables

When the two variables of concern are both categorical, we can still ask if they are associated, although we usually frame the issue as one of "independence." Suppose we were concerned with whether your preference for "sweet tea" was related to the region of the country in which you spent your "formative years." Suppose we drew a sample of 100 students from a university near (not in) Chapel Hill, one also known for its stellar basketball program (but not its football team). The students were asked how they liked their tea (sweetened, don't care, or unsweetened) and where they grew up (North or South). We could then "cross-tabulate" our data based on the two responses. The resulting table would consist of the number of students responding the "joint" responses for each cell; thus, the observations consist of counts. If you are thinking Pearson's χ^2, you are heading in the right direction. Often, this type of analysis is described as a *contingency table analysis*.

Imagine our "observed counts" appeared as those shown in Table 13.4. If we were to use Pearson's χ^2, we will also need to have "expected counts" for each cell. In the goodness-of-fit test described earlier, the expected values were based on our expectation of what the distribution would be, depending on our null hypothesis. In this situation, H_0 is that the two variables are independent. In order to understand the implications of "independence," we need to return to our discussion of probability, specifically, conditional probability. Recall that, if events A and B are independent, $P(A|B) = P(A)$. Applying that logic to our table, we see that 40 of the students are from the North and 60 are from the South. From that, we can estimate that $P(\text{North}) = .40$. If the two variables are independent, then $P(\text{North}|\text{Sweet})$ should also be .40. Thus, we would expect that 40% of the students who like their tea sweetened would be from the North. We can represent this as:

$$E_{\text{North|Sweetened}} = \frac{40}{100} \times 40 \qquad (13.25)$$

Stated differently, the expected value for a cell can be found by multiplying the respective row total by the respective column total, and then dividing by the total number of observations:

$$E_{ij} = \frac{R_i \times C_j}{T} \qquad (13.26)$$

Table 13.4 Observed results from cross-tabulating responses about tea preference and region of origin

Region of origin	Tea preference			
	Sweetened	Don't care	Unsweetened	Total
North	9	12	19	40
South	31	23	5	60
Total	40	35	25	100

The results of applying Equation 13.26 to the six cells in Table 13.4 are shown in Table 13.5.
We can now apply the formula for Pearson's χ^2 to the six cells:

$$\chi^2_{\text{obs}} = \sum_{i=1}^{2} \sum_{j=1}^{3} \frac{\left(O_{ij} - E_{ij}\right)^2}{E_{ij}} = \frac{(9-16)^2}{16} + \frac{(12-14)^2}{14} + \frac{(19-10)^2}{10} + \frac{(31-24)^2}{24}$$

$$+ \frac{(23-21)^2}{21} + \frac{(6-15)^2}{15} = 19.08 \tag{13.27}$$

In order to interpret this value, we need to compare it to the "critical value" from the χ^2 distribution. In order to do that, we must determine the appropriate *df*. Although 100 students were surveyed, we actually only have six observations (cell counts). Given the restriction that the totals in the margins are fixed, it turns out that only two of the cell counts are free to vary. That is, as soon as you specify the values in two cells, the rest are determined with reference to the totals in the margins. Generally, the *df* for a contingency table analysis can be derived as (No. of rows – 1) × (No. of columns – 1). In this case the result would be 2. Thus, we could look at the upper-tail of the χ^2 distribution with 2 *df* at the .05 level and find the tabulated value to be 5.99. In this case, our observed value was 19.08, so we would reject H_0; the two variables appear to be related.

In general, a contingency table can have any number of rows and any number of columns. However, keeping in mind that there is an assumption that the expected cell frequencies are 5 or greater, large tables can require very large samples. There is some basis in the literature for relaxing the assumption of minimum expected values a bit; if no more than 20% of the cells have expected frequencies less than 5, it is probably acceptable to move forward with the Pearson's χ^2 approximation.

There is also an alternative approach. According to Howell (2007), Fisher introduced what is now known as "Fisher's Exact Test" at the 1934 meeting of the Royal Statistical Society. In the case of a 2 × 2 table, Fisher proposed enumerating all possible arrangements of the cell counts, given fixed totals in the margins. Then, assuming independence, the probability of obtaining cell counts as "extreme" as the ones obtained could be found by looking at the proportion of all possible tables having cell counts as extreme, or more extreme, than those actually obtained. This approach is particularly useful when the cell counts are small, as the procedure does not rely on the χ^2 approximation. This procedure has been generalized to tables larger than 2 × 2 and it is available in R as the function **fisher.test( )**.

Table 13.5 Expected cell values based on responses about tea preference and region of origin

Region of origin	Tea preference			
	Sweetened	Don't care	Unsweetened	Total
North	16	14	10	40
South	24	21	15	60
Total	40	35	25	100

We will now turn our attention to using R for contingency table analysis. The function that we will use in R is the same **chisq.test( )** that we used before in the goodness-of-fit test, although the specifications are slightly different. The function is flexible in that it can be used on "raw" data; it will do the cross-tabulation if need be. Given two categorical variables in factor representation (e.g., f.region, f.tea), the form of the specification is **chisq.test**(f.region,f.tea). On the other hand, it is often the case that we have our data already tabulated, in which case we can supply a table or matrix to R. We have taken that approach to the previous example in Script 13.14.

The results are:

```
> tea.pref
        Sweetened Don't Care Unsweetened
North           9         12          19
South          31         23           6
> chisq.test(tea.pref)
        Pearson's Chi-squared test

data: tea.pref
X-squared = 19.0804, df = 2, p-value = 7.19e-05

> residuals(chisq.test(tea.pref))
        Sweetened Don't Care Unsweetened
North -1.750000 -0.5345225     2.84605
South  1.428869  0.4364358    -2.32379
```

As you can see, the results agree closely with what we calculated in Equation 13.27. In addition, we requested the cell residuals, which are in a z-score metric. Thus, you can see that the cells that are instrumental in yielding a statistically significant result are primarily in the "Prefer Unsweetened" group; the northerners are overrepresented and the southerners are underrepresented. The opposite pattern is present to a lesser degree in the "Prefer Sweetened" group.

For another example, let's look within the Native Hawaiian group to see if there is a relationship between level of SES (quintile) and whether or not the child ever spent any time in center-based day care. A cross-tabulation of the two variables resulted in Table 13.6.

Table 13.6 Results from cross-tabulating SES (quintile) and center-based day care

Center based		*SES quintile*				
		1	*2*	*3*	*4*	*5*
Day care	Yes	2	7	7	4	4
	No	7	3	10	1	1

Using R (see Script 13.15), we will first complete a conventional analysis using the Pearson's χ^2 approximation:

```
> day.care <- rbind(c(2,7,7,4,4),c(7,3,10,1,1))
> rownames(day.care) <- c("DayCare.Yes",
>    "DayCare.No")
```

```
> colnames(day.care) <- c("SESQ1", "SESQ2",
>   "SESQ3", "SESQ4", "SESQ5")
> day.care
            SESQ1 SESQ2 SESQ3 SESQ4 SESQ5
DayCare.Yes     2     7     7     4     4
DayCare.No      7     3    10     1     1

> chisq.test(day.care)

        Pearson's Chi-squared test

data:  day.care
X-squared = 8.4362, df = 4, p-value = 0.07685

Warning message:
In chisq.test(day.care) : Chi-squared approximation may be
incorrect
```

Note that, in this analysis, we received a warning message that the approximation may not be correct. This message was probably triggered by the small cell frequencies, thus we should probably be using the **fisher.test( )** function in this situation. We could also have used the resampling functionality of the **chisq.test( )** function:

```
> fisher.test(day.care)

        Fisher's Exact Test for Count Data

data:  day.care
p-value = 0.08613
alternative hypothesis: two.sided
```

Although the difference is not dramatic, the p-values for the two analyses differ by approximately .01. In both cases, we reach the same conclusion not to reject H_0, but in cases where there is disagreement, we would recommend the results from the **fisher.test( )**.

If we were to use the resampling approach with the **chisq.test( )** function:

```
> chisq.test(day.care, correct = FALSE,
>   simulate.p.value = TRUE, B = 100000)

Pearson's Chi-squared test with simulated p-value (based on
1e+05
        replicates)

data:  day.care
X-squared = 8.4362, df = NA, p-value = 0.07229
```

In closing, we should note that Pearson's χ^2, Fisher's Exact Test, and the Monte Carlo approach are quite close in terms of p-values. All three provide a test of the independence of two categorical variables, but none provides a descriptive measure similar to Pearson's r. Historically, some statisticians have recommended something called a "Contingency Coefficient" for this purpose, defined as:

$$C = \sqrt{\frac{\chi^2}{N}}$$ (13.28)

Theoretically, C can take on values from zero to one. However, as we noted in Chapter 6, the maximum value in any particular situation is a function of the marginal totals. Thus, it is nearly impossible to interpret the meaning of $C = .55$. That said, we do not recommend the use of the Contingency Coefficient.

As an alternative, we suggest using Cramer's V which was designed so that the upper bound of 1 would be attainable regardless of the row and column totals. As noted in Chapter 6, but probably more fully appreciated now, the formula for Cramer's V is:

$$V = \sqrt{\frac{\chi^2}{n(q-1)}}$$ (13.29)

where q is the lesser of i and j. For 2×2 tables, Cramer's V also has the nice property of being equal to the phi coefficient, which is easily interpreted as a correlation coefficient.

CHAPTER SUMMARY

We began this chapter with a focus on the characteristic of dispersion, introducing the χ^2 distribution as a tool to test a hypothesis about a variance. We completed our discussion of univariate distributional concerns with an explanation of Pearson's χ^2 test, applying it to test how well a set of counts in the cells of a categorical variable matched up with our expected counts.

Last, we turned our attention to looking at relationships between two variables measured on one sample. After looking at two different conditions ($\rho = 0$ and $\rho = \rho_0$) and testing hypotheses about linear relationships between two quantitative variables, we completed our presentation of the one-sample tests with an application of Pearson's χ^2 to look at the relationship between two categorical variables, where the lack of any relationship was expressed in terms of the two variables being independent.

Throughout all the discussions we presented alternatives to traditional tests of hypotheses which included confidence intervals and resampling methods. In addition, we showed you how R can be used to address the issue of statistical power.

In the next two chapters we will turn our attention to two-sample situations. We will continue with our basic approach, covering different issues such as means, proportions, variances, correlations, and regression coefficients. We will consider tests on means and other tests of location in Chapter 14 and tests on the other characteristics in Chapter 15. For each issue, we will first present the classical distribution-based approach to hypothesis testing (*parametric statistics*). We will then present the classical distribution-free approaches (non-parametric *statistics*), where available, which are considered by some to be the precursors of the more computer-intensive resampling methods, which we present last. We will also introduce the concept of independent versus dependent samples, which was not an issue when we were dealing with only one sample.

Key Terms

ν (nu)	Cross-tabulate
χ^2 distribution	Fisher's Exact Test
Contingency Coefficient	Fisher's r to r′ transformation
Contingency table	Goodness of fit
Cramer's V	Poisson distribution

REFERENCES

Althouse, L. A. (1997). Detecting departures from normality: A Monte Carlo simulation of a new omnibus test based on moments. (Unpublished doctoral dissertation.) University of North Carolina at Chapel Hill, Chapel Hill, NC.

Althouse, L. A., Ware, W. B., & Ferron, J. M. (1998, April). Detecting departures from normality: A Monte Carlo simulation of an omnibus test based on moments. Paper presented at the annual meeting of the American Educational Research Association.

D'Agostino, R. B., & Pearson, E. S. (1990). A suggestion for using powerful and informative tests of normality. *The American Statistician, 44*, 316–321.

Evans, M., Hastings, N., & Peacock, B. (1993). *Statistical distributions* (2nd ed.). New York: John Wiley.

Fisher, R. A. (1921). On the "probable error" of a coefficient of correlation deduced from a small sample. *Metron, 1*, pt. 4, 1–32.

Howell, D. C. (2007). *Statistical methods for psychology* (6th ed.). Belmont, CA: Thomson Higher Education.

Royston, J. P. (1982). An extension of Shapiro and Wilk's *W* test for normality to large samples. *Applied Statistics, 31*, 115–124.

Shapiro, S. S., & Wilk, M. B. (1965). An analysis of variance test for normality (complete samples). *Biometrika, 52*, 591–611.

Ware, W. B., & Althouse, L. A. (1999, April). A Monte Carlo simulation of an omnibus test based on probability plots: the line test. Paper presented at the Annual Meeting of the American Educational Research Association, Montréal, CA.

Ware, W. B., & Ferron, J. M. (1995, April). Skewness, kurtosis, and departures from normality. Paper presented at the annual meeting of the North Carolina Association for Research in Education, Greensboro, NC.

PRACTICE QUESTIONS

1. A researcher testing the null hypothesis that the population variance is 100 obtains a *p*-value equal to .15. Using an α-value of .05, the researcher should:

   a. reject the null hypothesis
   b. fail to reject the null hypothesis.

2. Suppose we wish to test the null hypothesis that the population variance is equal to 50. If we use a theoretical sampling distribution, which one would we be likely to use?

   a. *z*.
   b. *t*.
   c. χ^2.
   d. *p*.

3. If we sum squared z-values we will get a distribution that mimics which of the following distributions?

   a. z.
   b. t.
   c. χ^2.
   d. p.

4. Suppose we wish to test the null hypothesis that the population variance is equal to 50, but have concerns that the sampled population is not normal. We should use which of the following:

   a. z
   b. t
   c. χ^2
   d. bootstrap.

5. Under what circumstances would a researcher use Fisher's r to r' transformation?

   a. When testing the null hypothesis $\rho = 0$.
   b. When testing the null hypothesis $\rho = 10$.
   c. When testing the null hypothesis $\rho = .80$.

6. A researcher wishes to test the null hypothesis that the grade of middle-school students (sixth-, seventh-, or eighth-graders) is independent of whether or not they complete their math homework. It is observed that 40% of the whole sample complete their homework. If 50 of the students are sixth-graders, what is the expected value for sixth-graders completing the homework?

   a. 200.
   b. 50.
   c. 30.
   d. 20.

7. A researcher wishes to test the null hypothesis that the grade of middle-school students (sixth-, seventh-, or eighth) is independent of whether or not they complete their math homework. As the observed values get further and further from the expected values, the value of χ^2 becomes:

   a. a larger positive value
   b. a larger negative value
   c. a smaller positive value
   d. a smaller negative value.

EXERCISES

13.1. It has been shown that applicants who have taken a driver education course in high school have higher scores on the state licensing examination than do applicants who have not. It is reasonable to suspect that students completing the course may also exhibit less variability. Assume that the variance of the population of students not taking the course is 400. A sample of 15 students who completed the course was identified and their scores obtained from the Division of Motor Vehicles. Using the data below, determine whether the data support the hypothesis of less variance.

70 67 81 62 65 85 91 55 62 77 56 73 67 84 76

13.2. In a study designed to examine the relationship between creativity and anxiety, a random sample of 200 persons was selected. Each person was measured on both a test of creativity and a test of anxiety. The observed correlation coefficient was determined to be .24. Test the research hypothesis that the two variables are linearly related.

13.3. Suppose that it is known that the correlation between measures of verbal IQ at ages 6 and 16 years is .50. Given a random sample of size 150 drawn from a population of learning disabled students, it was found that the correlation was .29. Does this suggest that the stability of measured IQ is different from that in the general population?

13.4. A researcher in the rate department for an insurance company was attempting to determine whether there were differential accident rates for cars of different sizes. After randomly pulling files on 100 insurance claims within the past 2 years, she classified the cars as high-performance, full size, mid-size, and subcompact. The observed numbers of claims were as follows:

High performance	Full-size	Mid-size	Subcompact
38	20	15	27

Based on data provided by the American Automakers Association, the researcher determined that the distribution of car sales for the four types of car was 13%, 37%, 21%, and 29%, respectively. Can the researcher conclude that the pattern of accidents differs from what we might expect by chance?

13.5. A study was completed to examine the relationship between two different fertility drugs and the number of children conceived. The data below are the "counts" observed.

No. of children conceived	Drug A	Drug B
1	8	12
2	10	22
3	9	10
4 or more	18	6

14

Two-Sample Tests of Location

INTRODUCTION

In Chapters 12 and 13 we presented a number of one-sample procedures for addressing questions of location, spread, and relationship. We presented the traditional, distribution-based approaches, the non-parametric approaches where available, and the newer, computer-intensive resampling approaches. In this chapter we are going to follow the same paradigm, with the additional consideration of *independent* versus *dependent samples*. Independent samples may arise in a number of different ways. First, one might draw a random sample from a population and randomly assign the cases to one of two conditions. For example, we may assign half to an experimental group and half to a control group. In another situation, one might draw a random sample from a population of females and a separate random sample from a population of males. In each of these two cases, the observations in each of the two groups would be considered to be independent.

On the other hand, we might be interested in looking at the effects of some intervention on cognitive processing. We might identify a number of sets of identical twins, randomly assigning one of the pair to the intervention condition and the other to the control condition. Another possible study might involve the investigation of a new curriculum approach to teaching a difficult concept in mathematics. We could draw a random sample of fourth graders at the beginning of the year, obtain their end-of-grade mathematics scores from third grade, and pair them up. That is, the two highest scores would become Pair 1; the next two highest scores would become Pair 2, and so on. Then, one member of each pair would be randomly assigned to the new approach, while the other member of the pair would be assigned to the traditional approach. In these two latter situations, we would expect that there would be a relationship, either natural or constructed, between the two sets of scores. These samples would be described as dependent.

Before we address specific contexts, let's take a look at the basic paradigm using the specific issue of the classic experiment in which two samples are going to be compared to test a hypothesis about population means.

THE CLASSIC EXPERIMENTAL PARADIGM

In the classic experimental paradigm using an experimental group and a control group, a random sample is drawn from a population. Subsequently, the cases are randomly assigned to either the experimental group or the control group. In essence, two random samples of n cases have been drawn from the same population. For now, we will assume that the two groups are the same in terms of sample size. The process is depicted in Figure 14.1. We shall assume that the population of the random variable Y is normally distributed with mean μ and variance σ^2.

Thus, both sample means are estimates of the population mean μ. Now, we ask: What do we know about the distribution of the difference between the two sample means? That is, what would we expect if we repeatedly drew two samples in tandem and calculated the difference between them? The answer to this question rests on a number of assumptions. To begin, what do we know about the sum (and difference) between two random variables? First let's consider $V = X + Y$:

$$E(V) = E(X + Y) = E(X) + E(Y)$$

$$\text{(14.1)}$$

$$\text{var}(V) = \text{var}(X + Y) = \text{var}(X) + \text{var}(Y) + 2 \times \text{cov}(X, Y)$$

Of course we are also interested in the difference between two random variables:

$$E(V) = E(X - Y) = E(X) - E(Y)$$

$$\text{(14.2)}$$

$$\text{var}(V) = \text{var}(X - Y) = \text{var}(X) + \text{var}(Y) - 2 \times \text{cov}(X, Y)$$

We will take Equation 14.2 as our guide. Now, remember that we are dealing with two independent samples, in which case $\text{cov}(X, Y)$ would be expected to be zero. Thus,

$$\left(\bar{Y}_{.1} - \bar{Y}_{.2}\right) \sim N\left(\mu - \mu, \frac{\sigma^2}{n} + \frac{\sigma^2}{n}\right)$$

$$\text{(14.3)}$$

As you can see, the difference between the two sample means is itself a normally distributed random variable for which we know both the expected value and the variance. Based on our previous work, such a random variable lends itself to a z-test:

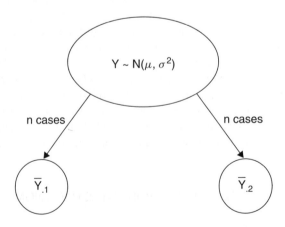

FIGURE 14.1   The paradigm of the classic experiment.

$$z_{obs} = \frac{\left(\bar{Y}_{.1} - \bar{Y}_{.2}\right) - \left(\mu - \mu\right)}{\sqrt{\left(\sigma^2/n\right) + \left(\sigma^2/n\right)}} = \frac{\left(\bar{Y}_{.1} - \bar{Y}_{.2}\right)}{\sqrt{\sigma^2\left[\left(1/n\right) + \left(1/n\right)\right]}} \qquad (14.4)$$

Thus, if we were to complete an experiment in which we assumed that the intervention had no effect, we could contrast the null hypothesis and alternate hypothesis as follows:

$$\begin{aligned} H_0 &: \mu_1 = \mu_2 \\ H_1 &: \mu_1 \neq \mu_2 \end{aligned} \qquad (14.5)$$

In this context, we have assumed that the population is normally distributed or that the sample size is sufficiently large to justify invoking the Central Limit Theorem. We have also stipulated that the samples are of equal size. Earlier, we described a situation in which we might draw separate and independent random samples from two different populations, as depicted in Figure 14.2. In this case, the two populations might have different means, different variances, and the two samples might differ in size. However, if we know the two population variances, we can assert:

$$\left(\bar{Y}_{.1} - \bar{Y}_{.2}\right) \sim N\left(\mu_1 - \mu_2, \frac{\sigma_1^2}{n_1} + \frac{\sigma_2^2}{n_2}\right) \qquad (14.6)$$

Again, given that the difference between the two sample means is a random variable with known expected value and variance, we can perform a z-test.

$$z_{obs} = \frac{\left(\bar{Y}_{.1} - \bar{Y}_{.2}\right) - \left(\mu_1 - \mu_2\right)}{\sqrt{\left(\sigma_1^2/n_1\right) + \left(\sigma_2^2/n_2\right)}} \qquad (14.7)$$

Furthermore, if we know that the two population variances are the same, Equation 14.7 simplifies to:

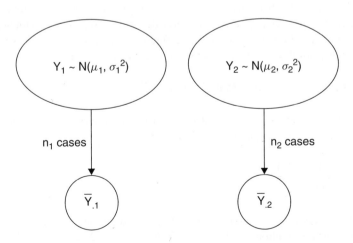

FIGURE 14.2   A modification of the classic experiment.

$$z_{obs} = \frac{\left(\bar{Y}_{.1} - \bar{Y}_{.2}\right) - \left(\mu_1 - \mu_2\right)}{\sqrt{\sigma^2\left[\left(1/n_1\right) + \left(1/n_2\right)\right]}} \tag{14.8}$$

If we assume H_0 as in Equation 14.5, then Equation 14.8 reduces to a variation of Equation 14.4 with an allowance for different sample sizes. To summarize, if we can assume that the populations are normally distributed, we can employ an appropriate form of the z-test to test the null hypothesis that the population means are equal. However, we have also assumed that we know the variances of the populations. It is time to ask ourselves how often we might expect to meet all of these assumptions. Unfortunately, the answer is, "not very often."

Before you begin to think that the material that you have just struggled through is a waste of time, let us assure you that it was not. Indeed, the process we just led you through provides a template for how we might proceed in situations in which we do not know the population variance(s). As you may recall from a similar situation in previous chapters, when faced with the need to estimate the population variance from the sample data, we could turn to the t-distribution and the associated t-test. We will do the same now, for the two-sample situation.

A MORE REALISTIC EXPERIMENTAL PARADIGM

When researchers conduct experiments in the real world, it is most often the case that they are working with dependent variables that do not have well-known distributions or with samples that are not randomly sampled from a population. Thus, in most situations in applied contexts, we are going to need to use the sample data to derive estimates of the population variances. Exactly how we should proceed, however, is one of the more thorny issues in applied statistics. The recommended solution depends on whether the samples come from populations with equal variances, whether the samples are the same size, and, if not, the disparity between the sample sizes and the variances.

In this chapter, we will proceed as though the circumstances are optimal: the samples come from normally distributed populations with the same variance and they are equal in size. In the next chapter, we will learn ways to assess whether or not it is reasonable to assume that the variances are the same. The condition of "sameness" is often called *homogeneity of variance*. We have modified Figure 14.2 in two ways, presenting the result in Figure 14.3. First, we deleted the subscript to reflect that the two populations do have the same variance. Unfortunately, we do not know its value. In that light, at the bottom of the figure we have added s_1^2 and s_2^2 to reflect that each of the obtained samples could be used to estimate the common σ^2.

A Derivation of the Two-Independent-Samples *t*-Test

Just as we did in the last chapter, we are going to rewrite the expression for the z-test, making the necessary substitutions. Thus, Equation 14.7 becomes:

$$t'_{obs} = \frac{\left(\bar{Y}_{.1} - \bar{Y}_{.2}\right) - \left(\mu_1 - \mu_2\right)}{\sqrt{\left(s_1^2/n_1\right) + \left(s_2^2/n_2\right)}} \tag{14.9}$$

We have used the notation t'_{obs} because, unfortunately, the distribution of the result of this calculation is similar to the distribution of t, but not with $df = n_1 + n_2 - 2$, as we might have anticipated. However, if we can assume that the two sample variances are both estimates of the common σ^2,

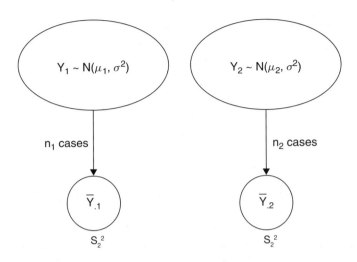

FIGURE 14.3   The realistic experimental paradigm.

then we might consider pooling them together. If the two sample sizes are equal, then we can simply average them. If the sample sizes are different, then we should take the sample sizes into account. To do this, we can find the weighted average by weighting each s^2 by the number of independent pieces of information in each, respectively. The weights are in fact the number of degrees of freedom (*df*) for each group. We show this as:

$$
\begin{aligned}
s^2_{\text{pooled}} &= \frac{(n_1-1)s_1^2 + (n_2-1)s_2^2}{n_1+n_2-2} \\[2mm]
&= \frac{\sum_{i=1}^{n_1}\left(Y_{i1}-\bar{Y}_{.1}\right)^2 + \sum_{i=1}^{n_2}\left(Y_{i2}-\bar{Y}_{.2}\right)^2}{n_1+n_2-2} \\[2mm]
&= \frac{SS_{wg_1} + SS_{wg_2}}{n_1+n_2-2}
\end{aligned}
\tag{14.10}
$$

As messy as that looks, it really boils down to a fairly simple computation (and remember that you will have a computer doing the "heavy lifting" for you). Conceptually, the pooled variance is simply the sum of the sum-of-squares within each group, divided by the total number of cases minus 2. Once we have obtained the pooled estimate, we can plug it into Equation 14.9, where we have the two separate estimates of variance. After factoring it out, we are left with:

$$
\begin{aligned}
t_{\text{obs}} &= \frac{\left(\bar{Y}_{.1}-\bar{Y}_{.2}\right)-\left(\mu_1-\mu_2\right)}{\sqrt{\left(s^2_{\text{pooled}}/n_1\right)+\left(s^2_{\text{pooled}}/n_2\right)}} \\[2mm]
&= \frac{\left(\bar{Y}_{.1}-\bar{Y}_{.2}\right)-\left(\mu_1-\mu_2\right)}{\sqrt{s^2_{\text{pooled}}\left[\left(1/n_1\right)+\left(1/n_2\right)\right]}}
\end{aligned}
\tag{14.11}
$$

Table 14.1 Summary data for two-independent samples *t*-test

	Low SES	High SES
ΣY	174.00	248.00
ΣY^2	3148.00	6708.00
n_j	10.00	10.00
$\bar{Y}_j$	17.40	24.80
SS_j	120.40	557.60
s_j	3.66	7.87

An Example of a Two-Independent-Samples *t*-Test Assuming Equal Variances

Suppose we were interested in looking at the level of reading performance for children entering kindergarten, comparing a random sample of 10 cases from the lowest quintile of socioeconomic status (SES) to a random sample of 10 cases from the highest quintile of SES. The scores for the low group were 13, 13, 21, 16, 22, 15, 18, 20, 22, and 14. The scores for the high group were 40, 28, 18, 32, 17, 27, 19, 21, 16, and 30. Using these data, we could develop the initial summary statistics as presented in Table 14.1.

Plugging these values into Equation 14.10, we find that s^2_{pooled} is equal to 37.67. In turn, plugging the values into Equation 14.11:

$$t_{obs} = \frac{\left(\bar{Y}_{.1} - \bar{Y}_{.2}\right) - \left(\mu_1 - \mu_2\right)}{\sqrt{s^2_{pooled}\left(\frac{1}{n_1} + \frac{1}{n_2}\right)}} = \frac{(17.4 - 24.8) - 0}{\sqrt{37.67\left(\frac{1}{10} + \frac{1}{10}\right)}} = \frac{-7.4}{2.745} = -2.696 \tag{14.12}$$

With *df* = 10 + 10 − 2 = 18, we can look at a *t*-table (Table A.3) to find the critical value of *t* to be ±2.10. Thus, we would reject the null hypothesis that these two populations (Low SES and High SES) have the same mean reading level at the beginning of kindergarten. If we want to use R to complete this *t*-test for us, we simply need to write the following statement:

```
t.test(low, high, var.equal = TRUE)
```

The results will be presented in the R console window:

```
> t.test(low, high, var.equal = TRUE)
        Two Sample t-test

data:  low and high
t = -2.6961, df = 18, p-value = 0.01477
alternative hypothesis: true difference in means is not equal
to 0
95 percent confidence interval:
 -13.166384  -1.633616
sample estimates:
mean of x    mean of y
     17.4        24.8
```

As you can see, R returns the same value for t that we had calculated by hand. In addition, it provides a p-value and a confidence interval. The confidence interval would be calculated as:

$$\left(\bar{Y}_{.1} - \bar{Y}_{.2}\right) - t_{\frac{\alpha}{2}, n_1 + n_2 - 2} \sqrt{s_{\text{pooled}}^2 \left(\frac{1}{n_1} + \frac{1}{n_2}\right)} \leq \mu_1 - \mu_2 \leq \left(\bar{Y}_{.1} - \bar{Y}_{.2}\right) + t_{\frac{\alpha}{2}, n_1 + n_2 - 2} \sqrt{s_{\text{pooled}}^2 \left(\frac{1}{n_1} + \frac{1}{n_2}\right)} \quad (14.13)$$

We could take you through the computation, but we'll leave that up to you. (When we did it, we obtained the same values that R provided.) As you can see in the R output, the confidence interval is (−13.166, −1.634) rounded to three decimal places. Any hypothetical value within the interval is reasonable at the 95% confidence level; any value not within the interval can be rejected at the .05 level of significance. Given that zero is not within the interval, we can reject the null hypothesis that the two samples have been drawn from one population, or two populations with the same mean. There are two other (related) issues that we should mention before moving on to a different way to analyze these data: effect size and power.

Effect Size and Power

In this example, the actual difference was 7.4 points, and the pooled standard deviation was $\sqrt{37.67} \approx 6.14$. We have used the pooled standard deviation as neither of the groups is a true control group. In situations with a control group, some statisticians recommend using the standard deviation of the control group. So, using Cohen's (1988) definition of *effect size*, we have observed a value of 7.4/6.14, or approximately 1.20. By any standard, that is a large effect. More formally, Cohen defined his effect size for comparing the means of two groups as d, where

$$d = \frac{\bar{Y}_{.1} - \bar{Y}_{.2}}{s} \quad (14.14)$$

Using the **power.t.test( )** function in R, we find that when testing the null hypothesis under these conditions ($n = 10$, $\alpha = .05$, two-tailed), the probability of our rejecting the null hypothesis (*power*) with a real difference of 1.2 standard deviations is approximately .72. For a moment, imagine that we are planning this study and we would like a power of .80 to detect a small effect (.2) at the .05 level. We can use the **power.t.test( )** function to find that we would need a sample size of approximately 400 cases in each group. The entire set of R commands for this example is included in Script 14.1 in the supplementary materials for this chapter that are contained on the book website.

To reiterate, all of the discussion pertaining to the two-independent-samples t-test is assuming that conditions are optimal: that the populations sampled are normally distributed with equal variances. Consider this for a moment. Very early in this book, we made the case that the first "four moments" captured the essence of any distribution. The four moments are the mean, the variance, skewness, and kurtosis. If you assume the distributions are normal, that covers both skewness and kurtosis. If you also assume the variances are the same, the only way the populations could possibly differ would be in terms of location.

In real life, things are often less than optimal. What if the populations are not normally distributed? What if the sample sizes are too small to justify the Central Limit Theorem? Historically, these concerns have been addressed by the application of non-parametric procedures, such as the Mann–Whitney U-test, which we will now describe. The non-parametric procedures are sometimes described as *small-sample statistics*.

The Mann–Whitney U-Test: An Alternative to the Two-Independent-Samples t-Test

Before computers were widely available, statisticians devised ways to deal with possible violations of assumptions necessary for the traditional parametric procedures. These procedures made fewer assumptions, particularly about the distribution of the population. Generally, the procedures involved converting the observed data values to ranks (the consecutive integers) and then enumerating the permutations of the ranks. Once the data were transformed to ranks, all data sets of two groups of 10 cases each were working with the same values, 1 through 20. Thus, the permutations only needed to be examined once, and tables of critical values could be constructed by looking at the proportion of permutations resulting in more extreme values of the test statistic. The Mann–Whitney U-test (Mann & Whitney, 1947) is one such procedure; it tests the null hypothesis that the two sets of scores come from the same population. If one can make the case that the two population distributions are similar, though not necessarily normal, then the test reduces to one of location. The Wilcoxon Rank Sum test, meanwhile, was derived independently and is algebraically equivalent to the Mann–Whitney U-test. Both are based on ways to compare the cumulative frequency distributions of the two samples. Remember ogives? We showed several in Figure 2.8. The Mann–Whitney U statistic is based on a way to compare the two ogives. If they are very similar (running neck-and-neck), then about half of the time one should be ahead of the other, and half the time the other one should be ahead. The process is based on an algorithm for finding the sum of consecutive integers; you may have encountered it in high-school algebra when you studied inductive proofs.

In the previous section, we used the conventional t-test to look at entering-kindergarten reading performance as a function of SES. We will now look at the same data with the Mann–Whitney U-test.

The Mann–Whitney U-Test: An Example

The process of completing the test requires several steps. First, the two samples are combined to give one set of observations. The observations are then ranked from smallest to largest. The procedure assumes that there are no tied observations, though it can be modified to accommodate tied scores. Typically, if two or more cases have the same value, each of them is assigned the average of positions occupied. For example, suppose we had a sequence of sorted scores such as 14, 17, 17, 18, etc. The value of 14 would receive a rank of 1, the two 17s would each be assigned a rank of 2.5 (the average of 2 and 3), and the 18 would be assigned a rank of 4, etc. Then the rank values are assigned back into the respective group from which they came, "replacing" the original scores. The ranks for each group are then summed, typically labeled as R_1 and R_2. We have written some R syntax to do this for the data in this example. We include the code here so that you can follow along.

```
# Define the groups
low <- c(13,13,21,16,22,15,18,20,22,14)
n1 <- length(low)
high <- c(40,28,18,32,17,27,19,21,16,30)
n2 <- length(high)
both <- c(low, high)
rank.both <-rank(both, ties.method = "average")
```

```
rank.both
ranks.low <-rank.both[1:n1]
first.2 <- n1 +1
last.2 <- n1 + n2
ranks.high <- rank.both[first.2:last.2]
ranks.high
r1 <- sum(ranks.low)
r2 <- sum(ranks.high)
r1; r2
> r1; r2
[1] 76.5
[1] 133.5
```

As you can see, we have found R_1 equal to 76.5 and R_2 equal to 133.5. If the groups are of the same size and they are random samples from the same population, we would expect the two sums to be approximately equal. However, if the two groups are different in the number of cases, we would no longer expect the two sums to be about the same. In order to account for this problem, calculate two values (U_1 and U_2) for U:

$$U_1 = n_1 n_2 + \frac{n_1(n_1+1)}{2} - R_1$$

$$U_2 = n_1 n_2 + \frac{n_2(n_2+1)}{2} - R_2$$

(14.15)

For our data, we would calculate as follows:

$$U_1 = 10 \times 10 + \frac{10(10+1)}{2} - 76.5 = 78.5$$

$$U_2 = 10 \times 10 + \frac{10(10+1)}{2} - 133.5 = 21.5$$

(14.16)

For an example with unequal sample sizes, suppose the five largest scores were in the first group and the 15 smallest scores in the second group, you would find R_1 to be equal to 90 and R_2 to be equal to 120.

$$U_1 = 5 \times 15 + \frac{5(5+1)}{2} - 90 = 0$$

$$U_2 = 5 \times 15 + \frac{15(15+1)}{2} - 120 = 75$$

(14.17)

Note that one of the U values is equal to 0; this will always be the case when the two sets of scores are non-overlapping. Now what? You take the smaller of the two U values to a table of critical values. You go with the smaller U because of the way that the tables are constructed. We have constructed a set of tables, which are included in Appendix A.

Let's assume that you want to complete the test as a two-tailed test at the .05 level. Extensive tables of the critical values of the Mann–Whitney U statistic may be found in Tables A.6.1 through A.6.4. Assuming a two-tailed test at the .05 level, go to Table A.6.2 and find the cell for $n_1 = 10$ and $n_2 = 10$. In that cell, you will see two rows: in the first row you see (**24**—0.0524) and in the second row you see (**23**—0.0432). The reason why you see two separate rows is because the distribution of U is discrete rather than continuous. The critical value of **24** cuts off a total of .0524 in the tails; the critical value of **23** cuts off a total of .0432 in the tails. There is no value of U that cuts off exactly .05 in the tails. We point this out as it can cause some confusion. Some statistical texts will present a table with the larger values; others present tables with the smaller values. They may appear to be typographic errors, but they are not. The discrepancy results from some statisticians or authors being liberal; they table the larger values. Conservative authors table the smaller values. Over the long haul, it probably does not make much difference. In any event, our smaller U value is 21.5, which is smaller than either **24** or **23**. Therefore, we reject the hypothesis. Remember that a value of zero represents the maximum difference that could be obtained between the two groups. Therefore, when we use tables, we reject the hypothesis when the value obtained is closer to zero than the tabulated value. In any event, most researchers will use a computer program like R to complete the analysis which will do it correctly. Furthermore, we expect that the Mann–Whitney U-test will be replaced by the newer resampling-based permutation tests. (For more on the Mann–Whitney test, see: http://en.wikipedia.org/wiki/Mann-Whitney_U.)

The Mann–Whitney U-Test with R

To our knowledge, the Mann–Whitney U-test is not available in R; however, its equivalent, the Wilcoxon Rank Sum test, is available in the base package and a variation that corrects for ties is in the **PASWR** package. The two different functions (**wilcox.test( )** and **wilcoxE.test( )**) report different test statistics, but the p-values are identical when there are no ties. The **wilcoxE.test( )** function has a built-in correction for ties. The R output from both functions is:

```
> wilcox.test(low, high, alternative = "two.sided",
>   exact = TRUE, correct = FALSE)

        Wilcoxon rank sum test

data:  low and high
W = 21.5, p-value = 0.03089
alternative hypothesis: true location shift is not equal to 0

Warning message:
In wilcox.test.default(low, high, alternative = "two.sided",
exact = TRUE,  :
  cannot compute exact p-value with ties
> wilcoxE.test(low, high, conf.level = .95)
```

Wilcoxon Rank Sum Test

```
data:  low and high
w = 76.5, p-value = 0.03023
alternative hypothesis: true median is not equal to 0
94.53008 percent confidence interval:
 -8 -5
sample estimates:
difference in location
                  -6
```

As you can see, both procedures lead us to the same conclusions reached by our hand calculation; we reject the hypothesis that these two sets of scores were sampled from the same population.

A Permutation Test for Means

With the computers and software now widely available, it is possible to use a resampling approach to comparing these two samples. We have written Script 14.3 to do so. The results are:

```
> diff
[1] -7.4
> pvalue
[1] 0.01444
```

As you can see, the p-value from the permutation test is quite close to the p-value from the t-test (0.01477).

To summarize, we have looked at three different ways to compare two groups with respect to location. Specifically, the conventional two-independent-samples t-test tests a hypothesis about the equivalence of two population means. However, the possibility of populations not being normally distributed, in combination with small sample sizes, led statisticians to develop procedures that compared two distributions based on ranks, including the algebraically equivalent Wilcoxon and the Mann–Whitney procedures. Third, we presented a resampling approach with a permutation test. After presenting tests for proportions and medians, we will end this chapter with some methods that are appropriate for dependent samples.

The Two-Independent-Samples Test for Proportions

A comparison between two groups with regard to a possible difference between two proportions is a fairly common research problem in our society. Think about possible differences between the two major political parties with respect to any of several "hot" issues. As we write, our society is immersed in controversies about healthcare reform, financial reform, regulation of off-shore drilling for oil, to name just a few. The hypotheses to be contrasted are:

$$H_0 : \pi_1 = \pi_2$$
$$H_1 : \pi_1 \neq \pi_2$$

(14.18)

Consider the following fictitious example applying a one-tailed analysis. Suppose we surveyed random samples ($n = 50$ each) of Republicans and Democrats regarding their opinion as to whether the full-benefit retirement age for Social Security should be raised. The alternate hypothesis would be $\pi_R > \pi_D$. Imagine the results as follows: 31 of the 50 Republicans indicated that they favored raising the age, and 19 of the 50 Democrats indicted the same. From this information, we can determine that $p_1 = 31/50$, or .62. Similarly, $p_2 = 19/50$, or .38. Do these two values differ by more than you might reasonably expect due to random sampling error? We can assess this possibility with a z-test:

$$z_{obs} = \frac{(p_1 - p_2) - (\pi_1 - \pi_2)}{\sqrt{(p_{pooled})(1 - p_{pooled})[(1/n_1) + (1/n_2)]}}$$

where

$$p_{pooled} = \frac{(n_1 p_1 + n_2 p_2)}{n_1 + n_2}$$

(14.19)

Equation 14.19 looks more difficult than it really is. The pooled estimate of π is nothing more than the total number of "in favor" responses divided by the total number of respondents. Thus,

$$z_{obs} = \frac{(.62 - .38)}{\sqrt{(.5)(.5)[(1/50) + (1/50)]}} = \frac{.24}{\sqrt{.25(2/50)}} = 2.40$$

where

$$p_{pooled} = \frac{(31 + 19)}{50 + 50} = \frac{50}{100} = .5$$

(14.20)

Given the z_{obs} of 2.4, we would reject H_0 at the .05 level, as z_{obs} is in the region of rejection (i.e., in excess of 1.645). Of course, this analysis can be completed in R as per Script 14.4:

```
> favor   <- c(31, 19)
> survey <- c(50, 50)
> prop.test(favor, survey, correct = FALSE,
>    alternative = "greater")

        2-sample test for equality of proportions without
continuity
        correction

data:  favor out of survey
X-squared = 5.76, df = 1, p-value = 0.008198
alternative hypothesis: greater
95 percent confidence interval:
 0.08032207 1.00000000
sample estimates:
```

```
prop 1 prop 2
   0.62   0.38
```

As you can see, the reported p-value is less than .05; the reported χ^2 statistic (5.76) is simply $(2.4)^2$. It is always reassuring when the computer results agree with our hand calculation.

The validity of the results of this test statistic depends on the sample sizes being sufficiently large to justify a sampling distribution of p that is essentially normally distributed. As with the one-sample test, there is a rule of thumb to assess this matter. As long as $n_1 p_1$, $n_1(1-p_1)$, $n_2 p_2$, and $n_2(1-p_2)$ are all equal to 5 or more, we can feel we are on safe ground. If these four conditions are not all met, we can resort to bootstrapping, as in Script 14.5. Reanalyzing the data from the previous example:

```
> cat("The observed difference is",diff1,
>    "and the p-value is",p.value,"\n")
The observed difference is 0.24 and the p-value is 0.01341
The quartiles for using CIs for hypothesis testing are:
 0.5%  2.5%    5%    95% 97.5% 99.5%
-0.24 -0.20 -0.16  0.16  0.20  0.24
```

As you can see, the p-value is a little larger than the one provided by the conventional z-test, but we reach the same conclusion: reject H_0. By the same token, to use the bootstrapped quartiles for a one-tailed (upper) test at .05, we would use the upper-tailed (95%) value of .16. Before we turn our attention to procedures for dependent samples, we will describe one last procedure for independent samples that allows us to compare two samples to assess whether they have been randomly drawn from populations with the same median.

A Two-Independent-Samples Test for Medians

In Chapter 12 we looked at an example of testing a hypothesis about a median using data from Raleigh, NC. In Exercise 12.3 we looked at the same process, using data from Chapel Hill, NC. Suppose that we wanted to compare the two housing markets to see if they seemed to reflect a common median. Unlike means, proportions, and many other parameters, the median does not have an easily defined sampling distribution. Thus, we cannot rely on traditional techniques that use the z- and t-distributions to obtain p-values. However, we can use logic somewhat like that used in the one-sample examples concerned with medians. That is, we can extend the Sign Test to the two-sample situation; this extension is often called the *Median Test*.

The Median Test

In Chapter 12, we looked at two examples dealing with medians based on two different real estate advertisements, one in Raleigh and the other in Chapel Hill, each testing the plausibility of the "local market" median. In this chapter, we will compare the two sets of house prices to assess whether (or not) they might have come from one population with regard to the median. As before, we will assume the null hypothesis that the two samples have come from one population with regard to the median. Thus, we will combine the two samples and find the common median. Continuing to assume no difference, it would seem reasonable to expect that about one-half of the observations in each sample would be above the common median; similarly, about one-half of the observations in each sample should be below the common median. We have written an R script to carry out this process (see Script 14.6 at the end of this chapter.) After running the first part of the script, we found that the common median was $357,500. In the Raleigh market advertisement (median = $449,900), there were 20 homes listed at prices above the common median, and 15 listed at prices below the common median. In the Chapel Hill market (median = $335,000) there were 12 homes listed at prices above the common median, and 17 homes listed below the common median. These counts were used to construct a 2 × 2 table, which was then analyzed using Fisher's Exact Test. Selected output was:

```
> median.table
            Above Below
Tate.Raleigh   20    15
Team.CH        12    17

> fisher.test(median.table)

        Fisher's Exact Test for Count Data

data:  median.table
p-value = 0.3152
```

As you can see, the obtained p-value of .3152 would suggest that these two samples may be considered to be two samples from one population with regard to the median. We can also apply resampling methods as we have done toward the end of Script 14.6. After defining the data for the two markets separately (*tate.price* and *team.price*), we combine the two samples into one variable, *house.price*, and resample many permutations. Of course, it is likely not reasonable that two sets of home prices represent random samples from the two respective markets. Thus, we present the technique for illustrative purposes only. Although the medians appear to be quite different—the Raleigh median is $449,900 and the Chapel Hill median is $335,000—the results from the permutation test suggest that they may differ only due to random error:

```
The difference in medians is 114900 and the p-value is
0.08327
```

Note that the p-value derived from the permutation test is quite a bit smaller than the corresponding p-value from Fisher's Exact Test. That difference is likely due to the greater power of the permutation test as it takes the magnitude into consideration, not just "above" or "below."

All of the procedures considered so far in this chapter have been concerned with situations in which the two samples are independent. We now turn our attention to two-sample situations in which the samples are dependent rather than independent.

AN ALTERNATIVE PARADIGM: DEPENDENT SAMPLES

Not all research involves independent samples. In some situations, the available data have come from dependent samples. In other situations, we may prospectively design a study based on dependent samples. There are good reasons for doing this, reasons that should become evident as we describe the paradigm.

Dependent samples may occur in several different ways, including natural aggregations. Earlier in this chapter, we mentioned the notion of identical twins being used in a study. The cases within a pair are likely to be more similar to one another than to a member of a different pair. That is, the cases within a pair are genetically matched. Extensions of this notion frequently occur within agricultural research in which members of a litter may be assigned to different conditions. The litters constitute a "blocking" variable, just as the pairs of twins. When you think about it, twins are actually litter mates. Earlier in the chapter, we also mentioned the process of matching cases. Here, the cases are not naturally occurring aggregations, but rather we proactively create pairs that are similar to one another with regard to some relevant characteristic, such as previous achievement in mathematics. A third way to create/obtain dependent samples is in what are called "repeated measures" designs. Literally, data are collected on the same cases under different conditions. One of the most frequent applications of this paradigm is the "pre-test/post-test" design.

One way to better understand the difference between independent and dependent samples is to consider the special case when the samples are of the same size. If you were to draw two random samples of size 10 and line the data up in two columns, you might be tempted to calculate the Pearson correlation (r) between the two columns. Were you to do so, we would expect the value of r to be quite close to zero, as the values within the columns are in random order. On the other hand, suppose that you had gone to the trouble of creating matched pairs as in the mathematics example. Let's say that the first pair consists of the individuals with the two highest end-of-third-grade math scores. The second pair would consist of the individuals with the third and fourth highest end-of-grade scores, etc. Thus, lined up in two columns, were you to calculate r, you would expect to find a fairly large, positive correlation between the two columns. At this point, you may be asking yourself: Why would anyone want to go to that much trouble?

Why Use Dependent-Samples Designs

The answer to this is actually fairly simple. Recall that earlier in the chapter we addressed the issue of the distribution of the difference between two random variables. We repeat the equation here:

$$E(V) = E(X - Y) = E(X) - E(Y)$$
$$\text{var}(V) = \text{var}(X - Y) = \text{var}(X) + \text{var}(Y) - 2 \times \text{cov}(X, Y) \tag{14.21}$$

In situations in which the samples are independent, the $\text{cov}(X, Y)$ is equal to zero, and we are able to construct the t-test formula as detailed in Equations 14.9 through 14.11. However, when the samples are dependent and the covariance between the two variables is positive, the variance of the difference between the two random variables will be smaller than the variance of the difference between the two random variables when the samples are independent. Reconsider the second part of Equation 14.11:

$$t_{\text{obs}} = \frac{\left(\bar{Y}_{.1} - \bar{Y}_{.2} \right) - \left(\mu_1 - \mu_2 \right)}{\sqrt{s_{\text{pooled}}^2 \left[\left(1 / n_1 \right) + \left(1 / n_2 \right) \right]}} \tag{14.22}$$

When the samples are dependent, we can expect that s^2_{pooled} will be smaller than it would be when the samples are independent. That is, the dependency between the samples introduces a correlation that can be used to reduce the estimate of the population variance. The effect of this reduction is to decrease the denominator of the t-test, which, in turn, increases the quotient, or t_{obs}. Another way to say this is that a dependent-samples t-test, when applied appropriately, will increase the statistical power of the analysis.

An Example of a Dependent-Samples t-Test

Suppose that we were interested in comparing the entry-level skills in reading and mathematics for Native American children at the beginning of kindergarten. Using the ECLS2577 data file, we selected 10 Native American children at random and extracted their T-scores in both reading and mathematics that were collected in the fall of their kindergarten year. Given that we are working with two different attributes, we are using the T-scores to assure comparable scales. The reading scores on the children were 58, 47, 38, 35, 43, 47, 34, 56, 53, and 44. The mathematics scores on the same children, respectively, were 43, 49, 40, 45, 38, 49, 38, 64, 52, and 49. Rather than try to estimate the covariance between the variables, we are going to use a little logic. If the two sets of scores have the same mean, then, algebraically, we can show that the mean of the differences in scores is zero. Thus, in completing a dependent-samples t-test, we will test the hypothesis that the mean of the differences is equal to zero. We have written Script 14.7 (see the supplementary materials for this chapter on the book website) to assist in this analysis. After entering the data, we find the 10 differences: 15, –2, –2, –10, 5, –2, –4, –8, 1, and –5. We find that the average difference (read–math) is –1.2 points. Using the symbol d for the difference, we find $\Sigma d = -12$ and $\Sigma d^2 = 468$. We plug these values into Equation 13.22 as follows, in essence a replication of the one-sample t-test:

$$t_{obs} = \frac{\bar{d} - 0}{\sqrt{s^2_d / n}} = \frac{-1.2}{\sqrt{\left(\left\{468 - \left[(-12)^2 / 10\right]\right\} / 9\right) / 10}} = \frac{-1.2}{2.25} = -0.53 \qquad (14.23)$$

You should be able to look at the resulting t_{obs} (–.53) and determine that it is not significant. Given that we were working with 10 differences, the df for this variation of a one-sample t-test would be $(n-1)$, or 9. The two-tailed critical value of t is ±2.26. The observed value of –.53 is well within the region of non-rejection, so we do not reject the null hypothesis. We could use the **t.test()** function in R to complete this analysis. Notice the additional specification of "paired=TRUE".

```
> t.test(read, math, paired=TRUE)

        Paired t-test

data:  read and math
t=-0.5345, df=9, p-value=0.6059
alternative hypothesis: true difference in means is not equal
to 0
95 percent confidence interval:
 -6.27853   3.87853
```

```
sample estimates:
mean of the differences
                 -1.2
```

At this point, you may be thinking about those 9 *df*. Had you done a two-sample *t*-test, you would have had 18 *df*. You know that more *df* is a good thing to have as it lowers the critical value of *t*, making it more likely that you will be able to reject the null hypothesis; thus more *df* tends to provide more statistical power. However, if you have "matched" on a variable that matters, this argument does not hold. Although you lose half of your degrees-of-freedom, you can take advantage of the dependency to reduce the random error. In effect, the loss of *df* can be considered as an "investment." As a case in point, suppose that we had treated this example as though it had been a two-independent-samples *t*-test:

```
> t.test(read, math, var.equal=TRUE)

        Two Sample t-test

data:  read and math
t=-0.3299, df=18, p-value=0.7453
alternative hypothesis: true difference in means is not equal
to 0
95 percent confidence interval:
 -8.841377  6.441377
sample estimates:
mean of x mean of y
    45.5      46.7
```

As you can see, you have recaptured your 9 *df*, but the *p*-value is larger; we have not taken advantage of the correlation between the two variables introduced by the dependent-samples design. Generally speaking, properly employed, the dependent-samples test will yield a smaller *p*-value as it is more powerful.

The Wilcoxon Matched-Pairs Signed-Ranks Test

Earlier in this chapter in our discussion of the two-independent-samples *t*-test, we presented an alternative non-parametric procedure, the Mann–Whitney *U*-test. In like fashion, there is a counterpart of the dependent-samples *t*-test; the Wilcoxon Matched-Pairs Signed-Ranks test. Again, the 10 differences between math and reading scores for entry-level Native American children were 15, –2, –2, –10, 5, –2, –4, –8, 1, and –5. Ranking these values, regardless of sign, and taking into account tied values, we would obtain ranks of 10, 3, 3, 9, 6.5, 3, 5, 8, 1, and 6.5. Reattaching the signs of the differences we would then have 10, –3, –3, –9, 6.5, –3, –5, –8, 1, and –6.5. We then count how many values there are of each sign; there are three positive values and seven negative values. At this point we could apply the Sign Test, obtaining a two-tailed *p*-value of .3438. (Hint: try the **binom.test( )** function in R.) However, the Sign Test only takes into consideration the direction of the differences, not both the direction and the magnitudes of the differences.

Returning to the Wilcoxon Matched-Pairs Signed-Ranks procedure, we focus on the ranks of the less frequent signs; there are only three ranks that are positive. Their sum is 17.5. It is that value, 17.5, which we take to the table of critical values (Table A.7). Given that we are working with 10 pairs and want a two-tailed test at the .05 level, we enter the table to find two critical values in that location, nine with an associated probability of .0643 and eight with an associated probability of .0487. Similar to the table for the Mann–Whitney critical values, we have provided two values, as we are working with a discrete distribution and there is no value that cuts off exactly .05 in the two tails. Similar to the Mann–Whitney table, Table A.7 has also been constructed in such a way that a value of zero would be obtained if all of the cases had the same sign. That is, if all of the cases were lower on reading than on math, all differences would have been negative. Given no positive differences, the sum of the ranks for the less frequent sign (positives) would be zero. Thus, in this application, we reject the null hypothesis if the observed value of the test statistic is less than the critical value (closer to zero). In our case, the obtained value of 17.5 is larger than either 8 or 9, so we do not reject the null hypothesis.

The Wilcoxon Matched-Pairs Signed-Ranks Test with R

As you may have anticipated, this example can also be completed with R. The appropriate commands are included within Script 14.7. Note the specification of "paired=TRUE". We used both the **wilcox.test( )** function in the base package and the **wilcoxE.test( )** function in the PASWR package. The results are as follows:

```
> wilcox.test(read, math, paired=TRUE,
>    correct=FALSE)
        Wilcoxon signed rank test
data:  read and math
V=17.5, p-value=0.3065
alternative hypothesis: true location shift is not equal to 0

Warning message:
In wilcox.test.default(read, math, paired=TRUE, cor-
rect=FALSE) :
  cannot compute exact p-value with ties

> wilcoxE.test(read, math, paired=TRUE)

        Wilcoxon Signed Rank Test (Dependent Samples)

data:  read and math
t+=17.5, p-value=0.334
alternative hypothesis: true median difference is not equal
to 0
95.3125 percent confidence interval:
 -6  5
```

All three of the non-parametric approaches yield a conclusion of no difference between the two sets of matched scores. Leaving no stone unturned, we now look at these same data with a resampling procedure. The commands are at the end of Script 14.7.

```
> cat("The mean difference is", mdiff, "and the
>   p-value is", pvalue2, "\n")
The mean difference is -1.2 and the p-value is 0.64165
```

As you can see, the two-sided p-value is approximately .64, relatively close to the value obtained with the dependent-samples t-test, but considerably larger than the p-values obtained with the non-parametric analyses of the data. As an explanation, we offer the observation that the largest difference (+15) is quite a bit larger than the next largest difference (−10), and that value is associated with the "less frequent" group. The magnitude of that value is lost by the Sign Test and the ranking by the Wilcoxon Matched-Pairs Signed-Ranks test. We now consider the situation in which you might want to test a difference in the proportions for dependent samples.

A Dependent-Sample Test for Proportions

There will be times when we might be interested in testing hypotheses within the context of dependent samples. For example, we might survey a group of legislators about their attitude toward healthcare reform during the debate in Congress. A year after the legislation was passed we might go back and survey the same group of legislators with a similar question about their attitudes. As another example in the field of educational measurement, we might be concerned with comparing the difficulty of two items on a test. In either case, the data may be arranged within a 2×2 table as shown in Figure 14.4. Note that there is a "reversal" in terms of labeling the rows and the columns. That is, in the attitude change example, the rows are labeled "For" and "Against," respectively. However, the columns are labeled "Against" and "For." This reversal is really unnecessary, but somewhat traditional. (We suspect that it has something to do with Western culture being oriented left-to-right and top-to-bottom.) Looking at either part of Figure 14.4, the frequencies that will be tabled in the upper-left cell and lower-right cell reflect the responses of participants who changed. The other two cells reflect the responses of participants who did not change. Given that we are interested in looking at the difference between the two proportions, the responses of participants who were consistent cannot contribute to any change. Thus, we are concerned with only two cells in the table (upper left and lower right.)

An Example of a Dependent-Samples Test on Proportions

Imagine that you are looking at two test items and want to see if they are of equal difficulty. Based on a sample of 50 students taking the exam, we found that 60% answered the first item correctly, while only 40% answered the second item correctly. We want to know if the two items are at the same level of difficulty. In order to assess this, we cast the data into a 2×2 table as in Figure 14.5. Note that of the 50 students, there were 12 who answered both items correctly and 12 who answered both items incorrectly. These students could not affect any degree of change. Rather, we focus on the 18 students who answered the first item correctly and the second item incorrectly and the 8 students who answered the first item incorrectly and the second item correctly. First consider that we are working with "count" data, which should make you think about χ^2.

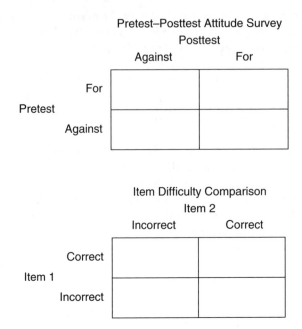

FIGURE 14.4   Data organization for a test on proportions with dependent samples.

Item Difficulty Comparison
Item 2

		Incorrect	Correct	
Item 1	Correct	18	12	30
	Incorrect	12	8	20
		30	20	50

FIGURE 14.5   Data for comparing the difficulty of two items arranged for hand calculation.

The values of 18 and 8 are the observed counts. In order to calculate the χ^2 statistic, we need the expected values. It would seem reasonable to argue that, if the two proportions are the same, the same number of people would change in both directions. Thus, the expected values for both cells would be $(18+8)/2$, or 13. Thus, we would calculate χ^2 as follows:

$$\chi^2_{\text{obs}} = \frac{(18-13)^2}{13} + \frac{(8-13)^2}{13} = 3.846 \qquad (14.24)$$

Given that there are only two cells, $df=1$ and the critical value for χ^2 with 1 df is 3.8415. Our observed value is in the region of rejection, so we would conclude that the two sample proportions, .60 and .40, are too far apart to reasonably conclude that the two items come from populations of items with equal difficulty. We have used R (see Script 14.8) to implement this analysis. The results are as follows:

```
> result

        Chi-squared test for given probabilities

data:  obs
X-squared=3.8462, df=1, p-value=0.04986
```

As you can see, the p-value is less than .05, leading us to reject the null hypothesis of no difference.

The formal name for this procedure is McNemar's Test for Dependent Proportions. If you are going to use the **mcnemar.test( )** function in R, the row/column relationship is not reversed as it usually is for hand computation. Rather, the data would be arranged as shown in Figure 14.6. The commands for implementing the test in R appear at the end of Script 14.8. The results from R are:

```
> item.diff
            2.Correct 2.Incorrect
1.Correct           12          18
1.Incorrect          8          12
> mcnemar.test(item.diff, correct=FALSE)

        McNemar's Chi-squared test

data:  item.diff
McNemar's chi-squared=3.8462, df=1, p-value=0.04986
```

Item Difficulty Comparison
Item 2

	Correct	Incorrect	
Correct	12	18	30
Incorrect	8	12	20
	30	20	50

FIGURE 14.6   Data for comparing the difficulty of two items arranged for the mcnemar.test( ) function in R.

As you can see, the results from **mcnemar.test( )** are identical to those from the χ^2 test that we constructed. The way in which you implement the test is a matter of personal preference, though you need to make sure to construct the 2×2 table accordingly.

CHAPTER SUMMARY

In this chapter, we have focused on procedures for two-sample tests of location. We have looked at the procedures for means, medians, and proportions within the frameworks of independent and dependent samples. Within each paradigm, we have presented the traditional approaches that use distribution-based theory and the non-parametric counterparts where appropriate, and we have offered resampling methods for your consideration.

Regarding the two-independent-samples t-test for means, there is more to consider than we have been able to present in this chapter. The additional considerations depend on the equivalence (or non-equivalence) of the sample estimates of population variance.

In the next chapter we will discuss two-sample procedures for considerations other than location (e.g., variability and relationship, both correlation and regression.) After the discussion of variability, we will revisit the two-independent-samples t-test for means. Similar to the organization of this chapter, we will examine traditional, non-parametric, and resampling approaches as appropriate.

Key Terms

Cohen's d	McNemar test
Dependent Samples	Median test
Blocking variable	Paired samples
Homogeneity of variance	Wilcoxon Matched-Pairs Signed-Ranks test
Independent samples	Wilcoxon Rank Sum test
Mann–Whitney U-test	

REFERENCES

Cohen, J. (1988). *Statistical power analysis for the behavioral sciences*. (2nd ed.). Hillsdale, NJ: Lawrence Erlbaum Associates.

Mann, H. B., & Whitney, D. R. (1947). On a test of whether one of two random variables is stochastically larger than the other. *Annals of Mathematical Statistics, 18*, 50–60.

PRACTICE QUESTIONS

1. A researcher comparing two groups computes a p-value of .037. If $\alpha = .05$, the statistical decision is to:

    a. reject the null hypothesis
    b. fail to reject the null hypothesis
    c. reject the alternative hypothesis
    d. fail to reject the alternative hypothesis.

2. A researcher made a comparison of two groups using an independent-samples t-test. The researcher noted two very low scores, one in each group. If the two low scores were less extreme but the difference between the means remained the same, the calculated t-value would be:

   a. lower
   b. the same
   c. higher.

3. A researcher comparing two groups with a t-test obtains a p-value of .19. The probability of getting:

   a. the obtained test statistic is .19 if the alternative hypothesis is true
   b. the obtained test statistic is .19 if the null hypothesis is true
   c. a test statistic as extreme or more extreme than the obtained test statistic is .19 if the alternative hypothesis is true
   d. a test statistic as extreme or more extreme than the obtained test statistic is .19 if the null hypothesis is true.

4. A colleague indicates that he wishes to compare two independent groups, but he knows the population is substantially skewed and is worried because his sample size is small. He asks you if you know of any options for testing that do not assume a normal distribution. What test would you recommend?

   a. z-test
   b. t-test
   c. Mann–Whitney U-test
   d. McNemar's test.

5. A researcher is considering how large a sample she should use in her study, which compares a treatment group to a control group. If she uses a large sample, this will tend to lead to:

   a. less chance of a Type I error
   b. a larger effect size
   c. greater power
   d. all of the above.

6. Suppose a researcher analyzes the data from a matched-pairs design using a dependent-samples t-test. Relative to conducting an independent-samples t-test that ignores the pairing, the dependent-samples test will tend to have:

   a. more degrees of freedom
   b. fewer degrees of freedom
   c. the same degrees of freedom.

7. Suppose a researcher analyzes the data from a matched-pairs design using a dependent-samples t-test. Relative to conducting an independent-samples t-test that ignores the pairing, the dependent-samples test will tend to have:

   a. more power
   b. less power
   c. the same power.

8. Suppose a colleague comes to you for advice about her research. She has conducted a study where she asked a sample of teachers whether they supported or opposed a new teacher merit program at two points in time (beginning of the school year and end of the school year). What test would you recommend for inferring whether the proportion of teachers favoring the program had changed?

    a. *t*-test.
    b. Median test.
    c. Mann–Whitney *U*-test.
    d. McNemar's test.

EXERCISES

14.1. An investigator has designed a study to determine if sensory stimulation will affect the level of intelligence of infants. A total of 36 infants were available for the study; 18 were assigned to each of the experimental and control groups, using a table of random numbers. After 18 months, the Bailey scale was administered to each of the 36 children. Using the data below, test the null hypothesis of no treatment effect.

	Experimental	*Control*
Mean	108.1	98.4
n	18.0	18.0
s	17.0	14.0
SS	4,913.0	3,332.0

14.2. In recent years the use of mental imagery to improve memory has been a popular topic of research. A psychologist prepared a list of 30 paired nouns (dog/car, broom/sidewalk, etc.). Subjects in Group 1 were given the list for 5 minutes and told to memorize the 30 noun pairs. Subjects in Group 2 were given the same list and instructions, but in addition, were told to form a mental image for each pair (e.g., a dog driving a car, a broom sweeping a sidewalk). After one week, the subjects were given a memory test. The data recorded below are the number of nouns correctly recalled by each subject. Is there any evidence to suggest that mental imagery affected memory?

Group 1 (number of nouns): 14, 13, 6, 7, 9, 3, 7, 10, 5, and 16.
Group 2 (number of nouns): 8, 9, 13, 19, 20, 21, 19, 16, 11, and 24.

14.3. Reanalyze the data which were presented in Exercise 14.2, using a computer package (R). Generate appropriate descriptive statistics and test the hypothesis of equal means for the two groups.

14.4. A developmental psychologist was interested in looking at social dominance in preschool children. A number of 3- and 4-year-olds were observed over a period of time totaling 10 hours, all in a preschool setting. For each child observed, the number of times a child dominated a social interaction was recorded. Afterwards, the data were partitioned by gender. Use the Mann–Whitney test to determine whether the data suggest a difference in social dominance between preschool boys and girls.

Boys' scores: 8, 17, 14, 21, 15, 23, 19.
Girls' scores: 18, 25, 36, 28, 22, 16, 30, 39, 24.

14.5. As our society moves toward two-working-parent families, it is reasonable to wonder if working mothers experience the same pressures as working fathers. One aspect of this question, "spare time," was recently examined. Believing that fewer working mothers feel that they have enough spare time for themselves, a researcher polled random samples of 100 working mothers and working fathers, respectively. The results are tabulated below. Do the data support the research hypothesis ($\alpha = .01$)?

	Working mothers	Working fathers
No. sampled	100	100
No. feeling they have enough time	38	55

14.6. In the text, we have used housing prices for our examples for procedures related to medians, as such data are notoriously skewed. Another example of a skewed variable might be salaries, especially in professional sports. For example, it is widely known that the salary of one New York Yankees player is more than the total payroll of the Tampa Bay Rays. So, we probably don't need to bother testing whether the salaries of those two teams come from populations with the same median. However, the Yankees have a traditional rivalry with the Boston Red Sox. Below are random samples of the 2010 salaries for players for each team. Test the hypothesis that these two samples come from populations with different medians.

Boston Red Sox	New York Yankees
$420,000	$435,000
$12,100,000	$9,000,000
$650,000	$487,975
$7,750,000	$5,500,000
$14,000,000	$22,600,000
$8,525,000	$4,000,000
$18,700,000	$1,200,000
$12,500,000	$11,750,000
$7,700,000	$15,000,000
$2,750,000	$33,000,000
$9,350,000	$6,850,000
$11,550,000	$900,000
$5,500,000	$1,100,000
$3,000,000	
$9,375,000	

14.7. A local, small, and somewhat destitute private college was considering an increase in class size to try to cut expenses. Wishing to effect this policy with a minimum of student protest, the Office of Student Affairs created a special film to enhance students' attitudes toward large classes. The attitudes of 10 students selected at random were assessed both before and after viewing the film. Test the hypothesis that the film was effective in improving students' attitudes.

Student	Attitude before film	Attitude after film
1	25	28
2	23	19
3	29	34
4	7	10
5	3	6

6	22	26
7	12	13
8	32	45
9	8	19
10	14	11

14.8. Reanalyze the data presented in Exercise 14.7 using R.

14.9. A quality-control expert for Scott Paper Company was conducting research on the softness of a particular product. A sample of 10 consumers was asked to rate one of the Scott products and a comparable product noted for its "squeeze attraction" on a 1 to 10 scale (with 1 being the least soft and 10 being the most soft). The results of the survey are presented below. Use these data to determine whether the two products are comparable in softness.

Consumer	Scott	Brand C
1	6	4
2	8	5
3	4	5
4	9	8
5	4	1
6	7	9
7	6	2
8	5	3
9	6	7
10	8	2

14.10. A random sample of 80 elected officials in the Senate and House were surveyed about their attitude toward presidential performance just prior to a vote on a major policy initiative coming from the White House. The same legislators were surveyed after the vote. Prior to the vote, 44 legislators indicated approval; 36 did not. After the legislation was passed, the survey indicated that 48 approved and 32 did not. When tabulated, the results were:

Before	After	
	Against	For
For	4	40
Against	28	8

Use the results to test the null hypothesis that there was no change in presidential approval over the time frame.

15

Other Two-Sample Tests: Variability and Relationships

INTRODUCTION

In the previous chapter we presented a variety of procedures for analyzing data from two samples, procedures that allow us to test hypotheses about location. Specifically, these procedures addressed hypotheses about means, proportions, and medians. We presented methods for both independent and dependent samples.

In this chapter, we continue to be concerned with situations having two samples. We will present techniques for comparing two variances, two correlation coefficients, and two regression coefficients. After looking at ways to compare two variances, we will revisit the t-test for two independent groups. Throughout the chapter, we will present methods for both independent and dependent samples, as appropriate. The material we present in this chapter is based on extensive work completed in the first part of the 20th century (Fisher, 1924; Snedecor, 1934). We will not dwell on the mathematics involved; for more detail see the references just cited, or for a summary of the developments, see Cowles (2001, pp. 121–123).

TESTS ON VARIANCES

In Chapter 14 we mentioned the issue of comparing two samples to see if they might have come from populations with the same variance. We did this in the context of the two-independent-samples t-test, where this concern is a precondition for the validity of the calculated t-statistic and its associated p-value. After our discussion of testing hypotheses about two variances, we will revisit our discussion of the independent-samples t-test. However, at this point, we are going to treat the two-independent-samples test for equivalent variance as a test in its own right.

In working through the logic of the t-test, we used Figures 14.1, 14.2, and 14.3 to develop an expectation of how the difference between the means of two random samples might be distributed. In Figure 14.3, we looked at a situation in which we were drawing two random samples of size n_1 and n_2 from populations that were normally distributed. At that point, we were concerned with the distribution of the means; but as we did not know the variances of the two respective populations, we calculated s_1^2 and s_2^2 to assist us in looking at the variance of the difference between the two sample means. Now, we focus on the two sample estimates of the respective population variances. We wish to test the null hypothesis against the alternate hypothesis as follows:

$$H_0 : \quad \sigma_1^2 = \sigma_2^2$$
$$H_1 : \quad \sigma_1^2 \neq \sigma_2^2$$

(15.1)

Of course, one could posit one-tailed hypotheses rather than two-tailed hypotheses. In our presentation of one-sample tests, we noted that variances are different from means in that their sampling distributions are skewed rather than symmetric. Thus, for the one-sample test on a variance, we needed to use the similarly skewed χ^2-distribution, rather than either of the symmetric z- or t-distributions.

Returning our focus to Figure 14.3, rather than looking at the difference between the two sample estimates of the population variances, let's look at the ratio of the two variances. Assuming that the two populations are normally distributed with equal variance, we developed an R script to simulate several scenarios, varying the sizes of the two samples (see Script 15.1) and running the script for each different scenario. The samples sizes were (5, 10), (5, 20), (10, 10), (10, 20), (15, 20), and (15, 30). All samples were random samples drawn from the unit-normal distribution. The results are shown in Table 15.1 and Figure 15.1.

Only the first four scenarios are shown in Figure 15.1. However, as you can see, all combinations yield positively skewed distributions, but the skewness seems to be reduced with larger sample sizes in the denominator. Also, in Table 15.1, note that the means for all six combinations are relatively close to 1.00, being closer for larger sample sizes in the denominator. We could show you more combinations of sample sizes, but we will spare you the suspense. We are looking at simulations of yet another mathematical probability distribution, the F-distribution. (Fisher completed most of the early developmental work, and Snedecor named it the F-distribution to honor Fisher.) Like the χ^2-distribution, the F-distribution is asymmetric so that the lower and upper tails must be tabled separately.

The F-Distribution

Like the t- and χ^2-distributions, the F-distribution is actually a family of distributions defined by two parameters, the number of degrees of freedom (df) for both the numerator and the denominator. Although it is theoretically defined as another special case of the gamma (γ) distribution, it can be more easily defined as the ratio of the variances of two independent samples of size n_1 and n_2, respectively, drawn from a normally distributed population. The particular member of the family is defined by the two df, where df_1 equals $(n_1 - 1)$ and df_2 equals $(n_2 - 1)$.

Table 15.1 Descriptive statistics for the ratio of two variances for different combinations of sample sizes based on 100,000 replications (n_1 = numerator sample size, n_2 = denominator sample size)

n_1	5	5	10	10	15	15
n_2	10	20	10	20	20	30
Minimum	.0031	.0049	.0239	.0675	.0737	.1019
Median	.9095	.8670	1.0070	.9693	.9864	.9737
Mean	1.3000	1.1070	1.2990	1.1210	1.1183	1.0713
Maximum	21.0400	11.9000	27.2000	7.8880	9.5030	7.9526
Variance	1.8380	.8337	1.2699	.4906	.3718	.2718
Skewness	3.7301	2.2499	4.5827	1.8245	1.8762	1.4777
Kurtosis	25.7140	9.7710	50.0807	6.0764	7.5777	4.4852

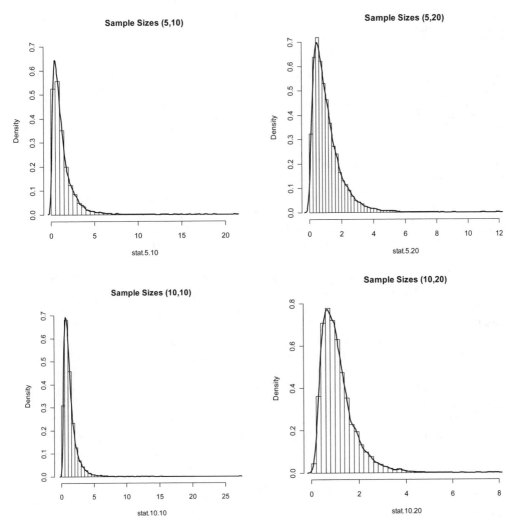

FIGURE 15.1   Simulated ratios of the variances of two samples of different sizes.

Typically, df_1 and df_2 are represented symbolically by v_1 and v_2 (pronounced "nu 1" and "nu 2"). The expected value (mean) and variance of the F-distribution are presented in Equations 15.2 and 15.3, respectively:

$$E[F] = \frac{v_2}{v_2 - 2} \tag{15.2}$$

$$\text{var}[F] = \frac{2v_2^2 (v_1 + v_2 - 2)}{v_1 (v_2 - 2)^2 (v_2 - 4)} \tag{15.3}$$

We wrote an R script (Script 15.2) to evaluate these two expressions for the various simulations that were summarized in Table 15.1. The results are presented in Table 15.2. As you can see, the means and variances of the simulated distributions of the ratio of two sample variances are

Table 15.2 Descriptive statistics (mean and variance) from the simulated scenarios and the expected values (mean and variance) based on Equations 15.2 and 15.3

n_1	5	5	10	10	15	15
n_2	10	20	10	20	20	30
Mean	1.3000	1.1070	1.2990	1.1210	1.1183	1.0713
Expected mean	1.2857	1.1176	1.2857	1.1176	1.1176	1.0741
Variance	1.8380	.8337	1.2699	.4906	.3718	.2718
Expected variance	1.8184	.8744	1.1755	.4811	.3688	.2703

in very close agreement with the expected values if we assume that the simulations follow the *F*-distribution.

We will now present the density distributions of several different members of the *F*-family, deliberately selecting some of the examples that were simulated and reported in Table 15.1. Specifically, we chose n_1 and n_2 to be (5, 10) to make the first distribution, (10, 20) to make the second distribution, and (15, 30) to make the third distribution. The three *F*-distributions are shown in Figure 15.2.

At this point, you should be convinced that the ratio of the variances of two independent samples drawn from normally distributed populations with the same variance should be distributed like the appropriate member of the *F*-distribution. Thus, the *F*-distribution may be used to test hypotheses as specified in Equation 15.1.

If we are going to use *F*-distributions to test hypotheses about variances, we will need a way to find the "critical values" for the appropriate probability distribution. Given that *F*-distributions are skewed, as noted earlier, we will need to consider the lower and upper tails separately, as with the χ^2-distribution. We have tabled selected values of the *F*-distribution for the lower and upper tails for both the .05 and .025 levels. That is, the values presented in Table A8.1 are those that "cut off" 5% of the area in the lower tail; the values presented in Table A8.2 cut off 5% of the area in the upper tail. Similarly, the values presented in Table A8.3 cut off 2.5% of the area in the

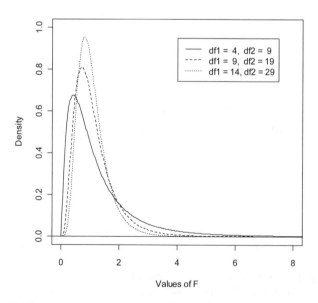

FIGURE 15.2   The density distributions of three different *F*-distributions.

lower tail; the values presented in Table A8.4 cut off 2.5% in the upper tail. Keep in mind that each of the four tables spans two pages; the second page is a continuation of the table, with the second page being lined up to the right of the first page. The **qf( )** function in R will allow you to find other values you may seek.

If we wanted to conduct a two-tailed hypothesis as indicated in Equation 15.1 at the .05 level, we would seek the critical values that cut off 2.5% in each tail, using Tables A8.3 and A8.4. If we wanted to test the one-tailed hypothesis

$$H_0: \ \sigma_1^2 \leq \sigma_2^2$$
$$H_1: \ \sigma_1^2 > \sigma_2^2$$

(15.4)

we would calculate our F-statistic with the variance from Sample 1 in the numerator, and find our critical value in Table A8.2. Can you explain why?

Some Properties of the F-Distribution

The F-distribution is the most general of the four mathematical probability distributions (z, t, χ^2, and F) that we cover in this book. Allow us to take a moment to present our case for this assertion. To begin, let's focus on the first column in Table A8.2, the column associated with one degree of freedom for the numerator. We will pick one of the rows arbitrarily, the one for $v_2 = 20$. You should be able to see the value 4.351. Now, go to the t-table and find the tabled value for a two-tailed t-test with $df = 20$. You can go to a table, or you can find the value easily with R:

```
qt(c(.025,.975),20)
[1] -2.085963 2.085963
```

As you can see, the critical values for the t-test would be ± 2.086. Now, find $(2.086)^2$ and you should obtain 4.3514. A coincidence? Hardly! The first column of the F-table contains squared values from the t-distribution.

At this point, recall that in the context of testing hypotheses about means, one distinction between the t-distribution and the z-distribution is whether you know the variance of the population or must estimate it from the sample data. If you have the entire population, the notion of degrees of freedom is not relevant; in essence your degrees of freedom are infinite. Now, look in the last row of the first column of Table A8.2 and you should find a value of 3.841. If you take the square root of 3.841, you should obtain 1.9598, within reasonable rounding error of 1.96. That is, the last row of the first column of the F-table contains values of z^2.

Let's try one more example; look at the bottom row of Table A8.2 and select one of the columns. Suppose we select the column for $v_1 = 8$. In the bottom row, we see an F-value of 1.938. Now, find the value of χ^2 with $df = 8$ that cuts off .05 in the upper tail. Let's use R:

```
> qchisq(.95,8)
[1] 15.50731
```

If you divide 15.5731 by 8, we obtain 1.938414. That is, the bottom row of the F-table contains the values of χ^2, divided by their respective df. We could present more examples, but hopefully, you are convinced that you could find the critical values of z, t, and χ^2 within the appropriate F-table. If you wish, try some more examples on your own. We will now present an example of the F-test.

An Example of an F-*Test for Two Variances*

Let's suppose that we are interested in comparing two ethnic groups with regard to the variability in their reading scores at the entry to kindergarten. Specifically, we are interested in comparing the populations of White and Asian students on the Item Response Theory (*irt*) reading scores. To do so, we have drawn two random samples ($n_1 = n_2 = 25$) from the ECLS2577 data file. We will not present the specific scores here, but you can see them in Script 15.4 on the book website. We now proceed to calculate the two sample variances by substituting the summarized data (Whites: $\Sigma Y = 566$, $\Sigma Y^2 = 13{,}748$; Asians: $\Sigma Y = 758$, $\Sigma Y^2 = 28{,}966$) into the following equation:

$$s_j^2 = \frac{\sum_{i=1}^{n_j} Y_{ij}^2 - \left[\left(\sum_{i=1}^{n_j} Y \right)^2 / n_j \right]}{n_j - 1} \tag{15.5}$$

For the White children, we obtain a value of 38.91, for the Asian children a value of 249.31. We can now define our test statistic as:

$$F_{\text{obs}} = \frac{s_1^2}{s_2^2} = \frac{38.91}{249.31} = .1560 \tag{15.6}$$

Given that both samples sizes are 25, we would want to compare our computed value to the critical values of the F-distribution with $df = (24, 24)$. As the question was stated, no direction was implied, so we would complete a two-tailed test. Assuming a level of significance (α) of .05, we would want to go to Table A8.3 to find the lower value of .441 and to Table A8.4 to find the upper value of 2.269. Of course, you can obtain these values with the probability functions included in R. The format for obtaining values of the F-distribution is:

```
qf(lower-tailed p-value, df for numerator,
df for denominator)
```

Thus, to get both the lower- and upper-tailed values for our example:

```
> qf(c(.025,.975),24,24)
[1] 0.4406689 2.2692773
```

Under the conditions for this test, values between .441 and 2.269 are reasonable to obtain under the null hypothesis of no difference. Values outside this range are more extreme than we would expect to see by chance; we obtained a value of .156, so we would reject the null hypothesis, concluding that these two populations appear to have different variances. We have depicted the regions of rejection and non-rejection in Figure 15.3.

THE EXAMPLE WITH R   All of what we have just presented can be completed with R. The additional statements are contained within Script 15.4. After loading the **car** package and our **functions** file, we read in the data with the **c( )** function. Then, we requested the two sample variances:

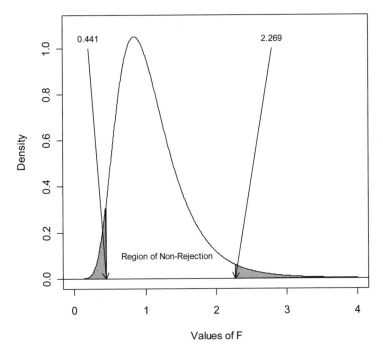

FIGURE 15.3   The regions of rejection and non-rejection for a two-tailed F-test on two variances at the .05 level when n_1 and n_2 are equal to 25.

```
> var(white)
[1] 38.90667
> var(asian)
[1] 249.31
```

As you can verify, the results from R match up with our hand calculations. We then employed the **var.test( )** function to complete the F-test:

```
> var.test(white, asian)
F test to compare two variances
data: white and asian
F=0.1561, num df=24, denom df=24, p-value=2.307e-05
alternative hypothesis: true ratio of variances is not equal
to 1
95 percent confidence interval:
0.06876964 0.35413748
sample estimates:
ratio of variances
0.1560574
```

Once again, you can see that the F-statistic in R matches ours, with a two-tailed p-value less than .05. Thus, we come to the same conclusion with regard to the null hypothesis. Recall that in our simulations of several F-distributions at the beginning of this chapter, we drew our sample from normally distributed populations. Indeed, the assumption of normally distributed populations is important to assure the appropriate interpretation of the p-value resulting from the F-test. Perhaps we should take a look at the legitimacy of this assumption. Returning to R,

```
> skewness(white)
[1] 0.4342019
> kurtosis(white)
[1] -0.1632085
> shapiro.test(white)
Shapiro-Wilk normality test
W=0.9671, p-value=0.5724
> skewness(asian)
[1] 0.9578602
> kurtosis(asian)
[1] 0.0123387
> shapiro.test(asian)
Shapiro-Wilk normality test
W=0.8958, p-value=0.01492
```

An inspection of these results suggests that the assumption of normality may be questionable for the sample of Asian children. Thus, we should perhaps consider other ways to compare two populations with regard to the equality of variance. For purposes of completeness, we will provide a historical perspective, describing some techniques that are no longer used. We will then consider some currently recommended approaches that do not require an assumption of normality.

Alternatives to the F-Statistic

One of the more widely known approaches to testing the equality of variances is the Bartlett (1937) χ^2 test statistic. Originally proposed for several groups, we show you the adaptation for two groups:

$$\chi^2_{obs} = \frac{2.30259}{C}\left[(n_1 + n_2 - 2)\log_{10} s^2_{pooled} - \sum_{j=1}^{2}(n_j - 1)\log_{10} s^2_j\right]$$

where

$$C = 1 + \left[\left(\frac{1}{n_1} + \frac{1}{n_2} - \frac{1}{n_1 + n_2 - 2}\right)/3\right]$$

(15.7)

The test statistic is approximately distributed as χ^2 with $df=1$ when sample sizes are both larger than 5. Unfortunately, this approach had two major drawbacks. First, without a calculator of some type, the formula is somewhat formidable. Second, the Bartlett test is also sensitive to departures from normality.

Other approaches have been suggested. One of those was proposed by Hartley (1940, 1950) and was known as Hartley's F_{max}-test. Like the Bartlett test, it was designed for any number of groups. The test simply involved finding s^2 for each of the groups and then forming the test statistic:

$$F_{max} = \frac{s^2_{largest}}{s^2_{smallest}} \tag{15.8}$$

The statistical significance of the observed test statistic was determined by comparing the observed result to the critical values in a special set of tables.

Another approach was proposed by Cochran (1941) and was known as Cochran's C.

$$C = \frac{s^2_{max}}{\sum_{i=1}^{k} s^2_j} \tag{15.9}$$

where k is the number of groups. As with the F_{max} test, a special table was used to determine the statistical significance of C. Although the two latter procedures are much simpler to calculate, they too are sensitive to departures from normality.

Currently Recommended Alternatives to the F-Statistic

With the widespread availability of high-speed computing and the associated software, there are several additional ways to test for the equality of variances, approaches which are less sensitive to departures from normality. One of the first of these was proposed by Levene (1960). Like so many creative contributions that build on simplicity, it is based on a measure of dispersion we described toward the beginning of this book: the average deviation. Recall that the average deviation is the mean of the absolute values of the differences between the observations and their mean. For a two-group situation, one would simply find the deviations for each of the groups from their respective means, take the absolute values, and then compare the means of the absolute values with a t-test. Levene (1960) proposed using deviations from the mean. Subsequently, Brown and Forsythe (1974) examined other possible measures of center: the median and trimmed mean. These variations are sometimes labeled as the Brown–Forsythe test, but more often than not, they are simply labeled as variations of the Levene test. For example, the **leveneTest( )** function in the **car** package uses the median as the default measure of center. There is an additional approach available in R known as the Fligner–Killeen test (**fligner.test( )**), based on work by Fligner and Killeen (1976) and extended by Conover, Johnson, and Johnson (1981). It also looks at absolute values of the deviations from the median, but differs because these values are ranked and then compared to the expected distribution of ranks under the null hypothesis. After creating a **data.frame** named *data.var* (see Script 15.4), the results from the two procedures are:

```
> leveneTest(read ~ group, data=data.var)
Levene's Test for Homogeneity of Variance (center=median)
Df F value Pr(>F)
group 1 9.2564 0.003798
48
```

```
> # Fligner-Killeen test
> fligner.test(read ~ group)
Fligner-Killeen test of homogeneity of variances
Fligner-Killeen:med chi-squared=7.626, df=1,
p-value=0.005753
```

At the beginning of this section, we described the conceptual basis of the Levene test as a *t*-test comparing the mean deviations of the two groups. As you can see immediately above, R reports the results of the **leveneTest** as an *F*-statistic, which makes things a little confusing as we have described the *F*-statistic as the ratio of two sample variances. The *F*-statistic that is reported by **leveneTest** is actually an extension of the *t*-statistic and hopefully will become clear in the next chapter on analysis-of-variance. In the interim, we have written an R script to implement the *t*-test version of Levene's test (Script 15.6) for our data on White and Asian children's *irt* scores. After finding the medians for the two groups, we found the deviations of the scores from their respective medians, took the absolute values of those deviations, and finally compared the means of the two sets of deviations with a *t*-test:

```
> t.test(devw, deva, var.equal=TRUE)
Two Sample t-test
data: devw and deva
t=-3.0424, df=48, p-value=0.003798
alternative hypothesis: true difference in means is not equal
to 0
95 percent confidence interval:
-11.758922 -2.401078
sample estimates:
mean of x mean of y
4.84 11.92
# Squaring the t-value
> (-3.0424)^2
[1] 9.256198
```

As you can see, the squared *t*-statistic comparing the means of the absolute values of the deviations from the medians is equal to 9.2562, virtually identical to the *F*-statistic of 9.2564 reported by the **leveneTest( )** function in R.

A Test to Compare Two Variances of Dependent Samples

Given situations in which there are two samples of observations, it is possible that the samples might be dependent. For example, one might design an intervention to reduce the amount of variability in some behavior. In this instance, we could collect data prior to the onset of the intervention. After the intervention, we would collect data on the same group. This pre-test/post-test design would produce dependent samples. In this case, we would want to employ a test statistic appropriate for the situation. A formula is provided in Kirk (1990, p. 414):

$$t_{obs} = \frac{s_1^2 - s_2^2}{\sqrt{\left[\left(4s_1^2 s_2^2\right)/\left(n-2\right)\right]\left(1-r_{12}^2\right)}} \tag{15.10}$$

where n is the number of paired observations and r_{12} is the Pearson correlation between the two sets of scores. Under the null hypothesis, the observed t-statistic is distributed as t with $(n-2)$ *df*.

At this point, we need to review what we have covered and relate this new information to some earlier material. In this chapter, we have considered several different ways to compare two samples of observations with respect to equivalent variances. We described the traditional F-test, noting that it was tied to an assumption of normality. We presented some other alternatives (Bartlett's χ^2, Hartley's F_{max}, and Cochran's C), which also were sensitive to departures from normality. We then turned our attention to some newer approaches, specifically Levene's test, its variation known as the Brown–Forsythe test, and the Fligner–Killeen test. These newer procedures are currently recommended as they are less sensitive to non-normality. We concluded with a presentation of a t-test to compare the variances for dependent samples.

Hypotheses about variances are hypotheses in their own right, although considerably less frequent than hypotheses about means. In the previous chapter, we spent considerable time and space on the two-independent-samples t-test for means. In our discussion, we noted that this test assumes that the samples are drawn from normally distributed populations with equal variances. The latter assumption is sometimes called *homogeneity of variance*. In our discussion, we presented some non-parametric alternatives to the t-test, specifically the Mann–Whitney U-test and the Wilcoxon Rank Sum test. We could not address adequately the assumption of equal variances at that time as we had not yet discussed ways to test for equal variances. However, we now turn our attention back to the t-test for means of independent samples, presenting a more complete discussion.

REVISITING THE TWO-INDEPENDENT-SAMPLES t-TEST FOR MEANS

In situations where we want to test hypotheses about two means, we may use Equation 14.11, which assumes normally distributed populations with equivalent variances. Due to the Central Limit Theorem, the t-test is fairly robust with respect to the assumption of normality when the sample sizes are sufficiently large. In the previous chapter, we presented the Mann–Whitney U-test and a permutation test as alternatives to employ with small samples. With respect to the pooling of the two samples estimates of variance as in Equations 14.9 through 14.11, it hardly makes sense to proceed in this fashion if the two populations have different variances. This problem is known as the Behrens–Fisher problem, and a number of approaches have been recommended.

Previous research has shown that the t-test is fairly insensitive (i.e., robust) to departures from homogeneity of variance when the two samples sizes are the same (Boneau, 1960; Box, 1953; Norton, 1952). However, as the sample sizes become more and more different, the assumption of equivalent variances becomes more important. If the large sample is paired with the large variance, then the weighted average (s^2_{pooled}) will be too large. On the other hand, if the large sample is paired with the small variance, then s^2_{pooled} will tend to be too small.

Although a number of solutions have been proposed, there does not appear to be widespread consensus on how to proceed. One approach uses the separate-sample estimate of t (see Equation 14.9):

$$t'_{obs} = \frac{(\bar{Y}_{.1} - \bar{Y}_{.2}) - (\mu_1 - \mu_2)}{\sqrt{(s_1^2 / n_1) + (s_2^2 / n_2)}} \tag{15.11}$$

When $\sigma_1^2 \neq \sigma_2^2$, t' is not distributed as t with $df = (n_1 + n_2 - 2)$. There have been several attempts to approximate the distribution of t'. One of the first solutions was proposed by Cochran and Cox (1957), who recommended deriving a critical value of t' by weighting the two critical values of t for $(n_1 - 1)$ and $(n_2 - 1)$ df by the two respective sample variances. Their approach is described in Johnson and Jackson (1959):

$$t' = \frac{t_1 (s_1^2 / n_1) + t_2 (s_2^2 / n_2)}{(s_1^2 / n_1) + (s_2^2 / n_2)} \tag{15.12}$$

where t_1 is the tabled value of t for $n_1 - 1$ df and t_2 is the tabled value of t for $n_2 - 1$ df, both at the desired level of statistical significance (α). Given that the df are for the separate samples rather than $(n_1 + n_2 - 2)$, this solution should be a conservative one. Another approach was independently derived by Welch (1938) and Satterthwaite (1946) and is implemented in many computer programs, including R. The separate-sample estimate of t' (Equation 15.11) is calculated and evaluated against the t-distribution with df equal to:

$$df' = \frac{\left[(s_1^2 / n_1) + (s_2^2 / n_2) \right]^2}{\left[(s_1^2 / n_1) / (n_1 - 1) \right] + \left[(s_2^2 / n_2)^2 / (n_2 - 1) \right]} \tag{15.13}$$

Returning to our example from Chapter 14 in which we looked at the level of reading performance for children entering kindergarten, comparing a random sample of 10 cases from the lowest quintile of socioeconomic status to a random sample of 10 cases from the highest quintile of socioeconomic status, we can implement this analysis quite easily with R as in Script 15.7:

```
> t.test(low, high, var.equal=FALSE)
Welch Two Sample t-test
data: low and high
t=-2.6961, df=12.714, p-value=0.01863
alternative hypothesis: true difference in means is not equal
to 0
95 percent confidence interval:
-13.343157    -1.456843
sample estimates:
mean of x    mean of y
   17.4         24.8
```

In this example, the sample sizes are equal so that the two t-statistics (pooled sample and separate sample) are the same. However, note that the degrees of freedom have been adjusted, leading to a slightly different p-value.

Our Recommendations

These recommendations are made against a background of research that shows the t-test to be robust against violations of the assumption of normality when the sample sizes are sufficiently large or when the samples appear to have similar, non-normal distributions. The research also shows that the procedure is robust with regard to violations of homogeneity of variance when the sample sizes are equal. That said, when confronted with the task of comparing two groups with regard to equivalent location, we think that, under the right conditions, a comparison of the two means may be the best way to proceed. However, the right conditions are not always present. Our recommendations reflect what we think to be the most widely held view. We believe that this view is, in part, encouraged by the desire to avoid dealing with Equation 15.13. However, with the correction available in the computer software, one might argue that the correction should always be applied.

As you may notice in the subsequent discussion, applied statistics is not an exact science; it involves a bit of artistic license too. First, consider the issue of normally distributed populations. Examine the data for each group separately with regard to shape. Specifically, you should generate graphic displays of your data (e.g., histograms, box plots) and measures of skewness and kurtosis. If the data appear reasonably normal, you are probably alright with regard to this assumption. If in doubt, you may want to apply the **shapiro.test( )** to each group. If the samples appear non-normal but similar, you are probably on firm ground. If the samples are relatively small, you may wish to employ the Mann–Whitney U-test or a permutation test.

Next, consider the sample sizes with regard to equality. If the sample sizes are the same and sufficiently large to justify the assumption of normality (Central Limit Theorem), you are also probably on safe ground to use the pooled-samples t-test which assumes homogeneity of variance. However, as we noted previously, as the sample sizes become increasingly different, the assumption of homogeneity of variance becomes increasingly more important. Rules of thumb have been offered, but they are only guidelines. Some "experts" have stated that, if the larger variance is less than twice the smaller variance, you can use the pooled-estimate version. Others mention a 1:4 ratio. When in doubt, you can apply the Levene test or the Fligner–Killeen test, but you will find that different experts recommend different levels of α to apply to the result, varying from .01 to .20, depending on the disparity between the sample sizes. If you decide that the variances are sufficiently similar, given the differences in the sample sizes, proceed with the pooled-samples estimate of t. On the other hand, if the sample sizes are quite different and the sample variances also appear different, you should probably employ the separate-sample estimate of t and the Welch–Satterthwaite correction for df.

Given this discussion, one cannot help but wonder if resampling methods might be applied here. In order to use a resampling approach, Good (2006) noted that there are some limitations on how to proceed, as the observations are not interchangeable if the variances differ. He stated that one can bootstrap the confidence interval for the difference between the two population means, but it must be done by drawing the bootstrap samples from the two original samples rather than drawing the bootstrap samples from a pooled sample. We wish it were that simple.

We have done some limited, very preliminary work, simulating data under optimal conditions, as follows: both populations normally distributed with both means equal to 50 and both variances equal to 100. With these specifications, we generated data based on several different sample sizes (i.e., 10 through 75, in increments of 5). For the bootstrapping and permutation tests, we generated 100,000 resamples. This was done 5,000 times with $\alpha = .05$. We compared the "actual" Type I error rates for the pooled-samples t-test, the separate-sample t-test with the Welch–Satterthwaite correction, the Cochran–Cox approximation, the pooled-bootstrap

Table 15.3 Actual type I error rate (5,000 replications) for a pooled-samples *t*-test (PST), separate-samples *t*-test with corrected *df* (SST), Cochran–Cox approximation (CCA), pooled-samples bootstrap (PSB), pooled-samples permutation test (PSP), and separate-sample bootstrap (SSB), with equal sample sizes and equal variances (nominal $\alpha = .05$)

Sample size	Method					
	PST	*SST*	*CCA*	*PSB*	*PSP*	*SSB*
10	.0516	.0502	.0366	.0552	.0526	.0848
15	.0478	.0470	.0398	.0496	.0476	.0668
20	.0488	.0486	.0430	.0498	.0490	.0624
25	.0528	.0524	.0466	.0536	.0524	.0614
30	.0492	.0488	.0440	.0498	.0494	.0586
35	.0498	.0494	.0460	.0502	.0496	.0558
40	.0534	.0534	.0502	.0554	.0534	.0608
45	.0476	.0476	.0446	.0488	.0476	.0528
50	.0528	.0528	.0418	.0538	.0534	.0582
55	.0456	.0454	.0430	.0460	.0452	.0490
60	.0506	.0502	.0482	.0508	.0504	.0542
65	.0446	.0446	.0442	.0456	.0450	.0448
70	.0538	.0538	.0526	.0544	.0544	.0578
75	.0468	.0468	.0450	.0472	.0464	.0516

approach, the permutation test, and the separate-sample bootstrapped approach recommended by Good (2006). We present the proportion of "significant" results for the six different approaches in Table 15.3; keep in mind that each significant result is a Type I error.

Looking at Table 15.3, you can see that, regardless of sample size, the first five approaches (traditional pooled-sample *t*, separate-sample *t* with Welch correction, Cochran–Cox approximation, pooled bootstrapping, and permutation test) yield Type I error rates in line with what we would expect. On the other hand, the separate-sample bootstrap approach recommended by Good seems to have an inflated Type I error rate, especially with smaller samples. In completing further analyses, we have simulated conditions of equal means and cell sizes, but varying the equality of the variances. Even when the variances were 100 and 1,600, respectively, we obtained similar results. All of the first five methods yield empirical Type I error rates close to the nominal rate of .05; the separate-sample bootstrapping procedure recommended by Good continued to provide upwardly biased empirical error rates, over .06 even with sample sizes of 40. When the conditions allowed the sample sizes to differ in a 1:4 ratio and the variances in a 1:4 ratio, the results were dramatic. When the smaller sample was paired with the smaller variance, both the separate-sample Welch correction and the Cochran–Cox approximation yielded empirical error rates that averaged .0516 and .0475, respectively. With the exception of the separate-sample bootstrapping, the other methods resulted in empirical Type I error rates consistently around .005. Only when the samples were as large as 30 and 120 did the procedure recommended by Good produce an error rate close to .05. When the smaller sample was paired with the larger variance, the results were such that the separate-sample Welch correction and the Cochran–Cox approximation yielded error rates of .0504 and .0493, respectively. The separate-sample bootstrapping recommended by Good produced an error rate of .0910 with sample sizes of 10 and 40, getting down reasonably close to .05 (.0538) when the sample sizes were 60 and 240. The other methods all produced empirical Type I error rates very close to .18. After additional work, we hope that we will be able to provide some definitive recommendations, but that remains to be seen; Good (2006) noted that this is a "problem whose exact solution has eluded statisticians for decades"

(p. 46). However, our results so far seem to suggest that the Welch correction might be the method of choice under any conditions; it always seems to work.

At this point, we are ready to return to the other main topic of this chapter, comparing two samples with regard to similarity of relationships. This topic will be treated in two parts: first with regard to the equivalence of correlation coefficients, and second with regard to the equivalence of regression coefficients.

COMPARING TWO CORRELATION COEFFICIENTS

Situations may arise in which we are interested in comparing two populations with regard to the strength of the linear relationship between variables. We begin with an example involving two independent samples, returning to the data used in Chapters 2 and 3 where we described samples of 100 White and 100 African American children on several traits. Assume that we are interested in looking at the relationship between end of first grade mathematics and beginning of kindergarten reading, separately by race. We might state a null hypothesis in the form:

$$H_0: \ \rho_{\text{w-rm}} = \rho_{\text{aa-rm}}$$
$$H_1: \ \rho_{\text{w-rm}} \neq \rho_{\text{aa-rm}}$$

(15.14)

We have generated the two sample correlations with Script 15.8, which is included on the book website with the supplementary materials for this chapter. The two correlations are .453 for Whites and .605 for African Americans. Clearly, these two coefficients are not the same, but do they differ by more than one might expect due to sampling error? Referring to Fisher's work on the r to r' transformation, we have a formula to calculate a test statistic:

$$z_{\text{obs}} = \frac{r_1' - r_2'}{\sqrt{\left[1/(n_1-3)\right]+\left[1/(n_2-3)\right]}}$$

(15.15)

Rounding the two coefficients to three decimal places and then using Table A.5, we find that $r_1' = .4885$ and $r_2' = .7010$. Entering these values into Equation 15.15 gives:

$$z_{\text{obs}} = \frac{.4885 - .7010}{\sqrt{\left[1/(100-3)\right]+\left[1/(100-3)\right]}} = \frac{-.2125}{\sqrt{.0206}} = \frac{-.2125}{.1436} = -1.480$$

(15.16)

Assuming $\alpha = .05$ with a two-tailed test, the critical values are yet again ± 1.96, and we do not reject H_0. That is, the two correlation coefficients do not differ by more than we might expect by chance.

Comparing Two Independent Correlation Coefficients with R

In Script 15.8, we have provided two options: the first works from raw data, while the second allows you to enter summary data. In any event, we ran the script based on raw data, and the results were as follows:

```
> r1 <- with(ecls200.white, cor(c1rrscal,
> c4rmscal))
> r1
[1] 0.4532125
> n1 <- with(ecls200.white, length(c1rrscal))
> n1
[1] 100
> r2 <- with(ecls200.aa, cor(c1rrscal, c4rmscal))
> r2
[1] 0.6049761
> n2 <- with(ecls200.aa, length(c1rrscal))
> n2
[1] 100
> r1.prime <- atanh(r1)
> r1.prime
[1] 0.4887359
> r2.prime <- atanh(r2)
> r2.prime
[1] 0.7009589
> # Calculate the test statistic
> z.obs <- (r1.prime - r2.prime)/sqrt((1/(n1-3))
> + (1/(n2-3)))
> z.obs
[1] -1.477963
> # Two tailed p-value
> 2*(1 - pnorm(abs(z.obs)))
[1] 0.1394178
> # One tailed p-value, confirm direction
> (1 - pnorm(abs(z.obs)))
[1] 0.0697089
```

The values of interest are identified in bold. As you can see, the value of z_{obs} is very close to the one that we calculated in Equation 15.16, and the two-tailed p-value exceeds .05.

Comparing Two Dependent (Overlapping) Correlations

The way in which dependent correlations is defined differs slightly from the way in which dependent groups were defined earlier. Recall that the dependent samples may result from naturally occurring aggregations (twins), matched cases, or repeated measures. With regard to correlations, there are actually two different ways in which the coefficients may be dependent. First, you may have data on several variables on one group. If you are interested in comparing how different variables (X and Y) correlate with a third variable, Z, you will compare r_{xz} with r_{yz}. Because the two coefficients share one variable, they are said to be dependent. The null and alternate hypotheses to be contrasted would be:

$$H_0: \rho_{xz} = \rho_{yz}$$
$$H_1: \rho_{xz} \neq \rho_{yz} \tag{15.17}$$

Many years ago, Hotelling (1931) presented a formula for calculating a test statistic:

$$t_{obs} = \left(r_{xz} - r_{yz}\right) \sqrt{\frac{\left(n-3\right)\left(1+r_{xy}\right)}{2\left(1-r_{zx}^2 - r_{zy}^2 - r_{xy}^2 + 2r_{zx}r_{zy}r_{xy}\right)}} \tag{15.18}$$

which is distributed with $df = n - 3$. Subsequently, Williams (1959) described what is generally regarded as a better test:

$$t_{obs} = \left(r_{xz} - r_{yz}\right) \sqrt{\frac{\left(n-1\right)\left(1+r_{xy}\right)}{2\left[\left(n-1\right)/\left(n-3\right)\right]|R| + \left[\left(r_{xz} + r_{yx}\right)^2 / 4\right]\left(1 - r_{xy}\right)^3}} \tag{15.19}$$

Where $|R|$ is the determinant of the 3×3 correlation matrix and is defined as:

$$|R| = 1 - r_{xz}^2 - r_{yz}^2 - r_{xy}^2 + 2r_{xz}r_{yz}r_{xy} \tag{15.20}$$

This test statistic is also distributed with $df = n - 3$.

An Example of Two Dependent Correlations with R

Suppose that we are interested in assessing two entry to kindergarten variables (reading and math) with respect to their strength of linear association with end-of-first-grade math for African American children. For purposes of the example, we shall define x as pre-kindergarten reading (*c1rrscal*), y as pre-kindergarten math (*c1rmscal*), and z as end-of-first-grade math (*c4rmscal*). There were 100 cases in the data file; the correlation between pre-kindergarten reading and end-of-first grade math was .605, the correlation between pre-kindergarten math and end-of-first grade math was .649, and the correlation between the two pre-kindergarten variables was .743. We have written Script 15.9 to implement the test, as suggested by Williams (1959). The script allows you to analyze both raw data and summary data.

Very abbreviated results are as follows:

```
> # Doing the test with R
> mat <- cbind(c1rrscal, c1rmscal, c4rmscal)
```

```
> r.mat <- cor(mat)
> r.mat
         c1rrscal  c1rmscal  c4rmscal
c1rrscal 1.0000000 0.7433614 0.6049761
c1rmscal 0.7433614 1.0000000 0.6492096
c4rmscal 0.6049761 0.6492096 1.0000000
> detR <- det(r.mat)
> t.obs <- (rxz - ryz)*sqrt(((n - 1)*
> (1 + rxy))/(2*((n - 1)/n - 3))*detR +
> (rxz + ryz)^2/4 *(1 - rxy)^3))
> t.obs
[1] -0.8182043
> # Two tailed p-value
> 2*(1 - pt(abs(t.obs), n - 3))
[1] 0.415246
> # One tailed p-value, confirm direction
> (1 - pt(abs(t.obs), n - 3))
[1] 0.207623
```

As you might have anticipated after seeing the sample correlation coefficients, there is no evidence to reject the null hypothesis.

Comparing Two Dependent (Non-Overlapping) Correlations

There is a second situation, less often encountered, in which one may be interested in comparing two correlations that are considered to be dependent. Similar to the first situation, you have one group for which you have several variables and their correlations. However, in this case, the correlations you want to compare do not share a common (overlapping) variable. Instead, you might be interested in comparing the correlation between the reading and math variables at the entry to kindergarten with the correlation between the reading and math variables at the end of first grade. The null and alternate hypotheses might be written as:

$$H_0: \rho_{r_k m_k} = \rho_{r_l m_l}$$
$$H_1: \rho_{r_k m_k} \neq \rho_{r_l m_l}$$

(15.21)

We will not provide a detailed treatment of this situation, but will refer you to Wuensch (2007) who has provided an example based on the work of Raghunathan, Rosenthal, and Rubin (1996).

At this point, we will turn our attention to another aspect of testing hypotheses about bivariate relationships. Correlations address the issue of "strength of relationship," but they do not tell you anything about the nature of the relationship. To address the question of whether one variable varies as a function of another the same way in two different populations, we turn our attention to testing hypotheses about regression coefficients (slopes).

COMPARING TWO INDEPENDENT REGRESSION COEFFICIENTS

There are several ways to compare two independent regression coefficients. In this book we will show you a way to compare the two coefficients using concepts and techniques that we have already presented. In subsequent coursework, you will probably learn a way to do this within the context of multiple regression, but that is beyond the scope of this text.

Earlier in this chapter we showed you how to compare two independent correlation coefficients. We now return to that example, but turn our focus to the regression of end-of-first-grade math on beginning-of-kindergarten reading, comparing the coefficients for White and African American children. We are interested in contrasting the null and alternate hypotheses as follows:

$$H_0 : \beta_{m.r_1} = \beta_{m.r_2}$$
$$H_1 : \beta_{m.r_1} \neq \beta_{m.r_2}$$

(15.22)

We have written Script 15.10 to help us with this example. We will start by using the script in a piecemeal fashion, obtaining some of the numbers we need. If we assume that the null hypothesis is true, the statistic $(b_{m.r1} - b_{m.r2})$ should follow a normal distribution with a standard error (se) of:

$$se_{b_1 - b_2} = \sqrt{se_{b_1}^2 + se_{b_2}^2}$$

(15.23)

Thus, we should be able to form a t-statistic as:

$$t_{obs} = \frac{b_{m.r_1} - b_{m.r_2}}{\sqrt{se_{b_1}^2 + se_{b_2}^2}}$$

(15.24)

First, we will use R to generate the two regression equations for the White and African American children's scores, respectively. First, for the White children:

```
> n.1 <- with(ecls200.white, length(c1rrscal))
> n.1
> lm.1 <- with(ecls200.white,
> lm(c4rmscal ~ c1rrscal))
> sum.1 <- summary(lm.1)
> sum.1
Call:
lm(formula=c4rmscal ~ c1rrscal)
Residuals:
     Min      1Q    Median      3Q      Max
  -20.969  -3.862    1.059   5.176   15.202
Coefficients:
```

```
              Estimate   Std. Error   t value      Pr(>|t|)
(Intercept) 37.16877      2.23894     16.601      < 2e-16
clrrscal     0.41432      0.08232      5.033      2.19e-06
Residual standard error: 7.136 on 98 degrees of freedom
Multiple R-squared: 0.2054, Adjusted R-squared: 0.1973
F-statistic: 25.33 on 1 and 98 DF, p-value: 2.191e-06
```

Of particular interest in the output above, we find $b_{m.r1}$ to be .41432 and $SE_{m.r1}$ to be .08232. In like fashion, we complete the regression analysis with the data from the African American children, finding:

```
> n.2 <- with(ecls200.aa, length(clrrscal))
> lm.2 <- with(ecls200.aa, lm(c4rmscal ~ clrrscal))
> sum.2 <- summary(lm.2)
> sum.2
Call:
lm(formula = c4rmscal ~ clrrscal)
Residuals:
    Min       1Q     Median      3Q        Max
-15.4423   -3.9109   0.0829    4.1165    15.9610
Coefficients:
              Estimate   Std. Error   t value      Pr(>|t|)
(Intercept) 26.73625      1.97663     13.526      < 2e-16
clrrscal     0.62186      0.08268      7.522      2.62e-11
Residual standard error: 6.253 on 98 degrees of freedom
Multiple R-squared: 0.366, Adjusted R-squared: 0.3595
F-statistic: 56.57 on 1 and 98 DF, p-value: 2.623e-11
```

In the output above, we find $b_{m.r1}$ to be .62186 and $SE_{m.r1}$ to be .08268. Given the results from these two separate regression analyses, we can substitute the appropriate values into Equation 15.24:

$$t_{obs} = \frac{b_{m.r_1} - b_{m.r_2}}{\sqrt{se_{b_1}^2 + se_{b_2}^2}} = \frac{.41432 - .62186}{\sqrt{.08232^2 + .08268^2}} = \frac{-.20754}{\sqrt{.01361}} = \frac{-.20754}{.11667} = -1.779 \qquad (15.25)$$

This t-statistic is distributed as t with $df = n_1 + n_2 - 4$, or 196. Using the **qt( )** function in R:

```
> qt(c(.025,.975), 196)
[1] -1.972141 1.972141
```

As you can see, the results suggest that the two regression coefficients are not sufficiently different to reject the null hypothesis.

Script 15.10 was actually written to run the necessary analyses, extract the relevant results, and compute the value of the t-statistic. Abbreviated output from the script is as follows:

```
> se.pooled
[1] 0.1166699
> t.obs <- (b.1 - b.2)/se.pooled
> t.obs
[1] -1.778828
>
> # Two tailed p-value
> 2*(1 - pt(abs(t.obs), n.1 + n.2 -4))
[1] 0.07681784
> # One tailed p-value
> (1 - pt(abs(t.obs), n.1 + n.2 -4))
[1] 0.03840892
```

As you can see, the results from the script are in agreement with our hand calculations. Interestingly, had we predicted that early reading ability might have been more important for later math achievement in African Americans (one-tailed test), we would have been able to reject H_0. But, we did not.

CHAPTER SUMMARY

In this chapter, we have completed our presentation of procedures for comparing two groups with respect to different characteristics. In Chapter 14, we focused on methods of comparing two groups with respect to location, presenting methods for means, proportions, and medians, along with some non-parametric procedures (Mann–Whitney U-test, Wilcoxon Matched-Pairs Signed-Ranks test, and the McNemar test). In this chapter we began with a presentation of approaches to compare two variances, first looking at the F-distribution and the associated F-ratio and then at a more recently developed test (Levene's test).

After considering ways to test for equality of variance, we presented a more complete explanation of the t-test for comparing the means of two independent samples, as the equality (homogeneity) of variance is an assumption for that test, particularly when sample sizes are not equal.

After making some recommendations about how one might proceed to employ the t-test under different conditions, we concluded the chapter with a presentation of ways to compare two groups with regard to the relationship between two variables. We showed ways to compare two groups with regard to strength of relationship (correlation) and nature of the relationship (regression).

In the next chapter, we will expand our perspective to consider ways to compare three or more groups with respect to location. Of course, two groups will turn out to be a special case of three or more groups.

Key Terms

Bartlett's χ^2	Fligner–Killeen test
Behrens–Fisher problem	Hartley's F_{max}
Cochran–Cox approximation	Homogeneity of variance
Cochran's C	Independent correlation coefficients
Dependent correlations coefficients	Independent regression coefficients
F-distribution	Levene's test
F-statistic	Welch–Satterthwaite correction

REFERENCES

Bartlett, M. S. (1937). Properties of sufficiency and statistical tests. *Proceedings of the Royal Society, A901, 160*, 268–282.

Boneau, C. A. (1960). The effects of violations of assumptions underlying the *t* test. *Psychological Bulletin, 57*, 49–64.

Box, G. E. P. (1953). Non-normality and tests on variance. *Biometrika, 40*, 318–335.

Brown, M. B. & Forsythe, A. B. (1974). *Robust tests for equality of variances. Journal of the American Statistical Association, 69*, 364–367.

Cochran, W. G. (1941). The distribution of the largest of a set of estimated variances as a fraction of their total. *Annals of Human Genetics, 11(1)*, 47–52.

Cochran, W. G., & Cox, G. M. (1957*). Experimental designs*. New York: John Wiley.

Conover, W. J., Johnson, M. E., & Johnson, M. M. (1981). A comparative study of tests for homogeneity of variances, with applications to the outer continental shelf bidding data. *Technometrics, 23*, 351–361.

Cowles, M. (2001). *Statistics in psychology* (2nd ed.). Mahwah, NJ: Lawrence Erlbaum Associates.

Fisher, R. A. (1924). On a distribution yielding the error functions of several well known statistics. *Proceedings of the International Congress of Mathematics, Toronto, 2*, 805–813.

Fligner, M. A., & Killeen, T. J. (1976). Distribution-free two-sample tests for scale. *Journal of the American Statistical Association, 71*, 210–213.

Good, P. I. (2006). *Resampling methods: A practical guide to data analysis* (3rd ed.). New York: Birkhäuser Boston.

Hartley, H. O. (1940). Testing the homogeneity of a set of variances. *Biometrika, 31*, 249–255.

Hartley, H. O. (1950). The maximum *F*-ratio as a short-cut test for heterogeneity of variance. *Biometrika, 37*, 308–312.

Hotelling, H. (1931). The generalization of Student's ratio. *Annals of Mathematical Statistics, 2*, 360–378.

Johnson, P. O., & Jackson, R. W. B. (1959). *Modern statistical methods: Descriptive and inductive*. Chicago, IL: Rand McNally.

Kirk, R. E. (1990). *Statistics: An introduction* (3rd ed.). Fort Worth, TX: Holt, Rinehart, and Winston.

Levene, H. (1960). *Robust tests for equality of variances*. In I. Olkin (Ed.), *Contributions to probability and statistics: Essays in honor of Harold Hotelling*. Palo Alto, CA: Stanford University Press.

Norton, D. W. (1952). *An empirical investigation of the effects of non-normality and heterogeneity upon the F-test of analysis of variance*. Unpublished doctoral dissertation, University of Iowa, Iowa City, IA.

Raghunathan, T. E., Rosenthal, R., & Rubin, D. B. (1996). Comparing correlated but non-overlapping correlations. *Psychological Methods, 1*, 178–183.

Satterthwaite, F. E. (1946). An approximate distribution of estimates of variance components. *Biometrics Bulletin, 2*, 110–114.

Snedecor, G. W. (1934). *Calculation and interpretation of analysis of variance and covariance*. Ames, IA: Collegiate Press.

Welch, B. L. (1938). The significance of the difference between two means when the population variances are unequal. *Biometrika, 29*, 350–362.

Williams, E. J. (1959). The comparison of regression variables. *Journal of the Royal Statistical Society (Series B), 21*, 396–399.

Wuensch, K. (2007). Comparing correlated but non-overlapping correlation coefficients. Retrieved from http://core.ecu.edu/psyc/wuenschk/stathelp/zpf.docx.

PRACTICE QUESTIONS

1. The *F*-distribution is:

   a. symmetric
   b. positively skewed
   c. negatively skewed.

2. When the null hypothesis that the variances are equal is true, the *F*-statistic tends to be close to:

   a. −1
   b. 0
   c. 1
   d. ∞.

3. A researcher wishes to compare the variances of two groups. If she suspects the distributions are not normal, which of the following tests would you recommend?

   a. Bartlett's χ^2.
   b. Cochran's *C*.
   c. Hartley's F_{max}.
   d. Levene's test.

4. Which of the following mathematical probability distributions is the most general?

   a. χ^2.
   b. *F*.
   c. *t*.
   d. *z*.

5. In comparing two means, under which of the following conditions would you be most motivated to use the separate samples *t*-test with Welch adjusted *df*?

   a. $n_1 = 30, n_2 = 30, s_1^2 = 100, s_2^2 = 100$.
   b. $n_1 = 30, n_2 = 60, s_1^2 = 100, s_2^2 = 100$.
   c. $n_1 = 30, n_2 = 30, s_1^2 = 100, s_2^2 = 200$.
   d. $n_1 = 30, n_2 = 60, s_1^2 = 100, s_2^2 = 200$.

6. Suppose you wish to compare two correlation coefficients: the correlation between attitude about school and mathematics achievement for a sample of fifth-grade boys and the correlation between attitude about school and mathematics achievement for a sample of fifth-grade girls. Which approach would you take?

   a. *z*-test for two independent correlations.

  b. Test for two dependent overlapping correlations.
  c. Test for two dependent non-overlapping correlations.

7. Suppose you wish to compare two correlation coefficients: the correlation between attitude about school and mathematics achievement for a sample of fifth-grade boys and the correlation between attitude about school and reading achievement for the same sample of fifth-grade boys. Which approach would you take?

  a. z-test for two independent correlations.
  b. Test for two dependent overlapping correlations.
  c. Test for two dependent non-overlapping correlations.

8. Suppose you were comparing two regression coefficients. The t-statistic tends to be greatest when:

  a. the first standard error is small and the second is large
  b. the first standard error is large and the second is small
  c. both standard errors are large
  d. both standard errors are small.

EXERCISES

15.1. A researcher wishes to compare the metabolic rates of mice which have been subjected to different drugs. The weights of the mice may affect such rates and thus introduce within-cell variability. In order to control for this, the experimenter wishes to obtain mice for the study that are relatively homogeneous in weight. Before ordering the 1,000 mice that will be necessary for the study, the researcher does a pilot study on some mice that are already available in the laboratory. After identifying 18 mice from Supply House A and 13 mice from Supply House B, the 31 mice are weighed, giving the results shown below. Do these data suggest ($\alpha = .10$) that the two suppliers differ in terms of homogeneity of weight?

	Supplier A	Supplier B
n	18	13
Mean	4.21 oz	4.18 oz
s	0.14 oz	0.22 oz

15.2. A researcher interested in the nature/nurture controversy posed the following question: "Are the IQs of identical twins reared together correlated any differently than the IQs of identical twins reared apart?" Data retrieved from the National Archives of Trivial Facts led to the following summary. What do the data suggest ($\alpha = .05$)?

	Reared together	Reared apart
r	0.93	0.83
n	80	30

15.3. Earlier in this chapter, we presented an example in which we compared the variances of pre-kindergarten reading scores for White and Asian students. Let's return to that example, slightly modified to compare the two groups with regard to central tendency. In the original example, there were 25 cases in each of the two samples. To make things interesting we have deleted randomly 13 cases from the White students group, so that there are now 12 White cases and 25 Asian cases. The scores for the two groups are:

White: 29, 32, 23, 23, 20, 24, 17, 20, 33, 29, 14, 24

Asian: 12, 26, 56, 11, 48, 19, 17, 40, 31, 12, 33, 20, 34, 54, 21, 24, 66, 24, 31, 33, 16, 21, 27, 20, 62

Using these data, compare the two groups with regard to central tendency. Read the data into R, explore the descriptive statistics, look at them with respect to the assumptions of normality and homogeneity of variance, and then run the traditional t-test, the separate-sample t-test, and the Mann–Whitney/Wilcoxon test. Compare the results. Which of them do you think is the most appropriate result and why?

Part V
k-SAMPLE TESTS

Up to this point, we have presented a number of procedures for testing hypotheses in situations in which we are dealing with one or two samples. In this last section, we extend our coverage to present procedures for comparing three or more samples in a hypothesis-testing context.

16

Tests on Location: Analysis of Variance and Other Selected Procedures

INTRODUCTION

In Chapter 14 we described several different ways to compare two groups with regard to central tendency, or location. The differences among the procedures related to issues of sample size, conformity to assumptions, and independent/dependent samples. In practice, studies often involve more than two groups, making the use of two-group procedures awkward, at best. In this chapter we will present several extensions of the two-group procedures. More specifically, we will describe the analysis-of-variance (ANOVA), the Kruskal–Wallis test, and randomization tests as each of them may be applied to the k-group situation. We want to remind you that group designs, such as the two-group situation addressed with the t-test and the k-group situation addressed with ANOVA, are really special cases of the more general matter of looking at the relationship between an independent variable and a dependent variable. Just because we employ statistical techniques such as t- and F-tests, we cannot necessarily draw stronger inferences about the possible causal relationship between the two variables. The major difference between group statistics (t-test, ANOVA) and correlational statistics (Pearson's r, regression) is related to the difference in which the variables are scaled (measured) in different situations. The "group" statistics are merely simplified computational routines to deal with the relationship between a numeric dependent variable and a categorical independent variable. In future statistics courses you will learn about the general linear model as an approach that subsumes many statistical procedures. Keeping this distinction between "design" and "statistical procedure" in mind, let us turn our attention to the k-group situation. For example, imagine that we want to compare White, African American, and Hispanic children with regard to their scores on the General Knowledge measure at the beginning of kindergarten. After introducing the conceptual basis and notation of ANOVA, we will complete an example that will show you how to make such a comparison.

The Argument for ANOVA

Recall the formula for a two-group t-test as presented in Chapter 14:

$$t = \frac{\bar{Y}_{.1} - \bar{Y}_{.2}}{\sqrt{s_{\text{pooled}}^2 \left[(1/n_1) + (1/n_2) \right]}} \tag{16.1}$$

A researcher who knows only about the *t*-test is confronted with a problem: there is no single difference among three groups that can be used in the numerator of the *t*-test. The researcher might be tempted to employ what appears to be a reasonable solution to the problem: use the *t*-test formula to conduct three different tests. That is, the researcher could compare Group 1 to Group 2, Group 1 to Group 3, and Group 2 to Group 3. While this approach may seem reasonable, there are some inherent problems. Perhaps the most important of these problems is the increased risk of making a Type I error (rejecting a true null hypothesis) when running several tests of significance. Each time a test is completed, there is a probability of making such an error. When three independent tests are completed at the .05 level, the probability that there is at least one Type I error is $(1 - .95^3)$, or .1426. In general, when a small number of independent tests are run, this error rate is approximately the α per test multiplied by the number of tests. In the aforementioned situation, the tests are not independent and it is very difficult to determine the probability of at least one Type I error, but suffice it to say, the probability is quite a bit larger than .05. One approach used by some researchers to deal with the inflated error rate problem is to conduct each test at a reduced level of significance. A popular adjustment is to divide the overall level of significance by the number of tests. In our case, we would divide .05 by 3, and thus conduct each *t*-test at the .0167 level. This approach is sometimes called the "Bonferroni technique."

Although widely used in other contexts to be discussed in Chapter 17, the Bonferroni technique is considered rather conservative. Furthermore, completing multiple *t*-tests is also problematic, as it does not fully consider the nature of the differences among the groups. A multiple *t*-test approach is predicated on the assumption that the differences are all pairwise in nature, or that those are the only differences in which the researcher is interested. However, it may be possible that the nature of the differences among groups is more complex. That is, it might be that the average of Groups 1 and 2 is different from the average of Group 3. Multiple *t*-tests would be relatively insensitive to this type of difference. Fortunately, Sir Ronald A. Fisher provided a solution to both of these problems that dates back to the mid-1920s. His approach not only permitted a single test for group differences, it also avoided the use of matrix algebra, which was necessary to solve most applications of the general linear model but very difficult to employ without computers. His approach is called the "analysis-of-variance" (ANOVA) and is the major topic of this chapter.

THE ANALYSIS OF VARIANCE (ANOVA)

While ANOVA is essentially an inferential procedure, we would like to again stress that an inferential procedure is relatively meaningless when reported in the absence of descriptive information about the data. This descriptive information should include the traditional descriptive statistics for each group (means and standard deviations) and the degree to which the data conform to the appropriate assumptions. In addition, one can present measures of effect size, which we discuss after our presentation of ANOVA. Both descriptive statistics and measures of effect size are critical pieces of information to have in order to determine the practical significance of the results.

Analysis of Variance Notation and Terminology

In the discussion of the *t*-test, we spent some time presenting the notational scheme for representing the data and the formulae. As ANOVA is an extension of the *t*-test, our notational scheme is merely an extension of that presented earlier. However, it is a bit more general and we thought that it was worth reviewing. First, recall that we use Y as a generic variable name. To identify particular cases, or values of Y, we use the subscripts i and j. ANOVA involves several groups; in general, we say that there are k groups. To denote a particular group, we talk about the jth group. Thus, j can take on the values from 1 to k. Within each of the k groups, there are multiple observations. If the group sizes are all equal to one another, then we say that there are n cases per group; if the group sizes are not equal, then we use n_j to denote the number of cases in the jth group. When we want to focus on a particular observation, we call it the ith case. The subscript i can take on values from 1 to n (or n_j). Thus, the notation is organized as shown in Table 16.1.

Note that the last row of Table 16.1 contains symbols for the column means. That is, a column mean is represented in general with the symbol $\bar{Y}_j$ and the mean of all the observations is denoted $\bar{Y}_{..}$. An understanding of this notation is extremely helpful to understand the remainder of this chapter. If you need more review, try looking again at Table 16.1.

The design depicted in Table 16.1 is called a *one-way analysis-of-variance* as it involves one grouping variable. It is also known as a *completely randomized design*. The grouping variable, or independent variable, is called a *factor*. The different groups represent different *levels* of the factor. Sometimes the groups are called *cells*. The observations within the groups are the *cases*, or *replications*.

Solution from Fisher

Our example comparing the entry-level General Knowledge scores of different ethnic groups deals with the question of the equality of means of the three groups. Fisher showed that the question of the equality of several groups can be expressed in terms of the variance among the group means. In essence, Fisher extended the work of Gosset to situations with more than two groups. To do this, he combined some fairly simple ideas in a new way, ideas that we have already discussed in this book. First, recall that in our presentation of variance, we stressed that the variance is an average squared difference from the mean and, as such, also a measure of the degree to which the values of the variable differ from each other. In like fashion, the variability of the group means can be interpreted as the degree to which the means differ from one another. The other simple idea employed by Fisher comes from what we know about the distribution of sample means relative to the distribution of the population.

You may recall that if a random variable Y is distributed as $Y \sim N(\mu, \sigma^2)$, then the distribution of sample means drawn from that population will be distributed as $\bar{Y} \sim N(\mu, \sigma^2/n)$. To see the implications of these fundamental ideas and the manner in which Fisher combined them, consider the situation in which a set of random samples is selected from a population, as depicted in Figure 16.1.

Table 16.1 Notational scheme for analysis of variance

Y_{11}	Y_{12}	Y_{13}	$\cdots$	Y_{1j}	$\cdots$	Y_{1k}
Y_{21}	Y_{22}	Y_{23}	$\cdots$	Y_{2j}	$\cdots$	Y_{2k}
Y_{31}	Y_{32}	Y_{33}	$\cdots$	Y_{3j}	$\cdots$	Y_{3k}
$\cdots$	$\cdots$	$\cdots$	$\cdots$	$\cdots$	$\cdots$	$\cdots$
Y_{i1}	Y_{i2}	Y_{i3}	$\cdots$	Y_{ij}	$\cdots$	Y_{ik}
$\cdots$	$\cdots$	$\cdots$	$\cdots$	$\cdots$	$\cdots$	$\cdots$
Y_{n1}	Y_{n2}	Y_{n3}	$\cdots$	Y_{nj}	$\cdots$	Y_{nk}
$\bar{Y}_{.1}$	$\bar{Y}_{.2}$	$\bar{Y}_{.3}$	$\cdots$	$\bar{Y}_{.j}$	$\cdots$	$\bar{Y}_{.k}$	$\bar{Y}_{..}$

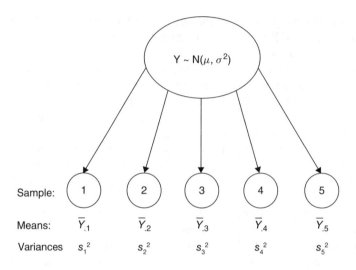

FIGURE 16.1   Schematic of four samples drawn at random from a population, with their means and variances.

First, let the mean of the population be equal to μ and the variance of the population be equal to σ^2. Thus, if these are four random samples drawn from the population, then each $\bar{Y}_{.j}$ is an estimator of μ. In turn, the variance of this sample of sample means is an estimator of the variance of the population of sample means, or σ^2/n. More formally, if there are k random samples drawn from a population, then we can calculate the sum-of-squares among the sample means, divide it by its degrees of freedom $(k-1)$, and we should have an estimate of the variance of the population of sample means. That is,

$$E\left[\frac{\sum_{j=1}^{k}\left(\bar{Y}_{.j}-\bar{Y}_{..}\right)^2}{k-1}\right]=\frac{\sigma^2}{n} \tag{16.2}$$

Then, by simple algebraic manipulation,

$$E\left[\frac{n\sum_{j=1}^{k}\left(\bar{Y}_{.j}-\bar{Y}_{..}\right)^2}{k-1}\right]=\sigma^2 \tag{16.3}$$

Thus, by looking at the variation of the sample means, we can derive an estimate of the population variance, σ^2.

Now consider the four sample variances, s_j^2, each of which is an estimator of σ^2. Following Gosset's logic in pooling the variances from two samples, Fisher argued that forming a weighted average of the several sample variances, s_j^2, would be an estimate of the population variance, σ^2. For four groups, more formally,

$$s_{\text{pooled}}^2 = \frac{(n_1 - 1)s_1^2 + (n_2 - 1)s_2^2 + (n_3 - 1)s_3^2 + (n_4 - 1)s_4^2}{(n_1 - 1) + (n_2 - 1) + (n_3 - 1) + (n_4 - 1)} \tag{16.4}$$

Thus,

$$s_{\text{pooled}}^2 = \frac{\sum\limits_{j=1}^{k}\sum\limits_{i=1}^{n}\left(Y_{ij} - \overline{Y}_{.j}\right)^2}{\sum\limits_{j=1}^{k} n_j - k} \tag{16.5}$$

and

$$E\left[s_{\text{pooled}}^2\right] = \sigma^2$$

We have just looked at two different (and independent) ways of estimating σ^2. Before proceeding, let us summarize the terms, the symbols, and the formulae in Table 16.2.

If the samples are indeed random samples from the same population, then both the mean squares among groups, MS_{ag} and MS_{wg}, estimate the same quantity, σ^2. Thus, as we considered in Chapter 15, their ratio should follow the F-distribution with degrees of freedom df_{ag} and df_{wg}, respectively.

Another Perspective

If the four samples are actually random samples from the same population, then it is reasonable to assume that $\mu_1 = \mu_2 = \mu_3 = \mu_4$, and their distributions might look like those depicted in Figure 16.2.

On the other hand, if the samples are drawn from populations with different means (at least one $\mu_j \neq \mu_{j'}$, where $j \neq j'$), then the distributions might look like those in Figure 16.3.

In the situation where the four random samples are from the same population (Figure 16.2), we noted that both the MS_{ag} and the MS_{wg} should be estimates of σ^2. In that case, we would expect the F-statistic to be about 1.0, a little more or a little less. As noted in Chapter 15, the expected value of F is $df_{\text{wg}}/(df_{\text{wg}} - 2)$ (Howell, 2007, p. 307).

Table 16.2 Terms, symbols, and formulae for analysis of variance

Term	Symbol	Formula
Sum-of-squares among groups	SS_{ag}	$n\sum\limits_{j=1}^{k}\left(\overline{Y}_{.j} - \overline{Y}_{..}\right)^2$
Degrees of freedom among groups	df_{ag}	$k-1$
Mean square among groups	MS_{ag}	SS_{ag}/df_{ag}
Sum-of-squares within groups	SS_{wg}	$\sum\limits_{j=1}^{k}\sum\limits_{i=1}^{n_j}\left(Y_{ij} - \overline{Y}_{.j}\right)^2$
Degrees of freedom within groups	df_{wg}	$k(n-1)$
Mean square within groups	MS_{wg}	SS_{wg}/df_{wg}

Note: The equations for SS_{ag} and df_{wg} assume equal sample sizes for the k groups.

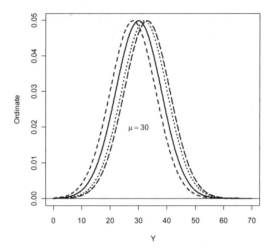

FIGURE 16.2   Four random samples from one population with $\mu = 30$.

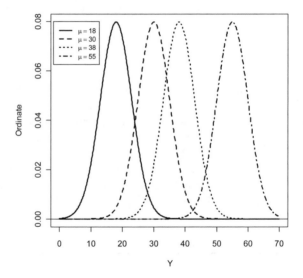

FIGURE 16.3   Four random samples from different populations.

Contrast this with the situation where the samples are not coming from the same population with regard to location, as in Figure 16.3. With the groups more spread out, the MS_{ag} should be larger than would be expected than when the groups are randomly sampled from one population. However, the MS_{wg} is not affected by differences among the groups, as it is calculated by looking at the spread within each of the groups separately. Thus, an F-statistic defined as MS_{ag}/MS_{wg} should be larger than 1.0 when the groups are different. On the other hand, F-statistics much less than 1.0 (close to 0) would suggest that the groups are more similar than would be expected by chance. Consequently, in ANOVA, a non-directional test on means translates to a directional test on variances, and we use the upper tail of the F-distribution to evaluate our findings. In other words, a set of hypotheses on means like the following:

$$H_0 : \mu_1 = \mu_2 = \cdots \mu_j = \cdots \mu_k \qquad (16.6)$$
$$H_1 : \mu_j \neq \mu_{j'} \text{ for some } j \neq j'$$

Actually, the null hypothesis can be false in any of several different ways. One group might be different from another group, as in Equation 16.6. Or perhaps the average of the first two groups is different from the mean of another group. The null hypothesis in Equation 16.6 is sometimes called the "omnibus hypothesis." The manner in which it is not true will be the topic of Chapter 17. In any event, the hypotheses about means translate into a set of hypotheses on variances, as follows:

$$H_0 : \sigma^2_{ag} \leq \sigma^2_{wg}$$
$$H_1 : \sigma^2_{ag} > \sigma^2_{wg} \qquad (16.7)$$

Thus, to test for differences among means, we can form our F-statistic as:

$$F_{obs} = \frac{MS_{ag}}{MS_{wg}} \qquad (16.8)$$

and compare our result to the critical value in the upper tail of the F-distribution for $k - 1$ and $\sum_{j=1}^{k} n_j - k$ (or $k(n-1)$ if the samples sizes are equal) degrees of freedom.

A Worked Example

At the beginning of this chapter we described a research situation comparing White, African American, and Hispanic children with respect to their scores on the General Knowledge test at the beginning of kindergarten. In this instance, the null hypothesis would be that $\mu_1 = \mu_2 = \mu_3$, and the alternate hypothesis would be that at least one of the population means was different than another. Ten children were randomly selected from each ethnic group from the *ecls2577* data set. The data are presented in Table 16.3.

In our presentation of the conceptual basis for ANOVA, we introduced the notions of the SS_{ag} and SS_{wg}. Recall that SS_{ag} looks at the variability of the group means about the grand mean and SS_{wg} looks at the variability of the individual scores about their respective group means. There is

Table 16.3 Pre-kindergarten general knowledge test scores for White, African American, and Hispanic children ($n = 10$)

White	African American	Hispanic
31	14	23
23	34	26
32	18	39
27	21	14
28	30	28
25	25	13
29	22	12
33	27	34
36	16	31
39	16	12

also a third *SS*, which we did not mention earlier, the *sum-of-squares total* (SS_{tot}), defined as the variability of the individual scores about the grand mean. It can be shown that the $SS_{tot} = SS_{ag} + SS_{wg}$. The interested reader can find a proof of this equality in Technical Note 16.1 at the end of this chapter.

Each of these *SS* terms has a definitional formula, as follows:

$$SS_{tot} = \sum_{j=1}^{k} \sum_{i=1}^{n_j} \left(Y_{ij} - \bar{Y}_{..} \right)^2 \tag{16.9}$$

$$SS_{ag} = \sum_{j=1}^{k} n_j \left(\bar{Y}_{.j} - \bar{Y}_{..} \right)^2 \tag{16.10}$$

and

$$SS_{wg} = \sum_{j=1}^{k} \sum_{i=1}^{n_j} \left(Y_{ij} - \bar{Y}_{.j} \right)^2 \tag{16.11}$$

Computations using these expressions are extremely laborious and contain more rounding error than is necessary, as the means are calculated early in the process. Calculating the means involves division, and division introduces rounding error, which is then compounded through the subsequent computation. Fortunately, each of these expressions can be algebraically modified to expressions which lend themselves to simpler computations. The derivations for these expressions are shown in Technical Note 16.2 at the end of this chapter; only the end results are presented here.

$$SS_{tot} = \sum_{j=1}^{k} \sum_{i=1}^{n_j} Y_{ij}^2 - \frac{\left(\sum_{j=1}^{k} \sum_{i=1}^{n_j} Y_{ij} \right)^2}{\sum_{j=1}^{k} n_j} \tag{16.12}$$

$$SS_{ag} = \sum_{j=1}^{k} \frac{\left(\sum_{i=1}^{n_j} Y_{ij} \right)^2}{n_j} - \frac{\left(\sum_{j=1}^{k} \sum_{i=1}^{n_j} Y_{ij} \right)^2}{\sum_{j=1}^{k} n_j} \tag{16.13}$$

and

$$SS_{wg} = SS_{tot} - SS_{ag} \tag{16.14}$$

Using these expressions for our computations necessitates that we do some initial summarizing of the raw data. In Script 16.4 in the supplementary materials for this chapter (see the book website), we show you syntax for generating the initial values, after reading in the data. The results using the data in Table 16.3 are shown in Table 16.4.

Using the summary values in the computational expressions leads to the following:

$$SS_{tot} = \sum_{j=1}^{k} \sum_{i=1}^{n_j} Y_{ij}^2 - \frac{\left(\sum_{j=1}^{k} \sum_{i=1}^{n_j} Y_{ij} \right)^2}{\sum_{j=1}^{k} n_j} = 21,046 - \frac{(758)^2}{30} = 1,893.87 \tag{16.15}$$

Table 16.4 Summary of the raw data in Table 16.3

	White	African American	Hispanic	Totals
$\sum_{i=1}^{n_j} Y_{ij}$	303	223	232	758
$\sum_{i=1}^{n_j} Y_{ij}^2$	9,399	5,367	6,280	21,046
$\bar{Y}_j$	30.3	22.3	23.2	$\bar{Y}.. = 25.60$
S_j^2	24.23	43.79	99.73	

Note: The grand mean is the mean of the group means only when the sample sizes are equal.

$$SS_{ag} = \sum_{j=1}^{k} \frac{\left(\sum_{i=1}^{n_j} Y_{ij}\right)^2}{n_j} - \frac{\left(\sum_{j=1}^{k}\sum_{i=1}^{n_j} Y_{ij}\right)^2}{\sum_{j=1}^{k} n_j} = \frac{(303)^2}{10} + \frac{(223)^2}{10} + \frac{(232)^2}{10} - \frac{(758)^2}{30}$$

(16.16)

$$= 9,180.9 + 4,972.9 + 5,382.4 - 19,152.13 = 384.07$$

and

$$SS_{wg} = SS_{tot} - SS_{ag} = 1893.87 - 384.07 = 1509.80$$

(16.17)

Alternatively, you could calculate the *SS* within each of the groups respectively, and then add them together as follows:

$$SS_{wg} = SS_{wg_1} + SS_{wg_2} + SS_{wg_3}$$

$$= \left[9,399 - \frac{303^2}{10}\right] + \left[5,367 - \frac{223^2}{10}\right] + \left[6,280 - \frac{232^2}{10}\right]$$

(16.18)

$$= 218.10 + 394.10 + 897.6$$

$$= 1,509.8$$

This last step is actually unnecessary, but it does give more meaning to the SS_{wg}, in addition to providing a check on our computation. When doing computations by hand, perhaps the most important check is to proof the data entry step, and we recommend that you develop the initial values of ΣY and ΣY^2 with Script 16.4.

Recall from our earlier discussion that we are interested in comparing two estimates of variance with an *F*-statistic. Thus, we must take our SS_{ag} and SS_{wg} and transform them into their respective MS_{ag} and MS_{wg}. We accomplish this transformation by dividing each of the *SS* by its appropriate *df*, as follows:

$$MS_{ag} = \frac{SS_{ag}}{df_{ag}} = \frac{384.07}{2} = 192.04$$

(16.19)

$$MS_{wg} = \frac{SS_{wg}}{df_{wg}} = \frac{1,509.8}{27} = 55.92$$

If the null hypothesis is true, then these two mean square values should be estimates of the same variance. That is, when the three samples are drawn from the same population (normal populations having the same mean and variance), the MS_{ag} and the MS_{wg} will be similar. You will also recall that, when the population means are different, the sample means will be more widely dispersed, and the variance estimated by the MS_{ag} will be larger than the variance estimated by the MS_{wg}. To assess which of the two situations is more plausible, we form an F-statistic as follows:

$$F_{obs} = \frac{MS_{ag}}{MS_{wg}} = \frac{192.04}{55.92} = 3.43 \tag{16.20}$$

In order for us to evaluate this observed F-statistic, we need to look up the critical value. We can use a table of the F-distribution (Table A.8), or we can use the **qf( )** function in R. If the null hypothesis is true, the observed F-statistic should be modeled by the F-distribution with 2 and 27 degrees of freedom, respectively. With R:

```
> qf(.95, 2, 27)
[1] 3.354131
```

As an alternative, you might use the **pf( )** function in R to find the p-value associated with the F_{obs}:

```
> pf(3.43, 2, 27, lower.tail=FALSE)
[1] 0.04705838
```

As the F-statistic which we observed (3.43) is larger than the critical F (i.e., 3.35), it would seem that the observed differences among the three means are larger than one would reasonably expect under the assumption of equal population means. Thus, at the .05 level, we reject the null hypothesis in favor of the alternate hypotheses. It would appear that at least one of the population means is different from at least one of the others. In turn, looking at the p-value (.047) we would reach the same decision that the probability of our obtaining means as different as we did under the assumption of random sampling is less than our level of significance, .05.

The F-statistic as we have presented it is sometimes called the "omnibus" F-test, as it suggests only that there is at least one difference, somewhere. That is, it tests the null hypothesis against a "family" of alternative hypotheses. It does not give us any information about which populations are different from which other populations. Procedures for completing follow-up analyses will be presented in Chapter 17.

Before showing you how to complete an ANOVA using one of the computer packages, we should point out that all of the computations we have shown above are often summarized in table format. Such a table is called a "summary table," and our results are summarized in Table 16.5.

Table 16.5 Summary table for the analysis of variance comparing the effects of three levels of incentives on school achievement

Source of variation	SS	df	MS	F-statistic	Critical value
Among groups	1,080.87	2	540.44	4.62	3.35
Within groups	3,158.10	27	116.97		
Total	4,238.97	29			

Until this point, we have discussed ANOVA in a fairly straightforward manner. That is, the results above suggest that there are differences among the groups. However, before proceeding to a computer example, we need to elaborate a bit. The interpretation you can make following an ANOVA actually depends, in part, on whether the data appear to meet the assumptions for the technique.

ASSUMPTIONS FOR ANALYSIS-OF-VARIANCE

The assumptions for ANOVA are similar to the assumptions for the *t*-test on the means of two groups. First, there is the assumption of a linear model: $Y_{ij} = \mu + \tau_j + \varepsilon_{ij}$. Within the context of ANOVA, the score for a case is considered to be composed of three parts: a component due to the population mean, μ; a component due to the "treatment effect" for the *j*th group, τ_j; and an error component which allows for individual differences and sampling error, ε_{ij}. Thus, if there are no differences among the groups, the appropriate model for the *i*th case in the *j*th group is $Y_{ij} = \mu + \varepsilon_{ij}$. The assumption of the linear model is important in the justification of the *F*-distribution as an appropriate criterion for the *F*-test. Recall that MS_{ag} and MS_{wg} are sample estimates of population variances. If the linear model assumption is met, then it can be shown that the expected values of MS_{ag} and MS_{wg} are as follows:

$$E\left(MS_{ag}\right) = \sigma_{\varepsilon}^2 + \frac{\sum_{j=1}^{k} n_j \tau_j^2}{k-1}$$

and

$$E\left(MS_{wg}\right) = \sigma_{\varepsilon}^2$$

(16.21)

The expected mean squares as presented above are based on the assumption that we are dealing with a *fixed-effects* model. That is, the different levels of the treatment are assumed to include all the levels in which you are interested. If you were to replicate the study, you would use the same levels each time. In contrast, there are situations in which you will deal with a *random-effects* model. In these situations, the levels of the factor represent a sample of the possible levels that could have been selected. In these situations, replications of the study will employ different samples of levels.

To help you see the distinction between the two types of effects, let's look as some examples. If we are interested in comparing different instructional strategies, we might select three different methods. Although these three methods might not be all the possible methods we could have chosen, they represent the methods in which we are interested, and we will confine our generalizations to the methods selected. In most applications of one-way designs, the independent variable is considered a fixed effect; we are interested in the differences among the levels of the factor. In some one-way designs, but more often in more complex designs, we use factors that are random effects, such as classrooms. We use classrooms as a variable to estimate the variance among classrooms so that we can control for it. (We are not particularly interested in differences between specific classrooms.) To reiterate, at this level, most one-way designs employ fixed effects and you will not need to worry about this distinction.

There are three other assumptions related to the linear model which are often summarized as: $\varepsilon_{ij} \sim NID(0, \sigma_{\varepsilon}^2)$. This notation can be deciphered to say that the error components of individual scores are normally distributed within each group, that the error components are independent of one another, and that the variances of the errors are the same in all groups. Typically, these assumptions are labeled as the assumptions of normality, independence, and homogeneity of variance.

If you are using the ANOVA to examine the data at hand for possible differences, these are the only assumptions which must be made. Rarely, if ever, is this the case. On the other hand, if you want to generalize the results beyond the immediate situation and to infer causality, then there are some additional assumptions. First, you must assume that the cases are random samples from the population and that they are randomly assigned to the treatment groups. If you are doing research with pre-existing groups, then you must assume that the cases are randomly drawn from the subpopulations. When you cannot assume that the cases have been randomly assigned to groups, causal inference is difficult, at best. Thus, the assumption of random selection enables generalization back to the population, and the assumption of random assignment allows for stronger assertions of causality.

Testing for Assumptions

In order to be able to interpret the results of an ANOVA within the appropriate context, you should have some sense of the degree to which the data conform to the assumptions. Regarding the assumption of the linear model, there is no direct test, but a violation of the assumption will usually show up as a violation of the assumption of normality or of homogeneous variances. Likewise, there is no simple (or readily available) test for the assumption of independence of errors. If you employ random sampling and random assignment, you will have done about all you can do to ensure that you have met this assumption. In addition, anything that can be done to implement the treatment on an individual basis will be helpful. If the data are collected from participants in pre-existing, intact groups such as classrooms, newsrooms, or clinics, you are likely to have violated the assumption of independence. There are statistical procedures for dealing with this problem (multilevel models), but they are beyond the scope of this book.

The assumptions of normality and homogeneity of variance are more easily tested. Various tests of normality are contained in different computer programs, e.g., the Shapiro–Wilk test, the Shapiro–Francia procedure, and a test based on skewness and kurtosis (D'Agostino, Belanger, & D'Agostino, 1990). Which test you might use will depend on which computer package you are using. In some packages, no test is available. In R, the Shapiro–Wilk procedure (**shapiro.test( )**) is in the base package and is often the test of choice. There is also a package (**nortest**) that contains several different tests for departures from normality.

At a minimum you can examine the distributions of each group visually. If the separate distributions are roughly symmetric and unimodal, you are probably close enough to normal distributions to satisfy the assumption. If your computer program gives you measures of skewness and kurtosis, you can generate these values for each of the groups. Looking at these measures can be quite tricky, particularly with small samples. The different computer programs each give you slightly different indices, and some of them are biased with small samples. The indices contained in our **functions** file are the ones provided by Fisher, which are also the ones used in SPSS and SAS.

With regard to homogeneity of variance, you can employ any one of several different tests. As noted earlier in Chapter 15, Levene's test is highly recommended.

Violations of Assumptions

The assumption of the linear model gives us the expected mean squares described in Equation 16.21. If there are no treatment effects ($\tau_j = 0$ for all values of j), then the MS_{ag} and the MS_{wg} have the same expected value. Thus, if the observed F-statistic exceeds the critical value from the

F-distribution, it is reasonable to infer the presence of treatment effects. If this assumption of a linear model is violated, the interpretation of the F-statistic becomes unclear, as a significant F-statistic may not be attributed to the presence of τ_j, but rather a violation of an assumption.

If the error components of the observations are not independent, then we run an increased risk of a Type I error (Glass & Hopkins, 1984). Lack of independence can occur when you have multiple observations on the same case, when the "treatment" is administered in a group setting, or when complex data are collected with cluster sampling. Kenny and Judd (1986) identified three categories of situations in which you are likely to encounter violations of the assumption of independence: groups, sequence, and space. We are not going to spend much time discussing non-independence due to sequence and space. Problems of sequence are addressed with time series analysis, a set of methods not covered in this book. Problems arising from spatial arrangements imply a quantitative measure of proximity, a notion not really relevant in the present context of examining differences among groups. Thus, the only category we address is the problem of non-independence due to grouping, a situation quite typical in educational research. Much applied research in education is conducted in the field, where students are already grouped into schools and classrooms within schools. Recall that in the additive model, the error component contains all of the variation not directly relevant to the research question. Irrelevant factors that occur within a classroom affect not just one student, but they may affect several students. Therefore, it seems logical that the error components of students within the same classroom are not independent. This problem is not confined to classrooms. In the interest of efficiency in data collection, many researchers administer "treatments" to groups of students (cases) assembled specifically for purposes of the study and/or collect outcome data in group situations, thus creating a potential problem with regard to independence of observations.

A number of different procedures/methods have been proposed for dealing with the problem of non-independence in group designs. Kirk (1995), Myers and Well (2003), and Winer, Brown, and Michels (1991) have described the use of hierarchal, or nested, designs when the independent variables are categorical. Raudenbush and Bryk (2002) and Hox (2010) have recommended using multi-level analyses, an approach which subsumes the earlier methods in a more flexible, but more complex, system. Both of these approaches have their advantages, but both are beyond the scope of this book. On the other hand, a relatively simple approach has been recommended by many people over the years, most recently by Kromrey and Dickinson (1996). When there may be potential problems of non-independence, whether these problems arise from using intact groups or from research procedures, they have suggested using "group" means as the unit of analysis. For example, if you are studying the relative effectiveness of three different instructional strategies, it is likely that each strategy will be used in several different classrooms. Suppose that each of the strategies has been used in ten different classrooms with about 25 students in each class. Although you have information on 750 cases ($3 \times 10 \times 25$), you would analyze the data as though you only have 30 cases. That is, within each class you would calculate the class average, and these 30 class means would be the data for your one-way ANOVA. This approach could be used by someone who might truncate their statistical education at this point. Now that the software is widely available, the approach suggested by Raudenbush and Bryk (2002) is preferred.

At this point, a clarification is in order. The discussion above may leave you somewhat confused between independence of cases and independence of errors. In our testing for differences in location between two groups, we introduced the dependent-samples t-test. This feature can be extended into an ANOVA context with three or more dependent samples. Obviously, *the observations* are not independent in matched-samples or repeated-measures designs. However, the linear model for this design contains another parameter, π, to allow for the case, or person, as follows:

$$Y_{ij} = \mu + \tau_j + \pi_i + \varepsilon_{ij} \tag{16.22}$$

The dependence of the observations is assumed to come from the parameter π, and thus the error components, ε_{ij}, may still be independent. In describing procedures for analyzing complex, repeated-measures designs, advanced statistics books (e.g., Kirk, 1995; Myers & Well, 2003; Winer, Brown, & Michels, 1991) discuss this issue in much greater detail and present statistical tests for the assumption of independence of error in a variety of designs. We mention the issue here only because we did not want to leave you with the misunderstanding that the use of dependent samples will necessarily lead you to problems of non-independence of error.

The assumptions of normality and homogeneity of variance are less problematic, particularly when the sample sizes are equal, or nearly so. When the sample sizes are large ($n > 30$), we can invoke the central limit theorem regarding the distribution of the sample means; when sample sizes are smaller, we need to examine this assumption more closely. Regarding the assumption of homogeneity of variance, you are on relatively safe ground when the sample sizes are equal and the largest group variance is no more than four times the smallest group variance. More complete discussions of the assumptions and the consequences of their violations can be found in Kirk (1995), Glass and Hopkins (1984), and Glass, Peckham, and Sanders (1972).

Given the literature on this issue, it is probably safe to say that ANOVA is *robust* with respect to violations of the assumptions of normality and homogeneity of variance, particularly when the sample sizes are large and equal, or nearly so. That is, violations of the assumptions do little to invalidate the use of the F-distribution as a criterion for evaluating the probability of our observed F-statistic. However, there are situations where ANOVA is not so robust, and cautious researchers may want to modify their data so that they more closely conform to the assumptions. These modifications are called "transformations."

Transformations of Data

Transformations may be employed to rectify any one of three types of assumption violations: linear model, normality, or homogeneity of variance. As it turns out, a transformation to fix any one of these problems usually may also fix other problems, if there are any. Before we give you some examples of specific problems and the appropriate transformations, we want to discuss transformations in general.

First, we acknowledge that transforming data changes the values, and that is precisely the purpose. From a pure measurement perspective in which the numerals have a clear relationship to the external world (i.e., ratio scales), transformations may become problematic as they change the units on which the variables are scaled. Thus, transformations of data pose problems for interpreting descriptive statistics. However, from an inferential perspective, changes in scale are not as important. Inferential statistics are employed to assess whether the pattern of variation is random or systematic. In this context, scales of measurement are essentially arbitrary. In fact, most scales of measurement in the social sciences are somewhat arbitrary. Physical scientists work with measures such as time, mass, and distance, all measures that are well standardized in meaningful units. In contrast, social scientists cannot visit the Smithsonian Institute to view the standard IQ point displayed under glass. Thus, our earlier argument concerning the relevance of scales of measurement to inferential statistics is merely extended here. We argue that changing the scale of measurement through transformations is legitimate, as long as the transformation does not change the rank ordering of the observations. Furthermore, we are not suggesting that you examine a number of different transformations to determine which one gives you the best value for your test statistic. Instead, we are suggesting that you may want to look at several transformations to determine which of them makes your data conform most closely to the required assumptions for the *one* test statistic that you will calculate.

If you find that your data do not meet the assumptions for ANOVA and that you are in a situation where you cannot argue for the robustness of the *F*-test, then you have a number of transformations to consider. First, we will show several "typical" distributions that are clear violations of the assumption of normality. Then we will describe briefly several of the more common transformations that can be employed to make your data "more normal." Some of the ways in which distributions can deviate from normality are shown in Figure 16.4; the three distributions differ in the degree of positive skewness.

We will first deal with positive skewness. The degree of skewness you detect will guide you in selecting an appropriate transformation. Before you try any of the transformations that we are about to describe, be certain that your data do not contain any negative values. If you find any such values, add to each value whatever constant is necessary so that all of your values are positive or zero.

When the distributions are positively skewed, transforming the data is relatively simple. If the degree of skewness is mild, you can use the **square root transformation**. Mild skewness is often present when the dependent variable is "count" data, particularly when the outcome has a small probability of happening. In such cases, you will often find that the group means are proportional to the group variances. The appropriate transformation is as follows:

$$Y' = \sqrt{Y} \tag{16.23}$$

However, if any value of Y is less than 10, it may be more appropriate to use a slightly different transformation:

$$Y' = \sqrt{Y} + \sqrt{Y+1} \tag{16.24}$$

When the degree of skewness is more pronounced, a **logarithmic transformation** may be employed. This transformation is often useful when the dependent variable is some measure of

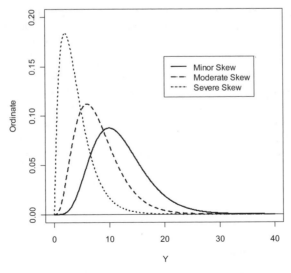

FIGURE 16.4   Distributions with differing degrees of skewness.

time to complete a task. In these situations, the group means will tend to be proportional to the group standard deviations, and an appropriate transformation is as follows:

$$Y' = \log_{10}(Y+1) \tag{16.25}$$

From time to time, you will encounter a dependent variable which is severely skewed. These situations may also occur when the dependent variable is a measure of time. In these instances, the group means will tend to be proportional to the square roots of the group standard deviations (or the squares of the group means will be proportional to the standard deviations). When this happens, you may want to try a **reciprocal transformation**:

$$Y' = \frac{1}{Y} \quad \text{or} \quad Y' = \frac{1}{Y+1} \tag{16.26}$$

If all of the values are greater than zero, you may use the first option. If some of the values of Y are zero, you must use the second option.

We have tried to present a few of the more common transformations, though others may be used. For a more complete discussion of transformations and their use, you are encouraged to examine Kirk (1995, pp. 103–107) or Howell (2007, pp. 318–324). Detailed presentations have been given also by Box and Cox (1964) and Mosteller and Tukey (1977).

Thus far, we have dealt only with situations in which there is positive skewness. The effect of any of the three transformations described is to disproportionately reduce the values in the right, or upper, tail. On the other hand, when the skewness is negative, you need to rein in the values in the lower tail. In order to do this, you must first reflect, or reverse score, the variable. That is, if the values of your dependent variable range from 37 to 81, create a new variable which is equal to 82 minus the value of the original variable. The low score of 37 will now become 45, and the high score of 81 will become 1. Once the variable has been reversed, you can then use any of the transformations we described earlier. One note of caution: You must remember that the scale has now been reversed in meaning when you try to interpret the results. If that causes a problem for you (and it often does), then you can take the transformed values and reflect them back to the original direction.

Selecting the right transformation for your data can be a frustrating experience. You may have to try several before you find the right one. Before jumping to the conclusion that we are recommending "playing" with the data, remember that you are looking for the transformation that makes your data most closely resemble samples from normal populations with homogeneous variances. You are *not* trying to find the transformation that makes your results come out the way that you want them to! Each time you try a transformation you can generate descriptive statistics on each of the groups to determine whether the within-group distributions appear normal with regard to skewness and kurtosis. At the same time, you can find the variances of the samples and then determine which transformation produces the most "normal"-appearing distributions. In a similar manner, Kirk (1995, p. 106) has described a procedure for selecting the best transformation for an analysis:

1. Apply each transformation under consideration to both the smallest value and the largest value in each group, respectively.
2. For each of the groups, determine the difference between the two transformed values (i.e., the "group range").
3. For each transformation, find the ratio of the largest "group range" to the smallest "group range."
4. Use the transformation that produces the smallest ratio.

Some notes of warning are in order. First, you need to know from the very beginning that there may be no transformation that is appropriate for your data. You cannot be selective in applying transformations. Whatever transformation you select, you must apply it to every observation in every group. If some of the groups are negatively skewed and other groups are positively skewed, then it is you who is "skewed." If no transformation appears to be appropriate, then you have two alternatives. You can analyze the data in their original form and be very cautious in your interpretation of the results. On the other hand, you may opt for one of the techniques that will be described later in this chapter: the Kruskal–Wallis ANOVA or randomization tests. Neither of these two approaches requires assumptions about normality.

If you do find yourself transforming your data prior to analysis, you have one more issue to confront: How do you report the results? After completing your statistical test on the transformed data, you would report your test statistic on the transformed values. The descriptive statistics which should accompany your results could be presented on the original scale or the transformed scale. There appears to be general agreement that the descriptive statistics should be on the original scale of measurement, particularly if the scale is meaningful. When you employ a transformation prior to calculating the ANOVA, your computer output should contain group statistics calculated on the transformed values. To report the descriptive statistics, you need to undo the transformation. If you used a square-root transformation, then you can take the group means on the transformed data and square them to get back to the original scale. However, these results will be different from those derived directly from the original data.

MEASURES OF EFFECT SIZE

Unrelated to transformations but related to reporting your study, it is often helpful to give the reader some sense of the practical significance of your results. These measures of practical significance are sometimes called measures of *effect size*. Historically, there are two different types of effect-size measures that have been used within the context of ANOVA. First, some measures that are correlational in nature have been recommended. While there is some disagreement as to whether correlational measures should be employed within the context of designs that involve fixed effects, we will present these measures as they are sometimes useful. Two correlational measures that have been recommended for fixed-effects designs are *eta-squared* (η^2) and *omega-squared* ($\hat{\omega}^2$). Both of these measures may be helpful in assessing the strength of association between the quantitative dependent variable and the categorical independent variable. Eta-squared is a descriptive measure of association for the sample, but recall that least-squares measures of association tend to overestimate population parameters. Thus, η^2 tends to overestimate the population value. On the other hand, $\hat{\omega}^2$ makes an adjustment, and thus is an unbiased estimator of the proportion of variation explained in the population. The formulae for the two measures are shown below. You may recognize η^2 as being rather similar to r^2 in regression, the proportion of variance in the dependent variable explained by the independent variable.

$$\eta^2 = \frac{SS_{ag}}{SS_{tot}} \quad \text{(positively biased)} \tag{16.27}$$

$$\hat{\omega}^2 = \frac{SS_{ag} - (k-1)\,MS_{wg}}{SS_{tot} + MS_{wg}} \quad \text{(unbiased)} \tag{16.28}$$

We place the "hat" over the ω to underscore the point that this value is an estimate of the proportion of variation explained in the population.

A slightly different measure of effect size has been employed by Cohen (1988), one which is similar to the measure of effect size we discussed within the context of the *t*-test. The expression given at that time was:

$$d = \frac{\bar{Y}_{.1} - \bar{Y}_{.2}}{\hat{\sigma}} \qquad (16.29)$$

The extension of this expression to a situation with *k* means requires a redefinition of the numerator to allow for multiple differences. The extension is analogous to that from the *t*-test to ANOVA. That is, rather than use a single difference, we use the standard deviation of the means, which summarizes all the differences among the means. Cohen (1988) substituted an *f* for the *d*, as follows:

$$f = \frac{\hat{\sigma}_{\bar{Y}}}{\hat{\sigma}} \quad \text{where} \quad \hat{\sigma}_{\bar{Y}} = \sqrt{\frac{\sum_{j=1}^{k}\left(\bar{Y}_{.j} - \bar{Y}_{..}\right)^2}{k}} \qquad (16.30)$$

Cohen attempted to give meaning to this index by saying that *f* = .10 is a *small* effect, *f* = .25 is a *medium* effect, and *f* = .40 is a *large* effect. Recall that Cohen had also suggested that *d* = .20 is a small effect, *d* = .50 is a medium effect, and *d* = .80 is a large effect; thus the scale for *f* is half that of *d*. This seems reasonable, if we consider the two-group case where the distance between a group mean and the grand mean (indexed by *f*) is half the distance between the two group means (indexed by *d*).

Effect Size and Power

Cohen's measure of effect size lends itself nicely to the estimation of power during the planning stages of a study. We have consistently taken the position that under ideal conditions, researchers should decide ahead of time how many cases they need in order to detect a minimally significant (clinically significant) effect with a desired power, given whatever level of significance they wish to employ. Cohen's measure allows us to express what we consider to be minimally significant effects as a summary measure of effect size, one that can be used to enter a table in order to determine an appropriate sample size. In order to accomplish this assessment, there are two pieces of information necessary. First, you must have some notion of what size differences you wish to detect; and, second, you need an estimate of the population standard deviation.

For example, if you are working with a well-known measure such as IQ, then you can use 15 as an estimate of the population standard deviation. If you are working with a measure that is not well known, then you can get an estimate of the population standard deviation from earlier studies. In effect, you just take the square root of the MS_{wg}.

Back to our example dealing with intelligence, suppose that you are working with three groups and you think that if the means differ in a pattern of 110, 115, and 120, then there is a minimally significant difference. Under these conditions, the measure of effect size is:

$$f = \frac{\sqrt{\left[(110 - 115)^2 + (115 - 115)^2 + (120 - 115)^2\right]/3}}{15} \qquad (16.31)$$

$$= .27$$

Using this value of .27, you can use a free, downloadable program for power analysis called G*Power 3 (available at: http://www.psycho.uni-duesseldorf.de/abteilungen/aap/gpower3).

For example, suppose you wanted to be able to detect such a pattern of differences with a power of .90 with a level of significance of .05 After starting G*Power 3, in the "Test family" box, select "F tests." Next, in the "Statistical test" box, select "Anova: Fixed effects, omnibus, one-way." Last, supply the values in the "Input parameters" area. Finally, click on "Calculate" in the lower right corner of the window. G*Power 3 returns a "Total sample size" of 177. Thus, we would need 177/3 cases per group, or 59 in each group.

For another example, suppose that you wished to detect a pattern of differences, or means, such as 105, 119, and 121. Assuming groups of equal sizes, the overall mean would be 115. Thus, the "effects" would be -10, $+4$, and $+6$. Using these values in the expression above, we would obtain the following results:

$$f = \frac{\sqrt{\left[(105-115)^2 + (119-115)^2 + (121-115)^2\right]/3}}{15} \tag{16.32}$$
$$= .47$$

Returning to G*Power 3, we would find that to detect this pattern and magnitude of differences with a power of .80 using $\alpha = .05$, you would need about 16 cases per group. To achieve the same power using $\alpha = .01$, you would need about 23 cases per group. Both of these examples are intended to give you a rough idea of how power, effect size, level of significance, and sample size relate to one another within a one-way ANOVA. For more information, you might refer to Cohen (1988) or Murphy and Myors (2004).

A COMPUTER EXAMPLE

To complete our discussion of ANOVA as applied to a one-way design, we will show you how the data from earlier in this chapter could be prepared for analysis and analyzed with R. First we insert our interpretations/comments in the output. The R script is given on the website in the supplementary materials for this chapter (Script 16.4). The script enters the data with the **c( )** function and shows you how to generate the values for hand computation. The next section builds a data frame, generates descriptive statistics, examines assumptions, and then completes the one-way ANOVA. It is this last section that is our focus here.

```
# Define the groups
w <- c(31,23,32,27,28,25,29,33,36,39)
a <- c(14,34,18,21,30,25,22,27,16,16)
h <- c(23,26,39,14,28,13,12,34,31,12)
n1 <- length(w)
n2 <- length(a)
n3 <- length(h)
gw <- rep(1,n1)
ga <- rep(2,n2)
gh <- rep(3,n3)
```

```
# Building a data.frame
dv <- c(w, a, h)
# Establish an id variable for each case
n <- length(dv)
id <- 1:n
group <- c(gw, ga, gh)
data16 <-data.frame(id, group, dv)
attach(data)
# Creating a factor-type representation of group
data16$f.group <- factor(group, levels = 1:3,
  labels = c("w", "a", "h"))
attach(data16)
> # Obtaining descriptive statistics
> tapply(dv, f.group, mean)
   w    a    h
30.3 22.3 23.2
> mean(dv)
[1] 25.26667
> round(tapply(dv, f.group, sd), 2)
   w    a    h
4.92 6.62 9.99
```

Inspecting the results, we can see that the mean for the White students appears to be higher than both the means for the African American and the Hispanic students. In examining the three group standard deviations, it appears that they may be different also. At this point, we should look at the three within-group distributions, first visually with box plots and then numerically with indices of skewness and kurtosis. Finally, we will use Levene's test from the **car** package to compare the three groups with respect to equivalent variability.

```
> boxplot(dv ~ f.group)
```

The box plot for the three groups is depicted in Figure 16.5. The pattern of means that we saw with the descriptive statistics is consistent with what we see in the medians in the plots. Also, the pattern for the standard deviations is similarly manifested in the interquartile ranges.

Let's turn our attention to a quantitative description of skewness and kurtosis.

```
> round(tapply(dv, f.group, skewness), 3)
    w     a     h
0.327 0.493 0.162
> round(tapply(dv, f.group, SEsk), 3)
    w     a     h
0.687 0.687 0.687
```

```
> round(tapply(dv, f.group, kurtosis), 3)
     w         a          h
-0.391    -0.807    -1.494
> round(tapply(dv, f.group, SEku), 3)
     w         a          h
 1.334    1.334     1.334
```

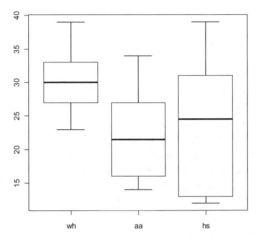

FIGURE 16.5   Box plot of within-group distributions of General Knowledge test scores of White, African American, and Hispanic children at entry to kindergarten.

Given the computer output, we examine it for several issues. First, with regard to the assumptions, we look at the descriptive statistics given for each group. Note that for $n = 10$, the standard errors of skewness and kurtosis are .687 and 1.334, respectively. Thus, any sample of $n = 10$ for which the measure of skewness falls within the range 0 ± 1.374 would be within ± 2 standard errors of symmetry, and thus could be considered symmetric. Similarly, if the measure of kurtosis fall within the range 0 ± 2.668, the sample could be considered mesokurtic. Any sample meeting both of these criteria could be considered to have come from a normal population. Using absolute criteria, if the actual measures of skewness are within the range ± 2 and kurtosis is less than 7 or so, the data may be considered sufficiently close to normal. Given the descriptive statistics on our three groups, it appears that all three samples may have come from normal populations. Thus, we can be fairly confident that our data conform to the assumption of normality.

Just to be extra cautious, let's look at both the issues of normality and homogeneity of variance in a more formal fashion, using the **shapiro.test( )** and **leveneTest( )** functions.

```
> tapply(dv, f.group ,shapiro. test)
$w
W = 0.9848, p-value = 0.9856

$a
W = 0.9488, p-value = 0.6546
```

```
$h
W = 0.9002, p-value = 0.2201
```

The three *p*-values all suggest that the assumption of normally distributed populations may be reasonable. Regarding homogeneity of variance,

```
> leveneTest(dv ~ f.group, data = data16)
Levene's Test for Homogeneity of Variance (center = median)
      Df F value  Pr(>F)
group  2  3.6214 0.04043
      27
```

If we are testing the assumption at the .05 level, we may have a problem. Given this possibility, we may want to look at the ANOVA from two perspectives, one assuming that the variances are equivalent, and the other assuming that they are not. There are two functions in R that will allow us to complete the ANOVA, **oneway.test( )** and **aov( )**. The first one will allow us to specify whether we want to assume equivalent variances (var.equal = TRUE) or not (var.equal = FALSE). However, **oneway.test( )** will give us the *F*-statistic, *df*, and *p*-value, but not the *SS* and *MS*. The **aov( )** function assumes that the variances are equivalent. Let's take a look. First, assuming equivalent variances:

```
> result1 <- oneway.test(dv ~ f.group, var.equal = TRUE)
> result1
        One-way analysis of means
data:  dv and f.group
F = 3.4342, num df = 2, denom df = 27, p-value = 0.0469
```

As you can see, the results are in close agreement with our hand calculations. Now, *not* assuming equivalent variances:

```
> result2 <- oneway.test(dv ~ f.group, var.equal = FALSE)
> result2
        One-way analysis of means (not assuming equal
variances)
data:  dv and f.group
F = 5.2787, num df = 2.000, denom df = 16.865, p-value =
0.01659
```

As you can see, these results are slightly different than those obtained under the assumption of equivalent variances. The results from the **aov( )** function are:

```
> result3 <- aov(dv ~ f.group)
> summary(result3)
```

```
              Df  Sum Sq Mean Sq F value Pr(>F)
f.group        2  384.07 192.033  3.4342 0.0469
Residuals     27 1509.80  55.919
```

The results from the **aov( )** function agree with those from both our hand calculations and the **oneway.test( )** function in which we assumed equivalent variances. There are other ways in which we might proceed, however.

ALTERNATIVES TO ONE-WAY ANOVA

The discussion of testing for differences in location presented thus far (in this chapter) has been predicated on the assumptions we have just discussed, although **oneway.test( )** does provide a way to accommodate non-equivalent variances. However, not all situations in the social sciences conform to these assumptions. In particular, often we have data from three or more groups with small sample sizes where the distributions within samples are decidedly non-normal. While the ANOVA has been shown to be robust with respect to violations of assumptions of normality and homogeneity of variance, it is not immune to extreme deviations from these assumptions. As noted earlier, several authors recommend techniques such as data transformations, adjustments to degrees of freedom, or modifications in the computation of the F-statistic. However, when sample sizes are particularly small, there are other procedures available which make fewer assumptions. We refer to rank-order statistics (Kruskal–Wallis ANOVA), bootstrapping, and permutation tests, all of which belong to the family of non-parametric statistics. These techniques are discussed in the following sections.

Kruskal–Wallis Analysis of Variance

In our earlier presentation of ways in which to compare two groups, we described the Mann–Whitney U-test as an alternative to the t-test. Similarly, the Kruskal–Wallis procedure may be considered a rank-order, non-parametric substitute for a one-way ANOVA. This approach is known as the "Kruskal–Wallis ANOVA on ranked data." It has been around since the early 1950s (Kruskal & Wallis, 1952), and quite simply, it is a permutation test on ranks, or consecutive integers.

Currently, this procedure is sometimes used as a substitute for a permutation test when appropriate computer software is not available. When the original data are actually ranks, it is the only test available for small samples. If the data are not in rank form, the first step of the procedure is to pool the data from all of the groups and to rank the observations from 1 to N. While rank-order statistics involve fewer assumptions than parametric tests, they do involve their own assumptions. One of these assumptions is that there are no ties. In the case of tied observations, the ranks are pooled and their average is assigned to each of the tied observations. As long as the number of tied observations is not extensive, you can complete the test as we show it below. More complete discussions of the test are given in Gibbons (1993), Gibbons and Chakraborti (2003), and Siegel and Castellan (1988). Let's consider how this procedure would be applied to a small data set for which it might be deemed appropriate.

The Situation

A researcher was interested in determining whether different incentives would differentially motivate third-grade children to achieve in school. Three different conditions were created: one group of children was rewarded with tokens that could be used to obtain toys, a second group of children was rewarded with tokens that could be used to "buy" unstructured playtime, and the third group served as a control group, receiving no special rewards. The study was conducted within a residential summer camp serving over 750 children between the ages of 7 and 10 years. Fifteen children who were rising third-graders were selected at random for all rising third-graders attending the camp. After obtaining informed consent from the parents, five children were randomly assigned to each of the three conditions. The scores to be used in the analysis were derived from teacher-made tests written by teachers working as counselors at the camp. The scores are contained in Table 16.6.

The situation just described is similar in structure to the previous example comparing the General Knowledge scores of White, African American, and Hispanic pre-kindergarteners. However, there are some important differences. First, the number of cases has been reduced. Second, the measure used cannot be expected to yield scores that are normally distributed. Thus, while the design lends itself to completing an ANOVA as we have presented in this chapter, the number of children and the nature of the measure suggest that we should be cautious. You may proceed to calculate a MS_{ag} and a MS_{wg}, followed by the calculation of the F-statistic, noting that an ANOVA proceeds from this point to compare the observed F-statistic to a critical value from the appropriate F-distribution. The legitimacy of this comparison rests upon the degree to which the data meet the attendant assumptions, and the data in this situation cannot be expected to meet the assumptions. In this instance, we might want to analyze the data differently.

The first step is to convert the data to ranks. We have presented a modified version of Table 16.6 in Table 16.7, showing both the original data and their respective ranks. Once the original data have been ranked, you sum the ranks for the observations in each group. These values are included in the bottom row of Table 16.7.

At this point, the "Sum of Ranks," group sizes (nj), and total sample size (N) are inserted in the following expression:

Table 16.6 Learning scores for three different groups of camp children based on different reward structures

Toy tokens	Playtime tokens	Control group
62	45	40
60	47	39
57	44	43
58	54	42
53	47	46

Table 16.7 Learning scores for three different groups of camp children based on different reward structures and their respective ranks

Toy tokens	Ranks	Playtime tokens	Ranks	Control group	Ranks
62	15	45	6	40	2
60	14	47	8.5	39	1
57	12	44	5	43	4
58	13	54	11	42	3
53	10	47	8.5	46	7
ΣRanks	64		39		17

$$H = \frac{12}{N(N+1)}\sum_{j=1}^{k}\frac{R_j^2}{n_j} - 3(N+1) \tag{16.33}$$

Substituting the values from our example, we obtain:

$$\begin{aligned} H &= \frac{12}{15(15+1)}\left(\frac{64^2}{5}+\frac{39^2}{5}+\frac{17^2}{5}\right) - 3(15+1) \\ &= \frac{12}{240}\left(\frac{4{,}096}{5}+\frac{1{,}521}{5}+\frac{289}{5}\right) - 48 \\ &= .05\left(\frac{5{,}906}{5}\right) - 48 \\ &= 11.06 \end{aligned} \tag{16.34}$$

The actual sampling distribution of H can be found by total enumeration using a randomization test program. However, under most conditions, the sampling distribution of H can be reasonably well approximated using the χ^2 distribution with $df = (k-1)$. This is what is done in most statistical packages. Thus, using a significance level of .05, we compare our observed result to the critical value of 5.99 which was obtained in R.

```
> qchisq(.95, 2)
[1] 5.991465
```

When $k = 3$ and each of the sample sizes is less than or equal to 5, the use of the χ^2 distribution with $(k-1)$ degrees of freedom is questionable, erring in the direction of being overly conservative. In these instances, you may wish to use randomization test software to determine whether the result is statistically significant, or you may compare the observed H-statistic to the tables provided by Kruskal and Wallis (1952).

Kruskal–Wallis Analysis of Variance with R

Script 16.5 is given on the book website and contains the commands to read in the data with the **c( )** function, create a grouping variable, and complete the **kruskal.test( )**. The results are:

```
> kruskal.test (score, g)
          Kruskal-Wallis rank sum test
data:  score and g
Kruskal-Wallis chi-squared = 11.0798, df = 2, p-value =
0.003927

> pchisq(11.0798, df = 2, lower.tail = FALSE)
[1] 0.003926920
```

As you can see, the computed χ^2 statistic is the same as our H, and it would appear that R is using the χ^2 distribution with $df = 2$ to compute the p-value. The Kruskal–Wallis test was, historically, the first alternative to the traditional ANOVA. However, with the computers we have now, we can use enumeration methods to derive exact p-values or use resampling methods to estimate them. We will now turn our attention to these procedures. Incidentally, if we apply the Kruskal–Wallis procedure to the General Knowledge scores of the three groups, the results come out as:

```
> kruskal.test(dv ~ f.group)
        Kruskal-Wallis rank sum test
data:  dv by f.group
Kruskal-Wallis chi-squared = 5.7496, df = 2, p-value =
0.05643
```

Randomization/Resampling Procedures

Earlier in this book we have given examples of resampling procedures, including both bootstrapping and permutation tests. If you are willing to assume the form of the population distribution, then you might employ a parametric bootstrap procedure. For example, if you are willing to assume that the population follows a normal distribution, then you could generate N random variates from the unit-normal distribution, compute the test statistic of interest, repeating this process many, many times. The distribution of the repeated test statistics can then be used to estimate the exact sampling distribution of the test statistic.

In the behavioral sciences, it is more often the case that we do not have sufficient information to assume a particular distribution of the population. In this instance, we might prefer to employ a non-parametric bootstrap procedure. There a two different ways in which we might proceed, either bootstrapping from the pooled samples with replacement or using a permutation approach. We will apply each of these approaches to the General Knowledge test scores. We will present a bootstrap approach, followed by a permutation approach.

A Bootstrap Approach

There are several different ways to implement a bootstrapping analysis for a one-way ANOVA. In Script 16.6 (see the supplementary materials for this chapter on the book website) we first found SS_{ag} for the actual arrangement of the data. We then "implemented" the null hypothesis of no difference by combining the three samples of 10 cases each into one "population" of 30 cases (**pop**). From **pop**, we drew, repeatedly, bootstrap samples of size 30, with replacement. Each bootstrap sample was divided into three groups of size 10. Each of the bootstrap replicates was analyzed to find the bootstrap sample SS_{ag}. We then counted the number of the 100,000 bootstrap replicates which yielded a SS_{ag} larger than the one for the actual data. Following the recommendations of Davison and Hinkley (1997, p. 177), we might have drawn 99,999 samples and calculated our p-value as (count + 1)/(N + 1). This was fairly standard procedure when computers were much slower and statisticians might draw 499 samples. However, with as many as 100,000 samples, the correction is negligible. The results from R are:

```
> cat("Based on 100,000 bootstrap samples, the p-value is",
   pvalue,"\n")
Based on 100,000 bootstrap samples, the p-value is 0.04602
```

A Permutation Approach

First, consider how many ways there are to arrange our 30 cases into three groups of 10 each. We can compute this fairly easily with R using the multinomial:

$$\frac{n!}{n_1! \, n_2! \, n_3!} = \frac{30!}{10! \, 10! \, 10!} = 5.550997 \times 10^{12} \tag{16.35}$$

```
> prod(1:30)/(prod(1:10)^3)
[1] 5.550997e+12
```

Now, there are 3! different orders in which the three groups could be arranged, so the number of permutations giving distinct results is:

```
> prod(1:30)/(6*prod(1:10)^3)
[1] 925166131890
```

Written in traditional notation, that is 925,166,131,890, or nearly one trillion different arrangements. Although there are computer programs that can actually generate all of these possible arrangements, the code is difficult to write and the programs take a very long time to execute. Therefore, it is more reasonable to take a large random sample with replacement from the nearly one trillion possible permutations of the data, and evaluate the probability of the actual arrangement of the data within the random sample of arrangements, perhaps as many as 100,000 or so. This approach of estimating the exact *p*-value by taking random samples of random arrangements yields what is sometimes called a "Monte Carlo *p*-value." We have written Script 16.7 to do this analysis (see the supplementary materials for this chapter on the book website). In the script, we enter the data, find SS_{ag} for the actual arrangement, generate 100,000 random arrangements of the data, and then count how many of the random arrangement yield a SS_{ag} value greater than the actual arrangement. The results are:

```
> cat("Based on 100,000 bootstrap samples, the p-value is",
    pvalue, "\n")
Based on 100,000 bootstrap samples, the p-value is 0.04861
```

A *k*-SAMPLE TEST FOR PROPORTIONS

In earlier chapters we have treated proportions as a special case of means. Thus, to be consistent, we should include a brief presentation in which we describe the process of testing the equivalence of *k*-sample proportions. As it turns out, it is simply a modified application of the χ^2 statistic to test for the relationship between two categorical variables. In our discussion of that procedure, we noted that one would draw a random sample from the defined population, "cross-tabulate" the cases on the two categorical variables, and then use the **chisq.test( )** function to test the null hypothesis of independence. This is sometimes described as *contingency table analysis*. In that discussion, we noted that the table could have any number of rows and any number of columns, although we noted that one might create a situation requiring a very large sample so that the expected values for the cells would be sufficiently large to justify the use of the χ^2 distribution with an appropriate *df*.

Now, let's consider a situation in which we might want to test the equivalence of k proportions. For example, the state of North Carolina is sometimes described as comprising three geographic areas: the coastal plain, the Piedmont, and the mountains. The state of Florida could be similarly thought of as comprising the southern peninsula, the panhandle, and the eastern area from the Georgia border down to Orlando. Consider North Carolina. Suppose a researcher was interested in comparing the three geographic regions with regard to the proportion of registered voters in favor of raising the age requirement for eligibility for social security benefits. A contingency table approach would be to draw a random sample of North Carolina registered voters and then cross-tabulate them according to their opinion (raise/not raise) and their region of residence.

A slightly different approach would be to test the equivalence of the three proportions. Rather than defining the state as the sampling frame, one would define three sampling frames, one for each geographic region. One would then draw a random sample from each of the three frames ($n = 100$?) and ascertain the opinion (raise/not raise). Both processes would result in a 2 × 3 contingency table, but the latter would be preferable to test proportions. However, once the 2 × 3 table has been constructed from the three sampling frames, one would use the same **chisq. test( )** function to generate the test statistic.

CHAPTER SUMMARY

In this chapter we have presented a great deal of material, all related to the matter of examining data for possible differences in location among groups where the central question is whether several groups come from the same population with respect to location or central tendency. Most of our focus was on ANOVA, a statistical technique that deals specifically with the question of whether the samples come from one population with regard to central tendency; in particular with respect to the mean. As such, ANOVA is a parametric technique. In our discussion of ANOVA, we provided an overview which included a conceptual presentation of the method, an example applied to a small prototypic set of data, and a detailed set of instructions for completing an ANOVA using R. We also modeled how the results should be interpreted after considering the degree to which the data meet the important assumptions. Finally, we provided examples of other statistical procedures for analyzing data in group designs; specifically the Kruskal–Wallis ANOVA and two randomization/resampling approaches. These latter methods are particularly useful when dealing with small samples and/or the data do not adequately meet the assumptions for ANOVA as derived by Fisher. When the data meet the assumptions for ANOVA, it is the most powerful of the techniques and should be employed.

ANOVA as described in this chapter only deals with the "omnibus" test of whether there are some differences among the groups, somewhere. In the next chapter, we will show you ways to test more specific questions within a one-way group design. These methods fall under the umbrella of what are called "multiple comparison procedures."

Key Terms

ANOVA
df_{ag}
df_{wg}
df_{tot}
Effect size
Eta-squared

Kruskal–Wallis test
MS_{ag}
MS_{wg}
Omega-squared
SS_{ag}
SS_{wg}

F
F-statistic

SS_{tot}

REFERENCES

Box, G. E. P.; Cox, D. R. (1964). An analysis of transformations. *Journal of the Royal Statistical Society, Series B, 26(2)*, 211–252.

Cohen, J. (1988). *Statistical power analysis for the behavioral sciences* (2nd ed.). Hillsdale, NJ: Lawrence Erlbaum Associates.

D'Agostino, R.B., Belanger, A., & D'Agostino, Jr., R.B. (1990). A suggestion for using powerful and informative tests of normality. *The American Statistician, 44*, 316–321.

Davison, A. C., & Hinkley, D. V. (1997). *Bootstrap methods and their application.* Cambridge, UK: Cambridge University Press.

Gibbons, J. D. (1993). *Nonparametric statistics: an introduction.* Newbury Park, CA: Sage.

Gibbons, J. D., & Chakraborti, S. (2003). *Nonparametric statistical inference* (4th ed.). New York: Marcel Dekker.

Glass, G. V., & Hopkins, K. D. (1984). *Statistical methods in education and psychology.* Englewood Cliffs, NJ: Prentice-Hall.

Glass, G. V, Peckham, P. D., & Sanders, J. R. (1972). Consequences of failure to meet assumptions underlying the fixed analysis of variance and covariance. *Review of Educational Research, 42*, 237–288.

Howell, D. C. (2007). *Statistical methods for psychology* (6th ed.). Belmont, CA: Thomson Wadsworth.

Hox, J. J. (2010). *Multilevel analysis: techniques and applications.* New York: Routledge.

Kenny, D. A., & Judd, C. M. (1986). Consequences of violating the independence assumption in analysis of variance. *Psychological Bulletin, 99*, 422–431.

Kirk, R. E. (1995). *Experimental design: Procedures for the behavioral sciences* (3rd ed.). Pacific Grove, CA: Brooks/Cole.

Kromrey, J. D., & Dickinson, W. B. (1996). Detecting unit of analysis problems in nested methods: Statistical power and Type I error rates of the F test for groups-within-treatments effects. *Educational and Psychological Measurement, 56*, 215–231.

Kruskal, W. H., & Wallis, W. A. (1952). Use of ranks in one-criterion variance analysis. *Journal of the American Statistical Association, 47,* 583–621.

Mosteller, F., & Tukey, J. W. (1977). *Data analysis and regression: a second course in statistics.* Reading, MA: Addison-Wesley.

Murphy, K. R., & Myors, B. (2004). *Statistical power analysis: a simple and general model for traditional and modern hypothesis tests* (2nd ed.). Mahwah, NJ: Lawrence Erlbaum Associates.

Myers, J. L., & Well, A. D. (2003). *Research design and statistical analysis* (2nd ed.). Mahwah, NJ: Lawrence Erlbaum Associates.

Raudenbush, S. W., & Bryk, A. S. (2002). *Hierarchical linear models: applications and data analysis methods* (2nd ed.). Thousand Oaks, CA: Sage.

Siegel, S., & Castellan, N. J. (1988). *Nonparametric statistics for the behavioral sciences* (2nd ed.). New York: McGraw-Hill.

Winer, B. J., Brown, D. R., & Michels, K. M. (1991). *Statistical principles of experimental design* (3rd ed.). New York: McGraw-Hill.

PRACTICE QUESTIONS

1. The means square within groups is based on deviations between:

   a. group means and other group means
   b. group means and the grand mean
   c. individual observations and the grand mean

    d. individual observations and group means.

2. When the null hypothesis for an ANOVA is false, the F-statistic tends to be:

    a. negative
    b. about 0
    c. about 1
    d. greater than 1.

3. A researcher conducting an ANOVA obtains a p-value of .0015. What should the researcher conclude about the population means?

    a. They are all different.
    b. At least one pair is different.
    c. They are all the same.
    d. At least one pair is the same.

4. You are reading about two different studies comparing two groups. The effect size for the first study is reported as $f = .5$. For the second study the effect size is reported as $d = .5$. The size of the effect is:

    a. equal in the two studies
    b. larger in Study 1
    c. larger in Study 2.

5. The means from three groups are 65, 72, and 84. The last group is found to have an outlier score of 49. Removing this outlier from the data set would:

    a. increase the standardized effect size
    b. decrease the standardized effect size
    c. have no effect on the standardized effect size
    d. change the standardized effect size in an unpredictable direction.

6. A researcher computes $SS_{ag} = 600$, $df_{ag} = 3$, $SS_{wg} = 5,000$, and $df_{wg} = 100$. The F-statistic is:

    a. 0
    b. 4
    c. 50
    d. 200.

7. Violation of which of the following assumptions is most problematic when conducting an ANOVA?

    a. Independence.
    b. Normality.
    c. Equality of variances.

8. In which of the following contexts would you recommend the researcher consider a non-parametric alternative to the ANOVA?

    a. Very large sample sizes coupled with non-normal distributions.
    b. Unequal sample sizes coupled with non-normal distributions.
    c. Very small sample sizes coupled with non-normal distributions.
    d. Equal sample sizes coupled with non-normal distributions.

9. With all other things being equal, which of the following pattern of means would lead to the

greatest power for an ANOVA?

    a. 10, 10, 10.
    b. 10, 11, 12.
    c. 10, 13, 15.
    d. 10, 15, 20.

10. With all other things being equal, which of the following sets of sample sizes would lead to the greatest power for an ANOVA?

    a. 10, 10, 10.
    b. 20, 30, 70.
    c. 50, 50, 50.
    d. 60, 62, 69.

EXERCISES

All three of the following exercises involve a comparison of several groups with regard to the level of performance on a quantitative variable. As you have learned in this chapter, there are three common choices for analyzing data having this structure: ANOVA, the Kruskal–Wallis procedure, and bootstrapping/permutation tests. With each of the exercises, examine the data, regarding the assumptions, and make a decision as to what analysis is most appropriate. Then analyze the data with R and interpret your findings in light of the analysis that you conducted.

16.1. A researcher was interested in comparing three different instructional models: individual tutoring (IT), programmed text (PT), and individual computer-assisted instruction (CAI). The instructional content was addition of fractions. A total of 45 fourth-graders were randomly assigned to one of the three treatments, 15 to each group. The instructional interventions were administered in individual settings. The outcome measure was the number of problems answered correctly on a test constructed by a panel of curriculum specialists. The data were as shown in Table 16.8. Using these data, test ($\alpha = .05$) the null hypothesis that these three groups are random samples from populations performing at the same level.

16.2. Recent changes in society have given reason to question the impact of day care on readi-

Table 16.8 Data for Exercise 16.1

IT	PT	CAI
12	9	11
14	12	17
16	10	15
11	13	5
11	13	16
11	15	12
9	13	10
10	13	7
13	10	10
13	7	14
16	15	15
15	16	11
6	6	11
12	14	10
13	7	12

ness for school. A researcher within a large school system pursued this question by comparing children entering kindergarten with regard to their preschool experience. Kindergarten teachers were asked to indicate whether children had come from a full day (FD) program, a half-day (HD) program, or had had no organized experience (NO). The data came from the preschool screening measure used by the local school district. Using the data provided in Table 16.9, determine ($\alpha = .05$) whether these three groups of children can be considered to be equivalent with regard to "readiness for school."

Table 16.9 Data for Exercise 16.2

FD	HD	NO
25	23	15
23	24	23
27	19	23
15	24	18
20	27	26
22	29	10
17	22	23
20	27	30
21	22	19
20	33	16
16	23	19
17		13
9		21
13		
27		

16.3. A researcher was interested in examining the relationship between academic content area and teaching evaluations made by high-school students. Ten teachers from the disciplines of math, science, language/arts, and social studies were rated by their students using a teaching evaluation form that had been constructed for this study. The ratings by members of the classes were aggregated into one measure on a scale from 0 to 100. Using the data presented in Table 16.10, are teachers in the different content areas rated differently by their students? Use a significance level of .05.

Table 16.10 Data for Exercise 16.3

Math	Science	Language/arts	Social studies
58	42	56	91
58	99	91	71
75	45	63	65
53	55	92	74
74	49	51	66
50	43	63	66
62	43	53	67
46	63	86	70
76	68	90	74
45	39	56	76

TECHNICAL NOTES

Technical Note 16.1: The Partitioning of the Total Sum-of-Squares

Given

$$SS_{\text{tot}} = \sum_{j=1}^{k}\sum_{i=1}^{n_j}\left(Y_{ij}-\bar{Y}_{..}\right)^2$$

it should be fairly easy to see that

$$\left(Y_{ij}-\bar{Y}_{..}\right) = \left(Y_{ij}-\bar{Y}_{..}\right)+\left(\bar{Y}_{.j}-\bar{Y}_{.j}\right) \qquad (a = a + 0)$$

Thus

$$\left(Y_{ij}-\bar{Y}_{..}\right) = \left(Y_{ij}-\bar{Y}_{.j}\right)+\left(\bar{Y}_{.j}-\bar{Y}_{..}\right) \qquad \text{(by regrouping)}$$

$$\left(Y_{ij}-\bar{Y}_{..}\right)^2 = \left[\left(Y_{ij}-\bar{Y}_{.j}\right)+\left(\bar{Y}_{.j}-\bar{Y}_{..}\right)\right]^2 \qquad (a^2 = a^2)$$

$$\left(Y_{ij}-\bar{Y}_{..}\right)^2 = \left(Y_{ij}-\bar{Y}_{.j}\right)^2 + \left(\bar{Y}_{.j}-\bar{Y}_{..}\right)^2 + 2\left(Y_{ij}-\bar{Y}_{.j}\right)\left(\bar{Y}_{.j}-\bar{Y}_{..}\right) \qquad \text{(squaring a binomial)}$$

$$\sum_{i=1}^{n_j}\left(Y_{ij}-\bar{Y}_{..}\right)^2 = \sum_{i=1}^{n_j}\left(Y_{ij}-\bar{Y}_{.j}\right)^2 + \sum_{i=1}^{n_j}\left(\bar{Y}_{.j}-\bar{Y}_{..}\right)^2 + \sum_{i=1}^{n_j}2\left(Y_{ij}-\bar{Y}_{.j}\right)\left(\bar{Y}_{.j}-\bar{Y}_{..}\right) \qquad \text{(rules of summation)}$$

$$\sum_{i=1}^{n_j}\left(Y_{ij}-\bar{Y}_{..}\right)^2 = \sum_{i=1}^{n_j}\left(Y_{ij}-\bar{Y}_{.j}\right)^2 + \sum_{i=1}^{n_j}\left(\bar{Y}_{.j}-\bar{Y}_{..}\right)^2 + 2\left(\bar{Y}_{.j}-\bar{Y}_{..}\right)\sum_{i=1}^{n_j}\left(Y_{ij}-\bar{Y}_{.j}\right) \qquad \text{(rules of summation)}$$

$$\sum_{i=1}^{n_j}\left(Y_{ij}-\bar{Y}_{..}\right)^2 = \sum_{i=1}^{n_j}\left(Y_{ij}-\bar{Y}_{.j}\right)^2 + \sum_{i=1}^{n_j}\left(\bar{Y}_{.j}-\bar{Y}_{..}\right)^2 + 2\left(\bar{Y}_{.j}-\bar{Y}_{..}\right)(0) \qquad \text{(deviations from mean sum to zero)}$$

$$\sum_{i=1}^{n_j}\left(Y_{ij}-\bar{Y}_{..}\right)^2 = \sum_{i=1}^{n_j}\left(Y_{ij}-\bar{Y}_{.j}\right)^2 + \sum_{i=1}^{n_j}\left(\bar{Y}_{.j}-\bar{Y}_{..}\right)^2 \qquad \text{(simplify the above)}$$

$$\sum_{i=1}^{n_j}\left(Y_{ij}-\bar{Y}_{..}\right)^2 = \sum_{i=1}^{n_j}\left(Y_{ij}-\bar{Y}_{.j}\right)^2 + n_j\left(\bar{Y}_{.j}-\bar{Y}_{..}\right)^2 \qquad \text{(summing a constant)}$$

$$\sum_{j=1}^{k}\sum_{i=1}^{n_j}\left(Y_{ij}-\bar{Y}_{..}\right)^2 = \sum_{j=1}^{k}\sum_{i=1}^{n_j}\left(Y_{ij}-\bar{Y}_{.j}\right)^2 + \sum_{j=1}^{k}n_j\left(\bar{Y}_{.j}-\bar{Y}_{..}\right)^2 \qquad \text{(rules of summation)}$$

Note that on the left side of the equals sign is the definitional formula for SS_{tot}. The first term to the right of the equal sign is the definitional formula for SS_{wg}. The second term on the right side of the equality is the definitional formula for SS_{ag}. Thus, $SS_{tot} = SS_{wg} + SS_{ag}$.

Technical Note 16.2: The Derivation of Computational Formulae for Sums-of-Squares

SS_{tot}

$$\sum_{j=1}^{k}\sum_{i=1}^{n_j}\left(Y_{ij}-\bar{Y}_{..}\right)^2 = \sum_{j=1}^{k}\sum_{i=1}^{n_j}\left[Y_{ij}^2 + \bar{Y}_{..}^2 - 2Y_{ij}\,\bar{Y}_{..}\right] \qquad \text{(squaring a binomial)}$$

$$= \sum_{j=1}^{k}\sum_{i=1}^{n_j}Y_{ij}^2 + \sum_{j=1}^{k}\sum_{i=1}^{n_j}\bar{Y}_{..}^2 - \sum_{j=1}^{k}\sum_{i-1}^{n_j}2Y_{ij}\,\bar{Y}_{..} \qquad \text{(rules of summation)}$$

$$= \sum_{j=1}^{k}\sum_{i=1}^{n_j}Y_{ij}^2 + \sum_{j=1}^{k}n_j\bar{Y}_{..}^2 - \sum_{j=1}^{k}\sum_{i=1}^{n_j}2Y_{ij}\,\bar{Y}_{..} \qquad \text{(rules of summation)}$$

$$= \sum_{j=1}^{k}\sum_{i=1}^{n_j}Y_{ij}^2 + \bar{Y}_{..}^2\sum_{j=1}^{k}n_j - 2\bar{Y}_{..}\sum_{j=1}^{k}\sum_{i=1}^{n_j}Y_{ij} \qquad \text{(rules of summation)}$$

$$= \sum_{j=1}^{k}\sum_{i=1}^{n_j}Y_{ij}^2 + \left[\frac{\sum_{j=1}^{k}\sum_{i=1}^{n_j}Y_{ij}}{\sum_{j=1}^{k}n_j}\right]^2\sum_{j=1}^{k}n_j - 2\left[\frac{\sum_{j=1}^{k}\sum_{i=1}^{n_j}Y_{ij}}{\sum_{j=1}^{k}n_j}\right]\sum_{j=1}^{k}\sum_{i=1}^{n_j}Y_{ij} \qquad \text{(substitution for } \bar{Y}_{..}\text{)}$$

$$= \sum_{j=1}^{k}\sum_{i=1}^{n_j}Y_{ij}^2 + \frac{\left(\sum_{j=1}^{k}\sum_{i=1}^{n_j}Y_{ij}\right)^2}{\sum_{j=1}^{k}n_j} - 2\frac{\left(\sum_{j=1}^{k}\sum_{i=1}^{n_j}Y_{ij}\right)^2}{\sum_{j=1}^{k}n_j} \qquad \text{(simple algebra)}$$

$$= \sum_{j=1}^{k}\sum_{i=1}^{n_j}Y_{ij}^2 - \frac{\left(\sum_{j=1}^{k}\sum_{i=1}^{n_j}Y_{ij}\right)^2}{\sum_{j=1}^{k}n_j} \qquad (a+b-2b=a-b)$$

SS_{ag}

$$\sum_{j=1}^{k}n_j\left(\bar{Y}_{.j}-\bar{Y}_{..}\right)^2 = \sum_{j=1}^{k}n_j\left(\bar{Y}_{.j}^2 + \bar{Y}_{..}^2 - 2\,\bar{Y}_{.j}\,\bar{Y}_{..}\right) \qquad \text{(squaring a binomial)}$$

$$= \sum_{j=1}^{k}n_j\bar{Y}_{.j}^2 + \sum_{j=1}^{k}n_j\bar{Y}_{..}^2 - \sum_{j=1}^{k}n_j 2\,\bar{Y}_{.j}\,\bar{Y}_{..} \qquad \text{(rules of summation)}$$

$$= \sum_{j=1}^{k} n_j \bar{Y}_{.j}^2 + \bar{Y}_{..}^2 \sum_{j=1}^{k} n_j - 2\bar{Y}_{..} \sum_{j=1}^{k} n_j \bar{Y}_{.j} \qquad \text{(rules of summation)}$$

$$= \sum_{j=1}^{k} n_j \left(\frac{\sum_{i=1}^{n_j} Y_{ij}}{n_j} \right)^2 + \left(\frac{\sum_{j=1}^{k} \sum_{i=1}^{n_j} Y_{ij}}{\sum_{j=1}^{k} n_j} \right)^2 \sum_{j=1}^{k} n_j - 2 \left(\frac{\sum_{j=1}^{k} \sum_{i=1}^{n_j} Y_{ij}}{\sum_{j=1}^{k} n_j} \right) \sum_{j=1}^{k} n_j \left(\frac{\sum_{i=1}^{n_j} Y_{ij}}{n_j} \right) \qquad \text{(substitution for } \bar{Y}_{..} \text{ and) } \bar{Y}_{.j}$$

$$= \sum_{j=1}^{k} n_j \frac{\left(\sum_{i=1}^{n_j} Y_{ij} \right)^2}{n_j^2} + \frac{\left(\sum_{j=1}^{k} \sum_{i=1}^{n_j} Y_{ij} \right)^2}{\left(\sum_{j=1}^{k} n_j \right)^2} \sum_{j=1}^{k} n_j - 2 \frac{\left(\sum_{j=1}^{k} \sum_{i=1}^{n_j} Y_{ij} \right)}{\sum_{j=1}^{k} n_j} \sum_{j=1}^{k} \frac{n_j}{n_j} \left(\sum_{i=1}^{n_j} Y_{ij} \right) \qquad \text{(simple algebra)}$$

$$= \sum_{j=1}^{k} \frac{\left(\sum_{i=1}^{n_j} Y_{ij} \right)^2}{n_j} + \frac{\left(\sum_{j=1}^{k} \sum_{i=1}^{n_j} Y_{ij} \right)^2}{\sum_{j=1}^{k} n_j} - 2 \frac{\left(\sum_{j=1}^{k} \sum_{i=1}^{n_j} Y_{ij} \right)^2}{\sum_{j=1}^{k} n_j} \qquad \text{(simple algebra)}$$

$$= \sum_{j=1}^{k} \frac{\left(\sum_{i=1}^{n_j} Y_{ij} \right)^2}{n_j} - \frac{\left(\sum_{j=1}^{k} \sum_{i=1}^{n_j} Y_{ij} \right)^2}{\sum_{j=1}^{k} n_j} \qquad (a + b - 2b = a - b)$$

Note: When the sample sizes are equal, these two computational formulae can be written more simply as:

$$SS_{\text{tot}} = \sum_{j=1}^{k} \sum_{i=1}^{n_j} Y_{ij}^2 - \frac{\left(\sum_{j=1}^{k} \sum_{i=1}^{n_j} Y_{ij} \right)^2}{kn},$$

and

$$SS_{\text{ag}} = \frac{1}{n} \sum_{j=1}^{k} \left(\sum_{i=1}^{n_j} Y_{ij} \right)^2 - \frac{\left(\sum_{j=1}^{k} \sum_{i=1}^{n_j} Y_{ij} \right)^2}{kn}$$

17

Multiple Comparison Procedures

INTRODUCTION

In the previous chapter we presented several different procedures for comparing more than two groups with regard to some aspect of location. The major part of the chapter focused on the one-way analysis of variance (ANOVA) for testing hypotheses about population means. We also described the Kruskal–Wallis procedure as a non-parametric alternative to ANOVA when the assumptions may be of concern. We then discussed some resampling approaches to the problem of comparing more than two groups, and concluded by mentioning the comparison of several groups with respect to proportions. Comparing several groups with regard to variances was treated previously (e.g., Levene's test, see Chapter 15).

All of these procedures address the overall question of whether there are any differences among the groups. The procedures described in Chapter 16 all address the omnibus null hypothesis: Are there differences somewhere within this set of groups? Although the result from the omnibus test provides evidence of whether there may be statistically significant differences, no information is provided regarding the nature of the differences. That is, which groups are different from which other groups? For example, it might be that the mean of Group 1 is different from that of Group 3, a *pairwise comparison*. On the other hand, it might be that the mean of Group 1 is different from the "mean of the means" of Groups 2 and 3 combined, *a complex comparison*. There are a number of procedures that one may employ to examine these more specific questions; the family of techniques is often labeled as *multiple comparison procedures* (MCPs), the focus of this chapter.

There are many different procedures for completing MCPs and many different contexts in which they can be employed. One decision to be made early in the analysis is whether the researcher is interested in the overall omnibus null hypothesis or in a small set of more specific hypotheses. If one wishes to examine the omnibus hypothesis and the results indicate non-significance, one would typically stop at that. However, if the omnibus null hypothesis is rejected, then the researcher would probably analyze the data further. In this case, the MCPs are labeled as *post hoc* comparisons. These MCPs are sometimes called "two-step procedures," in that one must reject the omnibus null hypothesis in order to proceed. Among the better known *post hoc* procedures are Fisher's Least Significant Difference test, the Studentized Newman–Keuls test, and Duncan's New Multiple Range test.

On the other hand, if one wishes to bypass the test of the omnibus null hypothesis and instead focus on a small set of hypotheses of particular interest, then the comparisons are completed and an adjustment is made on the error rate using some type of Bonferonni correction, which we will explain shortly in greater detail. Sometimes these contrasts are called *a priori* MCPs. There is a third category of MCPs known as "one-step tests," or *a posteriori* procedures, the nature of which is misunderstood by many researchers. Among these procedures are Tukey's Honestly Significant Difference (HSD) test, Scheffé's procedure, and Dunnett's Multiple Comparison test. These tests do not require an initial test of the omnibus null hypothesis to be significant. The HSD procedure tests all pairwise differences; Dunnett's procedure compares each of the treatment group means to a control group mean; and the Scheffé procedure allows us to test as many contrasts as you wish. For a more complete discussion of MCPs and some of the issues involved, see Kirk (1995, pp. 113–159) and/or Maxwell and Delaney (2000, pp. 129–160, 170–201). Other references include Toothaker (1991) and Winer, Brown, and Michels (1991). For a more theoretical treatment, you might look at Hochberg and Tamhane (1987).

As we noted at the beginning, conducting multiple tests will result in an inflated Type I error rate unless steps are taken to control for that. As we have suggested, there are a number of ways that have been devised to do this. We will classify these procedures into two categories. The first category consists of a general algebra of contrasts, along with the application of some Bonferroni-type approach to the control of the error rate. The second category consists of specific procedures that have been devised, most of which deal only with pairwise comparisons (e.g., Fisher's Least Significant Difference test, Duncan's New Multiple Range test, the Studentized Newman–Keuls test, Tukey's HSD test, Dunnett's procedure for comparing several means to a control group). Scheffé's procedure permits one to examine more complex contrasts. In this chapter, we will describe only a small subset of the techniques that are available.

First, we will present the algebra of multiple comparisons, sometimes called *contrasts*, followed by a discussion of different ways to control the Type I error rate. Typically, contrasts are completed within the context of *a priori* tests. In this case, the error rate is usually controlled with some form of Bonferroni procedure. If the contrasts are being completed in the context of *post hoc* exploration of possible differences, the usual approach is to employ Scheffé's approach to control error. We reiterate that Scheffé's procedure is actually a one-step procedure that does not require a significant omnibus test to proceed. An important point to note, however, is that it can be shown algebraically that, if the omnibus F-statistic is not significant, none of the possible Scheffé contrasts will be significant. Last, we will describe Tukey's HSD procedure, another one-step procedure. Like the Scheffé approach, it does not require a significant omnibus F-test, although it appears that most researchers apply it as a *post hoc* procedure. Unlike the Scheffé approach, Tukey's HSD test may result in significant pairwise differences, even though the omnibus F-statistic is not significant.

Explanations of these procedures will be accompanied by an example. After our presentation of each of the traditional approaches to multiple comparisons, we will consider resampling approaches when appropriate.

THE LOGIC AND ALGEBRA OF MULTIPLE COMPARISONS

In this section we will present the logic undergirding multiple comparisons and give a brief description of the mathematics involved. First, we need to define some terms. A *linear combination* is a weighted sum of values. Recall from your elementary school years being given a column of three or four numbers, with the task of adding them together. Actually, you were being asked to find a linear combination of the numbers, with the weights all being 1.0. Perhaps you recall the first day of a course in high school or college, during which the instructor may have announced that your final grade would be based on a weighting of homework, quizzes, the midterm exam, and the final exam. Perhaps the combination was 10% homework, 10% quizzes, 30% midterm exam, and 50% final exam. This, too, is a weighted composite or linear combination. Now, back to elementary school. Do you remember learning how to subtract? Imagine a simple problem like $(7 - 3) = ?$ This is a linear combination of two values where the weights are $+1$ and -1; linear combinations for which the sum of the weights equals zero are called *linear contrasts*. But wait! Do you recall that the numerator of the formula for the independent-samples t-test is the difference between two sample means? Thus, we could think of the numerator as a linear contrast between two means. The test of significance for the contrast is the ratio of the value of the contrast to the estimate of the standard error of the contrast. Hopefully, you also recall that the t-test is a special case of a one-way ANOVA.

Extending the t-Test to the k-Group Situation

Let's imagine sample data on four groups that we wish to compare in order to assess the hypothesis that the four groups are samples from the same population with regard to the mean:

$$H_0: \mu_1 = \mu_2 = \mu_3 = \mu_4 = \mu \tag{17.1}$$

On the other hand, suppose that we are not all that interested in the omnibus null hypothesis, but instead we wanted to test some specific *a priori* hypotheses:

$$H_0: \mu_1 = \mu_2 \tag{17.2}$$

$$H_0: \mu_1 = \frac{\mu_2 + \mu_3}{2} \tag{17.3}$$

$$H_0: \frac{\mu_1 + \mu_2 + \mu_3}{3} = \mu_4 \tag{17.4}$$

The hypothesis in Equation 17.2 could be rewritten as

$$H_0: \mu_1 - \mu_2 = 0 \tag{17.5}$$

If we look at Equation 17.5 carefully, hopefully we can see two weights; the coefficient for the first group is $+1$ and the coefficient for the second group is -1. As the third and fourth groups are not a part of this hypothesis, we will assign them both coefficients of 0. Thus, the complete set of coefficients is $(1, -1, 0, 0)$. In a similar fashion, we could rewrite Equation 17.3 and see that the set of weights (i.e., contrast coefficients) is $(1, -\frac{1}{2}, -\frac{1}{2}, 0)$. For Equation 17.4, we should be able to derive a set of coefficients $(\frac{1}{3}, \frac{1}{3}, \frac{1}{3}, -1)$. At this point, we can distinguish the first set of coefficients from the second and third set; the first set contains only two non-zero values, while the second and third contain more than two non-zero values. This implies that the first comparison involves only two groups, or is a pairwise comparison, while the second and third are complex comparisons involving more than two groups. Also, note that the coefficients for the pairwise comparison contains only integers, while those of the complex comparisons contain fractions. Unless you are one of the few students who enjoyed complex fractions in elementary school, it would be nice to convert everything to integers. Furthermore, the third set of coefficients contains fractions that contain "repeating decimals," which are difficult to represent to a computer program. Is ⅓ set to .33, .333, .3333, or what? Thus, it might be wise to rewrite the second set of coefficients to (2, –1, –1, 0) and the third set of coefficients to (1, 1, 1, –3). Thus we can avoid two problems: working with complex fractions and the rounding error created by repeating decimals.

As we progress we are going to deviate from the traditional notation, which uses the symbols ψ and $\hat{\psi}$ for the population and sample values of the contrast. To maintain the system that we detailed very early in this book (Greek characters for parameters and Latin characters for sample estimates), we will use δ (delta) for the parameter and d for the sample estimate of δ.

In the preceding paragraphs we have shown you how each of the three hypotheses of interest can be expressed as a set of coefficients. Those coefficients can be used to generate a t-test for each of the hypotheses as shown in Technical Note 17.1. Before we provide some computational examples, we need to address the issue of controlling the error rate.

Controlling the Type I Error Rate for MCPs

As we noted earlier, the use of MCPs creates a situation in which we are conducting several tests; the more tests we complete, the more likely it is that we will make one or more Type I errors. Thus, all of the various MCP procedures must employ some way to control for the inflated error rate. Following the example above, imagine that we have a study with several groups and that we want to test four specific hypotheses, rather than the omnibus hypothesis. These four hypotheses are detailed *a priori* and are sometimes called *planned comparisons*. One of the earliest techniques for error-rate control is the *Bonferroni technique*. There are several different ways to conceptualize the error-rate control, but one of the more common is the *familywise error rate*, the probability of making one or more Type I errors in making a number of tests. If you wanted to set the familywise error rate to .05, the Bonferroni technique would test each of the four hypotheses at an α' of .05/4, or .0125. Stated more formally,

$$\text{Familywise error rate } (\alpha) \leq \sum_{k=1}^{m} \alpha_k \tag{17.6}$$

where m is the number of planned comparisons. This correction for the error rate is based on Boole's inequality. The *less than or equal to sign* is the result of the tests not having to be independent. Independent (*orthogonal*) tests are those for which the results of one test do not inform you about the results of another test. For example, if we compare the mean of Group 1 to the mean of Group 2, the result does not give us any information about the result of a comparison of the means of Groups 3 and 4. On the other hand, if we compare the means of Groups 1 and 2, and then compare the mean of Group 1 to the mean of Groups 2 and 3 combined, these two tests are not independent, as the "1 to 2" difference is a part of both comparisons. If this is the case, we label the comparisons as *non-orthogonal*. As it turns out, the Bonferroni correction has been found to be overly conservative. With independent contrasts, it is a little too conservative. With dependent contrasts it is more substantially conservative, with the degree of conservatism depending on the degree of dependency in the contrasts. Consequently, several alternatives have been developed. One of these is the Šidák correction, which is restricted to situations in which the comparisons are all independent; we consider this overly restrictive and will not describe it here.

One of the first alternatives to the Bonferroni correction was the Bonferroni–Holm sequentially rejective procedure (Holm, 1979). This procedure controls the familywise error rate, α, by running the desired comparisons, rank ordering the p-values, and comparing the ranked p-values to a set of adjusted values of α. Specifically, let's assume that we are going to complete four planned comparisons with a familywise error rate set at .05. The smallest p-value is compared to $\alpha/4$, or .0125. If it is not significant, the process stops. However, if it is significant, the second smallest p-value is compared to $\alpha/3$, or .0167. In like fashion, if the second comparison is not significant, the process stops at this point. However, if the second comparison is significant, the next p-value is compared to $\alpha/2$, or .025. If the third comparison is significant, the last comparison is tested at $\alpha/1$, or .05. Thus, rather than making all four tests at the .0125 level as the Bonferroni correction would suggest, this sequential procedure provides us with more power if we get past the first comparison.

Another sequential procedure has been recommended by Benjamini and Hochberg (1995), and is sometimes called the *false discovery rate* (FDR) approach. It is similar to the Holm approach in that the p-values are ranked, but it differs slightly in the way in which the adjustment is made. Instead of decreasing the denominator at each stage, the numerator is adjusted. The first test is conducted at the $\alpha/4$ level, or .0125. If the first comparison is significant, the second comparison is tested at $2 \times \alpha/4$, or .025. The third comparison would be tested at $3 \times \alpha/4$, or .0375. The fourth comparison would be tested at the $4 \times \alpha/4$, or .05 level.

An Example

For our example we are going to reuse the data from the first example in Chapter 16, augmenting the data by adding a fourth sample of 10 Asian children. The data are contained in Table 17.1.

For this example, let's assume that we have labeled the White, African American, Hispanic, and Asian groups as 1, 2, 3, and 4, respectively, and that we have four specific questions we would like to pursue. We would like to compare the White group to the average of all of the others, the African American group to the Hispanic group, the Asian group to the average of all of the others, and the White group to the Asian group. The hypotheses stated formally are, respectively:

$$\mu_1 = \frac{\mu_2 + \mu_3 + \mu_4}{3} \tag{17.7}$$

$$\mu_2 = \mu_3 \tag{17.8}$$

$$\frac{\mu_1 + \mu_2 + \mu_3}{3} = \mu_4 \tag{17.9}$$

Table 17.1 Pre-kindergarten general knowledge test scores for White, African American, Hispanic, and Asian children ($n = 10$)

White	African American	Hispanic	Asian
31	14	23	11
23	34	26	21
32	18	39	26
27	21	14	28
28	30	28	18
25	25	13	24
29	22	12	19
33	27	34	18
36	16	31	12
39	16	12	11

$$\mu_1 = \mu_4 \tag{17.10}$$

For the first two comparisons, we will show you how to complete them by hand, after which we will show you an R script that will complete all four of the tests. At this point, we assume that you are able to read the data in Table 17.1 into R and obtain such things as the four sample means and sample sizes, in addition to the mean square among groups, MS_{wg}. We found the four group means to be 30.3, 22.3, 23.2, and 18.8, respectively. The MS_{wg} is 51.32. For the first comparison, we found d_1 to equal:

$$d_1 = (3)(30.3) + (-1)(22.3) + (-1)(23.2) + (-1)(18.8) = 26.6 \tag{17.11}$$

Based on the results in Technical Note 17.1, we found the variance of d_1 to be:

$$\text{var}(d_1) = MS_{wg} \sum_{j=1}^{k} \frac{c_j^2}{n_j} = 51.32\left(\frac{3^2}{10} + \frac{-1^2}{10} + \frac{-1^2}{10} + \frac{-1^2}{10}\right) = 61.58 \tag{17.12}$$

At this point, we can compute the value of the test statistic, either as t or F. We prefer the F-statistic as it makes it easier to derive the two-tailed p-value.

$$F_{obs} = \frac{26.6^2}{61.58} = 11.49 \tag{17.13}$$

With 1 and 36 degrees of freedom, the p-value is .0017. Now, moving to the second comparison,

$$d_2 = (0)(30.3) + (1)(22.3) + (-1)(23.2) + (0)(18.8) = -0.9 \tag{17.14}$$

$$\text{var}(d_2) = MS_{wg} \sum_{j=1}^{k} \frac{c_j^2}{n_j} = 51.32\left(\frac{0^2}{10} + \frac{1^2}{10} + \frac{-1^2}{10} + \frac{0^2}{10}\right) = 10.26 \tag{17.15}$$

$$F_{obs} = \frac{-.9^2}{10.26} = .079 \tag{17.16}$$

The corresponding p-value is .78. We now direct your attention to Script 17.1 (see the book website) in which we have written the commands to complete all four planned comparisons.

THE EXAMPLE WITH R   Running the commands in Script 17.1, we obtained the following results, which have been edited. The p-values are in bold. For additional material related to R, see Bretz, Hathorn, & Westfall (2011).

```
> # First Contrast
> c1 <- c(3, -1, -1, -1)
> d1
```

```
[1] 26.6
> fc1
[1] 11.49009
> cat("The p-value for the first contrast is", p1,
>    "\n")
The p-value for the first contrast is 0.001709669
>
> # Second Contrast
> c2 <- c(0, 1, -1, 0)
> d2
[1] -0.9
> fc2
[1] 0.07892173
> p2
> cat("The p-value for the second contrast is", p2,
>    "\n")
The p-value for the second contrast is 0.7803723
>
> #Third Contrast
> c3 <- c(1, 1, 1, -3)
> d3
[1] 19.4
> fc3
[1] 6.111725
> p3
> cat("The p-value for the third contrast is", p3,
>    "\n")
The p-value for the third contrast is 0.01828921
>
> #Fourth Contrast
> c4 <- c(1, 0, 0, -1)
> d4
[1] 11.5
> fc4
[1] 12.88568
> p4
> cat("The p-value for the fourth contrast is", p4,
>    "\n")
The p-value for the fourth contrast is 0.0009790635
```

As you can see, the four p-values are .0017, .7804, .0183, and .0009 respectively. Using the FDR approach for error-rate control, these four values would be ranked from smallest (.0009) to largest (.7804) and compared to an adjusted α as follows: .0125, .025, .0375, and .05 in order. Thus, the first, third, and fourth planned comparisons are significant; the second comparison is not significant.

We have provided Scripts 17.2, 17.3, and 17.4 as templates for you to complete as many as five contrasts on three, four, and five group designs; they are contained on the book website with the supplementary materials for this chapter. These scripts have been written with the assumption that you will be entering the data with the **c( )** function during the session. If, on the other hand, you are reading the data in from a text file and creating a **data.frame**, you would establish the cell sizes and cell means slightly differently, For example, let's assume that your problem has three groups. After reading in the data and creating the **f.group** variable:

```
cell.size <- table(f.group)
n1 <- cell.size[1]
n2 <- cell.size[2]
n3 <- cell.size[3]
means <- tapply(dv, f.group, mean)
```

We limited the number of contrasts to five as that appears to be a typical "maximum" number. If you wish to do more, you should be able to modify the scripts to do so. All you would need to do is to supply the data for the groups and the coefficients corresponding to the planned comparisons you wish to complete. At the end, you would need to apply the Bonferroni–Holm or FDR procedure for error-rate control. At the very end of the scripts, we provide for a Scheffé type of error-rate control. A more detailed explanation of the Scheffé type of correction is provided later in this chapter. As in previous chapters, we will now show you a resampling approach to planned comparisons.

Resampling Procedures for Planned Comparisons

The resampling approach relies on comparing our observed test statistic to an empirical distribution that is formed by computing the test statistic for many possible samples from the observed data set. Although this logic flows from the examples illustrated in previous chapters, a question arises. Should we resample observations from all the groups? Or should we restrict our sampling to the groups that were part of the contrast? If the groups which are not involved in the contrast have means which are quite different, their inclusion in the permutations will affect the distribution of the test statistic. Based on material presented in Hochberg and Tamhane (1987, p. 267), we recommend that you look at permutations involving only the groups involved in the contrast. Let's look at how we would use a resampling approach with the four contrasts in the previous section.

An Example

The first two contrasts previously examined were a comparison of the mean of the first group to the mean of the other three $(3, -1, -1, -1)$ and a comparison of the mean of the second group to the third group $(0, 1, -1, 0)$. The third contrast compared the mean of the fourth group to the mean of the other three groups $(-1, -1, -1, 3)$, and the fourth comparison compared the mean of the first group to the mean of the fourth group $(1, 0, 0, -1)$. We have written Script 17.5 to carry out these four tests. The critical point to note is that we have combined different subsets of groups, where each subset includes only the original data from the groups involved in the contrast. As the first and third contrast involve all four groups, we created the vector *dv1234*. The second contrast involves only the second and third groups, so we created the vector *dv23*; the fourth contrast involves only the first and fourth groups, hence *dv14*. We have written Script 17.5 to complete the testing of these contrasts with resampling/permutation procedures.

Running the script twice, each using a sample of one million permutations for each of the contrasts, we found Monte Carlo *p*-values for the first contrast of .00167 and .00162; for the first contrast, the classic, distribution-based *p*-value was .0017. Similarly, for the second contrast, .8334 and .8327 (distribution based = .7804); for the third contrast, .02854 and .02897 (distribution based = .0183); and for the fourth contrast, .00033 and .00030 (distribution based = .0009). As you can see, the resampled *p*-values are quite comparable to the distribution-based *p*-values for this particular example. Larger discrepancies would be anticipated in examples where the distributional assumptions are less appropriate. We now turn our attention to an alternative way to control the Type I error rate if you want to look at many comparisons.

Controlling the Error Rate for Many Comparisons: The Scheffé Approach

If there are many comparisons of interest, any of the Bonferroni adjustments may be overly conservative. For example, with four groups there are 25 different conventional contrasts that can be defined, and if one wants to use differential weights to define the contrasts as in Equation 17.17 the number of contrasts becomes infinite.

$$.2\mu_1 + .8\mu_2 = \mu_3 \tag{17.17}$$

Scheffé (1959) described a procedure based on simultaneous confidence intervals that allows researchers to conduct as many contrasts as they wish while controlling the familywise error rate at α. In order to effect this control, he recommended an adjusted critical value of the F-statistic, F', defined as

$$F' = (k-1)F_{\alpha, k-1, N-k}$$

or $$\tag{17.18}$$

$$t' = \sqrt{(k-1)F_{\alpha, k-1, N-k}}$$

In our example, we have four groups with 10 observations within each group, we could calculate F' as $(4 - 1) \times 2.866$, or 8.598. Thus, if we calculated the test statistics as F-statistics, we would test each result against a value of 8.598 rather than ranking the *p*-values as we did with *a priori* contrasts. The comparable adjusted value for *t*-statistics would be $\sqrt{8.598}$, or 2.932. We note in passing that this is equivalent to testing each Scheffé contrast at an adjusted α of .0029. In our presentation of *a priori* contrasts, we looked at four contrasts resulting in F-statistics of 11.49, .079, 6.11, and 12.88, respectively. Tested against the Scheffé standard, only the first and fourth contrasts would be determined to be significant, whereas the *a priori* standard would also find the third contrast to be significant. The underlying message is that, for a specific contrast, you have more statistical power if that contrast is included in a small set of planned contrasts rather than one of many *a posteriori* contrasts.

The last MCP procedure we wish to describe is Tukey's HSD. Tukey's HSD test does not use the algebra of contrasts and is confined to testing only pairwise differences. It is preferable to the Scheffé procedure in situations where the researcher wants to make all the pairwise comparisons, but no complex comparisons, because it has more power. Like the Scheffé procedure, it was designed as a one-step procedure, although many applied statisticians mistakenly believe that one must have a significant omnibus F-test before applying the HSD test.

Tukey's HSD Test

John W. Tukey (1915–2000) made numerous contributions to the fields of theoretical mathematics and applied statistics. It was he who "invented" the stem-and-leaf plot as well as the box-and-whiskers plot, now known as the "box plot." In addition, he coined the terms "software" and "bit" (binary digit). Our focus here is on his contribution to the literature of MCPs. After several years of considering the problem of inflated error rates in multiple tests, he presented a solution to the problem in a mimeographed monograph in 1953 (Tukey, 1953). Until it was published in one of a series of volumes known as *J. W. Tukey's Collected Works* during the mid-1980s and early 1990s, the work was reputed to be the most often cited work that had never been published.

Although we have no way of knowing the train of thought that led Tukey to develop the HSD procedure, we will pull together information that we have already presented to provide you with an understanding of the logic that he may have used.

First, recall the formula for the independent-samples t-test assuming equal variances:

$$t_{obs} = \frac{\bar{Y}_{.1} - \bar{Y}_{.2}}{\sqrt{s^2_{pooled}\left[(1/n_1)+(1/n_2)\right]}} \tag{17.19}$$

Given more than two groups, the omnibus test does not provide information about which groups might be different from which other groups. Assuming that we are only interested in comparing one group to another group in a pairwise fashion, a naïve approach would be to conduct multiple t-tests. As appealing as that appears, such an approach is subject to the same difficulty facing multiple contrasts; each comparison runs the risk of making a Type I error, and the more comparisons that are conducted, the more likely it is that one or more Type I errors will occur within the set of tests. If we were to complete four independent contrasts at the .05 level, the probability of making at least one Type I error would be equal to one minus the probability of making no errors, or $1 - (1 - .05)^4$, or about .185, which most people would regard as unacceptable.

Thinking back to another early point we made in discussing the range as a measure of dispersion, recall that we noted that a problem with the range is that it tends to increase with an increase in sample size. It turns out that there is a mathematical probability distribution that shares this property, the studentized range distribution. First, think of the set of means as a random sample of r independent sample means. We define R_{max} as the range of this set of means (largest mean − smallest mean). The studentized range (q_r) is defined as R_{max}/s, where s is our estimate of σ. For Tukey, the value of r was equal to k, the number of groups. Thus, assuming equal sample sizes, Tukey argued that Equation 17.19 could be revised to:

$$t_{obs} = \frac{\bar{Y}_{.j} - \bar{Y}_{.j'}}{\sqrt{s^2_{pooled}(2/n)}} \tag{17.20}$$

Now, imagining the world of statistics before computers and calculators, it would have been reasonable to try to reduce the amount of hand calculation. Thus, the factor of 2 was moved to the left side of the equation and the q-distribution was substituted for the t-distribution. In addition, the MS_{wg} was inserted as s^2_{pooled}:

$$q_{obs} = \frac{\overline{Y}_{.j} - \overline{Y}_{.j'}}{\sqrt{MS_{wg} / n}} \tag{17.21}$$

Equation 17.21 would be used to generate a q-statistic for each possible pair of sample means, and each observed value of q would be tested against the tabled value of q based on level of significance, number of means in the study (r), and the df_{wg}. That is, the critical value of q is the same value for every comparison made. In our example with four groups, we can find the number of unique pairwise comparisons using combinations; the number of combinations of four objects, taking two of them, is equal to six. Thus we would find the six calculated values of q and determine whether any of them exceeded the tabled value. Once again considering a world without easy access to calculators or computers, Tukey rewrote Equation 17.21 as:

$$\overline{Y}_{.j} - \overline{Y}_{.j'} = q_{obs}\sqrt{MS_{wg} / n} \tag{17.22}$$

Thus, if the observed difference was larger than the right side when $q_{\alpha,r,df}$ was substituted for q_{obs}, then the difference was larger than one would expect by chance. The critical difference was called the *Honestly Significant Difference* (*HSD*):

$$HSD = q_{\alpha,r,df_{wg}}\sqrt{\frac{MS_{wg}}{n}} \tag{17.23}$$

Looking at Equation 17.23, we can see that equal sample sizes are assumed. If the cell sizes are unequal, an adjustment is necessary. Years ago, it was recommended to find the harmonic mean of the samples sizes and insert the result in place of n. The harmonic mean is defined as the number of observations divided by the sum of the reciprocals of the observations. Kramer (1956) suggested an alternative, now the preferred approach, and the default included in most statistical software, including R. Rather than using the harmonic mean of all the sample sizes, Kramer suggested using the harmonic mean of the sizes of the two samples involved in each pairwise contrast. Thus, Equation 17.23 can be rewritten as:

$$HSD = q_{\alpha,r,df_{wg}}\sqrt{\left[MS_{wg}\left[\left(1/n_j\right) + \left(1/n_{j'}\right)\right]\right] / 2} \tag{17.24}$$

Of course, if the sample sizes are the same, Equation 17.24 simplifies to Equation 17.23.

We have included an abbreviated version of the studentized range distribution in Table A.9 in Appendix A. The values of the distribution are easily obtained in R with the **qtukey( )** function. Before we show how, let's take a quick look at the tabled values. Within any row, you will see that as the number of means increases, the critical values of q increase. Thus, the more means in the study, the larger the *HSD*, all other things held equal. Now turning to R, we will justify the move from Equation 17.20 to Equation 17.21. Think about a situation with only two groups, with 10 cases in each group. We could analyze the data with either a t-test or an ANOVA. The df for the t-test would be 18, the same value as the df_{wg} for the ANOVA. Looking at Table A.9, you can see that the value of q for two means and 18 df_{wg} is 2.971. In R,

```
> qtukey(.95, 2, 18)
[1] 2.971152
```

Now consider:

```
> sqrt(2)*qt(.975, 18)
[1] 2.971152
```

As you can see, the values in the first column of the table of the studentized range distribution are the values from the corresponding t-distribution, multiplied by $\sqrt{2}$.

An Example

Looking at the data from earlier in this chapter, the pre-kindergarten General Knowledge test scores for White, African American, Hispanic, and Asian children, we started with Script 17.1 to construct a **data.frame** and find the means. We also completed an ANOVA in order to obtain the MS_{wg}, which we need in order to calculate HSD. We reiterate that one need not look at the omnibus F-statistic prior to doing Tukey's test; Tukey's HSD test is a one-step procedure and could constitute the set of planned contrasts. The revised commands appear in Script 17.6 in the supplementary materials for this chapter (see the book website).

```
> tapply(dv, f.group, mean)
    w    b    h    a
 30.3 22.3 23.2 18.8
> model <- aov(dv ~ f.group, data = data)
> summary(model)
            Df Sum Sq Mean Sq F value   Pr(>F)
f.group      3  697.7 232.567   4.532 0.008531
Residuals   36 1847.4  51.317
```

First, we will show you how to calculate HSD by hand, after which we will implement the procedure in R. By tradition, the first step in completing Tukey's HSD test is to rank order the means from largest to smallest, and then find all the unique possible differences. We show the results in Table 17.2.

Table 17.2 Ranked group means and differences between means for White, Hispanic, African American, and Asian children on the pre-kindergarten general knowledge test

		White	Hispanic	African American	Asian
		30.3	23.2	22.3	18.8
White	30.3	NA	7.1	8.0	11.5
Hispanic	23.2		NA	0.9	4.4
African American	22.3			NA	3.5
Asian	18.8				NA

Given that the sample sizes are equal, we can use Equation 17.23 to find *HSD*. We need to find the critical value of the studentized range statistic from Table A.9 based on $r = 4$ and $df_{wg} = 36$. We note that there is no table entry of 36; we see the value for 35 is 3.814 and the value for 40 is 3.791. We could argue that the value for 36 should be about one-fifth of the way between those two values and use a process of linear interpolation to estimate the value to be 3.8094, or we could use R:

```
> qtukey(.95, 4, 36)
[1] 3.808798
```

If we round the value returned by R to three decimal places, we obtain 3.809 as our estimate of q. Using the value of the MS_{wg} (51.317) from above:

$$HSD = q_{\alpha,r,df_{wg}} \sqrt{\frac{MS_{wg}}{n}} = 3.809 \sqrt{\frac{51.317}{10}} = 8.63 \qquad (17.25)$$

Thus, we find that any difference between two means that equals or exceeds 8.63 should be declared a significant difference. Looking at the table of differences (Table 17.2), we see that the only difference larger than 8.63 is the difference between the White and Asian students (11.5). It is common practice to summarize these results in a table of homogeneous subsets as we have in Table 17.3. Groups appearing within the same column are not different from one another. Note that only the White and Asian groups do not appear within the same column.

Table 17.3 Summarizing the results from Tukey's HSD test with homogeneous subsets

Group	Homogeneous subset	
	1	2
White	30.3	
Hispanic	23.2	23.2
African American	22.3	22.3
Asian		18.8

Now, let's see how easy it is to get R to complete Tukey's HSD test. After creating the **data. frame**, we used the **aov( )** function to create an object named *model*.

```
> TukeyHSD(model)
  Tukey multiple comparisons of means
    95% family-wise confidence level

Fit: aov(formula = dv ~ f.group, data = data)

$f.group
      diff       lwr        upr      p adj
b-w   -8.0   -16.62814  0.6281404  0.0774065
h-w   -7.1   -15.72814  1.5281404  0.1381576
```

```
a-w  -11.5  -20.12814  -2.8718596  0.0051798
h-b    0.9   -7.72814   9.5281404  0.9921273
a-b   -3.5  -12.12814   5.1281404  0.6963040
a-h   -4.4  -13.02814   4.2281404  0.5237238
```

Looking at the column on the right, we note that the only adjusted p-value less than .05 is the one for the pairwise difference between the "a" (Asian) and "w" (White) groups. This is in perfect agreement with our hand computations.

CHAPTER SUMMARY

In this chapter, we have presented a number of techniques for looking at specific differences between/among groups within the context of three or more groups. Specifically, these procedures have been designed as supplements or alternatives to the omnibus F-statistic in one-way ANOVA.

There are a number of different ways in which one might proceed. At times, one is faced with a set of data for which there may be no specific questions of interest. In this case, we would advise that you conduct the omnibus F-statistic, and if it is not significant, stop. On the other hand, if the omnibus test indicates that there are differences among the groups in some way, then we would recommend that you apply either the Tukey HSD procedure for pairwise differences or the Scheffé procedure if you are interested in complex comparisons or some combination of both complex and pairwise comparisons.

At other times, one may be dealing with situations in which there is a relatively small set of questions that have been framed *a priori*. In this case, we recommend that you use the planned comparison approach, implementing some sort of control over the familywise error rate. While the Bonferroni approach is traditional, we would recommend one of the more recent developments, either the Bonferroni–Holm approach or the FDR approach; the latter is the more powerful of the two approaches.

Key Terms

A posteriori procedures	Linear contrasts
a priori procedures	Multiple comparison procedures
Benjamini–Hochberg FDR	Non-orthogonal comparisons
Bonferroni technique	Orthogonal comparisons
Bonferroni–Holm procedure	Pairwise comparisons
Complex comparison	Planned comparisons
Contrast coefficients	*Post hoc* comparisons
False discovery rate	Scheffé comparisons
Familywise error rate	Tukey's HSD test

REFERENCES

Benjamini, Y., & Hochberg, Y. (1995). Controlling the false discovery rate: a practical and powerful approach to multiple testing. *Journal of the Royal Statistical Society, Series B*, *57*, 289–300.

Bretz, F., Hathorn, T., & Westfall, P. (2011). *Multiple comparisons using R*. Boca Raton, FL: CRC Press.

Hochberg, Y., & Tamhane, A. C. (1987). *Multiple comparison procedures*. New York: John Wiley.

Holm, S. (1979). A simple sequentially rejective multiple test procedure. *Scandinavian Journal of Statistics*, *6*, 65–70.

Kirk, R. E. (1995). *Experimental design: Procedures for the behavioral sciences* (3rd ed.). Pacific Grove, CA: Brooks/Cole.

Kramer, C. Y. (1956). Extension of multiple range test to group means with unequal number of replications. *Biometrics*, *12*, 307–310.

Maxwell, S. E., & Delaney, H. D. (2000). *Designing experiments and analyzing data: a model comparison perspective*. Mahwah, NJ: Lawrence Erlbaum Associates.

Scheffé, H. (1959). *The analysis of variance*. New York: John Wiley.

Toothaker, L. E. (1991). *Multiple comparisons for researchers*. Newbury Park, CA: Sage.

Tukey, J. W. (1953). The problem of multiple comparisons. Unpublished manuscript reprinted in: *The collected works of John W. Tukey*, Volume 8, 1994, H. I. Braun (Ed.). New York: Chapman and Hall.

Winer, B. J., Brown, D. R., & Michels, K. M. (1991). *Statistical principles of experimental design* (3rd ed.). New York: McGraw-Hill.

PRACTICE QUESTIONS

1. A researcher is comparing four groups using a series of planned comparisons. If the researcher wishes to compare the first group to the average of the last two groups, the coefficients for this comparison would be:

    a. 1, 0, –1, –1
    b. 1, –1, 0, 0
    c. 0, 0, –1, –1
    d. 2, 0, –1, –1.

2. A researcher is making a set of planned comparisons. If the coefficients for the first comparison are 1, 0, –1 and the sample means are 70, 65, and 55, what is the estimated value of the contrast, d?

    a. 0.
    b. 5.
    c. 10.
    d. 15.
    e. 20.

3. A researcher is comparing four groups with equal sample sizes. Do the coefficients 1, –1, 0, 0 define a comparison that is independent of the one defined by the coefficients 0, 0, 1, –1?

    a. Yes.
    b. No.

4. If a researcher states that he controlled the overall Type I error rate to .05 by using a Bonferroni adjustment when making four planned comparisons, what value of α was used for each comparison?

    a. .20.
    b. .05.
    c. .025.

d. .0167.

e. .0125.

5. A researcher is making comparisons among groups. Consider the comparison of Group 1 to Group 2. An outlier in the third group would have what effect on the estimated contrast value, d?

    a. Increase the value of d.
    b. Decrease the value of d.
    c. No effect on the value of d.
    d. The direction of the effect on d cannot be determined.

6. A researcher is making comparisons among groups. Consider the comparison of Group 1 to Group 2. The presence of an outlier in the third group would have what effect on the F statistic from the distribution-based approach for testing the contrast?

    a. Increase the value of F.
    b. Decrease the value of F.
    c. No effect on the value of F.
    d. The direction of the effect on F cannot be determined.

7. Consider a researcher wishing to make all possible pairwise comparisons among five groups. Relative to the Tukey HSD test, the Scheffé procedure is:

    a. more likely to find differences
    b. less likely to find differences
    c. equally likely to find differences.

8. A researcher is making comparisons among five groups. She is interested in all of the possible pairwise comparisons, plus four complex comparisons. What analysis would you recommend?

    a. Planned comparisons with a Bonferroni adjustment.
    b. Planned comparisons with the Bonferroni–Holm sequentially rejective procedure.
    c. Scheffé procedure.
    d. Tukey's HSD test.

9. A researcher is making comparisons among five groups. She is interested in three specific comparisons (two complex comparisons and one pairwise comparison). Which of the following methods would you recommend?

    a. Planned comparisons with a Bonferroni adjustment.
    b. Planned comparisons with the Bonferroni–Holm sequentially rejective procedure.
    c. Scheffé procedure.
    d. Tukey procedure.

EXERCISES

The *ecls2755* data set was stratified by the child's composite race and 15 observations were drawn from the White, African American, Hispanic, Asian, and Native American groups using simple random sampling. The pre-kindergarten mathematics T-scores were extracted and are presented in Table 17.4. These data will be used to complete the exercises associated with this chapter.

Table 17.4 Pre-kindergarten mathematics test scores for White, African American, Hispanic, Asian, and Native American children ($n = 15$)

White	African American	Hispanic	Asian	Native American
72	45	69	40	54
59	54	60	62	56
53	56	63	50	66
65	66	43	49	56
65	52	52	61	62
55	37	28	55	63
46	39	56	55	64
56	63	51	38	57
52	35	53	58	49
54	42	64	40	55
59	53	55	43	36
56	60	63	46	56
62	47	58	49	81
45	62	59	38	76
46	51	47	56	53

17.1. Using these data, a researcher was interested in completing four planned contrasts to address specific questions. In particular, she was interested in comparing the mean of the White group to the mean of all of the other groups, the mean of the White group to the mean of the Asian group, the mean of the African American and Hispanic groups to the mean of the Native American group, and the mean of the mean of the Asian group to the mean of the Native American group. Use the data from Table 17.4 and R to complete and evaluate these four planned contrasts.

17.2. A different researcher with access to the same data file did not have specific questions to address. His analytic strategy was to examine the omnibus hypothesis of possible group differences and then, if group differences were found, probe the data. Using the data from Table 17.4 and R, test the omnibus null hypothesis of no differences among the means. Assuming that you will find some indication of differences, test the same contrasts as indicated in Exercise 17.1 using Scheffé's procedure. Summarize your results.

17.3. A third researcher wished to approach the data set with yet another strategy. She was interested *a priori* in examining all possible pairwise differences. Using the data, conduct all possible comparisons for the five groups and summarize the results.

TECHNICAL NOTES

Technical Note 17.1. The Variance of a Linear Contrast

A contrast is the representation of a hypothesis regarding the population(s). For example, in the context of a four-group completely randomized one-way ANOVA, one might want to test the hypothesis that:

$$H_0: \quad \mu_1 = \frac{\mu_3 + \mu_4}{2} \tag{17.26}$$

If this null hypothesis is true, then it is also true that:

$$\delta = \sum_{j=1}^{4} c_j \mu_j = 1 \times \mu_1 + 0 \times \mu_2 - \frac{1}{2}\mu_3 - \frac{1}{2}\mu_4 = 0 \tag{17.27}$$

Using sample means as estimates of population means, we would estimate this contrast as:

$$d = \sum_{j=1}^{4} c_j \bar{Y}_{.j} = 1 \times \bar{Y}_{.1} + 0 \times \bar{Y}_{.2} - \frac{1}{2}\bar{Y}_{.3} - \frac{1}{2}\bar{Y}_{.4} \tag{17.28}$$

Assuming the null hypothesis, we could expect the value of to be close to zero. More formally,

$$E(d) = 0 \tag{17.29}$$

Assuming normal distributions and equivalent population variances,

$$\frac{d - 0}{sd(d)} \tag{17.30}$$

should be distributed as a t-distribution with the appropriate df, based on sample sizes. Actually these test statistics may be calculated as t-statistics with df_{wg} or as F-statistics with 1 and df_{wg} degrees of freedom. Thus, the key is to derive the variance of d. First, in the case of k groups, we define d as:

$$d = \sum_{j=1}^{k} c_j \bar{Y}_{.j} = c_1 \bar{Y}_{.1} + c_2 \bar{Y}_{.2} + c_3 \bar{Y}_{.3} + \dots + c_j \bar{Y}_{.j} + \dots + c_k \bar{Y}_{.k} \tag{17.31}$$

Thus,

$$\text{var}(d) = \text{var}\left(c_1 \bar{Y}_{.1} + c_2 \bar{Y}_{.2} + c_3 \bar{Y}_{.3} + \dots + c_j \bar{Y}_{.j} + \dots + c_k \bar{Y}_{.k}\right) \tag{17.32}$$

Assuming that the samples are independent,

$$\text{var}(d) = \text{var}\left(c_1 \bar{Y}_{.1}\right) + \text{var}\left(c_2 \bar{Y}_{.2}\right) + \dots + \text{var}\left(c_j \bar{Y}_{.j}\right) + \dots + \text{var}\left(c_k \bar{Y}_{.k}\right) \tag{17.33}$$

which can be rewritten as

$$\text{var}(d) = c_1^2 \, \text{var}\left(\bar{Y}_{.1}\right) + c_2^2 \, \text{var}\left(\bar{Y}_{.2}\right) + \dots + c_j^2 \, \text{var}\left(\bar{Y}_{.j}\right) + \dots + c_k^2 \, \text{var}\left(\bar{Y}_{.k}\right) \tag{17.34}$$

In turn,

$$\text{var}(d) = c_1^2 \frac{\sigma_1^2}{n_1} + c_2^2 \frac{\sigma_2^2}{n_2} + \dots + c_j^2 \frac{\sigma_j^2}{n_j} + \dots + c_k^2 \frac{\sigma_k^2}{n_k} \tag{17.35}$$

If we assume homogeneity of population variances,

$$\operatorname{var}(d) = c_1^2 \frac{\sigma^2}{n_1} + c_2^2 \frac{\sigma^2}{n_2} + \ldots + c_j^2 \frac{\sigma^2}{n_j} + \ldots + c_k^2 \frac{\sigma^2}{n_k} \tag{17.36}$$

We can then factor out the σ^2:

$$\operatorname{var}(d) = \sigma^2 \left(\frac{c_1^2}{n_1} + \frac{c_2^2}{n_2} + \ldots + \frac{c_j^2}{n_j} + \ldots + \frac{c_k^2}{n_k} \right) = \sigma^2 \sum_{j=1}^{k} \frac{c_j^2}{n_j} \tag{17.37}$$

Within the context of a one-way ANOVA, the MS_{wg} is our estimator of σ^2, so we can write:

$$\operatorname{var}(d) = MS_{wg} \sum_{j=1}^{k} \frac{c_j^2}{n_j} \tag{17.38}$$

Here, it important to note that d is a sample difference; even though it may be based on several groups, the several groups are themselves "grouped" into only two groups, the groups with positive coefficients and the groups with negative coefficients. Thus, we could expect that

$$\frac{d}{\sqrt{\operatorname{var}(d)}} = \frac{d}{\sqrt{MS_{wg} \sum_{j=1}^{k} \frac{c_j^2}{n_j}}} \tag{17.39}$$

should be distributed as the t-distribution with df_{wg} degrees of freedom. Thus, we could rewrite Equation 17.19 as

$$t_{obs} = \frac{d}{\sqrt{\operatorname{var}(d)}} = \frac{d}{\sqrt{MS_{wg} \sum_{j=1}^{k} \frac{c_j^2}{n_j}}} \tag{17.40}$$

An equivalent form would be

$$F_{obs} = t_{obs}^2 = \frac{d^2}{\operatorname{var}(d)} \tag{17.41}$$

18

Looking Back ... and Beyond

INTRODUCTION

If you are still reading this text, you are aware of the volume of material we have covered. At best, we have piqued your interest, and you are considering taking more classes in applied statistics. At worst, you have realized that statistics is not for you; we've had a good time together, but you are done. Either way we hope you have gained a basic understanding of statistical concepts and harbor no ill will toward the authors of this text.

In this chapter, we are going to review quickly where we have been. We will follow this with a look at some more advanced topics that you might consider for future coursework.

LOOKING BACK

In this book, we started by presenting methods of descriptive statistics, with the goal being to summarize information in meaningful ways. To demonstrate, we began with a set of scores to introduce the concept of a frequency distribution; that is, a summary of the scores in terms of the possible values and how many times each occurred. The scores consisted of measurements of attributes of entities which might be quantitative or categorical. For example, quantitative variables might be test scores, years of education, family income, etc. Categorical variables might be gender, ethnicity, college major, etc. Although there are some minor differences in the way we might proceed (e.g., histogram vs. bar graph), the goal is the same; we want to present the information in a manner that does not overwhelm the recipient.

We looked at frequency distributions in both table and graphic form, noting that there are some characteristics that can be used to differentiate one distribution from another. In particular (for quantitative variables), we noted that distributions may differ in regard to how they tend to center (mode, median, mean), how far apart they seem to be from one another (range, interquartile range, mean deviation, variance, standard deviation), and their shape (skewness and kurtosis). We then introduced bivariate distributions and developed indices to describe their "joint" distribution in terms of strength (correlation) and nature (regression).

Nearly all of this discussion was within the context of describing the scores at hand, considering them to be a population. We moved to the population/sample paradigm in which we might want to use the data at hand (sample) to make reasonable statements about a population, not immediately observable (inferential statistics). First, we presented some basic notions related to probability, moving quickly to the idea of a sampling distribution. We saw that the sampling distributions of statistics could be described in ways similar to those used to describe frequency distributions. That is, sampling distributions have a center (expected value), a spread (standard error), and shape. We presented two probability distributions (binomial and normal) that allow us to predict what might be reasonable to observe when sampling from some presumed (hypothesized) population. We used "flipping a coin" and the distribution of the sample mean to demonstrate these concepts.

Next, we discussed systems for making inferences about populations based on sample data. There are two popular approaches (hypothesis testing and confidence intervals), which in many ways yield equivalent information. We also introduced the notion of resampling methods as an alternative to the more traditional use of mathematical probability distributions; resampling methods can be used to generate exact p-values, Monte Carlo estimates of p-values, or confidence intervals. We applied these procedures in a wide variety of situations that differed in terms of the statistic (mean, proportion, median, variance, correlation, etc.) and the specifics of the situation (one sample, two samples, k samples, independent samples, dependent samples, etc.) and showed that the process was fundamentally the same.

Looking back over what has been presented, you may be under the impression that statistical procedures can be classified into two categories: those that deal with relationships and those that deal with group differences. To oversimplify, on the one hand, we have the correlational procedures that grew out of the work of Galton and Pearson; on the other hand, we have the group-difference procedures that were developed by Gosset and Fisher. If that misconception exists, we need to correct it.

Virtually all statistical analyses are directed toward assessing the degree of relationship between two sets of information. For example, in Pearson correlation, we are looking at the relationship between X and Y. If we are willing to declare one of the variables as the independent variable and the other one as the dependent variable, we can complete a regression analysis. Similarly, in the t-test or analysis-of-variance (ANOVA), we are looking for possible differences between or among groups. That is, we are assessing whether the response variable differs/varies as a function of the grouping variable. If that sounds a little like regression, it should. It is! In fact, regression, ANOVA, and many other inferential statistical procedures are manifestations of what is called the *general linear model*.

THE GENERAL LINEAR MODEL

It is the general linear model that allows us to extend our discussion of the statistical procedures available. We will not present the mathematics underlying the model, but rather attempt to give you a conceptual understanding of the model. In simple linear regression, we had one quantitative X variable and one quantitative Y variable. Consider extending the situation to one in which there might be more than one X variable and also more than one Y variable. Now consider the possibility that any of the X variables could be either quantitative or categorical. That said, the names of the particular statistical techniques have been assigned depending on the number and the nature of the X variables and the number of Y variables. Regardless of the particular name, these techniques are subsumed under the general linear model.

EVEN MORE GENERAL MODELS

Although the general linear model is flexible enough to handle analyses from many research contexts, there are cases where it is too restrictive. If the researcher has a categorical Y variable, then an extension of the general linear model known as "generalized linear models" is appropriate. If the researcher has observations that have resulted from sampling at multiple levels (e.g., sampling schools, and then sampling students within those schools), then a multilevel extension of the general linear model or of generalized linear models is needed; and if the researcher needs to examine not a single model but a system of interrelated models, then structural equation modeling would be fitting. In that spirit, we now proceed to give you some very brief presentations of a number of more advanced techniques, each of which can be seen as a special case of, or an extension of, the general linear model.

LOOKING BEYOND: ONE DEPENDENT VARIABLE

In this section, we will describe a number of techniques more advanced than those we have presented in this book. For each of them, we will describe the number and nature of both the independent and dependent variables, present a conceptual description of the technique, and give you an example.

Multiple Regression

Previously, we described simple linear regression in which a quantitative variable Y is regressed on quantitative variable X. Now suppose that we have more than one quantitative X variable. For example, suppose that we want to predict first-year Grade Point Average (GPA) in college using both the high-school GPA and the SAT total score. In this case, we have two quantitative independent variables and one quantitative dependent variable. The underlying idea is to find the weights that can be used to form a linear combination of the two independent variables, such that the combination $\hat{Y}$ correlates maximally with the Y variable. Just as r^2 is the proportion of variation in Y explained by X, in multiple regression there is a corresponding value R^2 that provides the proportion of variation in Y that is explained by the linear combination of the X variables. Mathematically, there is no limit to the number of Xs that can be used, as long as that number is less than the number of observations minus one. In practice, one actually wants to have many more cases than there are Xs. In addition to obtaining the R^2 and its test of significance, each of the X variables comes with its own test of significance which assesses the additional amount of variation explained by that variable when added to the other variables in the model. This contribution is sometimes called the "partial contribution of X," or the contribution of X after controlling for the other independent variables.

Logistic Regression

A variation of regression occurs when the dependent variable is categorical. For example, in medical research, the patient may show a positive response to a pharmacological intervention, or not. In such a case, the response variable is dichotomous, or binary. In other situations, the response variable may have more than two categories. The independent variables may be a mixture of categorical and quantitative variables. In this instance, one should consider using logistic regression. In cases when all of the variables are categorical, one might employ log-linear analysis.

Analysis-of-Variance

In actuality, ANOVA is often considered a special case of regression. That is, there is one quantitative dependent variable Y, and the X variables are categorical rather than quantitative. In the simplest examples, imagine that we have two groups as we might in a t-test situation. Rather than completing a t-test as we have shown you previously, you could create a code for group membership and then regress Y on the coded variable X. That is, you could code all of the cases in the first group to have an X-value of 1 and all the cases in the second group to have an X-value of 0. Then, if you regressed Y on X, you would obtain virtually the same result that you would obtain if you had completed a t-test.

One-Way ANOVA

If there are more than two groups, then the coding schemes that are created are more elaborate. You may learn how to do that in a more advanced course, but you can also allow the statistical package to do that for you. Thus, the ANOVA that we presented in Chapter 16 can be done with regression analysis.

Factorial ANOVA

On occasion, we design studies to examine the effects of more than one categorical independent variable. For example, we might want to compare three different pedagogical approaches to reading instruction in first grade and see how the three methods compare for both boys and girls. If the design is constructed in such a way that it can be cast as a rectangle with two rows and three columns, there will be six boxes, or cells. Each of the six cells would contain the observations for each of the six combinations resulting from the crossing of the two genders with the three methods. With a factorial design, one can test for row (i.e., gender) effects, column (pedagogical approach) effects, and their interaction. There is an interaction present when the row effects are not constant across the columns. For example, if boys did better than girls with Approach 1, girls did better than boys with Approach 2, and there was no difference between boys and girls with Approach 3, there would be an interaction. Such an effect is sometimes called a "moderation effect."

Analysis of Covariance

There may be situations in which we have a quantitative dependent variable and a mixture of quantitative and categorical independent variables. The categorical variables constitute the design and the quantitative independent variable is used as a control variable, or covariate. If certain assumptions are met, one may examine the effects of the categorical variables after controlling for the effects of the quantitative independent variable. For example, we might want to look for possible differences due to three different ways to teach students how to solve mathematics word problems. In this case, we might have access to scores reflecting previous achievement in mathematics; these scores could be used to "equate" the groups for initial random differences, while at the same time reducing the within group variation and thus making the analysis more sensitive or powerful. The measure of previous achievement in mathematics is called the "covariate."

In all of the options just presented, there has been only one dependent variable. Now let's consider situations with more than one dependent variable. These situations are described as "multivariate."

LOOKING BEYOND: TWO OR MORE DEPENDENT VARIABLES

Correlational Methods

With multiple variables on both the independent and dependent sides, there are several approaches to consider. In the correlation/regression tradition, one might consider canonical variate analysis

(CVA) or multivariate multiple regression (MMR). If the situation is one in which neither set of variables is to be considered as the dependent set, you might employ CVA. For example, many years ago, the lead author came across an example which analyzed the nature of the soil (nitrogen, phosphorus, potassium, organic material, etc.) as it might relate to the properties of tobacco leaves grown in the soil (sugar, tar, nicotine, burn rate, etc.). In essence, the analysis is done in such a way that it finds paired linear combinations from each side that correlate maximally. The linear/weighted combinations are called "canonical variates" and the correlations for each pair are called "canonical correlations."

On the other hand, if one of the sets of variables is considered to be the dependent set, one might use MMR. The dependent variables are regressed simultaneously on the independent variables. For example, one might want to look at patterns of school achievement (language arts, mathematics, science, and social studies) as a function of background variables (socioeconomic status, parental involvement, and level of motivation).

Group Membership Analyses

Similar to univariate ANOVA, suppose that one set of variables contains quantitative variables and the other set contains information about group membership (categorical variables). If you are interested in assessing whether the quantitative variables vary as a function of group membership, you would probably conduct a multivariate analysis of variance (MANOVA). For example suppose that you wanted to compare three different curricular approaches to teaching reading in first grade. Specifically, you wanted to look for differential effects on reading comprehension and reading speed. One approach, although not the best, might be to conduct two ANOVAs, one for each of the two reading variables. A better approach would be to complete a MANOVA, in which one seeks weighted/linear combinations of the reading variables on which the groups might be different. If a significant effect is indicated, then one might want to assess which groups are different from which other groups on which combinations. The combinations are referred to as "discriminant functions," and analyzing them is referred to as a "descriptive discriminant function analysis."

On occasion, one might want to predict group membership based on a set of quantitative variables. This could be done using logistic regression, as previously mentioned, or it could be done using predictive discriminant function analysis. In essence, this is the reversal of MANOVA; the group variables (coded) are the dependent variables and the quantitative variables are the independent variables.

If you are having a little difficulty keeping things straight at this point, don't be alarmed. All of these statistical techniques are special cases or extensions of the general linear model. Indeed, the distinctions among them are somewhat artificial and most likely the result of the specific techniques having been developed by different statisticians at different times. At this point, we would like to call your attention to some additional methods that, at first, may not seem to be related to the general linear model, although they are.

Principal Components and Exploratory Factor Analysis

There will be times when you might be confronted with only one set of variables. The way in which you would proceed will depend on the goals of the analysis. Although the two techniques (principal components analysis and exploratory factor analysis) have many similarities in the way they appear, we see the two types of analyses as distinctly different. Principal components analysis is actually a mathematical rotation in which one seeks linear combinations of the variables that preserve the maximum amount of individual difference information in the smallest number of composites. For example, suppose you have variables that include income in dollars, years of education, and occupational prestige. These variables would probably be correlated in such a way that you might be able to derive one composite variable that contains most of the information in the original three variables that would allow you to separate the cases.

Now let's consider a different situation; you have administered a questionnaire/survey to a large number of children. The survey contains 50 questions that ask them to indicate the degree to which they agree with the items concerning several different domains. For example, some of the items related to their physical appearance (e.g., "I like the way I look", "I am too short", "I am ugly", etc.), to their social skills (e.g., "I have lots of friends", "People like me", "I am shy in large groups", etc.), to their academic abilities (e.g., "I do well in school", "I am very smart", " I do poorly on tests", etc.). All of the items seem to be related to how they feel about themselves; the responses to the items seem to be correlated with one another. You find yourself wondering about the number and nature of the underlying variables that might explain the correlations between pairs of items. The underlying variables are sometimes called "factors" or "latent variables." In this case, you might want to conduct an exploratory factor analysis (EFA). You might think about the situation as one in which you have been given a set of dependent variables and your task as being one of trying to derive a plausible set of independent variables that explain them. Many different solutions may be generated and examined; ultimately the one that makes the most sense is advanced.

There are two more statistical analyses that we want to mention before we leave you: structural equations and multilevel analyses.

Structural Equations: Combining CFA and Path Analysis

Structural equations, or structural equation modeling, is a family of techniques that seems to have grown out of the correlational traditions of factor analysis and regression analysis. It is sometimes seen as being composed of path analysis, confirmatory factor analysis (CFA), and a blending of both. The use of structural equations calls for a change of mindset. In virtually all of the examples of inferential statistics we have covered, one has a research hypothesis, contradicts it with a null hypothesis, and then hopes to show that the data are inconsistent with the null hypothesis, thus providing indirect support for the null hypothesis. In structural equation modeling, the researcher posits a theoretical model that represents the hypothesized causal relationships among the variables. After estimating the parameters represented in the model, the parameter values are used to reconstruct the variances and covariances for the original variables. If the model fits the data well, the reconstructed variance–covariance matrix should be very similar to the actual variance–covariance matrix. The two matrices are compared for equivalence, and one hopes that the null hypothesis is *not* rejected.

Path Analysis

As a starting place, let's revisit multiple regression; the dependent variable is considered to be a function of some set of independent variables. However, there is no attempt to explain how the independent variables affect one another; they simply are allowed to correlate. Path analysis is a technique that attempts to specify a model of how the variables in the set affect other variables in the set. This technique appears to have originated in the 1920s and was seen as a way of examining possible casual relationships with correlations.

Confirmatory Factor Analysis

To better understand this technique, let's go back to explanatory factor analysis. Rather than trying several solutions, with CFA one hypothesizes (or predicts) the number of latent variables and the specific variables that are functions of these latent variables. The model is specified and tested.

Combining CFA and Path Analysis

The result of combining both techniques goes by many names, including hybrid models and full structural models. You might think of it as having two parts, a measurement model and a path model. The measurement model is sometimes called the "outer model," and it relates the observed variables to the latent constructs. The "inner model" is the path model, and it details specific relationships between the latent variables.

The last technique we will introduce is multilevel modeling, otherwise known as "hierarchical linear models" (HLMs).

MULTILEVEL MODELS

In virtually all of the techniques mentioned in this book thus far, the techniques have assumed that the observations are independent of each other; a reasonable assumption when simple random sampling is employed and any intervention/treatments and data collection are done on an individual basis. However, this is not often the case. Early in the book, we described a sampling method which we called "cluster sampling," which is becoming increasingly popular as we now tend to generate large, national data sets. We might begin with a listing (sample frame) of zip codes and draw a random sample of 100 codes. Within each zip code, we might draw a random sample of elementary schools, and within each school, draw two third-grade classrooms, and within each classroom draw a random sample of 10 students. The data set so generated is said to have a "complex sampling structure," or a "nested structure;" students are nested within classrooms, classrooms are nested within schools, and schools are nested within zip codes. When sampling is done in this manner, we tend to introduce dependencies in the data. Let's take a simpler example.

There are 100 different counties in North Carolina. Consider a sampling design in which we draw a random sample of 30 different counties, and within each of the 30 counties, we draw a random sample of 10 elementary classrooms. It has been shown that children within a classroom tend to be more similar to one another than they are to children in other classrooms in other counties. The essence of the problem is that, when such dependencies exist, the number of independent observations is less than the actual number of cases. Thus, when dividing by the number of degrees of freedom (df), the standard errors of our estimates are negatively biased, resulting in positively biased test statistics.

For an example, let's assume we are interested in examining the relationship between intellectual ability as measured by IQ and school achievement. Although not exactly mathematically correct, it may be helpful to think about completing 300 separate regressions, one within each classroom. Thus, each classroom is allowed to have its own intercept and slope. This would be called the "level-one model." Subsequently, we might have a variable at the classroom level (e.g., years of teacher experience) which we could use to try to explain the variability in the slopes with a level-two model. It might be reasonable to expect that within-classrooms slopes might decrease with increasing years of teaching experience.

CHAPTER SUMMARY

In this chapter we have reviewed some of the material covered in the previous chapters in an effort to give you the big picture. We have also introduced many more advanced techniques that you may encounter in additional statistics courses. The mastery of the content in the first 17 chapters of this book should provide you with a firm foundation to proceed beyond this text. We hope that your experience with our book has given you both the curiosity and the desire to take more applied statistics courses.

Appendix A
Statistical Tables

Table A.1 9600 Random Digits

	1	2	3	4	5	6	7	8	9	10	11	12
1	22041	71081	14249	06627	90258	33013	01571	31475	62368	31021	58495	08139
2	33153	19927	44872	58214	29309	44402	72829	80880	69670	94774	09570	99243
3	14264	43354	68734	63906	25191	76307	69846	22707	91992	15463	60769	90677
4	09863	83802	61109	51391	00127	25986	71914	90509	03327	24576	62558	70058
5	46977	63839	26197	35996	73604	45885	93957	04055	24095	07446	51753	46587
6	52699	05643	63089	75190	65975	27342	36737	94452	72487	39733	12705	10018
7	72178	50821	00769	95820	95445	24169	84053	73423	58327	89868	15932	54680
8	53306	95201	39871	79564	37786	73927	20590	16769	51384	51128	67993	13524
9	09119	70808	39391	97574	62798	89091	41430	86830	75454	55066	37410	04620
10	19300	56153	81200	92760	64249	36031	99666	58392	08260	05804	13381	78960
11	77483	15886	42167	52636	41540	52677	49272	24706	02340	06520	17168	76216
12	51451	17888	38945	15070	82954	58307	03759	01618	75436	35055	77403	53002
13	73096	30776	06657	18389	32249	04178	64177	13387	51567	07698	75435	79204
14	15590	03670	62478	25791	80268	33259	33513	34088	61266	32070	16484	74728
15	25323	93591	78518	81264	75689	02647	97735	91874	46329	00178	93953	43463
16	63926	62791	18099	32270	12955	65128	37993	62589	52482	21729	90342	68866
17	06265	22845	97926	50207	74994	05212	94768	15378	76489	20609	64458	57797
18	46169	26202	58124	23482	21363	14120	67841	46657	29633	28774	93643	30362
19	80261	53826	77199	11255	44902	11456	31678	70907	22833	34266	30260	20259
20	73668	03024	78755	91012	94337	63781	06998	13274	09573	28124	97410	26360
21	34743	92065	68712	35266	39469	17304	19503	10123	43287	33193	31880	81932
22	97032	83742	35119	89823	97607	71133	14067	14153	72081	95204	65893	62093
23	47782	27526	17376	42409	63030	63585	78079	58969	81884	01521	35497	83818
24	60518	78579	13684	11598	26976	57760	55507	38230	99163	80363	62493	86495
25	14197	53834	28557	53521	20863	42625	10254	76007	05689	26146	40145	34371
26	22123	50283	47726	50954	81151	34546	59279	81886	99175	08385	09688	10834
27	89533	67310	32058	32675	69154	18233	86476	18947	18316	41512	24236	50491
28	95160	14302	24354	84121	86338	57933	03287	21839	00092	36136	17530	83794
29	64065	93163	14620	92017	11024	89081	04121	60944	24447	22862	29464	31626
30	71957	51383	64600	29444	83479	82178	11282	43702	24158	99955	67864	28675
31	08591	47086	88135	62393	31931	40506	93004	83627	41194	25848	74142	48040
32	28534	94195	52580	75127	06750	26728	71807	69732	61801	42563	39369	82038
33	90423	54897	08041	14250	69418	56426	40683	84908	51449	93241	54738	74344
34	88227	98032	80831	82766	70722	04315	94007	04071	80411	11161	91657	44208
35	54237	65803	39952	42493	31168	18751	44916	81123	25347	03939	10009	20394
36	89712	13949	00646	85862	41120	92127	78226	97125	30460	37418	19035	49229
37	45847	12000	06361	02044	61772	60135	92511	41120	47773	96326	62749	27105
38	22837	08643	38517	73169	38139	83293	34130	48738	87725	62938	02010	33580
39	62304	19765	96187	47896	95714	28599	59570	07527	32249	43682	91098	65811
40	47038	56732	17232	88010	66519	01718	72254	15504	85481	09538	39995	52512

Table A.1 Continued

	13	14	15	16	17	18	19	20	21	22	23	24
1	31740	86480	62508	22671	66964	75418	59367	66671	97910	19637	23778	13007
2	94133	51149	22425	45612	76435	13862	17911	96963	16869	57888	41285	48010
3	68115	19885	16585	37345	26990	88750	67936	95656	13750	27688	60439	96869
4	47462	28907	71646	90726	55680	33793	13965	34340	04036	01593	82573	96829
5	19036	54041	05451	51730	39937	20043	34021	74782	52581	77598	05030	14022
6	37921	84072	94481	73537	66280	07251	58846	39971	40868	71286	58419	74583
7	53370	66391	01004	01220	42362	88699	93087	99850	05244	99156	70122	92719
8	05664	69976	56268	22819	18731	35164	40342	04469	34206	76743	13154	06774
9	81792	95092	31876	80994	73635	21744	05762	09197	49337	10148	38594	42679
10	28783	25006	09231	27548	37191	90496	98139	33295	09862	84828	39889	55683
11	36026	40887	41670	10253	47502	67883	45052	30778	27035	19362	48833	03505
12	50118	39229	51470	77894	23274	75516	10088	60037	09993	14432	59917	82327
13	36946	59962	91821	36378	82922	35134	79340	96483	31378	90289	55680	23380
14	59333	91303	57108	50061	78077	68985	43998	85359	22974	32852	88731	97492
15	29876	58952	39276	40804	29704	98678	60495	80223	90096	32826	29252	97641
16	46715	38415	18313	79212	69854	72613	10693	87602	38734	53707	18448	38916
17	30282	60984	70779	36556	01162	02392	35427	67441	21846	72324	23442	91053
18	38496	01790	19834	33861	88820	66847	89052	44449	97320	31951	03078	45098
19	58353	70996	69680	97399	80020	93988	17531	12692	36514	98507	86597	89265
20	33714	36247	41297	10584	87531	78417	79057	14822	73249	82078	41073	49116
21	09425	29550	18496	37297	66997	96688	94746	89199	02682	69551	26751	50178
22	08181	31437	09026	43836	74460	00723	34616	22859	52598	07379	78116	25313
23	10709	95485	44653	76619	45620	33286	35210	29252	38257	30834	08509	90899
24	19414	73172	94784	11914	25678	70388	36036	46664	12562	44197	79300	86849
25	15381	93341	01149	54355	32088	05773	84959	80425	68457	33401	56352	83757
26	41411	29981	00844	37320	05990	59195	18136	10883	73216	70889	03977	97098
27	06346	94335	14521	66493	43755	78213	72896	47434	65332	32490	01706	22630
28	60655	73239	96906	99379	72754	37423	41814	60487	25809	17526	96119	16552
29	77411	11346	17948	97104	47070	70898	97306	00016	93619	96581	90712	48143
30	49413	67999	09055	19104	28773	29500	30590	73717	55645	84250	34136	89135
31	69072	79030	29079	49521	05592	62548	04812	63599	89573	33318	10077	55008
32	20702	25449	58201	56095	81104	78090	01841	95758	79380	40262	41949	86509
33	48910	04798	79554	90477	93761	12318	68421	56439	43003	87466	34604	68766
34	96197	25343	01367	13668	75700	51878	57227	36568	23951	40262	17148	27600
35	53687	16534	43773	15776	53124	91266	29832	26905	34147	18832	58507	86943
36	38346	33162	80991	59749	94205	82650	87111	81724	95302	12429	19729	22842
37	13850	70459	46064	58496	60398	58059	86288	42813	08709	95034	33108	40770
38	85191	20363	66437	47397	84320	41507	35075	75386	55504	64221	35862	26819
39	53957	10540	47644	66505	62731	87362	46097	09400	01733	88227	29707	96612
40	80251	35501	94814	81827	85332	96213	14319	75421	79516	76606	50889	90276

Table A.1 Continued

	25	26	27	28	29	30	31	32	33	34	35	36
1	00036	11716	13931	79268	52691	68155	93651	09823	98618	14773	27912	46367
2	41157	63705	37009	28643	37506	82087	41400	22956	73999	81645	11156	45920
3	98495	09248	15407	64696	78092	98845	52012	73675	27376	61008	67666	13592
4	98377	15352	36168	36385	57850	30065	58469	05890	53368	77627	24424	64527
5	09563	74904	60585	63868	55023	47182	16075	44513	06119	62223	56423	58831
6	26252	81034	99681	75606	76264	31449	97838	25362	27443	63231	49148	91428
7	24518	31250	02035	50699	03681	36662	35339	66744	28854	73193	45287	22631
8	60287	63343	70208	28817	82516	55333	15497	81231	33526	33368	43939	52660
9	83853	28272	58929	24031	19967	50791	37627	30932	82887	23687	18358	81267
10	70140	28263	44395	30075	65099	25672	24773	89815	96715	59078	31295	65931
11	09719	24474	85056	64780	86227	81878	45157	98671	65661	57696	54020	00371
12	04085	00417	06092	51610	47846	03869	89210	06321	71702	44837	67329	66787
13	84039	91160	07985	36297	37647	66060	09223	83738	44689	96155	15758	30096
14	47668	26497	21048	94819	55593	50296	45067	53655	90127	97868	25546	49319
15	13763	27036	18166	31365	35396	32891	71861	87789	49939	61302	62762	81280
16	56623	80853	72977	73625	43706	90616	39827	15857	56387	12304	85285	21171
17	13912	68143	53402	59084	84087	89655	14644	33813	95852	22091	71735	68096
18	92893	00448	88732	88559	98844	60793	10773	58316	91635	16909	59678	67153
19	62342	88970	65690	85118	69319	57977	22667	11587	99992	62381	55458	67003
20	01433	38451	33930	80844	38625	99819	34854	09592	32201	83389	86292	50828
21	00093	25178	91338	44458	13580	46610	89018	18161	40694	98467	55304	41137
22	60029	38953	87388	17639	25373	60662	86278	83891	03739	23963	51006	39471
23	91333	98453	08958	97326	86715	77749	41232	57877	39577	46473	51079	72284
24	71555	74257	23015	60789	22670	84398	57980	23932	23539	66964	64194	93237
25	29590	68592	25132	80038	80809	88185	80093	04441	31366	04276	16593	57931
26	37599	23331	09998	82740	56824	38424	14551	24133	27233	51895	23731	41521
27	02436	18727	66856	71463	24693	95065	47231	67563	21839	28101	31262	70139
28	42070	90957	43338	95648	84106	56092	03858	47127	20592	22174	22090	62995
29	00386	21490	48500	34222	37600	58349	24598	99012	90435	53548	94279	23610
30	53694	18702	98891	32651	53988	35401	84398	89188	44190	98519	06820	91357
31	06574	30970	47532	77308	06200	62584	57467	83057	33196	95056	50240	77960
32	16748	59092	26452	34771	58083	36452	82559	77391	17380	14708	65750	36464
33	42097	39743	60338	93338	96169	47801	63286	82485	45986	11682	22022	48051
34	59976	34980	94097	27792	29003	02389	98988	69670	66321	08231	23928	82916
35	42855	43146	21885	80111	99419	28414	55964	81192	20846	65475	24908	91382
36	14218	07660	38639	18142	62342	97790	14650	82423	95644	65372	73466	36952
37	92100	19493	69903	56763	78702	97548	26450	15565	35235	25919	96426	98421
38	82746	94584	76512	87153	85690	73419	26765	44898	04206	74070	66071	39706
39	55450	00959	54718	43896	47376	54966	16823	98283	03486	99190	17412	44037
40	65736	99065	73012	26115	66718	82944	40995	59005	67338	24429	48787	11275

Table A.1 Continued

	37	38	39	40	41	42	43	44	45	46	47	48
1	65036	12681	08554	01648	68752	18140	95580	24786	19240	78297	65882	03732
2	59893	03944	01397	32612	72501	08245	01975	85993	85390	95100	28328	60371
3	37309	92103	96183	12758	80979	84830	48359	52186	40456	57457	49350	89588
4	95815	18323	63343	19167	17411	26085	87105	96679	39528	42369	15290	28464
5	73844	85567	39062	69521	41775	70047	09917	34505	47504	82692	47179	71617
6	40328	61672	01861	23809	13083	68704	69134	04028	00893	36448	39984	77336
7	55103	13235	89069	21022	79635	12886	87120	58669	69897	71166	66034	00251
8	22309	91349	11359	00394	37388	23523	40240	92734	69450	39926	68124	13355
9	31535	49923	71236	19731	08518	89732	42148	26740	75188	05953	01608	62588
10	73197	38296	00445	94840	40879	91474	99070	99376	36438	73058	30894	75509
11	16353	45502	12478	05407	90759	51190	41813	50581	36729	17540	21323	10078
12	54574	82027	18672	77143	05791	59472	80827	33311	65047	42425	93157	08232
13	03409	15536	63079	99913	16658	39747	60448	70663	19157	13441	87288	22710
14	29124	48947	52276	23130	16636	05922	86562	74780	30749	62259	14426	00152
15	91735	46458	09161	80887	77149	31782	86060	01374	27810	69894	73759	90067
16	81323	63803	64564	12605	18284	74389	10909	46940	14404	30798	28735	26378
17	67038	02431	38630	76790	97849	50159	31900	63897	91568	37367	25778	28696
18	78508	45575	66224	37490	41413	58478	07675	28339	90323	36916	14315	38065
19	97049	81990	01037	56773	91828	66338	06631	06107	49004	71450	47125	27256
20	92192	32385	91283	97510	10963	65719	47781	52560	08405	87470	51601	56778
21	28988	03456	92760	74610	82033	80269	69428	51889	49589	72141	69329	45852
22	39075	53307	38586	04898	28450	31854	03788	83310	56025	79779	25891	04717
23	67464	01655	06011	27240	34500	99439	14945	45844	35569	47120	79520	49405
24	27089	46548	89329	59982	93075	40609	91450	54626	50319	02032	59093	98558
25	82712	09896	45376	78109	10842	33056	36532	08358	08174	20210	34645	00463
26	24666	57889	93288	02904	45050	72520	48715	55561	14962	15918	82031	31936
27	58449	08941	92520	11932	71357	93534	74850	26511	63794	24271	38272	68719
28	21915	78823	47723	53437	75348	77305	33802	96814	44725	76839	36629	48722
29	56121	90292	50667	34257	79243	52854	59620	61521	21002	39189	81672	50012
30	68751	44525	45478	77157	68844	94615	65183	48290	29957	57416	61098	12284
31	33214	10572	81517	81196	75145	44353	72155	10366	35121	54069	66710	25751
32	36644	64487	34516	93758	49341	15116	64604	83792	97935	66659	45848	01787
33	04871	95375	25721	54639	69617	01453	98471	74820	57357	62791	81522	75765
34	01185	76630	03245	30099	09387	02267	09309	50458	28064	34564	87498	81324
35	49273	31773	32008	29782	33265	83603	05340	95130	74311	55885	09039	82383
36	82854	48004	99962	22952	07722	32408	23222	49870	84588	61859	51965	67791
37	71645	91828	12657	40371	49135	30677	30771	52300	63167	68255	57429
38	71372	02111	99698	32522	02358	28384	40703	50144	03507	40620	87217	10661
39	56081	45745	15596	34737	14255	09024	01884	15612	33125	13800	38737	00815
40	94659	73756	05906	14583	32493	56288	43922	45294	21345	09926	11341	70612

Table A.2 The unit-normal distribution (z)

z score	area to mean	area beyond	ordinate	z score	area to mean	area beyond	ordinate
0.00	.00000	.50000	.39894	0.53	.20194	.29806	.34667
0.01	.00399	.49601	.39892	0.54	.20540	.29460	.34482
0.02	.00798	.49202	.39886	0.55	.20884	.29116	.34294
0.03	.01197	.48803	.39876	0.56	.21226	.28774	.34105
0.04	.01595	.48405	.39862	0.57	.21566	.28434	.33912
0.05	.01994	.48006	.39844	0.58	.21904	.28096	.33718
0.06	.02392	.47608	.39822	0.59	.22240	.27760	.33521
0.07	.02790	.47210	.39797	0.60	.22575	.27425	.33322
0.08	.03188	.46812	.39767	0.61	.22907	.27093	.33121
0.09	.03586	.46414	.39733	0.62	.23237	.26763	.32918
0.10	.03983	.46017	.39695	0.63	.23565	.26435	.32713
0.11	.04380	.45620	.39654	0.64	.23891	.26109	.32506
0.12	.04776	.45224	.39608	0.65	.24215	.25785	.32297
0.13	.05172	.44828	.39559	0.66	.24537	.25463	.32086
0.14	.05567	.44433	.39505	0.67	.24857	.25143	.31874
0.15	.05962	.44038	.39448	0.68	.25175	.24825	.31659
0.16	.06356	.43644	.39387	0.69	.25490	.24510	.31443
0.17	.06749	.43251	.39322	0.70	.25804	.24196	.31225
0.18	.07142	.42858	.39253	0.71	.26115	.23885	.31006
0.19	.07535	.42465	.39181	0.72	.26424	.23576	.30785
0.20	.07926	.42074	.39104	0.73	.26730	.23270	.30563
0.21	.08317	.41683	.39024	0.74	.27035	.22965	.30339
0.22	.08706	.41294	.38940	0.75	.27337	.22663	.30114
0.23	.09095	.40905	.38853	0.76	.27637	.22363	.29887
0.24	.09483	.40517	.38762	0.77	.27935	.22065	.29659
0.25	.09871	.40129	.38667	0.78	.28230	.21770	.29431
0.26	.10257	.39743	.38568	0.79	.28524	.21476	.29200
0.27	.10642	.39358	.38466	0.80	.28814	.21186	.28969
0.28	.11026	.38974	.38361	0.81	.29103	.20897	.28737
0.29	.11409	.38591	.38251	0.82	.29389	.20611	.28504
0.30	.11791	.38209	.38139	0.83	.29673	.20327	.28269
0.31	.12172	.37828	.38023	0.84	.29955	.20045	.28034
0.32	.12552	.37448	.37903	0.85	.30234	.19766	.27798
0.33	.12930	.37070	.37780	0.86	.30511	.19489	.27562
0.34	.13307	.36693	.37654	0.87	.30785	.19215	.27324
0.35	.13683	.36317	.37524	0.88	.31057	.18943	.27086
0.36	.14058	.35942	.37391	0.89	.31327	.18673	.26848
0.37	.14431	.35569	.37255	0.90	.31594	.18406	.26609
0.38	.14803	.35197	.37115	0.91	.31859	.18141	.26369
0.39	.15173	.34827	.36973	0.92	.32121	.17879	.26129
0.40	.15542	.34458	.36827	0.93	.32381	.17619	.25888
0.41	.15910	.34090	.36678	0.94	.32639	.17361	.25647
0.42	.16276	.33724	.36526	0.95	.32894	.17106	.25406
0.43	.16640	.33360	.36371	0.96	.33147	.16853	.25164
0.44	.17003	.32997	.36213	0.97	.33398	.16602	.24923
0.45	.17364	.32636	.36053	0.98	.33646	.16354	.24681
0.46	.17724	.32276	.35889	0.99	.33891	.16109	.24439
0.47	.18082	.31918	.35723	1.00	.34134	.15866	.24197
0.48	.18439	.31561	.35553	1.01	.34375	.15625	.23955
0.49	.18793	.31207	.35381	1.02	.34614	.15386	.23713
0.50	.19146	.30854	.35207	1.03	.34849	.15151	.23471
0.51	.19497	.30503	.35029	1.04	.35083	.14917	.23230
0.52	.19847	.30153	.34849	1.05	.35314	.14686	.22988

Table A.2 Continued

z score	area to mean	area beyond	ordinate	z score	area to mean	area beyond	ordinate
1.06	.35543	.14457	.22747	1.59	.44408	.05592	.11270
1.07	.35769	.14231	.22506	1.60	.44520	.05480	.11092
1.08	.35993	.14007	.22265	1.61	.44630	.05370	.10915
1.09	.36214	.13786	.22025	1.62	.44738	.05262	.10741
1.10	.36433	.13567	.21785	1.63	.44845	.05155	.10567
1.11	.36650	.13350	.21546	1.64	.44950	.05050	.10396
1.12	.36864	.13136	.21307	1.65	.45053	.04947	.10226
1.13	.37076	.12924	.21069	1.66	.45154	.04846	.10059
1.14	.37286	.12714	.20831	1.67	.45254	.04746	.09893
1.15	.37493	.12507	.20594	1.68	.45352	.04648	.09728
1.16	.37698	.12302	.20357	1.69	.45449	.04551	.09566
1.17	.37900	.12100	.20121	1.70	.45543	.04457	.09405
1.18	.38100	.11900	.19886	1.71	.45637	.04363	.09246
1.19	.38298	.11702	.19652	1.72	.45728	.04272	.09089
1.20	.38493	.11507	.19419	1.73	.45818	.04182	.08933
1.21	.38686	.11314	.19186	1.74	.45907	.04093	.08780
1.22	.38877	.11123	.18954	1.75	.45994	.04006	.08628
1.23	.39065	.10935	.18724	1.76	.46080	.03920	.08478
1.24	.39251	.10749	.18494	1.77	.46164	.03836	.08329
1.25	.39435	.10565	.18265	1.78	.46246	.03754	.08183
1.26	.39617	.10383	.18037	1.79	.46327	.03673	.08038
1.27	.39796	.10204	.17810	1.80	.46407	.03593	.07895
1.28	.39973	.10027	.17585	1.81	.46485	.03515	.07754
1.29	.40147	.09853	.17360	1.82	.46562	.03438	.07614
1.30	.40320	.09680	.17137	1.83	.46638	.03362	.07477
1.31	.40490	.09510	.16915	1.84	.46712	.03288	.07341
1.32	.40658	.09342	.16694	1.85	.46784	.03216	.07206
1.33	.40824	.09176	.16474	1.86	.46856	.03144	.07074
1.34	.40988	.09012	.16256	1.87	.46926	.03074	.06943
1.35	.41149	.08851	.16038	1.88	.46995	.03005	.06814
1.36	.41309	.08691	.15822	1.89	.47062	.02938	.06687
1.37	.41466	.08534	.15608	1.90	.47128	.02872	.06562
1.38	.41621	.08379	.15395	1.91	.47193	.02807	.06438
1.39	.41774	.08226	.15183	1.92	.47257	.02743	.06316
1.40	.41924	.08076	.14973	1.93	.47320	.02680	.06195
1.41	.42073	.07927	.14764	1.94	.47381	.02619	.06077
1.42	.42220	.07780	.14556	1.95	.47441	.02559	.05959
1.43	.42364	.07636	.14350	1.96	.47500	.02500	.05844
1.44	.42507	.07493	.14146	1.97	.47558	.02442	.05730
1.45	.42647	.07353	.13943	1.98	.47615	.02385	.05618
1.46	.42785	.07215	.13742	1.99	.47670	.02330	.05508
1.47	.42922	.07078	.13542	2.00	.47725	.02275	.05396
1.48	.43056	.06944	.13344	2.01	.47778	.02222	.05292
1.49	.43189	.06811	.13147	2.02	.47831	.02169	.05186
1.50	.43319	.06681	.12952	2.03	.47882	.02118	.05082
1.51	.43448	.06552	.12758	2.04	.47932	.02068	.04980
1.52	.43574	.06426	.12566	2.05	.47982	.02018	.04879
1.53	.43699	.06301	.12376	2.06	.48030	.01970	.04780
1.54	.43822	.06178	.12188	2.07	.48077	.01923	.04682
1.55	.43943	.06057	.12001	2.08	.48124	.01876	.04586
1.56	.44062	.05938	.11816	2.09	.48169	.01831	.04491
1.57	.44179	.05821	.11632	2.10	.48214	.01786	.04398
1.58	.44295	.05705	.11450	2.11	.48257	.01743	.04307

z score	area to mean	area beyond	ordinate	z score	area to mean	area beyond	ordinate
2.12	.48300	.01700	.04217	2.61	.49547	.00453	.01323
2.13	.48341	.01659	.04128	2.62	.49560	.00440	.01289
2.14	.48382	.01618	.04041	2.63	.49573	.00427	.01256
2.15	.48422	.01578	.03955	2.64	.49585	.00415	.01223
2.16	.48461	.01539	.03871	2.65	.49598	.00402	.01191
2.17	.48500	.01500	.03788	2.66	.49609	.00391	.01160
2.18	.48537	.01463	.03706	2.67	.49621	.00379	.01130
2.19	.48574	.01426	.03626	2.68	.49632	.00368	.01100
2.20	.48610	.01390	.03547	2.69	.49643	.00357	.01071
2.21	.48645	.01355	.03470	2.70	.49653	.00347	.01042
2.22	.48679	.01321	.03394	2.71	.49664	.00336	.01014
2.23	.48713	.01287	.03319	2.72	.49674	.00326	.00987
2.24	.48745	.01255	.03246	2.73	.49683	.00317	.00961
2.25	.48778	.01222	.03174	2.74	.49693	.00307	.00935
2.26	.48809	.01191	.03103	2.75	.49702	.00298	.00909
2.27	.48840	.01160	.03034	2.76	.49711	.00289	.00885
2.28	.48870	.01130	.02965	2.77	.49720	.00280	.00861
2.29	.48899	.01101	.02898	2.78	.49728	.00272	.00837
2.30	.48928	.01072	.02833	2.79	.49736	.00264	.00814
2.31	.48956	.01044	.02768	2.80	.49744	.00256	.00792
2.32	.48983	.01017	.02705	2.81	.49752	.00248	.00770
2.33	.49010	.00990	.02643	2.82	.49760	.00240	.00748
2.34	.49036	.00964	.02582	2.83	.49767	.00233	.00727
2.35	.49061	.00939	.02522	2.84	.49774	.00226	.00707
2.36	.49086	.00914	.02463	2.85	.49781	.00219	.00687
2.37	.49111	.00889	.02406	2.86	.49788	.00212	.00668
2.38	.49134	.00866	.02349	2.87	.49795	.00205	.00649
2.39	.49158	.00842	.02294	2.88	.49801	.00199	.00631
2.40	.49180	.00820	.02239	2.89	.49807	.00193	.00613
2.41	.49202	.00798	.02186	2.90	.49813	.00187	.00595
2.42	.49224	.00776	.02134	2.91	.49819	.00181	.00578
2.43	.49245	.00755	.02083	2.92	.49825	.00175	.00562
2.44	.49266	.00734	.02033	2.93	.49831	.00169	.00545
2.45	.49286	.00714	.01984	2.94	.49836	.00164	.00530
2.46	.49305	.00695	.01936	2.95	.49841	.00159	.00514
2.47	.49324	.00676	.01888	2.96	.49846	.00154	.00499
2.48	.49343	.00657	.01842	2.97	.49851	.00149	.00485
2.49	.49361	.00639	.01797	2.98	.49856	.00144	.00470
2.50	.49379	.00621	.01753	2.99	.49861	.00139	.00457
2.51	.49396	.00604	.01709	3.00	.49865	.00135	.00443
2.52	.49413	.00587	.01667	3.10	.49903	.00097	.00327
2.53	.49430	.00570	.01625	3.20	.49931	.00069	.00238
2.54	.49446	.00554	.01585	3.30	.49952	.00048	.00172
2.55	.49461	.00539	.01545	3.40	.49966	.00034	.00123
2.56	.49477	.00523	.01506	3.50	.49977	.00023	.00087
2.57	.49492	.00508	.01468	4.00	.49997	.00003	.00018
2.58	.49506	.00494	.01431	4.50	.50000	.00000	.00002
2.59	.49520	.00480	.01394				
2.60	.49534	.00466	.01358				

Source: Compiled by the authors using SYSTAT.

Table A.3 Selected critical values of *t*

	Level of significance for a one-tailed test								
.	10000	.05000	.02500	.01250	.01000	.00833	.00625	.00500	.00050
	Level of significance for a two-tailed test								
v	*.20000*	*.10000*	*.05000*	*.02500*	*.02000*	*.01667*	*.01250*	*.01000*	*.00100*
1	3.0777	6.3138	12.7060	25.4520	31.8200	38.1880	50.9230	63.6570	636.6200
2	1.8856	2.9200	4.3027	6.2053	6.9646	7.6488	8.8602	9.9248	31.5990
3	1.6377	2.3534	3.1824	4.1765	4.5407	4.8566	5.3919	5.8409	12.9240
4	1.5332	2.1318	2.7764	3.4954	3.7469	3.9608	4.3147	4.6041	8.6103
5	1.4759	2.0150	2.5706	3.1634	3.3649	3.5341	3.8100	4.0321	6.8688
6	1.4398	1.9432	2.4469	2.9687	3.1427	3.2874	3.5212	3.7074	5.9588
7	1.4149	1.8946	2.3646	2.8412	2.9980	3.1275	3.3353	3.4995	5.4079
8	1.3968	1.8595	2.3060	2.7515	2.8965	3.0158	3.2060	3.3554	5.0413
9	1.3830	1.8331	2.2622	2.6850	2.8214	2.9333	3.1109	3.2498	4.7809
10	1.3722	1.8125	2.2281	2.6338	2.7638	2.8701	3.0382	3.1693	4.5869
11	1.3634	1.7959	2.2010	2.5931	2.7181	2.8200	2.9809	3.1058	4.4370
12	1.3562	1.7823	2.1788	2.5600	2.6810	2.7795	2.9345	3.0545	4.3178
13	1.3502	1.7709	2.1604	2.5326	2.6503	2.7459	2.8961	3.0123	4.2208
14	1.3450	1.7613	2.1448	2.5096	2.6245	2.7178	2.8640	2.9768	4.1405
15	1.3406	1.7531	2.1314	2.4899	2.6025	2.6937	2.8366	2.9467	4.0728
16	1.3368	1.7459	2.1199	2.4729	2.5835	2.6730	2.8131	2.9208	4.0150
17	1.3334	1.7396	2.1098	2.4581	2.5669	2.6550	2.7925	2.8982	3.9651
18	1.3304	1.7341	2.1009	2.4450	2.5524	2.6391	2.7745	2.8784	3.9216
19	1.3277	1.7291	2.0930	2.4334	2.5395	2.6251	2.7586	2.8609	3.8834
20	1.3253	1.7247	2.0860	2.4231	2.5280	2.6126	2.7444	2.8453	3.8495
21	1.3232	1.7207	2.0796	2.4138	2.5176	2.6013	2.7316	2.8314	3.8193
22	1.3212	1.7171	2.0739	2.4055	2.5083	2.5912	2.7201	2.8188	3.7921
23	1.3195	1.7139	2.0687	2.3979	2.4999	2.5820	2.7097	2.8073	3.7676
24	1.3178	1.7109	2.0639	2.3909	2.4922	2.5736	2.7002	2.7969	3.7454
25	1.3163	1.7081	2.0595	2.3846	2.4851	2.5660	2.6916	2.7874	3.7251
26	1.3150	1.7056	2.0555	2.3788	2.4786	2.5589	2.6836	2.7787	3.7066
27	1.3137	1.7033	2.0518	2.3734	2.4727	2.5525	2.6763	2.7707	3.6896
28	1.3125	1.7011	2.0484	2.3685	2.4671	2.5465	2.6695	2.7633	3.6739
29	1.3114	1.6991	2.0452	2.3638	2.4620	2.5409	2.6632	2.7564	3.6594
30	1.3104	1.6973	2.0423	2.3596	2.4573	2.5357	2.6574	2.7500	3.6460
35	1.3062	1.6896	2.0301	2.3420	2.4377	2.5145	2.6334	2.7238	3.5911
40	1.3031	1.6839	2.0211	2.3289	2.4233	2.4989	2.6157	2.7045	3.5510
45	1.3006	1.6794	2.0141	2.3189	2.4121	2.4868	2.6021	2.6896	3.5203
50	1.2987	1.6759	2.0086	2.3109	2.4033	2.4772	2.5913	2.6778	3.4960
55	1.2971	1.6730	2.0040	2.3044	2.3961	2.4694	2.5825	2.6682	3.4764
60	1.2958	1.6706	2.0003	2.2990	2.3901	2.4629	2.5752	2.6603	3.4602
80	1.2922	1.6641	1.9901	2.2844	2.3739	2.4454	2.5554	2.6387	3.4163
100	1.2901	1.6602	1.9840	2.2757	2.3642	2.4349	2.5437	2.6259	3.3905
120	1.2886	1.6577	1.9799	2.2699	2.3578	2.4280	2.5359	2.6174	3.3735
200	1.2858	1.6525	1.9719	2.2584	2.3451	2.4143	2.5205	2.6006	3.3398
500	1.2832	1.6479	1.9647	2.2482	2.3338	2.4021	2.5068	2.5857	3.3101
∞	1.2816	1.6449	1.9600	2.2414	2.3263	2.3940	2.4977	2.5758	3.2905

Source: Compiled by the authors using SYSTAT.

Table A.4 The critical values of χ^2

		Lower-tailed critical values of the chi-squared (χ^2) distribution				
df	*0.005*	*0.010*	*0.025*	*0.050*	*0.100*	*0.200*
1	0.0000	0.0002	0.0010	0.0039	0.0158	0.0642
2	0.0100	0.0201	0.0506	0.1026	0.2107	0.4463
3	0.0717	0.1148	0.2158	0.3518	0.5844	1.0052
4	0.2070	0.2971	0.4844	0.7107	1.0636	1.6488
5	0.4117	0.5543	0.8312	1.1455	1.6103	2.3425
6	0.6757	0.8721	1.2373	1.6354	2.2041	3.0701
7	0.9893	1.2390	1.6899	2.1673	2.8331	3.8223
8	1.3444	1.6465	2.1797	2.7326	3.4895	4.5936
9	1.7349	2.0879	2.7004	3.3251	4.1682	5.3801
10	2.1559	2.5582	3.2470	3.9403	4.8652	6.1791
11	2.6032	3.0535	3.8157	4.5748	5.5778	6.9887
12	3.0738	3.5706	4.4038	5.2260	6.3038	7.8073
13	3.5650	4.1069	5.0088	5.8919	7.0415	8.6339
14	4.0747	4.6604	5.6287	6.5706	7.7895	9.4673
15	4.6009	5.2293	6.2621	7.2609	8.5468	10.3070
16	5.1422	5.8122	6.9077	7.9616	9.3122	11.1521
17	5.6972	6.4078	7.5642	8.6718	10.0852	12.0023
18	6.2648	7.0149	8.2307	9.3905	10.8649	12.8570
19	6.8440	7.6327	8.9065	10.1170	11.6509	13.7158
20	7.4338	8.2604	9.5908	10.8508	12.4426	14.5784
21	8.0337	8.8972	10.2829	11.5913	13.2396	15.4446
22	8.6427	9.5425	10.9823	12.3380	14.0415	16.3140
23	9.2604	10.1957	11.6886	13.0905	14.8480	17.1865
24	9.8862	10.8564	12.4012	13.8484	15.6587	18.0618
25	10.5197	11.5240	13.1197	14.6114	16.4734	18.9398
26	11.1602	12.1981	13.8439	15.3792	17.2919	19.8202
27	11.8076	12.8785	14.5734	16.1514	18.1139	20.7030
28	12.4613	13.5647	15.3079	16.9279	18.9392	21.5880
29	13.1211	14.2565	16.0471	17.7084	19.7677	22.4751
30	13.7867	14.9535	16.7908	18.4927	20.5992	23.3641
35	17.1918	18.5089	20.5694	22.4650	24.7967	27.8359
40	20.7065	22.1643	24.4330	26.5093	29.0505	32.3450
45	24.3110	25.9013	28.3662	30.6123	33.3504	36.8844
50	27.9907	29.7067	32.3574	34.7643	37.6886	41.4492
55	31.7348	33.5705	36.3981	38.9580	42.0596	46.0356
60	35.5345	37.4849	40.4817	43.1880	46.4589	50.6406
65	39.3831	41.4436	44.6030	47.4496	50.8829	55.2620
70	43.2752	45.4417	48.7576	51.7393	55.3289	59.8978
75	47.2060	49.4750	52.9419	56.0541	59.7946	64.5466
80	51.1719	53.5401	57.1532	60.3915	64.2778	69.2069
85	55.1696	57.6339	61.3888	64.7494	68.7772	73.8779
90	59.1963	61.7541	65.6466	69.1260	73.2911	78.5584
95	63.2496	65.8984	69.9249	73.5198	77.8184	83.2478
100	67.3276	70.0649	74.2219	77.9295	82.3581	87.9453
200	152.2410	156.4320	162.7280	168.2786	174.8353	183.0028
300	240.6492	245.9637	253.9093	260.8784	269.0702	279.2172
400	330.8905	337.1477	346.4792	354.6413	364.2095	376.0243
500	422.2924	429.3808	439.9338	449.1471	459.9280	473.2121

Source: Compiled by the authors using SYSTAT.

Table A.4 Continued

	Upper-tailed critical values of the chi-squared (χ^2) distribution					
df	*0.200*	*0.100*	*0.050*	*0.025*	*0.010*	*0.005*
1	1.6424	2.7055	3.8415	5.0239	6.6349	7.8794
2	3.2189	4.6052	5.9915	7.3778	9.2103	10.5966
3	4.6416	6.2514	7.8147	9.3484	11.3449	12.8382
4	5.9886	7.7794	9.4877	11.1433	13.2767	14.8603
5	7.2893	9.2364	11.0705	12.8325	15.0863	16.7496
6	8.5581	10.6446	12.5916	14.4494	16.8119	18.5476
7	9.8032	12.0170	14.0671	16.0128	18.4753	20.2777
8	11.0301	13.3616	15.5073	17.5345	20.0902	21.9550
9	12.2421	14.6837	16.9190	19.0228	21.6660	23.5894
10	13.4420	15.9872	18.3070	20.4832	23.2093	25.1882
11	14.6314	17.2750	19.6751	21.9200	24.7250	26.7569
12	15.8120	18.5493	21.0261	23.3367	26.2170	28.2995
13	16.9848	19.8119	22.3620	24.7356	27.6883	29.8195
14	18.1508	21.0641	23.6848	26.1189	29.1412	31.3193
15	19.3107	22.3071	24.9958	27.4884	30.5779	32.8013
16	20.4651	23.5418	26.2962	28.8454	31.9999	34.2672
17	21.6146	24.7690	27.5871	30.1910	33.4087	35.7185
18	22.7595	25.9894	28.8693	31.5264	34.8053	37.1565
19	23.9004	27.2036	30.1435	32.8523	36.1909	38.5823
20	25.0375	28.4120	31.4104	34.1696	37.5662	39.9968
21	26.1711	29.6151	32.6706	35.4789	38.9322	41.4011
22	27.3015	30.8133	33.9244	36.7807	40.2894	42.7957
23	28.4288	32.0069	35.1725	38.0756	41.6384	44.1813
24	29.5533	33.1962	36.4150	39.3641	42.9798	45.5585
25	30.6752	34.3816	37.6525	40.6465	44.3141	46.9279
26	31.7946	35.5632	38.8851	41.9232	45.6417	48.2899
27	32.9117	36.7412	40.1133	43.1945	46.9629	49.6449
28	34.0266	37.9159	41.3371	44.4608	48.2782	50.9934
29	35.1394	39.0875	42.5570	45.7223	49.5879	52.3356
30	36.2502	40.2560	43.7730	46.9792	50.8922	53.6720
35	41.7780	46.0588	49.8018	53.2033	57.3421	60.2748
40	47.2685	51.8051	55.7585	59.3417	63.6907	66.7660
45	52.7288	57.5053	61.6562	65.4102	69.9568	73.1661
50	58.1638	63.1671	67.5048	71.4202	76.1539	79.4900
55	63.5772	68.7962	73.3115	77.3805	82.2921	85.7490
60	68.9721	74.3970	79.0819	83.2977	88.3794	91.9517
65	74.3506	79.9730	84.8206	89.1771	94.4221	98.1051
70	79.7146	85.5270	90.5312	95.0232	100.4252	104.2149
75	85.0658	91.0615	96.2167	100.8393	106.3929	110.2856
80	90.4053	96.5782	101.8795	106.6286	112.3288	116.3211
85	95.7343	102.0789	107.5217	112.3934	118.2357	122.3246
90	101.0537	107.5650	113.1453	118.1359	124.1163	128.2989
95	106.3643	113.0377	118.7516	123.8580	129.9727	134.2465
100	111.6667	118.4980	124.3421	129.5612	135.8067	140.1695
200	216.6088	226.0210	233.9943	241.0579	249.4451	255.2642
300	320.3942	331.7856	341.3940	349.8765	359.9145	366.8584
400	423.5870	436.6465	447.6315	457.3073	468.7315	476.6186
500	526.3992	540.9281	553.1260	563.8532	576.4991	585.2175

Source: Compiled by the authors using SYSTAT.

Table A.5 Fisher's *r* to *r'* transformation

	Fisher's Natural Logarithmic Transformation of r to r' (Thousands place)								
	0.000	*0.001*	*0.002*	*0.003*	*0.004*	*0.005*	*0.006*	*0.007*	*0.008*	*0.009*
0.00	0.0000	0.0010	0.0020	0.0030	0.0040	0.0050	0.0060	0.0070	0.0080	0.0090
0.01	0.0100	0.0110	0.0120	0.0130	0.0140	0.0150	0.0160	0.0170	0.0180	0.0190
0.02	0.0200	0.0210	0.0220	0.0230	0.0240	0.0250	0.0260	0.0270	0.0280	0.0290
0.03	0.0300	0.0310	0.0320	0.0330	0.0340	0.0350	0.0360	0.0370	0.0380	0.0390
0.04	0.0400	0.0410	0.0420	0.0430	0.0440	0.0450	0.0460	0.0470	0.0480	0.0490
0.05	0.0500	0.0510	0.0520	0.0530	0.0541	0.0551	0.0561	0.0571	0.0581	0.0591
0.06	0.0601	0.0611	0.0621	0.0631	0.0641	0.0651	0.0661	0.0671	0.0681	0.0691
0.07	0.0701	0.0711	0.0721	0.0731	0.0741	0.0751	0.0761	0.0772	0.0782	0.0792
0.08	0.0802	0.0812	0.0822	0.0832	0.0842	0.0852	0.0862	0.0872	0.0882	0.0892
0.09	0.0902	0.0913	0.0923	0.0933	0.0943	0.0953	0.0963	0.0973	0.0983	0.0993
0.10	0.1003	0.1013	0.1024	0.1034	0.1044	0.1054	0.1064	0.1074	0.1084	0.1094
0.11	0.1104	0.1115	0.1125	0.1135	0.1145	0.1155	0.1165	0.1175	0.1186	0.1196
0.12	0.1206	0.1216	0.1226	0.1236	0.1246	0.1257	0.1267	0.1277	0.1287	0.1297
0.13	0.1307	0.1318	0.1328	0.1338	0.1348	0.1358	0.1368	0.1379	0.1389	0.1399
0.14	0.1409	0.1419	0.1430	0.1440	0.1450	0.1460	0.1471	0.1481	0.1491	0.1501
0.15	0.1511	0.1522	0.1532	0.1542	0.1552	0.1563	0.1573	0.1583	0.1593	0.1604
0.16	0.1614	0.1624	0.1634	0.1645	0.1655	0.1665	0.1676	0.1686	0.1696	0.1706
0.17	0.1717	0.1727	0.1737	0.1748	0.1758	0.1768	0.1779	0.1789	0.1799	0.1809
0.18	0.1820	0.1830	0.1841	0.1851	0.1861	0.1872	0.1882	0.1892	0.1903	0.1913
0.19	0.1923	0.1934	0.1944	0.1955	0.1965	0.1975	0.1986	0.1996	0.2007	0.2017
0.20	0.2027	0.2038	0.2048	0.2059	0.2069	0.2079	0.2090	0.2100	0.2111	0.2121
0.21	0.2132	0.2142	0.2153	0.2163	0.2174	0.2184	0.2195	0.2205	0.2216	0.2226
0.22	0.2237	0.2247	0.2258	0.2268	0.2279	0.2289	0.2300	0.2310	0.2321	0.2331
0.23	0.2342	0.2352	0.2363	0.2374	0.2384	0.2395	0.2405	0.2416	0.2427	0.2437
0.24	0.2448	0.2458	0.2469	0.2480	0.2490	0.2501	0.2512	0.2522	0.2533	0.2543
0.25	0.2554	0.2565	0.2575	0.2586	0.2597	0.2608	0.2618	0.2629	0.2640	0.2650
0.26	0.2661	0.2672	0.2683	0.2693	0.2704	0.2715	0.2726	0.2736	0.2747	0.2758
0.27	0.2769	0.2779	0.2790	0.2801	0.2812	0.2823	0.2833	0.2844	0.2855	0.2866
0.28	0.2877	0.2888	0.2899	0.2909	0.2920	0.2931	0.2942	0.2953	0.2964	0.2975
0.29	0.2986	0.2997	0.3008	0.3018	0.3029	0.3040	0.3051	0.3062	0.3073	0.3084
0.30	0.3095	0.3106	0.3117	0.3128	0.3139	0.3150	0.3161	0.3172	0.3183	0.3194
0.31	0.3205	0.3217	0.3228	0.3239	0.3250	0.3261	0.3272	0.3283	0.3294	0.3305
0.32	0.3316	0.3328	0.3339	0.3350	0.3361	0.3372	0.3383	0.3395	0.3406	0.3417
0.33	0.3428	0.3440	0.3451	0.3462	0.3473	0.3484	0.3496	0.3507	0.3518	0.3530
0.34	0.3541	0.3552	0.3564	0.3575	0.3586	0.3598	0.3609	0.3620	0.3632	0.3643
0.35	0.3654	0.3666	0.3677	0.3689	0.3700	0.3712	0.3723	0.3734	0.3746	0.3757
0.36	0.3769	0.3780	0.3792	0.3803	0.3815	0.3826	0.3838	0.3850	0.3861	0.3873
0.37	0.3884	0.3896	0.3907	0.3919	0.3931	0.3942	0.3954	0.3966	0.3977	0.3989
0.38	0.4001	0.4012	0.4024	0.4036	0.4047	0.4059	0.4071	0.4083	0.4094	0.4106
0.39	0.4118	0.4130	0.4142	0.4153	0.4165	0.4177	0.4189	0.4201	0.4213	0.4225
0.40	0.4236	0.4248	0.4260	0.4272	0.4284	0.4296	0.4308	0.4320	0.4332	0.4344
0.41	0.4356	0.4368	0.4380	0.4392	0.4404	0.4416	0.4428	0.4441	0.4453	0.4465
0.42	0.4477	0.4489	0.4501	0.4513	0.4526	0.4538	0.4550	0.4562	0.4574	0.4587
0.43	0.4599	0.4611	0.4624	0.4636	0.4648	0.4660	0.4673	0.4685	0.4698	0.4710
0.44	0.4722	0.4735	0.4747	0.4760	0.4772	0.4784	0.4797	0.4809	0.4822	0.4834
0.45	0.4847	0.4860	0.4872	0.4885	0.4897	0.4910	0.4922	0.4935	0.4948	0.4960
0.46	0.4973	0.4986	0.4999	0.5011	0.5024	0.5037	0.5049	0.5062	0.5075	0.5088
0.47	0.5101	0.5114	0.5126	0.5139	0.5152	0.5165	0.5178	0.5191	0.5204	0.5217
0.48	0.5230	0.5243	0.5256	0.5269	0.5282	0.5295	0.5308	0.5321	0.5334	0.5347
0.49	0.5361	0.5374	0.5387	0.5400	0.5413	0.5427	0.5440	0.5453	0.5466	0.5480
0.50	0.5493	0.5506	0.5520	0.5533	0.5547	0.5560	0.5573	0.5587	0.5600	0.5614

Table A.5 Continued

Fisher's Natural Logarithmic Transformation of r to r'

	0.000	0.001	0.002	0.003	0.004	0.005	0.006	0.007	0.008	0.009
0.51	0.5627	0.5641	0.5654	0.5668	0.5682	0.5695	0.5709	0.5722	0.5736	0.5750
0.52	0.5763	0.5777	0.5791	0.5805	0.5818	0.5832	0.5846	0.5860	0.5874	0.5888
0.53	0.5901	0.5915	0.5929	0.5943	0.5957	0.5971	0.5985	0.5999	0.6013	0.6027
0.54	0.6042	0.6056	0.6070	0.6084	0.6098	0.6112	0.6127	0.6141	0.6155	0.6169
0.55	0.6184	0.6198	0.6213	0.6227	0.6241	0.6256	0.6270	0.6285	0.6299	0.6314
0.56	0.6328	0.6343	0.6358	0.6372	0.6387	0.6401	0.6416	0.6431	0.6446	0.6460
0.57	0.6475	0.6490	0.6505	0.6520	0.6535	0.6550	0.6565	0.6580	0.6595	0.6610
0.58	0.6625	0.6640	0.6655	0.6670	0.6685	0.6700	0.6716	0.6731	0.6746	0.6761
0.59	0.6777	0.6792	0.6807	0.6823	0.6838	0.6854	0.6869	0.6885	0.6900	0.6916
0.60	0.6931	0.6947	0.6963	0.6978	0.6994	0.7010	0.7026	0.7042	0.7057	0.7073
0.61	0.7089	0.7105	0.7121	0.7137	0.7153	0.7169	0.7185	0.7201	0.7218	0.7234
0.62	0.7250	0.7266	0.7283	0.7299	0.7315	0.7332	0.7348	0.7365	0.7381	0.7398
0.63	0.7414	0.7431	0.7447	0.7464	0.7481	0.7498	0.7514	0.7531	0.7548	0.7565
0.64	0.7582	0.7599	0.7616	0.7633	0.7650	0.7667	0.7684	0.7701	0.7718	0.7736
0.65	0.7753	0.7770	0.7788	0.7805	0.7823	0.7840	0.7858	0.7875	0.7893	0.7910
0.66	0.7928	0.7946	0.7964	0.7981	0.7999	0.8017	0.8035	0.8053	0.8071	0.8089
0.67	0.8107	0.8126	0.8144	0.8162	0.8180	0.8199	0.8217	0.8236	0.8254	0.8273
0.68	0.8291	0.8310	0.8328	0.8347	0.8366	0.8385	0.8404	0.8423	0.8441	0.8460
0.69	0.8480	0.8499	0.8518	0.8537	0.8556	0.8576	0.8595	0.8614	0.8634	0.8653
0.70	0.8673	0.8693	0.8712	0.8732	0.8752	0.8772	0.8792	0.8812	0.8832	0.8852
0.71	0.8872	0.8892	0.8912	0.8933	0.8953	0.8973	0.8994	0.9014	0.9035	0.9056
0.72	0.9076	0.9097	0.9118	0.9139	0.9160	0.9181	0.9202	0.9223	0.9245	0.9266
0.73	0.9287	0.9309	0.9330	0.9352	0.9373	0.9395	0.9417	0.9439	0.9461	0.9483
0.74	0.9505	0.9527	0.9549	0.9571	0.9594	0.9616	0.9639	0.9661	0.9684	0.9707
0.75	0.9730	0.9752	0.9775	0.9798	0.9822	0.9845	0.9868	0.9892	0.9915	0.9939
0.76	0.9962	0.9986	1.0010	1.0034	1.0058	1.0082	1.0106	1.0130	1.0154	1.0179
0.77	1.0203	1.0228	1.0253	1.0277	1.0302	1.0327	1.0352	1.0378	1.0403	1.0428
0.78	1.0454	1.0479	1.0505	1.0531	1.0557	1.0583	1.0609	1.0635	1.0661	1.0688
0.79	1.0714	1.0741	1.0768	1.0795	1.0822	1.0849	1.0876	1.0903	1.0931	1.0958
0.80	1.0986	1.1014	1.1042	1.1070	1.1098	1.1127	1.1155	1.1184	1.1212	1.1241
0.81	1.1270	1.1299	1.1329	1.1358	1.1388	1.1417	1.1447	1.1477	1.1507	1.1538
0.82	1.1568	1.1599	1.1630	1.1660	1.1692	1.1723	1.1754	1.1786	1.1817	1.1849
0.83	1.1881	1.1914	1.1946	1.1979	1.2011	1.2044	1.2077	1.2111	1.2144	1.2178
0.84	1.2212	1.2246	1.2280	1.2315	1.2349	1.2384	1.2419	1.2454	1.2490	1.2526
0.85	1.2562	1.2598	1.2634	1.2671	1.2707	1.2745	1.2782	1.2819	1.2857	1.2895
0.86	1.2933	1.2972	1.3011	1.3050	1.3089	1.3129	1.3169	1.3209	1.3249	1.3290
0.87	1.3331	1.3372	1.3414	1.3456	1.3498	1.3540	1.3583	1.3626	1.3670	1.3714
0.88	1.3758	1.3802	1.3847	1.3892	1.3938	1.3984	1.4030	1.4077	1.4124	1.4171
0.89	1.4219	1.4268	1.4316	1.4365	1.4415	1.4465	1.4516	1.4566	1.4618	1.4670
0.90	1.4722	1.4775	1.4828	1.4882	1.4937	1.4992	1.5047	1.5103	1.5160	1.5217
0.91	1.5275	1.5334	1.5393	1.5453	1.5513	1.5574	1.5636	1.5698	1.5762	1.5826
0.92	1.5890	1.5956	1.6022	1.6089	1.6157	1.6226	1.6296	1.6366	1.6438	1.6510
0.93	1.6584	1.6658	1.6734	1.6811	1.6888	1.6967	1.7047	1.7129	1.7211	1.7295
0.94	1.7380	1.7467	1.7555	1.7645	1.7736	1.7828	1.7923	1.8019	1.8117	1.8216
0.95	1.8318	1.8421	1.8527	1.8635	1.8745	1.8857	1.8972	1.9090	1.9210	1.9333
0.96	1.9459	1.9588	1.9721	1.9857	1.9996	2.0139	2.0287	2.0439	2.0595	2.0756
0.97	2.0923	2.1095	2.1273	2.1457	2.1649	2.1847	2.2054	2.2269	2.2494	2.2729
0.98	2.2976	2.3235	2.3507	2.3796	2.4101	2.4427	2.4774	2.5147	2.5550	2.5987
0.99	2.6467	2.6996	2.7587	2.8257	2.9031	2.9945	3.1063	3.2504	3.4534	3.8002

Source: Compiled by the authors using SYSTAT.

Table A.6.1 Liberal and conservative critical values for the **Mann–Whitney** *U-test* for two-tailed tests at the 0.10 level (one-tailed at the 0.05 level) and their estimated probabilities. Probabilities estimated with 1,000,000 random permutations using Resampling Stats

n_1	n_2=5	6	7	8	9	10	11	12
5	**5** .1513 **4** .0953	**6** .1259 **5** .0825	**7** .1064 **6** .0736	**9** .1271 **8** .0926	**10** .1117 **9** .0827	**12** .1289 **11** .0992	**13** .1149 **12** .0900	**14** .1036 **13** .0817
6	—	**8** .1322 **7** .0932	**9** .1019 **8** .0738	**11** .1077 **10** .0810	**13** .1138 **12** .0882	**15** .1180 **14** .0935	**17** .1216 **16** .0982	**18** .1031 **17** .0836
7	—	—	**12** .1280 **11** .0970	**14** .1211 **13** .0943	**16** .1142 **15** .0908	**18** .1091 **17** .0880	**20** .1039 **19** .0848	**22** .1006 **21** .0834
8	—	—	—	**16** .1050 **15** .0831	**19** .1131 **18** .0922	**21** .1011 **20** .0831	**24** .1087 **23** .0910	**27** .1154 **26** .0979
9	—	—	—	—	**22** .1129 **21** .0935	**25** .1122 **24** .0943	**28** .1120 **27** .0950	**31** .1111 **30** .0955
10	—	—	—	—	—	**28** .1049 **27** .0891	**32** .1144 **31** .0985	**35** .1068 **34** .0930
11	—	—	—	—	—	—	**35** .1013 **34** .0879	**39** .1039 **38** .0911
12	—	—	—	—	—	—	—	**43** .1004 **42** .0886
13	—	—	—	—	—	—	—	—
14	—	—	—	—	—	—	—	—
15	—	—	—	—	—	—	—	—
16	—	—	—	—	—	—	—	—
17	—	—	—	—	—	—	—	—
18	—	—	—	—	—	—	—	—
19	—	—	—	—	—	—	—	—
20	—	—	—	—	—	—	—	—

Table A.6.1 Continued

					n_2			
n_1	13	14	15	16	17	18	19	20
5	**16** .1175	**17** .1067	**19** .1183	**20** .1094	**21** .1013	**23** .1110	**24** .1013	**26** .1123
	15 .0948	**16** .0870	**18** .0979	**19** .0912	**20** .0850	**22** .0943	**23** .0850	**25** .0969
6	**20** .1057	**22** .1097	**24** .1118	**26** .1146	**27** .1008	**29** .1038	**31** .1061	**33** .1086
	19 .0871	**21** .0917	**23** .0944	**25** .0976	**26** .0865	**28** .0897	**30** .0926	**32** .0954
7	**25** .1153	**27** .1099	**29** .1057	**31** .1022	**34** .1137	**36** .1102	**38** .1065	**40** .1042
	24 .0976	**26** .0936	**28** .0910	**30** .0886	**33** .0995	**35** .0968	**37** .0940	**39** .0925
8	**29** .1041	**32** .1097	**34** .1007	**37** .1055	**40** .1099	**42** .1023	**45** .1064	**48** .1105
	28 .0890	**31** .0948	**33** .0874	**36** .0925	**39** .0969	**41** .0906	**44** .0949	**47** .0992
9	**34** .1102	**37** .1091	**40** .1078	**43** .1078	**46** .1070	**49** .1060	**52** .1056	**55** .1050
	33 .0956	**36** .0954	**39** .0948	**42** .0955	**45** .0954	**48** .0951	**51** .0952	**54** .0951
10	**38** .1005	**42** .1084	**45** .1024	**49** .1084	**52** .1037	**56** .1093	**59** .1037	**63** .1093
	37 .0879	**41** .0959	**44** .0909	**48** .0968	**51** .0931	**55** .0986	**58** .0941	**62** .0995
11	**43** .1057	**47** .1068	**51** .1082	**55** .1093	**58** .1007	**62** .1011	**66** .1028	**70** .1033
	42 .0933	**46** .0951	**50** .0970	**54** .0985	**57** .0911	**61** .0918	**67** .0939	**69** .0946
12	**48** .1098	**52** .1063	**56** .1030	**61** .1100	**65** .1068	**69** .1044	**73** .1013	**78** .1068
	47 .0977	**51** .0954	**55** .0925	**60** .0996	**64** .0971	**68** .0953	**72** .0930	**77** .0984
13	**52** .1014	**57** .1047	**62** .1079	**66** .1007	**71** .1032	**76** .1055	**81** .1076	**85** .1009
	51 .0908	**56** .0946	**61** .0979	**65** .0918	**70** .0944	**75** .0971	**80** .0992	**84** .0934
14	—	**62** .1034	**67** .1023	**72** .1012	**78** .1083	**83** .1066	**88** .1054	**93** .1045
	—	**61** .0939	**66** .0932	**71** .0926	**77** .0997	**82** .0983	**87** .0974	**92** .0971
15	—	—	**73** .1066	**78** .1016	**84** .1046	**89** .1001	**95** .1037	**101** .1068
	—	—	**72** .0977	**77** .0934	**83** .0965	**88** .0925	**94** .0964	**100** .0997
16	—	—	—	**84** .1018	**90** .1019	**96** .1019	**102** .1015	**108** .1014
	—	—	—	**83** .0940	**89** .0943	**95** .0947	**101** .0944	**107** .0948
17	—	—	—	—	**97** .1063	**103** .1032	**110** .1068	**116** .1036
	—	—	—	—	**96** .0989	**102** .0963	**109** .0999	**115** .0972
18	—	—	—	—	—	**110** .1039	**117** .1048	**124** .1054
	—	—	—	—	—	**109** .0971	**116** .0984	**123** .0990
19	—	—	—	—	—	—	**124** .1027	**131** .1006
	—	—	—	—	—	—	**123** .0965	**130** .0948
20	—	—	—	—	—	—	—	**139** .1020
	—	—	—	—	—	—	—	**138** .0964

Table A.6.2 Liberal and conservative critical values for the **Mann–Whitney** *U-test* for two-tailed tests at the .05 level (one-tailed at the 0.025 level) and their estimated probabilities. Probabilities estimated with 1,000,000 random permutations using Resampling Stats

									n_2								
n_1	5		6		7		8		9		10		11		12	
5	3	.0553	4	.0522	6	.0736	7	.0648	8	.0598	9	.0552	10	.0521	12	.0636
	2	.0316	3	.0304	5	.0482	6	.0446	7	.0418	8	.0400	9	.0384	11	.0486
6	—	—	6	.0652	7	.0515	9	.0590	11	.0667	12	.0560	14	.0615	15	.0535
	—	—	5	.0412	6	.0352	8	.0425	10	.0499	11	.0422	13	.0476	14	.0421
7	—	—	—	—	9	.0529	11	.0545	13	.0550	15	.0554	17	.0551	19	.0555
	—	—	—	—	8	.0376	10	.0402	12	.0420	14	.0431	16	.0438	18	.0447
8	—	—	—	—	—	—	14	.0650	16	.0588	18	.0544	20	.0507	23	.0575
	—	—	—	—	—	—	13	.0499	15	.0460	17	.0433	19	.0409	22	.0474
9	—	—	—	—	—	—	—	—	18	.0508	21	.0530	24	.0562	27	.0585
	—	—	—	—	—	—	—	—	17	.0404	20	.0430	23	.0464	26	.0490
10	—	—	—	—	—	—	—	—	—	—	24	.0524	27	.0513	30	.0501
	—	—	—	—	—	—	—	—	—	—	23	.0432	26	.0429	29	.0423
11	—	—	—	—	—	—	—	—	—	—	—	—	31	.0558	34	.0514
	—	—	—	—	—	—	—	—	—	—	—	—	30	.0474	33	.0440
12	—	—	—	—	—	—	—	—	—	—	—	—	—	—	38	.0519
	—	—	—	—	—	—	—	—	—	—	—	—	—	—	37	.0450
13	—	—	—	—	—	—	—	—	—	—	—	—	—	—	—	—
14	—	—	—	—	—	—	—	—	—	—	—	—	—	—	—	—
15	—	—	—	—	—	—	—	—	—	—	—	—	—	—	—	—
16	—	—	—	—	—	—	—	—	—	—	—	—	—	—	—	—
17	—	—	—	—	—	—	—	—	—	—	—	—	—	—	—	—
18	—	—	—	—	—	—	—	—	—	—	—	—	—	—	—	—
19	—	—	—	—	—	—	—	—	—	—	—	—	—	—	—	—
20	—	—	—	—	—	—	—	—	—	—	—	—	—	—	—	—

Table A.6.2 Continued

n_1	n_2=13		14		15		16		17		18		19		20	
5	13	.0595	14	.0554	15	.0522	16	.0503	18	.0585	19	.0555	20	.0585	21	.0505
	12	.0463	13	.0435	14	.0414	15	.0402	17	.0476	18	.0458	19	.0476	20	.0423
6	17	.0575	18	.0510	20	.0547	22	.0585	23	.0521	25	.0562	26	.0508	28	.0541
	16	.0462	17	.0411	19	.0449	21	.0485	22	.0435	24	.0476	25	.0430	27	.0463
7	21	.0564	23	.0560	25	.0557	27	.0552	29	.0552	31	.0549	33	.0546	35	.0554
	20	.0462	22	.0460	24	.0466	26	.0466	28	.0469	30	.0473	32	.0471	34	.0481
8	25	.0532	27	.0500	30	.0557	32	.0523	35	.0570	37	.0538	39	.0514	42	.0553
	24	.0446	26	.0419	29	.0475	31	.0447	34	.0495	36	.0470	38	.0449	41	.0489
9	29	.0512	32	.0532	35	.0547	38	.0570	40	.0513	43	.0524	46	.0540	49	.0556
	28	.0434	31	.0455	34	.0472	37	.0495	39	.0448	42	.0461	45	.0479	48	.0496
10	34	.0569	37	.0562	40	.0546	43	.0528	46	.0522	49	.0510	53	.0555	56	.0546
	33	.0489	36	.0486	39	.0478	42	.0462	45	.0459	48	.0452	52	.0498	55	.0492
11	38	.0548	41	.0505	45	.0534	48	.0500	52	.0526	56	.0548	59	.0520	63	.0538
	37	.0474	40	.0441	44	.0470	47	.0440	51	.0470	55	.0491	58	.0466	62	.0486
12	42	.0524	46	.0526	50	.0527	54	.0529	58	.0530	62	.0533	66	.0532	70	.0531
	41	.0458	45	.0462	49	.0467	53	.0472	57	.0476	61	.0480	65	.0481	69	.0484
13	46	.0500	51	.0543	55	.0521	60	.0555	64	.0535	68	.0513	73	.0541	77	.0521
	45	.0440	50	.0481	54	.0466	59	.0499	63	.0483	67	.0466	72	.0493	76	.0477
14	—	—	56	.0557	60	.0509	65	.0521	70	.0534	75	.0540	79	.0500	84	.513
	—	—	55	.0497	59	.0457	64	.0470	69	.0484	74	.0493	78	.0456	83	.0470
15	—	—	—	—	65	.0505	71	.0546	76	.0531	81	.0519	86	.0517	91	.0503
	—	—	—	—	64	.0455	70	.0496	75	.0486	80	.0477	85	.0475	90	.0464
16	—	—	—	—	—	—	76	.0515	82	.0534	87	.0505	93	.0514	99	.0533
	—	—	—	—	—	—	75	.0471	81	.0490	86	.0464	92	.0475	98	.0494
17	—	—	—	—	—	—	—	—	88	.0534	94	.0527	100	.0525	106	.0520
	—	—	—	—	—	—	—	—	87	.0489	93	.0488	99	.0486	105	.0483
18	—	—	—	—	—	—	—	—	—	—	100	.0508	107	.0530	113	.0511
	—	—	—	—	—	—	—	—	—	—	99	.0472	106	.0493	112	.0476
19	—	—	—	—	—	—	—	—	—	—	—	—	114	.0534	120	.0501
	—	—	—	—	—	—	—	—	—	—	—	—	113	.0497	119	.0478
20	—	—	—	—	—	—	—	—	—	—	—	—	—	—	128	.0522
	—	—	—	—	—	—	—	—	—	—	—	—	—	—	127	.0489

Table A.6.3 Liberal and conservative critical values for the **Mann-Whitney** *U-test* for two-tailed tests at the .02 level (one-tailed at the 0.01 level) and their estimated probabilities. Probabilities estimated with 1,000,000 random permutations using Resampling Stats

n_1		5	6	7	8	9	10	11	12
						n_2			
5		**2** .0316	**3** .0304	**4** .0303	**5** .0293	**6** .0289	**7** .0280	**8** .0276	**9** .0269
		1 .0158	**2** .0172	**3** .0176	**4** .0184	**5** .0190	**6** .0193	**7** .0193	**8** .0194
6		—	**4** .0259	**5** .0221	**7** .0293	**8** .0258	**9** .0228	**10** .0202	**12** .0247
		—	**3** .0151	**4** .0140	**6** .0199	**7** .0178	**8** .0162	**9** .0145	**11** .0183
7		—	—	**7** .0260	**8** .0207	**10** .0230	**12** .0251	**13** .0202	**15** .0218
		—	—	**6** .0175	**7** .0139	**9** .0165	**11** .0186	**12** .0152	**14** .0169
8		—	—	—	**10** .0207	**12** .0205	**14** .0203	**16** .0203	**18** .0200
		—	—	—	**9** .0148	**11** .0151	**13** .0153	**15** .0157	**17** .0157
9		—	—	—	—	**15** .0244	**17** .0221	**19** .0201	**22** .0228
		—	—	—	—	**14** .0187	**16** .0172	**18** .0160	**21** .0184
10		—	—	—	—	—	**20** .0230	**23** .0241	**25** .0203
		—	—	—	—	—	**19** .0183	**22** .0196	**24** .0167
11		—	—	—	—	—	—	**26** .0235	**29** .0225
		—	—	—	—	—	—	**25** .0195	**28** .0187
12		—	—	—	—	—	—	—	**32** .0204
		—	—	—	—	—	—	—	**31** .0172
13		—	—	—	—	—	—	—	—
14		—	—	—	—	—	—	—	—
15		—	—	—	—	—	—	—	—
16		—	—	—	—	—	—	—	—
17		—	—	—	—	—	—	—	—
18		—	—	—	—	—	—	—	—
19		—	—	—	—	—	—	—	—
20		—	—	—	—	—	—	—	—

Table A.6.3 Continued

		n_2 = 13	14	15	16	17	18	19	20
n_1 = 5		10 .0267	11 .0257	12 .0253	13 .0250	14 .0247	15 .0242	16 .0247	17 .0236
		9 .0196	10 .0192	11 .0193	12 .0194	13 .0193	14 .0192	15 .0193	16 .0190
6		13 .0222	14 .0200	16 .0231	17 .0213	19 .0242	20 .0226	21 .0211	23 .0234
		12 .0169	13 .0154	15 .0182	16 .0170	18 .0196	19 .0149	20 .0173	22 .0194
7		17 .0238	18 .0200	20 .0213	22 .0224	24 .0233	25 .0205	27 .0214	29 .0223
		16 .0188	17 .0158	19 .0173	21 .0183	23 .0193	24 .0171	26 .0180	28 .0189
8		21 .0247	23 .0238	25 .0235	27 .0229	29 .0225	31 .0219	33 .0219	35 .0213
		20 .0200	22 .0196	24 .0196	26 .0192	28 .0189	30 .0186	32 .0188	34 .0182
9		24 .0208	27 .0229	29 .0208	32 .0232	34 .0215	37 .0230	39 .0215	41 .0204
		23 .0171	26 .0190	28 .0174	31 .0196	33 .0185	36 .0198	38 .0186	40 .0177
10		28 .0212	31 .0221	34 .0226	37 .0229	39 .0203	42 .0209	45 .0210	48 .0214
		27 .0176	30 .0187	33 .0191	36 .0196	38 .0176	41 .0181	44 .0184	47 .0189
11		32 .0217	35 .0211	38 .0205	42 .0226	45 .0219	48 .0212	51 .0209	54 .0201
		31 .0183	34 .0180	37 .0176	41 .0196	44 .0192	47 .0186	50 .0184	53 .0177
12		36 .0221	39 .0201	43 .0214	47 .0225	50 .0207	54 .0219	57 .0203	61 .0211
		35 .0188	38 .0173	42 .0186	46 .0197	49 .0181	53 .0193	56 .0180	60 .0189
13		40 .0219	44 .0220	48 .0222	52 .0220	56 .0223	60 .0221	64 .0221	68 .0217
		39 .0190	43 .0191	47 .0195	51 .0195	55 .0199	59 .0196	63 .0198	67 .0196
14		—	48 .0211	52 .0202	57 .0216	61 .0211	66 .0220	70 .0211	74 .0204
		—	47 .0185	51 .0178	56 .0192	60 .0189	65 .0198	69 .0189	73 .0184
15		—	—	57 .0209	62 .0215	67 .0219	71 .0201	76 .0209	81 .0211
		—	—	56 .0185	61 .0193	66 .0197	70 .0181	75 .0190	80 .0193
16		—	—	—	67 .0211	72 .0210	77 .0205	83 .0219	88 .0214
		—	—	—	66 .0190	71 .0189	76 .0185	82 .0199	87 .0195
17		—	—	—	—	78 .0216	83 .0203	89 .0212	94 .0201
		—	—	—	—	77 .0196	82 .0186	88 .0194	93 .0185
18		—	—	—	—	—	89 .0204	95 .0205	101 .0206
		—	—	—	—	—	88 .0187	94 .0188	100 .0190
19		—	—	—	—	—	—	102 .0217	108 .0209
		—	—	—	—	—	—	101 .0198	107 .0193
20		—	—	—	—	—	—	—	115 .0210
		—	—	—	—	—	—	—	114 .0195

Table A.6.4 Liberal and conservative critical values for the **Mann–Whitney** *U-test* for two-tailed tests at the .01 level (one-tailed at the 0.005 level) and their estimated probabilities. Probabilities estimated with 1,000,000 random permutations using Resampling Stats

n_1		n_2 = 5	6	7	8	9	10	11	12
5	liberal	**1** .0158	**2** .0172	**2** .0100	**3** .0108	**4** .0121	**5** .0126	**6** .0133	**7** .0136
	conservative	**0** .0079	**1** .0086	**1** .0050	**2** .0062	**3** .0071	**4** .0080	**5** .0088	**6** .0094
6	liberal	—	**3** .0151	**4** .0140	**5** .0126	**6** .0122	**7** .0111	**8** .0103	**10** .0135
	conservative	—	**2** .0087	**3** .0081	**4** .0079	**5** .0077	**6** .0077	**7** .0071	**9** .0096
7	liberal	—	—	**5** .0112	**7** .0139	**8** .0117	**10** .0136	**11** .0112	**13** .0130
	conservative	—	—	**4** .0071	**6** .0093	**7** .0079	**9** .0098	**10** .0082	**12** .0098
8	liberal	—	—	—	**8** .0106	**10** .0111	**12** .0115	**14** .0121	**16** .0123
	conservative	—	—	—	**7** .0072	**9** .0080	**11** .0085	**13** .0091	**15** .0096
9	liberal	—	—	—	—	**12** .0106	**14** .0100	**17** .0125	**19** .0118
	conservative	—	—	—	—	**11** .0078	**13** .0075	**16** .0098	**18** .0093
10	liberal	—	—	—	—	—	**17** .0113	**19** .0100	**22** .0110
	conservative	—	—	—	—	—	**16** .0088	**18** .0079	**21** .0088
11	liberal	—	—	—	—	—	—	**22** .0105	**25** .0106
	conservative	—	—	—	—	—	—	**21** .0084	**24** .0087
12	liberal	—	—	—	—	—	—	—	**28** .0100
	conservative	—	—	—	—	—	—	—	**27** .0083
13		—	—	—	—	—	—	—	—
14		—	—	—	—	—	—	—	—
15		—	—	—	—	—	—	—	—
16		—	—	—	—	—	—	—	—
17		—	—	—	—	—	—	—	—
18		—	—	—	—	—	—	—	—
19		—	—	—	—	—	—	—	—
20		—	—	—	—	—	—	—	—

Table A.6.4 Continued

n_1	13	14	15	16	17	18	19	20
5	**8** .0141	**8** .0102	**9** .0108	**10** .0112	**11** .0116	**12** .0117	**13** .0116	**14** .0102
	7 .0098	**7** .0071	**8** .0078	**9** .0883	**10** .0086	**11** .0090	**12** .0086	**13** .0094
6	**11** .0126	**12** .0118	**13** .0109	**14** .0104	**16** .0125	**17** .0120	**18** .0114	**19** .0107
	10 .0093	**11** .0088	**12** .0083	**13** .0080	**15** .0099	**16** .0096	**17** .0091	**18** .0086
7	**14** .0112	**16** .0123	**17** .0109	**19** .0118	**20** .0104	**22** .0116	**23** .0102	**25** .0113
	13 .0086	**15** .0095	**16** .0085	**18** .0094	**19** .0084	**21** .0094	**22** .0083	**24** .0093
8	**18** .0127	**19** .0103	**21** .0107	**23** .0107	**25** .0110	**27** .0110	**29** .0113	**31** .0113
	17 .0100	**18** .0083	**20** .0087	**22** .0087	**24** .0091	**26** .0091	**29** .0095	**30** .0096
9	**21** .0110	**23** .0105	**25** .0101	**28** .0116	**30** .0112	**32** .0105	**34** .0101	**37** .0115
	20 .0088	**22** .0085	**24** .0081	**27** .0096	**29** .0093	**31** .0088	**33** .0085	**36** .0098
10	**25** .0120	**27** .0108	**30** .0114	**32** .0102	**35** .0111	**38** .0116	**40** .0104	**43** .0111
	24 .0098	**26** .0089	**29** .0095	**31** .0086	**34** .0094	**37** .0099	**39** .0090	**42** .0096
11	**28** .0107	**31** .0108	**34** .0108	**37** .0108	**40** .0109	**43** .0108	**46** .0109	**49** .0108
	27 .0088	**30** .0090	**33** .0091	**36** .0092	**39** .0094	**42** .0093	**45** .0095	**48** .0094
12	**32** .0114	**35** .0108	**38** .0102	**42** .0112	**45** .0106	**48** .0100	**52** .0110	**55** .0105
	31 .0096	**34** .0091	**37** .0087	**41** .0097	**44** .0092	**47** .0088	**51** .0096	**54** .0092
13	**35** .0101	**39** .0105	**43** .0111	**46** .0100	**50** .0106	**54** .0107	**57** .0100	**61** .0100
	34 .0085	**38** .0090	**42** .0095	**45** .0086	**49** .0092	**53** .0094	**56** .0087	**60** .0089
14	—	**43** .0106	**47** .0104	**51** .0102	**55** .0103	**59** .0100	**64** .0109	**68** .0109
	—	**42** .0091	**46** .0089	**50** .0089	**54** .0090	**58** .0089	**63** .0097	**67** .0098
15	—	—	**52** .0112	**56** .0107	**61** .0113	**65** .0105	**70** .0113	**74** .0105
	—	—	**51** .0099	**55** .0094	**60** .0100	**64** .0094	**69** .0099	**73** .0095
16	—	—	—	**61** .0108	**66** .0110	**71** .0110	**75** .0100	**80** .0100
	—	—	—	**60** .0096	**65** .0099	**70** .0099	**74** .0089	**79** .0090
17	—	—	—	—	**71** .0106	**76** .0102	**82** .0110	**87** .0107
	—	—	—	—	**70** .0096	**75** .0092	**81** .0099	**86** .0097
18	—	—	—	—	—	**82** .0107	**88** .0108	**93** .0104
	—	—	—	—	—	**81** .0097	**87** .0098	**92** .0095
19	—	—	—	—	—	—	**94** .0111	**100** .0107
	—	—	—	—	—	—	**93** .0099	**99** .0098
20	—	—	—	—	—	—	—	**106** .0103
	—	—	—	—	—	—	—	**105** .0094

n_2

Table A.7 Liberal and conservative critical values for the **Wilcoxon matched-pairs signed-ranks test** for two-tailed tests at the .10, .05, .02, and .01 level (one-tailed at the .05, .025, .01, and .005 level) and their estimated probabilities. Probabilities estimated with 1,000,000 random permutations using Resampling Stats

| | | \| Nominal level of α | | | | | | |
| | | .10 | | .05 | | .02 | | .01 | |
		T	p	T	p	T	p	T	p
	5	1	.1250	–	–	–	–	–	–
		0	.0625	–	–	–	–	–	–
	6	3	.1561	1	.0626	–	–	–	–
		2	.0937	0	.0314	–	–	–	–
	7	4	.1099	3	.0785	1	.0314	–	–
		3	.0785	2	.0472	0	.0157	–	–
	8	6	.1094	4	.0546	2	.0233	1	.0155
		5	.0781	3	.0390	1	.0155	0	.0077
	9	9	.1288	6	.0547	4	.0274	2	.0118
		8	.0977	5	.0391	3	.0196	1	.0078
	10	11	.1053	9	.0643	6	.0272	4	.0137
		10	.0838	8	.0487	5	.0195	3	.0097
	11	14	.1014	11	.0536	8	.0243	6	.0135
		13	.0829	10	.0418	7	.0184	5	.0097
	12	18	.1095	14	.0520	10	.0208	8	.0122
		17	.0920	13	.0423	9	.0161	7	.0093
	13	22	.1098	18	.0573	13	.0216	10	.0107
		21	.0942	17	.0479	12	.0172	9	.0083
N	14	26	.1038	22	.0580	16	.0203	13	.0107
		25	.0903	21	.0494	15	.0166	12	.0085
	15	31	.1068	26	.0552	20	.0216	16	.0103
		30	.0944	25	.0477	19	.0182	15	.0084
	16	36	.1043	30	.0506	24	.0214	16	.0103
		35	.0933	29	.0442	23	.0182	15	.0084
	17	42	.1089	35	.0509	28	.0202	24	.0110
		41	.0983	34	.0451	27	.0174	23	.0094
	18	48	.1085	41	.0540	33	.0208	28	.0150
		47	.0988	40	.0484	32	.0182	27	.0090
	19	54	.1047	47	.0551	38	.0207	33	.0110
		53	.0960	46	.0499	37	.0185	32	.0096
	20	61	.1056	53	.0533	44	.0217	38	.0107
		60	.0976	52	.0486	43	.0195	37	.0095
	21	68	.1031	59	.0501	50	.0214	43	.0100
		67	.0955	58	.0457	49	.0193	42	.0089
	22	76	.1056	66	.0502	56	.0210	49	.0150
		75	.0986	65	.0463	55	.0191	48	.0094

Table A.7 Continued

			.10		.05		.02		.01
		T	p	T	p	T	p	T	p
	23	84	.1049	74	.0525	63	.0215	55	.0102
		83	.0984	73	.0487	62	.0197	54	.0092
	24	92	.1014	82	.0526	70	.0290	62	.0103
		91	.0952	81	.0490	69	.0192	61	.0094
	25	101	.1018	90	.0519	77	.0205	69	.0106
		100	.0962	89	.0485	76	.0190	68	.0098
	26	111	.1046	99	.0525	85	.0205	76	.0102
		110	.0991	98	.0493	84	.0191	75	.0094
	27	120	.1007	108	.0521	93	.0201	84	.0103
		119	.0958	107	.0490	92	.0187	83	.0096
	28	131	.1043	117	.0506	102	.0204	92	.0103
		130	.0993	116	.0480	101	.0191	91	.0096
	29	141	.1010	127	.0511	111	.0206	101	.0108
		140	.0965	126	.0486	110	.0193	100	.0099
	30	152	.1008	138	.0525	121	.0211	110	.0107
		151	.0964	137	.0499	120	.0198	109	.0099
	31	164	.1025	148	.0505	131	.0211	119	.0104
		163	.0985	147	.0482	130	.0198	118	.0098
N	32	176	.1027	160	.0523	141	.0207	129	.0107
		175	.0988	159	.0499	140	.0197	128	.0099
	33	188	.1004	171	.0506	152	.0208	139	.0103
		187	.0967	170	.0484	151	.0197	138	.0097
	34	201	.1008	183	.0502	163	.0204	149	.0101
		200	.0971	182	.0481	162	.0195	148	.0096
	35	214	.1032	196	.0513	174	.0200	160	.0101
		213	.0997	195	.0494	173	.0191	159	.0096
	36	228	.1011	209	.0520	186	.0204	172	.0106
		227	.0978	208	.0499	185	.0195	171	.0099
	37	242	.1008	222	.0510	199	.0207	183	.0101
		241	.0976	221	.0492	198	.0198	182	.0097
	38	257	.1024	236	.0515	212	.0207	195	.0100
		256	.0993	235	.0497	211	.0199	194	.0094
	39	272	.1013	250	.0508	225	.0204	208	.0102
		271	.0984	249	.0492	224	.0196	207	.0098
	40	287	.1001	265	.0512	239	.0207	221	.0102
		286	.0974	264	.0496	238	.0199	220	.0098

Table A.8.1 The lower-tailed F-distribution ($\alpha = .05$)

	v_1												
v_2	1	2	3	4	5	6	7	8	9	10	12	14	16
1	0.006	0.054	0.099	0.130	0.151	0.167	0.179	0.188	0.195	0.201	0.211	0.217	0.223
2	0.005	0.053	0.105	0.144	0.173	0.194	0.211	0.224	0.235	0.244	0.257	0.267	0.275
3	0.005	0.052	0.108	0.152	0.185	0.210	0.230	0.246	0.259	0.270	0.287	0.299	0.309
4	0.004	0.052	0.110	0.157	0.193	0.221	0.243	0.261	0.275	0.288	0.307	0.321	0.333
5	0.004	0.052	0.111	0.160	0.198	0.228	0.252	0.271	0.287	0.301	0.322	0.338	0.351
6	0.004	0.052	0.112	0.162	0.202	0.233	0.259	0.279	0.296	0.311	0.334	0.351	0.365
7	0.004	0.052	0.113	0.164	0.205	0.238	0.264	0.286	0.304	0.319	0.343	0.362	0.376
8	0.004	0.052	0.113	0.166	0.208	0.241	0.268	0.291	0.310	0.326	0.351	0.371	0.386
9	0.004	0.052	0.113	0.167	0.210	0.244	0.272	0.295	0.315	0.331	0.358	0.378	0.394
10	0.004	0.052	0.114	0.168	0.211	0.246	0.275	0.299	0.319	0.336	0.363	0.384	0.401
11	0.004	0.052	0.114	0.168	0.213	0.248	0.278	0.302	0.322	0.340	0.368	0.390	0.407
12	0.004	0.052	0.114	0.169	0.214	0.250	0.280	0.305	0.325	0.343	0.372	0.395	0.412
13	0.004	0.051	0.115	0.170	0.215	0.251	0.282	0.307	0.328	0.346	0.376	0.399	0.417
14	0.004	0.051	0.115	0.170	0.216	0.253	0.283	0.309	0.331	0.349	0.379	0.403	0.421
15	0.004	0.051	0.115	0.171	0.217	0.254	0.285	0.311	0.333	0.351	0.382	0.406	0.425
16	0.004	0.051	0.115	0.171	0.217	0.255	0.286	0.312	0.335	0.354	0.385	0.409	0.429
17	0.004	0.051	0.115	0.171	0.218	0.256	0.287	0.314	0.336	0.356	0.387	0.412	0.432
18	0.004	0.051	0.115	0.172	0.218	0.257	0.288	0.315	0.338	0.357	0.389	0.414	0.434
19	0.004	0.051	0.115	0.172	0.219	0.257	0.289	0.316	0.339	0.359	0.391	0.417	0.437
20	0.004	0.051	0.115	0.172	0.219	0.258	0.290	0.317	0.341	0.360	0.393	0.419	0.439
22	0.004	0.051	0.116	0.173	0.220	0.259	0.292	0.319	0.343	0.363	0.396	0.423	0.444
24	0.004	0.051	0.116	0.173	0.221	0.260	0.293	0.321	0.345	0.365	0.399	0.426	0.447
26	0.004	0.051	0.116	0.174	0.221	0.261	0.294	0.322	0.346	0.367	0.402	0.429	0.451
28	0.004	0.051	0.116	0.174	0.222	0.262	0.295	0.324	0.348	0.369	0.404	0.431	0.453
30	0.004	0.051	0.116	0.174	0.222	0.263	0.296	0.325	0.349	0.370	0.405	0.433	0.456
40	0.004	0.051	0.116	0.175	0.224	0.265	0.299	0.329	0.354	0.376	0.412	0.441	0.465
50	0.004	0.051	0.117	0.175	0.225	0.266	0.301	0.331	0.357	0.379	0.416	0.446	0.471
60	0.004	0.051	0.117	0.176	0.226	0.267	0.303	0.333	0.359	0.382	0.419	0.450	0.475
80	0.004	0.051	0.117	0.176	0.227	0.269	0.304	0.335	0.361	0.385	0.423	0.454	0.480
100	0.004	0.051	0.117	0.177	0.227	0.269	0.305	0.336	0.363	0.386	0.426	0.457	0.483
120	0.004	0.051	0.117	0.177	0.227	0.270	0.306	0.337	0.364	0.388	0.427	0.459	0.486
200	0.004	0.051	0.117	0.177	0.228	0.271	0.307	0.339	0.366	0.390	0.430	0.463	0.490
500	0.004	0.051	0.117	0.178	0.229	0.272	0.309	0.340	0.368	0.392	0.433	0.467	0.495

Note: v_1 and v_2 are degrees of freedom for the numerator and denominator, respectively.

Source: Compiled by the authors using SYSTAT.

Table A.8.1 Continued

	v_1												
v_2	18	20	22	24	30	40	50	60	100	120	200	500	1000
1	0.227	0.230	0.233	0.235	0.240	0.245	0.248	0.250	0.254	0.255	0.257	0.259	0.260
2	0.281	0.286	0.290	0.294	0.302	0.309	0.314	0.317	0.324	0.326	0.329	0.332	0.333
3	0.316	0.323	0.328	0.332	0.342	0.352	0.358	0.363	0.371	0.373	0.377	0.381	0.383
4	0.342	0.349	0.355	0.360	0.372	0.384	0.391	0.396	0.406	0.409	0.414	0.418	0.420
5	0.361	0.369	0.376	0.382	0.395	0.408	0.417	0.422	0.434	0.437	0.443	0.448	0.450
6	0.376	0.385	0.392	0.399	0.413	0.428	0.437	0.444	0.456	0.460	0.466	0.472	0.474
7	0.388	0.398	0.406	0.413	0.428	0.445	0.455	0.462	0.476	0.479	0.486	0.493	0.495
8	0.398	0.409	0.417	0.425	0.441	0.459	0.470	0.477	0.492	0.496	0.504	0.511	0.513
9	0.407	0.418	0.427	0.435	0.452	0.471	0.482	0.490	0.506	0.511	0.519	0.527	0.529
10	0.415	0.426	0.435	0.444	0.462	0.481	0.494	0.502	0.519	0.523	0.532	0.541	0.543
11	0.421	0.433	0.443	0.451	0.470	0.491	0.504	0.512	0.530	0.535	0.544	0.553	0.556
12	0.427	0.439	0.449	0.458	0.478	0.499	0.512	0.522	0.540	0.545	0.555	0.564	0.568
13	0.432	0.445	0.455	0.464	0.485	0.507	0.520	0.530	0.550	0.555	0.565	0.575	0.578
14	0.437	0.449	0.460	0.470	0.491	0.513	0.528	0.538	0.558	0.563	0.574	0.584	0.588
15	0.441	0.454	0.465	0.474	0.496	0.520	0.534	0.545	0.566	0.571	0.583	0.593	0.597
16	0.445	0.458	0.469	0.479	0.501	0.525	0.540	0.551	0.573	0.579	0.590	0.601	0.605
17	0.448	0.462	0.473	0.483	0.506	0.530	0.546	0.557	0.579	0.585	0.597	0.609	0.612
18	0.451	0.465	0.477	0.487	0.510	0.535	0.551	0.562	0.586	0.592	0.604	0.616	0.620
19	0.454	0.468	0.480	0.490	0.514	0.540	0.556	0.567	0.591	0.597	0.610	0.622	0.626
20	0.456	0.471	0.483	0.493	0.518	0.544	0.560	0.572	0.597	0.603	0.616	0.628	0.632
22	0.461	0.476	0.488	0.499	0.524	0.551	0.569	0.581	0.606	0.613	0.627	0.640	0.644
24	0.465	0.480	0.493	0.504	0.530	0.558	0.576	0.588	0.615	0.622	0.636	0.650	0.654
26	0.469	0.484	0.497	0.508	0.535	0.564	0.582	0.595	0.622	0.630	0.645	0.659	0.664
28	0.472	0.487	0.501	0.512	0.539	0.569	0.588	0.601	0.629	0.637	0.652	0.667	0.672
30	0.475	0.490	0.504	0.516	0.543	0.573	0.593	0.606	0.636	0.643	0.659	0.675	0.680
40	0.485	0.502	0.516	0.529	0.558	0.591	0.612	0.627	0.660	0.669	0.687	0.705	0.711
50	0.491	0.509	0.524	0.537	0.568	0.602	0.625	0.641	0.677	0.687	0.707	0.727	0.734
60	0.496	0.514	0.529	0.543	0.575	0.611	0.635	0.652	0.689	0.700	0.722	0.743	0.751
80	0.502	0.520	0.536	0.551	0.584	0.622	0.647	0.666	0.707	0.718	0.743	0.767	0.776
100	0.506	0.525	0.541	0.555	0.590	0.629	0.656	0.675	0.719	0.731	0.757	0.784	0.794
120	0.508	0.527	0.544	0.559	0.594	0.634	0.662	0.682	0.727	0.740	0.768	0.797	0.807
200	0.513	0.533	0.551	0.566	0.603	0.645	0.674	0.696	0.745	0.760	0.792	0.827	0.840
500	0.518	0.539	0.557	0.572	0.611	0.655	0.686	0.710	0.765	0.781	0.819	0.863	0.882
1000	0.522	0.543	0.561	0.577	0.616	0.663	0.695	0.720	0.779	0.798	0.841	0.898	0.928

Note: v_1 and v_2 are degrees of freedom for the numerator and denominator, respectively.
Source: Compiled by the authors using SYSTAT.

Table A.8.2 The upper-tailed F-distribution ($\alpha = .05$)

v_2	\multicolumn{13}{c}{v_1}
	1	2	3	4	5	6	7	8	9	10	12	14	16
1	161.400	199.500	215.700	224.500	230.100	233.900	236.700	238.800	240.500	241.800	243.900	245.300	246.400
2	18.510	19.000	19.160	19.240	19.290	19.330	19.350	19.370	19.380	19.390	19.410	19.420	19.430
3	10.120	9.552	9.277	9.117	9.013	8.941	8.887	8.845	8.812	8.786	8.745	8.715	8.692
4	7.709	6.944	6.591	6.388	6.256	6.163	6.094	6.041	5.999	5.964	5.912	5.873	5.844
5	6.608	5.786	5.409	5.192	5.050	4.950	4.876	4.818	4.772	4.735	4.678	4.636	4.604
6	5.987	5.143	4.757	4.534	4.387	4.284	4.207	4.147	4.099	4.060	4.000	3.956	3.922
7	5.591	4.737	4.347	4.120	3.972	3.866	3.787	3.726	3.677	3.637	3.575	3.529	3.494
8	5.318	4.459	4.066	3.838	3.687	3.581	3.500	3.438	3.388	3.347	3.284	3.237	3.202
9	5.117	4.256	3.863	3.633	3.482	3.374	3.293	3.230	3.179	3.137	3.073	3.025	2.989
10	4.965	4.103	3.708	3.478	3.326	3.217	3.135	3.072	3.020	2.978	2.913	2.865	2.828
11	4.844	3.982	3.587	3.357	3.204	3.095	3.012	2.948	2.896	2.854	2.788	2.739	2.701
12	4.747	3.885	3.490	3.259	3.106	2.996	2.913	2.849	2.796	2.753	2.687	2.637	2.599
13	4.667	3.806	3.411	3.179	3.025	2.915	2.832	2.767	2.714	2.671	2.604	2.554	2.515
14	4.600	3.739	3.344	3.112	2.958	2.848	2.764	2.699	2.646	2.602	2.534	2.484	2.445
15	4.543	3.682	3.287	3.056	2.901	2.790	2.707	2.641	2.588	2.544	2.475	2.424	2.385
16	4.494	3.634	3.239	3.007	2.852	2.741	2.657	2.591	2.538	2.494	2.425	2.373	2.333
17	4.451	3.592	3.197	2.965	2.810	2.699	2.614	2.548	2.494	2.450	2.381	2.329	2.289
18	4.414	3.555	3.160	2.928	2.773	2.661	2.577	2.510	2.456	2.412	2.342	2.290	2.250
19	4.381	3.522	3.127	2.895	2.740	2.628	2.544	2.477	2.423	2.378	2.308	2.256	2.215
20	4.351	3.493	3.098	2.866	2.711	2.599	2.514	2.447	2.393	2.348	2.278	2.225	2.184
22	4.301	3.443	3.049	2.817	2.661	2.549	2.464	2.397	2.342	2.297	2.226	2.173	2.131
24	4.260	3.403	3.009	2.776	2.621	2.508	2.423	2.355	2.300	2.255	2.183	2.130	2.088
26	4.225	3.369	2.975	2.743	2.587	2.474	2.388	2.321	2.265	2.220	2.148	2.094	2.052
28	4.196	3.340	2.947	2.714	2.558	2.445	2.359	2.291	2.236	2.190	2.118	2.064	2.021
30	4.171	3.316	2.922	2.690	2.534	2.421	2.334	2.266	2.211	2.165	2.092	2.037	1.995
40	4.085	3.232	2.839	2.606	2.449	2.336	2.249	2.180	2.124	2.077	2.003	1.948	1.904
50	4.034	3.183	2.790	2.557	2.400	2.286	2.199	2.130	2.073	2.026	1.952	1.895	1.850
60	4.001	3.150	2.758	2.525	2.368	2.254	2.167	2.097	2.040	1.993	1.917	1.860	1.815
80	3.960	3.111	2.719	2.486	2.329	2.214	2.126	2.056	1.999	1.951	1.875	1.817	1.772
100	3.936	3.087	2.696	2.463	2.305	2.191	2.103	2.032	1.975	1.927	1.850	1.792	1.746
120	3.920	3.072	2.680	2.447	2.290	2.175	2.087	2.016	1.959	1.910	1.834	1.775	1.728
200	3.888	3.041	2.650	2.417	2.259	2.144	2.056	1.985	1.927	1.878	1.801	1.742	1.694
500	3.860	3.014	2.623	2.390	2.232	2.117	2.028	1.957	1.899	1.850	1.772	1.712	1.664
	3.841	2.996	2.605	2.372	2.214	2.099	2.010	1.938	1.880	1.831	1.752	1.692	1.644

Note: v_1 and v_2 are degrees of freedom for the numerator and denominator, respectively.

Table A.8.2 Continued

| | v_1 | | | | | | | | | | | | |
v_2	18	20	22	24	30	40	50	60	100	120	200	500	1000
1	247.300	248.000	248.600	249.100	250.100	251.100	251.800	252.200	253.000	253.200	253.700	254.100	254.200
2	19.440	19.450	19.450	19.450	19.460	19.470	19.480	19.480	19.490	19.490	19.490	19.490	19.500
3	8.675	8.660	8.648	8.639	8.617	8.594	8.581	8.572	8.554	8.549	8.540	8.532	8.529
4	5.821	5.803	5.787	5.774	5.746	5.717	5.699	5.688	5.664	5.658	5.646	5.635	5.632
5	4.579	4.558	4.541	4.527	4.496	4.464	4.444	4.431	4.405	4.398	4.385	4.373	4.369
6	3.896	3.874	3.856	3.841	3.808	3.774	3.754	3.740	3.712	3.705	3.690	3.678	3.673
7	3.467	3.445	3.426	3.410	3.376	3.340	3.319	3.304	3.275	3.267	3.252	3.239	3.234
8	3.173	3.150	3.131	3.115	3.079	3.043	3.020	3.005	2.975	2.967	2.951	2.937	2.932
9	2.960	2.936	2.917	2.900	2.864	2.826	2.803	2.787	2.756	2.748	2.731	2.717	2.712
10	2.798	2.774	2.754	2.737	2.700	2.661	2.637	2.621	2.588	2.580	2.563	2.548	2.543
11	2.671	2.646	2.626	2.609	2.570	2.531	2.507	2.490	2.457	2.448	2.431	2.415	2.410
12	2.568	2.544	2.523	2.505	2.466	2.426	2.401	2.384	2.350	2.341	2.323	2.307	2.302
13	2.484	2.459	2.438	2.420	2.380	2.339	2.314	2.297	2.261	2.252	2.234	2.218	2.212
14	2.413	2.388	2.367	2.349	2.308	2.262	2.241	2.223	2.187	2.178	2.159	2.142	2.136
15	2.353	2.328	2.306	2.288	2.247	2.204	2.178	2.160	2.123	2.114	2.095	2.078	2.072
16	2.302	2.276	2.254	2.235	2.194	2.151	2.124	2.106	2.068	2.059	2.039	2.022	2.016
17	2.257	2.230	2.208	2.190	2.148	2.104	2.077	2.058	2.020	2.011	1.991	1.973	1.967
18	2.217	2.191	2.168	2.150	2.107	2.063	2.035	2.017	1.978	1.968	1.948	1.929	1.923
19	2.182	2.155	2.133	2.114	2.071	2.026	1.999	1.980	1.940	1.930	1.910	1.891	1.884
20	2.151	2.124	2.102	2.082	2.039	1.994	1.966	1.946	1.907	1.896	1.875	1.856	1.850
22	2.098	2.071	2.048	2.028	1.984	1.938	1.909	1.889	1.849	1.838	1.817	1.797	1.790
24	2.054	2.027	2.003	1.984	1.939	1.892	1.863	1.842	1.800	1.790	1.768	1.747	1.740
26	2.018	1.990	1.966	1.946	1.901	1.853	1.823	1.803	1.760	1.749	1.726	1.705	1.698
28	1.987	1.959	1.935	1.915	1.869	1.820	1.790	1.769	1.725	1.714	1.691	1.669	1.662
30	1.960	1.932	1.908	1.887	1.841	1.792	1.761	1.740	1.695	1.683	1.660	1.637	1.630
40	1.868	1.839	1.814	1.793	1.744	1.693	1.660	1.637	1.589	1.577	1.551	1.526	1.517
60	1.778	1.748	1.722	1.700	1.649	1.594	1.559	1.534	1.481	1.467	1.438	1.409	1.399
120	1.690	1.659	1.632	1.608	1.554	1.495	1.457	1.429	1.369	1.352	1.316	1.280	1.267
200	1.656	1.623	1.596	1.572	1.516	1.455	1.415	1.386	1.321	1.302	1.263	1.221	1.205
500	1.625	1.592	1.563	1.539	1.482	1.419	1.376	1.345	1.275	1.255	1.210	1.159	1.138
1000	1.604	1.571	1.542	1.517	1.459	1.394	1.350	1.318	1.243	1.221	1.170	1.106	1.075

Note: v_1 and v_2 are degrees of freedom for the numerator and denominator, respectively.

Source: Compiled by the authors using SYSTAT. Copyright © 2012 by W. B. Ware, J. M. Ferron, and B. M. Miller. All rights reserved.

Table A.8.3 The lower-tailed F-distribution (α = .025)

	v_1												
v_2	1	2	3	4	5	6	7	8	9	10	12	14	16
1	0.002	0.026	0.057	0.082	0.100	0.113	0.124	0.132	0.139	0.144	0.153	0.159	0.164
2	0.001	0.026	0.062	0.094	0.119	0.138	0.153	0.165	0.175	0.183	0.196	0.206	0.213
3	0.001	0.026	0.065	0.100	0.129	0.152	0.170	0.185	0.197	0.207	0.224	0.236	0.245
4	0.001	0.025	0.066	0.104	0.135	0.161	0.181	0.198	0.212	0.224	0.243	0.257	0.268
5	0.001	0.025	0.067	0.107	0.140	0.167	0.189	0.208	0.223	0.236	0.257	0.273	0.286
6	0.001	0.025	0.068	0.109	0.143	0.172	0.195	0.215	0.231	0.246	0.268	0.286	0.299
7	0.001	0.025	0.068	0.110	0.146	0.176	0.200	0.221	0.238	0.253	0.277	0.296	0.311
8	0.001	0.025	0.069	0.111	0.148	0.179	0.204	0.226	0.244	0.259	0.285	0.304	0.320
9	0.001	0.025	0.069	0.112	0.150	0.181	0.207	0.230	0.248	0.265	0.291	0.312	0.328
10	0.001	0.025	0.069	0.113	0.151	0.183	0.210	0.233	0.252	0.269	0.296	0.318	0.335
11	0.001	0.025	0.070	0.114	0.152	0.185	0.212	0.236	0.256	0.273	0.301	0.323	0.341
12	0.001	0.025	0.070	0.114	0.153	0.186	0.214	0.238	0.259	0.276	0.305	0.328	0.346
13	0.001	0.025	0.070	0.115	0.154	0.188	0.216	0.240	0.261	0.279	0.309	0.332	0.351
14	0.001	0.025	0.070	0.115	0.155	0.189	0.218	0.242	0.263	0.282	0.312	0.336	0.355
15	0.001	0.025	0.070	0.116	0.156	0.190	0.219	0.244	0.265	0.284	0.315	0.339	0.359
16	0.001	0.025	0.070	0.116	0.156	0.191	0.220	0.245	0.267	0.286	0.317	0.342	0.362
17	0.001	0.025	0.070	0.116	0.157	0.192	0.221	0.247	0.269	0.288	0.320	0.345	0.365
18	0.001	0.025	0.070	0.116	0.157	0.192	0.222	0.248	0.270	0.290	0.322	0.347	0.368
19	0.001	0.025	0.071	0.117	0.158	0.193	0.223	0.249	0.271	0.291	0.324	0.350	0.371
20	0.001	0.025	0.071	0.117	0.158	0.193	0.224	0.250	0.273	0.293	0.325	0.352	0.373
22	0.001	0.025	0.071	0.117	0.159	0.195	0.225	0.252	0.275	0.295	0.329	0.355	0.377
24	0.001	0.025	0.071	0.117	0.159	0.195	0.227	0.253	0.277	0.297	0.331	0.359	0.381
26	0.001	0.025	0.071	0.118	0.160	0.196	0.228	0.255	0.278	0.299	0.334	0.361	0.384
28	0.001	0.025	0.071	0.118	0.160	0.197	0.228	0.256	0.280	0.301	0.336	0.364	0.387
30	0.001	0.025	0.071	0.118	0.161	0.197	0.229	0.257	0.281	0.302	0.337	0.366	0.389
40	0.001	0.025	0.071	0.119	0.162	0.200	0.232	0.260	0.285	0.307	0.344	0.374	0.399
50	0.001	0.025	0.071	0.119	0.163	0.201	0.234	0.263	0.288	0.310	0.348	0.379	0.405
60	0.001	0.025	0.071	0.120	0.163	0.202	0.235	0.264	0.290	0.313	0.351	0.383	0.409
80	0.001	0.025	0.071	0.120	0.164	0.203	0.237	0.266	0.292	0.316	0.355	0.387	0.414
100	0.001	0.025	0.072	0.120	0.164	0.203	0.238	0.267	0.294	0.317	0.357	0.390	0.417
120	0.001	0.025	0.072	0.120	0.165	0.204	0.238	0.268	0.295	0.318	0.359	0.392	0.420
200	0.001	0.025	0.072	0.121	0.165	0.205	0.239	0.270	0.297	0.321	0.362	0.396	0.424
500	0.001	0.025	0.072	0.121	0.166	0.206	0.241	0.271	0.299	0.323	0.365	0.400	0.429

Note: v_1 and v_2 are degrees of freedom for the numerator and denominator, respectively.

v_1

v_2	18	20	22	24	30	40	50	60	100	120	200	500	1000
1	0.167	0.170	0.173	0.175	0.180	0.184	0.187	0.189	0.193	0.194	0.196	0.198	0.198
2	0.219	0.224	0.228	0.232	0.239	0.247	0.252	0.255	0.261	0.263	0.266	0.269	0.270
3	0.253	0.259	0.264	0.269	0.279	0.289	0.295	0.299	0.308	0.310	0.314	0.318	0.320
4	0.277	0.285	0.291	0.296	0.308	0.320	0.327	0.332	0.343	0.346	0.351	0.356	0.357
5	0.296	0.304	0.311	0.317	0.330	0.344	0.353	0.359	0.371	0.374	0.380	0.386	0.388
6	0.310	0.320	0.327	0.334	0.349	0.364	0.374	0.381	0.394	0.398	0.405	0.411	0.413
7	0.323	0.333	0.341	0.348	0.364	0.381	0.392	0.399	0.414	0.418	0.425	0.432	0.435
8	0.333	0.343	0.352	0.360	0.377	0.395	0.407	0.415	0.431	0.435	0.443	0.451	0.454
9	0.341	0.353	0.362	0.370	0.388	0.408	0.420	0.428	0.446	0.450	0.459	0.467	0.470
10	0.349	0.361	0.370	0.379	0.398	0.419	0.432	0.440	0.459	0.464	0.473	0.482	0.485
11	0.355	0.368	0.378	0.387	0.407	0.428	0.442	0.451	0.471	0.476	0.486	0.495	0.499
12	0.361	0.374	0.384	0.394	0.415	0.437	0.451	0.461	0.481	0.487	0.497	0.507	0.511
13	0.366	0.379	0.390	0.400	0.422	0.445	0.460	0.470	0.491	0.497	0.508	0.518	0.522
14	0.371	0.384	0.395	0.405	0.428	0.452	0.467	0.478	0.500	0.506	0.518	0.529	0.532
15	0.375	0.389	0.400	0.410	0.433	0.458	0.474	0.485	0.508	0.514	0.526	0.538	0.542
16	0.379	0.393	0.405	0.415	0.439	0.464	0.481	0.492	0.516	0.522	0.535	0.547	0.551
17	0.382	0.396	0.409	0.419	0.443	0.470	0.486	0.498	0.523	0.529	0.542	0.555	0.559
18	0.385	0.400	0.412	0.423	0.448	0.475	0.492	0.504	0.529	0.536	0.549	0.562	0.567
19	0.388	0.403	0.416	0.426	0.452	0.479	0.497	0.509	0.535	0.542	0.556	0.569	0.574
20	0.391	0.406	0.419	0.430	0.456	0.484	0.502	0.514	0.541	0.548	0.562	0.576	0.581
22	0.395	0.411	0.424	0.436	0.462	0.491	0.510	0.523	0.551	0.559	0.574	0.588	0.593
24	0.400	0.415	0.429	0.441	0.468	0.498	0.518	0.531	0.561	0.568	0.584	0.599	0.604
26	0.403	0.419	0.433	0.445	0.473	0.504	0.524	0.539	0.569	0.577	0.594	0.609	0.615
28	0.406	0.423	0.437	0.449	0.478	0.510	0.530	0.545	0.576	0.585	0.602	0.618	0.624
30	0.409	0.426	0.440	0.453	0.482	0.515	0.536	0.551	0.583	0.592	0.610	0.627	0.633
40	0.419	0.437	0.453	0.466	0.498	0.533	0.557	0.573	0.610	0.620	0.640	0.660	0.667
50	0.426	0.445	0.461	0.475	0.508	0.546	0.571	0.589	0.628	0.639	0.662	0.684	0.692
60	0.431	0.450	0.466	0.481	0.515	0.555	0.581	0.600	0.642	0.654	0.678	0.703	0.711
80	0.437	0.457	0.474	0.489	0.525	0.567	0.595	0.615	0.661	0.674	0.702	0.730	0.740
100	0.441	0.461	0.478	0.494	0.531	0.575	0.604	0.625	0.674	0.688	0.718	0.749	0.760
120	0.443	0.464	0.482	0.498	0.536	0.580	0.610	0.632	0.683	0.698	0.730	0.763	0.775
200	0.449	0.470	0.488	0.505	0.545	0.592	0.624	0.648	0.704	0.720	0.757	0.797	0.813
500	0.454	0.476	0.495	0.512	0.554	0.603	0.637	0.663	0.726	0.744	0.788	0.839	0.861
1000	0.457	0.480	0.499	0.517	0.560	0.611	0.647	0.675	0.742	0.763	0.814	0.880	0.914

Note: v_1 and v_2 are degrees of freedom for the numerator and denominator, respectively.
Source: Compiled by the authors using SYSTAT.

Table A.8.4 The upper-tailed F-distribution ($\alpha = .025$)

v_2	v_1 = 1	2	3	4	5	6	7	8	9	10	12	14	16
1	647.800	799.500	864.200	899.600	921.800	937.100	948.200	956.700	963.300	968.600	976.700	982.500	986.900
2	38.510	39.000	39.160	39.250	39.300	39.330	39.360	39.370	39.390	39.400	39.420	39.430	39.440
3	17.440	16.040	15.440	15.100	14.880	14.740	14.620	14.540	14.470	14.420	14.340	14.280	14.230
4	12.220	10.650	9.979	9.605	9.364	9.197	9.074	8.980	8.905	8.844	8.751	8.684	8.633
5	10.010	8.434	7.764	7.388	7.146	6.978	6.853	6.757	6.681	6.619	6.525	6.456	6.403
6	8.813	7.260	6.599	6.227	5.988	5.820	5.695	5.600	5.523	5.461	5.366	5.297	5.244
7	8.073	6.542	5.890	5.523	5.285	5.119	4.995	4.899	4.823	4.761	4.666	4.596	4.543
8	7.571	6.059	5.416	5.053	4.817	4.652	4.529	4.433	4.357	4.295	4.200	4.130	4.076
9	7.209	5.715	5.078	4.718	4.484	4.320	4.197	4.102	4.026	3.964	3.868	3.798	3.744
10	6.937	5.456	4.826	4.468	4.236	4.072	3.950	3.855	3.779	3.717	3.621	3.550	3.496
11	6.724	5.256	4.630	4.275	4.044	3.881	3.759	3.664	3.588	3.526	3.430	3.359	3.304
12	6.554	5.096	4.474	4.121	3.891	3.728	3.607	3.512	3.436	3.374	3.277	3.206	3.152
13	6.414	4.965	4.347	3.996	3.767	3.604	3.483	3.388	3.312	3.250	3.153	3.082	3.027
14	6.298	4.857	4.242	3.892	3.663	3.501	3.380	3.285	3.209	3.147	3.050	2.979	2.923
15	6.200	4.765	4.153	3.804	3.576	3.415	3.293	3.199	3.123	3.060	2.963	2.891	2.836
16	6.115	4.687	4.077	3.729	3.502	3.341	3.219	3.125	3.049	2.986	2.889	2.817	2.761
17	6.042	4.619	4.011	3.665	3.438	3.277	3.156	3.061	2.985	2.922	2.825	2.753	2.697
18	5.978	4.560	3.954	3.608	3.382	3.221	3.100	3.005	2.929	2.866	2.769	2.696	2.640
19	5.922	4.508	3.903	3.559	3.333	3.172	3.051	2.956	2.880	2.817	2.720	2.647	2.591
20	5.871	4.461	3.859	3.515	3.289	3.128	3.007	2.913	2.837	2.774	2.676	2.603	2.547
22	5.786	4.383	3.783	3.440	3.215	3.055	2.934	2.839	2.763	2.700	2.602	2.528	2.472
24	5.717	4.319	3.721	3.379	3.155	2.995	2.874	2.779	2.703	2.640	2.541	2.468	2.411
26	5.659	4.265	3.670	3.329	3.105	2.945	2.824	2.729	2.653	2.590	2.491	2.417	2.360
28	5.610	4.221	3.626	3.286	3.063	2.903	2.782	2.687	2.611	2.547	2.448	2.374	2.317
30	5.568	4.182	3.589	3.250	3.026	2.867	2.746	2.651	2.575	2.511	2.412	2.338	2.280
40	5.424	4.051	3.463	3.126	2.904	2.744	2.624	2.529	2.452	2.388	2.288	2.213	2.154
50	5.340	3.975	3.390	3.054	2.833	2.674	2.553	2.458	2.381	2.317	2.216	2.140	2.081
60	5.286	3.925	3.343	3.008	2.786	2.627	2.507	2.412	2.334	2.270	2.169	2.093	2.033
80	5.218	3.864	3.284	2.950	2.730	2.571	2.450	2.355	2.277	2.213	2.111	2.035	1.974
100	5.179	3.828	3.250	2.917	2.696	2.537	2.417	2.321	2.244	2.179	2.077	2.000	1.939
120	5.152	3.805	3.227	2.894	2.674	2.515	2.395	2.299	2.222	2.157	2.055	1.977	1.916
200	5.100	3.758	3.182	2.850	2.630	2.472	2.351	2.256	2.178	2.113	2.010	1.932	1.870
500	5.054	3.716	3.142	2.811	2.592	2.434	2.313	2.217	2.139	2.074	1.971	1.892	1.830
1000	5.024	3.689	3.116	2.786	2.567	2.408	2.288	2.192	2.114	2.048	1.945	1.866	1.803

Note: v_1 and v_2 are degrees of freedom for the numerator and denominator, respectively.

Table A.8.4 Continued

	v_1												
v_2	18	20	22	24	30	40	50	60	100	120	200	500	1000
1	990.300	993.100	995.400	997.200	1001.000	1006.000	1008.000	1010.000	1013.000	1014.000	1016.000	1017.000	1018.000
2	39.440	39.450	39.450	39.460	39.460	39.470	39.480	39.480	39.490	39.490	39.490	39.500	39.500
3	14.200	14.170	14.140	14.120	14.080	14.040	14.010	13.990	13.960	13.950	13.930	13.910	13.910
4	8.592	8.560	8.533	8.511	8.461	8.411	8.381	8.360	8.319	8.309	8.289	8.270	8.264
5	6.362	6.329	6.301	6.278	6.227	6.175	6.144	6.123	6.080	6.069	6.048	6.028	6.022
6	5.202	5.168	5.141	5.117	5.065	5.012	4.980	4.959	4.915	4.904	4.882	4.862	4.856
7	4.501	4.467	4.439	4.415	4.362	4.309	4.276	4.254	4.210	4.199	4.176	4.156	4.149
8	4.034	3.999	3.971	3.947	3.894	3.840	3.807	3.784	3.739	3.728	3.705	3.684	3.677
9	3.701	3.667	3.638	3.614	3.560	3.505	3.472	3.449	3.403	3.392	3.368	3.347	3.340
10	3.453	3.419	3.390	3.365	3.311	3.255	3.221	3.198	3.152	3.140	3.116	3.094	3.087
11	3.261	3.226	3.197	3.173	3.118	3.061	3.027	3.004	2.956	2.944	2.920	2.898	2.890
12	3.108	3.073	3.043	3.019	2.963	2.906	2.871	2.848	2.800	2.787	2.763	2.740	2.733
13	2.983	2.948	2.918	2.893	2.837	2.780	2.744	2.720	2.671	2.659	2.634	2.611	2.603
14	2.879	2.844	2.814	2.789	2.732	2.674	2.638	2.614	2.565	2.552	2.526	2.503	2.495
15	2.792	2.756	2.726	2.701	2.644	2.585	2.549	2.524	2.474	2.461	2.435	2.411	2.403
16	2.717	2.681	2.651	2.625	2.568	2.509	2.472	2.447	2.396	2.383	2.357	2.333	2.324
17	2.652	2.616	2.585	2.560	2.502	2.442	2.405	2.380	2.329	2.315	2.289	2.264	2.256
18	2.596	2.559	2.529	2.503	2.445	2.384	2.347	2.321	2.269	2.256	2.229	2.204	2.195
19	2.546	2.509	2.478	2.452	2.394	2.333	2.295	2.270	2.217	2.203	2.176	2.150	2.142
20	2.501	2.464	2.434	2.408	2.349	2.287	2.249	2.223	2.170	2.156	2.128	2.103	2.094
22	2.426	2.389	2.358	2.331	2.272	2.210	2.171	2.145	2.090	2.076	2.047	2.021	2.012
24	2.365	2.327	2.296	2.269	2.209	2.146	2.107	2.080	2.024	2.010	1.981	1.954	1.945
26	2.314	2.276	2.244	2.217	2.157	2.093	2.053	2.026	1.969	1.954	1.925	1.897	1.888
28	2.270	2.232	2.201	2.174	2.112	2.048	2.007	1.980	1.922	1.907	1.877	1.848	1.839
30	2.233	2.195	2.163	2.136	2.074	2.009	1.968	1.940	1.882	1.866	1.835	1.806	1.797
40	2.107	2.068	2.035	2.007	1.943	1.875	1.832	1.803	1.741	1.724	1.691	1.659	1.648
50	2.033	1.993	1.960	1.931	1.866	1.796	1.752	1.721	1.656	1.639	1.603	1.569	1.557
60	1.985	1.944	1.911	1.882	1.815	1.744	1.699	1.667	1.599	1.581	1.543	1.507	1.495
80	1.925	1.884	1.850	1.820	1.752	1.679	1.632	1.599	1.527	1.508	1.467	1.428	1.414
100	1.890	1.849	1.814	1.784	1.715	1.640	1.592	1.558	1.483	1.463	1.420	1.378	1.363
120	1.866	1.825	1.790	1.760	1.690	1.614	1.565	1.530	1.454	1.433	1.388	1.343	1.327
200	1.820	1.778	1.742	1.712	1.640	1.562	1.511	1.474	1.393	1.370	1.320	1.269	1.250
500	1.779	1.736	1.700	1.669	1.596	1.515	1.462	1.423	1.336	1.311	1.254	1.192	1.166
1000	1.751	1.708	1.672	1.640	1.566	1.484	1.428	1.388	1.296	1.268	1.205	1.128	1.090

Note: v_1 and v_2 are degrees of freedom for the numerator and denominator, respectively.

Source: Compiled by the authors using SYSTAT.

Table A.9 Abbreviated table of the critical values of the studentized range statistic ($\alpha = .05$)

Error df	r = number of means or number of steps between ordered means								
	2	3	4	5	6	7	8	9	10
2	6.080	8.331	9.799	10.881	11.734	12.435	13.028	13.542	13.994
3	4.501	5.910	6.825	7.502	8.037	8.478	8.852	9.177	9.462
4	3.927	5.040	5.757	6.287	6.706	7.053	7.347	7.602	7.826
5	3.635	4.602	5.218	5.673	6.033	6.330	6.582	6.801	6.995
6	3.460	4.339	4.896	5.305	5.628	5.895	6.122	6.319	6.493
7	3.344	4.165	4.681	5.060	5.359	5.606	5.815	5.997	6.158
8	3.261	4.041	4.529	4.886	5.167	5.399	5.596	5.767	5.918
9	3.199	3.948	4.415	4.755	5.024	5.244	5.432	5.595	5.738
10	3.151	3.877	4.327	4.654	4.912	5.124	5.304	5.460	5.598
11	3.113	3.820	4.256	4.574	4.823	5.028	5.202	5.353	5.486
12	3.081	3.773	4.199	4.508	4.750	4.950	5.119	5.265	5.395
13	3.055	3.734	4.151	4.453	4.690	4.884	5.049	5.192	5.318
14	3.033	3.701	4.111	4.407	4.639	4.829	4.990	5.130	5.253
15	3.014	3.673	4.076	4.367	4.595	4.782	4.940	5.077	5.198
16	2.998	3.649	4.046	4.333	4.557	4.741	4.896	5.031	5.150
17	2.984	3.628	4.020	4.303	4.524	4.705	4.858	4.991	5.108
18	2.971	3.609	3.997	4.276	4.494	4.673	4.824	4.955	5.071
19	2.960	3.593	3.977	4.253	4.468	4.645	4.794	4.924	5.037
20	2.950	3.578	3.958	4.232	4.445	4.620	4.768	4.895	5.008
21	2.941	3.565	3.942	4.213	4.424	4.597	4.743	4.870	4.981
22	2.933	3.553	3.927	4.196	4.405	4.577	4.722	4.847	4.957
23	2.926	3.542	3.914	4.180	4.388	4.558	4.702	4.826	4.935
24	2.919	3.532	3.901	4.166	4.373	4.541	4.684	4.807	4.915
25	2.913	3.523	3.890	4.153	4.358	4.526	4.667	4.789	4.897
26	2.907	3.514	3.880	4.141	4.345	4.511	4.652	4.773	4.880
27	2.902	3.506	3.870	4.130	4.333	4.498	4.638	4.758	4.864
28	2.897	3.499	3.861	4.120	4.322	4.486	4.625	4.745	4.850
29	2.892	3.493	3.853	4.111	4.311	4.475	4.613	4.732	4.837
30	2.888	3.486	3.845	4.102	4.301	4.464	4.601	4.720	4.824
35	2.871	3.461	3.814	4.066	4.261	4.421	4.555	4.671	4.773
40	2.858	3.442	3.791	4.039	4.232	4.388	4.521	4.634	4.735
45	2.848	3.428	3.773	4.018	4.209	4.364	4.494	4.606	4.705
50	2.841	3.416	3.758	4.002	4.190	4.344	4.473	4.584	4.681
55	2.834	3.406	3.747	3.989	4.176	4.328	4.455	4.566	4.662
60	2.829	3.399	3.737	3.977	4.163	4.314	4.441	4.550	4.646
70	2.821	3.386	3.722	3.960	4.144	4.293	4.419	4.527	4.621
80	2.814	3.377	3.711	3.947	4.129	4.277	4.402	4.509	4.603
90	2.810	3.370	3.702	3.937	4.118	4.265	4.389	4.495	4.588
100	2.806	3.365	3.695	3.929	4.109	4.256	4.379	4.484	4.577
120	2.800	3.356	3.685	3.917	4.096	4.241	4.363	4.468	4.560
200	2.789	3.339	3.664	3.893	4.069	4.212	4.332	4.435	4.525
500	2.779	3.324	3.645	3.872	4.046	4.187	4.305	4.406	4.494

Source: Compiled by the authors using R 2.13.1.

Appendix B
An Introduction to R

Virtually all courses in applied statistics, even those taught at the introductory level, employ one or more statistical packages for completing the analyses of data. Among the most popular are SAS, SPSS, Stata, and Systat. These packages are integrated statistical environments that allow the user to manage data, analyze data, and produce graphics. The latter three packages all employ a typical graphical user interface (GUI) with pull-down menus that allow the user to point-and-click to generate the results that they desire. On the other hand, the Windows version of SAS is much like the old mainframe version, with three primary windows. One window (Editor) allows the user to type in the commands, another window (Output) displays the results, and the third window (Log) displays the history of commands, provides information about the execution of the commands, and displays warnings and error messages.

For many, many years, the first author has used SPSS in his classes so that students can avoid the tedious task of typing commands. However, over time, he became more and more convinced that this may not be in the best interests of students. There are several concerns. First, the location of the desired command within the pull-down menus is not always intuitive. Second, there are some particular tasks that are not available in the point-and-click interface. And third, he had a growing sense that students who construct sets of commands gain a better understanding of the material. Thus, we are making a change for this book; we are moving to support another program, R (R Development Core Team, 2011).

WHAT IS R?

R is a programming environment closely related to S, a program developed at Bell Labs in the mid-1970s. Currently, S is marketed commercially as S-PLUS by the Insightful Corporation. On the other hand, R is available for free downloading from the Comprehensive R Archive Network (CRAN) website (http://cran.r-project.org). At the time of this writing, the current version for Windows is R 2.15.0. In addition to the extensive base package, there are over 3,700 other packages that can be downloaded, enabling the user to complete virtually any statistical analysis known.

WHY R?

As noted above, it is free; although this, in itself, is not sufficient reason to advocate its use. There are several reasons for making the switch from other programs. To begin, there are different versions of R that run on different platforms; it can run on Windows, Macintosh, and Linux/Unix-type machines. In addition, there is a virtual explosion of new statistics books featuring R, and it is beginning to show up in articles published in major journals. For us, there is yet another reason. Most introductory courses are designed to introduce students to ways to describe sets of numbers (descriptive statistics) and ways to suggest whether different sets of scores are really different (inferential statistics). The traditional methods of inferential statistics are based on classical probability theory, which makes some rather restrictive assumptions about the nature of the data. Historically, violations of assumptions have been addressed by non-parametric techniques, which make fewer assumptions than do the classical methods. Currently, with the advances in computer technology, there are even better ways to address situations where the assumptions have been violated. These newer techniques are typically described as one of the following: randomization tests, bootstrapping, or permutation tests.

With R, we can do all of the above in one statistical program. In addition, we can construct simulations to show students the sampling distribution of many statistics. The trade-off in moving away from a GUI program such as SPSS is that you will have to type the commands, and you may object to that. We have two counter arguments. First, virtually all of the R commands that have been used in conjunction with this book are available in a Word document and also as separate R script files that are available on the book website. Second, and perhaps more cogent, you are the generation of email and text messaging; so we know you like to type! ☺

OBTAINING AND INSTALLING R

As noted above, R is available for downloading at the CRAN website. Either do a Google search for "cran," or go directly to the website (http://cran.r-project.org). Once there, you can select the platform you use: Linux, Mac, or Windows. If you select Windows, you will be routed to the next page, where you will choose "base." The next page lists several files; you want to select R-2.15.0 (or the most current version), which includes a 32-bit and 64-bit version. During the install process, the best one for your machine will be selected and installed. Follow the directions for downloading the file. Once downloaded, a click on the file will extract and install the program in the usual way. You may be asked to select a "mirror site" from which to download the file. In our experience, the "mirror site" at CA1 is quite quick; we have had good luck with clicking on the file name and downloading from CRAN or from CA1, rather than the "mirror site" that is closest.

The base package actually contains several packages and libraries. From time to time you will want to use some procedures that are available in other packages and not part of the base package. Once you have installed R, you should find an icon/shortcut on the desktop for R. Click on it to start the program; shortly the program will open and the console window shown in Figure B.1 will appear. In this window, you can type commands, and the results will appear immediately.

There are two other types of windows for use in R. One of these is a "script" window. These are windows in which you can enter several commands and then submit them for execution all at once. Script windows have the advantage of being "savable." Essentially, they are text files that you can save, open, and use again. When you save one of your script files, be sure to add a **.r**

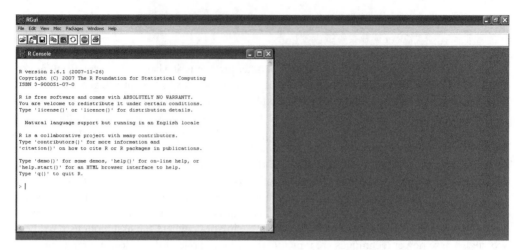

FIGURE B.1   The console window for accessing packages that are not part of the base package of R.

extension on the file name so that R can find it easily. These script files provide a distinct advantage of maintaining a record of what you have done. The third type of window is the graphics window, which displays the graphic outputs from your commands.

With the console window open, go up to the toolbar and click on the "Packages" item. When the menu appears, you will see several options that are available, two of which will be important in the future. One of the guiding principles in the writing of R is that computer resources should not be unnecessarily overloaded. We have noticed in recent years that it takes longer and longer to open a program like SPSS, and longer and longer to execute the procedures. In contrast, when you open the R program, only the bare essentials are loaded. The two options in the Packages menu of particular interest are "Load package ..." and "Install package(s) ...". The "Load package" option will make available packages that were installed when you installed R, but that are not loaded when you start R. To see what packages are installed on your computer, click on "Load packages ..." and you will see a window that lists all of the packages/libraries that were installed, not all of which are loaded when you start R. For example, if you want to access the bootstrapping package, you can load it using the GUI interface, or you can simply type

>**library**(*boot*)

in the console and hit Enter. If the procedure that you want is contained in a package not yet installed, click on the "Install package(s) ..." option and you will be prompted to select a CRAN mirror site. We usually go to the USA(CA1) site. Once there, you can obtain the package(s) that you want. For example, later in the course we will be using procedures that are available in the **car** and **PASWR** packages, to name two. Supposing that you want to install the **car** package, you could also type

>**install.packages**(*car*)

in the Console, and the package will be installed. It will not be automatically loaded when you start R, so you will need to use a **library(***car***)** command to load it for the current session.

THE R CONSOLE

Like most other computer programs, R has a few quirks, but overall it is pretty easy to learn and use. When you open R you will see the R console. Here you can type your commands, and the results will immediately appear either in the console or in the graphics window, depending on what you requested.

Let's begin by seeing how R can be used to calculate with numbers. At the prompt, type "3 + 4" without the quotes. After you hit the enter key, the console will look like:

```
> 3+4
[1] 7
```

The command that you typed is repeated in the console as part of the output. The [1] simply indicates that this is the first result of all the results you requested.

Here are some additional results:

```
> 2^3
[1] 8
> (2 - 4)*4
[1] -8
> sqrt(5)
[1] 2.236068
> pi
[1] 3.141593
> exp(1)
[1] 2.718282
> log(20)
[1] 2.995732
> log(100, base = 10)
[1] 2
```

"Assignment" can be done in several ways. Traditionalists use <-, while others may use the equals sign. For example:

```
> x <- 4 + 5
> x
[1] 9
> x = 4 + 5
> x
[1] 9
```

If you need help with a command, you can simply type the following and the help files will open:

```
>?command
```

READING DATA INTO R

This part of the presentation may be somewhat oversimplified, though we believe it sufficient to get you started with R. Basically, R stores data in several different ways; we will describe two of the more common forms. You can have one or more single variables or vectors that are not linked to one another. Or you can have a data set, or **data.frame**, which is the conventional way to organize data with each column containing the values of a variable and each row containing all the variable values for a case. That said, there are many ways to enter data into the system. At this point, a brief discussion of variable names is appropriate. Variable names in R can contain letters, numerals, and decimal points (periods). Generally, we encourage you to use variable names that start with letters, are mnemonic, and avoid any special characters other than the period. It is important to know that "case" is important. That is, "Year" is not the same variable as "year."

With small sets of data, it is sometimes easiest to simply enter the data from the keyboard, either directly into the console or in a script file. Two common commands for doing this are the **scan( )** function and the **c( )** function. The most straightforward way to do it is with the **c( )** function. For example, let's suppose that you want to enter some values for a variable to be named "y:"

```
> y <- c(1,3,4,6,11,5)
> y
[1]  1  3  4  6  11  5
```

Note that the values within the parentheses must be separated by commas. Another way to read data in is with the **scan( )** function. After typing the variable name and **scan( )**, you simply enter the values one at a time and hit the Enter key after each value. To end the process, you hit the Enter key twice. For example, let's say you want to read in some values for a variable to be named "x:"

```
> x<- scan()
1: 1
2: 3
3: 4
4: 5
5: 13
6: 9
7: 4
8:
Read 7 items
> x
[1]  1  3  4  5  13  9  4
```

If you want to create a **data.frame**, it is possible to do so from the keyboard in at least two ways. First, let's say you have two variables (height and weight) on five cases that you want to link together in a **data.frame** called "physical:"

```
physical <- data.frame(ht = c(,,,,),
   wt = c(,,,, ))
```

will do the trick. If the data set gets much larger, you might want to use the "spreadsheet-like" editor in R, albeit fairly primitive. To do this, you would enter the following command:

```
#Comments start with #
#Open a blank data editor
dsn <- edit(as.data.frame(NULL))
```

Another option to open a blank data editor is:

```
dsn <- data.frame()
fix(dsn)
```

Either way, you will be presented with a window containing the data editor (Figure B.2).

By clicking on the variable names supplied (var1, var2, etc.), you can change the variable names and declare the variables to be either numeric or character. We recommend entering everything first as numeric; it gives you more options later on. When you have finished entering the data, you close the window. R creates a **data.frame** with the name used in the earlier **edit** or "assignment" command. Then, in order to make that data.frame the active data set, you type:

```
attach(dsn)
```

and then you will have access to the data set. If you want to use a different data file, it is a good idea to close the one you have been using with a **detach**(*dsn*) command.

When you are done, you will probably want to save the data file as a "permanent" text file:

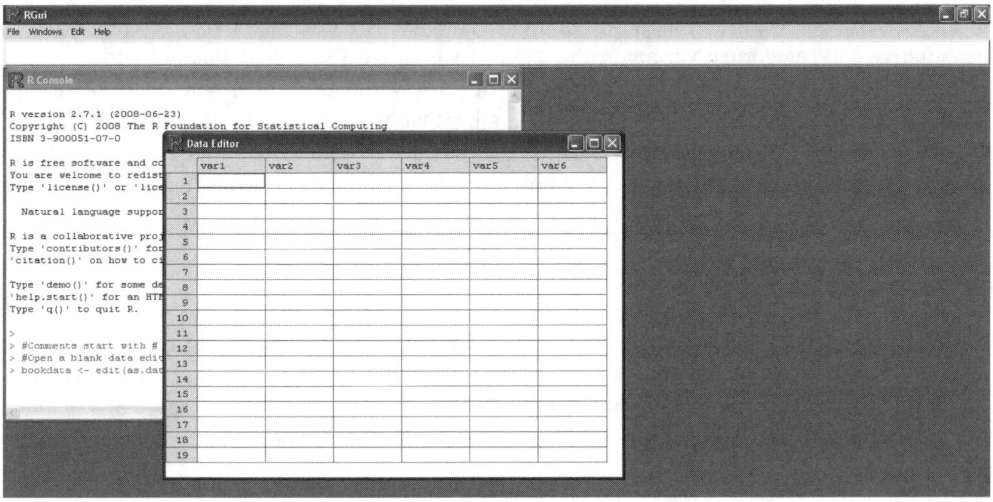

FIGURE B.2   The data editor window.

```
#After entering data, save the file
write.table(dsn, "c:/filepath/dsn.txt")
```

The **write.table** command creates a tab-delimited ASCII/text file in the directory specified in the file path, with the variable names in the first row. When you want to read that file back into R, type

```
dsn <- read.table("c:/filepath/dsn.txt",
  header = TRUE)
```

If you find the data editor in R a bit clunky, you can enter your data in an Excel spreadsheet, typing the variable names in the first row. After entering the data for each case in a separate row, you can save it as both an Excel file and a tab-delimited text file, and then read it into R with a **read.table** command. Generalizing, you can create your data file in any program of your choosing as long as you can save it as a **.txt** file. A trick to then find your text file is to use the following command:

```
dsn <- read.table(file = file.choose())
```

The last option is to use the **foreign** package to read the data in from another program. Suppose you are given an SPSS data file, *dsn.sav*. You can read this file directly into R with the following commands:

```
library(foreign)
dsn <- read.spss("c:/filepath/dsn.sav")
```

MANAGING YOUR DATA

Data management is not heavily emphasized in this first course, but there are a few skills that are very useful. First, as noted earlier, we recommend that, when creating a data set, you code all of the values as numerals, even the categorical variables. R recognizes the difference between quantitative and categorical variables, the latter of which are also called "factor" variables. For example, if you are entering data regarding gender, we would advise that you enter the data as quantitative and use the numerals "1" and "2", rather than the letters "F" and "M". It affords you greater flexibility. However, the drawback is that you need to remember which is which. That is, did you use "1" for males or females? A simplistic way to handle this is to add a comment to your script, which can serve as a reminder note to yourself:

```
# Gender 1 = Female, 2 = Male
```

A more elegant solution is to create labels for the variable values so that the labels appear on the output. After creating the labels, you should probably save the file with the labels under a new file name, using the **write.table** command. First, let's assume that we have read in a text file *classdata* with two categorical variables, *gender* and *major*. The variables were originally coded in the file as:

Gender: 1 = Female, 2 = Male

Major: 1 = Business, 2 = Humanities, 3 = Mathematics, 4 = Natural Science, and 5 = Social Science.

There is more than one way to create the value labels. Let's look at two different ways to create the labels for gender. First, you should decide whether you want to create a new variable or modify the original variable. We lean toward creating new variable names to preserve the original structure of the file, and we suggest using names that help you keep track of which is which. Here is one way to do that:

```
classdata$f.gender <- factor(classdata$gender,
  levels = 1:2, labels = c("Female", "Male"))
```

Note: All quotation marks were vertical in the statement above when originally typed in Word. After entering the text in R the quotation marks were shown with a bit of a tilt. If you write your commands in Word and then paste them into an R script file, the special characters used for quotes in Word may not be recognized by R. If R does not recognize these characters as quotes, it returns a warning to the effect that an "unrecognized character" was encountered. If that occurs, check for quotation marks in your code and retype them within the R environment.

If you simply want to modify the original variable, you would start with

```
classdata$gender <- factor(...
```

The last part of the statement, ordered = TRUE, is important if you want to keep the levels of the factor in the original order. R, like most programs, will put the factor labels in alphabetical order, which may confuse things down the road. Here is an alternative way to create the labels for gender.

```
gender.vals = c("Female" = 1, "Male" = 2)
classdata$f.gender <- factor(classdata$gender,
  levels = gender.vals,
  labels = names(gender.vals))
```

There are occasions when you might have several items, all measured on a four-point Likert-type scale, where the values have been entered as 1–4, but they correspond to "Strongly agree," "Agree," "Disagree," and "Strongly disagree." Let's assume that the variable names are *item1*, *item2*, etc. To create new variables:

```
item.names <- c("SA", "A", "D", "SD")
classdata$i1 <- factor(classdata$item1,
  levels = 1:length(item.names),
  labels = item.names, ordered = TRUE)
classdata$i2 <- factor(classdata$item2,
  levels = 1:length(item.names),
  labels = item.names, ordered = TRUE)
etc.
```

Now, at this point, things can get a little confusing. Once the value labels have been linked to the levels of the original categorical variables, you would like to keep the "order" of the levels consistent. R does not make this easy. Your first thought might be to write out the file and then read it back in when you need it. You could do this with:

```
write.table(ecls200,
    file = "c:/rbook/f.ecls200.txt")
```

This command would write a new text file, *f.ecls200.txt*. However, when you read the file back in, any commands involving the categorical factors will result in output having the labels alphabetized; the "ordered" property is not retained. We offer two solutions to this problem. First, you could use a "prefix" for your labels. Rather than using "Male" and "Female," you could use "1. Male" and "2. Female." A second option is to save the script file that you used to create the value labels, and always use it to read in the original text file which did not have the labels. As long as you stay in R, the order of the labels will be maintained. We actually prefer this second option, as your computer does not become cluttered with a lot of files.

Another issue with data management is the accessing of files and subfiles. As noted earlier, R is very frugal with regard to the use of memory. Although you may have read more than one data file in a session, only one of them is accessible at any given time. Indeed, none of them may be accessible. After reading a file, you must attach it with an **attach(***dsn***)** command in order to use it. Also as noted earlier, when you are finished with that file, you should "clean up" with a **detach(***dsn***)** command. When you are moving from one file to another that has the same variable names, you need check to make sure that the switch has become effective. There is another way to make a file accessible that essentially combines the **attach( )** and **detach( )** functions, and the **with( )** command. For example, **with**(*dsn, command*) will **attach** the particular data set, execute the R command specified, and then **detach** the data set. If you are going to be moving from data set to data set, this works well. However, if you are going to be executing many functions on the same data frame, it is probably more efficient to **attach( )** it, execute the several commands, and then **detach( )** it. We would be remiss if we did not point out that the **attach( )/detach( )** option is not without controversy. Some R programmers prefer combining the **data.frame** name and the variable name to specify the location of the variables. For example, to create a frequency distribution of gender with labels:

```
table(classdata$f.gender)
```

We agree that this option does remove any ambiguity, but it does require typing the **data.frame** name every time.

A similar logic pertains to working with subsets of a data frame. For example, suppose that we want to generate information on subfiles. We have a file that contains both females and males, and we wish to generate the same information on each of the subgroups. Again, we have several options. If you just want to do a small number of analyses, we could use a **with** command as follows:

```
with(classdata, subset=gender=="1",mean(math))
```

to obtain the average math score for the females. However, if you are going to complete lots of analyses on the subgroups, it is probably better to create new data frames:

```
classdata.female <- subset(classdata,
  subset=gender=="1")
classdata.male <- subset(classdata,
  subset=gender=="2")
```

You will now have two additional **data.frames**, one for each gender group, and you can **attach( )** and **detach( )** at will. You might even want to write each of them out as a text file.

Another quick heads-up note: In R, there are distinctions made between parentheses, brackets, and braces. They are not interchangeable! Parentheses **( )** are used for function arguments, brackets **[ ]** are used for indexing (like subscripts) and braces **{ }** are used for functions and loops. For now, just focus on the parentheses and brackets.

In conjunction with this book, we have written a number of our own functions for calculating some statistics that are not readily available in R. They are contained in a text file named "*functions.txt*" on the book website. In order to be able to use these functions, you will need to download that file from the website and save it as a text file on your hard drive. We recommend that you put it somewhere "near the top" of the directory structure. For example, we created a directory on our c:/drive named R and saved the *functions.txt* file to that directory. At the beginning of each session, we execute the following command, which makes the function available to us:

```
source("C:/R/functions.txt")
```

We would be the first to acknowledge that this very brief introduction does not take you very far. It is our intent not to overload you with information at this point, but rather to provide you with enough information to get you up and running with R. You will be learning much more about R as you proceed through this book. And remember, all of the script files used in the book are available as both R script files (.r) and within Word files for each chapter. We have also listed below a number of references/resources that we have found very helpful in our own learning about R.

REFERENCES

Adler, J. (2010). *R in a nutshell: A desktop quick reference.* Sepastapol, CA: O'Reilly Media.

Fox, J., & Weisberg, S. (2011). *An R companion to applied regression* (2nd ed.). Thousand Oaks, CA: Sage.

Kabacoff, R. I. (2011). *R in action: Data analysis and graphics with R.* Shelter Island, NY: Manning.

R Development Core Team (2011). R: A language and environment for statistical computing. R Foundation for Statistical Computing, Vienna, Austria. ISBN 3-900051-07-0; URL http://www.R-project.org.

Teetor, P. (2011). *R cookbook.* Sepastapol, CA: O'Reilly Media.

Verzani, J. (2005). *Using R for introductory statistics.* Boca Raton, FL: Chapman & Hall/CRC Press.

SUBJECT INDEX

AUTHOR INDEX